The John Doe Associates

The John Doe Associates

BACKDOOR DIPLOMACY FOR PEACE, 1941

R. J. C. BUTOW

STANFORD UNIVERSITY PRESS, STANFORD, CALIFORNIA
1974

Stanford University Press, Stanford, California
© 1974 by the Board of Trustees of the
Leland Stanford Junior University
Printed in the United States of America
ISBN 0-8047-0852-5   LC 73-89857

For my daughter Stephanie

A Note to the Reader

THIS BOOK deals with a major endeavor for peace in 1941 that has remained virtually unknown and unexplored through all these intervening years. It is the story of the "John Doe Associates"—a priest, a colonel, and a banker—who persistently tried to maneuver the United States and Japan into a settlement of their differences, short of war, through manipulations behind the scenes on both sides of the Pacific.

In Part One events unfold largely as they were seen during the early stages of the affair by the President and the Secretary of State. Only occasionally is something revealed that was not within their knowledge at the time. Parts Two, Three, and Four explore a prolonged period of secret activity that ended in disillusionment on a Sunday morning in December, as smoke blackened the sky over Oahu. Here, in the main body of the book, appearances and reality grow further and further apart —denouement culminating in disaster.

Although the John Doe Associates did not succeed in what they set out to do, their intrusion into policy formulation and decision-making in 1941 adds a new dimension to the diplomatic prelude to Pearl Harbor—a dimension that alters the historical perspective with which one of the most critical confrontations of the twentieth century must be viewed. The John Doe venture also reaches into the present and the future. It is not merely something that happened a generation ago in the Japanese-American arena of high politics; it is an experience of the past that will remain relevant to the human condition as long as international rivalries are a basic concern and private efforts for peace an irresistible temptation.

R.J.C.B.

Contents

PART FOUR. DISASTER

The John Doe Associates

The acts and decisions of statesmanship will seldom be found entirely intelligible if viewed apart from the immediate context of time and circumstance—information, associates, pressures, prejudices, impulses, and momentary necessities—in which they occur. . . . There is none who understands fully the stuff of which international affairs are made, none whose mind can embrace and calculate all its complexities, none who is not being constantly surprised by the turns it actually takes.

GEORGE F. KENNAN, *Russia Leaves the War*

Most political action can be summed up as the business of encountering, grappling with, and resolving or evading a series of more or less difficult dilemmas. . . . It is seldom a case of choice between good and bad, or right and wrong, but between things that are partly desirable and partly undesirable, and there is no easy way of weighing the relative advantages. . . . If people generally understood that this type of perplexity is the normal daily fare of statesmen, they would perhaps be more charitable in their judgments about them.

FREDERICK S. DUNN, *Peace-Making and the Settlement with Japan*

General Marshall used to say that the rarest gift the gods ever give to man is the capacity for decision. At the top there are no easy choices. All are between evils, the consequences of which are hard to judge.

DEAN ACHESON, *Present at the Creation*

"In the Midst of Swift Happenings"

I N THE NEWS of the week that began on Monday, January 20, 1941, the inauguration of Franklin Delano Roosevelt for an unprecedented third term captures the eye of the reader and his imagination. Even a hasty review of the press reveals the context of the times—a context of growing public concern over international affairs and problems of foreign policy. Stories of every description, long and short, significant and insignificant, fill the neat rows of type into which they were once ushered to help convey to the man-in-the-street a sense of what was happening in the world: Wendell L. Willkie and Joseph P. Kennedy ... A Nazi flag in San Francisco ... Air raid tests in the New York–New England area ... Developments in Europe and the Mediterranean ... A "pioneer of the clouds" afflicted with the "will to lose" ... And finally, but by no means least, some disturbing dispatches from far-off Japan.

Seen in retrospect and taken in at a glance, these items impart a definite mood to the week in which FDR undertook to lead the nation, God willing, for another four years. It is a mood that illuminates the atmosphere prevailing in the United States as 1941, which was to culminate in war for the American people, got under way.

Willkie and Kennedy (the defeated Republican candidate for President and the Administration's retiring ambassador to Great Britain) had made headlines over the weekend and were to remain in the news for several days thereafter. In addressing themselves to H.R. 1776, the Lend-Lease Bill then before Congress, they had provided an interesting bird's-eye view of the American political process.

In the face of mounting opposition to the bill among some Republicans, Willkie had surprised an audience in New York by urging his party's representatives in Washington to refrain from action that would render America or its Chief Executive impotent to preserve liberty in Britain. The American way of life could not be preserved, Willkie argued, if Britain fell.

Kennedy, on the other hand, had come out against passage of the bill as it then stood. In a nationwide broadcast he had expressed views that ran counter to the position of the President whose reelection he had only recently supported.

American defense needs should come first, Kennedy had declared; after that, aid to Britain, but this aid must not go to the point where war became inevitable: "It is said that we cannot exist in a world where totalitarianism rules. I grant you it is a terrible future to contemplate. But why should anyone think that our getting into a war would preserve our ideals, a war which would then practically leave Russia alone outside the war area getting stronger while the rest of the world approached exhaustion?"*

Despite his dissatisfaction with the bill, Kennedy had stopped short of offering any specific recommendations. In England there was a sigh of relief. The Ambassador's speech, which had been awaited there with some misgivings, had proved to be nothing more than "a damp squib."

The Italian Foreign Office news service, Aroi, offered a rather different interpretation. Assessing both the speech and Kennedy's subsequent Congressional testimony, Aroi twisted everything to Axis advantage, its gloating praise of the Ambassador adding gloss to the concoction.

According to Aroi, Kennedy had made it plain that Britain could not win the war. He had ridiculed the "fable" that the British were fighting for freedom, democracy, Christianity, and the welfare of mankind. They were fighting to keep their empire; freedom had nothing to do with it. Aroi felt that Kennedy had spoken with "unusual" courage in a country that was "the target of the most frantic British propaganda, backed by the most powerful and hysterical financial and political forces of world Jewry."

In the Golden Gate city of San Francisco, meanwhile, an incident had occurred on the day of the Willkie-Kennedy speeches that revealed the temper of one segment of the population—a segment that was to grow, in time, into a majority of Americans. Anger had exploded when a Nazi flag was displayed outside the ninth-floor offices of what later proved to be the German Consulate General. A crowd of some 2,000 persons milling in the streets gasped, held its breath, then cheered as a small raiding party cut the swastika loose. A tug-of-war ensued, with the spectators roaring their approval as the sinister emblem, minus a corner and ripped down the middle, finally disappeared into the building.

German officials in Berlin indignantly denounced "this violation of

---

* All source and discussion notes are printed at the back of the book; they are keyed to the pages of the text to which they apply.

the most sacrosanct rights of hospitality . . . observed even in the depths of the jungle." The Nazi-controlled press alternately bleated and growled over the incident. It was called an "impudent insult" caused by the "hatred against Germany" that had been fanned by the American Government. In a front-page editorial *Der Montag* trumpeted: "Only in democratic countries can a war-mongering clique gain such influence over the masses."

Although many Americans still hoped that the United States would not have to participate in the war in Europe, the country as a whole supported the idea of greater preparedness to meet any eventuality. In his inaugural address, the President expressed his determination "to protect and to perpetuate the integrity of democracy"—to safeguard what George Washington had called in 1789 "the sacred fire of liberty."

In Washington's day the task of the people was to create and weld together a nation.

In Lincoln's day the task of the people was to preserve that nation from disruption from within.

In this day the task of the people is to save that nation and its institutions from disruption from without.

The President emphasized that Americans were living "in the midst of swift happenings." The time had come for them to take stock—to recall what their place in history had been and to rediscover what they were and what they might be.

Although the swearing-in ceremonies were bracketed with prayers for peace, the keynote of the inaugural parade was defense—tanks and planes roaring a "stirring echo to the President's words" while the nation's fighting forces marched past "in a brief thundering swirl of power."

The importance of preparedness was highlighted later in the week by other newsworthy items. Despite the shrinking of distances that had been taking place in the world, the average American still regarded himself as rather remote from the sources of danger. How a man felt in this respect, however, often depended on where he lived. The vastness of the Atlantic was some consolation, but Nazi blitzkrieg methods, submarine warfare, and surprise attacks from the air made the old idea "It can't happen here" sound rather hollow.

In apparent recognition of this, the nation's first Air Defense Command launched a four-day test in an 18,000-square-mile zone stretching "from Coney Island to Cape Cod." The object was to gain experience that would be useful in developing a warning network for the eastern seaboard and the best possible air defense system for the rest of the country.

The test had been planned as a round-the-clock affair, but the general in charge limited all activity to the hours between 6:00 A.M. and 11:00 P.M. as a concession to winter. He subsequently made public a letter from an irate chief observer in Massachusetts, who declared: "With all due respect to the Army and its officer personnel, I must say this is a hell of a time to be changing your mind." The American people had to wake up to the situation confronting them; they had to realize that their freedom and democracy could not be preserved unless they were prepared to make sacrifices; there was "too much luxury and soft living" in the country; even soldiers were being "molly-coddled"; the defeat of the French Army was an example of where this could lead. The chief observer wanted to see the original schedule restored. He was awaiting this, he wrote, "with obedience and a disgusted frame of mind."

The general's critic was being rather officious, but he did have a point. Some Americans were acting as though they were on another planet far removed from the holocaust taking place on earth. Even during this air defense exercise it was deemed proper to declare a truce at noon so that friend and foe could land for lunch. When snow and sleet brought a sudden end to all flying in midafternoon on the last day, some pilots who had been forced down short of their bases became indignant on learning that two-ton trucks would be sent to retrieve them instead of staff cars with heaters.

The fact of war may not have registered with all Americans but it was real enough in Europe and the Mediterranean. On the day of Roosevelt's inauguration the British drove more than thirty miles into Eritrea, their mobile units pursuing the retreating forces of Il Duce, the Fascist dictator in Rome.

While Kennedy was testifying before Congress, British imperial troops smashed through the defenses of the Libyan port of Tobruk, which had been under siege for a fortnight, thus adding to the troubles of the Italians, who were also finding it difficult to launch a counteroffensive in Albania against the Greeks.

Along with these developments came an announcement that Washington had lifted its "moral embargo" against the Soviet Union. The ban had been imposed in 1939 when the Russians, taking advantage of the Nonaggression Pact they had concluded with Berlin, mounted an attack on Finland that led to the bombing of civilian centers in that beleaguered country. By early 1941, however, the international situation had changed so completely that the President was prepared to reverse himself. The ending of the ban—a conciliatory move toward Moscow—left the Empire of Japan in high relief as the only nation against which the embargo still applied.

On the day Tobruk fell to the British, a revolt broke out in Rumania. Although this was quickly suppressed with the aid of the Germans, events there as elsewhere gave some hope that the Axis powers did not have matters quite so well in hand as their propaganda alleged.

And yet the war, already seventeen months old, was to last another four years—well into 1945. Indeed, even before these Axis reverses had taken place, Adolf Hitler and Benito Mussolini had secretly met at an undisclosed place presumably to map and coordinate new strategic surprises. Such conferences had usually been touted by Axis publicity as though they represented "a conjunction of Mars and Saturn," but on this occasion the news blackout was so complete that speculation darted in many directions.

*

"Which side do you want to win?" was a question not often heard in the United States in those days, but when it was put to Colonel Charles A. Lindbergh, he replied "neither side." Testifying before the House Foreign Affairs Committee during its hearings on H.R. 1776, Lindbergh propounded his belief that the conflict in Europe was simply over the balance of power; that responsibility for the war and "the causes of it" were "about evenly divided"; that "it would be better for us, and for every nation in Europe," if the fighting ended "without a conclusive victory"; and that, in his opinion, "a negotiated peace" would be in the "best interests" of the United States.

The one-time American hero—an "ex-hero" to some—ranged over many topics, speaking before the largest crowd of spectators drawn by the hearings to date. His statements touched off vigorous support from a host of admirers, who lent distortion to the scene through noisy demonstrations on behalf of their prophet.

When Lindbergh was asked whether it would be necessary for the United States "to come to a friendly agreement" with Hitler if the Germans succeeded in establishing a "New Order" in Europe, the Colonel was heartily applauded when he replied, "Somewhat the same as we have with Russia, sir." Uttering the credo of isolationism, Lindbergh declared: "I believe we can endure in this hemisphere, or on this continent, regardless of what happens abroad."

Reactions to Lindbergh's assertions ran the gamut. A Foreign Office spokesman in Berlin hailed his testimony as "courageous," saying that it called for "Hats off!" In the United States a quietly angry editor revealed that he had a question for the witness. If the opportunity arose, he wanted Lindbergh to be reminded that he had also said Americans should prepare to defend themselves. The question was "Against whom?"

Just what kind of a negotiated peace could be arranged with the Nazis holding all of the cards? What were the chances of American survival in a world in which Hitler was supreme? The *New York Times* provided some answers: German success in Europe would make of every nation west of Russia "a vassal of the German Reich"; Nazi control would embrace the Mediterranean and the resources of Africa; South America would be forced to enter into barter agreements on terms with which Americans could not compete. German success would also mean "a Japanese victory in China and Japanese hegemony over a vast Asiatic area" on which the United States depended for essential raw materials.

In an appearance before the House Foreign Affairs Committee prior to the inauguration, Secretary of State Cordell Hull had denounced Japan, Italy, and Germany for "their determination to repudiate and destroy the very foundations of a civilized world order under law and to enter upon the road of armed conquest, of subjugation of other nations, and of tyrannical rule over their victims." The American Government, according to Hull, had repeatedly tried to persuade Japan that she should develop friendly relations with all nations who believed in "orderly and peaceful processes." Japan's response was a matter of record. In September 1940 she had become the ally of Germany and Italy, thus establishing, by means of the Tripartite Pact, a Rome-Berlin-Tokyo axis. Mankind was therefore confronted, "not with regional wars or isolated conflicts, but with an organized, ruthless, and implacable movement of steadily expanding conquest." The United States could ignore this movement only at the risk of her own survival.

In Tokyo at this time, speeches in the Diet by the Premier, Prince Fumimaro Konoye, and by the Foreign Minister, Yōsuke Matsuoka, stressed Japan's firm commitment to the Axis alliance and to the "New Order" concept. The civil and military leaders of Japan clearly understood that their policy might result in war in the Pacific. Matsuoka thought that this in turn could bring about the collapse of civilization; he therefore wanted the *United States* to take steps to prevent such a catastrophe. He believed that the Axis powers would certainly achieve their goal "if only given time," and if only the *American Government* would exert every effort to forestall a collision.

Men like Matsuoka kept expecting Washington to remain "reasonable" in 1941, even though Japan's use of force in the Far East during the preceding decade had greatly aggravated the very crisis to civilization that Roosevelt and Hull were now supposed to alleviate by belatedly giving Tokyo the blank check the United States had earlier withheld.

The shape of the future could be discerned in a Cabinet decision to approve a proposal designed to encourage every family to have five children so that Japan's population, currently at the 67,000,000 mark, would reach 100,000,000 by 1960. Four objectives were announced: "First, to maintain a perpetual increase; second, to outrival other nations in the rate of increase and quality; third, to supply the military and industrial manpower required by the State; fourth, to distribute the population properly to maintain Japan's leadership in Asia."

A large number of tanks and planes would serve no useful purpose, one official said, unless there were enough men to operate them. The Japanese people had to abandon their current, "individualistic tendency to 'avoid pregnancy and enjoy their own lives only.'" This comment caught the eye of the editor of the *New York Times*, whose lead the next day was "Empire in Wonderland":

> About a generation and a half ago Japan began to take territory away from her weaker neighbors. She took Korea; then, after an interval, Manchuria; then, after another interval, the northeastern provinces of China. She is now in the fourth year of an attempt to take the rest of eastern China. The principal reason for this activity, as it is explained by the Japanese, is that the population of the Japanese islands was beginning to exceed the capacity of the islands to support them.
>
> It has now been discovered that since 1920 the Japanese birthrate has dropped from 36 a thousand to 27 a thousand—or just a little more than the American birthrate of a quarter of a century ago. A plan has therefore been set on foot in Tokyo to persuade Japanese women to have five children apiece instead of "enjoying their own lives only." The reason for this proposal, as explained by the Japanese, is that more Japanese are needed in order to occupy and administer the new conquests.
>
> Perhaps one of these explanations is valid. And perhaps the author of "Alice in Wonderland," if he were still alive, would be able to get the Mad Hatter to fit them together.

Fitting the pieces of the contemporary puzzle together was not really so difficult. Axis propagandists were performing that function all of the time. As the week of January 20 drew to a close, a periodical that spoke for the German Foreign Office issued a blast at the newly inaugurated American President, charging him with "aggression," with having "consciously and systematically poisoned relations between Germany and the United States," and with harboring "plans for Anglo-Saxon world domination." Roosevelt's only worry, according to this source, was the refusal of the Axis powers to lend themselves to his malevolent designs: "Germany, Italy, and Japan do not permit themselves to be provoked. ...They do not do him the favor of letting him play the frightened American lamb surrounded by the German-Italian-Japanese wolf...."

They refuse to relieve him of even one ounce of the responsibility for whipping up his people without reasonable grounds against three great powers."

Such tortured thoughts, a specialty of the Axis camp, nevertheless provide revealing insights. As Secretary Hull had already noted, the situation facing the American people at the beginning of 1941 did not inspire optimism. In Europe and in Asia the United States was beset by major threats to her security. Nowhere was this clearer than in the Far Eastern sector of the world, where the Japanese-American quarrel over methods and goals was showing signs of getting out of hand. Recognition of this by members of the ruling elite in Tokyo had led to the designation of a new ambassador to the United States, Admiral Kichisaburō Nomura, a hale and hearty type of simple sailor. It was hoped that his "genial personality and sincere desire for peace would miraculously change Japanese-American relations"—in short, that he would be able to charm his "old friend," the President, into a more "reasonable" frame of mind favorable to Japan.

Although Nomura had been invested by the Emperor in November 1940, the Ambassador did not leave for the United States until two months later. By that time the Japanese press was in a "gloomy mood." There seemed to be a growing realization that the Japanese-American crisis had arisen not from a single misunderstanding, which might be easily talked away, but rather from "a clash of national policies," complex in its origins and development.

The "program" Nomura was reportedly bringing with him did not suggest that he would succeed in his mission, for he had been given the task of repeating an old refrain: Tokyo's diplomacy centered on the Axis alliance; Japan must be recognized as a "stabilizing force" in the Far East; within the limitations imposed by these concepts, Japan would endeavor to improve relations with the United States.

The obstacles in the way of successful negotiation were clear enough. They were Japan's adherence to the Tripartite Pact, her continuation of the war in China, and her apparent ambition to absorb all of Southeast Asia. Nothing that the Japanese had thus far said officially, or off-the-record for that matter, provided any basis for thinking that a change in Japanese policy might be imminent.

Imagine, then, the surprise with which President Roosevelt and Secretary Hull now listened to a private evaluation to the effect that the Japanese Government was ready to move in an entirely different direction.

The setting was the President's office at the White House, the date

Thursday, January 23, 1941—the day on which Ambassador Nomura left Tokyo for Washington and Colonel Lindbergh aired his opinions on the Hill. The President's callers were two American clergymen—the distinguished Superior General of the Catholic Foreign Mission Society of America at Maryknoll, New York, Bishop James E. Walsh, and his second-in-command, Vicar General Father James M. Drought. Their meeting with the President, who was the goal of many persons with special information to report or causes to espouse, had been arranged primarily by Postmaster General Frank C. Walker—one of the most prominent Catholics in the Administration and the only other person present at the interview.

Walsh and Drought had just returned from a month-long visit to Japan during which they had looked into the effects of a recent decree requiring all Christian institutions to replace foreign executives with Japanese nationals. The visit, although brief, had broadened their understanding of the Japanese position. Drought, in particular, had learned a great deal from conversations with a number of important persons, including some influential members of the government.

Roosevelt was emphatically told by Drought that a new day was dawning. American diplomacy, economic pressure, and defense preparations had been so successful that Japan was ready to execute an about-face. An opportunity now existed to effect "a complete reversal of Japan's place within the Axis Alliance," to secure a settlement of the fighting in China, and to prevent the war in Europe from spreading to the Far East.

The civil and military authorities in Tokyo, although willing to proceed along these lines, were afraid to disclose their intentions because of the danger of assassination. Once all the arrangements had been made, however, the two sides could simultaneously propose a conference at which they would publicly announce that they had already concluded an agreement. This fait accompli would destroy the power of the extremists in Japan.

If a Japanese-American accord were not reached, Drought said, and if American pressure on Japan were maintained, the extremists would predominate. The people of Japan would then accept the Axis alliance as "their only hope," and "through emotional despair" would "rush headlong into a war with the United States." A speedy Japanese-American settlement, on the other hand, might dissuade the Germans from attempting an invasion of England. A settlement would also be of great benefit to the Chinese. If handled properly, it would eliminate the Soviet Union as a potential ally of Germany in China.

The steps to be taken toward these goals had to be kept secret, Drought warned. Piecemeal revelation would give pressure groups a chance to misrepresent the objective. So long as this did not happen, the President would be able to achieve what the Department of State and the Forcign Office of Japan could not possibly accomplish: a guaranteed peace in the Pacific acceptable to the United States and a realignment of power that would startle American as well as world opinion. In this way, Father Drought declared, Hitler could be "rolled up politically and economically from the back door of the Far East."

To persons uninitiatcd in the complexities of international relations, this prospect might have been appealing, but Roosevelt and Hull—toughened in the school of practical experience—were not swept off their feet. They listened and asked questions but remained unconvinced. And yet they were patient and friendly; they did not retreat on the plea of "pressing commitments" or attempt in any other way to curtail the interview. The fifteen minutes originally allotted for the meeting grew into one hour and then into two, an indication, perhaps, that the President was interested.

"What the Catholic priests were telling us," Hull later noted, "was in drastic contrast to what Matsuoka and many official leaders of Japan were proclaiming to the world. . . . We could therefore view the approach of Bishop Walsh and Father Drought only with caution. But they insisted that the proposal they had outlined was acceptable to many high Japanese officials and could be agreed to in Japan. The President and I [felt that] we could not afford to neglect any chance to avoid a war in the Pacific. The menace of Hitlerism from across the Atlantic was sufficient to induce us to take any steps we could to keep our other flank peaceful."

Roosevelt and Hull wanted to learn, first of all, what Ambassador Nomura had to offer. At the same time, they could see no harm in letting Walsh and Drought maintain contact "on a purely private basis" with the Japanese with whom they had been in touch. In this way the two clergymen might be able "to reduce to writing" what the Japanese had in mind.

Through this discreet but favorable response, Roosevelt and Hull unwittingly gave impetus to an extraordinary private endeavor for peace that was to produce diplomatic ramifications of a magnitude unimagined at the time. It was an endeavor that unobtrusively permeated the endless conversations the Secretary of State held with the Japanese Ambassador through the remainder of 1941, repeatedly impinging upon their painstaking search for a settlement capable of banishing, for years to come, the burgeoning danger of war in the Pacific.

PART ONE

APPEARANCES

CHAPTER ONE

A Bid for a Friendly Settlement

THREE DAYS AFTER being told that Hitler could be rolled up politically and economically from the back door of the Far East, the President sent Secretary Hull a brief note marked Personal: "Here is the memorandum that was handed to us the other day by the Reverend Bishop. What do you think we should do?"

The "Strictly Confidential Memo" appended to this note repeated in writing many of the points Walsh and Drought had made orally at the White House on January 23. It contained the conclusions they had drawn from conversations with some of the highest civil and military leaders of Japan. It also contained the text of an "Agreement" outlining the legal, political, and economic bases on which the United States and Japan could reach an understanding.

The "Conservative authorities" in Tokyo, the memo declared, needed support. If they could win a "safe" position for their country through diplomacy, public opinion would restore them to "complete control." Premier Konoye had said, "I am riding the horses until I can stop them." Foreign Minister Matsuoka had been even more outspoken: "To call the present war in China a Holy War is a blasphemy. . . . To call the Treaty with Wang Ching-Wei an equal treaty is a lie."*

The next step was up to the President. If he would send a personal representative to Tokyo, a settlement could be reached with "the controlling elements in Japan, including the Emperor." This settlement "would bring some order in the Far East" and would make it possible for Mr. Roosevelt "to immunize the Pacific for at least three years." If the President decided to pursue the matter, Bishop Walsh and Father Drought "would be willing to cooperate with his representative for the

---

* The reference here is to various arrangements concluded with a puppet regime that had been established at Nanking under Japanese auspices by Wang Ching-wei (a defector from Chungking, the seat of the Nationalist Government of China headed by Chiang Kai-shek).

safeguarding of the Japanese officials, and the verification of their statements."

Before the Secretary of State had an opportunity to respond to the President's question of January 26, "What do you think we should do?," the White House forwarded a letter that Walsh had sent to Walker on the twenty-seventh. This letter reported that a cable had just been received at Maryknoll indicating the Japanese Government was "ready to send a trusted representative to discuss the terms of a projected agreement."

Walsh and Drought still felt that the President should dispatch his own emissary to Japan, but they were very much encouraged by Tokyo's decision. "Of even more significance," Walsh wrote, "is the fact that the most recent statements from ———— are *exactly* in accordance with the plan which we worked out with those people before leaving their country. Their very statements are intended to indicate their consent. The harsh talk is for home consumption, lest that Government be supplanted by a group of Extremists. A bid for friendly settlement is being clearly made."

Walsh thought that Drought should "remain on call" in Washington for "a week or so" in order to keep the record straight and place matters in proper perspective. "Father Drought knows their plan," Walsh advised Walker, "and could interpret the day-to-day developments accordingly; whereas, their moves may otherwise puzzle, or completely deceive, anyone not previously informed of their true character."

This time, the President's covering note to Hull, marked Private and Confidential, consisted of a single sentence: "What should I do next?"

Replies to both queries were given on February 5 in three separate State Department memoranda. The first and shortest of these was drafted by Stanley K. Hornbeck, an adviser on political relations, who posed a very pertinent question: "Inasmuch as the Japanese Government is sending a new Ambassador, who is due to arrive here shortly, would it not seem desirable to await arrival of and contact with that Ambassador before taking any action regarding any suggestions offered through indirect channels?"

The other two memoranda were written by the chief of the Division of Far Eastern Affairs, Maxwell M. Hamilton. They were approved by Hornbeck and passed along to the President by Hull as representing his own views. "It seems clear," the White House was told, "that Japan's military leaders are bent on conquest—just as are Germany's. They demand that this country make concessions: that we give up principles, rights, interests: that we stand aside while Japan proceeds by force to subjugate neighboring areas and . . . in partnership with Germany, contributes to the establishing of a new 'world order': even that we facilitate their efforts by promising to give them financial assistance for the exploitation of areas which they expect to conquer."

Anyone who wished to think in conciliatory terms had to bear in mind that the people of China were fighting for their very existence. If they lost, Japan would in all probability become an ever greater menace to the United States. If American mediation were to help extricate Japan from China, "the likelihood would be that Japan would extend and accelerate her aggressions" to the resource-rich areas of Southeast Asia "rather than that Japan would change her present course of aggression to one of peaceful procedures."

The State Department frankly questioned the feasibility of taking any action at the moment along the lines suggested by Walsh and Drought, for there seemed to be very little chance that the Japanese would accept, in good faith, an "Agreement" of the type proposed. An effort had been made, the President was told, to consider the "Agreement" in its broad aspects, to evaluate the ideas underlying the plan, and to appraise it in perspective. A number of items were "definitely not practicable" as they stood. It seemed doubtful that the Japanese Government would undertake some of the commitments outlined in the "Agreement" or consent to a rephrasing of others that would make them acceptable to the United States or China.

One problem would be the Japanese desire to fight communism in Asia. The Chinese had consistently interpreted this as "merely a mask" for Japanese military occupation of their country. The failure of Japan in the past to honor contractual obligations had caused the Chinese to insist that they could not enter into negotiations with Japan without first being shown evidence of her good faith. The evidence they wanted was the withdrawal of Japanese troops from China. "It may be assumed," Hull informed FDR, "that this specification on the part of the Chinese need not be regarded as absolute: a complete withdrawal by Japan of her forces need not be regarded as the condition precedent; but some clear indication of a change of heart and of intention on Japan's part would seem to be a *sine qua non.*"

The State Department "would not wish to be doctrinaire" regarding some of the difficulties, but all aspects of the matter had to be considered. The one prerequisite for any agreement was that Japan forsake the course of conquest she had been following since 1931.

The best policy now, the Department felt, would be to await the arrival of Nomura, who was expected within a week. The President should not resort to "other agents and channels" before talking with the Admiral. Since it was also possible to work through Joseph C. Grew, the American ambassador in Tokyo, there was even less reason to use private avenues of approach of an unknown character.

Nomura might have something to offer. At any rate, he should be given a careful hearing. Once this had been done, an effort could be made to convince him that Japan ought to move in a different direction for her own good. "Should we succeed in convincing him," Hull concluded, "the next question will be can he convince his own Government and people?"

The man on whom the Secretary's attention was now focused had in the meantime been making his way across the Pacific on board the *Kamakura-maru*. As Nomura's ship approached Hawaii, two American destroyers escorted her into port—a gesture of respect toward a fellow officer who was well known within the top echelons of the U.S. Navy.

The welcome given to Nomura in San Francisco was even more impressive than the one he had received at Honolulu—leaving him in good spirits and "radiating confidence that the United States and Japan would remain at peace." Despite a busy schedule, the Ambassador spent more than an hour alone with an old Navy friend, Captain Ellis M. Zacharias, who was later to achieve prominence as an intelligence/propaganda expert on Japan. The meeting had been arranged by Zacharias in an effort to determine the purpose behind Nomura's mission and "to explore, if possible, the latitude which might be in his hands."

After a frank exchange, Zacharias concluded that Japan already regretted being a partner of Hitler and Mussolini. There had been a sharp division of opinion over the Tripartite Pact, Nomura told Zacharias, with only a slight balance of influence in its favor. The mistake had now been realized, but to cancel the alliance would be practically impossible; it would have to die a natural death.

Before talking with Nomura, Zacharias had toyed with the idea that the Admiral was being sent to the United States to "rock us to sleep" while Japanese military forces plunged into Southeast Asia. After the meeting, however, Zacharias rejected this completely. Nomura's mission was to find the best bargain available. He was going to try to prevent the United States from placing an embargo on the oil and other strategic materials that Japan was still obtaining from American suppliers. He was also going to try to dissuade the United States from extending further aid to Chiang Kai-shek. If Nomura proved unsuccessful, he would then explore other means of bringing about peace in China. War between Japan and the United States could be avoided, Zacharias felt, if Nomura were given a "sufficient basis" for an approach to the leaders of Japan.

Zacharias forwarded these judgments to Admiral Harold R. Stark, the chief of naval operations. Stark found the Captain's report so "intensely interesting and illuminating" that he sent the original to the President and earmarked a copy for Secretary Hull. Thus one more item was added to the record, including what amounted to a difference of opinion between the Japanese Ambassador, on the one hand, and Bishop Walsh and Father Drought, on the other, over the chances of doing something about the Tripartite Pact.

*

In departing from San Francisco Nomura left behind the thought that he was undertaking his diplomatic duties with "great hope." A large man, plain and sincere, the Admiral easily made a good impression. Veteran correspondent Hugh Byas, who had interviewed him in Tokyo and whose report now appeared in the *New York Times*, described him as a "straightforward fellow."

Brought up in a rural background, the sixty-three-year-old Nomura had first visited the United States in 1899 as a midshipman on a training cruise. During World War I he had served as Japan's naval attaché in Washington; there he had become acquainted with a number of important men, including Woodrow Wilson's Assistant Secretary of the Navy, Franklin D. Roosevelt.

Unlike Foreign Minister Matsuoka, whose eloquence Byas likened to the rolling of the Mississippi, Nomura was not a monologist. He was rather given to ruminating silences and to short answers delivered with a simplicity that was quite appealing. He refused to further the illusion that a "six-footer able to inspire trust and confidence" could perform miracles by exercising "personal magnetism."

Matsuoka and the Japanese press were insisting that the choice of a "sympathetic" ambassador was "a grand gesture"; it should convince the American people that Japan did not want war. But the Tripartite Pact, Byas argued, "was no gesture; it was national policy." Its avowed purpose was to keep the struggle in Europe from spreading to the Pacific, but no one in Japan was even pretending that Washington would ever be responsible for such a catastrophe. It was the Japanese Government that threatened to launch hostilities in the Pacific if the United States intervened in Europe. Peace in the Far East had been made to depend upon something that might happen in the Atlantic. "Prince Konoye and Mr. Matsuoka," Byas wrote, "have tied the destiny of East Asia to that of Germany."

*

Public reactions to Nomura had reportedly grown colder as he had traveled east, but his first contacts in Washington were warm and friendly. The Ambassador's initial call on the Secretary of State established a record for brevity, but the shortness of the interview, which lasted exactly four minutes, cannot be attributed to any hostility on Hull's part. The visit was a purely formal one during which Nomura may have felt constrained by the knowledge that he had not as yet handed his credentials to the President. This ceremony took place two days later, on Friday, February 14, with Hull personally doing the honors that were normally handled by the chief of protocol.

Through the usual medium of memoranda Hull had already sent several suggestions to the White House outlining what the President might say to the Ambassador. The Secretary's main thought was to leave the diplomatic door open for a full and frank examination of "points of divergence" between the two countries in the hope that Nomura would walk through the open door. This did not mean, however, that Hull was ready to enter into negotiations—a stage that could be reached only much later, after preliminary conversations had cleared up a number of issues.

As to the "tone" to be employed, Hull thought it might be "advisable ... to 'speak softly' (carefully avoiding any word that might to a wishful thinker imply that we would consider offers of 'compromise')." At the same time, the fact of American determination should be underscored by action in the Pacific that would provide "new glimpses of diplomatic, economic, and naval 'big sticks.' "

Most of Hull's advice was discernible in the President's remarks on February 14, but there were some distinctive personal touches—the whole thing being carried off with FDR's usual aplomb. He greeted Nomura with great cordiality, saying that he did not look any the worse for wear despite the intervening years and the unfortunate loss of an eye.

It was as clear as could be, the President declared, that Japanese-American relations were deteriorating. The American people were "thoroughly and seriously concerned and to a more or less increasing extent" over the course Japan was following—specifically, Japan's movement southward and her alliance with the European Axis. The day might come when some incident like the sinking of the *Maine* or the attack on the *Panay* could easily result in a sudden clamor of American sentiment against the perpetrators of the deed, "regardless of the exact facts or details as to the cause."*

The President was therefore very glad (and he mentioned this several times) that Japan was now to be represented by Admiral Nomura so "that the two of them could in the friendliest and frankest manner talk out to the best advantage of both countries ways and means of dealing with such [inflammatory] circumstances and with methods to avoid them." He hoped Nomura would also be willing to go over the last four or five years of Japanese-American relations with Hull. By ascertaining when and how "points of divergence" had developed, the Secretary and the Ambassador might be able to come up with ideas that would eliminate further friction. After all, the President said (repeating the words with emphasis), *there is plenty of room in the Pacific for everyone.*

Throughout these remarks Hull watched Nomura closely to gauge his reaction. The Ambassador did a lot of bowing as though he agreed with everything that was being said, but he was obviously not at home in the English language. He therefore kept his own remarks to a minimum, commenting briefly, and in a general way, "about the existence of unsatisfactory relations, the need for their improvement, and his every disposition to say and do anything possible to that end."

In essence this was the response Hull received again several weeks later, Nomura indicating that he was willing to review Japanese-American relations but not specifying when or with whom he would like to do so. Although Hull did not realize this at the time, Nomura had by then already fallen under the influence of the "John Doe Associates"— a sobriquet subsequently coined by Stanley Hornbeck to describe a group of Japanese individuals, of not fully revealed identity or authority, who were trying to capture the attention of the American Government by employing Bishop Walsh and Father Drought as their spokesmen.

John Doe and his friends were not the only persons who wanted to influence policy in the Pacific. There were others—both Japanese and Americans—who importuned the State Department from time to time

---

* The sinking of the U.S.S. *Maine* in Havana harbor in 1898 provided the spark that touched off the Spanish-American War. On December 12, 1937, the gunboat *Panay*, assigned to the Yangtze Patrol of the U.S. Asiatic Fleet, was bombed by Japanese planes and sunk, with colors flying, twenty-seven miles above Nanking while evacuating American diplomatic personnel from the doomed city.

or who tried to reach the White House with one scheme or another. None of these potential "competitors," however, possessed the organization, connections, persistence, and imagination that gave the John Doe Associates their great advantage. It is consequently not surprising that it was to be the John Doe bid for a friendly settlement, rather than anything Nomura had to offer, that would determine the course of Japanese-American diplomacy in the months ahead.

CHAPTER TWO

Envoys Extraordinary in Washington

I N A LETTER written a few days after Bishop Walsh and Father Drought had talked with the President in January, Frank Walker had indicated that he had been "only too happy" to lend himself, "even though in small fashion," to the "very important mission" that had brought the two Maryknollers to the nation's capital. "I will always be anxious to be of help to you," Walker had promised. "Do not hesitate to call at any time."

Now, one month later, on Friday, February 28, 1941, Walsh and Drought were back in town with news that the Postmaster General promptly conveyed to the Secretary of State and to the President. The contact with Hull was by telephone, but Walker went personally to the White House, carrying a John Doe memorandum to the effect that "a Plenipotentiary Representative of the Japanese Government" had arrived in Washington "empowered to negotiate concrete terms for a settlement of all outstanding Far Eastern questions vis-à-vis the United States."

According to this memorandum, the Japanese were ready "to invite the President ... personally to initiate mediation" of the Sino-Japanese conflict. They were also prepared to "nullify" their participation in the Axis alliance "by a refusal to send any supplies to Germany and by the assumption of an obligation to keep the Germans out of the Far East, by military force, if necessary." John Doe hoped the President would appoint a personal representative immediately "to work out, privately, with the Japanese Plenipotentiary, a draft of agreement." The Japanese Government would then "indicate" its approval of the terms. As soon as this had been done, the President "could call a public conference (preferably at Tokyo)" to ratify the agreement that had "really been consummated previously."

In his office at the State Department, Stanley Hornbeck reacted with a surge of questions as he read the memorandum the Postmaster General had carried to the White House on February 28. Had Hornbeck been the President or the Secretary of State, he would have put the matter squarely to "Mr. F. W.": Who is this Plenipotentiary Representative?, Hornbeck would have asked. What is his name? Whom does he represent? Is he in Washington with the knowledge and approval of the Japanese Ambassador?

The message delivered by Walker contained a fundamental weakness in Hornbeck's opinion; the "proposers" were not taking a realistic view of the current policies and practices of Japan or of the policies, objectives, and practices of the United States. The procedure they were advocating was simply "not adapted to the facts of the situation."

What was the issue between Japan and China that these people wanted the President to mediate? As far as Hornbeck was concerned, the issue was not legal or economic; it was political: who was to have control in China, the *Japanese* or the *Chinese*?

What was the issue between Japan and the United States? Hornbeck believed it to be force and conquest versus legitimate rights and orderly processes. It was an issue, he implied, that had been created by Japan's unilateral actions; it could be resolved by Japan "on her own initiative, without any agreement with anybody."

Where in Japan did effective authority lie? It rested with the leaders of the military element. Any settlement concluded with Japan would have to satisfy those leaders. But if *they* were satisfied, what would the American people say?

Hornbeck had the habit of asking questions to which he did not always supply answers, but when he left a point in midair the logic of the situation acted with the force of gravity in bringing it down to earth. In this instance he was saying in effect, "First things first." A diplomatic undertaking that did not have the support of the Japanese military was unlikely to reach the "Agreement" stage. If by some chance it did, stiff resistance might develop within the United States Senate unless a significant change in Japanese policy provided the reassurance needed to garner votes for ratification.

The Far Eastern imbroglio was assuming alarming proportions. Diplomacy might be able to map a detour around the danger of war, but only long and arduous negotiations could determine a route acceptable to all the parties concerned. No useful purpose would be served by indulging in fanciful schemes offered by outsiders. It would be far better, Hornbeck thought, to let Ambassador Nomura have his say, whatever that might be.

John Doe, on the other hand, was becoming impatient. On Tuesday,

March 4, Walsh and Drought again got in touch with the Postmaster General. He in turn arranged to call on Secretary Hull later in the day. The next evening Walker received a new memorandum consisting of thirteen "Principal Items" that John Doe and his colleagues wanted to "discuss and reach agreement upon." This document, which was passed to Hull on March 6, was a conglomeration in every sense of the word. It was the product of a mind whose thoughts occasionally outran their author's ability to express what he wished to say.

The overall effect was that of a shotgun blast—the target was covered with holes but the shooting was indiscriminate. Since it showed no signs of abating, however, the composition of the John Doe group now became a subject of greater interest than it had previously been.

On March 6, the day on which the "Principal Items" memorandum was delivered to Hull, Hornbeck conferred with Donald W. Smith, an assistant commercial attaché who had just returned home from Japan on emergency leave. The subject of their conversation was a letter that Smith had mailed to the Department of State from Vancouver, British Columbia, right after his ship, the *Hikawa-maru*, had put into port.

Smith had an interesting story to tell about a fellow passenger named Tadao Wikawa.* Before leaving Japan in mid-February, Smith had stopped by the Tokyo branch of the National City Bank of New York. The manager there had talked to him about a Mr. Wikawa who had been in the bank earlier and who, like Smith, was headed for Washington. The manager had gotten the impression that there was something politically important about Wikawa's trip. Currency and travel restrictions being what they were, he could hardly be going to the United States for reasons of health or pleasure.

After mulling the matter over for a while, Smith had decided to see what he could find out about Wikawa by engaging him in conversation during the long voyage across the Pacific. The picture that had emerged was rather interesting: Wikawa was a man in his mid-forties, "apparently a sincere and ardent Christian ... believed to be married to an American woman"; he had used his desire to see his daughter, who was currently attending Columbia University, as his "reason" for visiting the United States; he himself had once worked in New York as an assistant to the Japanese financial commissioner; later he had served in the Finance Ministry in Tokyo; more recently he had been the chief executive officer of the Central Bank of Co-operative Societies, "the second largest depository in Japan."

* The spelling Ikawa is also possible; the initial vowel should be pronounced with the value of the "e" in "edict."

Even more significant was Wikawa's revelation that he was supposed to prepare, in some way, for the arrival of a Colonel Hideo Iwakuro, whom he described as a "driving force" in the Japanese Army—the one man who could exercise control over its various elements. It was anticipated that Iwakuro would leave Japan early in March, that Wikawa would meet him in San Francisco on or about March 20, and that the two of them would then travel together across the country, with stopovers along the way.

Iwakuro's purpose in visiting the United States remained somewhat obscure, but word had in the meantime reached the Department from Grew that a colonel by the name of Iwakuro—an officer who enjoyed "the complete confidence of the Minister of War"—was being dispatched to Washington as a "special adviser" to Nomura.

In chatting with Smith, Wikawa had indicated that Iwakuro would probably bring concrete proposals from the Japanese Army touching on relations with the United States. It seemed that both men would work closely with Nomura, and that they would stay in Washington for about six months.

Wikawa himself had apparently been encouraged to travel to the United States by certain Americans with whom he was on friendly terms, but when Smith had tried to find out who they might be Wikawa had dodged the question. All he would say was, "The present Administration has its Colonel House."*

In a round-table discussion held on board ship, Wikawa had plumped for diplomacy, arguing that all problems outstanding between Japan and the United States could be solved by this means. Privately, however, he had told Smith that if Iwakuro's mission failed there would be no hope of reaching an amicable settlement.

*

The information that Hornbeck had obtained from talking to Smith and from reading his letter could mean only one thing: the "Plenipotentiary Representative" to whom reference had been made in the John Doe memorandum of February 28 and the bank executive to whom Smith had devoted so much attention during the voyage of the *Hikawamaru* from Yokohama to Vancouver must be one and the same man.

Confirmation of this was not long in coming. On Friday, March 7, the Postmaster General forwarded a new memorandum that he had just received from Father Drought. Without the slightest explanation of any kind, this memorandum referred to "the authority of Mr. Wikawa" as

---

* Woodrow Wilson's close friend and adviser, Edward M. House.

though his position and his right to speak for the Japanese Government were clearly established and unassailable facts.

"It would be imperilling, as well as useless," the State Department was told, "to project, at this time, progressive diplomatic conversations with members of the Japanese Embassy." Premier Konoye, the Privy Council, and the leaders of the Army and Navy had all "agreed with the Emperor" on "a conditional reversal of policy." If this were to become known, however, before any real progress had been made, some of these men might be "assassinated as 'traitors' and their contemplated agreement with the United States nullified."

The "inner Cabinet group with the Army and Navy leaders" had already decided on "a formula for relinquishing active participation in the Axis Alliance," but "neither this central fact nor any other major items of policy" had been communicated to Ambassador Nomura or his second-in-command, Minister-Counselor Kaname Wakasugi. Nomura had not even been told by his government that Hitler had been informed within the last few days of "the Japanese intention 'to shake hands with the United States.'" The American Government should consequently not waste its time, or endanger the contemplated settlement, by getting involved with the Japanese Embassy.

In submitting this advice on March 7, John Doe knew that Secretary Hull was scheduled to meet with Ambassador Nomura the next day. John Doe also knew that he could not prevent this meeting from taking place. His purpose at this moment, therefore, was to isolate the Japanese Embassy (though not necessarily the Ambassador) in order to keep the Foreign Office "clique" from interfering in an effort for peace that was to be conducted outside regular channels and on a level more rarefied than the one at which the career men usually operated.

Hornbeck, on the other hand, wanted Hull to confer only with the Japanese Ambassador or with a high-ranking member of his staff; under no circumstances should the Secretary run the risk of talking with private persons of undetermined authority.

This was a view shared by Maxwell Hamilton. Both men wanted the game of diplomacy to begin in earnest, on a professional level, and in accordance with traditional rules of procedure. They felt that there should be no sign of "perplexity, uneasiness, apprehension, or eagerness" on the part of the American Government. They wanted Hull to play diplomatic poker by not disclosing his position regarding any proposals Nomura might put forward. If the Ambassador raised the question of "a negotiation," a vague but encouraging reply would suffice. This would afford time to develop an appropriate response.

Hull probably did not need this advice. He was a man "given to sifting a difference into its smallest particles; to enduring a strained situation long. And all the while, and every hour, subtly he tugged at the cords of trouble so that it might unravel as he wanted. . . . Years of Senate Committee hearings had trained him to endure prolonged and watchful talk. A viscosity of speech covered, as those who dealt with him long enough found out, insight and set purpose."

The Secretary of State was going to be more than a match for Admiral Nomura and the John Doe Associates.

*

Three weeks had now passed since the President had urged the Japanese Ambassador to reexamine, with Hull, every important phase of Japanese-American relations so that ways and means could be found of bringing about an improvement. Instead of acting on this invitation, Nomura had stayed away from the State Department. It was his belief that nothing was to be gained by indiscriminate haste. Minister Wakasugi agreed with the Ambassador in this regard.

Since John Doe did not want the Japanese Embassy to interfere with what he was secretly planning, he should have been pleased that Nomura and Wakasugi were acting so cautiously. Instead, he was distressed, for he knew that sooner or later the John Doe Associates would have to make use of Nomura to achieve their goals. If the State Department remained adamant—refusing to deal with anyone but Japan's officially accredited envoy—Nomura's participation would be essential. Even if the Department proved to be pliable, having Nomura play a more active role would be advantageous. If difficulties developed, his powers of persuasion—on both sides—might spell the difference between success and failure. A too-meddlesome Nomura would be bad, but a too-casual Nomura would not be any better.

The Ambassador's relaxed attitude, which was a matter of concern to John Doe, was a distinctive part of Nomura's charm. His public and private statements, although unremarkable for the most part, may nevertheless be compared to a cool and refreshing breeze suddenly felt in an arid atmosphere. While Foreign Minister Matsuoka and others in Japan were making matters worse with tough-tongued pronouncements, Nomura was creating a good impression by being reasonable in what he said. Only much later would it become apparent that the Japanese Ambassador to the United States spoke more for himself than for the government he supposedly represented.

Secretary Hull was prepared to take up the subject of Japanese-

American relations with Nomura at any time, but Hull felt that the prospects for a settlement were far from encouraging. As he saw it, "there was not one chance of success in twenty or one in fifty or even one in a hundred." And yet he hoped to prevent the outbreak of war in the Pacific, and so did the President.

They knew they would have to be patient. Even if the Japanese Government proved willing to reverse its course, Tokyo would not be able to do so abruptly. Much time would be needed for the implementation of promises made by Japan in any peaceful agreement that might emerge from the forthcoming conversations.

Hull understood this completely, but he had no idea how soon his task would be complicated by the activities of agents whose influence seemed at times to transcend the authority vested in the Japanese Ambassador. Hull expected to deal with Admiral Nomura—the envoy chosen by his government to grapple with the problems that were exacerbating Japan's relations with the United States. Hull did not know that he would also have to contend with "Plenipotentiary Representative" Wikawa and "Special Adviser" Iwakuro—a very eager two-man team coached by a zealous John Doe, who was none other than Father James M. Drought of Maryknoll, New York, the author of all of the memoranda that had been delivered by Frank Walker to date.

Had the Secretary of State been able to see into the future, he might have been even more pessimistic in calculating the chances of achieving success. But Hull could not predict what was in store for him. The presence of Wikawa in Washington and the imminent arrival of Iwakuro from Japan indicated that there might be more to the John Doe peace effort than had at first seemed likely. So long as the State Department confined itself to dealing only with Ambassador Nomura, Hull was willing to let Walsh and Drought submit, through Walker, whatever the John Doe Associates had to offer. Perhaps something might come of it after all. In the meantime, despite the unfavorable odds that he had projected, Hull was determined to devote his own energies to the laborious task of unraveling the "cords of trouble" in which the United States and Japan had by now become dangerously ensnarled.

CHAPTER THREE

"The End of the Axis Alliance! Alleluia!"

T HE HULL-NOMURA conversations that were ultimately to provide an exhaustive record of American policy toward Japan in the year 1941 began in an atmosphere of mystery. The first encounter took place on Saturday, March 8, in the study of Hull's apartment at the Carlton Hotel, to which Nomura repaired as inconspicuously as he could, using a back staircase to the proper floor.

The rendezvous had been set up by an "indirect arrangement" based on "equal and joint initiative." Since there had been some uncertainty on both sides, each man was pleased to find that everything had gone according to plan. From the Ambassador's response to his warm greeting, the Secretary of State gathered that Nomura had been anxious to have a meeting but had not wanted to appear to be making the first move.

The ensuing conversation proved to be rather one-sided. At the very outset Hull referred to the John Doe Associates, although not by that name. At all times, he said, most countries had some fine, responsible, capable citizens who tried earnestly and patriotically to encourage better relations between nations. In the present case he deeply appreciated what "these good people" were endeavoring to do and had sent word to them to that effect. He had also informed them, however, that he could not deal with them personally unless the Ambassador took the initiative in this regard, and also the responsibility. Hull "made this very definite" so that there could be no misunderstanding, repeating the point more than once, but Nomura merely bowed in reply. Hull consequently concluded that his meaning was clear.

At ease in his own language and never at a loss for words, the Secretary of State assumed the aspect of a man who was trying to be both judge and prosecutor in a courtroom in which later generations would sit as the jury. In the role of judge, Hull asked questions that still demanded answers, even though each side had already supplied its own version of what those answers should be. In the role of prosecutor, Hull insinuated the conclusions he had drawn from the evidence at hand, concrete and circumstantial. As judge and prosecutor combined, Hull seemed to personify the present looking at the past but thinking of the future.

He called Nomura's attention to the terms of the Tripartite Pact and to the public declarations of Hitler, Matsuoka, and other high authorities to the effect that Germany and Japan were out to establish a New Order for the entire world. The Ambassador, Hull said, might place whatever interpretation he wished on such utterances and on current military activities in harmony with them. The fact was that the American people, who had been complacent for so long, had recently become thoroughly aroused as a result of what they saw happening around them.

Nomura tried to convince the Secretary that everything would be all right in the case of Japan, but in his eight years as head of the State Department Hull had listened to assurances of this type ad infinitum. They had often been delivered with conviction by sincere men, and yet time and again the Japanese Army had revealed its intransigence by committing some new outrage or by persisting in some current perversity. Hull therefore replied with emphasis, trying to kindle an awareness in Nomura of the truth of the situation and of the workings of the American mind.

With Japanese military forces clambering all over China, with Japanese troops and ships and aircraft operating as far south as French Indochina and Thailand, accompanied by such threatening declarations as Japanese statesmen were in the habit of making week after week, nations that were vitally interested in seeing world conquest and barbaric methods of government brought to a halt could not but become increasingly concerned. If Japan could prove that she intended in good faith to abandon expansion through force, all would be well. Nothing would be gained, however, if Japan's military leaders were to make new avowals now only to break them later on, as they had so frequently done in the past.

As the meeting progressed, Hull discovered that Nomura had little to contribute. He was ill-prepared for the kind of talk that was essential to a full exposure of the many issues that required settlement by mutual agreement. In the two hours or more that he spent with Hull, Nomura at no time promised that his government would take steps to halt its program of expansion in Asia while discussion proceeded in Washington. And yet, how could the projected conversations serve any purpose if they were to take place against a background of continuing preparations for a Japanese offensive southward?

On the other major issues—the war in China and the alliance with

Germany and Italy—Hull learned nothing of value. Whatever Nomura personally thought about these matters—whatever he knew of his government's attitude toward them—he kept to himself.

The inconclusive nature of the tête-à-tête at the Carlton seemed to bear out the predictions contained in the John Doe memorandum of March 7. The Japanese Ambassador, according to Drought, had not been informed by his government that a "conditional reversal of policy" had taken place following his departure from Tokyo; it would be "imperilling as well as useless" to enter into negotiations with a man who did not know what was going on; it would be far better to entrust everything to the John Doe Associates.

Drought's arguments had failed to make an impression at the State Department, but he did not feel discouraged. From Washington he traveled to New York, checking into the Berkshire Hotel with Tadao Wikawa. Through a special arrangement with the manager, they could be reached only by number and not by name: PLaza 3-5800, Room 1812. The net result of their stay in New York was a new memorandum that Drought gave to the Postmaster General for transmission to the President and the Secretary of State.

Hull might have gloomy thoughts about the chances of settling American differences with Japan. Hornbeck might reinforce his chief by demanding proof of the pudding before the eating—who, when, where, what, and why. Yet here were Drought and Wikawa looking forward with great expectations to the arrival of an Imperial Army colonel who allegedly held the key to everything.

According to Drought, Iwakuro would be able to offer the latest information on Sino-Japanese relations; he would also be carrying a prescription to be used in treating the Tripartite Pact malady. He had already cabled through a friend: "Don't worry. Bringing detailed instructions Axis formula." In the meantime, Wikawa had given his full backing to the "Berkshire" memorandum; he had read it and agreed to it "with the stipulation that it must remain *absolutely confidential* to [Walker] and the two other persons thus far concerned [Roosevelt and Hull]."

But the matter was not quite so simple, for the delivery of the new memorandum to the State Department coincided with the news of Matsuoka's imminent departure for Europe on a junket of dubious purpose—a pilgrimage to Berlin and Rome, with Moscow thrown in for good measure. How could the Foreign Minister's determination to pay his respects to Hitler and Mussolini be reconciled with John Doe's contention that the Japanese Government was prepared to "substitute" the United States for Germany, to "nullify" Japan's role in the Axis, and to enter into a "mutual pledge of peace" with the American Government that would effectively replace the Tripartite Pact?

These assertions had appeared in memoranda submitted by Drought on January 23, February 28, and March 5. On March 7 he had written that the authorities in Tokyo had decided on "a formula for relinquishing active participation" in the alliance with the European dictatorships. None of this jibed with Matsuoka's forthcoming trip, which was being hailed in Berlin as an important step toward strengthening Axis cooperation.

But Drought took a different position. "The journey of Foreign Minister Matsuoka," he wrote, "is interpreted as a maneuver (1) to keep the German door open and (2) to get Matsuoka out of the way so Prince Konoye himself may conveniently exercise more direct control should negotiations with the United States take place."

This explanation, which had been supplied by Wikawa, fitted in with a warning from Nomura that fifth columnists in Japan were endeavoring to undermine his government's desire to seek a settlement in the Pacific. It also rendered Iwakuro's pre-embarkation cable more meaningful. The Colonel had said not to worry; he was bringing detailed instructions. Whatever Matsuoka might have in mind, the problem of Japan's relationship with the Axis powers would soon be solved.

＊

As the Foreign Minister was preparing to leave Tokyo to connect with the Trans-Siberian Railway on the Soviet-Manchukuo border, Father Drought began building up the momentum needed to carry his efforts for peace to the next logical stage. The final sentence of his "Berkshire" memorandum had read, "I shall keep you informed by typed memo most every day," and that is what he now proceeded to do. One report followed another in rapid succession over the next week; all were sent to Frank Walker for submission to the President and the Secretary of State.

The first of the batch (the longer of two items dated March 13) covered three and one-half, single-spaced typewritten pages consisting of seventeen paragraphs and four p.s.'s, one of which naïvely declared: "Prince Konoye has hung on the wall of his private bedroom a photograph of President Roosevelt."

The opening note was optimistic, but qualifications quickly appeared along with some alleged dangers. One of these was that Generalissimo Chiang Kai-shek would "now volubly oppose . . . for trading purposes" the de facto recognition of Manchukuo that he had "already conceded" in "secret truce terms." Despite this development, Drought claimed that "recent coded-cable communications from Tokyo" provided a basis for "increasing confidence" that an agreement could be worked out with Japan. As a means of making this possible, Konoye had been asked to instruct the Japanese Embassy in Washington not to request any more official interviews until Wikawa gave the go-ahead signal (Minister Wakasugi seemed to be "talking too much"). Drought now needed to know the thinking of the President and the Secretary of State—he needed a list of objectives that were of vital interest to the American Government.

As Hull had already told Nomura, matters of this kind could be communicated only to the Japanese Ambassador. Either Drought had not been informed of Hull's position or he had chosen to ignore the hint. Active and energetic, a man of intense personality and great dedication, he had long since developed an interest in politics and diplomacy that had taken him beyond the bounds other men might see as the frontier of his priestly duties. Although this was not Drought's first venture into the field of Far Eastern affairs, his involvement with Wikawa in pursuit of peace in the Pacific represented the greatest commitment of his career. He certainly was not going to let the "hidebound" approach of the State Department stand in his way.

In this instance Drought decided that his lengthy March 13 memorandum did not quite say all that needed saying. He therefore immediately wrote a second and much shorter "Special Memo" that served as a covering note for a "ticker report," which he described as "exactly what was predicted and communicated to you some days ago." The report was to the effect that Matsuoka, upon departing from Japan, had said that he was leaving "with an open mind" and would be willing to extend his tour to include Washington and London, if he were invited to do so. Matsuoka's chief secretary had then remarked that the best way to solve Japanese-American differences would be for the President or the Secretary of State "to meet the Foreign Minister at Hawaii and thresh out the whole problem."

To Father Drought, this report indicated that Matsuoka had belatedly realized Konoye was sending him to Berlin "to get him out of the way." The Premier did not trust the Foreign Minister. Of all the code and plain cables sent to Konoye during recent weeks (Drought declared), only one had been shown to Matsuoka. Wikawa had asked Konoye to take over the Foreign Affairs portfolio and to instruct the Japanese Embassy not to say anything to the State Department about inviting Matsuoka to Washington.

According to Drought, Minister Wakasugi was again providing cause for concern. He claimed to be "preparing business for the U.S. State Department" when in fact he knew "very little" at all about the "real intentions" of his government.

Who did know what the leaders in Tokyo were planning? The answer is implicit: Iwakuro, Wikawa, and Drought.

This was the message on March 13 and had been the message all along. "If you will only leave everything to us," Drought was saying in effect, "we can deliver a settlement that will mark the dawn of a new age in the Pacific."

In contrast to Drought, who was full of ideas and suggestions, Nomura had nothing to offer. On Friday, March 14, he called at the White House for a talk with the President, who was joined for the occasion by Secretary Hull. The meeting was most disappointing. No matter how the conversation turned, Japan's adherence to the Axis alliance and her war against China remained stumbling blocks of major proportions.

Although this second encounter between the President and the Ambassador would later stand in the record as a way station in the long line of conversations that stretched between March and December, the hub of Japanese-American relations at the moment was in New York, not in Washington. Being absent from the capital did not hamper Drought at all, for he continued to draw on an immense amount of information that he processed into memoranda with increasing energy.

On the day Nomura went to the White House, Drought composed still another message aimed at Roosevelt and Hull. The opening paragraph did not waste any words: "If, at this time, substantial conversations are carried on between our State Department and the Japanese Embassy, the Japanese will conclude that they are being taken advantage of."

He had promised, Drought wrote, and Wikawa had assured Konoye by cable, that the conversations Wikawa was having with Drought would be reported only to Roosevelt, Hull, and Walker. These three Americans were supposed to reach a "confidential decision" before bringing either the State Department or the Japanese Foreign Office into play. "Can I repeat to Mr. Wikawa," Drought asked, "that this procedure is being followed?"

In the meantime, an "Agreement in Principle" would be drafted in New York and would be sent to the leaders of both countries "for possible modification." If Iwakuro and Wikawa concurred on the substance of this proposal, then "acceptance" by Japan and the United States could "be indicated through existing unofficial channels." After that, the State Department and the Foreign Office could take over.

Two days later, on Sunday, March 16, Drought reported his latest achievement: "Incredible as it may seem, Mr. Wikawa has substantially approved an 'Agreement in Principle' " containing certain points "so important and critical that they should reach you, in summary form, at once."

There were nine items in all—for the most part merely repeating what had already been proposed. As had been the case earlier, there was a marked fuzziness about the offering. Secret terms would be "confided exclusively to the United States for the settlement of the China War." If these terms met with the President's approval, there would be "provision" for his "intermediation." A "vast economic opportunity" would then be inaugurated in Eastern Asia, making Japan so "subservient" to the United States that "political antagonism would be suicidal."

It was "morally certain, though as yet not positively confirmed by private cable," Drought asserted, that Matsuoka was going to Berlin to tell the Germans that an agreement with the United States was in the offing. Konoye considered it "most necessary to synchronize" the signing of this agreement with Japan's "renouncement" of the Axis. "Indeed," Drought wrote, "[the two actions] must be synchronized if assassinations are to be avoided."

Wikawa planned to confer with Iwakuro as soon as the Colonel arrived. Some modification of the nine points might result, but "no substantial change" would be made. A bilateral conference should therefore be convened at the earliest moment "to specify the economics and limitations" of the "Agreement in Principle." The presence of Konoye and Roosevelt at this conference would "signalize" not only "the inauguration of a new era of Peace in the Pacific," but also "the end of the Axis Alliance! Alleluia!"

CHAPTER FOUR

An Excess of "Plenipotentiaries"

B Y MONDAY, March 17, 1941, Father Drought's memoranda offensive against President Roosevelt and Secretary Hull had grown in intensity on a wide front. As the new week began—the week in which Colonel Iwakuro's arrival from Japan would at last bring the John Doe forces in the United States to full strength—Hull's "mailman," Frank Walker, delivered two communications that Drought had entrusted to his care. Both dealt with the "Preliminary Draft of 'Agreement in Principle' " that Drought and Wikawa had been concocting in New York.

This document, according to Drought, amounted to "a proclamation of a revolution in Japanese 'ideology' and policy." Wikawa had called it a "180° change." It was "proof," Drought declared, "of the complete success of American statesmanship." Any delay now would greatly increase the chances of failure. Prince Konoye and the other leaders in Tokyo who wanted to reach a settlement with the United States could not manage it "piecemeal"; they were running the risk of assassination.

If Washington chose to procrastinate, the fifth columnists in Japan would proceed at once to "cement" the Axis alliance through Matsuoka, who was already on his way to Berlin. Roosevelt and Hull should act immediately on the "Agreement." They should either suggest changes or indicate their approval.

Once the proposal had been accepted by the United States, Tokyo and Washington could publicly reveal that an "Agreement in Principle" had been reached; in Japan this announcement would have the Emperor's sanction.

Drought was as positive and specific as he could be: "If an authoritative approval of substance is privately, but categorically, given to me by the two persons [Roosevelt and Hull], we will request the Japanese leaders to instruct . . . Admiral Nomura to present personally to Mr. Hull the Draft of the 'Agreement in Principle.' If this is not done [by April 1], we can properly doubt the sincerity of the Japanese. I have such confidential information that I am thoroughly satisfied *we must help the Japanese to 'put it over.'* "

The document in question—fourteen, single-spaced typewritten pages —was duly delivered in Washington two days later. With the help of his friend Wikawa, Drought had attacked the problem of Japanese-American relations like a mountain climber plotting an assault on his objective. Ledges and crannies that could be exploited to good advantage had been carefully mapped with one thought in mind—to reach the summit and to plant there the flag of peace.

Every major aspect was covered: Japan's role in the Axis alliance, the war in China, commercial relations with the United States, and a Monroe Doctrine for the Far East. These were matters that were thenceforth to be constantly at issue between Secretary Hull and Ambassador Nomura—between Washington and Tokyo. Through the "Agreement in Principle" Drought thus introduced his own very definite views on all of the problems that required solution.

Despite Drought's desire to "wrap everything up" as quickly as possible, Hull and his advisers were not going to be rushed into a decision. Hamilton had earlier suggested telling the Postmaster General that nothing further would be done until Iwakuro arrived. Hornbeck was even more specific. He wanted to "short-circuit the informality of the approach." The suggestions that had been put forward by the John Doe Associates would have to be discussed with the proposers, and this ought to be done "in, by, and through official channels."

As a consequence of this advice, and perhaps because Drought was currently seeking a personal meeting, the Secretary of State asked Joseph W. Ballantine, a Japanese-speaking Foreign Service officer on special assignment in Washington, to rendezvous with Colonel Iwakuro in New York for the purpose of finding out what he and the others had in mind.

Thus it came to pass that on Monday morning, March 24, 1941, Ballantine called on Drought at the Berkshire Hotel, preparatory to meeting Iwakuro and Wikawa, who were expected that evening on a flight from San Francisco. Drought briefed his visitor on the background of the "business" that had brought them together. He explained that he had gone to Tokyo with Bishop Walsh in November 1940 to discuss with the authorities there the adverse impact their recent religious legislation would have on Maryknoll activities in Japan. In the course of these discussions, the subject of Japanese-American relations had arisen. Foreign Minister Matsuoka had said that "if he could only see the President for an hour" he was sure he would be able to bring about an improvement in the situation. He had asked the two churchmen to make his desire for peace known to the White House.

Walsh and Drought had subsequently been introduced to "numerous Japanese leaders outside the Foreign Office group." Their "principal contact" had been Tadao Wikawa, who seemed to be on close terms with "persons in the higher political circles, both civilian and military." It was in conferences with these leaders that most of the points were discussed that had now been incorporated into the "Preliminary Draft of 'Agreement in Principle.' "

After seeing the President in January, Drought said, he and the Bishop had sent word to Matsuoka, through the Japanese Consulate General in New York, that his message had been delivered to the White House. Drought had also communicated with Wikawa. Soon thereafter, Drought had heard from him that he was coming to the United States. During the past few weeks, the two of them had been busy preparing the "Draft."

Ballantine had expected to confer with Iwakuro and Wikawa either that day or the next, but Drought had just received a call from San Francisco telling him that the Colonel wanted to travel by train rather than by plane because he had become ill on the boat. There would consequently be some delay. Wikawa, however, had agreed to stick to the original plan—he would fly east while Iwakuro followed by rail.

After being grounded at Albuquerque by bad weather, Wikawa finally reached New York two days later. The next morning, March 27, Ballantine again went to the Berkshire Hotel. Drought told him that a hitch had occurred because the German ambassador in Tokyo had learned of Iwakuro's departure from Japan a few hours after he had sailed. Berlin had now taken countermeasures of a type the Japanese had not foreseen. Drought would not disclose what these measures were, but "he said that the situation would necessitate a complete change in plans as far as procedure was concerned." He felt certain, however, that this development would not substantially affect the terms of the "Draft."

Drought then took Ballantine to Wikawa's room, where he introduced the two men to each other. Ballantine spent the next four hours alone with Wikawa, listening to a detailed account of his career and of his relations with various Japanese leaders, including a "cousin," Baron Reijirō Wakatsuki, who had twice served as the Premier of Japan and who was still influential in circles close to the Throne. Wikawa himself, through his position in the banking world, claimed to represent "55 percent of the entire population of Japan and 90 percent of the agricultural and fishing populations."

Wikawa described Colonel Iwakuro as a "driving force" in the Army —"a prodigious worker" who had the "complete confidence" of both Hideki Tōjō, the Minister of War, and Akira Mutō, the chief of the Military Affairs Bureau of the War Ministry. All factions in the Army,

Wikawa said, looked on Iwakuro with favor; he was also well regarded in civilian circles.

According to Wikawa, the Germans had conducted their propaganda campaign in Japan with scientific thoroughness. Berlin's special representative, who had negotiated the Tripartite Pact with Matsuoka, had taken advantage of American action against Japan to persuade the Foreign Minister and others to fall into step beside Hitler and Mussolini. The Germans had promised, in return, to prevail upon the Russians to enter into a political agreement with Tokyo. The new Japanese ambassador to Moscow had even anticipated that all he would have to do when he got there would be to sign on the dotted line. There had been considerable disappointment over the Axis alliance when the agreement with the Soviet Union had failed to materialize.

As Wikawa talked on, Ballantine began forming impressions of the man Drought had called a Plenipotentiary Representative. He seemed to be a person of "character, force, and intelligence," but Ballantine did not quite share Drought's optimistic view that Iwakuro and Wikawa would be ready to agree, then and there, to a settlement of the Far Eastern situation along the lines indicated in the "Preliminary Draft." The Japanese would have to make adjustments to the new situation. While they were doing that, they would "divulge their ideas and plans only a little at a time" in the hope of finding out just how eager the State Department was to come to terms with them.

Since Iwakuro would not arrive in New York for several days yet, Ballantine decided to return to Washington. Wikawa cautioned him not to say anything to the Japanese Embassy about their conversation. Wikawa did not have any confidence in Japan's career diplomats; he felt that the negotiations should be in more experienced hands than theirs. Nomura's staff was out of touch with politics at home and did not know what was going on—Minister Wakasugi was a good example.

The implication was that Colonel Iwakuro, who had left Tokyo only a few weeks before, was the man to see.

Drought himself believed this to be the case and was looking forward to Iwakuro's arrival. Shortly after their first meeting, which took place at St. Patrick's Cathedral in New York on March 31, Drought checked into the Wardman Park Hotel in Washington. This marked the beginning of a number of extended visits to the capital that permitted him to keep his fingers directly on the pulse of developments for a period amounting to five of the eight months—from April to December—during which Secretary Hull and Ambassador Nomura maintained their search for a diplomatic solution.

The situation in early April was especially interesting, for Iwakuro and Wikawa were also registered at the Wardman Park. Since Frank Walker had been a long-time resident and Secretary Hull had recently moved there from the Carlton, the John Doe Associates could not have picked a better place to converge.

On Thursday, April 3, Drought got in touch with Walker by telephone and later lunched with the Postmaster General in his office. Still later Drought brought Wikawa in, so that the three of them could confer. Secretary Hull phoned Walker at least once—possibly twice. The next day the Postmaster General handed Hull an unsigned memorandum that had been written by Drought:

> After some delays, caused by new German offers to Mr. Matsuoka and by certain items in the "Preliminary Draft," Colonel Iwakuro came to New York and gave his "unofficial" consent to every substantial point—viz:
>
> (1) No military action against the U.S., if our Government decides on "protective defensive action against Germany";
>
> (2) Mediation of President Roosevelt for China-Japan peace on basis offered to and accepted by President Roosevelt as just and prudent;
>
> (3) Acceptance of U.S. credit that would involve Japanese business in a substantial dependent alliance with the U.S.;
>
> (4) Release of high percentage of Japanese merchant marine [for charter by American marine brokers or shipping companies];
>
> (5) Mutual pledge of Pacific peace and appropriate Naval placements;
>
> (6) Conference at Honolulu [to be] opened by President Roosevelt.*

Drought did not reveal which items in the "Preliminary Draft" had caused delay, but he did say the Colonel felt it would be impossible to effect a 180° change politically unless he could show his government that it would obtain "substantial benefits." Iwakuro was thinking in terms of "Japanese ownership" of some of the oil, rubber, and tin found in Southeast Asia, along with the "removal of Hong Kong and Singapore as doorways to further political encroachment by the British in the Far East."

According to Drought, the Colonel was now working with Wikawa and the Japanese Ambassador, preparing a "short statement" that would incorporate all of the points previously mentioned. This new draft would be completed within a few days. "The Japanese," Drought wrote, "desire to have their draft shown unofficially to Mr. Hull in the expectation that Mr. Hull will unofficially inform a third party whether such a draft would be accepted or rejected substantially."† If accepted, the draft would be presented immediately to Secretary Hull by Ambassador No-

---

* Although Drought had originally promoted the idea of a meeting to be held in Tokyo, he had recently begun shifting his attention to Honolulu.

† A "third party" probably means Frank Walker (or possibly Drought himself).

mura. A joint announcement could then be issued to the effect that the United States and Japan were "negotiating for the establishment of Peace in the Pacific."

"It is desired," Drought declared, "to counter-balance, as quickly as possible, the German offers to Mr. Matsuoka. If these negotiations with the U.S. fail, the Japanese authorities are certain that they will lose control and a war in the Southwestern Pacific will be started."

As soon as this John Doe memorandum reached Stanley Hornbeck, he began at once to analyze its contents. Throughout his step-by-step dissection Hornbeck remained as skeptical and hardheaded as he had been in February and March when he had first been consulted. An announcement of the type Drought had in mind would be equivalent, Hornbeck believed, to detonating "a super-colossal political bombshell: tremendous repercussions in all directions."

It was Saturday, April 5, when Hornbeck wrote these words, but the arrival of the weekend did not diminish the intensity with which Drought sought to press the advantage he had already obtained. At some point early in the day, Hull received a portion of the new "short statement" that Drought had said Iwakuro, Wikawa, and Nomura were preparing. Although incomplete, it covered the major issues. An attempt by Hull to reach the Postmaster General by telephone proved unsuccessful, but the Secretary of State left a message that was recorded rather elliptically at the other end of the line:

Secretary Hull called at 2 o'clock.
He thinks it better to let the matter go over until the first of the week—Monday—unless the folks who spoke to him should be disposed to have Mr. Ballantine have another conference to include the Colonel who hadn't been included yet.*
Asked Mr. Hull if I could reach Mr. Walker at the hotel and have them talk but he said that he was on his way to his apartment . . . and can be reached there.

Two days later, on Monday, April 7, Ballantine visited Drought at the Wardman Park by prearrangement. Drought virtually repeated what he had already said in his latest report: the situation had changed since their meeting at the Berkshire; Iwakuro and Wikawa were now working with the Japanese Ambassador; Nomura would probably have a new draft ready by the next evening that Drought would very likely have an opportunity to see; before the Japanese presented their draft officially, however, they would want some intimation that the American Govern-

---

* In other words, Hull thought that the matter could wait until the beginning of the week unless Drought and Wikawa, who had spoken with Ballantine in New York, wanted another meeting with him—this one to include Iwakuro, who had only just arrived on the scene.

ment would regard their offering as "substantially acceptable"; as soon as such an assurance had been given, Prince Konoye's Cabinet would act on the matter and would instruct Nomura to present the draft formally in Washington.

It was important that this be done prior to Matsuoka's return from Berlin, Drought said, for otherwise the Foreign Minister might create difficulties. The Japanese armed services were behind the proposals. If prompt action were now taken, Matsuoka would be faced with a fait accompli. He would have to accept it or resign. Theoretically, the Japanese authorities could relieve Matsuoka of his post before he got back to Tokyo, but they wanted to avoid doing this if at all possible.

Having thus provided Ballantine with the latest information, Drought picked up the telephone. Moments later Wikawa appeared at the door. He greeted Ballantine very effusively and then escorted him to another room where the Colonel was waiting.

In the conversation that ensued, Iwakuro did most of the talking. He had "an attractive and vigorous personality" but seemed determined to avoid subjects of any consequence.

Ballantine had been forewarned by Drought that Iwakuro and Wikawa were fearful a premature leak might endanger their lives. Drought had said they probably would not want to discuss any details until the new proposal had been presented officially by Nomura. Ballantine had replied that so far as he was concerned the meeting would be purely "social."

And that is what it turned out to be. Despite a pinprick here and there, amicability prevailed. At no point in the conversation, however, did either Iwakuro or Wikawa say a word about the mission that had brought them to the United States.

From April 7 to April 17 Drought remained in close touch with Walker as the John Doe effort for peace moved into high gear. On Wednesday, April 9, the incomplete proposal of the preceding Saturday was suddenly supplanted by a full and revised "Draft Understanding," which was personally delivered to Secretary Hull by Father Drought. They spent thirty-five minutes together, and the following afternoon they met again for an additional fifteen minutes of talk.

The Division of Far Eastern Affairs and Stanley Hornbeck immediately began studying the contents of the "Draft Understanding." A memorandum of comment was prepared by "Far East" on April 10 for the Secretary's benefit. This was followed, twenty-four hours later, by a tentative counterdraft that incorporated as much of the John Doe offering as Hornbeck thought the American Government could accept.

In a second memorandum, written that same day (April 11), Hornbeck warned that hasty diplomatic action at this juncture might lead to a further deterioration of the situation in the Pacific unless the United States disabused Japan of any misconceptions she might have in regard to American intentions. Hornbeck wanted to encourage Tokyo to believe that Japan could obtain "a fair deal" without having to make conquests in order to get it, but he did not want the Japanese to draw the wrong conclusions. "It is most desirable," he argued, "that we should cultivate rather than destroy an impression on their part that adventure southward by them would meet with armed resistance on our part."

The day on which Hornbeck wrote these words happened to be Good Friday. Drought would normally have returned to Maryknoll for the Easter weekend, but now he was stuck in Washington, uncertain whether he would be able to get away or not. "Father Drought phoned this afternoon," Bishop Walsh informed the members of his governing council, ". . . to say that the white-haired man from Tennessee [Hull] has asked him to remain near the Potomac for a few days longer while our govt. is making its final decision about the submitted agreement. Verbal reports are favorable to speedy acceptance but Fr. D. expects to be held over Easter—maybe for a few days of next week."

Despite this report, Drought managed to get to Maryknoll after all. While there, he drafted a telegram to Wikawa: "Have arranged meeting for Monday. You and your companion will have an interview with one or two of the persons on Tuesday. It now seems probable that our guess was correct as to the cause of the delay but I have been assured we may have confidence in good result. Will inform you further after meeting on Monday. Kindest regards to your companion. Happy Easter. James."*

On Sunday, April 13, Walker telephoned Hull from New York over "the White House line," but found that he was not immediately available; Hull called back later, however, and talked to the Postmaster General.

At the Wardman Park Hotel, meanwhile, Wikawa assembled a "little token" of souvenirs from Japan for Walker and his family. In a covering note, to which Iwakuro added his signature, Wikawa wrote: "We wish you to know that we are appreciatively mindful of your great devotion to the cause of peace, for which we beg you to accept our humble congratulations."

On April 14 Secretary Hull asked Ambassador Nomura to come to his

* Drought is claiming credit here for having arranged a Hull-Nomura meeting for Monday, April 14. He is also saying that Iwakuro and Wikawa can expect to see Hull or Walker, or both, on April 15.

apartment for a talk (they had not seen each other for a month). That same day Hornbeck made some further changes in his counterdraft of April 11, adding a word of caution by way of advice to the Secretary of State.

On April 15 Drought called on Hull—their third meeting in six days. Drought also visited Walker, and he in turn received Iwakuro and Wikawa.

On Wednesday, April 16, Hull and Nomura held their most important conversation to date, the Secretary having in the meantime been briefed by his advisers. Two of the memoranda submitted to him dealt specifically with what he might say to the Japanese Ambassador. A third went even further: it represented a pooling of thoughts on the part of Hamilton and Ballantine, who had been studying Hornbeck's proposals of April 11 and 14. The result was a document for State Department use only—"a tentative basis for a possible counterdraft" to offset "the Japanese draft of April 9."

At the Wardman Park Hotel on April 17, Wikawa wrote a letter similar to the one he had sent to Frank Walker on Easter Sunday. Iwakuro again added his signature, but the addressee this time was Cordell Hull:

Dear Mr. Secretary:
We desire cordially to express to your Excellency our genuine esteem for your devoted efforts to achieve peaceful relations not only between your great nation and ours, but also among all nations.
Whatever the outcome of our present efforts may be, our hearty admiration for your peaceful noble motive will remain steadfast and unchanging.
We beg you and Hon. Mrs. Hull to accept for each of you a slight souvenir from our home land as a token of our deep esteem which no circumstances can alter.

> Respectfully yours,
> H. Iwakuro
> Tadao Wikawa

What did all this mean? It signified the successful termination of the initial phase of John Doe's plan. The period of preparation was over; the assault on the summit was about to begin. Studied in retrospect, the portents are ominous indeed—more ominous than they appeared at the time, for no one could then have foreseen what the consequences would be.

In the Preamble to his "Preliminary Draft" of mid-March 1941, Father Drought had envisaged Japan and the United States marching side by side, "in a spirit of high resolve," toward a new era of peace in the Pacific.

April, May, June, and July were to be spent by the John Doe Associates in a vigorous effort to make this dream come true. Even the movement of Japanese military forces into southern French Indochina in midsummer—an act that evoked a Presidential order freezing Japanese assets—did not do more than cause a brief pause and a somewhat revised approach.

During the final months of 1941, from August to December, Drought and Wikawa continued to strive for success—the one in Washington, the other in Tokyo. Colonel Iwakuro would no doubt have done his share also, had he not been posted to a military command in Indochina.

In a moment of zeal during the early stages of the affair, Drought had referred to the extraordinary progress that had already been made. His assertion then had been premature, but by mid-April he might easily have repeated his claim. What he had done since the interview at the White House on January 23, 1941, was indeed unbelievable.

At no time did this incredible priest ever reveal the background circumstances that alone could explain his dual role as James Drought and John Doe. Presumably he felt that a Japanese-American settlement would be more difficult to achieve if he were to divulge too much. The overriding consideration in his mind was to bring Japan and the United States together. He was afraid that their differences might otherwise culminate in war in the Pacific, and that communism would emerge the victor by absorbing all of Asia.

As the "Draft Understanding" of April 9 passed into the hands of Secretary Hull, Drought was pleased that after so much effort on his part the goal was finally in sight. And yet it was not to be quite that simple. Appearances were one thing and reality another.

During the ten months that elapsed between Nomura's first visit with Hull on February 12, 1941, and his final call on December 7, the Japanese Ambassador and the American Secretary of State conferred with each other approximately forty-five times. During that same period Nomura saw Acting Secretary of State Sumner Welles on six occasions and had nine interviews with the President (with either Hull or Welles in attendance)—a grand total of at least sixty substantive meetings between the Japanese envoy and the highest American authorities concerned with the conduct of foreign affairs.

From start to finish this prolonged search for peace in Washington and all corresponding contacts in Tokyo were consistently under the pernicious influence of the misbegotten actions of the John Doe Associates operating behind the scenes. During all that time, from the warm and hopeful beginning in the spring to the bitter and denunciatory ending in midwinter, each and every proposal offered either formally or informally by the two sides, fourteen documents in a period of seven months, *derived directly from the "Draft Understanding" of April 9*—a John Doe creation, pure and simple, conceived at the Wardman Park Hotel in Washington, D.C., with the knowledge and blessings of Ambassador Nomura, by none other than James Drought, Hideo Iwakuro, and Tadao Wikawa.

The Japanese-American quest for peace was entirely at the mercy of these three individuals—each a self-appointed diplomatic "Mr. Fix-it." The erroneous conclusions that sprang from the words and deeds of the John Doe Associates, working singly and in concert, exerted a most harmful effect, especially on the Japanese side. The confusion the Associates spread over the issues they sought to clarify was compounded with the passage of time, thus further snarling an already tangled situation.

Even the endless round of talk to which Hull and Nomura returned again and again proved incapable of overcoming the difficulties that arose from the continuing ministrations of Drought, Iwakuro, and Wikawa. It is indeed ironic that despite their intentions and desires these three "patriots for peace" nevertheless so managed the affair that their activities actually worked against, rather than for, the goals they had in mind.

To understand the nature of the misconceptions that prevailed and their disruptive aftereffects, one must go back to the beginning—to the reality that never emerged at any time in 1941, even though the effort to maintain appearances ultimately ended in failure. How Father Drought became John Doe, what he tried to achieve, the means he employed, and the results he obtained lead inevitably to the cliché that fact can be stranger than fiction.

PART TWO

REALITY

CHAPTER FIVE

The Historical John Doe

BORN IN New York City on November 18, 1896—the third of five children—James Matthew Drought advanced through the usual stages of a Catholic education, receiving in the process an "impetus ... to piety and learning" that was to carry him eventually to the priesthood. Following the death of his mother from a heart condition when he was seventeen, various "extravagances" in his mode of life began affecting his health. He spent his days in "indiscriminate 'goings abroad'" and his nights devouring one book after another. An "induced nervous state" was the price he paid for reading until dawn. He became moody, shy, and sensitive, but after a summer in the mountains he returned sufficiently refreshed to begin the life of a seminarian.

Following a long sick leave in 1919 prompted by "melancholy and scruples," James Drought reached the conclusion that he wished to lead "the life of a messenger of 'glad tidings of great joy,' of a saviour, through Christ, of men." It was this decision that brought him to Maryknoll in 1920.

From 1924 to 1929 he labored in the Far East, first in South China and then in the Philippines. In 1932, having in the meantime been elected assistant treasurer of the Maryknoll Society, Drought was chosen to represent the Archbishop of Manila in special financial negotiations in Rome—a difficult assignment but one in which he achieved his first notable success. The following year he was named "Extraordinary Visitor to the Missions." He was thus able to survey Maryknoll's work in fields afar and to see for himself the state of the world in remote places.

In 1934, at age thirty-eight, Drought was elected Vicar General and also Treasurer General, posts that he retained thereafter, along with certain other duties, including Public Relations Planning. The declining health of the Father General, who was to die two years later, meant that much of the burden of administering the Society was now borne by his second-in-command.

The year in which "JMD" began moving toward the apex of his career at Maryknoll is significant in other respects as well. In the spring a Japanese Foreign Office spokesman touched off a diplomatic hullabaloo with a statement that attempted to arrogate exclusive responsibility to Japan for the preservation of peace in the Far East. Other nations were told, in effect, to refrain from any measures of assistance to China that Japan might find objectionable. Soon after the uproar created by this statement had subsided, reports in the press intimated that President Roosevelt wanted to meet high Japanese officials during a forthcoming visit to Hawaii. The State Department issued a denial, but stories of impending "deep sea conferences" in the vicinity of Honolulu continued to appear in the newspapers.

In the late summer of 1934, having just returned from a visit to China, Korea, and "Manchukuo," Father Drought posted a letter to the president of the Foreign Policy Association in New York to complain about some articles on Asia that had appeared under the Association's imprint. These pieces had caused Drought "growing dismay" because of the "bias" and "journalistic baiting" many of them displayed.

"It is my studied belief," Drought wrote, "after years of experience in the Far East, that the ordinary American attitude on things Japanese is a serious obstacle to a diplomatic and commercial development that could bring power and profit to the United States." There was "too much of the Big Bad Wolf psychology" in current American comment on the Orient, "and not enough intelligent American self-interest." The time had come to conclude a secret nonaggression pact with Japan and a commercial reciprocity agreement. Such a move "would help to stabilize the Far East and benefit both countries considerably."

Drought was also in favor of "de facto recognition of Manchukuo" on historical as well as political grounds, and for reasons of expediency. He anticipated that Chiang Kai-shek would eventually have to extend such recognition himself.

Soon after Drought expressed these sentiments, naval conversations were begun in London between Great Britain, Japan, and the United States. The Japanese wanted agreements that would permit the Imperial Navy to build up to the level maintained by the other powers— a position that was unacceptable to Britain and America because equality of strength for Japan in naval armaments would work to their disadvantage in maintaining the security of their possessions in the Far East.

Writing in his diary at this time, Jay Pierrepont Moffat, chief of the Western European Division of the State Department, noted that there was "a unanimity of opinion" in the United States, "all the way over to any but the most pacifist circles," that the Japanese were adopting "an unreasonable, not to say offensive, position." They clearly desired one thing, "overlordship in the Far East," and that meant the expulsion of American rights and the closing of the Open Door.

Drought, on the other hand, held very different views in this regard— views that he carried to the White House on November 1, 1934, in the form of a memorandum given to Stephen Early, an assistant secretary to the President. Drought wanted the United States to offer parity to Japan. He believed that the Japanese would otherwise withdraw from the conversations in London, and that the British would then say the American Government was to blame. If the United States took the initiative in granting parity, however, the way would be clear for a non-aggression pact, and the American people would be able to achieve their "real objective—namely, peace." Prompt action by Washington would therefore give the United States a rightful and merited "position . . . of dominance with Japan in the affairs of the Far East."

Surviving records do not reveal whether these recommendations were made known to the President, but Early subsequently sent Drought's memorandum to the State Department, where it was read by Stanley Hornbeck and Maxwell Hamilton.

During a visit to the Department, Drought told Hamilton that the Chinese were going to come to terms with the Japanese and would permit Japan to have control over Chinese affairs. In talking with Moffat, Drought stressed his belief that the American delegation in London should negotiate with the Japanese behind the backs of the British, "preparatory to confronting them with a fait accompli."

In Tokyo, meanwhile, Ambassador Joseph C. Grew was looking forward to the day when the United States would reach the maximum naval strength allowed under existing agreements—a development that would give American diplomacy a backbone of national preparedness. Turning to his diary at the end of 1934, Grew paraphrased some thoughts that he had just sent to Washington: "It would be helpful if those [Americans who want to accord parity to Japan in the belief that this is the way to avoid war] could hear and read some of the things that are constantly being said and written in Japan, to the effect that Japan's destiny is to subjugate and rule the world (*sic*),* and could realize the expansionist ambitions which lie not far from the surface in the minds of certain elements. . . ."

"I wish that more Americans would come out here and live here,"

* The *sic* is Grew's and is apparently equivalent to an exclamation point.

Grew added, "and gradually come to sense the real potential risks and dangers of the situation instead of speaking and writing academically on a subject which they know nothing whatever about, thereby contributing ammunition to the Japanese military and extremists who are stronger than they have been for many a day. The idea that a great body of liberal thought lying just beneath the surface since 1931 would be sufficiently strong to emerge and assume control with a little foreign encouragement is thoroughly mistaken. The liberal thought is there, but it is inarticulate and largely impotent, and in all probability will remain so for some time to come."

The opinions expressed by Ambassador Grew in his diary touched on aspects of the situation in Japan that Father Drought would have done well to ponder, but to expect a judicious approach from him is to misunderstand his nature. He was a man of such forceful character that virtually nothing could restrain him—even lack of prior experience—once he had committed himself to a given task.

Nowhere is this side of Drought more clearly illustrated than in the part he played, during the final months of 1935, in arranging a special convocation at the University of Notre Dame to celebrate the birth of the new Commonwealth of the Philippines. One of Drought's purposes in organizing this affair was to obtain an honorary degree for Carlos P. Romulo, a prominent Catholic journalist and public servant whom he had known since his days in Manila.

The distance between Philippine Day at Notre Dame in 1935 and Drought's role as John Doe in 1941 is not nearly so great as one might think, for in the earlier episode Drought not only exhibited his ability as an entrepreneur but also employed techniques that he was to use again later on. As a consequence, certain phases of his performance are noteworthy for what they reveal about his methods, motives, and thoughts.

From the beginning, Drought made it clear that he intended to remain in the background. He showed no concern for personal advantage, and yet he assumed responsibility for practically everything—he was the puppeteer who pulled the strings from behind the scenes. Energy, determination, knack, gall, skill, and luck were all present in varying degrees, and were constantly at work.

Drought not only persuaded Notre Dame to award a degree but also contributed a flowery citation that he hoped would be read, word for word, on the day Romulo received his honorary doctorate. But this was not all; Drought did even more. When Romulo's efforts to compose an acceptance speech ended up sounding political and reading like an editorial, Drought came to the rescue with an address, "The Mind of a New Commonwealth," that he considered worthy of the occasion.

When Romulo later indicated that the limited time available for radio coverage might force him to shorten his remarks, Drought would not hear of it. "Once you begin to speak," he told Romulo, "nobody can stop you. . . . Do not consider . . . curtailing your address in any way. If worse comes to worst and you are allotted fifteen minutes, accept the allotment but go ahead and make the speech even if it takes an hour. I mean this quite seriously and quite finally. You must please keep it in mind that we are running the show and have no intention of losing sight of the fact."

"We want Catholic-Philippine-Romulo emphasis," Drought declared, "and we are going to get it! That is that."

"Our objectives, for the University and for the Church," Drought informed Father John F. O'Hara, the president of Notre Dame, "are clearly defined and should be seized; not shied away from through timidity, or the nervous meekness that overpowers some when they are faced with a critical situation."

Acting on this principle, Drought did not hesitate to give Notre Dame one "tip" after another, butting in whenever he thought it necessary— "Pardon the presumption that prompts further suggestions!"

He was full of ideas for the program, and was anxious to use it to broadcast his views to the world. "Politically," he told O'Hara, "any reference to the possible encroachment of Japan should be avoided scrupulously. . . . The belief should be expressed that Japan will be a good neighbor if treated with a spirit of dignified equality and an absence of suspicious fear. The jingoism of alarmists should be condemned and confidence expressed in the good intention of the Japanese with respect to the Philippines."

"The more I think of it," Drought advised O'Hara, "the more I suspect that President Roosevelt himself would be glad to take the opportunity to send some kind of an expression [of congratulations]. He enjoys playing the role of benefactor. If you do not care to handle this end of it directly, you or I could ask . . . the President of the Illinois Central to ask Mr. John Pelly, the director of the Railway Administration, to put the idea to Marvin McIntyre, the Secretary of President Roosevelt. Pelly and McIntyre are good friends. I know all of them and will handle it if you wish."

A few days later Drought returned to this theme. "If Mr. Frank Walker needs any help, Monsignor Robert Keegan, of the New York Charities, is an influential friend of the President (Woe is me!)."

In communicating with a fellow Maryknoller at this time, Drought spoke of the "many angles" he was developing. "It is not unlikely," he declared, "that President Roosevelt will be asked to open the affair with a radio message. If he accepts, I will put cotton in my ears; but it will be good propaganda. I will get [Postmaster General James A.] Farley or Keegan or Marvin McIntyre to ask him."

When it developed that the President might personally attend the Philippine Day ceremonies rather than merely extend greetings from Washington, Drought was not persuaded that this would be in Romulo's interest. Roosevelt would drain attention away from everyone else, including Drought's protégé, who was a rising star but not yet a luminous one. "I have just returned to Maryknoll," Drought wrote to O'Hara after the matter was settled, "and am very much surprised—nearly fell off my chair in fact—to read a notice in the papers to the effect that Notre Dame has arranged the [Philippine Day] affair . . . in order to present the President with an honorary degree!"

Drought wondered whether this was "just a mistake on the part of the reporters or whether it was the outcome of sympathetic charity for a fallen hero." He felt that "the raison d'etre of the affair" had been "completely obscured." It would take "strong publicity effort and control to stop Roosevelt" from capitalizing on the ceremonies by pretending that the occasion had been organized for "his own particular glorification."

All Drought could do was make the best of it. Confronted by a change in circumstances, he would alter his tactics but not his objectives. Romulo was still going to be the first speaker; the President would follow him. If Romulo overshot his allotted time, the National Broadcasting Company might not carry Roosevelt along; that would suit Drought "perfectly."

As the big day approached, Drought had 1,500 copies of "The Mind of a New Commonwealth" run off at a printer's in New York. Concurrently, a press conference was arranged for Romulo by a Madison Avenue agency whose motto was "Proper Publicity is Career Insurance."

When the time came for Romulo to deliver his address, he talked for as long as all the other speakers combined and three times as long as any other man on the podium, including the President of the United States. *The Notre Dame Scholastic* later reported that campus opinion was unanimous: Romulo's speech had been "one of the best ever delivered at the University." Especially remembered was a line in which communism in the Far East was dismissed as "an illegitimate hope for unearned increment."

In a letter to O'Hara, Drought was unstinting in the praise he bestowed on Notre Dame. He was also candid about himself. "Mine is an impatient soul," he wrote, "and the memory of such an occasion perceptibly quickens my impetuous desires that the Catholics here and elsewhere should be more responsive, I mean conclusively responsive, to the opportunities which are offered daily for displaying or strengthening the Faith."

*

Impatience, imagination, and zeal made Drought a prodigious worker who was totally unsparing of himself. He chain-smoked his way through many a night of hard labor on whatever currently held his interest. His self-confidence was so impelling that he was often able to succeed at schemes other men might not have attempted or might soon have discarded as impractical. Like Don Quixote, Father Drought was forever finding a new challenge beckoning on the horizon—a moving giant goading the passing knight to spur his steed to full gallop, tilting his lance to the attack position.

The year 1936 was not far advanced when Drought experienced just such an encounter, the moment coming into being as a result of a Senate speech in which Key Pittman of Nevada, the chairman of the Foreign Relations Committee, had some harsh things to say about Japan and the Japanese.

The Foreign Office in Tokyo reacted with a "Let him roar" statement, but when word arrived from the head of the Maryknoll mission in Japan, Father Patrick J. Byrne, that it was "imperative [to] strangle Pittman immediately," Drought rushed forward to do battle.

In a telegram sent to Carl W. Ackerman, a New York friend, Drought declared that Pittman's "frenetic outbursts against Japan" had caused "great damage there to peaceful and political relations." "Could some publicity be developed to discredit Pittman's views . . . ?" Drought asked. "Can anything be done to prevent repetition or obtain retraction?"

As dean of the School of Journalism at Columbia University, Ackerman was accustomed to thinking in terms of the press. He therefore recommended a public rebuttal to be signed by as many prominent Americans as could be persuaded to lend their names to the project.

It so happened that the Premier of Japan, Kōki Hirota, chose this moment to hold a reception in Tokyo for foreign correspondents. Repeating earlier assurances that there would be no war while he was in office, Hirota spoke of fostering "cordial relations" with all nations "with a view to contributing toward international peace and [the] advancement of human welfare."

These remarks, which were reported in the *New York Times*, were noted by both Drought and Ackerman. It was thus natural that they should decide to "strangle Pittman" with the silken cord of a goodwill message to the Premier of Japan.

Drought immediately began drafting the text of a cablegram phrased in what he called "a rather oriental manner." By this he meant that words like "dignity," "esteem," and "respect" would be purposely inserted "for Japanese consumption." "I thought it necessary," he later informed Ackerman, "to avoid any reference to peace because of its belligerent implications."

When Ackerman suggested seeking the support of certain men in Washington, Drought expressed reservations: "If we are not to go there in a spirit of attack, my feeling is that we should not enlist their cooperation.... I think your idea is too good to be entrusted to a blundering, selfish Administration."

Concurrently Drought advised Father Byrne by telegram that a "movement" had been inaugurated "for [a] more sympathetic and intelligent understanding with Japan," and that "American notables" had promised to "cooperate."

In a follow-up letter to Byrne, Drought summarized the steps being taken to indicate to the people of Japan that the "loud-spoken and dangerous" senator from Nevada did not represent public opinion in the United States. "I am sure you are fully aware," Drought wrote, "that I have always pursued a policy of making clear our friendly attitude toward the Japanese. You know, of course, that the friendly statement issued by President Roosevelt in 1934 was dictated verbally at the White House by myself."

Now, however, the scenario was different. "We do not intend," Drought advised Byrne, "to use the facilities of the [American] Government at all since we believe that the Government's policy on Far Eastern affairs needs to be absolutely repudiated by intelligent Americans." To address the goodwill message directly to Premier Hirota, "without using the channels of Government," was a "revolutionary" diplomatic measure. "It would be so understood here," Drought declared, "and I look for considerable opposition from the Administration at Washington. As a matter of fact, when this message is actually sent, I will be glad to invite the opposition of the Administration and give [out] whatever statements may be necessary to make clear to the Japanese that Maryknoll entertains in their regard nothing but the most friendly and cordial attitude."

In a letter to the Very Reverend John J. Burke, the general secretary of the National Catholic Welfare Conference, Drought revealed some further thoughts: "If we were concerned only with the international relationship, I would not be inclined to invite public condemnation of Pittman's views. But the fact is that we are concerned with the continuity of our missions and the lives of our men. Accordingly, if a sharp antagonism is to be developed between the Japanese and Americans, we must feel bound to do all in our power to protect our own group even to the extent of making it clear to the Japanese authorities that we of Maryknoll do not share the political animosity which may actuate others."

"I do not consider," Drought added, "that we are any less American in that we are persistently Catholic."

The United States would find it "relatively easy" to conquer Japan, Drought thought, but to do so "would prove fruitless, unprofitable, and untenable."

"Did I tell you," Drought asked in a letter to Byrne, "that on the basis of our complaint Father Burke saw Secretary Hull personally and conveyed to him our opinions as to the foolish utterances of Senator Pittman? Secretary Hull was very nice about it and agreed to report the complaint in good fashion. Father Burke did not know at the time that we were getting up a round-robin cablegram, so, happily, he could not tell [Hull] of it, though he may have told him since."

On the Catholic side of the matter, there had been the usual rigmarole of getting permission "from the top down," talking the matter through "Chanceries, Delegations, Archbishops, and so forth." Someone had thought that perhaps the Apostolic Delegate in Japan should be consulted, but Drought had managed "to stave that off."

Aiding the Catholic cause as he saw it, and especially Maryknoll's share of it, was one of Drought's motivations, as was a desire to revamp American diplomacy—to make it more independent of European influences and more "constructive."

"Official American diplomacy in the Far East," Drought told his friend Lewis L. Strauss, "is too much the creature of the motives of Continental Powers. . . . I think it is idle to hope for any constructive move from our present State Dept. and I have recently declined a request to consult with them. Peace is the true battlefield of progress and we Americans can never make progress in the Far East so long as we permit the continuance of insecurity."

To the Bishop of Reno, Nevada, who had arranged through local people close to Pittman to bring to his attention the difficulties confronting the Maryknoll Fathers in the Japanese Empire, Drought was also outspoken: "Quite apart from such damage as intemperate statements might cause to our missioners, it is my feeling that, as American citizens, we should not permit ourselves to be misled by the subtle diplomacy of the

British and French and Russians into acting as the police agent for the protection of their own interests in the Far East."

In assembling signatures for his goodwill cable to Hirota, Drought had the help not only of Ackerman but also of a number of others, including a lawyer friend, William E. Cotter, and a onetime ambassador to Germany, James W. Gerard. Not everyone who was approached, however, fell into line. Among those who refused to go along with the idea was Mrs. William Brown Meloney of the *New York Herald Tribune,* who had "a prejudice against signatures on form messages."

"There is a tendency in this country," she advised Drought, "to follow the famous cowboy legend. He promised his mother to pray every night. He hung a copy of a prayer above his bed and squared his conscience by saying . . . 'There, mother, them's my sentiments.'"

Drought replied that he respected the lady's bias against signing form letters and shared it "rather violently." That was precisely why he wanted American relations in the Pacific to be "less Rotary-minded." The cable to be sent to Hirota was "warmed by exasperation with the cowboy method of prayer and thinking." "I feel it is time," Drought declared, "for another prayer card! If people insist on thinking the way Congressmen vote, I am in favor of giving them something sensible to say Amen to."

When James R. Angell, the president of Yale, was asked for his support, he expressed reservations of a different sort. "I am entirely willing to sign the cablegram," he wrote in reply to Gerard's solicitation, ". . . provided I may have some adequate assurance that its dispatch will not be objectionable to the Department of State. Your long diplomatic experience will, of course, make you sensitive to this phase of the proposal. I should like therefore to request some assurance on this score before authorizing the use of my name."

Gerard thought that Angell had a point. But after consulting Ackerman and Drought, Gerard changed his mind. This was explained to Angell by Drought in a letter that shows how he dealt with such difficulties: "Mr. Ackerman and Mr. Gerard have discussed the proposition from the point of view of the State Dept., and have concluded, from evidence on hand, that the State Dept. might be better pleased if it were not consulted especially since the cable itself, in effect, can only help American interests. We have reason to know that the Department is aware of the project. Under the circumstances, the absence of unfavorable comment is interpreted by those who have considered the matter [Ackerman, Gerard, and Drought] as implied consent. . . . Our State Department desires only such relations with other nations as will make for progress in every line of national development. Unless the officials of the Department saw such possibilities in the move, of which some of them are aware, they would have indicated their fears of it as hindering the goal to which they strive to bring the nation."

Angell remained unconvinced and consequently did not participate in the venture. How Drought could seriously have offered such arguments is hard to explain. There appears to have been no basis for what he was saying despite his reference to "evidence on hand." His own attitude toward the authorities in Washington had been hypercritical. In addition, Ackerman had recently sent Drought a copy of a hard-hitting letter from Tyler Dennett, the president of Williams College:

Japan stands faithless before the world. She has broken solemn treaties in the most barefaced manner. Our government is placed in a very awkward position. Any gesture of this sort would be used by the Japanese Government to indicate that a group of people endorse what Japan has done and disapprove of the present policy of our Department of State.

I gravely doubt whether there is at present in Japan any substantial group which can be depended upon to develop within the country a different kind of public opinion on international [affairs].

Indeed I feel so strongly on this subject that I should deplore the sending of such a telegram as you have in mind. I am confident that it would be misused.

Ackerman and Drought did not let this denunciation divert them from continuing their project, even though they subsequently learned, on excellent authority, that Dennett was "perhaps as well acquainted as anyone in the country with the political and diplomatic aspects of international affairs in the Far East, being on a par with Hornbeck of the Department of State."

Instead of stopping Drought, Dennett's letter prompted him to act with greater determination. "It is very important," he wrote to a fellow priest, "that we exercise unremitting haste because opposition is already gathering against the move on the part of some sinophiles and other Americans who seem to be afraid of Japan. If they make their voice heard too loudly and too soon, some of the effect of our move will be lost."

The necessary arrangements were therefore quickly completed. On Saturday, April 11, 1936, a cable of goodwill, addressed to the Premier of Japan over the names of twenty-seven individuals, was given to Western Union.

"I have had a difficult yet interesting ten days of effort," Drought informed Ackerman, "in attempting to obtain desirable signatures, while using every possible means to keep far enough in the background to avoid giving the impression that our message was tinged with some kind of ecclesiasticism. Believe me, there are times when being a Padre is a liability. I enjoy direct forth-right action and find myself exasperatingly hampered when I have to approach an objective circuitously."

Drought was in favor of briefing the Japanese Embassy in Washington, especially since Tokyo would probably ask the ambassador to verify the "genuineness" of the goodwill cable. "I can see no need of advising our own State Dept.," Drought declared, "particularly as, having given the matter considerable thought, I feel the State Dept. may be quite gratified at the message."

Although the goodwill cable to Hirota was not very quotable, several New York papers subsequently carried substantial accounts, text and all. Still later, an unsigned article appeared in the *Japan Times and Mail*, in which importance was attached to the fact that the signers of the message—newspapermen, industrialists, financiers, educators, and statesmen —had "no direct connection with Japan" and therefore could be regarded as "impartial third parties." The *Times and Mail* frankly admitted editorially that "few things could have been more unexpected" or "more welcome" than the friendly message Hirota had received expressing hope that "a 'new era' in Japanese-American relations based upon the 'common sentiments of both nations'" would now be inaugurated. "Not a single official of the American Government" was among the signatories, the editorial declared, "and it is extremely doubtful whether the American Department of State knew anything of the plan until the morning papers publishing its text were delivered. It is one of the most striking instances of 'people's diplomacy' that the world has seen, and of the employment of such diplomacy in the way that it can function best—by the building up of friendly public opinion."

*

With this further success coming so soon after the Philippine Day achievement, there is no telling what Drought might have done next to exert his influence in the policy-making field, but relentless circumstances intervened.

During the summer of 1936 Drought participated in an Extraordinary General Chapter held in Hong Kong for the purpose of finding a successor to the Father General, who had died in the spring.* The result of this convocation was that James Edward Walsh was elected to head the Maryknoll Society. Drought, who had been serving as Vicar General, was chosen by the Chapter to continue in that post; later, the members of

---

* A Chapter is an assembly of delegates charged with deciding matters of concern to Maryknoll.

the Bishop's Council decided that JMD should also stay on in the job of Treasurer General.

Work at the "Knoll" seemed on the point of settling back to "normal" when suddenly, while returning to the United States by way of Europe, Father Drought very nearly lost his life. He was en route from Alexandria to Athens on an Imperial Airways flying boat when the plane crashed into the sea off the island of Crete while coming in for a refueling stop at Mirabella Bay.

Drought suffered a fractured spine, a rib injury, and embolisms of both the heart and the lungs, but his spirits remained high, and the nurses who cared for him in Athens found him "très charmant." When it was safe for him to travel, he was brought back to New York, where he spent months in the hospital. Even then his health was so precarious that his doctors ordered a long rest cure abroad. It was thus nearly the end of 1937 before he was able to resume his duties at Maryknoll.

It is characteristic of Drought's energy and determination, however, that less than two months after his "Icarus" accident (as he liked to call it) he was already involving himself, by mail, in the 1936 Presidential campaign. His opening move was an eight-page letter to Lewis Strauss outlining a made-to-order strategy for the Republican contender, Alfred M. Landon. "As a circus ring-master," Drought wrote, "he cannot compete with Roosevelt. Accordingly, [Landon] should deepen the contrast so as to make Roosevelt appear a loquacious charlatan."

Drought was so eager to put his own words into Landon's mouth that he provided a "Credo" for the candidate. To help Landon further, Drought drew up a list of potential Cabinet appointees.

In acknowledging Drought's long letter, Strauss found time for only one sentence of reply, but in that brief space of words he indicated that he had put the matter into the hands of the man he believed to be Landon's closest personal friend.

Almost a year later, in September 1937, with Roosevelt still in the White House and Drought still convalescing, a fellow priest wrote to a prominent Catholic Democrat asking the gentleman in question, Frank Walker, to do whatever he personally could to persuade the State Department to intercede on Drought's behalf with the British Government, which had a financial interest in Imperial Airways. Drought's solicitors in London were planning to take the airline to court for failing to cover his medical expenses in full. To press their claim they needed the release of a classified report pertaining to the accident at Mirabella Bay.

It was February 1938 before Walker received a reply to his inquiries. Despite action by the Department through the American Embassy in

London, the British Government maintained that the Air Ministry could not furnish the report because it was a confidential document "rendered for official use only."

Nine months later, with his health once again "in a rather precarious condition," Drought was persuaded to take an extended cruise to Caribbean ports in order to obtain a complete rest. Being somewhat sensitive about the matter, he was reluctant to admit that he was not a well man. He might even have refused to go had he not been assured that he could look into certain investments of the Society in Venezuela, if he felt up to doing so.

After his arrival in Caracas, Drought met a number of officials, including the President of Venezuela, Eleazar López Contreras. In response to a plan outlined by Drought, the President and others expressed interest in having a group of American Catholic experts in the field of social service visit their country to suggest ways and means of introducing a welfare program. Six months later, in June 1939, the wish became a reality when Drought returned to Caracas as the moving spirit behind a Social Service Commission that included some old friends—Carl W. Ackerman, William E. Cotter, and John F. O'Hara.

One member of the group, who was deeply impressed by Drought's energy, later described him as "a human dynamo with the vision of a poet."

By the time Drought got back to New York from Venezuela, the war that had been raging in China since July 1937 had already entered upon its third year. As this so-called Incident had progressed, and as the zone of Sino-Japanese hostilities had expanded, Maryknoll had found itself in an increasingly difficult position. Maintaining an attitude of neutrality with respect to the belligerents was essential to the continuation of the Society's activities in the Far East, but theory and practice could not always be aligned with absolute precision.

Since Maryknoll's work would suffer if impediments arose from any quarter, Bishop Walsh ultimately decided to explain the Society's policy to the Secretary of State. In a letter sent to Hull in early 1940, Walsh noted that Maryknoll missions in the Far East had customarily reported damages sustained as a result of the fighting in China. The Society wished to reserve to itself, however, the question of what to do about its losses. It did not want the State Department to press claims for restitution without a specific request from the authorities at Maryknoll.

The Japanese Ambassador, Kensuke Horinouchi, was also told about this policy and was given a copy of the statement Walsh had sent to Hull. "As Missioners friendly to Japan and to China," Drought advised Horinouchi, "we submit ourselves to the existing conditions in those countries, and to the goodwill of the respective Governments. We do not wish that any circumstances of our living, or even of our dying, shall be taken as occasion for political intervention by the American Government on the basis of our citizenship."

This subject was of such importance to Maryknoll that Drought sent copies of his letter to Horinouchi (and of Walsh's earlier communication to Hull) to the Japanese consuls in Los Angeles and Seattle, and to Kaname Wakasugi, then the consul general in New York. For his part, Horinouchi passed along the "valuable information" he had received from Maryknoll. "To be sure," he informed Drought, "my Government will appreciate the stand taken by your Society." It was his "prayerful hope," Horinouchi added, that Maryknoll would enjoy "a providential year in all parts of the Far East."

Whatever 1940 may have been for Maryknoll, the new year was definitely not providential for a great part of the world. In Europe, Hitler's spring offensive shocked his opponents into a sudden recognition of their predicament as Denmark, Norway, the Netherlands, Belgium, Luxembourg, and France each fell in turn before the Nazi onslaught and was trampled underfoot. In the Far East, Foreign Minister Matsuoka made his bid for greatness by allying Japan with the Rome-Berlin axis. Concurrently, Japanese military forces moved into northern French Indochina. In the United States, an awareness of the increased threat to the nation's security led to popular demands for rearmament and to the conscription of men for military service. The danger from Nazi Germany caused many Americans to favor greater support for England, but there were also dissenters who remained hostile to the President and his policies. There were even some who saw Hitler as a much maligned statesman striving to gain justice for the German nation.

Nineteen-forty was an election year, and Father Drought, for one, wanted to make the most of it. "I grow daily more concerned," he wrote to Lewis Strauss in late February, "lest Mr. Roosevelt should capture a third term. Would it be possible to attack him as leading the country into war?"

Several weeks later Drought thought he saw an opportunity for action in the estrangement of James A. Farley, who had once been very close to the President. "In the field of our own national politics," Drought informed Strauss, "it appears that the gravest issue may be that of the Third Term. If Mr. Farley could be persuaded to hold off until and if Roosevelt is nominated, Farley could then make a dramatic appeal to the country for the preservation of democracy and the rejection of

Roosevelt . . . on the basis of patriotism and not [on the grounds of] personal animosity. Farley would ruin him. Roosevelt would then appear not only ambitious, but much worse, ungrateful."

When the Republican Convention adopted a platform containing a foreign policy plank that announced the party's opposition to American involvement in "foreign wars," Drought sent a telegram to William Cotter that bluntly stated Drought's opinion: "Foreign plank unbelievably stupid. Evidently Hoover wants third term in control of Republican Party. Unless his clique is stopped the Republican Party will be."

Following the nomination of Wendell Willkie, a onetime Democrat imbued with Wilsonian internationalism, Drought stepped up his efforts to help bring about a Republican victory in November, duplicating but going beyond the part he had played four years earlier in the Landon campaign. In early August Drought forwarded "a rough summary of thoughts" to John W. Hanes, a former Under Secretary of the Treasury who had bolted the Democratic Party to work for the election of Willkie. Toward the end of August Drought offered more ideas. He urged that they "be developed into many articles and rounded out and applied in one great speech" to be delivered immediately by Willkie—preferably on Labor Day, which "would afford an admirable occasion for an exposition of the American principle of the freedom and dignity of the individual."

A month later Drought sent Hanes a nine-page, singled-spaced typewritten "strategic analysis" entitled "Electoral Campaign of Mr. Willkie"—a memorandum that contained Drought's advice concerning the best way to maneuver the Republican challenger into the Presidency of the United States. Included in this memorandum were Drought's personal choices for Cabinet appointments. For Postmaster General, he felt that "it might be daring, but might prove a boomerang, to suggest the name of Alfred E. Smith," who had lost to Hoover in 1928 and who—like Farley—had parted company with Roosevelt.

As if this were not enough, Drought submitted eight additional pages —"A Sketch Draft on a Popular Presentation of Campaign Issues Made to Revolve Around the Question of the Third Term." This had been "so devised in style and paragraphing," he informed Hanes, "that it should be easy to listen to."

Drought was once again trying to put his words into someone else's mouth. He had written a speech for Willkie—a speech that reflected the various points contained in the "strategic analysis." Drought wanted Willkie to stress Roosevelt's "incompetence," his "dilettante inexperience," and his "disloyalty" to Farley and the Democratic Party.

"During the past eight years," Willkie was supposed to tell the American people, "Roosevelt has announced more emergencies than all his predecessors put together. At first, every domestic problem, which the 'brain trust' did not have a prescription for, became an emergency which required a fat appropriation and a further concession to one man rule. . . . At present, all our emergencies have acquired a foreign origin. . . . These events [abroad] may well portend peril for the United States; a peril against which we must prepare with all possible speed and efficiency. But the United States is not the League of Nations—nor is Mr. Roosevelt the President of the League of Nations. . . . Must we dance to every rumbling of foreign drums?"

Drought's answer was emphatically in the negative, but he did not let the matter rest there. He had already composed (and was now circulating) an essay on "The Nature of the War," to which he appended thirty-four "Informational and Propaganda Directives."

It is clear from these documents of August-September 1940 that Drought would have been very pleased to see the Democratic Party sent packing. And yet the same Drought who could think of giving Al Smith the job of Postmaster General under Willkie could concurrently write a letter of congratulations to Frank Walker, who had recently been nominated by FDR to replace Farley.

"I am particularly pleased," Drought informed Walker, "not only because of my personal regard and esteem for you but also because I frankly feel that the Administration in Washington needs you, and more like you." It was his hope, Drought said, that Walker's counsel and guidance would be accepted not only in Post Office affairs but also in those "larger issues" that were of "such critical importance" to the nation and the world.

As election day drew nearer, Drought began bombarding various Republican friends with copies of the items he had earlier forwarded to Hanes. Drought was confident that William Cotter would be interested in these memoranda and thought "it might be helpful" if he would "pass them around" where they would do some good.

"If a clear mind, a keen desire, and a conscientious presentation of a campaign can contribute to the election of Mr. Willkie," Carl Ackerman wrote from Columbia, "the memos you sent me will be effective."

And yet Willkie lost the race in November, and so Father Drought, who was soon to become John Doe, turned his attention elsewhere. He began making preparations for a visit to Japan, a venture that would subsequently bring him to the doorstep of Willkie's successful opponent, Franklin D. Roosevelt, with the surprising news that it now lay within the capability of the President of the United States to achieve—by a series of quick, secret strokes—what the State Department and the Japanese Foreign Office could not possibly accomplish on their own: a guaranteed peace in the Pacific and a realignment of power in the Far East that would startle American as well as world opinion.

CHAPTER SIX

To"The Land of the Gods"

FOLLOWING THE outbreak of the China Incident in July 1937—a war in fact though not in name—a grimness compounded of growing austerity and of increasing emphasis on duty and sacrifice had settled on the islands of Japan like fog rolling in from the sea. The vision of the Japanese people had gradually become restricted as continuous propaganda inculcated the virtues of *Nippon seishin*—a unique spirit that allegedly would permit Japan to conquer all obstacles in her path. Among the more difficult of these was a fundamental lack of the material means to create a "New Order in East Asia." This self-imposed mission, despite the murder, rape, and pillage it entailed, was somehow to become Japan's contribution to the maintenance of peace in the world.

Hitler's resort to war in Europe in September 1939 had stirred new worries and old ambitions. If the Nazis were victorious, they might gobble up the Far Eastern colonies of the defeated powers—England, the Netherlands, and France. Japan would then be unable to realize her dream of establishing a Greater East Asia Co-prosperity Sphere; she therefore had to act quickly to safeguard her own interests.

As a consequence of such reasoning, and notwithstanding its deep military involvement in China, the Japanese Government within the space of a single year had cast its lot with Germany and Italy, a decision that staked the people of Japan to the greatest gamble in their history. Trained to obedience, the subjects of His Majesty the Emperor, the 124th descendant of an august imperial line, loyally supported an opportunistic policy that was to have a disastrous impact on their lives and on the lives of their children.

Foremost among the delusions in which the Japanese people took increasing comfort was a mystical belief in the "divine" origin of their dynasty. Plans had long been in the making to celebrate the 2,600th anniversary of the founding of the nation. The arbitrary designation of 660 B.C. as the year in which the first Emperor had ascended the Throne rendered 1940 the target date for the inevitable organizing committee. And so it came to pass that ceremonies were held throughout the land, in early November, to commemorate a heritage so unique that it did not need the support of myth at all—an absurd impertinence perpetrated for chauvinistic purposes.

It was to the capital of Japan that all eyes turned as the masses were briefly permitted to experience some feelings of gladness. Colorful flags, lighted lanterns, Shintō rites, and neighborhood parades contributed to the occasion, as did a small task force of flower-bedecked streetcars bearing such inspirational inscriptions as "Banzai for the Emperor," "Universal Brotherhood," and "Joy Upon the Four Seas."

There had once been talk of holding an international exposition, with Tokyo playing host to the Olympic Games as well. Other events and festivities had been promised, but by 1940 there was little room in wartime Japan for anything smacking of frivolity. The police and Kenpeitai (a Gestapo-like gendarmerie) were cracking down on all who dared hinder the progress of the "New Structure." Japanese were becoming reluctant to associate with foreigners—a term almost synonymous with spies. Rotarians throughout the country were searching their souls for a way out of the dilemma: they could disband of their own "free will and accord," try to "Japanize" their clubs, or simply ask foreign members to stop coming to the weekly meetings.

Discipline and sacrifice were the bywords as "self-abnegation" set in. Department store windows that had once beckoned customers with a glittering assortment of fancy goods were now reduced to more somber displays: a schoolboy's knapsack pasted together from pieces of cardboard and a little cloth, ersatz shoes of sharkskin masquerading as leather, posters and banners exhorting the people of Japan to invest in the nation's future by buying "patriotic bonds."

Inside the stores the same theme prevailed. Wives could order blackout curtains "to measure" while their husbands tried on the new national uniform that not only economized on materials and labor but also made every civilian look like a soldier. A father toting his small son in a sailor suit could let him select a toy from a large assortment of machines of war made of wood because metal had been diverted to more critical uses. If money happened to be scarce, the boy could at least go away waving a miniature German, Italian, or Japanese flag, an inexpensive reminder of the "glorious" New Order that Japan and her Axis partners were in the process of "constructing." "Comfort kits" could be bought at a counter set up for that purpose, and mailed to servicemen overseas. While mother saw to this, father could look at bows and arrows —the martial sport of archery, a legacy of the samurai past, having come into favor once again. The son, his eyes filled with wonder, could follow dutifully along as father pulled at one bow and then another, letting imaginary arrows fly at targets of choice. Then, caught up in the spirit of it all, this innocent little warrior of the future could suddenly charge willy-nilly down the aisle into his own world of make-believe.

On their way home, the family could bow in front of the Imperial Palace or visit a shrine dedicated to the spirits of the war dead. Mother might even pause for a moment, in response to public solicitation, to add her contribution to a *senninbari,* a belt of a thousand stitches sewn by faithful hands. The young men of Japan were far from home, fighting in China. The belts being made by the women they had left behind were supposed to offer protection against the bullets and bayonets of the enemy, a prevalent superstition that was soon transformed into a harsh battlefield joke: men lucky enough to survive an engagement with their belts intact often discovered that their thousand stitches were infested with a thousand lice.

Within Japan itself, scarcely a week now passed without new restrictions making their appearance in meticulous detail. The Cabinet Planning Board published "guidance rules" to check extravagance and to encourage a vigorous, healthy life among the people. Leaders of the "Spiritual Mobilization Movement" joined with women's organizations to expatiate on the handling of ceremonies connected with birth, marriage, and death. Economy was the keynote; everything was to be simple, solemn, and cheap. Far-reaching regulations were mixed in with trivial ones, and among these in turn were items that were droll: mistresses were not to have telephones anymore, and that was that.

The noble game of golf, a passion among members of the aristocracy (and proof of their degeneracy), fell under special stricture. Indirect pressure was employed along with open fiat until the "voluntary" acts of individuals reinforced the prohibitions of the government. Golf was to be tolerated only if pursued for the purpose of developing physical stamina. Competition for trophies, playing on weekdays, and the hiring of caddies were henceforth forbidden. Cups and plaques already won were to be melted down for the good of the state (a precursor of similar contributions to come: the sacrificial offering of personal jewelry and silver to help support Japan's "holy war"). No one under twenty was to be allowed on the courses. To arrive in an automobile was to proclaim one's lack of patriotism; cars were to be used for official business only. Men who perversely insisted on sticking to the game were told to travel by train or tram, but they had to be careful of how they dressed: there must be no wearing of knickerbockers in public.

If the athleticism of golf could be called into question, how much more proper it was to exterminate a form of exercise that might make the heart beat faster, but for all of the wrong reasons: the leaping and stepping in unison with music with which persons harboring incorrect thoughts endeavored to while away the few lonely hours they could still call their own. And so, as bleakness slowly spread from one sector of life to another, the decline and fall of the big city dance halls came as a symbolic turning point that seems to have appealed more to the foreign than to the Japanese sense of humor.

"Off with the dance," wrote the British-owned *Japan Weekly Chronicle* with a wry smile, "its joys are unrefined! . . . The orchestras [have] blared and moaned for the last time. . . . There has not been much dignity about the ball-room dance these last few years. It was all right for foreigners perhaps, but it emphatically was not the thing for anyone else. . . . On the whole this is perhaps no time for dancing, but one can still be pardoned for mourning the fact of it."

There was, of course, much else to mourn of far greater consequence, but "no time for dancing" succinctly expresses the mood prevailing in Japan as His Majesty's subjects, wherever situated, simultaneously marked their 2,600th year by rendering homage to the Emperor—BANZAI! . . . BANZAI! . . . BANZAI! The boom of cannon accentuated the solemn silence that followed as the multitude seemed briefly to reflect upon the significance of the moment. At Hsinking in "Manchukuo," the puppet Emperor K'ang-te (better known in the Western press as Henry P'u-yi), "in thoughtful consideration of the inseparable relations" he maintained with Japan, "was graciously pleased to step out into the inner garden" of his palace so that he could join in the celebrations by bowing in the direction of the nation he served as a pawn.

Only those foreigners who had immersed themselves in the language and culture of Japan could hope to understand, in the circumstances of 1940, what it meant to be a Japanese. Occasionally, however, an explanation was offered to the outside world: "Ancestor worship, tracing from lineage to lineage, made the Imperial family the fountainhead of the whole nation. To us the country is more than land and soil from which to mine gold or reap grain—it is the sacred abode of the gods, the spirits of our forefathers; to us the Emperor . . . is the bodily representative of Heaven on earth, blending in his person its power and its mercy."

What did this Emperor want for himself and his people? By all accounts that may be considered reliable he wanted a life free of turmoil and war. How sad it is, even so long after the events of that awful time, to reflect upon the death and misery, the blood and tears, that stain the record of his reign. Even the name by which history will remember him, Shōwa—Enlightened Peace—unintentionally mocks the shimmering goal toward which Hirohito continued to strive while successive governments of uninspired men and many false prophets in search of glory inexorably led his people to a distant and bitter awakening that finally came only when it was too late.

Among the ceremonies over which His Majesty presided during the 2,600th anniversary celebrations was the reading of a congratulatory address by the American Ambassador, the doyen of the diplomatic corps. Those close enough to observe what was happening were surprised to see the Emperor, who had until then remained properly expressionless, suddenly respond visibly to Grew's statements, nodding vigorously when the hope was expressed that the Japanese nation would "ever increasingly contribute to the general culture and well-being of mankind."

In a conversation with Grew the next day, the French Ambassador suggested that the Imperial nods of approval had been meant to indicate the Emperor desired peace. Grew's colleague was so certain of this that he regarded the episode as an important political event.

Hugh Byas, in a dispatch to the *New York Times*, noted that in the Japanese Court, where etiquette was synonymous with rigid formality, such incidents attracted and deserved attention. "To some eminent guests it seemed like a ray of light amid the gloomy apprehensions that the . . . government's foreign policy had aroused. They construed it as a sign of hope that peace was still cherished in the highest quarters."

In periods of crisis it is human to grasp at a straw, to look for a sign. But if men allow reason to prevail, the signs suddenly multiply, and it can be seen that they point in many directions. How unrealistic and implausible it now seems that anyone should then have found in the nod of a head a promise of peace.

And yet, it was to this Japan—mindful of the past but uncertain of the future, a country of contradictions that often defied interpretation even by those well versed in Japanese affairs—that Bishop James E. Walsh and Father James M. Drought now turned their attention in connection with the work of their Society and their Church.

＊

Father Drought's decision to involve himself in matters outside his religious calling by doing something personally about Japanese-American relations—a decision that was consistent with earlier activities of a politically intrusive nature—seems to have been the culmination of growing concern on his part over developments in the Far East. Bishop Walsh had been planning to set out on one of the periodic visitations that permitted him to maintain closer liaison with work "in the field" than might otherwise have been possible. He tended to look upon these triennial tours of inspection as "the only consolation prize" in his "headache of a job." The timing of his departure on this occasion, however, and his desire to have Drought assist him were tied directly to news that Maryknoll had received from the Far East. The Japanese Government had announced a change in policy toward Christian institutions within its jurisdiction, and the Apostolic Delegate in Tokyo had responded to this change in a way that left the future in doubt. On top of this had come word that Japan had joined the Axis alliance.

Normally the Vicar General would have remained close to home during the absence of the Superior General, but in this instance Walsh felt that Drought should accompany him as far as Japan. If problems arose concerning Maryknoll's activities in the Far East, the Bishop would be able to turn to his principal assistant for help. How much either man could have hoped to accomplish at this particular juncture in dealing with the Japanese Government seems rather doubtful in retrospect, especially since neither one of them had had any prior extensive experience in Japan.

This did not stop Father Drought. Like anyone else planning a trip, he obtained the names of people, places, and things from friends and acquaintances, but in his quest for information he soon went beyond the point where the average tourist would have stopped. The response was varied, ranging from formal letters of introduction (written by persons with Japanese connections) to tongue-in-cheek tips from a fellow Maryknoller on using the language: *Benjo*—first door to the left."

On the serious side, Drought's colleague reported that the New York agent of the Nippon Yūsen Kaisha had been unable to find any record of passage having been booked from the West Coast on the *Nitta-maru*. The vessel was sold out; there were no accommodations. In an effort to oblige, however, the agent (who was a Catholic) had wired the San Francisco office of the company to the effect that Bishop Walsh was undertaking a mission of assurance—he would urge Maryknollers to remain at their posts.* The agent had asked that a special first-class stateroom, normally held for "last-minute diplomats," be assigned to the Bishop and that another cabin be found for Father Drought.

Early in November, with passage finally secured and departure from Maryknoll only hours away, Drought hurriedly wrote to an influential friend to brief him on the trip and to solicit his assistance:

* The State Department had recently advised all Americans in the Far East to return home as soon as they could arrange their affairs.

It would be extraordinarily helpful if we could have from yourself a personal letter of introduction to Mr. Matsuoka, the Foreign Minister of Japan. I do not desire at all any letters from our State Department if such formal introduction would give a diplomatic color which I am anxious to avoid. I do not know what the practice of Mr. Roosevelt may be; specifically, I do not know if he would ever give a letter of personal introduction. I should say, however, that our effort, which may yield so much during years to come for the spread of our Catholic Faith, would be sharply facilitated if Mr. Roosevelt would commend us personally to the Premier of Japan.

The man to whom Drought sent this appeal was none other than the Postmaster General of the United States, Frank Walker.

That same day, November 8, 1940, Drought also turned to Frank Murphy, an associate justice of the Supreme Court, who had been governor-general of the Philippines at the time of the Notre Dame affair and who had later served as high commissioner. "I am presuming to impose upon your devout interest in the work of the Church," Drought declared, "by enclosing for your perusal a copy of a letter which I have just addressed to Mr. Frank C. Walker. I would gratefully appreciate any comment or advice which you might care to give me, and would be happy also if you could, without inconvenience or impropriety, commend me to some of your important Japanese friends."

The following day Drought sent a similar appeal to William Cotter in New York: "Perhaps you may consider that a word from you would be helpful or possibly a word from Nelson Rockefeller. What I am really after of course is to get an influential personal introduction to Mr. Matsuoka. Maybe some of your RKO [Radio-Keith-Orpheum Corporation] friends would know him."

Apparently they did not, and neither it seems did Murphy or Walker. An approach made to Joseph P. Kennedy also proved unproductive. A radiogram to Honolulu, where the *Nitta-maru* briefly put into port, brought word that Kennedy did not have any Japanese connections.

*

The arrival in Japan of Bishop Walsh and Father Drought toward the end of November 1940 did not go unnoticed—at least in the English-language press. To the reporters who interviewed him, Walsh spoke in a friendly manner. Although he had come to investigate the new strictures that required all Christian institutions to be headed by Japanese nationals, he was the essence of tact.

"The first aim of Maryknoll," Walsh said, "is the creation and development of a Japanese clergy to minister to the Japanese people. Therefore, it is the culmination of our efforts and our greatest triumph when

... a Japanese Superior can be placed over missioners and assume full responsibility. . . . After all, we work to perpetuate the Faith, not ourselves."

"Why should we leave?" he asked. "It is our duty to remain. . . . We take no orders of any sort from the United States government. We are here as guests of the country, and our work is for Japan. . . . I love the Japanese people as I love my own . . . and I shall do all I can for their benefit. Politics and religion are two different things, and I am working for religion."

During the month that followed, Bishop Walsh did primarily that, but he had time enough left over to be drawn into meetings with business and government leaders at which the war in China, the alliance with Germany, and Japanese relations with the United States came under discussion. The man responsible for this larger activity in which Walsh found himself engaged was his companion and helper, Father Drought.

Men influence men, and men shape events. This was the theory on which Drought operated. Walsh might believe that politics and religion were two different things, but Drought did not see them as mutually exclusive entities. Despite this, he was not being consciously disloyal to the Father General, to Maryknoll, or to the Church. Instead, he was trying to serve all three within the context of his own personality. He was incurably addicted to fanciful schemes—imaginative, intense, and resourceful—full of shifts and devices to meet any contingency. His complete dedication to whatever cause he was serving at the moment left little room for discretion and discrimination, for these were soon overcome by onslaughts of enthusiasm that made him quite ready to take on any and all comers. In the role of John Doe, James Drought would have done well to heed Talleyrand's advice to fledgling diplomats: "Et surtout, messieurs, pas trop de zèle."

Although Drought's efforts to secure help from Walker, Murphy, Cotter, and Kennedy had been unsuccessful, he did not arrive in Japan empty-handed. From Carl Ackerman at Columbia he had obtained a letter of introduction to Shingorō Takaishi, the editor-in-chief of the *Ōsaka Mainichi* and the *Tōkyō Nichi-Nichi*, which together represented a circulation in the neighborhood of 3,000,000. To this prominent newspaper executive, who had been sent to the United States in 1937 and '38 as a so-called People's Envoy charged with explaining his country to American audiences, Ackerman had written: "Father Drought is one of my very good friends. He is coming to Japan on a special mission for his Church. I commend him to you both as a gentleman and as a realist. If you can give him the opportunity of calling on you I know that you will find him a most interesting visitor."

Ackerman had also provided a glowing endorsement addressed to Kensuke Horinouchi, who had recently returned home from his ambassadorial post in Washington. "[Father Drought] is a man whom I trust implicitly. He is as honest as he is direct. . . . He is one of the young intellectual giants of the Roman Catholic Church and a charming gentleman."

Of even more value than Ackerman's recommendations, however, was a special packet of nine letters, identical in wording, that Drought had received from another New York friend—the highly successful financier Lewis Strauss, a man with excellent Japanese connections. Written on the stationery of the prestigious international banking house of Kuhn, Loeb and Company, these letters were to function as passports into the exclusive enclave of Tokyo's elite:

November 8, 1940

Dear ———,

I take the liberty of giving this letter of introduction to you of one of my dearest personal friends, Reverend Father James Drought, Vicar General of the Maryknoll Fathers. This great Catholic religious Order is doubtless known to you and its splendid humanitarian work necessitates no description from me.

May I bespeak for Father Drought the kindnesses you customarily extend and assure you of my deep appreciation for any courtesies he may receive. He brings you my personal greetings and I hope, through him, to have news of you when he returns to the United States.

In the hope that the coming year may see the restoration of goodwill among men and nations and, particularly, the maintenance of friendship between our own lands and with the most cordial regards, I am, as ever,

Faithfully yours,

Four days after his arrival in Japan, Drought put his generous supply of "Kuhn, Loeb" letters into the mail, enclosing with each a covering note written at the Imperial Hotel, where he and Walsh were staying. The manner in which Drought gave a fillip to what had been intended as ordinary fare shows something of the method he was to employ throughout the venture he was now beginning:

Nov. 29, 1940

My dear Sir:

At the instance of Mr. Lewis Strauss, I am forwarding to you by enclosure a letter of personal introduction.

Mr. Strauss considers you with most cordial esteem and feels confident that you will be readily inclined to foster, with us, the speedy resumption of amicable relations between our peoples; founded, this time, on a realistic appreciation of the true facts and circumstances underlying the Far Eastern situation.

I anticipate that I shall remain in Tokyo at this address for two or three weeks. I would be both pleased and privileged to make your acquaintance, to convey the regards of our mutual friend and to discuss with you the steps which may be taken toward reaching the horizon of a better understanding and lively friendship.

I have the honor to be,

Sincerely yours,

The most prominent of the nine individuals to whom Drought addressed this message was Baron Reijirō Wakatsuki, who had held the Premiership on two occasions, but the most responsive proved to be a man whom Strauss had known in New York in the 1920's—Tadao (Paul) Wikawa.

It was in this way, through the good offices of Lewis Strauss, an old friend of both, that John Doe and the "Plenipotentiary Representative" who was to be one of his closest "Associates" first became acquainted, discovering in each other a rapport that was to see them through the many vicissitudes they were to encounter during the year ahead. Although a very special relationship was to develop from the discussions they had together in Tokyo in December 1940, Drought seems only gradually to have realized the extent to which Wikawa could fit into his scheme for a Japanese-American rapprochement. Drought consequently spared no effort during his stay in Japan to explore as many leads as possible and to develop a variety of contacts, some of which were quite unusual. A partial log of what he and the Bishop did during their month-long visit would read as follows:

Nov. 25 Docked at Yokohama; checked into the Imperial Hotel in Tokyo.

Nov. 26 Called on the Chief of the American Bureau of the Foreign Office, Tarō Terasaki (a Catholic).

Nov. 27 Saw Setsuzō Sawada; began working on the memo.

Nov. 30 Dinner at the Sawadas' [followed by home] movies of Maryknoll [taken by our host]; talked some more about the current situation.

Dec. 3 Dinner with Mr. and Mrs. Terasaki.

Dec. 5 Tea with Foreign Minister Matsuoka (unforgettable exposition of policy); handed over the full memo on strategy (the translation should be ready tomorrow or Saturday).

Dec. 6 Further discussion with Terasaki.

Dec. 10 Dinner with the Vice-Minister of Foreign Affairs (Sawada and Terasaki were also present); talked about the speech.

Dec. 11 Mr. Wikawa (our second meeting).

Dec. 17 Talked with Wikawa; Sawada called at the hotel.

Dec. 19 America-Japan Society luncheon (Matsuoka's speech—an historic occasion); gaucherie of the American Ambassador.

Dec. 21 Lunch with Sawada, Terasaki, and others (Departmental flutterings); invited them to dinner—speeches and *saké* galore.

Dec. 23 Lunch with Matsuoka at his private residence; dinner with Wikawa.

Dec. 25 Christmas—clear, chill, sunny.

Dec. 27 Saw General Mutō at the War Ministry (Mr. Wikawa acted as our interpreter).

Dec. 28 Packing to leave; many callers, messages, presents; went to Prince Konoye's residence but his secretary told us the Premier had not yet returned; to Yokohama by car—a crowd to see us off; sailed at 3:00 P.M.; a lovely sunset for "sayo-nara" to Japan.

Before departing from Maryknoll for the Far East, Drought had tried his best to obtain a high-level letter of introduction to Foreign Minister Matsuoka. When his efforts had produced no results, he had left instructions regarding a cable to be sent to Setsuzō Sawada, a senior Japanese diplomat who had visited Maryknoll on several occasions earlier in his career (his wife and children were Catholics): "Would government officials invite Maryknoll superiors to discuss at Tokyo situation of their American missioners now in Japan? Purpose would be to create favorable impression on large groups in this country. No expenses necessary."

Following Drought's arrival in San Francisco, a fellow Maryknoller had handed him a short memo entitled "Japanese Friends in Nippon." The list included several Foreign Office men who had held consular rank in the United States at one time or another. The foremost among these, although this was not apparent from the memo, was a "high" official who was said to be "a very good friend of Maryknoll." A more accurate description would have been Chūichi Ōhashi, Vice-Minister of Foreign Affairs and a close associate of Mr. Matsuoka.

While Drought was crossing the Pacific, the instructions he had left behind were carried out. The cable he had drafted (or one very similar to it in wording) had come in due course into the hands of Sawada. It had been dispatched over the name of a Catholic friend of many years' standing, Robert J. Cuddihy (one of the signers of the goodwill cable to Hirota). Cuddihy was known to Sawada as a benefactor of Maryknoll and as a man deeply interested in the problem of world peace. Sawada had immediately discussed Cuddihy's telegram with several members of the Konoye Cabinet who might have a jurisdictional interest. The Foreign Minister, in particular, had indicated that he would be willing to confer with the Maryknollers when they got to Japan.

After their arrival in Tokyo, Walsh and Drought talked first with Terasaki and then with Sawada (both men had a good command of English). Terasaki's reaction to what Walsh and Drought had to say is not known, but Sawada felt that their proposals were so "serious and delicate" in nature they ought to be committed to paper "so that there would be no mistake." Drought did not need further urging. Once back at the Imperial Hotel, he labored through the night organizing his thoughts into what soon became a long memorandum.

A week later, on December 4, Drought wrote to Terasaki to thank him for his "most gracious courtesy" the previous evening and to follow through on a matter Drought had raised: "I am sending down two copies of the memo.* If you will be in your office tomorrow morning, I will have more copies and the complete memo on policy and strategy. ... Mr. Kabayama will prepare the translation and [will] probably have it ready on Friday or Saturday. Will you kindly advise him to whom he should give the translated copies so as to expedite our business. ... P.S. You may, of course, give these copies to anyone you wish."

The next day Walsh and Drought were ushered into the presence of the Foreign Minister. After greeting his visitors politely, Matsuoka plunged into a tirade against the fighting in China. Instead of defending Japanese policy, he denounced it. He spoke in the strongest terms about the injustice of the war and about the harm it was doing to the Chinese people. If only some way could be found to bring it to an end!

Matsuoka then revealed that he wanted to enlist the aid of the United States in restoring peace to the Far East by means of a special treaty. Just how far he went in outlining what he had in mind is not entirely clear. In recalling the experience many years later, however, Bishop Walsh felt that the terms of the proposed treaty—when they were ultimately spelled out—"seemed almost too good to be true."

For his part Drought took advantage of this meeting with Matsuoka to thrust a copy of his own "memo on policy and strategy" into the hands of the Foreign Minister, along with a summary he had prepared of the main points. Drought had written both pieces *as though he were a Japanese.* Unlike the full memo, which was very long, the summary went straight to the point:

Despite contrary appearances, the present emotional tension between Japan and the United States affords ... an opportunity for an epochal diplomatic stroke that will appreciably divide American opinion and may bring about American acknowledgment of our Far Eastern hegemony and the recognition of our status as paralleling that of the United States. ... A "Working Analysis" (herewith submitted) ... states our position comprehensively and indicates how, without relinquishing a single, important gain or prospect, we may reverse completely the unfavorable American trend and consolidate for years to come our security vis-à-vis the United States.

"An effort could be made," the summary declared, "through a well-staged and psychologically-American speech ... to decisively reach pub-

* Drought is referring here to a summary of the document he had drafted in response to Sawada's request for something in writing.

lic opinion. . . . We could then project a secret, non-diplomatic suggestion of a plenipotentiary conference of Japanese and American delegates at Tokyo (preferably) or at Honolulu (concessively). If our speech and ensuing publicity are successful, American public opinion, particularly business and finance, would be inclined to feel that such a conference had become logically and practically compulsory."

"[With the exception of] our Axis Alliance," Drought argued, "we could propose . . . that the Agenda comprise all subjects of outstanding differences. . . . In reaching our Agenda conclusions and agreements, we must shrewdly allow President Roosevelt to assume some credit for 'Peace in the Pacific.' If the United States Government refuses to move simultaneously toward an Understanding, we could then reveal our proposed Agenda to the American Press and thereby embarrass the American Government and weaken proportionately the fast-growing American sentiment that war with Japan may prove inevitable."

With this much on paper, how far did Drought dare to go in person? Probably no one will ever know (the mind boggles at the possibilities), but in a letter written the next day, he pulled out all of the stops:

It was a privilege to visit the Minister of Foreign Affairs—but it was an inspiration to visit Mr. Matsuoka. May God bless and strengthen your Excellency!

Your Excellency has taken the diplomatic initiative for peace. Will you not keep it? Encouraged by your character and vision, we should like, humbly, to remark that the admirable tactic designed by your Excellency to restrict the war might cause it to spread unless other *equally* wise and dramatic moves are currently made. Both wars are now territorially localized. Could they not also be emotionally and politically localized? Your Excellency, with others, might then *compel* the arbitration of a just and realistic peace. . . .

According to all the rules, Mr. Roosevelt plans to enter the military war. Yet, it is quite possible that his threatening attitude (which has already served its domestic, political purpose) is also prompted by the same motives as your own. He may be striving to localize war, from another direction. Mr. Roosevelt is a political genius who does not follow the established rules. He is also a very cunning gambler who really likes plain people and vainly loves their gratitude. The spirit that animates hakkoichiu is not unlike the spirit . . . that promoted the League of Nations. Mr. Roosevelt shared that spirit at Versailles. He needs only to be captivated again. We believe he can be: and we are not unacquainted with his character or circumstances.*

The December 5 meeting with Matsuoka proved to be one of the highlights of the Walsh-Drought visit to Japan, but nowhere did they find a

---

* By "admirable tactic" Drought meant Japan's entry into the Axis alliance through the Tripartite Pact. The reference to "both wars" is to the war in Europe and the war in China. *Hakkō-ichiu* ("the eight corners of the world under one roof") signified "universal brotherhood," according to the Japanese (but "domination of the world," according to their "brothers").

more attentive listener or a more willing helper than in the person of Tadao Paul Wikawa.

The initiative, which had been Drought's from the very beginning, was to remain largely in his hands thereafter, though this is not to say that he was always in command of the situation. Wikawa was not lacking in ideas, nor was he prepared to play only a passive role. He had connections in high places and knew how to make the most of an opportunity. He had a reputation among his Japanese colleagues as a clever, ambitious, and pushy fellow, a manipulator who would not let scruples stand in the way of gaining an advantage.

Wikawa was well aware of the differences in personality between the forty-nine-year-old Bishop and the forty-four-year-old priest—the devout and quiet nature of the one contrasting with the energetic and business-like approach of the other. As a man of affairs himself, three years older than Drought and a Christian besides, Wikawa was pleased at suddenly finding himself face to face with an American priest, obviously friendly to Japan, who had some plan or other aimed at restoring the balance that had once existed in Japanese-American relations.

And yet Wikawa felt that he would have to be careful. If an ulterior motive lay behind the Walsh-Drought desire to help ease existing tensions, he would only be endangering himself by getting involved. This thought caused him to consult a colonel in the War Ministry with whom he was acquainted. The officer in question, Hideo Iwakuro, occupied an important position: he was the chief of the Army Affairs Section of the powerful Military Affairs Bureau, which served as a link between the Army and the Cabinet.

Upon hearing Wikawa's story, Iwakuro went to his superior, Major General Akira Mutō. The upshot was a decision to let Wikawa listen—purely as a private individual—to what the American priest had to say. Orders would be issued to the Kenpeitai and the Metropolitan Police "to close their eyes" to what was going on.

Having acquired this guarantee against interference from the most likely source, Wikawa felt free to introduce himself more deeply into the undertaking. He did this by means of a letter addressed to another acquaintance of his, Prince Fumimaro Konoye, the Premier of Japan.

Writing on the evening of Saturday, December 7, 1940, Wikawa summarized what had occurred to date, including his visit to the War Ministry. By way of documentation, he enclosed copies of Strauss's letter of introduction and Drought's covering note.

Wikawa described Strauss as one of the most influential directors of Kuhn, Loeb and Company, the firm that had helped Japan float loans in the European and American markets at the time of the Russo-Japanese War. Strauss had once served as a confidential secretary to Herbert Hoover and (according to Wikawa) was very anti-British. On a visit to Japan in the 1920's, Strauss had been feted at a formal dinner by the then Premier, Baron Wakatsuki, and had been granted an audience at Court. Strauss had frequently told Wikawa that he hoped someday to be able to repay the kindness extended to him during his stay in Japan.

Wikawa had come to the conclusion, and so informed Konoye, that Drought had received instructions from Kuhn, Loeb and Company before leaving for Japan. When Wikawa had tried to find out, however, whether the firm might have some connection with the American Government or be acting for it, Drought had sidestepped the question by saying, "Don't ask me to tell you too much." Wikawa believed that this reply, barren on the surface, was nevertheless full of meaning.

Wikawa admitted that nothing might come of the affair, but he wanted to pursue it nevertheless. If Drought really had something to offer, the Foreign Office or some other appropriate agency could then open negotiations. In the meantime Wikawa would learn what he could and would keep Konoye advised of developments.

"It was indeed a pleasant surprise," Wikawa wrote to Strauss the next day, "that I should receive from Father Drought such a nice letter as the enclosed copy shows, together with your letter of introduction dated November 8. I lost no time in calling on him and we really had very interesting talks. My first impression of him was nothing but superlative. You certainly have a good and trustworthy friend in him, and I am sure I shall share the same fortune with you by making him our mutual friend."

Drought was in Kyoto at the moment, but as soon as he returned to Tokyo Wikawa was going to discuss with him "the necessary steps" mentioned in Drought's covering note. "I earnestly pray," Wikawa informed Strauss, "that such may lead to laying one of the corner stones for the restoration of peace and establishment of new order on earth as you wished in the last paragraph of your letter."

The developments anticipated by Wikawa in his report to Konoye quickly materialized. On Wednesday, December 11, Drought took his new friend Paul more fully into his confidence. The next day Wikawa dutifully informed Konoye of this second meeting in a letter that has yet to be found. On December 14 Wikawa again communicated with the Premier. The subject this time was a document in English that Wikawa had received from Drought. It was rather ponderously entitled "Working Analysis of Our (Japanese) Position & Policy in the Far East, With Particular Reference to the United States."

Wikawa suspected that influential forces were pulling the strings from behind the scenes; he did not think the "Analysis" could be the product of Drought's mind alone. For one thing, there was the deliberate way in which various delicate matters were divulged, including the true motives of President Roosevelt. For another, the terminology employed in the document and the information it contained did not sound like something a priest would write.

The short letter in which Wikawa reported these conclusions to Konoye was all but swallowed up by an enclosure that ran to thirteen tightly packed, single-spaced pages: a typewritten copy, on Wikawa's office letterhead, of the document he had received from Drought. Despite Wikawa's doubts, this extraordinary submission was actually Drought's own blueprint for peace in the Pacific—a personal memorandum on policy and strategy—the very same that he had handed to Foreign Minister Matsuoka on December 5. It covered at great length what Drought's earlier summary had presented in a few paragraphs. From beginning to end, the presentation was forceful:

> Japan is so far distant, its actions have been so grossly misrepresented, its policy so badly understood, its incidents of diplomatic conflict so frequent, that the United States Government shrewdly estimates what its people unconsciously feel, viz. that a relieving explosion of sentiment against Japan will compensate for their own lack of unified and decisive action toward Europe and thereby unite them on at least one aspect of foreign policy.

What Japan needed now, Drought argued, was a carefully designed strategy, along with "emotional rather than legal diplomacy."

Writing as one Japanese to another, he warmed to the task: we must "keep in reserve and make no present concessions" on "our military and political position in China" and "our Axis Alliance"; in East, Central, and North China we can, "without any loss whatever, permit the Americans to talk of some sort of political structure which would leave our position substantially unchanged but which could be presented acceptably to American public opinion."

"If they are at all fair," Drought's "Working Analysis" declared, "(and Americans, when not emotionally aroused, are inclined to be very fair) the Americans will admit that they have run into a cul-de-sac." Care had to be taken, however, to manipulate the current situation to advantage: "It should be our aim to so dispose affairs that the calling of a plenipotentiary Japan–United States conference at Tokyo, or at Honolulu (but not at Washington) would seem reasonable and desirable in the mind of American public opinion: if not in the mind of the Roosevelt Government."

Drought favored "a bold manoeuvre," for even if it were only "moderately successful" it would "break down the present tension *and permit Japan to consolidate her position, with or without American approbation."*

What did Drought have in mind? What would be "strategically advisable"? His answer was a "special address" to be delivered to some large and representative group by Premier Konoye or Foreign Minister Matsuoka. The purpose would be to "outline Japan's position" in a way that would capture the attention of the American people.

To guarantee a propitious outcome, Drought promised to draft "a psychological and diplomatic speech" of the type he had in mind. It ought to be given, he said, before Ambassador Nomura took up his post in the United States. A good time would be around December 20, "when the Christmas spirit of 'peace on earth to men of goodwill' " permeated the American scene.

Every effort had to be made to secure the widest possible publicity, including immediate distribution in the United States of newsreels in English covering the event. The press associations should be alerted twenty-four hours in advance and also the State Department, "but not any sooner lest the . . . Department devise some counter-publicity."

The speech itself "should be so thorough and moving as to insure favorable comment." The fundamental aim would be "to force the hand of the American Government" so that it would have to agree to participate in a "plenipotentiary conference" with Japan.

To help matters along, Drought even included a sample agenda. "Constructive discussion" of this agenda at the conference, he said, should "force" the Americans "to discontinue their 'rear-guard action' diplomacy: and force them, also, to abandon their tactic of trying to fit new circumstances into old legal phrases."

Drought felt that the conference should take place "as soon as possible after the proposed speech of December 20." Once the two governments had agreed to meet, they should refrain from any controversial actions. "This would immobilize the United States until the conference had been concluded."

It would be very advantageous to us [Japanese] if the Americans could be persuaded to come to Tokyo. As such a concession might be represented in America as "appeasement" we must be prepared to *make every effort* to overcome objections by pointing out the propriety of our acting as the conference hosts for a Far Eastern bilateral conference. It would be a diplomatic victory, and assure a good start, if we can secure Tokyo as the place of meeting. To this end, we must take the practical, though not the diplomatic, initiative. Japanese courtesy, cherry-blossom time, a fine hotel, golf courses, the moving pageantry of kimonos against the backdrop of national sacrifice—all of these should prove helpfully disposing circumstances. If we fail to agree on Tokyo, we could reluctantly accept Honolulu because of its symbolic significance and as a subtle indication of our own policies.

For the first time in nearly a century, Drought declared, Japanese-American relations need not be "entangled" by bringing Europeans into the picture. Guarding against the twin evils of imperialism and communism was essential. A Japanese-American settlement of the type contemplated would place both countries "in so dominant a position as to minimize the importance of the European area for years to come."

If such a settlement could be reached, Drought wrote, "we would not only prevent the Far Eastern extension of the European conflict, but we would *immunize the Far East* against it. It is even possible that our two countries might become the final arbitrators of the outcome of the European War. Moreover, by such common action and agreement, we would create a friendly and intimate American relationship which would eliminate the likelihood of armed conflict with the United States and thereby strengthen our position against Russia which will remain, for years or generations, a doubtful quantity."

"If [the Japanese-American conference] is successful," Drought argued, "no one would dare to object; and if it fails, no one will quarrel with us."

Probably nowhere in the annals of diplomacy does a more fantastic document exist. By reading it one can in some measure look into the mind and personality of Father Drought. He eagerly plunged into the world of high politics with complete confidence in his ability to mold national destinies, all the while utterly disregarding the existing state of affairs, for which there was no dearth of evidence.

In *Japan News-Week*, an American-owned paper Drought took to reading while he was in Tokyo, Editor Charles Nelson Spinks described the nature of the problem:

> The ill-feeling and distrust which characterizes American sentiment toward Japan today has been generated by a great variety of causes. There is the conviction that Japan has deliberately invaded China for the purpose of territorial aggrandizement, that Japan has wilfully violated treaties and disregarded the rights of others merely because these happened to stand in her way. There is the feeling that Japan has unreasonably injured and jeopardized American rights and interests in China, not as an unavoidable and temporary aspect of a military campaign, but as part of a preconceived plan to oust American and all foreign interests from China. More recently, these disturbing convictions have been intensified by the belief that Japan's recent activity in China is but a prelude to the general domination of Asia, that this alleged program now constitutes an actual menace to American security—not the security of the relatively

small American stake in the Orient, but the security of America's position in the Western Hemisphere. Fantastic as this may at first seem, it must be admitted that Japan's recent military alliance with Germany and Italy has provided a powerful stimulant to such a belief.

The people of the United States might be wrong in their judgment that Japan's "New Order" would be detrimental to their safety and therefore had to be opposed. Japan might have some substantial arguments on her side. If so, Spinks thought she would serve her cause better by putting an end to the vague generalities constantly offered by way of explanation. Americans wanted straight answers to straight questions, not more mumbo jumbo about Japan's mission to make the world one big happy household.

Spinks had not minced words, but he had tried to be fair in a situation in which being fair was becoming more and more difficult. He knew that a crisis was in the making—that the future was precarious indeed. His views gained authority from the accumulated observations of five years of residence in Japan.

Drought, on the other hand, had only recently arrived in this unfamiliar country—this "land of the gods"—and yet he had already formulated conclusions of his own, conclusions that he presented with conviction. As he saw it, relations between Japan and the United States had "moved beyond the cool mathematics of diplomacy." In these circumstances he believed that more could be accomplished in a short time by a "dramatic reversal . . . than could be gained by years of normal effort"; the prevailing "emotional atmosphere" made "a radical solution in either direction" not only possible but necessary.

In short, the time had now come for "the greatest diplomatic stroke in a generation." Needless to say, Father James M. Drought of Maryknoll, New York, was more than ready to deliver it.

CHAPTER SEVEN

The Language of Diplomacy Unveiled

EDITOR SPINKS was right. The day was long past when the generalities offered by Japanese apologists could serve the cause of their nation. Even Foreign Minister Matsuoka seemed to realize this, for on coming to his high office in mid-1940 he had told the press that "deeds not words" represented the principle he would follow in handling his responsibilities. Propaganda could well be left to other nations, he had said, for a talkative diplomat was generally a lying diplomat.

What an extraordinary remark from the mouth of a man whose "chief outward characteristic" was his "extreme loquaciousness."

Opinions differed on whether Matsuoka should be described as "a famous or a notorious conversationalist"—the reason being that "a conversation with him [was] generally like listening to a monologue." There was a story to the effect that persons who called on him for the first time were advised to enter the room talking, and to keep right on talking until they had finished whatever it was they had come to say, for if Matsuoka got the "jump" on them it was unlikely that they would ever make any headway "against his steady, irresistible flow of words."

The British Ambassador, Sir Robert Craigie, felt that he had never met anyone who spoke so much and said so little, but behind this garrulousness was the mind and the will of a sixty-year-old product of two cultures—Matsuoka's youth having been spent in school and college in the United States, an experience that helps to explain why he was later regarded by some of his contemporaries as an "American expert."

Matsuoka's performance at the League of Nations in 1933 as Japan's "Refuter-in-Chief" had made him famous throughout the world. By 1940 he had apparently grown so eager to take charge of the Foreign Office that he had expressed his readiness to be Konoye's *zōri-tori*, a reference to an anecdote of the sixteenth century when the low-born but clever Hideyoshi had allegedly gotten his start in life through his willingness to accept the menial task of carrying the sandals of the all-powerful Nobunaga (the master of Japan whom Hideyoshi ultimately succeeded and surpassed).

In the twentieth century, Matsuoka and Konoye were as different in their own way as Hideyoshi and Nobunaga had been. A close subordinate of the Foreign Minister later wrote: "If Konoye was a shy squirrel sheltered in the deep forests, Matsuoka was the stormy petrel that delights to spread its wings over the foaming sea. It is doubtful if the two ever understood one another."

A Japanese reporter, who knew the Foreign Minister well, subsequently remembered a man whose love of posing had kept him from exercising good judgment. Matsuoka might be "painfully candid in conversation with a single individual, but when two or more were present, he seemed constitutionally incapable of candor and resorted to a hypocritical kind of showing off."

The very prolixity of Matsuoka's language often made it difficult for his listeners to carry away clear-cut impressions from conversations with him. Foremost among those who had to deal with this problem was the American Ambassador. Despite Matsuoka's tendency to make a display of himself, Grew knew that he was not to be dismissed lightly. To engage in combat with him was to become involved in a battle of wits across ground that changed hands many times before the immediate objective was won or lost. During the in-fighting that resulted great skill was needed to parry or thrust, as the circumstances required.

German victories in Europe in the spring of 1940 had acted on Matsuoka and many of his countrymen "like strong wine." The effects were soon noticeable. In a midsummer conversation with Wilfrid Fleisher, an experienced correspondent, the new Foreign Minister had revealed thoughts that anyone else in his position would have kept to himself. Speaking for background and not for attribution, Matsuoka had insisted that totalitarianism would win without question; the era of democracy was finished. Matsuoka's elaboration of this theme had provided such a clear view of his philosophy that he seemed "more intensely pro-Axis than any other Japanese" with whom Fleisher had talked.

With Vice-Minister Chūichi Ōhashi supplying assistance and support, Matsuoka had quickly made his presence felt at the Foreign Office through the most drastic personnel shake-up in the history of the Kasumi-ga-seki.* The "Matsuoka cyclone" was going to blow out the

---

* This word is a metonym for Gaimushō (the Japanese Ministry of Foreign Affairs), which is located in a section of Tokyo that served as a checkpoint during Tokugawa days. Since ground fog was a common occurrence there, the area came to be known as Kasumi-ga-seki (literally, "the misty barrier").

old and blow in the new. The object of the purge was to get rid of bureaucrats who did not appreciate "the spirit of the times." There was to be no room for "conservatism" or "bachelor of law diplomacy." Career officials with legal training and considerable practical experience were to make way for men who would help transform Japan into a nation on fire capable of consuming every obstacle in its path.

According to Matsuoka, many of those who were to be ousted had "gone Western"—they had lost touch with the Japanese point of view. "Western" meant pro-British and pro-American, for with Matsuoka in the Foreign Office Japan had rushed "hell-bent toward the Axis." The result was a striking change in the Japanese people. Eugene H. Dooman, Grew's Counselor of Embassy, felt he was dealing with a land that he had once thought he understood fairly well but that he now regarded as "utterly strange."

Everywhere there was talk of the "golden opportunity" awaiting Japan. As Dooman saw it, this meant that she would take advantage of countries that had been friendly to her and with whom she had no quarrel. With France badly beaten, with the Netherlands overrun by the enemy, and with Great Britain fighting for her survival, the Japanese were going to grab whatever they could in the way of privileges from the Far Eastern possessions of the European powers. The Imperial Army and Navy might even attempt to seize the colonies by force.

The Japanese were hoping that the Germans would be successful in Europe. If they were not, Japan would presumably moderate her attitude toward the British, the French, and the Dutch. By the time the Japanese got around to changing their stand, however, they might find that they had "forfeited the right to have accepted by the world on its face value any policy of moderation" they might then belatedly adopt.

This was indeed a danger, but it did not deter Matsuoka. He plunged ahead with his policy of tying a Japanese tail to the German kite, developing in the process a "style" as Foreign Minister that made him unique.

Whenever an opportunity offered itself, Matsuoka displayed his thoughts indiscriminately, like a street-vendor hawking gewgaws at night on the Ginza. In one of his meetings with Ambassador Grew, for example, he pointedly referred to an article he had written for a Japanese magazine. Since it was full of the "frank and direct speaking" Matsuoka had been advocating, Grew had the piece translated and sent to Washington. It made such an impression within the State Department that copies were soon on their way to Army and Navy Intelligence. Beneath a good deal of froth rested some substance of a type that could not but be of concern to American officials (despite a certain quaintness in the translation that served as their text).

The League of Nations from which Matsuoka had led the Japanese delegation in 1933 was "excellent as an ideal," the Foreign Minister believed, but it was "only a 'Utopia' in the present stage of the development of mankind"—a "Tower of Babel." International politics could not be regulated by the kind of idealism that found expression in the League, a "false idealism" that "camouflaged" actual conditions, "a trick of those favoring the maintenance of the status quo."

A distinction had to be made, Matsuoka insisted, between the end and the means—between Japan's "final goal . . . and the road (usually called 'diplomacy')" by which Japan would reach that goal.

Even when Japan's aim is to cooperate with a certain country, Japan may fight that country on the way to the accomplishment of that end. Japan may even wage a war with that country. Such action is, however, a road to cooperation.

In other cases, owing to actual international conditions, Japan may be compelled to court temporarily the favor of a certain country, which Japan thinks that it must destroy as its enemy. There may be a case in which Japan shall be compelled even to shake hands with such a country.

All of this, however, is not inconsistency. It is a way to defeat that country as our enemy. It is only a different form of . . . war.

And yet Matsuoka—a practicing Christian who ultimately embraced Catholicism—was not opposed to having a moral spirit serve as the foundation for relations between nations. The actual state of diplomacy being what it was, however, it would be "absurd" for Japan alone to adopt a moral approach. Diplomacy did not differ in essence from fighting with actual weapons. It meant combat at the "intellectual" level; the object was to win.

With such thoughts churning in his mind, the Foreign Minister of Japan set out to prove that he personally recognized what was happening in the world and could rise to meet the occasion. By the time Bishop Walsh and Father Drought had arrived in Tokyo in late November 1940, Matsuoka had demonstrated his capacity in this regard through the conclusion of an alliance with Hitler and Mussolini. His pride in this achievement was marred only by the vigor of the American reaction, for which he was entirely unprepared.

Confronted by this development, Matsuoka had to resort to countermeasures. Shifting his stance whenever that seemed necessary, he blandly denied evil intent but continued to threaten the United States with the consequences should any situation arise to which Article 3 of the Tripartite Pact might apply. Under this stipulation, Germany, Italy, and Japan would assist each other with "all political, economic, and military means" at their disposal in case one of the contracting parties was *attacked* by a power not currently involved in the war in Europe or in the fighting in China. The only room for interpretation in this commitment seemed to lie in the verb.

Sir Robert Craigie judged that Matsuoka's primary purpose was to frighten the American Government into stopping its aid to Britain. "Cajolery having failed, America was now, under the Matsuoka policy, to be threatened." It soon became clear to Craigie, however, that the Japanese Foreign Minister could not have done Britain a better turn. By taking Japan into the Axis camp, he had prejudiced all future efforts to settle Japanese-American differences by peaceful means.

Grew was of the same opinion. Like other members of his Embassy, he had become increasingly disturbed by what he saw happening around him. Some two weeks before the conclusion of the Tripartite Pact he had deemed it wise to dispatch a "Green Light" telegram to Washington, his aim being "to express the opinion that while a strong policy would inevitably involve the risk of war, a laissez-faire policy, on the other hand, risked bringing American-Japanese relations into an increasingly precarious state and was therefore 'hopeless.'"

Japan had become a predatory power. She had "submerged all moral and ethical sense" and had "frankly and unashamedly" become opportunistic, "seeking at every turn to profit by the weakness of others."

Japan had thus far been deterred from taking "greater liberties" only out of respect for the potential power of the United States. The Japanese had trampled on American rights in the past "in precise ratio to the strength" of their conviction that "the American people would not permit that power to be used." If the Japanese now learned that the United States was determined to rouse herself against further aggression by Japan, diplomacy might again be able to operate effectively in the arena of Japanese-American relations.

"I have worked for eight years," Grew wrote in his diary, "to minimize the possibility of war; but I recognize that under present circumstances, our unwillingness to contemplate war might well lead to a future catastrophe of far greater proportions than any catastrophe which now confronts us."

Grew felt that Japan's word of honor could be trusted no further than Hitler's. The promises of the government might generally be based "on an overoptimistic frame of mind rather than on any studied intention to mislead," but this was "a purely academic point." Whenever an assurance given by the Japanese Foreign Minister was not carried out, the United States could legitimately charge Japan with breaking her word. Experience had taught the Ambassador a lesson: the Japanese Government had found it "all too easy," in the past, to resort to the "time-worn excuse" that the conditions prevailing when the promise was made had in the meantime "changed."

Conditions were always changing—sometimes quite drastically. New stresses might result, but also new opportunities. Matsuoka seemed to pay very little attention to this vital aspect of foreign relations. He was forever rummaging around in the kit of diplomatic stratagems he had brought with him to the Foreign Office. One day he would declare that the Axis alliance was the "pivot" of Japan's policy and would warn the American Government to watch its step. Another day he would assert that the alliance was defensive in nature; it was not aimed at the United States or any other nation. The Tripartite Pact was designed to keep the war in Europe from spreading to the Pacific; it was a noble effort to save civilization from destruction. By linking Japan to the Axis, he was preventing the United States from falling into the evil course of war with Japan.

Coping with such a man at any level—private or official—was no easy task. It certainly was not a mission that someone like Father Drought should have undertaken. Grew and Dooman acting for the United States, Craigie at the British Embassy, Editor Spinks of *Japan News-Week,* and every other knowledgeable person in a position to keep an eye on developments recognized Matsuoka's double-talk for what it was. Compared with Drought—a raw volunteer on the battlefield of diplomacy—Grew and Dooman were seasoned veterans. They were quite unaware, however, that a soldier of the cloth had somehow found his way into the trenches. If only they had known that he was there, they might have been able to prevent him from foolishly venturing into the no-man's-land that already grimly separated the opposing forces.

*

In writing to Matsuoka on December 6, Drought had suggested that the Foreign Minister, "with others," might now be able to bring about a "realistic peace" in the Far East. The very steps he had taken thus far had brought him to "the threshold of a magnificent triumph for contemporary humanity." One more move was necessary, however, "a complicated one but far from impossible."

The move Drought had in mind was the "special address" he had proposed in his "Working Analysis." He had not previously forced the issue of who should deliver the speech (the Premier of Japan or the Foreign Minister), but his success in reaching Matsuoka—together with another fortuitous development, a forthcoming America-Japan Society luncheon at the Imperial Hotel with the Foreign Minister as the principal speaker—soon settled that question. The occasion would be ideal, since the purpose of the luncheon was to honor the new Japanese envoy to the United States, Kichisaburō Nomura.

Drought had already begun drafting the kind of talk—"psychological and diplomatic"—that he felt the circumstances required. He had also conferred again with Setsuzō Sawada, asking him specifically whether the Japanese Government would publicly state that the proposals contained in the "Working Analysis" were "substantially acceptable."

After clearing the matter through the Foreign Office, Sawada had informed Drought that Matsuoka might be disposed to offer assurances of the type desired when he addressed the America-Japan Society luncheon on December 19.

Drought had then indicated that as soon as the assurances were given he would cable his friend Frank Walker in Washington. In this way it would be possible to get the Foreign Minister's remarks before the American people prior to Christmas.

Various Japanese had been telling Drought that they could not make any progress dealing with the American Embassy because Grew and his staff kept lodging protest after protest against the conduct of the Japanese Army in China but never said a word about "fundamentals." Drought had concluded from these complaints that Japan badly needed an "intelligible" presentation of her case in America—a presentation that would help convince public opinion that Matsuoka had been right when he had said the United States and Japan were "natural Allies."

In drafting remarks that would serve this purpose, Drought had endeavored to "set forth rather clearly the policy of Japan" and to "indicate, without loss of face, the willing desire of Japan to 'talk things over.' " The speech he concocted, however, was a poor product. It was far too long and involved—eight single-spaced, typewritten pages marred by phrases fashioned in an odd and awkward manner and by sentences aimlessly meandering through a labyrinth of thoughts that were often formless in shape and empty of meaning.

Drought had gone at matters too amateurishly. He had incorporated elements so un-Japanese that they would not have rolled well off the tongue of even a Matsuoka. Although the Foreign Minister looked at the speech Drought had written for him, he cast it aside.

Matsuoka had his own ideas, his own manner of speaking, and his own sources of advice. Indeed, he was about to deliver one of his most memorable performances. He would appear as *bucinator novi temporis*

—the trumpeter of a new age in which Japan, Germany, and Italy (three partners with a common aim) would achieve the mastery they felt they deserved.

*

The arguments in favor of adopting a stronger policy toward Japan that Ambassador Grew had presented in his "Green Light" telegram to the State Department in September 1940 had loomed larger with the passage of time. By mid-December, when Father Drought was trying to pump his ideas into Matsuoka and other Japanese leaders, Grew had grown sufficiently concerned over recent developments to write one of the "Dear Frank" letters with which he sometimes conveyed his views directly to President Roosevelt regarding matters that the Embassy deemed to be of critical importance to the security of the United States.

Ever since 1932, when Grew had taken up his post in Japan, he had lived with an "area problem" of a specific nature. Following the outbreak of the European war, however, and especially after Japan had joined the Axis, Grew had realized that the Far Eastern question was no longer a separate entity. It had become, instead, "an integral part of the world crisis created by Adolf Hitler's bid for world domination."

"After eight years of effort to build up something permanently constructive in American-Japanese relations," Grew informed Roosevelt, "I find that diplomacy has been defeated by trends and forces utterly beyond its control, and that our work has been swept away as if by a typhoon with little or nothing remaining to show for it. Japan has become openly and unashamedly one of the predatory nations and part of a system which aims to wreck about everything that the United States stands for. Only insuperable obstacles will now prevent the Japanese from digging in permanently in China and from pushing the southward advance, with economic control as a preliminary to political domination in the areas marked down."

Unless the American people were prepared "to withdraw bag and baggage from the entire sphere of 'Greater East Asia including the South Seas,'" the United States was "bound eventually to come to a head-on clash with Japan."

"It is important constantly to bear in mind," Grew added, "... that if we take measures 'short of war' with no real intention to carry those measures to their final conclusion if necessary, such lack of intention will be all too obvious to the Japanese who will proceed undeterred, and even with greater incentive, on their way. Only if they become certain that we mean to fight if called upon to do so will our preliminary measures stand some chance of proving effective and of removing the necessity for war."

The day on which the Ambassador wrote this letter to the President—December 14, 1940—happened to be the Saturday on which Drought's new friend Paul Wikawa sent Konoye a copy of the "Working Analysis." This document was already available to Matsuoka and key members of his staff—as was the "psychologically-American speech" that Drought had drafted over the preceding weekend. December 14 seems also to have been the day on which Matsuoka first dictated some notes to one of his subordinates for inclusion in the public address he was to deliver at the Imperial Hotel five days later—an address that would be quite unlike the one Father Drought had in mind.

The America-Japan Society, which was acting as host for the occasion, embraced many individuals who professed a common interest: perpetuation of harmonious relations between their respective nations. Meetings of the Society therefore constituted a forum of significance.

As guest speaker on December 19, Matsuoka made the most of the opportunity. His audience numbered well over three hundred persons, described by the *Japan Times and Advertiser* as "the most distinguished gathering of Americans and Japanese held in Tokyo in recent years."

Even now, so long after the event, the words uttered by Matsuoka on that day, and the reactions they produced, are a powerful echo of the past reverberating through the monumental canyons of history.

Matsuoka's opening remarks were all charm and good humor—his occasionally awkward phrasing in English adding a flavor of its own. Professing pleasure at being accorded "a free luncheon" during a period "of stress and strictly managed economy," the Foreign Minister proceeded to confide "a bit of private information" about the difficulties he had encountered in persuading an "adamant" Nomura to represent Japan in the United States: "At first it looked hopeless. . . . But I refused to be scared away. I went back at him again and again. . . . Finally, at the end of three months' siege and attack, this stubborn Admiral capitulated. Certainly I was proud of my victory. However, I came very soon to realize that I [had] fought the battle on my own ground, i.e. terra firma, and not in the sailor's element. That was not fair for the Admiral, but it was a thing on which Japan is to be congratulated and may be for America, too. In any case, I wouldn't see myself compelled to meet him on the high seas!"

In the mimeographed copies of Matsuoka's speech distributed in advance of the luncheon, the sentence following the "high seas" remark had been painted out with India ink. This tantalizing obliteration, which appeared total to the naked eye, was later to yield a legible text to resourceful and irreverent types who took the trouble to use strong lamps and other devices to pluck Matsuoka's suppressed thought from the obscurity to which it had been consigned. "And I wonder," the Foreign Minister had planned to say, "if the President or the Secretary of the United States of America would show a liking to meet such an Admiral in the Pacific waters and take chance."

According to Matsuoka, some Americans—"wilfully or otherwise"—had misunderstood Japan's purpose in joining the Axis alliance. Japan was consequently being accused of "harboring hostile intentions towards America." Nothing could be "more absurd and untrue." Japan had no desire to antagonize America or any other nation. Japan wanted to be "left alone" to carry on her "constructive work unhindered." She wanted "to see the trouble in China and the war in Europe brought speedily to an end, without adding more participants, particularly such a powerful one as America."

Imagine just for a moment that America joined the European war or came to a clash with Japan in the Pacific. What then? If any bit of human feeling or an atom of instinct for self-preservation is left in you, ladies and gentlemen, wouldn't you shudder at the very thought? Would not a kind of ice-water shoot down your spine?

There would loom up every chance of facing at last the Armageddon that would end in a total destruction of our culture and civilization. I do beseech my American friends to think twice, thrice, nay, ten, hundred or thousand times before they take a leap that may prove fatal to all Humanity.

Although Matsuoka may not have been aware of it, many Americans were beginning to give a great deal of thought to the uncertainties of the world in which they lived and to the relative merits of action versus inaction. The evil of Hitler and all his works could no longer be ignored by sensible people, no matter how strongly they desired to close their eyes to the sight, and yet here was the Foreign Minister of Japan wringing his hands in public over the fate that might befall "humanity" if the United States tried to stand in the way of the "New Order" Japan, Germany, and Italy were in the process of "constructing."

"I wish to leave no doubt whatever in the mind of any American citizen," Matsuoka declared, "... that Japan is, and will remain, loyal to her Allies; that Japan's foreign policy will revolve in the future around the [Tripartite] Pact as its pivot, as it did around the pivot of the Anglo-Japanese Alliance in the past.... This, of course, implies no threat. It is a simple statement of truism made in order to prevent possible misapprehension. For, an illusion on an issue like this will bring no good to anyone."

According to Matsuoka, the other major issue of the moment—the fate of China—was largely a matter of "sentiment" to the American people. To the Japanese, on the other hand, whatever happened on the Asian mainland was "truly vital" because events there affected the "very existence" of the Empire. The "new Chinese Central Government at Nanking" (headed by Wang Ching-wei) was "the harbinger of better times," an example of "daffodils that come before the swallow dares."

"My proposition," Matsuoka said, "is that we . . . shall not blink at realities, however unpalatable they happen to be, but shall try earnestly and honestly to understand each other's position with sympathy and in a spirit of mutual accommodation. For this, we must clear our mind of cant and avoid the folly of 'rubbing the sore when one should bring the plaster' which sometimes thoughtless, not to say malevolent, people are apt to do."

Japan was sending Nomura to the United States to usher in "a happier period of mutual trust and better understanding." The Admiral might not be a professional diplomat, but he was "a skillful and tried seaman" who would take the ship of state safely into port. Lying unseen in the hold was the ballast needed for stability. "That ballast," Matsuoka declared, "is the common sense of our two peoples."

And so I close this address with an earnest appeal . . . to maintain calm judgment and quiet self-restraint. . . . Let us go slow and take time. . . . Eternity before us, why over-hurry? Half a century is but a passing moment and will fill merely one brief paragraph in a history book.

Is it too much for Japan to ask for so much of a minute, just half a century or even less, in which to prove herself to the world? Time is the great curer of human travail. Let us all have a bit of patience. This is my appeal.

The members of the America-Japan Society, having been shaken collectively by the shoulders into an awareness of where matters stood, were now being eased gently back into their seats to mull it over. Giddy minds and foreign affairs, Matsuoka had said, did not go well together. Neither did an olive branch extended with the left hand while a sword was being brandished in the right. Earnest appeals to common sense were all well and good, but in late 1940 common sense at any level—government, press, or public—was a precious commodity that simply could not be wished into existence. No useful purpose would be served by the leaders of one nation urging broad vision and good judgment on their counterparts in another while at the very same time conducting themselves as though they alone possessed a talisman that permitted them to run wild with impunity.

Poor Admiral Nomura—to be cast adrift in this manner on a sea so stormy and unfamiliar. Bobbing in the wake of Matsuoka at the luncheon in the Imperial Hotel would be one thing; steering the Japanese ship of state into a distant diplomatic haven would be quite another.

Speaking in his turn to the assembled guests, this "plain sailor ... brought up amid tall masts and crowded sails ... a complete stranger to the elegant society, its speech and its manner," candidly told his listeners, "I am not meant to be an Ambassador." A sailor on land, Nomura said, is "quite helpless. ... He is reduced to perfect impotence, like a stranded boat. In the tangled wood of diplomacy, he would be just as good as lost."

Nomura's realization of this had caused him to hesitate for a long time before succumbing to the pressure exerted by a number of men, including officers in the Imperial Navy, who wished to send him to the United States to charm the President and the American people into an acceptance of Japan's program. "Swim or sink, survive or perish, I do not care," the Admiral declared. "Only am I anxious to serve—serve the cause of better understanding between our two nations."

Nomura's soothing words could not compete, however, with the strong message the Foreign Minister had delivered moments before. Stripped of its sugar coating, the pill that Matsuoka had dispensed to the America-Japan Society would taste bitter in most American mouths.

Ambassador Grew found that he was no exception. As honorary president of the Society, he had been asked in advance of the event to chair the luncheon. He had agreed to do so but had insisted that he would keep his remarks to a minimum. "This is no time for good-will speeches," he had written in his diary, "and when I preside ... I shall ... carefully avoid any soft-soaping whatsoever. As I constantly say to those Japanese with whom I come into contact, the time has gone by when statements, assurances, promises, or pious expressions of hope can do any good; nothing can count now but facts, actions, and realities."

On the morning of December 19, forewarned of what was coming by an advance copy of Matsuoka's text, Grew had learned that the newly elected head of the Society had already tried—unsuccessfully—to persuade Matsuoka to alter parts of his speech. "So I had to go to the luncheon 'loaded for bear,' " Grew later wrote, "and the Minister got both barrels."

The Ambassador did not believe in provocative utterances that would cause unnecessary irritation, but he felt that he could not just sit there and let Matsuoka carry the day, without saying anything in reply. Grew therefore responded briefly and in a "perfectly friendly tone," observing that the Foreign Minister had brought out certain points with which everyone had to agree, especially his "expressed desire for peace, his appeal for calm judgment, and his good wishes for the success of Admiral Nomura's mission."

Other points, however, were of a "controversial nature." The Ambassador could not deal with each of these individually, but "with all due respect" he felt compelled to "relieve the Minister of his misapprehension that the interest of the American people in China [was] largely sentimental."

Mr. Matsuoka had lived long enough in the United States, Grew said, to know that the American people were "firmly determined" to look after their obligations as well as their rights. "In the present state of world affairs," he added, "we must inevitably realize that what counts in international relationships today . . . is the concrete evidence of facts and actions, regardless of the persuasive garb in which such facts and actions may be dressed. Let us say of nations as of men: 'By their fruits ye shall know them.'"

Grew's purpose in making this remark was to tell Matsuoka in polite terms: "You can't hoodwink the hard-headed American from Missouri or from any other part of our country by trying to camouflage bare-faced acts of aggression under high-sounding slogans and pious talk about promoting the brotherhood of man."

Diplomatic colleagues in the audience who were friendly to the cause were virtually "rubbing their hands with glee" over Grew's comeback at Matsuoka. During a subsequent function at the Spanish Legation, the Minister—who had a reputation for being rather crotchety—proposed Grew's health in a short speech in which he said that the Ambassador's remarks had undoubtedly been "inspired by God."

Grew had had other help as well, for Matsuoka had left himself unprotected at several points and was therefore an easy target. He had been heavy-handed in explaining the Axis alliance and had blundered in his treatment of the China problem. The historical record might provide Japan with some legitimate grounds for complaint, but this same record would also reveal that Matsuoka and many of his colleagues had been living in a dangerous miasma arising from the swampy soil of a decade or more of pernicious influences within their own country. Instead of giving diplomacy a fair chance to redress any international imbalance, the leaders of Japan in the 1930's had all too often sanctioned the use of force because they believed they were capable of imposing their will in this way. Matsuoka cannot be blamed for inheriting such a legacy, but neither can he escape censure for gambling with the destiny of his country while serving as Foreign Minister.

In 1940 and '41 Matsuoka was anxious to protect and expand the gains that had already been made on the continent of Asia; he was eager to pursue the "golden opportunity" he thought he saw in Nazi victories in Europe; he ignored the possibility that he might simply be dragging a thirsty Japan across a searing desert in pursuit of nothing but a mirage.

There were points in Matsuoka's progress at which he could have turned back, but he pressed on instead. During his year at the Foreign Office he added greatly to the distrust with which Japan was regarded by the American Government and people. He thereby increased the chances that the Armageddon against which he uttered warnings from time to time would in the end take place.

*

The vigor of Grew's response to Matsuoka had made a distinct impression on the luncheon audience. As the gathering was breaking up, one of Drought's acquaintances, Tarō Terasaki, chief of the American Bureau of the Foreign Office, buttonholed a member of Grew's staff to ask whether the Ambassador had seen the Foreign Minister's speech in advance. Upon being given an affirmative answer, Terasaki remarked that the Ambassador did not seem to be working any longer for Japanese-American friendship.

Grew regarded this gibe as "completely typical." Anyone who did not accept the Japanese point of view "hook, bait, and sinker" was immediately charged with being unfriendly.

Father Drought, whose presence in the banquet room was known to the Ambassador but whose thoughts were not, was already formulating his own reactions to what he had seen and heard. If he had been required to choose sides, he would have lined up behind Terasaki rather than behind Grew, thus undermining the universality of the Ambassador's judgment that *all* the Americans at the luncheon, including "even the missionaries," wholeheartedly supported his response to the Foreign Minister.

That Drought should be an exception to this generalization is not surprising. He was currently bending over backwards in his effort to look at matters as the Japanese did. He was consequently not at all pleased with Grew's rebuttal. Drought was also annoyed with Matsuoka. Instead of delivering the address Drought had written for him, he had given a speech that would remain "open to misinterpretation." Drought wondered (as Grew did also) how the press would handle the whole affair.

The coverage in Japan proved typical in some respects but surprising in others. The vernacular papers chose to omit the opening paragraphs of the Foreign Minister's speech. This permitted them to begin on a forceful note, introduced by a subheading that read "Must Think Big." There were also other deletions, including more than 50 percent of the three final paragraphs in which Matsuoka had "most fervently" prayed that Nomura would succeed in ushering in "a happier period of mutual trust and better understanding."

Of perhaps even greater significance than the omissions was the extent to which certain Japanese papers found fault with the Foreign Minister's approach. The Ōsaka Mainichi and the Tōkyō Nichi-Nichi (the two newspapers guided by Dean Ackerman's friend Shingorō Takaishi) were among those that were critical.

According to the Mainichi, the Roosevelt Administration was acting by design for the express purpose of restraining Japan. The Nichi-Nichi also followed this line but was more openly annoyed with Matsuoka for having taken only a lukewarm attitude; he did not do what the average Japanese would most likely have done—he did not denounce American Far Eastern policy as a deliberate attempt to checkmate Japan.

Grew's rebuttal of Matsuoka was not published in the Japanese press, though some of the Ambassador's statements did appear in the Japan Times and Advertiser "in distorted form." To combat this news blackout, Grew decided that his reply to the Foreign Minister should be released by the State Department. American correspondents in Tokyo had filed full reports, but no one knew whether their stories had passed the Japanese censor. Grew was consequently concerned about the way in which the speeches made at the Imperial Hotel on December 19 would be handled in the United States.

Drought was also thinking about this problem. The result was a cable to Maryknoll, New York: "Matsuoka speech today should be given good publicity."

Actually, there was far-reaching coverage in the United States but not of the type Drought desired. From north to south and east to west, up and down and across the length and breadth of the country, in cities and towns and in places in between, the words of the two opponents— Matsuoka for Japan, Grew for the United States—clashed in verbal combat on the pages of one newspaper after another, and the Ambassador was declared "THE WINNER!"

"JOSEPH GREW 'TELLS 'EM' IN TOKYO"
"STRAIGHT TALK TO JAPAN"
"CANDOR WORKS IN THE ORIENT"
"OUR BLUNT MR. GREW"

In Augusta, Maine, and McKeesport, Pennsylvania; in Worcester and in Boston; in Minneapolis and Milwaukee; in Fargo, North Dakota; in Denver, Topeka, and St. Louis; in Knoxville, Louisville, and Greenville; in Norfolk and Lynchburg; in Charlotte, Atlanta, and Houston; in Los Angeles, San Francisco, and Seattle; in Baltimore, Philadelphia, Newark, and New York, Ambassador Grew was supported and cheered—a source of gratification to him as one clipping after another arrived in Japan.

Of the thirty-odd items he received, only two—both from Ohio—were negative in content. The *Columbus Dispatch* expressed concern over the timing and "uncompromising tone" of Grew's "surprisingly blunt statement"—"an ultimatum to Nippon" warning her to stay put. The *Canton Repository* was even more outspoken. It referred critically to persons who believed firmly in "the cherished theory of preventing trouble by promising to go more than halfway to meet it." This was called "speaking the only language the Japanese [could] understand." Unless Grew and other subscribers to this theory knew what they were talking about, "war headlines in the near future [might] contain the names of something besides cities in Greece and England and desert outposts in Libya."

To the *Philadelphia Inquirer,* on the other hand, Grew's "forthright reply to the honeyed words of the Japanese Foreign Minister" was just what Americans had come to expect from their "sturdy Ambassador." The *Washington Star* was of the same opinion: Grew was an "ace" diplomat, who knew "how to say the right thing at the right time." In South Carolina the *Greenville News* was also pleased with Grew's response. How could anyone accept Matsuoka's assertion that Japan was engaged in a "moral crusade" in China when all the evidence was to the contrary? "And the great wonder is that Japanese statesmen continue to believe that their reiteration of such absurdities will have some effect upon the American mind."

In Wisconsin the editor of the *Milwaukee Journal* attempted to link the past with the present in a relationship of cause and effect:

The main trouble today is in the *manner* in which Japan has gone about making two basic decisions. The first had to do with chaotic conditions in China, reaching back a decade. Let it be granted that Japan had a right to be weary of the warlord robbing and the manhandling of Japanese nationals. What should she have done about it? She was committed [by treaty] to . . . calling a conference of the treaty nations and laying before them a course of action.

Instead Japan attacked China and began to grab Chinese territory. She opened war on defenseless civilians. Then she proclaimed a "new order" and asked Americans to endorse it. We had every right to refuse to approve Japan's course of action.

Then look at the manner in which Japan went about her recent commitments. She signed a treaty with Germany and Italy which ranges her with our potential enemies. That made matters infinitely worse. It made impossible our speaking to Japan as an ancient friend. She had gone to the camp of those opposed to us.

Now the Japanese foreign minister "hopes" the United States will not force Japan to live up to her Axis commitment and thus drag all the world into war. That's silly. We didn't force her to sign with Hitler. Japan ought to have thought about that before she signed the treaty, not afterward. Again it was a thing done in a manner that not only offended and outraged us but which was designed to threaten us. Yet we are supposed to accept and "understand" it. The bluff will not work.

If bluff would not work, what would? The *Journal*'s answer was that "straight talk" seemed to be "the only method left" capable of keeping the two nations from "drifting into conflict." In this respect Grew was making "an important contribution." If relations were ever to improve, however, Japan would have to change her "manner" of doing things in Asia.

Many other editors seemed to agree. Despite variations here and there, Grew found that one of his statements had consistently been quoted with approval: "What counts in international relationships today . . . is the concrete evidence of facts and actions, regardless of the persuasive garb in which such facts and actions may by dressed."

Apparently no one remembered that Matsuoka had said virtually the same thing—"deeds not words"—when he had assumed the post of Foreign Minister six months earlier. The chasm separating the two nations had in the meantime grown wider and deeper. It would never be bridged by the kind of deeds Matsuoka had in mind.

CHAPTER EIGHT

An Impresario from Abroad

FATHER DROUGHT had a great deal on his mind as the day approached
when he and Bishop Walsh would leave for home. There were some
men he had not met yet, and others whom he wanted to visit a second or
third time. He had been pleased when one of the letters of introduction
written by Lewis Strauss had led to an interview with Baron Wakatsuki.
The results had been disappointing, however, because the interpreter
had done a poor job. Wakatsuki had apologized, and had indicated how
sorry he was that Tadao Wikawa had been unable to help out, as he
usually did whenever the Baron needed him.

The meeting had taken place in the offices of the Society for International Cultural Relations, with which Wakatsuki was connected. Old
Japan Hands knew that such organizations were not always quite what
they seemed to be—that they might serve a purpose other than the one
to which they were nominally committed—but Drought was an "innocent abroad," grazing in unfamiliar pastures.

As December drew to a close he found that he could not fit everything
in. During a luncheon at the Tokyo Club earlier in the month, to which
he and the Bishop had been invited by a Privy Councilor who was another of Strauss's friends, Drought had chatted with a number of influential persons. Among them was a businessman from Osaka, who had
subsequently reported the conversation to Masatsune Ogura, director
general of the Sumitomo zaibatsu. Ogura had been so intrigued by what
he had thus heard of Drought's "mission" that a messenger had been
sent to Tokyo with a letter asking Drought to travel to Osaka for a talk
with Ogura and "a few chosen friends."

Although Drought had to decline, he suggested that he and Ogura
might be able to get together on some future occasion either in Japan
or in the United States. "It was really a great regret," Ogura replied,
"that I could not meet you. . . . I hope you will come back again and stay
longer with us. You will please, when you visit us next time, include it

in your schedule a visit to our district. I pray the year would bring the blessings to the humanity."

Less than four months later, as the John Doe Associates were preparing to submit their "Draft Understanding" to Secretary Hull and Ambassador Nomura, Drought would have occasion to recall this correspondence, for he learned then that Ogura had just been appointed to Prince Konoye's Cabinet.

The day on which Drought had to turn down the invitation to Osaka happened to be the day after the America-Japan Society luncheon at the Imperial Hotel. After checking the coverage in Tokyo's English-language press, Drought decided to keep several of the papers for future reference. As mementos of the past, they offer some revealing glimpses of Axis Japan at work and at play—glimpses that leave little to the imagination.

Take, for example, the figure cut by Toshi Gō, the president and editor of the *Japan Times and Advertiser* (a Foreign Office "rag"), as he bows to his morning readers on December 20 with an editorial entitled "Warning and Advice."

According to Gō, Foreign Minister Matsuoka had clearly revealed Japan's intentions: she wanted to be "left alone" so that she could carry on her "constructive work" unhindered; she wanted to see "the trouble in China and the war in Europe" brought quickly to an end. "The essence of that sentence," Gō explained, "is American hands off China. [Mr. Matsuoka] used the term 'trouble' for what is going on in China, and 'war' for the conflict in Europe. Perhaps he meant that even more dreadful things could happen in China, and in all the Pacific, if Japan were provoked past all endurance, and a clash with America exploded."

This was certainly plain enough, and it did not greatly matter whether the term "advice" was used, or "warning," to encompass the threat. Even Gō admitted that the prospect was "distressing," but he took heart from the fact that Japan was an ally of Germany and Italy. The goal of the Tripartite Pact (Matsuoka had said) was "justice and equity."

Alas, that there could be a nation so divorced from the world that the masses could be made to regard an alliance with Hitler and Mussolini as having justice and equity as its goal.

It was a time of grimness. Take another look at Japan in December 1940, as portrayed in Gō's paper. Beside a picture of Admiral Nomura radiating charm at the America-Japan Society luncheon is a sobering photograph showing a blind soldier participating in ceremonies that ought to have made some people stop and think. The soldier was one of many who had lost their sight in the service of the state. They were now getting something back in return—a present, a token, a trinket. The Empress Dowager had been prevailed upon to play a part, unseen but no less felt. "Out of her gracious sympathy with the war blind," she had been "pleased to make a gift of a blind man's watch" to each member of a group of soldiers and sailors whose combined experience reached back to the Russo-Japanese War at the beginning of the century. The watches had been especially designed so that the recipients would be able to "touch" the time of day.

Perhaps these veterans could be helped by such largess, but what could be done for the millions of their countrymen who were equally blind even though they could in fact see?

There were plain indications that Tokyo was strengthening Japan's Axis commitment. A subject of front-page importance was the reappointment of Lieutenant General Hiroshi Ōshima as ambassador to Germany. He had long been a proponent of marching forward, arm in arm, with Hitler and Mussolini. In order to keep the knot that tied Japan to Germany as tight as possible, he was now going back to Berlin. Ōshima's presence in the Third Reich would supposedly reassure Hitler that his Japanese allies could be trusted, even though Herr Matsuoka was about to send "an old friend of President Roosevelt's" to Washington to improve relations with the United States.

Japan's eagerness to help warm the Axis bed could also be seen in a War Ministry release noting that a military mission would soon depart for Germany and Italy "to study the war tactics of the Axis powers at first hand."

The Cabinet Information Bureau in Tokyo and the official German News Agency in Berlin concurrently declared that Germany, Italy, and Japan had decided to set up special commissions in their respective capitals in order to bring the Tripartite Pact "into operation." Some observers judged that this particular move was meant "as a reminder to the United States of the hazards of giving limitless aid" to the British. No authorized spokesman in Berlin would confirm this, but informally it was said, "It is an action that speaks for itself." And that seemed to mean the same thing.

With the defeat of Britain being forecast by the Germans, what would Japan do? She would watch, wait, and prepare, taking whatever advantage opportunity afforded, trying all the while to use diplomacy to gain her ends so that she would not have to fight to achieve the hegemony she was seeking in "Greater East Asia."

Japan would work hard and play hard, but pure recreation—doing something for the fun of it—was unpatriotic. Only activities that developed strong bodies or special skills were to be encouraged—the designing and testing of model airplanes, for example. While Matsuoka and Grew had publicly exchanged shots through the clatter of coffee cups in a smoke-filled banquet room at the Imperial Hotel, a large gathering of boys, their individual identities submerged by the dull sameness of their school uniforms, had eagerly competed against each other at a military parade ground in the capital. Government agencies and private groups had been promoting this "sport" among the youth of the country—the nation's soldiers and sailors and airmen to be—and now the ultimate moment had arrived. Excitement and tension mounted as each plane soared aloft, carrying its builder's hopes and dreams. How happy those few boys must have been who could take home with them that evening the prizes they had won for producing aircraft that had "performed well over long distances."

Into this atmosphere, in which war loomed ever larger in the consciousness of the Japanese people, Bishop Walsh and Father Drought inserted a note of peace. The occasion was a luncheon of the Pan-Pacific Club of Tokyo, meeting at the Imperial Hotel on December 20, the day after the Matsuoka-Grew encounter.

"The world is a bountiful place," Walsh told his audience, "and was so fashioned by its Creator. It contains enough for everybody. There is no apparent reason why all the people of the earth cannot be supplied with all that they need for their well-being and security and happiness and peace, if the proper spirit is present and the proper adjustments are made."

How could this be achieved? Through "common brotherhood," through "patience and understanding," through "a sympathetic study of each other's problems," and through a continual search on the part of all governments for the elusive "formulae of security and peace."

"I am not one of those," Walsh declared, "who think that amateur individuals are more likely to solve these problems than are the responsible officers of government whose specialty this is. . . . It is incumbent on us all to have confidence in those statesmen who are conspicuously striving to solve these problems. . . . We ought to try to understand their policies and uphold them."

This was advice that Drought might have heeded, but he did not. When his turn came to speak, he compared the fatalism of a Japanese poet of old, who "could find no solution of life's conflict but in the grave," with the pessimism of Rudyard Kipling, whose throbbing line "Oh, East is East, and West is West, and never the twain shall meet" had "done more harm to the proper growth of international relations than [had] the words of any diplomat, the incautious utterances of any statesman, or the objectionable practices of any traders."

Drought had no patience with either the Japanese poet or Kipling. East and West *would* meet; they *would* achieve a harmonious relationship in which a simultaneous interchange of learning and teaching would take place. "And that," Drought declared, "is the consummation devoutly to be wished for. It is a consummation that is to be striven for —no less ardently than wished, and pursued with confidence and courage."

The next day, December 21, Drought talked with Sawada, Terasaki, and others during a luncheon meeting in which Walsh also participated. That evening they all got together again for dinner. Matsuoka had been invited, but he was unable to come because of a prior engagement; Vice-Minister Ōhashi, however, turned up for the occasion.

On Monday, December 23, the Foreign Minister played host to the two Maryknollers. Among the guests were Setsuzō Sawada, Tadao Wikawa, and Kaname Wakasugi (who had recently returned to Tokyo from New York).

Walsh and Drought had first met Matsuoka on December 5. At the America-Japan Society affair on the nineteenth they had been afforded a second opportunity to listen to his views. Now, on the twenty-third, they were seeing him for the third time—over lunch at his private residence.

Although the Foreign Minister may not have been very definite on December 5 about the terms of the "peace treaty" that he wanted to "negotiate" with the United States, "other officials and spokesmen" had supplied the missing details in conversations conducted primarily with Father Drought. The "most assiduous" of these "spokesmen" had been Tadao Wikawa—a man who seemed so close to Konoye that Walsh and Drought took him to be the Premier's "confidential agent."

As time passed, Walsh had learned from Drought that the Japanese had two basic proposals in mind: "(1) a guarantee to nullify their participation in the Axis Pact, if not by public repudiation, at least in some definite manner that would be effective and complete, and (2) a guarantee to recall all military forces from China and to restore to China its geographic and political integrity."

Why should a matter of this nature be entrusted to two unknown clergymen when regular channels existed for the exchange of communications between the Japanese and American governments? Bishop Walsh, who had expressed concern about this very point, was told that a cabled report from the American Embassy would be picked up and decoded by the Japanese Army. If a radiogram were sent, the agents of a half dozen other countries would be able to read the message as well. In either case, the project would be doomed before it ever came to the attention of the President. It was therefore necessary to convey Japan's "peace overture," by word of mouth, to Washington.

This put Walsh in an awkward position. He did not want to go back to the United States until he had visited all the Maryknoll missions in the Far East. This had been his intention from the beginning. He therefore suggested that Father Drought return alone across the Pacific to report on Japan's desire for peace, but this idea was rejected by the "officials and spokesmen" with whom Drought talked. It seems that everyone was very keen on having the two of them go together. No reasons were given, but Walsh gathered that "the proponents of the plan" would feel greater "assurance" if he accompanied Drought to Washington. The Bishop accordingly decided he would have to interrupt his tour of the missions in order to perform the "little task" that had been requested of him in the interest of peace. He did make a point, however, of asking for pledges from the Imperial Army and Navy to the effect that there was "unanimity of purpose" on the part of all elements in the Japanese Government with respect to reaching an agreement with the United States, and carrying it out.

If Walsh had been a politically minded man, he might not have been satisfied with the explanations he had received, for it is obvious that some basic questions remained unresolved. If lack of security in communications posed a problem, why not let Admiral Nomura do the job that Walsh and Drought were being urged to perform? Nomura could be briefed before he left Tokyo for Washington. His arrival there with a proposal for a settlement would have far more impact on the American Government than anything Walsh and Drought might say to Roosevelt and Hull.

Why turn to private individuals? Was Matsuoka afraid that the Imperial Army and Navy would sabotage a "peace offensive"? Did he think that a message of amity addressed to Washington might be leaked to Berlin by Axis sympathizers among the members of his own staff? Or was Matsuoka simply taking advantage of the Walsh-Drought visit to Japan to blow the pipes of peace without having to dance to the tune?

Such a strategy would have fitted into his conception of diplomacy as a game of trickery in which the most successful players were those with the least scruples.

*

The coming of Christmas, with its connotations of "peace on earth to men of goodwill," provided a time for contemplation and spiritual communion, but the moment of rest was brief. On Thursday, December 26, Walsh and Drought paid their respects at the American Embassy. Having already pledged themselves to secrecy, they did not tell Ambassador Grew that they had been asked to carry a "message" to President Roosevelt.

That same day Drought began writing farewell letters to a number of Japanese, including Matsuoka, Ōhashi, and Terasaki: "I am confident that efforts promoted by goodwill must prove ultimately successful. It is my earnest hope that the acquaintance begun here in Tokyo may mature with the fruits of accomplishment."

On Friday, December 27, the condition interposed earlier in regard to Army-Navy assurances of "unanimity of purpose" was met. With only some twenty-four hours remaining before their ship sailed, Walsh and Drought were taken by Wikawa to the office of Major General Akira Mutō, the chief of the Military Affairs Bureau, which functioned as the War Minister's political and diplomatic braintrust. The appointment had been arranged by Wikawa through Colonel Iwakuro, who headed one of the Sections into which the Bureau was divided. Iwakuro, however, was not present at the interview.

Since Mutō did not seem to know any English, Wikawa filled in as interpreter. The result was a conversation lasting some twenty minutes, perhaps a half hour, during which Walsh and Drought learned that the General "was pledging himself—and, as far as it lay in his power, the Army he represented—to concurrence in the proposed undertaking." Speaking through Wikawa, Mutō made it clear "that he and his associates in the Japanese Army were in accord with the efforts to reach a peace agreement," and that he personally would do all he could to further those efforts.

In writing about this meeting some years later, Walsh could not remember whether the actual terms of an agreement were discussed, but he did recall, "though rather vaguely," that Father Drought had previously seen a representative of the Japanese Navy and had received assurances from him similar to those offered by Mutō.

Walsh and Drought had been told (mainly by Wikawa but also by others) that the "peace proposals" not only had the full support of Premier Konoye but were in fact largely a result of his own doing. They had also been informed that if they agreed to act as messengers they would have an opportunity to talk with the Prince before they set sail. Ultimately an appointment was arranged for them on the very day of their departure, but when they arrived on the scene Konoye was not there—he had been called away, suddenly, by pressing business elsewhere. And so Walsh and Drought had to leave Japan on board the

Nitta-maru on December 28 without ever having seen the man who had by now emerged in their thoughts as Japan's principal advocate of peace.

*

Only seven weeks had passed since the two Maryknollers had sailed through the Golden Gate bound for Yokohama. The date had been November 11—the anniversary of the Armistice that had brought World War I to an end. "A peaceful day for a peaceful mission," Drought had said in a letter to Frank Walker, but if peace was anywhere in sight as the year 1940 drew to a close no one in authority in Washington was aware of it.

In the Far East in the months ahead, the American Government would continue to help China resist Japan through measures short of war. In Europe a pro-British policy would prevail, but Roosevelt would go further in aiding Britain against Nazi Germany than he would in his support of China.

The direction in which the United States was moving was clearly indicated on December 29 when the President addressed his fellow citizens in a fireside chat that was to become a landmark of American foreign policy.

"Thinking in terms of today and tomorrow," he declared, "I make the direct statement to the American people that there is far less chance of the United States getting into war if we do all we can now to support the nations defending themselves against attack by the Axis than if we acquiesce in their defeat, submit tamely to an Axis victory, and wait our turn to be the object of attack in another war later on. . . . We must be the great arsenal of democracy. For us this is an emergency as serious as war itself. We must apply ourselves to our task with the same resolution, the same sense of urgency, the same spirit of patriotism and sacrifice, as we would show were we at war."

It would be unfair to describe James Drought as a member of the "see no evil, hear no evil" minority of Americans to whom the President drew attention in the course of his speech. Drought was alive to the Nazi menace in Europe and consequently wanted to entice Japan away from Hitler's embrace. In a letter written earlier in the year he had declared, "I would like myself to believe that Lindbergh . . . is right. But I am profoundly convinced that he is mistaken."

In his own way, however, Father Drought was also mistaken; he was as wrong about Japan as any person could be. If he had been more perceptive and knowledgeable, if he had been able to view Japan in a larger context than his limited experience provided, he would have seen, as did an alert American consul in Osaka, that a disturbing aspect of the situation in late 1940 was a growing trend toward "unqualified endorsement of current Japanese foreign policy by the liberal and moderate elements which [had] formerly comprised a passive but substantial opposition."

These elements were now emphatically asserting in private that the United States must acquiesce in Japan's program. Prominent among the men who were making such demands were Masatsune Ogura of the Sumitomo zaibatsu (with whom Drought had corresponded) and Shingorō Takaishi of the *Ōsaka Mainichi* and the *Tōkyō Nichi-Nichi* (to whom Dean Ackerman had written on Drought's behalf). And yet Ogura, Takaishi, and many others who were currently climbing on the "bandwagon" had once upon a time, in 1937 and '38, "confidentially voiced regrets" over the course of Japanese policy, and had sometimes even uttered "mild apologies."

Many Japanese Christians were now going through a similar "process of rationalization" that enabled them "to justify in their own eyes (on the grounds of 'ultimate good') the aggressive aims of the Japanese Government, and to reject some of the altruism inherent in Western Christianity." Teachers all over Japan from the elementary school level up through the universities were dedicating themselves "to the task of indoctrinating students with the current state philosophy while suppressing freedom of thought ever more rigidly." Japanese leaders in all walks of life were increasingly fearful of the Kenpeitai and other police forces, and were exhibiting "a more supine acceptance of their narrow point of view."

Elements in Japan who had once dissented were doing so no longer. They believed that the die had been cast, and that resistance at this stage "would be unpatriotic if not treasonable." They now shared "with the bolder groups" in control of the government "a dangerous conviction" that rapprochement with the United States could take place only through "a reorientation of American policy, with little or no deviation by Japan from the 'immutable' line" she had adopted in her relations with other nations.

The Japanese press, not to be left behind, was becoming more and more anti-American in tone. Newspapers like the *Asahi* and the *Mainichi*, which had been "conservative" in outlook, were far more amenable now than ever before to the wishes of governmental agencies concerned with the "molding" of public opinion.

Despite Drought's optimistic judgments, the Japanese Government was not prepared to set out in any new directions at this time. In writing to the President about the prevailing situation, Grew had advised against harboring any illusions on this score. As matters then stood, it seemed to him that "no Japanese leader or group of leaders could reverse the expansionist program and hope to survive." Only if those responsible for the policies of Japan could be discredited by positive action on the part of the United States was there any chance that "a regeneration of thought" might ultimately take place, thus permitting the resumption of normal relations and an adjustment of the entire Far Eastern problem.

Grew was jubilant over the fireside chat of December 29—"the best New Year's message" that could have come out of "a grim and cruel year." He had heard the speech over the radio and had later read it five times, until he knew it practically by heart. He was going to drive the President's message home to as many influential Japanese as possible.

Although the Ambassador had once described himself as "an original Willkie man," he was now convinced that his former schoolmate at Groton and Harvard was "precisely the right man in the right place at the right time." The American people were "highly fortunate" to have FDR directing their foreign affairs during such a critical period. Grew was pleased that 71 percent of his fellow citizens, according to a recent Gallup poll, shared his judgment.

Father Drought, who was much more of "an original Willkie man" than Grew, belonged somewhere in the categories that accounted for the other 29 percent, and yet Drought knew where power rested in the United States; he knew that somehow or other he must capture the attention of the President.

As the *Nitta-maru* crossed the Pacific, Drought drafted several brief but suggestive messages. To Lewis Strauss: "Expect to see you soon as possible." To Maryknoll: "Both of us encouraged returning." To Dean Ackerman of Columbia: "Returning hopeful of your cooperation."

Upon reaching San Francisco, Drought placed a long-distance call to Strauss to solicit his help. Strauss thought that it would be a good idea to seek the advice of Herbert Hoover. The former President concluded, in turn, that a report should be conveyed to the White House at once. Because of "the barriers to communication" that existed between him and Roosevelt, however, Hoover did not feel he could provide an entrée. He therefore suggested that the matter be taken up with someone like Frank Walker, a man who had been close to FDR for a number of years.

This is essentially the route Drought traveled in his journey to Washington, but he did not limit himself to relying solely on his Jewish and Republican friend Strauss or on his Catholic and Democratic friend Walker. Following his arrival at Maryknoll, Drought telephoned Cecil

W. Gray, an assistant to Secretary Hull. Three days later, on January 16, 1941, Drought talked to the retiring ambassador to Great Britain, Joseph P. Kennedy.

A fragmentary reconstruction of the week that followed, as seen from Frank Walker's desk, reveals the progress Drought made toward his goal:

Jan. 16 Fr. Drought called Mr. Walker from New York; Mr. Cronin [William F. Cronin, special assistant to Walker] spoke with Fr. Drought.

Jan. 17 Fr. Drought called and talked to Mr. Cronin; Fr. Drought saw the Postmaster General.

Jan. 18 Mr. Walker talked with Bp. Walsh who called from Poughkeepsie; Fr. Drought phoned Mr. Walker at noon, as requested, and will call back shortly; Fr. Drought saw the PMG [Postmaster General].

Jan. 21 Fr. Drought is at the Willard, Rm. 832; he would like Mr. Cronin to call him. He said the PMG expects a message from him.

Mr. Walker has an appointment with the President at noon.

2:30 P.M.—Mr. Cronin returned Fr. Drought's call and left word at the Hotel that he was to come over to see Mr. Walker at 3:45.

Fr. Drought saw the PMG.

Jan. 22 Fr. Drought called from the Willard Hotel and talked to Mr. Cronin.

Mr. Cronin spoke to Fr. Drought.

Fr. Drought and Bp. Walsh saw Mr. Walker.

Fr. Drought will call on Mr. Walker at 10 o'clock tomorrow morning.

Jan. 23 10:45 A.M.—Bp. Walsh and Fr. Drought are to see the President.

Kennedy in the meantime had gone unexpectedly to the White House on January 16. He had also been busy presenting his views on Lend-Lease and related matters to the American people at large—first by means of a radio address and subsequently in testimony before the House Committee on Foreign Affairs. Among the messages he received following his broadcast was a telegram from Drought: "Congratulations on your unassailable speech. Thank you for Washington arrangements. Will be pleased if we could see you also on Tuesday."

Dispatched at exactly the same time on Sunday, January 19, was an unsigned cable consisting of one word—"Good"—that reached Tadao Wikawa in Tokyo on Monday, a few hours before Drought sent a second, equally cryptic report reading "Satisfactory."

That same Monday morning Bishop Walsh filed a telegram to Kennedy: "Father Drought and I would be grateful if you and Mr. Walker would arrange to be present at our meeting on Tuesday or Wednesday according as it may be decided."

What did all this mean?

It meant that Kennedy, like Walker, had come to the aid of Walsh and Drought; it meant that arrangements for a meeting with the President were in progress, a meeting that would take place as soon as time could be found to fit the two clergymen into Roosevelt's busy inaugural schedule; it meant that Walsh and Drought hoped to be accompanied to the White House by both Kennedy and Walker; and, finally, it meant that an inkling of what was taking place was being reported to Tokyo in a simple, homemade code.

Before leaving Japan Drought had worked out the details with Wikawa. A few days after Drought had sailed, Wikawa had written to Mutō, Iwakuro's superior in the War Ministry, to brief him on the code. Konoye was also informed.

The key words were "Difficult," "Good," "Satisfactory," and "Complete." The Japanese equivalent of "Difficult" was *Mikomi nashi*: no prospect of accomplishing anything. "Good" stood for *Kaku hōmen junchō shinkō-chū*: everything going well in all quarters. "Satisfactory" translated into *Daitōryō kōryo-chū*: under consideration by the President. "Complete"—*Junbi kansei*—would be the best news of all, signifying that the preparation phase was over, that the time to negotiate a settlement was at hand.

In cabling Wikawa on Monday, January 20, that the President had the matter "under consideration," Drought was stretching the point, for it was not until three days later, on Thursday, January 23, that FDR talked with Walsh and Drought and learned directly from them what they had to offer.

Unaware of this, Wikawa was impressed by the speed with which results were being obtained. On January 22 he sent an answering cable, "My trip depending your next wireless," and on January 23 (the day of the White House meeting and of Nomura's departure for the United States) Wikawa posted a long letter that not only revealed his mood but also reported some interesting developments. Although the letter was written in English, the phrasing smacked of Japanese:

Dear Father Drought:
    ... You could hardly imagine how pleased I was with [your two wireless messages], especially at this very moment when, judging from very gloomy news despatches from Washington, I had no other expecatation [sic] than to receive from you the worst code meaning hopeless. I lost no time in bringing them to our Premier, Foreign Minister, General Muto and Count Arima's attention, of course, to their pleasant surprise.*

---

* Count Yoriyasu Arima was serving as secretary general of the Imperial Rule Assistance Association, which was regarded in some quarters as the spearhead of the totalitarian movement in Japan. In the "Strictly Confidential Memo" that Drought took to the White House, however, Arima was described as one of the "Conservative authorities" who would be restored to "complete control" if they could win "a safe economic and international position" for Japan by diplomatic means. The other "Conservatives" mentioned by Drought were the Emperor, Premier Konoye, Foreign Minister Matsuoka, and General Mutō.

Let me congratulate you on rushing things so rapidly to the President's consideration. And I am quite confident now, that it will not take too much time before I hear from you the third code, which will herald the dawn of the new Pacific Age based on the firm determination for peace everlasting among the peoples' minds of the two great nation on both sides of the Pacific.* If so, the noble efforts of Father Drought and Bishop Walsh, coupled with your great President's prudence, shall forever be remembered in the World History. I shall keep on praying the Almighty God for His wise guidance on the leading statesmen of both countries.

The War Office has decided to send Colonel Iwakuro, Chief of Political Section of Military Affairs Bureau, to Washington as the Military Attaché. . . . He is the right-hand man of General Muto, and is one of the so-called driving force of our Army. His selection to that important position has much significance. . . . Everybody well informed with our politics has not even the slightest doubt as to his ability in handling the very delicate affairs pending between the two governments.

I have been urged by leaders of our politics to go over to America on the similar mission with yours. I have not yet made up my mind, as I think it better to wait until I here [*sic*] from you the third message. So everything depends on it, which I shall be looking forward to receive before this letter reaches you.

After every consideration, I have come to this conclusion that it would be wiser for you to get in touch with none in our regular diplomatic service until I notify you the proper time for it.

How is Bishop Walsh? Is he making much progress on his line?† May I trouble you to give my best wishes to him?

At the America-Japan Society tea party given this afternoon at the Tokyo Club, I was introduced to [a bishop from the] San Francisco Area named James Chamberlain Baker. This old Methodist told me that he came here two weeks ago on the similar mission with that of yours, and is leaving for America . . . on the same boat our new Ambassador travels. I am sorry he came a little too late, for things will be prepared satisfactorily before he gets back there. . . .

With much prayer for your success for the sake of humanity, I remain, Father Drought,

> Very faithfully yours,
> T. Wikawa

Whatever Bishop Baker had in mind, Father Drought was more than one step ahead of any "competition" that was likely to materialize, whether of an ecclesiastical or of a secular nature. Having conducted himself in Tokyo in a way that had caused a number of his Japanese contacts to conclude he had access to the President of the United States, Drought was now going to appear at the White House in the role of a messenger and spokesman for the civil and military leaders of the Empire of Japan.

---

* The reference to the third code should be interpreted to mean the final message in the group reporting success: "Good," "Satisfactory," "Complete." When this message arrived, Wikawa would know that the time to negotiate was at hand.

† This could mean "along the lines we discussed."

A great deal depended on the meeting with Roosevelt. Drought would have to "sell" him on the whole idea or the Walsh-Drought mission would fail.

After checking into the Willard Hotel on January 21, Drought began jotting down snatches of conversation from his stay in Tokyo that he thought might be useful. These and other items, scribbled hastily on pieces of hotel stationery and on anything else that came to hand at odd moments, were about to be pieced together, edited, and transformed by Drought into a secret peace overture, which he would attribute to the Japanese Government:

> [Matsuoka's] Dec. 19th speech was really an Orientally phrased bid for a conference. [It was] a big risk.... If Matsuoka (almost fanatically peace-loving) does not succeed quickly he will be followed by a radical and extremist cabinet....
>
> Absolutely necessity of
>   (1) moving secretly
>   (2) acting through Mr. R.
>   (3) speed
>
> *Significant statements* (conversations over a month; what was said):
> "One hour with Mr. R.; I am certain I could convince him"; "Killed if known [we have made overtures to the U.S.]—foolish if to no purpose"; "Extremist minority will obtain control if we suffer defeat"; "We don't want war with the U.S.; it would be a catastrophe"; "We are natural allies."*
>
> *Program for agreement*:
> Any China settlement... could not require more than a regional autonomy for Ch. K. Sh. [It] must stipulate that communism will be attacked [and must include] conditional recognition of Manchukuo.†
>
> Discussion with U.S. of all points of conflict but no Jap. govern. could last through a piecemeal discussion unless subtantial points had been agreed to in advance.

If Drought could just get Roosevelt and Hull to say that the "Agreement" outlined in his "Strictly Confidential Memo" was "substantially acceptable," he would be able to cable their "assurances" to his friends in Japan and thus get the wheels of his peace effort moving at last.

The "Agreement" that Drought was about to submit to the President, however, was not what it appeared to be; it was not a proposal from the Japanese government at all. It was a proposal from Father Drought. He had composed this "Agreement" just prior to the White House interview, using as raw material whatever he could remember from the con-

---

* In talking with the President, Drought probably attributed all of these statements to Matsuoka.

† Elsewhere in his notes Drought stated this more clearly as "retention of present status of Manchukuo."

versations he had had with various persons in Tokyo, putting "two and two" together, so to speak, in a way that he considered meaningful.

Drought's lack of diplomatic experience and the limitations of his prose style produced a document (the first of many) that was amateurish in content and fuzzy in phraseology. And yet he succeeded in making a place for himself simply by taking advantage of the existing situation: there was a crisis in Japanese-American relations that threatened to result in war; both governments wanted to reach a settlement through negotiation. In these circumstances, Drought claimed to possess unique information that would help Japan and the United States break the deadlock.

In an early draft of his "Strictly Confidential Memo" for the President, Drought had included a partial explanation of what had occurred during his stay in Japan with Bishop Walsh:

Realizing that Mr. Roosevelt's pressure technique, and the Italian losses in the Mediterranean, had created a remarkable opportunity for solidifying the Far Eastern situation in our favor, we worked out with the Japanese a plan of procedure, which they are apparently now following, for cooperation with the United States. Mr. Matsuoka designed his speech of December 19 as an indication of this intention. He could not repudiate the Axis Alliance without bringing about the fall of his Government; but a careful analysis will reveal his real intention. We are certain of this because the very idea and content of the speech was suggested by ourselves and, at first, opposed by Mr. Matsuoka. Though the Japanese were dismayed, it was a happy diplomatic circumstance that Mr. Grew chose to rebut the objectionable features. The Japanese, however, as Orientals, caught the real change in direction (obviously we could not tell Mr. Grew in Tokyo).

In re-reading his draft, however, Drought had decided to eliminate virtually all of this explanation, leaving only two sentences that gave no indication of the role he had played.

Drought had also originally intended to explain to the President that Japan's alliance with Hitler and Mussolini would have "to be broken realistically, while being retained legally and officially," but he had subsequently altered his statement to read, "The Japanese feel that their alliance with the Axis will have to be nullified realistically before it can be broken legally and officially."

"The Japanese do not want to be forced to strive for territorial exploitation of China proper" had become, in the process of revision, "No territorial aggrandizement in China proper."

The sending of a Presidential emissary to Tokyo to work out an agreement that would "put within the power of Mr. Roosevelt the opportunity to immunize Japan [for] at least three years, and conceivably to use Japan, after one year, against Hitler" was transformed into immunization *of the Pacific* rather than of Japan.

The sharp edges of reality were blunted as a consequence of these changes in wording.

In his "Strictly Confidential Memo" Drought did not refer to the "Working Analysis" he had written in Tokyo from a purely Japanese point of view. Roosevelt and Hull would consequently never learn that Drought had already offered his own personal blueprint for peace to the leaders of a nation with which the United States was critically at odds.

Roosevelt and Hull would never discover that Drought had advised the Japanese Government not to make any concessions (for the time being at least) on Japan's military and political position in China or on the Axis alliance.

The President and the Secretary of State would never find out that Drought had in effect told his friends in Japan he could help them maneuver the United States into making the various commitments he had suggested in the "Working Analysis," thus permitting a consolidation of Japan's position in the Far East whether the United States liked it or not.

Roosevelt and Hull would never have an opportunity to read what Drought had written with Konoye and Matsuoka in mind: "It should be our aim to so dispose affairs that the calling of a plenipotentiary Japan–United States conference at Tokyo, or at Honolulu (but not at Washington) would seem reasonable and desirable in the mind of American public opinion: if not in the mind of the Roosevelt Government."

*

The meeting with the President that John Doe had so earnestly been seeking was arranged with care to avoid publicity. There is no mention of Walsh and Drought in either of the President's principal appointment diaries, nor is there anything in a third source—a combination "desk diary" and "itinerary." It is only in a fourth appointment book, which was the responsibility of the White House Office of Social Entertainments, that a handwritten entry in ink provides the missing information for January 23, 1941: "10:45 Secy State, P.M. General, Bishop Walsh, Father Drout [sic]—12:05—To office." Other evidence suggests that adjustments had to be made in the President's schedule for that day to accommodate a much longer session with the two Maryknollers than had originally been contemplated.

A penciled entry in Hull's desk diary for January 23 reveals that he was to go to the White House at 10:30 A.M. Written across the end of this entry is an instruction reading "DO NOT ENTER ON CALENDAR."

The most likely explanation of all this is that Drought had convinced Walker of the need for secrecy; and the Postmaster General in turn had asked the White House and the State Department to bear this in mind.

Although the President chose his words carefully in responding to the desire of his visitors to be of assistance, Drought was nevertheless gratified by the results of the interview. On January 24 he cabled Wikawa: "Visit accomplished; encouraging progress; expect developments." Drought also communicated once again with Joseph P. Kennedy, this time by letter: "You will be pleased, I am sure, to learn that we had a most interesting visit with our friend and his First Assistant in the Department concerned [FDR and Hull]. What will come of it, I cannot say, but the indications are favorable, particularly the fact that the interview consumed nearly two hours."

In Tokyo, meanwhile, Wikawa interpreted Drought's latest message as an answer to his own earlier communication, "My trip depending your next wireless." Since he wanted to be sure, however, he now asked: "Is my immediate sailing advisable?" Drought replied on January 27: "Await developments within next week."

That same day Walsh wrote to Walker suggesting that it might be helpful if Drought were "to remain on call" in Washington in order to brief the President and the Secretary of State on what was happening. John Doe's method of operation can be seen in the opening sentence of this letter: "Today we received word by cable that the [Japanese] Government are now ready to send a trusted representative to discuss the terms of a projected agreement." *This* is what Drought had read into Wikawa's simple question, "Is my immediate sailing advisable?" In writing to Walker, Walsh was merely repeating what Drought had told him.

Although Drought wanted to get negotiations started as quickly as possible, he still thought the parleying should take place in Tokyo rather than in Washington. He had already urged the President to send a personal agent to Japan to work out the details of a settlement. This was to be done "in cooperation with the controlling elements . . . including the Emperor," and with the "utmost speed and secrecy."

This recommendation had been made prior to the arrival, on January 27, of Wikawa's message indicating his readiness to sail at once for the United States. Since there had been no word from the White House or the State Department that the President might be prepared to follow the advice he had received, Drought decided to let a few more days go by before making any move. He did not want Wikawa to leave Japan until this issue had been settled.

That Drought could have refrained from personally nominating someone to act for Roosevelt seems almost out of character. Perhaps he was undecided in his own mind, but it is not difficult to include among the possibilities such men as Harry Hopkins, Herbert Hoover, Lewis Strauss, Wendell Willkie, Joseph P. Kennedy, and Frank Walker. Of these six, however, only Hopkins and Walker could have qualified under the criteria Drought had laid down in describing the "ideal" Presidential representative: he had to be someone Roosevelt knew and trusted intimately, a man fully apprised of American aims in the Orient; he had to be keenly aware that the Germans would ruthlessly attempt to prevent a Japanese-American agreement; he ought not to be a member of the State Department.

With further word from Drought likely to arrive in Tokyo at any moment, Wikawa busied himself with preparations for his mission to the United States. On January 31 he sent an enthusiastic letter to Drought: "Oh! How glad I am to think that I shall be able to see both of you there some time next month, though such ought to be kept in secret even from my daughter from every respect, especially to give her a pleasant surprise. . . . I regret there is no Clipper service between Japan and America!"

"I learnt from my friend in Foreign Office," Wikawa reported, "that our consul in New York wirelessed almost the same effect rather in detail, by which we knew that the visit was made both by you and Bishop Walsh to the President. Anyhow, there is only one more message lacking, that is, 'complete,' with which I shall be sailing on the Pacific, complaining the boat's slow speed."

Five days later, on February 5, the strain of no response from Drought was beginning to show. "You could hardly imagine," Wikawa confided, "how anxiously I have been these days awaiting your fifth good wireless message. Indeed, it seems to me as if the whole world's happiness is hanging on it."

Wikawa had previously noted that Foreign Minister Matsuoka had emphasized in the Diet that *his* dictionary did not contain the word "hopeless" with respect to Japanese-American diplomacy. "And I do pray," Wikawa had written, "that he meant it earnestly!" Matsuoka had also declared in the Diet, Wikawa now reported, that a Japanese-American war would mean the end of civilization. "If so," Wikawa informed Drought, "your success in averting it will be nothing but salvation of modern civilization. That is the very reason I have almost made up my mind to cross over the Pacific at my own expense, as such was in your case, and cooperate with you in the noble battle against the fatal war."

Wikawa hoped to hear from Drought in time to leave for Seattle on the *Hikawa-maru* on February 13. If he missed that departure date, there would be other vessels sailing later to Los Angeles and San Francisco. Wikawa did not care to which port he went so long as he could reach one of them as soon as possible. He was already thinking of flying the rest of the way, and he therefore asked Drought to assist him in getting a plane reservation. "We have to hurry up everything," he wrote, "if we are to carry out our plan of holding an international conference in April in Tokyo or Honolulu."

In Japan, all was going according to schedule—or so Wikawa implied. Iwakuro's "nomination to the new post" had been publicly announced that very day. Wikawa hoped he and the Colonel could arrange to travel together so there would be "ample time" to discuss various problems. Iwakuro might not be able to leave that quickly, however, because of "his dental treatment." In that event Wikawa would go on ahead. If anyone asked him why he was leaving for the United States, he would say he was going there to study the cooperative movement in Japanese-owned enterprises.

"Of course," Wikawa confided to Drought, "such is an excuse, as you know. I am trying to sail from Yokohama secretly if possible in order to avoid any unnecessary friction. If you have any advise [*sic*] to give me in connection with it, please do not hesitate to do so, as I have to act in every respect according to your friendly advises, as the reverse was the case with you while you were here."

Even now, with thousands of miles separating them, Wikawa felt it best to warn Drought to be on his guard: "Our consul [in New York] wirelessed to the Foreign Office something about your activities, which we think very undiplomatic. But such is always the case with our bureaucrats. They ought to be more trustful in your ability and kinder to you while they received you here. Now that you have shown some success in your noble effort, they have become more enthusiastic than before. Anyhow, it will be wiser for you not to discuss the matter with them until proper time comes."

Although Wikawa may not have known this as yet, Drought had his own suspicions where "bureaucrats" were concerned, especially when it came to his fellow Americans in the State Department.

Since Drought had not thus far received any official response to his most recent overtures, he was in a somewhat precarious position at the moment. But he was not without resources. Among his friends at Kuhn, Loeb and Company was Sir William Wiseman, whom he had known for a number of years. As the central figure in British Secret Service operations in the United States during World War I, Sir William had been handpicked by President Wilson and Colonel House as their liaison officer with the British Government. Wiseman had become "virtually a private secretary" to House and had been able to see Wilson at any time.

Drought now took Sir William into his confidence and later sent him a copy of the "Memo" that had been left at the White House on January 23. "I am very anxious about this matter," Drought wrote, "since I am completely confident that quick action would bring the result desired whereas delay may lead to a radical change in the Japanese Cabinet."

Wiseman found Drought's memorandum "very interesting." He promised to "re-cast it along the lines" they had discussed and to see that it got into the "proper hands."

Drought also turned once again to Frank Walker. After telephoning him twice on February 5, only to learn that he was out, Drought finally managed to establish contact. On February 6 an unsigned cable left Maryknoll for Tokyo (Drought's fifth message to Wikawa in less than three weeks): "Consulted with Satisfactory last night again. Increasingly encouraging."

These eight words fulfilled all of Wikawa's dreams. Since "Satisfactory" was the code word that signified "under consideration by the President," Drought's cable could mean only one thing to Wikawa: Walsh and Drought had gotten to the President a second time—and with "increasingly encouraging" results. Why delay any longer?

Why indeed?

Wikawa hurriedly filed his reply: "Arriving Seattle on twenty-fifth by Hikawa-maru." Within a week, Drought's "Plenipotentiary Representative" would be on his way to the United States at long last. The Foreign Office men to the contrary notwithstanding, the Reverend Father had proved his worth as a diplomatic impresario of extraordinary capabilities. Perhaps the bureaucrats in the Kasumi-ga-seki would now pay attention to what Wikawa and Drought had been trying to tell them all along; perhaps they would now realize that the dawn of a promising new day was on the verge of breaking over the dark and stormy Pacific.

CHAPTER NINE

"Harsh Talk Is for Home Consumption"

IN WRITING TO the Postmaster General in late January 1941, several days after the White House meeting at which Walker had been present, Bishop Walsh had declared that the most recent statements from Japan were "*exactly* in accordance with the plan" worked out with "those people" during the Walsh-Drought sojourn in the Japanese capital a month earlier. Father Drought knew this plan and could interpret developments accordingly. Without his help, the moves being made might "puzzle, or completely deceive, anyone not previously informed of their true character."

Walsh was convinced that the Japanese Government was sincerely seeking an amicable solution. The inflammatory utterances that were being reported in the United States had not been intended for export. Prince Konoye and his colleagues had to permit a certain amount of harsh talk at home or they would lose out to a group of "Extremists." Officials in Washington should ignore such talk—they should respond as quickly as possible to Tokyo's bid for a friendly settlement.

At the State Department, however, Stanley Hornbeck was of an altogether different opinion: he regarded the "bluster and threats" of the Japanese press and the Hitleresque "table pounding" of Foreign Minister Matsuoka as "attempts to intimidate the United States." In Hornbeck's view, the Japanese wanted to diminish the amount of aid flowing to Great Britain; they wanted to nourish isolationism within the United States and paralyze the American Government in its relations with Germany; they wanted to force the American people "to stand silent and idle" while Japan proceeded with her "program of aggression in the Far East."

At the American Embassy in Tokyo, Ambassador Grew could hear the strident noises being made by Japanese advocates of a "tough" policy, but he knew that there were other sounds in the air suggestive of compromise and conciliation. He had to decide whether to pay more attention to the shrilling of the birds of prey or to the cooing of the doves of peace. Grew had to distinguish, as Sir Robert Craigie later wrote of his own mission, "between dangers that were real and those that were imaginary"; he had "to avoid being alarmist in a situation that was full of alarums."

On the day on which Walsh wrote his optimistic letter to Walker, Grew had dispatched several messages that pointed to the likelihood of a further decline in Japanese-American relations. One of his telegrams had gone far beyond that: "My Peruvian colleague told a member of my staff that he had heard from many sources including a Japanese source that the Japanese military forces planned, in the event of trouble with the United States, to attempt a surprise mass attack on Pearl Harbor using all of their military facilities. He added that although the project seemed fantastic the fact that he had heard it from many sources prompted him to pass on the information."

The Japanese people were reliably reported to be fully determined, regardless of the cost, to proceed with their drive for leadership in East Asia—a goal that was described as "vital" to Japan. Rapprochement with the United States appeared to hinge on an American willingness to allow Japan an entirely free hand. If the United States refused, relations would deteriorate even more.

Foreign Minister Matsuoka had just told a committee in the Diet that Japan had been extremely generous in dealing with China but that this generosity had made the Chinese think Japan would suffer all manner of insults. The United States wanted Japan to withdraw her troops from China and to forgo her advance southward. "Not one Japanese in the Empire would assent to the abandonment of these policies."

It was absolutely necessary for Japan to dominate the Western Pacific:

My use of the word "dominate" may seem extreme [Matsuoka had said] and while we have no such designs, still in a sense we do wish to dominate and there is no need to hide the fact. Has America any right to object if Japan does dominate the Western Pacific? As Minister of Foreign Affairs, I hate to make such an assertion, but I wish to declare that if America does not understand Japan's rightful claims and actions, then there is not the slightest hope for [an] improvement of Japanese-American relations.

In reply to subsequent interpellations, Matsuoka declared that Chiang Kai-shek, Britain, and the United States "must be made to know" that economic pressure could "never halt Japan's determined course." If Japan's lifeline were endangered by a further strengthening of Anglo-American military bases in the Pacific, Article 3 of the Tripartite Pact might come into play. Matsuoka "emphasized that his statements were not irresponsible remarks but were based on careful thought." His bold words were just what his American listeners needed, for "American illusions regarding Japan" had to be dissipated. Every effort ought to be made, of course, "to avoid a Japanese-American clash."

*

Vagueness, uncertainty, contradictory reports, and highly personal ways of looking at the same set of circumstances are among the kaleidoscopic components of the diplomatic process. The judgment of the viewer is affected by each change in images. No single day or week is instructive. Only prolonged observation can provide insight into the shape and color of the times.

Incompatible elements must somehow be assessed and a value assigned to each; this must frequently be done in circumstances that are far from ideal. Up-to-the-minute information keeps arriving, sometimes before earlier items have received full attention. As new pieces are added, a shift in emphasis is likely to occur. The process is endless and can become increasingly difficult when the work takes place (as is often the case) under the pressure of events that do not stand still while men attempt to find solutions.

Despite various indications that the so-called moderates in Japan were trying to cope with the fanatics, not even Grew, who wanted to believe in the existence of a conciliatory group, could find any justification for assuming they would be successful. In point of fact, the "southward advance" was being pushed with all the energy the armed services could command. Japan was endeavoring to secure a predominant economic position in the Netherlands East Indies; she was involved in mediating a border dispute between Thailand and French Indochina to the disadvantage of the colonial rights and interests of France; Japan's military intrusion upon Indochina was increasing in intensity; in addition to all this, Japanese efforts to acquire a naval base in Camranh Bay for use against Singapore were becoming more marked with the passage of time. In short, the extremists—not the moderates—were in charge. The outlook for the future of Japanese-American relations, Grew felt, had "never been darker."

Indeed, the month of February 1941 was to see a serious case of war "jitters" arising out of the belief, especially strong in London, that Japan was about to launch a major offensive in Southeast Asia (to be coordinated with a German attack on Britain). Intelligence reports indicated that Japanese ships were being recalled to their home ports and that Japan would soon demand military bases in southern Indochina and on the west coast of Thailand. This would put the Imperial Navy in a position to cut communications with Singapore at will. A substantial naval force was said to be gathering off Saigon, with other units assembling in the vicinity of Hainan Island. Military operations against Singapore were expected within a matter of weeks.

Although the United States was already on the road to becoming "the great arsenal of democracy," Britain needed food, reinforcements, and innumerable "primary commodities" that could best come from Australia, New Zealand, and India. Singapore was essential to the maintenance of communications with and between the disconnected parts of the British Empire. The fall of this "Gibraltar of the East" would undermine the American policy of all-out aid to Great Britain; it would make available to Nazi Germany, via the Persian Gulf, the very supplies Britain so desperately needed, thus diminishing her chances of survival; the loss of Singapore "would render almost certain the collapse of China," would "seriously prejudice" the defense of the Philippines, and in addition would jeopardize the safety of Australia, New Zealand, and the Netherlands East Indies.

Reports reaching Washington of impending Japanese action against Singapore caused a "flurry of excitement" that led to hasty consultation at the White House regarding the strategy the United States should adopt. It was precisely in this period of uncertainty and growing tension that Hull and his top aides responded to the President's request for advice concerning the Walsh-Drought overture; it was in this period also that Roosevelt instructed one of his secretaries to convey to the Postmaster General the comments received from the State Department in reply; finally, it was in this very period that Hull told the President it might be advisable to "speak softly" to Nomura during the initial phases of contact with him while simultaneously making sure that United States action in the Pacific gave Japan some "new glimpses of [America's] diplomatic, economic, and naval 'big sticks.'"

The State Department did not need Father Drought's services in Washington or anywhere else. Official channels of communication were regarded as far more reliable than private avenues of approach of an unknown character.

Undaunted by this negative stand, Drought went right ahead with his own plans. From Maryknoll, on February 11, he wired his personal greetings to Ambassador Nomura, to whom he had been introduced in Tokyo by Setsuzō Sawada: "Welcome. May Divine Providence guide you as the emissary of a triumphant peace."

Two days later Drought received Nomura's reply: "Thanks for your kind telegram. I expect to see you in the near future."

Drought had by this time written to Sawada, asking him to report to Foreign Minister Matsuoka and Vice-Minister Ōhashi that the "peaceful mission" undertaken by the two Maryknollers had developed "with a rapidity that no one could have anticipated, and with a success that few could have imagined."

"You will have noticed during the past two weeks particularly," Drought's letter read, "a succession of small but very significant incidents that reflect, I have reason to believe, a change of viewpoint and an honest intention for constructive peaceful relations on the part of our President."

You will appreciate that it is impossible for me to write of the circumstances or the character of our activities since returning. The very nature of our mission compels secrecy. Moreover, we are not at liberty to disclose in correspondence the scope of our extended conversations with President Roosevelt and Mr. Hull. . . . I can only say now that I entertain the liveliest confidence in their good will and in their deep desire for a constructive peace that will bring blessings not only to this country but to the Far East. You may assure the Foreign Minister that we carefully explained that Prince Konoye and Mr. Matsuoka were animated by a desire for a realistic peace based on justice and the equity of life opportunity.

"Mr. Roosevelt," Drought added, "is not an enemy of Japan, and if in some respects he may not understand fully the purposes and policies of your Government, it must be admitted that he is not alone responsible for this."

Since the matter had been left in the hands of the President, "the best policy for the present," Drought advised Sawada, would be "to await some decisive favorable action" by Roosevelt. "This would be more effective than reams of propaganda. . . . May I repeat, in order that you may infer what I cannot write, that our activity in this country has been extraordinarily successful."

In Tokyo, meanwhile, Ambassador Grew was feeling very much "out on a limb" concerning "many matters of high policy, intelligence, and tentative plans to meet hypothetical developments." He thought it "simply silly" to argue that such developments could not be approached until they had arrived. If ambassadors were to be "something more than messenger boys," they must be allowed "to see behind the scenes."

Grew's desire to learn what his government was planning to do about Japan had caused him to try to clear the way for his counselor of embassy, Eugene Dooman, to report personally at the White House while he was in the United States on home leave. Prior to Dooman's departure from Tokyo, Grew had given him a letter of introduction to the President. Grew had subsequently followed up on this by sending FDR a personal telegram indicating that Dooman had his "complete confidence."

When Dooman got back to Tokyo early in February, however, he still had Grew's letter of introduction, neatly folded and enclosed in the original envelope. Walsh and Drought, who were unversed in diplomatic matters, had talked with Roosevelt for two hours at the White House, but Dooman, a Foreign Service officer "whose long experience in Japan, mature advice, and incisive diagnosis of political developments" made him invaluable to Grew, had not even been able to set foot inside the door.

Feeling that he should go through channels, Dooman had asked Hull's permission to make an appointment to see the President. In reply Hull had launched into "a long harangue, the burden of which was the sanctity of treaties . . . and the condition precedent to a settlement—the withdrawal of Japanese forces from China." In the course of these remarks, Hull had made it plain that he did not want Dooman to go to the White House.

Dooman had later spent a few days with members of the Far Eastern Division, but they had handed him "the same line" he had already gotten from Hull. The men with whom he had talked "knew nothing of the Administration's thinking." All he had learned was that sooner or later some economic action would be taken against Japan unless the situation improved. The nature of that action "had not as yet been determined."

Despite his inability to find out anything, Dooman had returned to Tokyo with some definite personal views on the imbroglio with Japan and on the policy that would prevail in certain eventualities. On February 14, the day on which the President welcomed Nomura to Washington in a relaxed and friendly manner, Dooman spoke in very forceful terms to Japan's Vice-Minister of Foreign Affairs.

With Grew's prior knowledge and approval, Dooman emphasized the determination of the American people to assist Britain to the limit of their capacity even at the risk of becoming involved in the European war. He then proceeded to show how this bore on relations with Japan: "It would be absurd to suppose that the American people, while pouring munitions into Britain, would look with complacency upon the cutting of communications" between Britain and her dominions and colonies overseas. If Japan or any other nation "were to prejudice the safety of those communications, she would have to expect to come into conflict with the United States."

Although normally "sparing of words," Ōhashi responded with "an impassioned apologia" covering Japanese policies in recent years. When the Vice-Minister finished, Dooman told him that he had presented his case with the "eloquence" of a man "suffering under a sense of grievance." "We do not deny that Japan has grievances," Dooman said, "but we object to the methods pursued by Japan to rectify those grievances." The United States did not want to clash with Japan over China, "but at the same time . . . it would be idle and extravagant to believe that, so long as Japan remained a partner of Germany and Italy and so long as she was unable to resolve her troubles with China on a mutually satisfactory and equitable basis, a stabilization of relations between the United States and Japan could be hoped for."

Ōhashi wanted to know whether he had understood Dooman to say that war could be prevented only if Japan stood still and allowed herself to be tied hand and foot by the United States and Britain. Dooman replied that it had not been his intention to tell the Vice-Minister "what Japan should or should not do," but it was his opinion "that if Japan did not exercise the same degree of restraint and forbearance as that being exercised by the United States, it was very difficult to see how a war could be averted."

Dooman's explanation of the American position and of the philosophy behind it seemed to astonish the Vice-Minister. He "remained perfectly quiet for an appreciable space of time and then burst forth with the question 'Do you mean to say that if Japan were to attack Singapore there would be war with the United States?' " "The logic of the situation," Dooman replied, "would inevitably raise that question."

The Australian Minister to Japan, who was ushered into Ōhashi's presence a few minutes after Dooman had left, found the Vice-Minister inexplicably "agitated and distrait." And well he might have been, for Dooman's statements were "the frankest and most direct admonition thus far made to the Japanese Government" by any American official.

Ōhashi could not know that this démarche had been initiated solely by the American Embassy on its own responsibility rather than by order of the State Department. He could not know that Grew and Dooman were expressing views well in advance of the "spineless program" then being discussed in Washington.

The Dooman-Ōhashi tête-à-tête was duly reported to the Department, and later in the month Grew sent Matsuoka a copy of Dooman's memorandum of the conversation. Matsuoka subsequently told Dooman that he had found the memorandum interesting. All this talk of war between Japan and the United States, Matsuoka said, was a lot of nonsense. There were, of course, "some very tough fellows in the Diet," and when confronted by them he had to speak "rather nationalistically and belligerently." Whenever he was with his "intimate friends," however, he always emphasized to them that war with the United States was "unnecessary and inconceivable."

*

The idea that Japan might have designs upon Southeast Asia was not a figment of a hostile imagination. A settlement of the war in China could bring peace to the Pacific, but it could also bring new and greater danger, sparked by a concerted drive to the south, where resources to satisfy Japan's hunger could be found in abundance. If that was her goal, she would have every reason to seek a termination of the conflict in China.

Information reaching the State Department emphasized that this was indeed a possibility. There were even suggestions that secret negotiations were about to take place between Tokyo and Chungking. A solution leading to Sino-Japanese cooperation in the suppression of communism in China could thus clear the way for a Japanese debouchment into Southeast Asia that could be synchronized with a German invasion of England.

Ambassador Grew felt that Japan was making rapid progress in her policy of advancing to the south. An "acute threat" against the Philippines would touch the United States directly; a Japanese attack on Singapore would affect American security "indirectly but not the less seriously." It would be much more dangerous, Grew and his staff believed, to allow the Japanese to continue their advance indefinitely, and without restraint, than to call a timely halt to their nibbling movement toward the south.

The importance of Singapore in the war against Hitler and the probable vulnerability of the island to attack were well appreciated by the Japanese Government, and yet it continued to denounce Britain and the United States for bolstering their defenses in the western Pacific.

Not Admiral Nomura. Sitting in the ballroom of the Japanese Embassy in Washington—affable and cordial, surrounded by some fifty correspondents—Nomura spent nearly three-quarters of an hour freely answering questions put to him right and left. There was no hint of apology in anything he said with reference to the actions of Japan to date, but neither was there any truculence or defiance. Nomura did not flinch at the questions or try to dodge them; he had fair words for everyone.

The Ambassador would not go so far as to say that his country would refrain from war if she failed to obtain what she wanted by other means, but he argued that Japan's goal was peaceful economic expansion. She wanted to keep the European conflict from spreading to the Far East; she wanted to avoid war with the United States.

Despite Nomura's sincerity, his assurances fell on deaf ears in the State Department and at the White House. If a man is seen crawling across a rooftop on a dark night, it is better to assume he is up to some mischief than to conclude that he is merely out for a breath of fresh air.

Nomura soon found that it was this kind of a situation. His country was the man on the roof who was up to no good. Nomura also found that there was little he could do about it, although perhaps this was something he learned only much later.

The Foreign Minister of Japan did not make the Ambassador's task any easier. Matsuoka fashioned the fabric of his talk to the style of his audience; as a consequence he produced a varied line. To the British Government he suggested that the situation in the Far East would be "very much mitigated" if the United States "could only be persuaded" to restrict her activities to the Western Hemisphere, thus prudently avoiding the danger of causing Japan "unnecessary anxiety." Matsuoka also recommended "a wise and courageous statesmanship willing to display an accommodating and generous spirit" in listening to what others had to say. But less than a month earlier he had declared in the Diet: "We have no recourse but to proceed toward our goal; we cannot change our convictions to accommodate the American viewpoint."

This was the same Matsuoka who had talked peace with Walsh and Drought in December 1940—a man of unstable temperament whose dexterity in juggling words won him applause from his admirers even when his performance was lacking in substance.

One of Matsuoka's assistants remembers him as a dynamic but erratic genius. "His mind worked as swiftly as lightning. People were dazzled by his brilliance. He was eloquent and could plead a cause with passion. Many were impressed by the vigor of his utterances and were carried away by them. But he often contradicted himself." To Matsuoka, as to Ralph Waldo Emerson, consistency was "the hobgoblin of little minds."

Aware of the contradictions but not that a comparison would be made with Emerson, Secretary Hull felt confirmed in his long-standing judgment that Matsuoka was "as crooked as a basket of fishhooks."

Without interpretation of the type mentioned by Bishop Walsh in his letter to Frank Walker, Matsuoka's myriad pronouncements (even if adorned occasionally with a lulling phrase or two) might indeed puzzle or deceive a person not carefully briefed regarding their "true character."

On the surface, the evidence was against Japan, but what lay under the surface might tell a different story, and it was precisely this "other story" that Father Drought was now hoping to present in Washington.

CHAPTER TEN

The John Doe Associates Converge

PRIVATE PERSONS who aspire to participate in the settling of international disputes must have sizable funds at their disposal. Often they must travel long distances—sometimes halfway around the world—living in a style consistent with their self-imposed mission; or at least they must maintain extensive communications, using the telephone and sending telegrams whenever an occasion arises that demands speed rather than economy. They may have a heavy correspondence and can become involved in drafting lengthy documents; these tasks will generally require the assistance of a stenographer-typist, who must be paid for her services. The entertainment of key individuals can add another item to the mounting bill; and sometimes the unexpected will occur and further, unanticipated expenses must then be met. If the money for all this is not at hand, the peace maneuver may suffer a serious loss of momentum—possibly at a critical moment.

Father Drought was fortunate in being able to draw on the resources of Maryknoll. Whatever he spent in his capacity as John Doe could be regarded as ultimately contributing to the work of the Church. Peace in the Far East would permit a vigorous resumption of Catholic missionary activity in areas where it had encountered difficulties as a result of the war between Japan and China. A return to "normalcy" would presumably also provide a better opportunity to combat communism in Asia. These desiderata made the disbursement of any reasonable amount entirely worthwhile from Drought's point of view.

Tadao Wikawa, by comparison, was not well situated. Confronted by this fact, he turned to Iwakuro for help. As chief of the Army Affairs Section of the Military Affairs Bureau of the War Ministry, the Colonel was in a position to render assistance. After hearing what Wikawa had to say, Iwakuro consulted two businessmen who were trying to get the Ford Motor Company to take part in a venture of importance to Japan. They were acquainted with Wikawa and apparently believed that he could be useful; they therefore offered to help pay for his trip "as a patriotic gesture." When Matsuoka learned of this arrangement, he questioned War Minister Hideki Tōjō about it. Matsuoka suspected that the money would come from secret funds available to the Army for special projects. When Tōjō made inquiries, however, Iwakuro assured him that this was not the case. Matsuoka then let the matter drop.

But money was only one of Wikawa's problems. By early 1941 excursions abroad had become virtually impossible for private persons unless they happened to be traveling for a purpose deemed to be of benefit to the state. Thus, once Wikawa had obtained financial backing for his American venture, he had to persuade the Foreign Office to issue him a passport. He encountered less difficulty than might have been anticipated, largely because Iwakuro once again interceded on his behalf. Vice-Minister Ōhashi knew that Wikawa had approached Konoye concerning Japanese relations with the United States; he also knew that Iwakuro had been ordered to Washington to assist Ambassador Nomura. Now the Vice-Minister was told that the Colonel would serve as a consultant in the Ford Motor Company project, and that he was going to use Wikawa as his interpreter.

Although Ōhashi had misgivings, he agreed to authorize the issuance of a passport that bestowed quasi-official standing on Wikawa as a *Gaimushō shokutaku*—a temporary, non-regular staff member of the Foreign Office (this term was translated into "Extra Secretary of the Ministry of Foreign Affairs" when Wikawa applied for a visa to enter the United States).

Having secured a passport and the financial backing he needed for his trip, Wikawa faced one more hurdle. To obtain a permit that would authorize him to convert yen into dollars, he had to submit an application to the Finance Ministry. Although he had told various people that he was leaving for New York to see his daughter and to arrange a property settlement with his estranged wife, Wikawa informed the authorities at the Finance Ministry that the purpose of his trip was to study industrial cooperatives and credit associations formed by Japanese living in the United States—a purpose that was consistent with the position Wikawa currently held in the banking world. He estimated that he would spend five months abroad, and that he would require $1,000 per month for his expenses (plus some extra money for local travel within the United States).

Since Wikawa was a *Gaimushō shokutaku*, no one saw any reason to deny his request. With the permit in hand, Wikawa went to the Tokyo branch of the National City Bank, where he purchased $5,750 worth of traveler's checks—nearly all of the funds he had gathered together for his American venture. The impression Wikawa made during this trans-action helps to explain why the bank manager subsequently spoke about him to Donald Smith of the American Embassy, who stopped by the bank soon thereafter.

Twenty-four hours prior to sailing for the United States, Wikawa went to see Premier Konoye. The Prince may have asked Wikawa to report back whatever seemed of interest or value, but he did no more than that. Wikawa was not empowered to act for the Japanese Government; he was not a personal envoy dispatched by the Premier. He was simply a private individual who shared Drought's desire to dabble in diplomacy. Like Drought, he was an amateur with no special qualifi-cations to play the part of an international emissary and with no official patent of any kind. The only claim Wikawa could legitimately make at the moment was that he had gotten on well with two American clergy-men who were friendly to Japan and who apparently had access to President Roosevelt and other important figures in the United States.

By the time of Wikawa's departure for Washington, Iwakuro's rela-tionship to the Walsh-Drought affair had changed considerably. The Colonel had not consorted with the two Americans while they were in Tokyo, for it had not occurred to him that he might be going to the United States. He had arranged a meeting for Walsh and Drought with the chief of the Military Affairs Bureau, but he had not been present at the interview. He had merely heard later what had transpired in Mutō's office.

After word had come that Walsh and Drought had seen the Presi-dent, Iwakuro had looked more closely into the matter. He had then asked Wikawa to precede him to the United States. In this way a be-ginning could be made prior to his own arrival, which would not be for at least another month. Wikawa had not only agreed to do this but had also consented to serve as the Colonel's interpreter.

Iwakuro and Wikawa had no intention of taking part in any nego-tiations with the Ford Motor Company; that was merely camouflage. They would participate, instead, in a backdoor maneuver to secure a diplomatic settlement that would eliminate the need to resort to force in the Pacific. In a very real sense, therefore, it was the Colonel, and not Prince Konoye, who was sending Wikawa to the United States. So far as Iwakuro was concerned, Wikawa was going to Washington as his personal agent.

*

As the *Hikawa-maru* put out to sea, Wikawa's mood of elation found expression in a message sent to an American friend of recent standing.

Cover and concealment combined with economy to trim Wikawa's thoughts to a few words: "Am calming down the Pacific. Regards to Bishop." When this unsigned radiogram reached Maryknoll, New York, Father Drought knew at once from whom it came. "Happy landing and safe pleasant trip east," he wired in reply. "May the full joy of peace crown your hopes."

Since Wikawa wanted to cover the last leg of his journey by plane, he had already asked Drought for help in obtaining a reservation. Five days out of Yokohama, Wikawa decided that he had better be more specific: "Reaching Vancouver Monday morning [February 24]. Kindly arrange flying therefrom saving one day without Canadian visa. Baggages bonded."

When this request arrived at Maryknoll, Bishop Walsh had to deal with the matter personally, for Drought was then in Atlanta, Georgia. The Society's representative in Seattle, Father Leopold H. Tibesar, was promptly instructed to make plane reservations for a Japanese banker named Wikawa. "Divulge his name to nobody," Walsh warned, "except airplane company."

Walsh then turned to the immigration authorities in Ottawa for assistance: "May I inquire if personal friend Japanese citizen arriving Vancouver without Canadian visa on Japanese boat bound Seattle can be allowed to save one day travel by disembarking at Vancouver and immediately taking first plane available Vancouver to New York."

Having thus set the wheels in motion, Walsh dispatched a radiogram to the *Hikawa-maru* to let Wikawa know that efforts were being made on his behalf. Walsh also sent a telegram to Drought to brief him on developments and to assure him that he would be alerted if anything occurred requiring his attention.

Over the next five days communications passed back and forth between the principals as complications arose or problems were resolved. Tibesar was kept busy coping with some conflicting advice and a change or two in plans. At one point he reported that Wikawa was now booked on two flights—one out of Vancouver and the other out of Seattle. Walsh relayed this to Drought, who immediately sent an answering telegram: "I think Tibesar better advise Wikawa to accept Seattle reservation. One day will hardly make any difference as the Potomac has stopped moving."*

When word was received that the authorities in Ottawa were willing

* Drought was referring here to the wait-and-see attitude the President and Secretary Hull had adopted.

to accede to the request of the "Lord Bishop" of Maryknoll, Walsh asked Tibesar to meet Wikawa in Vancouver and to assist him in every way possible. Tibesar, who could scarcely imagine what all the fuss was about, saw no point in doing this, since the airline people had offered to send someone to the boat. Walsh felt that this was not good enough: "Must insist you meet him Vancouver. . . . Highly important show Wikawa every possible attention even if no practical result gained."

When the *Hikawa-maru* docked at Vancouver on schedule, Wikawa was admitted by the local officials as a non-immigrant. He departed the next morning on a flight that gave him brief glimpses of Seattle and Chicago, where his plane landed en route. Thus the man who had sailed from Yokohama on February 13 as Colonel Iwakuro's agent and interpreter flew into New York on February 26 as a "Plenipotentiary Representative of the Japanese Government" and was welcomed as such by Bishop Walsh and Father Drought.

*

While all this had been taking place across land and sea, Admiral Nomura had arrived in Washington and had paid his first visit to the White House. Despite the President's recommendation that he meet with Secretary Hull to eliminate "points of divergence," Nomura did not go near the State Department. Why did he hold back?

The reasons are various, but perhaps foremost among them is the important fact that the Ambassador had been dispatched from Tokyo with nothing to offer in the way of new proposals. The instructions he had received from Matsuoka at the outset of his mission were so narrowly conceived that Nomura would have exceeded his authority had he suggested even so much as a willingness on the part of his government to consider altering the policies Japan had followed to date. The United States, Matsuoka had declared, must be prevented from going to war with Japan and from participating in the European conflict. If coercion or intimidation were needed to accomplish this purpose, then they would be used. The future policy of Japan would turn on the axis of the Tripartite Pact, just as in earlier years the pivoting point had been Japan's alliance with England. If Roosevelt joined forces with Churchill in the war against Hitler and Mussolini, the United States would have to face the Japanese consequences.

This was the threat—the means by which Matsuoka intended to bend the American Government to his will.

When the President subsequently had an opportunity to read what he called "the purported instructions from Foreign Minister Matsuoka to

Ambassador Nomura," he took them to be "the product of a mind" that was "deeply disturbed and unable to think quietly or logically."

Matsuoka believed that Japan should adhere to the Tripartite Pact; he also believed that his country should continue to expand in Asia. These convictions were shared by Konoye and other leaders in Tokyo. Friendly relations with the United States would therefore be possible only if the American Government recognized and accepted the Japanese stand. Although Nomura knew that this was the attitude of his government, he disagreed with it. He was not in favor of an armed advance southward or of war with the United States. He saw what Matsuoka and others chose to ignore: to seek an improvement in Japanese-American relations while strengthening Japan's ties with Hitler was like trying to chase two rabbits at the same time.

Nomura had not wanted the ambassadorship; he had agreed to take the post only as a matter of duty after considerable pressure had been brought to bear upon him. In the process, he had talked to Matsuoka, Konoye, and many others—especially to friends in the Imperial Navy. Almost to a man they had expressed their concurrence with his views, or had spoken in such a vague manner that Nomura came away feeling he had their "understanding." Thus he had concluded—falsely as it turned out—that he had far more support in Tokyo than he actually had. This fact explains why he could later be so positive that everything would turn out all right in the end.

Following his arrival in Washington, Nomura decided not to rush matters. He wanted to study the situation before inching too far out on "the tightrope of diplomacy." He therefore engaged in nothing more strenuous than a few courtesy calls.

Nomura thought in terms of the way things were done in Japan where go-betweens were a standard feature of any delicate endeavor. His plan was to reestablish contact with old American friends—Navy men in particular. Once these preliminaries were out of the way, he would face up to the issues. This plan, however, overlooked an important possibility: events might move too rapidly to permit Nomura to employ such a leisurely approach. This is indeed what happened. Before Nomura was ready to deal with concrete problems, the initiative he should have exercised as the Japanese ambassador to the United States had passed into other hands.

On February 28, 1941, the day on which Secretary Hull and the President learned of the presence in Washington of "a Plenipotentiary Representative of the Japanese Government," Tadao Wikawa called on the Envoy Extraordinary and Ambassador Plenipotentiary already installed in the Japanese Embassy on Massachusetts Avenue. Several days later

Wikawa turned up again. He found that "although the store was open it wasn't doing any business." This was to be of great help to the John Doe Associates in launching their own enterprise.

During these initial visits to the Embassy, Wikawa "dropped" the names of Konoye, Matsuoka, Iwakuro, and other men of affairs in Tokyo with whom he claimed to be on good terms. He also spoke of a developing relationship with certain Americans who were close to President Roosevelt and who were anxious to help bring about a settlement with Japan.

Nomura was impressed by all this, especially by an exchange of views that Wikawa had already had with Postmaster General Frank Walker. According to Wikawa, Walker had suggested that a secret meeting take place between Hull and Nomura to permit them to confer with each other without arousing the interest of members of the press. The Ambassador was to go to the Carlton Hotel on Saturday, March 8, for a heart-to-heart talk with Hull. It would be advisable, Wikawa said, to use a rear staircase to the proper floor. The door to Hull's apartment would be open; Nomura was to enter without knocking.

Minister Wakasugi and others at the Embassy scoffed at Wikawa's claims, for his proposal smacked of the kind of melodrama found in third-rate novels. The whole scheme was ridiculous—a man in Hull's position would not ask the Japanese Ambassador to tiptoe up the backstairs of the Carlton like a paramour sneaking into the bedroom of his mistress. At best Nomura would find no one home; at worst he would become the butt of a joke that could laugh him out of Washington.

Nomura hesitated at first but then decided to take a chance. If Wikawa was telling the truth, it would be the height of discourtesy toward Hull not to keep the appointment. And so on March 8, scarcely knowing what to expect, Nomura went to Hull's apartment. As soon as he crossed the threshold, he discovered that Wikawa had been as good as his word. Hull was there; Nomura saw him and talked with him; they agreed to meet again. Nomura was glad he had kept the appointment despite the forebodings of his staff; he was glad he had listened to Wikawa after all.

Thus did Nomura acquire confidence in a man whose connections in the United States were so excellent that within days of his arrival he had been able to arrange a "backstairs meeting" between the Secretary of State and the Japanese Ambassador.

*

Walsh and Drought had introduced Wikawa to Walker in New York on February 27. The Postmaster General had been sincere and friendly.

He had assured his three visitors that he would aid them in any way he could. He had suggested that they put their heads together in an effort to find a means of adjusting Japanese-American relations. In the course of the conversation, Walker had noted that the distinguishing characteristic of American diplomacy at the moment was the use being made of "shirtsleeve diplomats"—the implication being that amateurs could sometimes succeed where professionals might fail.

It is easy to imagine how a word here and a word there on February 27 became transformed into a suggestion, made several days later in Washington, that Hull and Nomura should secretly get together at the Secretary's apartment, where a meeting could take place without the knowledge of the press.

The memorandum brought to the White House by Walker on February 28, containing Drought's assertion that "a Plenipotentiary Representative of the Japanese Government" had arrived in Washington "empowered to negotiate concrete terms for a settlement of all outstanding Far Eastern questions vis-à-vis the United States," represented a blending of the "facts" Drought had gathered in Tokyo in December with the "up-to-date information" Wikawa had brought from Japan. The proposals for a Japanese-American settlement that were made in this memorandum, and in every document that followed throughout the month of March, were entirely worthless as an indication of the intentions of the leaders of Japan. No one in the Japanese Government had drafted such proposals or had authorized either Wikawa or Drought to engage in a maneuver of this kind. No one in Tokyo was prepared to enter into any such settlement, and yet—strangely enough—each new assertion spun out by Father Drought, whether orally or in writing, imperceptibly strengthened the web of his conspiracy for peace.

Hornbeck's reaction to the document submitted on February 28— his negative view of the offering as a whole and his desire to know more about the mystery-man who had suddenly turned up in Washington with negotiating powers—was correct in every respect. As Hornbeck pointed out at the time, the "proposers" were not realistically evaluating the current policies and practices of Japan or the policies, objectives, and practices of the United States. The procedure they were advocating was simply "not adapted to the facts of the situation."

Despite the encouragement that had been given to Drought at the White House in January, the recommendations made by Hornbeck and by Hamilton early in March were followed to a large extent. The State Department's handling of the John Doe affair was consequently quite proper at this stage (caution being the order of the day), and yet the front-line position held by Hornbeck, Hamilton, and Hull was constantly harassed by the memoranda barrage that Drought laid down upon the American Government—ten items in all in a period of two weeks from March 5 to March 19, culminating in the "Preliminary Draft of 'Agreement in Principle,' " which was simply a glorified presentation of the views Drought had discussed with his "fellow Japanese" in Tokyo in December 1940.

By the time this proposal was delivered in Washington, the basis had been laid for claiming that Colonel Iwakuro, who was to reach San Francisco on March 20, held the key to everything. Wikawa planned to consult him immediately in regard to the "Preliminary Draft of 'Agreement in Principle.' " If Iwakuro seconded the approval already expressed by "Plenipotentiary" Wikawa, then "acceptance" of the "Agreement in Principle" could be "indicated" by the two governments "through existing unofficial channels" and the further conduct of the negotiations turned over to the State Department and the Japanese Foreign Office—"public announcement to be made as soon as possible thereafter" at a Konoye-Roosevelt conference to be convened in Honolulu.

Drought's eagerness had again run away with his imagination, permitting him to place the most favorable construction on everything and to ignore some very fundamental impediments to what he proposed. On the basis of the information supplied by Wikawa, Drought judged that Iwakuro was coming to Washington with instructions from his Army superiors to expedite the settlement Drought had in mind. According to Iwakuro's own postwar statements, however, there was no connection between the Walsh-Drought visit to Japan and the orders he received posting him to the United States; the two circumstances were purely coincidental. His only specific assignment was to assist Nomura in whatever way he could.

Commissioned as an infantry officer late in 1918, Iwakuro had served with the Kwantung Army in the early 1930's in Manchuria and had later graduated to the General Staff in Tokyo. In August 1938 he had been assigned to the Army Affairs Section of the Military Affairs Bureau of the War Ministry. In February 1939 he had become the chief of that Section, a post in which he had demonstrated his interest in political matters. He had advocated an alliance with Germany and had allegedly been involved, in the spring of 1940, in a scheme to overthrow a recalcitrant Cabinet. He had been picked for duty in Washington because Admiral Nomura, whom he did not know personally, had asked the Army to provide an officer who was a "China expert."

Iwakuro had been surprised by the news that he was going to the

United States; he did not regard himself as an authority on Chinese affairs. He was in fact so amazed by his orders that he began wondering whether the "top brass" might be easing him out of Tokyo because he had been too active there.

It was presumably because of the Colonel's influence in the "right places," however, that Wikawa had originally turned to him for help. If Iwakuro had lost favor in Tokyo, Wikawa was unaware of it. In his eyes, the Colonel was still a key man in the Army—a member of the "nucleus clique" of officers who had gradually achieved a predominant position in the shaping of high policy through manipulations behind the scenes.

Ambassador Grew also thought of Iwakuro as an important figure. During a courtesy visit to the American Embassy, the Colonel had been "perfectly candid in observing that the center of politics in Japan [lay] in the Army and not in the Foreign Office."

Dooman had obtained an even fuller view of the Colonel's candor, for Iwakuro had suggested to him that the pro-British attitude of the United States could be attributed to her desire to join with Great Britain in monopolizing the resources of the world. Dooman had tried to explain to Iwakuro that Americans were not making sacrifices, which would require a radical revision of their own economic and social systems, merely to acquire more wealth.

Dooman had also tried to elucidate the "transcendental importance" of human liberties in the thinking of the American people, but the task had seemed hopeless. Dooman had concluded that his remarks were as unintelligible to Iwakuro as were Japanese attempts to explain to foreigners the meaning of *hakkō-ichiu* (the "eight corners of the world under one roof") and all the other mummery then current in Japan. Dooman could not help wondering just how much Iwakuro could possibly learn about the philosophy of the American people, and yet he was being posted to the United States to serve as Nomura's "right-hand military man."

What could be the purpose of having an officer of the Colonel's background and reputation take up residence in Washington? Were his superiors in Tokyo so anxious to get rid of a *bōryaku no meijin*—"a past master of plots and stratagems"—that they would use Nomura's request for a "China expert" as an excuse to unload Iwakuro on the Ambassador, even though the Colonel did not meet Nomura's specifications? Were the War Minister and the chief of the Military Affairs Bureau so irresponsible that they would send such a "cunning" Colonel to the capital of a nation with which Japan's relations were strained to the point where war in the Pacific was a distinct possibility? Did they think that a "born plotter" who had engaged in intrigue in Tokyo would not do so in Washington?

Or did they perhaps have something else in mind?

Was there a connection between the Walsh-Drought visit to Japan and the orders that took Iwakuro to Washington? Was the Army employing the Colonel as a secret agent to negotiate a settlement with the United States—a settlement favorable to Japan? Or was the Army playing a different role? Was Iwakuro being dispatched on an intelligence-surveillance mission? Was he supposed to prevent Nomura from doing anything that might undermine the Tripartite Pact?

On one point there is no doubt: the authorities in Tokyo intended to adhere to that treaty. Hitler's victories in Europe had created a "golden opportunity" for Japan in the Far East; her only fear was that she might "miss the bus" while being detained by the United States. Neither the Japanese Government nor Colonel Iwakuro was going to support a Japanese-American settlement that would impinge upon relations with the Axis powers or hamper the Japanese program for a New Order in East Asia.

Among Iwakuro's fellow passengers on board the *Tatsuta-maru* was a Dōmei correspondent named Masuo Katō.* Unaware that the Colonel might be the victim of a purge from within, Katō regarded the sending of Iwakuro to Washington as "an encouraging sign"; it meant that "even the Army was anxious to reach an agreement that would avoid war." In their contacts on the ship and later, Katō found Iwakuro to be "engagingly frank." He was a man "of great energy . . . with an alert brain," who possessed "boundless enthusiasm" for his work.

When Iwakuro wanted to know with whom he could deal most effectively in the United States, Katō told him: "In that country Mr. Roosevelt is everything. You should negotiate with him directly."

At Hawaii Iwakuro was interviewed by members of the Japanese press, who had already heard of his coming through a front-page story in an English-language newspaper that gave the impression he was carrying "a flag of truce." In an article that subsequently appeared in the *Hawaii Hōchi*, reference was made to Iwakuro's reputation as a man of talent so esteemed by his colleagues that he was likely to become the Army's representative in the Cabinet at some future date. The Colonel had been open in answering questions. He had said that a Japanese-American war would be completely nonsensical but that it might break out never-

---

* Dōmei was Japan's official news agency.

theless, especially if the United States prevented Japan from pursuing her policies in the Far East or if the Americans ended up fighting the Germans. Hostilities would also occur if the American Government applied economic pressure and other "war measures" to the point where Japan and the United States grew so antagonistic toward each other that some small incident could produce an explosion. Both sides must therefore exercise discretion so as to calm down the waves of the Pacific.

With this as his parting comment, Iwakuro continued his journey to San Francisco. On hand to greet him when the *Tatsuta-maru* reached port on March 20 was Tadao Wikawa, who had flown to the West Coast from Washington. Wikawa told Iwakuro that Walsh and Drought were earnestly working to bring about a Japanese-American settlement, that President Roosevelt was fully cognizant of their efforts, and that the Postmaster General was acting as a middleman in the "negotiations." Walker was coming to California ostensibly on a speaking tour, Wikawa said, but actually for the purpose of conferring with the Colonel.

That same day Wikawa dispatched a telegram to Drought: "Arriving New York Sunday [March] 30th ... by train due to [Iwakuro's] much-needed rest and thoroughgoing study of the paper though generally he is pleased with it."*

By the time this message was relayed from Maryknoll to the Wardman Park in Washington, Drought was on the point of leaving the hotel to go to New York, where a meeting with Ballantine was scheduled to take place as soon as Iwakuro and Wikawa arrived. It was therefore March 22 before a reply reached San Francisco, addressed to the Japanese consul general and signed Murphy (the name of Drought's current secretary): "Would you kindly advise Mr. Wikawa to telephone friend at hotel in New York immediately. Matter most important and urgent."

Upon receiving this message, Wikawa promptly complied, but the issue remained unsettled. On March 24, after stopping briefly with Iwakuro at Yosemite Valley en route to Los Angeles, Wikawa wired Drought at the Berkshire: "Could it be postponed as everything would become speedier by our study on train and his getting first object lesson on America?"†

Drought quickly replied: "Party came to New York today to meet you. I apologized but said you would probably be here tomorrow. If I send him back to wait until the 30th you will certainly lose your present ad-

* Wikawa was referring here to Iwakuro's reaction to the "Preliminary Draft of 'Agreement in Principle'" (fourteen single-spaced typewritten pages in a language the Colonel did not understand).

† Wikawa was suggesting that the meeting with Ballantine be deferred.

vantage and lose also the great benefit of the bargaining position which the Trumpet's visit gives you.* Moreover unless you yourself come you will have embarrassed me extremely. So long as conversation starts you can delay and postpone as much as you think wise. Please phone me immediately and advise because the situation is really serious."

Further consultation by telephone finally produced a compromise that was revealed, in part, to Ballantine: Wikawa would fly on ahead; Iwakuro would follow by train.

This change in travel arrangements ruled out a visit to the Grand Canyon that the two men had been planning. The rendezvous with Walker also had to be postponed. After talking with Ballantine at the Berkshire, Wikawa would fly to Chicago to meet Iwakuro's train. By taking a plane from there, he and the Colonel could be in New York by March 30 ready to move in whatever direction seemed most likely to produce the best results in the shortest possible time.

*

Although Nomura had fallen in with Wikawa's proposal regarding the March 8 meeting with Hull at the Carlton, Minister Wakasugi and the other "regulars" on the Ambassador's staff had remained uncooperative, treating Wikawa with the suspicion that professionals are inclined to feel toward any amateur who is brash enough to plunge thoughtlessly into a venture their experience tells them should be tackled with great care, or not at all. As a consequence, Wakasugi had flatly refused to allow Wikawa to use the facilities of the Embassy to transmit the progress-reports he wished to cable to Tokyo.

Wikawa had complained of his troubles to Drought, and he in turn had included a number of slighting references to members of the Japanese Embassy—to Wakasugi in particular—in memoranda delivered to the State Department by Frank Walker early in March.

Wikawa, for his part, had decided to outflank Wakasugi by working through the office of the financial commissioner in New York—an office in which he himself had served in the early 1920's and where the current incumbent, Tsutomu Nishiyama, was willing to be helpful. For several critical weeks in March Wikawa had thus been able to circumvent Wakasugi through the simple device of having Nishiyama send special telegrams to the Minister of Finance in Tokyo (to whom the commissioner normally reported), requesting that these messages be conveyed to Premier Konoye without delay.

---

* Drought was reminding Wikawa that Foreign Minister Matsuoka was on his way to Europe, with solo performances slated for Moscow, Berlin, and Rome.

Although this had solved the immediate problem, Wikawa's position had remained somewhat precarious. Nomura had reported to Matsuoka, on March 1, that Wikawa was engaged in some sort of maneuver with Walsh and Drought aimed at maintaining direct contact with Roosevelt, the idea being that this might lead to a Japanese-American conference in the near future. Nomura had asked about Wikawa's backing in Tokyo and had indicated he would await instructions before forwarding a long cable addressed to Matsuoka that Wikawa wanted him to send to the Foreign Minister.

Five days later, on March 6, Matsuoka had sent an answering telegram that touched briefly on some of Wikawa's activities in Tokyo prior to his departure for the United States. Nomura was not to discourage the Walsh-Drought "maneuver" outright, but at the same time he was supposed to handle the matter carefully (the idea being to keep Wikawa from doing as he pleased).

Nine days later, on March 15, a follow-up telegram had left Tokyo warning the Ambassador that very unfavorable rumors were circulating in regard to Wikawa. Nomura was advised that a stage had been reached where there was no need for Wikawa to remain active. He was to cease and desist. This was the wish of Premier Konoye himself. There would be no harm, however, in maintaining contact with Walsh and Drought.

Two days later, on March 17, a third and far more stringent instruction had been dispatched. Nomura was informed that neither Konoye nor Matsuoka had "any connection whatsoever" with Wikawa; that Wikawa's behavior in requesting help from Konoye was outrageous; that under no circumstances was anyone to give Roosevelt or others the impression Japan might be moving toward mediation of the European war in cooperation with the United States; that to do so would constitute a betrayal of Japan's obligations toward her Axis allies, Germany and Italy; and that Nomura should not only admonish Wikawa but should strictly order him to stop interfering. Nomura was also told that Walsh and Drought had never been commissioned to speak in such a way for the Japanese Government.

In a cable sent that same day to Nishiyama in New York, an even clearer picture was given of the liberties Wikawa had taken: investigation in Tokyo had revealed that he had no authority for what he was doing; the men with whom he had talked before his departure, including Konoye, had expressed the view that every effort should be made to avoid war in the Pacific; no one had ever asked Wikawa, however, to enter into negotiations in Washington; he was merely supposed to get in touch with "the persons close to the President" (Walsh, Drought, Walker) and report what they had in mind; from the standpoint of Japanese relations with Germany and for other reasons as well, it was extremely undesirable to allow Wikawa or anyone else to convey the impression that he had been sent to the United States to represent Konoye; finally, during Matsuoka's forthcoming visit to Europe, Wikawa should say nothing of a concrete nature—he should restrict himself to trying to determine the intentions of the American side.

If Matsuoka's postwar recollections are correct, Nomura had by this time already received another telegram in which the Foreign Minister told him to have nothing to do with Wikawa. Matsuoka had sent this telegram after receiving a request from Father Drought, forwarded through Nomura, asking not only for authorization to report to Roosevelt what Matsuoka had said to Walsh and Drought in Tokyo in December 1940, but also for permission to convey these remarks in the form of a personal message from the Foreign Minister of Japan to the President of the United States. Matsuoka had immediately replied that he did not know which statements Drought wanted to repeat at the White House, but that he was absolutely opposed to the whole idea.

Despite this background, Nomura maintained his connections with Wikawa and Drought. They were almost total strangers to him, but he listened to them nevertheless. He did so because he thought that he could use the kind of help they promised to supply. He also found their rosy outlook very much to his liking. Nomura was incurably optimistic; he could not believe that his government would remain as "immovable" as it did, or that the United States would stand firm in dealing with Japan.

With the arrival of Iwakuro in Washington, Nomura would acquire still another assistant from outside the ranks of the Foreign Office. As a "Special Adviser," the Colonel would be officially accredited to the Embassy; he would be in a position to play a vital part in the conduct of Nomura's mission. The Ambassador would trust Iwakuro because he had been sent in response to Nomura's request for a "China expert." Iwakuro in turn would support Nomura in his use of Wikawa, effectively blocking any rearguard action by Wakasugi. The Colonel would do this because he needed Wikawa as his interpreter, and because—like Nomura—Iwakuro wanted to take advantage of Wikawa's friendship with Drought to ride the "inside track" to the White House that ran through the office of the Postmaster General.

The misconceptions that had already permeated the minds of Drought and Wikawa were now going to spread in many directions, like creeping vines imperceptibly reaching out to secure a firm hold on their existence.

The situation might have been somewhat less serious if Matsuoka had given Nomura specific instructions on how to negotiate with Roosevelt and Hull, or if the Foreign Minister had adhered to what seems to have been his original plan—to appear personally on the scene to cultivate a settlement after the Ambassador had prepared the soil.

With neither of these prospects in sight, Nomura was left to his own devices. In allowing the John Doe Associates to mastermind his strategy and to draw him into ill-conceived maneuvers that were kept secret from the Japanese Government, he helped to undermine, little by little, whatever chance he might otherwise have had to create a basis for negotiations.

Nomura was a man of many admirable qualities, but he had no business being where he was. Prior to his departure for the United States, he had been regarded in some quarters as Japan's "last trump card," and yet the painful truth is that he was a greenhorn at the game of diplomacy. From beginning to end in Washington, he played his hand so poorly that he might just as well have been trumping his own side.

CHAPTER ELEVEN

Shirtsleeve Diplomats at Work

I N A LETTER sent to Father Drought from San Francisco shortly after Iwakuro's arrival from Japan, Wikawa had hinted that the Colonel's reaction to the "Preliminary Draft of 'Agreement in Principle' " had not been entirely favorable. Wikawa's "impression" was that "on the whole" Iwakuro was "pleased with it" and would come "to some compromise on the very delicate points therein." The main thing now was to let the Colonel acquire a "perfect understanding" of the proposal before he reached Washington; he would then be in a better position "to persuade Admiral Nomura." "Anyway," Wikawa had written by way of encouragement, "things are not at all bad. We have already achieved something toward humanity."

Drought had not expected such lukewarm tidings. He had just submitted several memoranda to Frank Walker in which he had spoken in glowing terms of the "Agreement in Principle." Although he had personally drafted this proposal with the help of Wikawa, Drought had presented it as "a proclamation of a revolution in Japanese 'ideology' and policy." He had declared that "some modification" might result after Wikawa had consulted Iwakuro, but that there would be "no substantial change."

Drought had called for immediate action on the part of the United States Government, warning that delay now would greatly increase the chances of failure. He had insisted that Prince Konoye and several other like-minded men in Japan (none of whom knew anything at all about the "Preliminary Draft" as yet) would be unable to manage it "piecemeal." He had declared that they were running the risk of assassination, and that the lives of Iwakuro and Wikawa were also in danger. He had repeatedly solicited top-level assurances that the "Agreement in Principle" was "substantially acceptable" to the President and the Secretary of State. He had claimed that if he could so advise Tokyo the Japanese would quickly cable "their formulation" of the "Agreement" to Ambassador Nomura, instructing him to submit it officially to Roosevelt and Hull.

"If this is not done [by April 1]," Drought had written, "we can properly doubt the sincerity of the Japanese."

"I have such confidential information," he had added, "that I am thoroughly satisfied *we must help the Japanese to 'put it over.'*"

Having said all this, Drought was now faced with the problem of explaining why everything was not going according to plan. The excuse he offered to Ballantine was that the German Government, having learned of Iwakuro's departure from Tokyo, had taken countermeasures of a type the Japanese had not anticipated, and that as a consequence a complete change in procedure would be necessary. Drought assured Ballantine, however, that this development would not seriously affect the terms of the "Preliminary Draft."

Prior to making these statements to Ballantine, Drought had been briefed by Wikawa regarding Iwakuro's objections to the "Agreement in Principle." Wikawa may have had some difficulty in putting the text of the "Preliminary Draft" into Japanese, but the Colonel had learned enough of its contents to comment on the main issues—the alliance with Hitler, trade relations with the United States, the war in China, and the Japanese advance southward.

Confronted by Iwakuro's dissatisfaction with some of the features of his "Agreement in Principle," Drought rushed to the defense of his brainchild. On March 27, the day Ballantine talked with Wikawa in New York, Drought produced eight and one-half, single-spaced typewritten pages of point-by-point explanation that he hoped Wikawa would convey to Iwakuro. Once again, as in the "Working Analysis" of December 1940, Drought went over to the Japanese side. If Ballantine had seen Drought's memorandum of comment, the undesirability of permitting him to maintain any connection with officials of the American Government or with members of the Japanese Embassy would have been apparent.

It is the role Drought was playing at this time rather than the "solution" he was proposing that merits attention. He was suggesting ways and means of leading the United States Government into a settlement that he regarded as an intelligent answer to the Japanese-American impasse—an answer that the deaf and the blind who inhabited the State Department of his imagination would never comprehend unless they were given the assistance their handicapped condition required.

Drought's purpose now was to persuade Iwakuro that he had failed to appreciate how much Japan would gain from an acceptance of the "Preliminary Draft of 'Agreement in Principle.' " Drought consequently supplied Wikawa with one argument after another to use on the Colonel.

According to Drought, the eleven "Rules for Nations" that he had laid down in the "Preliminary Draft" were "deliberately intended to compel from the Americans a fundamental admission of the propriety and justice of the Japanese position." A careful reading, with this in mind, would lead to the conclusion that these "Rules" constituted "a real, substantial element of a complete Japanese victory in diplomacy." "Diplomatically," Drought declared, "it is always advantageous to make the other person eat his own words and taste a meaning that he did not foresee when he uttered them."

Care had to be exercised, however, in translating the "Rules" into Japanese. "They should not be translated *literally*" but "according to substance, in a language appropriate to the psychology of the Japanese people." It would then become "perfectly clear" that the "Rules," together with some corresponding "Aids to Peace," were "entirely more favorable to the Japanese position than . . . to the American position." As soon as they were accepted and promulgated, they would "establish Japan's political . . . hegemony over the Far East." They have been "very carefully designed," Drought wrote, "to accomplish this purpose and have, accordingly, been put in language that would be attractive to the Americans and to the American public, who would not, of course, realize the full meaning and the inevitable consequence that I have described above. Accordingly, I feel that we must not only insist upon these 'Rules,' etc., but that we must move quickly for their acceptance before the Americans themselves try to change them in the realization that they 'cut both ways.' . . . From the viewpoint of diplomacy and [the] fundamental realities of Japan's own case, I am convinced that *these 'Rules' now favor Japan in every way* but serve to put the United States diplomatically on the defensive."

In substance, everything that Japan wanted had been given "except immediate oil control," and even that would "certainly develop" out of the "Agreement in Principle," once the two nations had entered into it.

"The [Preliminary] Draft," Drought declared, ". . . indirectly but firmly provides a fundamental alliance of the United States and Japan against Russia and Communism." "I have proceeded throughout," he explained, "with the deep conviction that Soviet Russia, like Tsarist Russia, is the convinced enemy of Japan. I further considered that there are only two Powers capable, either now or in the near future, of a military attack upon Japan; these Powers are Russia and the United States. If we eliminate the United States and set up Japanese political and economic hegemony in the Far Eastern region, and at the same time indirectly ally the United States against Russia, the menace from either is completely removed."

"The Leftist elements in the United States," Drought added, "must be deprived of their ammunition against Japan. The [Preliminary] Draft ... leaves them rather helpless."

The "mildness" of the terms proposed with regard to China was more apparent than real. "The Japanese could offer these terms very sincerely," Drought suggested, "and they could very sincerely hope that conditions in China will so change as to make the actual realization of such terms possible ... even though their practical judgment and factual knowledge convince them that conditions in China are such that the *Chinese themselves* could not meet such terms. When it becomes evident that the Chinese cannot meet the terms, the Japanese will have won another diplomatic and actual victory without firing a shot."

There was no need to announce that American aid to China would cease as soon as the President invited China and Japan to negotiate their differences. To introduce a stipulation to that effect, Drought said, would be to give the impression that the United States was making "some sort of a concession" in stopping aid to China. The Japanese would then be expected to make "some comparable concession." It would be smarter to "get the result without asking for it" and "without giving anything in return."

"In negotiations of this kind," Drought declared, "it seems to me [more] important to apparently make concessions while obtaining, in reality, exactly what you want, than to approach the other parties with demands which put them on the defensive and prompt them to [lodge] counter-demands in an effort to out-match you in trading skill."

"I think we have lost a little ground during the last few days," Drought concluded, "due not only to the delay [caused by the Colonel's decision to travel by train] but also to the psychological factor that the Americans have had an interval to think over our proposals from different angles. Until these last few days we had been pushing them and insisting that they had to make a choice quickly.... I am in favor of resuming [this] type of pressure ... as soon as possible, even though the ultimate authorities in Japan may not wish to move so quickly. The advantage is always with the person who deliberately creates an atmosphere of 'crisis' and knows perfectly well what he is doing."

Having provided Wikawa with arguments to use on Iwakuro, Drought decided that Konoye and others in Japan might be equally in need of advice that would encourage them to respond favorably to the "Agreement in Principle." As a consequence, on March 29, the day before the Colonel was scheduled to arrive in New York, Drought put the finishing touches on still another memorandum, "written exclusively from the Japanese viewpoint"—a memorandum to be sent to the Premier of Japan.

"Our fundamental objective," Drought declared, "is Japan's legitimate national interest—regardless of the consequences to the Anglo-Saxons, or the Germans, or the Chinese."

Japan had reached a decisive moment in her history. She could gamble on choosing the winning side in the European struggle; she could launch hostilities in the Far East to attain her goals; or she could achieve the same result, and simultaneously keep the war in Europe out of the Pacific, by employing a diplomatic maneuver that would force the United States to go along with Japan.

As Drought saw it, only the last of these alternatives represented a sensible decision. If the maneuver he had in mind was "carefully managed and conceived in a spirit of 'high statesmanship,'" Japan would be able to "solidify her legitimate political and economic position in the Far East," win full American support for that position, put an end to the British role in Asia, "settle the China Incident advantageously," and "avoid giving direct challenge either to Britain or Germany."

According to Drought, Japan would also be able to keep the victors in Europe from absorbing the Far East as "spoils of war." Japan would be able to create regional security, "recover her financial strength," and establish herself both realistically and legally "as an equal of the great Powers of the world."

How could Japan achieve all this? The answer was obvious: through the "Preliminary Draft of 'Agreement in Principle.'" "We can think of no other way," Drought wrote, "to accomplish so much while sacrificing so little. Nor can we think of any other way better calculated to insure future peace as opposed to the certainty of future conflict."

*

Exactly what was said when Iwakuro and Wikawa finally got together with Walsh and Drought in New York on March 31 cannot be determined, for no record was made of the conversation at the time. It appears, however, that the Colonel held his ground on all major issues. It also seems likely that he and Drought did most of the talking. Since they did not share a common tongue, they had to converse through Wikawa —a practice that remained standard throughout their association.

Of all the languages in the world, Japanese is one of the least amenable to on-the-spot translation. Even in the best of circumstances a blurring of nuances may occur. Wikawa's English was passable in everyday situations, but Drought was not always easy to follow. There is reason to believe, therefore, that Wikawa may occasionally have made some honest mistakes. He may also have resorted, at times, to trimming the edges of the dialogue between the Colonel and the priest so that each man would hear what he wanted to hear.

Although Drought knew by this time that his "Agreement in Principle" might have to be discarded to make way for a document more in harmony with the Japanese viewpoint, he nevertheless claimed, in an April 4 memorandum aimed at the White House and the State Deparment, that Iwakuro had consented—unofficially—to every principal point contained in the "Agreement." A 180° change could not be achieved, however, unless Tokyo were given "some substantial benefits." As a consequence, a new proposal incorporating everything that had previously been mentioned was now being prepared by Iwakuro, Wikawa, and Nomura. This proposal, Drought said, would be shown to him "during the course of preparation." The Japanese also planned to let Hull see their draft in the hope that he and the President would find it acceptable. "It is desired," Drought added, "to counter-balance, as quickly as possible, the German offers to Mr. Matsuoka. If these negotiations with the U.S. fail, the Japanese authorities are certain that they will lose control and a war in the Southwestern Pacific will be started."

Drought's report to the effect that he would be "shown" the new proposal while his Japanese friends were putting it together was misleading, for he was already elbow-deep in sorting out his differences with Iwakuro over the stipulations it would contain. With Wikawa's help, Drought was at this very moment composing an English text that would reflect the Colonel's wishes to a large extent.

When this proposal was finally ready on April 5, Hull was not the only recipient. Nomura was also given a copy. He immediately sat down with Iwakuro and Wikawa to study the document. Included in this meeting were several members of Nomura's regular staff—Minister Wakasugi, the military and naval attachés, and an Embassy treaty expert. All of these men were under the impression that Roosevelt and Hull were similarly engaged, but this was not in fact the case. Iwakuro and Drought had simply agreed that their "first draft" probably contained a number of shortcomings, and that the best way to eliminate these defects would be to prepare a second draft after sounding out the opinions of the Ambassador and the President. There is no evidence, however, to indicate that the April 5 proposal reached the White House or that anyone at the State Department did more than read through the document.

Nations that are far apart on fundamental issues must approach their differences with deliberation, unhurriedly exploring all aspects of the situation in the hope of finding some common ground. Subjects of dispute must be discussed at length until compromises are reached that will provide the cement needed to hold a final agreement together.

In attempting to bypass this process, Drought soon discovered that his efforts to hasten a settlement, although readily absorbed at the State Department, were quickly squeezed out again like water from a sponge. He learned with mounting chagrin that Secretary Hull and his Far Eastern advisers were men of more than ordinary prudence—imperturbable, analytical, unrelenting in their moral judgments, and collectively endowed with the brooding patience and inscrutability of a sphinx.

Hornbeck "[did] not for one moment believe" that "the real authorities in Japan," whoever they might be, would embark upon war in the southwestern Pacific "because of lack of success in a 'negotiation' with the United States in the near future."

"This method of approach," he wrote, "with an offer of a reward in one hand and a threat of a penalty in the other hand . . . needs always to be met with a calm and cold scrutiny of [the] realities in the situation."

Hull was equally determined not to allow himself to be stampeded into abrupt action. On Saturday, April 5, he decided that the John Doe matter could be postponed until the first of the week unless Drought and Wikawa, who had already spoken to Ballantine in New York, desired another conference "to include the Colonel who hadn't been included yet."

Two days later, the John Doe Associates reconvened to piece together the "second draft." That same day—April 7—Drought told Ballantine that Iwakuro and Wikawa "were now working with the Japanese Ambassador"; Nomura would probably soon produce a document, which he, Drought, would have an opportunity to see; before presenting this document "officially," however, the Japanese would want "some intimation" that their proposals "would be substantially acceptable to [the American] Government."

From the John Doe material Hornbeck had read thus far, he judged that a nonaggression pact was being put forward. This meant that Japan desired simultaneously to remain a member of the Axis alliance while enjoying the benefits of an American pledge to refrain from hostilities against any of the Axis powers unless one or more of them committed an act of war against the United States. Hornbeck thought that "there might be virtue" in a simple nonaggression treaty if several other nations were included, notably China, Britain, and the Netherlands. John Doe's limited proposal, however, "would be far more to Japan's advantage than to that of the United States."

The agreement being offered was "perhaps even more unsatisfactory from another point of view." Its provisions were "highly complicated" and contained "an extraordinary number and variety of qualifying words, phrases, and clauses." Each and every government that became a party to such an undertaking would interpret those qualifiers to suit itself. "Japan's record in such matters," Hornbeck noted, "is not good."

All the same, Hornbeck was willing to admit that the suggestions John Doe had made concerning mediation of the Sino-Japanese war were "by no means without merit." Important changes had taken place, however, between 1937 and 1941. The fighting in China had become part of a world conflict from which it could not now be isolated. So long as Japan remained in the Axis camp, "it would not be in the interest of the United States or in the interest of Great Britain" to have Sino-Japanese hostilities brought to an end "by any process [that would leave] Japan's military machine undefeated (undiscredited) and intact." To help Axis Japan out of the war in China, without giving "intensively careful thought" to what the Japanese might be able to do as a consequence of being relieved of the burden of hostilities on the mainland, would amount to creating a situation in which they would be free to strike elsewhere in the Far East at will.

Why not test Japan's good faith before plunging into a program as potentially dangerous as the one being advocated by John Doe? Why not indicate that before any negotiations could be started "some concrete evidence" was needed to show the world Japan had "turned toward peace"? Why not suggest that one practical manifestation might be the cessation of all Japanese bombing in China, coupled with no new offensive operations on land or sea?

The John Doe Associates claimed they were speaking for the Army and Navy authorities in Japan. If this claim squared with fact, those authorities ought to be able to control the movement of Japan's armed forces in the Far East—they ought to be able to give their word that those forces would now forgo "activities inconsistent with the representations" John Doe and his friends were making in Washington.

Had Hornbeck's test been proposed to the Japanese Government, the results might have been illuminating, but the "truce" concept died in the files of the State Department. It is a fate that befalls many position-papers—either because the ideas they contain do not seem currently feasible to the men who help make policy or because these men are engulfed, and sometimes overwhelmed, by the onrush of events.

International affairs do not stand still. Postponement of a decision at any given moment may mean that the decision-makers will later be confronted by a situation in which they would like to proceed according to an earlier plan but in which they cannot reasonably do so. The change in circumstances that has taken place in the interim will not permit them to initiate now what they might once have done with relative ease.

In this instance, Father Drought was thus able to proceed with his own plans without having to prove anything to anyone.

With Admiral Nomura reportedly participating in a recasting of Drought's earlier "Agreement in Principle," the distinction the State Department had wished to maintain between private drafts and official proposals was breaking down. Hull could hardly turn his back on an ambassador who was willing to accept responsibility for what was taking place behind the scenes.

Although the Colonel and the priest would each later claim the honors of authorship, the "Draft Understanding" of April 9 was a collaborative effort that incorporated revisions made at the Japanese Embassy. As a result, the *quid pro quo* essence of this proposal, which was to become the key document in the Hull-Nomura conversations of 1941, largely reflected the views of Iwakuro, whereas the window-dressing phraseology used to present these views retained the characteristics of Drought's distinctive style—a circumstance that helps explain why each man would subsequently feel that credit should be given where credit was due.

Thus Drought could assert that he had "recast" Iwakuro's counterdraft; if the April 9 proposal were "properly managed," it would put the Japanese in American hands even though it contained "their original terms." Iwakuro, for his part, could feel relieved that the second draft, despite changes made by the "American side," had turned out to be 90 to 95 percent identical with the outline he had had in mind before leaving Tokyo. Because the document was favorable to his country, the Colonel could even take pride in publicly identifying himself, in postwar Japan, as "the actual author of the 'Draft Understanding.'" So far as Iwakuro was concerned, it was *a Japanese proposal*.

Here is the significant fact in this entire affair. Not a single paragraph, sentence, or word in the "Draft Understanding" of April 9, 1941, had come from anyone in the American Government.

Drought had repeatedly failed to obtain the "substantially acceptable" commitment he had been seeking from Roosevelt and Hull, but he had

conducted himself so confidently in the presence of Iwakuro and Wikawa that they did not realize where matters stood. They thought the
"Boss" in the White House and his "principal assistant" in the State Department were prepared to open negotiations with Japan on the basis being offered—an erroneous conclusion that Admiral Nomura swallowed
with one gulp.

Nothing that he was told later, on far better authority than that of
Father Drought, made any lasting impression on the Japanese Ambassador. As 1941 progressed, the discrepancy between appearances and
reality gradually grew greater until the damage that was done ultimately
passed beyond the point of easy repair, thus making it less and less likely
that a mutually satisfactory formula for peace in the Pacific would ever
be found.

CHAPTER TWELVE

A Mission Is Placed in Jeopardy

THE ARRIVAL ON April 9, 1941, of a "proposal presented to the Department of State through the medium of private American and Japanese individuals" plunged Hull's Far Eastern advisers into a week of extraordinary activity during which they produced eight memoranda and three counterdrafts all revolving around John Doe's latest offering. Hull and his staff felt keenly disappointed as they studied the document the Department had received from Father Drought. "It was much less accommodating," the Secretary later wrote, "than we had been led to believe it would be, and most of its provisions were all that the ardent Japanese imperialists could want."

The assurances that had been given earlier concerning Japan's willingness to divorce herself from the Axis alliance were nowhere to be found.

In regard to China, the presence of a stipulation calling for "joint defense against communistic activities" meant that Japan did not contemplate retreating from a very objectionable feature of the treaty she had signed in November 1940 with Wang Ching-wei. In addition, the John Doe Associates were trying to bring the President of the United States into play. They wanted him to look at certain "general terms" that were to serve as a basis for peace between Japan and China ("concrete terms" would be submitted later to the Chinese). As soon as FDR had "approved" Tokyo's "general terms," and they had been "guaranteed" by the Japanese Government, the President was supposed to ask "the Chiang-Kai-Chek regime" to negotiate peace with Japan.

If Chiang proved amenable to this idea, Tokyo would commence "direct peace negotiations." These talks would not be with Chiang alone, however; they would be with a "newly coalesced Chinese Government" consisting of both the Chiang and the Wang forces.

What if the Generalissimo refused? What then? The "Draft Understanding" dealt decisively with this possibility: "Should the Chiang-Kai-

Chek regime reject the request of President Roosevelt, the United States Government shall discontinue assistance to the Chinese."

Confronted by provisions of this nature, the Division of Far Eastern Affairs felt the time had come for the Secretary of State to raise "certain fundamental questions" with Ambassador Nomura, which he in turn could put to his government. Until clarification had been obtained in regard to these questions, Hull should refuse to be drawn into a discussion of the John Doe proposals.

"Negotiations of any sort between would-be aggressors and persons or groups who wish to exercise a restraining influence," Hornbeck warned, "are of greater advantage to the former than to the latter, by virtue of the fact that in the process of a negotiation the would-be aggressor gains information regarding what is or is not in the hands and in the minds of those whom he is seeking to outwit or to defeat."

Although he was unoptimistic in his expectations, Hornbeck nevertheless dictated a complete counterdraft. "I have tried," he wrote, "to include as much of what is proposed in the John Doe draft as it would be possible, in my opinion, for this Government to agree to. I regard [my] draft as a rough outline and not a complete setting forth of our position. The Japanese draftsmen have had months in which to prepare their draft. I have had only a few hours in which to dictate this possible 'counterdraft.'"

Hornbeck's proposal of April 11 was for State Department use only. It followed the format of the "Draft Understanding" of April 9 and was surprisingly close, at times, to the original wording. Sufficient changes were introduced, however, to bring the text into harmony with the basic principles and policies of the United States.

Hornbeck continued to believe that a firm attitude was needed—the Japanese must be made to understand that the American Government was prepared to use force to oppose any further acts of aggression on their part.

The threat to Malaya and the Netherlands East Indies was uppermost in Hornbeck's mind, for he was convinced that the security of the United States would be impaired if Japan absorbed these areas.

Hornbeck's colleague, Maxwell Hamilton, was aware of this danger, but despite this he thought the American Government should try to take advantage of the opportunity created by "the Japanese draft" of April 9 to begin the discussions with Nomura that the President had recommended during his first meeting with the Ambassador on February 14.

Hull saw the sense in this advice. "The state of our relations with Japan was such," he subsequently wrote, "and the requirements of our policy of extensive aid to Britain were such, that I felt no opportunity should be overlooked that might lead to broad-scale conversations with Japan."

American military leaders could not have agreed more, for secret Anglo-American staff conferences in Washington had just reaffirmed the principle that "everything possible should be done to forestall hostilities in the Pacific."

And so Hull decided to ask the Japanese Ambassador to drop by the Wardman Park Hotel for a talk.

Their meeting took place on Monday, April 14. The Secretary of State was a model of circumspection. Nomura was less tongue-tied than before, but he did not seem equal to holding up his end of the conversation. Since no one else was present—not even an interpreter—the results fell short of being satisfactory.

Hull referred at the outset to reports he had received to the effect that "certain of the Ambassador's compatriots [had] been working on the formulation of proposals and plans for improving relations" with the United States;* he had been told that these men had been in touch with the Ambassador, and that Admiral Nomura had "participated in and associated himself" with their plans; whether or not these reports were "entirely accurate," the fact remained that the State Department could deal only with the Ambassador.

Hull wanted to find out how much Nomura knew about the document received by the State Department on April 9 from "those Americans and Japanese who [were] collaborating as individuals in an effort to make some sort of contribution to better relations" between the United States and Japan.† The Secretary also wanted to determine "whether it was [Ambassador Nomura's] desire to present that [document] officially as a first step in negotiations between the two Governments."

The Ambassador promptly replied that he knew all about the document, that "he had collaborated more or less with the individual Japanese and Americans referred to, and that he would be disposed to present it as a basis for negotiations."

Having obtained these assurances, Hull began to speak about the improvement that had taken place in recent years in Pan-American relations. The Secretary regarded this as a good illustration of what could be achieved if only the nations of the world would agree to abide by

---

* "Certain of the Ambassador's compatriots" meant Iwakuro and Wikawa.

† This was a reference to Walsh, Drought, Iwakuro, and Wikawa. Hull did not know that Walsh was inactive at this time.

certain fundamental principles in their conduct toward each other. Nomura was unable to follow what Hull was saying and had to be set right.
Finally, the Ambassador "seemed to understand and to get the point."

Two days later, on April 16, Hull laboriously led Nomura over virtually the same ground in order to make sure he was thoroughly familiar
with the hurdles that would have to be cleared if Japan and the United
States were to run the course successfully. Hull told Nomura that the
April 9 document "on which the Ambassador and the private group of
individual Americans and Japanese were collaborating" contained "numerous proposals" with which the United States "could readily agree."
At the same time, some of the items in that document would have to be
modified or eliminated. In addition, the American Government would
want to offer "some new and separate suggestions" of its own.

There was one paramount, preliminary matter, however, that had to
take precedence over everything else: the United States wanted to know,
once and for all, whether the Japanese Government was prepared "to
abandon its present doctrine of military conquest," to relinquish title
to "all property and territories seized," and to forsake "the use of force
as an instrument of policy." Hull also wanted to know whether Tokyo
was ready to adopt Four Principles that the American Government regarded as "the foundation on which all relations between nations should
properly rest":

Respect for the territorial integrity and the sovereignty of each and all nations.
Support of the principle of noninterference in the internal affairs of other
countries.
Support of the principle of equality, including equality of commercial opportunity.
Nondisturbance of the status quo in the Pacific except as the status quo may
be altered by peaceful means.

"You can answer [these] questions," Hull told Nomura, "or submit
them to your Government for its answer through you, as you prefer. You
understand that we both agree that we have in no sense reached the
stage of negotiations; that we are only exploring in a purely preliminary
and unofficial way what action might pave the way for negotiations later.
You tell me that you have not [yet] submitted the [April 9] document
... to your Government, but that you desire to do so. Naturally, you are
at the fullest liberty to do this, but, of course, this does not imply any
commitment whatever on the part of this Government with respect to
the provisions of the document in case it should be approved by your
Government."

If Tokyo instructed Nomura to present the document officially, the authorities in Washington would then feel free to offer "counterpropos-als" as well as "independent proposals," and these—"in conjunction with the Japanese proposal"—would then be "fully discussed and talked out to a conclusion in one way or the other."

For a few minutes Nomura said nothing. He studied the text of the Four Principles that Hull had handed him, letting the meaning of the words sink in. Then he suggested that the third point—the principle of equality—might be discussed "in connection with the negotiations." He thus touched on a matter so fundamental that the Secretary could not even conceive of entering into negotiations if Nomura's government should hesitate to agree to this point.

Hull maintained that no nation would benefit more from the princi-ple of equality than Japan would. To drive his argument home, he again referred to recent developments in Latin America. He handed Nomura a copy of the "Declaration of American Principles" that had been adopted at a conference held in Lima, Peru, in December 1938. Hull said that this eight-point declaration represented "the well-defined atti-tude" of the American Government and would consequently be at the forefront of his thinking throughout any conversations he might have with the Japanese Ambassador.

Blocked in this direction by the nature of Hull's reply, Nomura turned to the Secretary's fourth point, nondisturbance of the status quo except by peaceful means. Nomura believed that acceptance of this principle would interfere with the Manchurian situation, but Hull disagreed. He said "the question of nonrecognition . . . would be discussed in connec-tion with the negotiations and dealt with at that stage." His status quo principle "would not . . . affect 'Manchukuo' "; it "was intended to ap-ply to the future from the time of the adoption of a general settlement."

As the conversation continued, Hull became so troubled by Nomura's marginal command of English that he began to speak more slowly, and to repeat himself. Even then, he was not sure whether the Ambassador fully understood the discussion relating to the Four Principles.

Nomura wanted the Secretary to indicate whether he would approve, for the most part, the proposals contained in the April 9 document. Hull had already answered this question, but in order to be helpful he reiter-ated his position.

"The Ambassador seemed not to understand," Hull later wrote, "why I could not now agree to some of these proposals in his document.* I

---

* Drought had claimed, on two occasions, that Nomura had played a part in for-mulating the "Draft Understanding." In talking to Hull on April 14, the Ambassador had admitted he had been "more or less" involved. Hull consequently referred to that proposal, on April 16, as though Nomura were responsible for it (as though it were "his document").

sought repeatedly to make clear to him, in the first place, that we have not reached the stage of negotiations, he himself agreeing that he thus far has no authority from his Government to negotiate; and in the second place, that if I should thus out of turn agree to a number of important proposals in the document and these proposals should be sent to Japan and the military or extremist groups should ignore them, I and my Government would be very much embarrassed."

Nomura then said he understood the situation fully. He made it plain, or so Hull thought, that he would now proceed to consult the authorities in Tokyo in regard to the "Draft Understanding," and that he would seek clarification concerning the various matters Hull had raised, including the question of the Four Principles.

*

Upon leaving the Secretary's apartment at the Wardman Park Hotel on April 16, Nomura had a clear duty to perform. He should have reported to Tokyo that Iwakuro, Wikawa, and Drought had drafted a proposal for the consideration of both governments, that Hull had indicated a willingness to discuss this proposal under certain conditions, and that in the meantime the Secretary of State was more than ready to proceed with purely preliminary conversations designed to determine whether a basis for negotiations existed.

Nomura should have revealed the extent of his collaboration with Iwakuro, Wikawa, and Drought. He should have emphasized that Hull regarded the "Draft Understanding" as an informal offering "presented to the Department of State through the medium of private American and Japanese individuals" who were interested in furthering the cause of peace in the Pacific. Tokyo should have been told that Hull would not explore the matter with the Japanese Ambassador until Nomura had been authorized by his government to present the proposal officially to the Secretary of State, and that even then the American Government would consider itself free to develop its own ideas.

Nomura should also have quoted Hull to the effect that the "Draft Understanding" contained numerous provisions with which the United States "could readily agree" but that others would have to be modified or eliminated, and that, in addition, the American Government would want to offer "some new and separate suggestions" and some counterproposals of its own.

Finally, the Ambassador should have cabled Hull's Four Principles to Tokyo along with the eight points of the Lima Declaration; he should have conveyed to the Foreign Office, as Hull had to him, the transcendental importance of the Four Principles, for they were the bedrock on which the structure of Japanese-American relations would henceforth stand upright and secure, or upon which it would fall in a thousand shattering pieces.

Nomura did none of these things. He followed, instead, a course that completely misled his government. He behaved as he did partly because he had been taken in by the words and deeds of the John Doe Associates and partly because he had not fully comprehended everything the Secretary of State had said to him.

Another factor in Nomura's conduct was his desire to succeed in his mission. He let himself be persuaded that a settlement could be achieved only if the decision-makers on both sides of the Pacific were *enticed* into it. This was a view that duplicated Father Drought's thinking; it was also a view to which Colonel Iwakuro subscribed.

As a consequence, hardly a single word that had been uttered by Hull trickled through to Tokyo. In reporting to the Foreign Office, Nomura sent a distorted account of what had transpired in Washington. The phrasing he employed tended to suggest that the "Draft Understanding" was an American offering prepared in response to various inside moves with which he and his staff had been associated, that the Secretary of State had personally been involved, and that the *United States Government was now taking the initiative in making a proposal to Japan!*

There was no mention of Hull's Four Principles. In fact, it was not until May 8 that Nomura got around to quoting them to Tokyo. He did so then only in passing, toward the end of a long telegram in which he declared that the "U.S. side" had stubbornly advocated these four points during discussions relating to the "Draft Understanding." He had proposed instead (he told the Foreign Office) that the two countries should avoid becoming involved in arguments over principles in order to concentrate on finding solutions to practical problems.

The conclusion Tokyo drew from these statements was that Nomura had successfully shelved the issue. In actuality, as the Japanese Government belatedly learned several months later, the Secretary's Four Principles were the *sine qua non* of the Japanese-American conversations so far as Roosevelt and Hull were concerned.

In a telegram that reached the military authorities in Tokyo on April 18, Colonel Iwakuro joined Nomura in urging the Japanese Government to proceed with the negotiations on the basis being offered. Everyone at the Embassy, he said, shared the view that the current controversy could be settled by diplomacy only if Japan acted decisively—an overall solution achieved with a single stroke was needed. An opening had recently been found through "maneuvers conducted behind the scenes." Father Drought, "an influential Catholic priest with rare political ability," had been involved in these maneuvers, as had Bishop Walsh, "a man of lofty character" admired by Roosevelt. Postmaster General Walker, who was "one of the most trusted individuals" in the President's entourage, had also played a part.

According to Iwakuro, results had been obtained quickly because of the progress Wikawa had made in "preparing the ground"; the "first draft" of the proposal that was now being cabled to Tokyo had been written by the "U.S. side," which had accepted most of the demands lodged on behalf of Japan; this proposal had been studied at the Embassy, where a "second draft" had been prepared to sound out American intentions; when the Embassy had learned that the "U.S. side" had "in general no objections" to the stipulations contained in this draft, a decision had been made to accept a suggestion to the effect that the matter should be taken up by Nomura and Hull without further delay; Roosevelt had already approved the "Draft Understanding"; all that was needed to bring it to fruition, therefore, was speedy action by the Japanese Government.

In a section-by-section explanation of the "Draft Understanding" sent to the Foreign Office at this juncture, Nomura added emphasis to the claims he and Iwakuro had already made. The Axis alliance, Nomura reported, would remain untouched; the United States would find it more difficult to participate in the war in Europe, but Japan would be able to pursue her policy of collaboration with Hitler and Mussolini unhindered; the European powers would be put on notice that neither the United States nor Japan would acquiesce in any transfer of territory in the Far East or the southwestern Pacific that might be written into a European peace settlement; the hands of the European powers would be tied, but Japan would remain free to do as she pleased.

Through the "good offices" of President Roosevelt, Japanese terms would be imposed on China. If the "Chiang regime" refused to accept the President's advice to sign on the dotted line, the United States would stop aiding Chungking (this could not be put into the "Draft" right at the moment, Nomura said, but this was the American intention).

Japan would have to undertake not to advance into Southeast Asia by military force, Nomura added, but in return for this guarantee Japan would be permitted to penetrate the area economically with the backing of the United States.

In reading these reports from Nomura and Iwakuro, the authorities in Tokyo could not possibly know that the Ambassador and the Colonel were basing their assertions on what they had learned from Drought through Wikawa rather than on impressions received directly from Roosevelt or Hull. Since the "Draft Understanding" seemed to offer a way out with regard to many problems (the most urgent being the war in China), Konoye and his colleagues decided to study the matter further; they would postpone responding to the "American proposal" until after the Foreign Minister had returned from Europe; in the meantime, clarification would be sought from Nomura on a number of key points.

Regardless of the angle of approach or of the questions raised, the Admiral stood squarely behind the "Draft Understanding," bestowing upon it the sanction of his authority as Japan's Envoy Extraordinary and Ambassador Plenipotentiary to the United States. The jeopardy in which Nomura thus placed his mission was very soon to be matched by the hazards created by Matsuoka's rapidly accelerating pro-Axis policy. Despite repeated assurances that his country had no such designs, the Japanese Foreign Minister was looking forward to the time when the Imperial Army and Navy would be able to attack Singapore. The day would also come when he would call for a Japanese invasion of the Soviet Far East—the Neutrality Pact he had just concluded in Moscow assuming then the character of a readily expendable scrap of paper.

So long as the Empire of Japan had a Foreign Minister with such ideas, war with the United States would become ever more likely unless Roosevelt and Hull ultimately proved willing to capitulate to Japanese demands—a prospect that seemed as remote in the spring of 1941 as the possibility that a new breed of American pioneers would one day land on the moon.

PART THREE

DENOUEMENT

CHAPTER THIRTEEN

Into a Quagmire of Confusion

THE RETURN OF the Japanese Foreign Minister to Tokyo on April 22, 1941, after a European junket that had lasted forty-two days, generated excitement throughout the country and tension within the ranks of the government. As "the man of the hour," Matsuoka burst upon the scene like a "conquering hero," as proud as he could be of his recent accomplishments. Not since 1933, when he had led the Japanese delegation out of the League of Nations, had he been accorded so much public attention.

The *Japan Times and Advertiser* saw in Matsuoka's homecoming "a triumphant close [to] one of the most notable chapters in Japanese diplomacy." The Neutrality Pact he had brought back from Moscow provided "abundant evidence," the paper said, that the Empire of Japan—"under the vigorous impulse of positivism"—was capable of reaching new heights of diplomatic achievement.

During a "blitz interview" given to the foreign press, Matsuoka verified the truth of the proverb "Seeing is believing." He felt he could now speak "with better authority" about the situation in Western Europe, "having ascertained on the spot many a doubtful point." He attributed the conclusion of the treaty with the Soviet Union to a sudden decision by "Mr. Stalin" during the final phase of the negotiations; it was an example, Matsuoka said, of the way in which outstanding leaders were expeditiously settling affairs of great moment at a time when the international situation was "so full of swift and surprising changes." "Vacillation and hesitation," the Foreign Minister added, "are, indeed, fatal. We, too, must be quick in action in order to cope with the momentous need of the times."

For a man who was stressing the importance of decisiveness in the handling of diplomatic affairs, Matsuoka proved to be amazingly slow when it came to doing something about the "Draft Understanding." Premier Konoye had conveyed the news of this development to him over the telephone after he had reached Dairen on the final leg of his journey back to Japan. Matsuoka had thereupon jumped to the conclusion that several trial balloons he had released earlier were now bringing results. On arriving in Tokyo, however, the Foreign Minister discovered "to his amazement" that the "American proposal" had no connection whatsoever with any initiative on his part; it was an entirely independent development that had occurred as a result of various maneuvers undertaken by Ambassador Nomura working in concert with certain Japanese and American individuals who had operated outside regular channels in Washington.

All this had been done behind Matsuoka's back without so much as a "by your leave." The ensuing disenchantment soon produced some very distinct consequences that seem to have gathered force from the Foreign Minister's ambition to become Japan's next Premier.

Konoye had intended to brief Matsuoka on the "Draft Understanding" while riding into Tokyo from the airport, where he had gone to meet the returning "hero." The Prince abandoned this plan, however, upon learning that Matsuoka desired to drive to the plaza in front of the Imperial Palace to "pay his respects" publicly to an Emperor he was scheduled to see privately later in the day. To indulge Matsuoka in what was essentially a publicity stunt would mean getting out of the limousine and bowing in the direction of the Palace, which lay out of sight beyond a wide moat and a dense stand of trees. Having no stomach for this kind of display, Konoye let the Foreign Minister ride with Vice-Minister Ōhashi instead.

On the basis of what Ōhashi told him, Matsuoka believed that the proposal Nomura had sent from Washington came from the American Government. The Foreign Minister did not realize that the "Draft Understanding" was the private concoction of Iwakuro, Wikawa, and Drought; he knew only that they had been involved, in some way, behind the scenes.

Matsuoka suspected that the aim of the "Draft Understanding" was to neutralize Japan—the object was to assure the United States that she would not have to worry about an attack in the Pacific in case she became involved in the war in Europe. To fall in with such a scheme would be equivalent to throwing overboard the policy he had been following for months. He had no intention of doing so.

At a Liaison Roundtable Conference held that evening, the Foreign Minister curtly dismissed the "American proposal" as representing 30 percent goodwill and 70 percent evil intent (an extraordinary evaluation in view of the role Iwakuro and Wikawa had played in manipulating

Drought's ideas to the advantage of Japan). Matsuoka declared that the "Draft Understanding" was quite different from anything he had ever had in mind. His idea had been to have the American Government tell Chiang to make peace. A readjustment of the entire relationship between the United States and Japan had not been under consideration. He therefore wanted time to study the proposal; two weeks, a month, perhaps even two months might be needed.

During a private conversation with Konoye the next day, Matsuoka again insisted that he be allowed to decide the matter at a later date—after he had gotten his European experiences "out of his system." From remarks the Foreign Minister had made the previous evening, it was clear to Konoye that Matsuoka did not intend to take any action at all until he could consult his German colleague in Berlin, Foreign Minister Joachim von Ribbentrop.

*

In dispatching the "Draft Understanding" to Tokyo in mid-April, Ambassador Nomura had anticipated that an answer would come within a week. He had subsequently felt encouraged upon learning that secret funds amounting to $50,000 were being remitted by the Foreign Office for use in the "negotiations." A cable from the Navy had also provided grounds for optimism. The message was to the effect that there was general agreement in favor of adjusting Japanese-American relations along the lines of the "Draft Understanding," but that instructions would not be forthcoming until Matsuoka got back from Europe.

Iwakuro had subsequently sent a telegram of welcome to the Foreign Minister containing a thinly disguised request for a speedy and favorable response to the so-called American proposal: "I offer you my heartfelt congratulations for your brilliant triumphal return. I am anticipating receiving your very appropriate and generous present here. Accept kind regards from Wikawa also."

When the news media in Japan learned of the "Draft Understanding," Matsuoka warned Nomura to be careful in talking to Japanese correspondents in the United States, but the Foreign Minister gave no hint of where he stood with regard to the proposal itself.

Some days later a message from Tokyo addressed to Iwakuro attributed the delay in the dispatch of instructions to the indisposition of the Foreign Minister and the Premier—the one had suffered an attack of chronic bronchitis, the other was in bed with a cold.

By the end of the month, Nomura's optimism had faded, and he was feeling very concerned. On April 28 he reported that Postmaster General Walker had said Secretary Hull tended to be slow in coming to grips with a decision but once he made up his mind he seldom changed it. Consequently, in the present instance, if the "Draft Understanding" were drastically revised by Japan, the whole thing might fall through.

The next day, Iwakuro and Wikawa went to New York. After checking into the Berkshire Hotel, the Colonel placed a call to Matsuoka in Tokyo, urging him to hurry up and cook *the dried fish* that had been sent to him from Washington *before it spoiled*. Everyone at the Embassy, Iwakuro added, was impatiently looking forward to hearing *how it tasted* to the Foreign Minister. Matsuoka's reply left nothing to the imagination; he was clearly not going to be rushed into anything.

Before returning to Washington with the "bad news," Iwakuro and Wikawa took a train to Ossining, New York, to pay their respects at Maryknoll. While being shown around the premises, they learned from Father Drought that his efforts to promote a Japanese-American settlement had kept him so busy he had been neglecting his responsibilities at home.

Since Drought had spent nearly the entire month of April at the Wardman Park Hotel, he could hardly have kept abreast of his duties at Maryknoll. Not content with what he had already done, he had sought ways and means of making further progress. Frank Walker had borne the brunt of this activity, for Drought had been a frequent caller both in person and on the telephone. He had also dispatched letters and telegrams, and had composed new and insistent memoranda.

Waiting for an answer from Tokyo was getting on Drought's nerves. His mood kept changing during this period, veering in different directions. One day he would feel mad at the Americans, another day at the Japanese.

Drought was particularly annoyed with the Secretary of State. Hull had made an awful botch of it; Nomura had wanted to take up the "Draft Understanding" in mid-April, when the two of them had met at Hull's apartment, but the Secretary had "put him off: would not discuss it even." The Japanese had "definitely committed themselves," and then Hull had come along with his Four Principles. "One more mistake like that" would "finish it."

Something had to be done, Drought felt, to overcome the suspicion caused by that move. Perhaps he could persuade Hull to let him work everything out with Hamilton. Hull would be unable to get anywhere with Nomura because half the time the Ambassador did not understand the Secretary's English.

Another possibility was to involve the President directly. In roughing out a letter to be sent to Frank Walker, Drought argued that it was "urgently necessary" to show the "Draft Understanding" to Roosevelt: "It attains what the President called a 'ten strike.' No one can excel him in executing it with dramatic finesse. He could put the Far East 'in his pocket' and change totally, overnight, the aspect of the European War. He can inspire the Far East with American idealism: the legalistic diplomats inspire only suspicion (Their prudence is in their cautious memories; not in their creative vision)."

According to Drought, the "Draft Understanding" would permit the President to "capture the 'seven seas' in one magnificent stroke of statesmanship." He would be able to support the Chinese completely and yet win the "undying loyalty" of the Japanese. The former were "real pragmatists and extremely intelligent," whereas the latter were "incurably emotional and therefore tenacious and stupid in ideas."

The Chinese were going to claim that the peace terms were unsatisfactory. "They would say that, no matter what the terms were." They would resort to delaying tactics, refusing to see that they had the United States to thank for the offer being as good as it was.

The "China Affair" was virtually over. If Roosevelt could still get the terms outlined in the "Draft Understanding," he would be a "miracle worker." If the Chinese did not accept the conditions, the Japanese armed forces would "move southward and then return to finish China—in full cooperation with the Nazis."

The "preaching tactics" of the bureaucrats in the State Department had "always lost opportunities for them." The Japanese were not going to stand still forever. There would be trouble unless some encouragement were forthcoming from the United States.

Still, the indecision of the Japanese themselves was "certainly exasperating." The "Draft Understanding" had been a "bloodless victory," and they should have followed up on it immediately. It was only because of his own efforts that such a solution was even available to them, for he had "literally imposed the whole thing on their government." Nomura had better not call on Hull again until there was "something definite in the way of an approved plan & solution." Otherwise the State Department would say the Japanese were "stalling," and would accuse them of engaging in a "peace offensive."

If only the Japanese would announce that they had agreed to the "Draft Understanding," Konoye and Roosevelt would then be able to go ahead with the Honolulu meeting. The Japanese delegation would be handpicked by Iwakuro and Wikawa. These two men were "far more important than the Ambassador & most of the Cabinet Ministers (over half of whom they nominated)." Roosevelt would simply have to attend; his presence would be "worth ten battles."

Drought could not decide whether Matsuoka would be a help or a hindrance. The Foreign Minister had made an excellent impression on him in Tokyo, but now Wikawa was saying he did not trust the man. Drought wondered whether Matsuoka could be switched with Home Minister Kiichirō Hiranuma, and then dropped from the Cabinet later on. This would permit Hiranuma to "preside" as Foreign Minister at the Honolulu Conference.

Matsuoka was "a perfect fool" if he thought he could trust either Germany and Italy or the Soviet Union ("Has he no knowledge of past history?"). If he were "really clever," he would see that he currently had an opportunity to make Japan and the United States "the dominant world powers."

"Matsuoka wants the credit," Drought informed Walker toward the end of April, "and is delaying to find a place for himself. Two days ago, he hinted again at a trip to America which he would use to pretend that he himself had managed the 'Understanding.' This is what he did with the Russian Pact. However, he will be asked to give his O.K. before Tuesday next [May 6], or to resign. . . . If Mr. Hull were to say that he himself would preside at the [Honolulu] conference, there would be no doubt about Mr. Matsuoka's speedy approval."

On May 1 Drought supplied still more details in a memorandum that reached Hull through the Postmaster General: an effort would be made to get Matsuoka to resign, but the matter would have to be referred to the Emperor; the Army and Navy authorities and Baron Hiranuma had cabled that their position on the "Draft Understanding" was unchanged; the Japanese in Washington were "thoroughly confident" that it would be approved; "an open cable" sent to Konoye "from the Wardman Park Hotel" had "advised that 'Matsuoka should cooperate with the rest of the Government and cease acting out of vanity.' "

Despite Father Drought's assertions, Matsuoka was not about to be replaced as Foreign Minister, nor was the Japanese Government prepared to accept the "Draft Understanding." Matsuoka remained what he had previously been—a "stormy petrel" whose sentiments as Foreign Minister were anything but favorable from the point of view of Washington. When one of Nomura's friends in the United States Navy asked about Matsuoka's hostility, the Ambassador replied that the Minister should not be judged entirely by his public statements. According to Nomura, Matsuoka was a disciple of the American political method of saying a great many things to see their effect, but what he had in his heart might be quite another matter.

The only trouble with this explanation was that no one could ever know—at any given moment—exactly what Matsuoka had in his "heart."

*

Two weeks had now passed since the text of the "Draft Understanding" had arrived in the Japanese capital, and Nomura was still waiting for word from his government. On Friday, May 2, he informed Hull that "a favorable reply" was expected "within a few days." The delay had been caused, the Ambassador said, by politics back home.

It was not until the following afternoon in Tokyo, however, that Foreign Minister Matsuoka finally broached the subject of relations with the United States. In discussing the matter with his Liaison Conference colleagues, he insisted that an adjustment would have to contribute to a solution of the war in China. Beyond that, Japan should not take any action that would run counter to her obligations under the Tripartite Pact or lead to a charge that she was "breaking faith" with Germany.

Matsuoka thus favored a strict application of the Tripartite Pact at a time when others thought a broad interpretation might be more in the nation's interest. The Foreign Minister did not go so far as to reject the idea of a settlement with the United States, but he wanted an agreement phrased in a way that would permit Japan to implement the objectives he had outlined. He therefore submitted an amended "Draft Understanding" to be sent to the United States in the form of a "counterproposal." He made it clear, however, that he first wanted to obtain the views of Berlin and Rome. In the meantime he would instruct Nomura to hand over an "Oral Statement" as an interim measure.

Matsuoka also intended to have Nomura suggest to Hull that a Japanese-American settlement might be facilitated if the two nations were to start off by signing a Neutrality Pact, just as Japan and the Soviet Union had done.

The Foreign Minister's colleagues did not think well of this plan. They recognized that the United States would probably not respond favorably. Someone even pointed out that Nomura was not endowed with the mind and manner of the Foreign Minister, and therefore could not be expected to achieve in Washington results similar to those secured in Moscow. But Matsuoka said this did not matter since he would write everything out in detail and would simply tell Nomura to read it all to Secretary Hull.

When Konoye tried to persuade Matsuoka to forget about proposing a Neutrality Pact to the United States, the Foreign Minister hedged in reply. He wanted to think about it some more, he said; perhaps the way to handle it would be to have Nomura bring up the subject spontaneously as though the idea had just popped into his head on the spur of the moment. In any event, the question required more thought.

The Foreign Minister's answer implied there would be further consultation at a later meeting, but that very evening—prior to leaving for a visit to the Grand Shrine at Ise—Matsuoka sent instructions to Washington that reflected the policy he had outlined during the afternoon. Included in these instructions were the "Oral Statement" to be handed to Hull and the Neutrality Pact proposal, a proposal he now described to Nomura as "a sort of diplomatic blitzkrieg" aimed at the United States.

During Matsuoka's absence from Tokyo, the chief of the European and Asiatic Bureau of the Foreign Office, acting on Matsuoka's orders, confidentially advised the German and Italian Ambassadors of what had taken place thus far. The German envoy, Major General Eugen Ott, immediately cabled a report to Berlin, informing the authorities there that he had just been told *the American Government* had offered an "agreement" to Japan in mid-April.

Following Matsuoka's return from Ise, Ott learned that the Foreign Minister was planning to seek clarification in regard to two questions. One was, "Would America pledge herself not to enter the European war?" The other was, "Would America pledge herself to induce Chiang Kai-shek to enter into direct negotiations with Japan without the participation of the United States?" If Washington gave a "yes" answer to both questions, Japan would be willing to begin discussing the "American proposal."

Ott tried to obtain the text of the mid-April "agreement," but Matsuoka replied that "to his extreme regret, in consequence of the promise of secrecy, he did not feel in a position" to hand over a copy of the "American proposal." The Foreign Minister emphasized, however, that he would not be a party to negotiations that might in any way adversely affect the Tripartite Pact, the New Order in Greater East Asia, or the interests of Germany and Italy.

In Washington, meanwhile, Father Drought was reporting to Hull, in a memorandum transmitted by Walker, that Nomura was under instructions to propose a Japanese-American Neutrality Pact. The Ambassador *wanted to be told*, Drought declared, that such an arrangement would be "out of the question." This would "stop Matsuoka."

According to Drought, Japan's "Super-Cabinet" had already approved the "Draft Understanding."* Matsuoka had accepted this decision "to avoid resigning," but he had asked to be allowed to handle "present procedure." Although this concession had been made "temporarily," the Army and Navy authorities had "insisted that he act promptly." Having agreed to this, Matsuoka would remain as Foreign Minister for the time being, "but hardly for long."

Drought advised Hull to pay no attention to an "Oral Statement" Nomura was supposed to hand to the Secretary of State. "This is intended for home consumption face-saving," Drought wrote, "and as a little bit of poker-playing. The Japanese here ridiculed this cable and did not wish to present it. I have advised them to present it, while indicating to Mr. Hull its true character."

The next day, May 7, Nomura turned up at Hull's apartment. After some preliminary remarks, he strongly implied once again that politicians in Japan, including the Foreign Minister, were responsible for the delay. Although Matsuoka did not want a nonaggression clause to be included in his Neutrality Pact proposal and had so informed Nomura, Hull got the impression that the Ambassador, acting under instructions from his government, was trying to get the United States to join Japan in just such an arrangement!

From Nomura's further comments, Hull judged that the Admiral had "something in the way of a manuscript" to present, and that it came "either directly or indirectly from Matsuoka." Nomura told Hull that many things in the "paper" were "wrong" but he would hand it over anyway, if the Secretary would be willing to receive it.

Since the item in question contained so many things that were "wrong," Hull replied, the Ambassador might just as well hold onto it if he had the authority to do so, especially since it appeared, from his remarks, to veto much of the proposal for a settlement that had been offered to the State Department in April.

Hull could afford to react in this way because he already knew what Nomura's "paper" contained. The Secretary's knowledge came from "Magic," a remarkable, top-secret, cryptographic achievement that permitted a small group of officials in Washington to read, from time to time, a number of the messages exchanged between the Japanese Government and its diplomatic representatives abroad—messages that had

---

* "Super-Cabinet" was Drought's way of describing the May 3 meeting of the Liaison Roundtable Conference at which Matsuoka had divulged his plans to his colleagues.

been intercepted, decoded, and translated by United States Army and Navy Intelligence personnel.

Nomura did not have the authority to withhold the document he had brought with him to Hull's apartment, but he acted as though he did. He consequently retained in his possession the "Oral Statement" Matsuoka had wanted him to deliver as an interim measure. Instead of obeying his instructions, Nomura merely read aloud "some lines of greeting"— none of which Hull could clearly understand—and then wound up, "on the first half of the first page," with what sounded like a pledge that everything would develop favorably in line with the "Draft Understanding." Hull knew, however, that this assertion did not square with what he had seen in the text supplied by "Magic."

Since Matsuoka had taken Ott into his confidence, Ribbentrop and his staff in Berlin were also able to read what the Japanese Foreign Minister had to say to Roosevelt and Hull on this occasion: "The German and Italian leaders are determined never to have peace by negotiation; they demand capitulation. They seem to regard that the war is as good as won. . . . These leaders feel that . . . American entry into the war will not materially affect the final issue, although they are ready to admit that in that event the war is likely to become protracted. . . . I need hardly add that Japan cannot and will not do anything that might in the least degree adversely affect the position of Germany and Italy to whom Japan is in honour bound as an ally under the Tripartite Pact."

In the months that had passed since the conclusion of the Axis alliance in September 1940, Matsuoka had so consistently emphasized Japan's loyalty to Germany and Italy that neither Roosevelt nor Hull could possibly have had any doubts in that regard. Only in the topsy-turvy world of postwar revisionism would the old canard be trotted out, once again, that Matsuoka never planned to act in conformity with the pro-Axis policies he proclaimed, that his true intentions were of an entirely different sort, that in his heart he harbored a genuine desire for peace, and that the United States was at fault in not trusting him.

Matsuoka may have hoped to reap the profits implicit in the Tripartite Pact without having to make good on the investment it demanded, but no one in Washington could ever be certain that the loyalty he preached toward his German and Italian allies would turn out to be treachery in practice. If Roosevelt and Hull could have been certain of this, then they would logically have had to ask themselves, When will *our* turn come?

It was far more sensible to base American policy on an acceptance of Matsuoka's pronouncements, which invariably stressed Japanese obligations under the Tripartite Pact, than to toy with the security of the United States by perversely believing that the Foreign Minister of Japan was always saying one thing while really meaning another.

In trying to deal with the world in which he lived, Cordell Hull may have overstressed the utopian moral principles with which his name has become synonymous, but there was more to the Secretary of State than the image he projected in public. The determination and stamina of a stubborn old fighter combating a far-ranging movement of conquest governed his actions, not the quivering rhetoric of an ineffective sermonizer shaking his finger at a group of indifferent transgressors. Safeguarding the vital interests of the United States came first; promoting the concept of a planet on which nations would abide by a chosen set of rules designed to maintain peace with justice, without the threat of war, came second.

Hull spoke at great length to Nomura on May 7, repeating much of what he had covered on previous occasions. After weeks of fruitless waiting for an indication of the views of the Japanese Government, the Secretary now felt he "could not give any assurances of further patience in the event of further delay." Matsuoka and others in Japan had been "talking loudly and acting aggressively." Their conduct was contrary to the "entire spirit" of the John Doe proposal that Nomura had recently sent to the Foreign Office in Tokyo.

"The Ambassador, without talking but a word here and there," Hull later noted, "was constantly bowing and smiling and certainly endeavoring to make me think at least that he was himself approving my statements. In fact, from time to time he would give expression to his approval."

Nomura wanted Hull to commit himself concerning the possibility of reaching an agreement on the basis of the "Draft Understanding," but Hull patiently repeated what he had already made plain three weeks earlier. He emphasized that no matter what Nomura might have done with that document, or what he might yet intend to do, the United States Government "remained entirely free from any commitments." The Ambassador seemed to comprehend this, but Hull was not absolutely sure. "I never know for certain," he wrote, "how fully and accurately we understand each other in given instances."

Four days later, on Sunday, May 11, Nomura handed Hull a set of documents he had received from Tokyo. Speaking very slowly for the Ambassador's benefit, Hull again referred to the "numerous unfriendly remarks" that the Foreign Minister of Japan, "in a purely gratuitous way," had recently been quoted as making. Matsuoka had announced "ideas and doctrines diametrically opposed to most of the fundamental principles" set forth in the proposal the Ambassador had "prepared" early in April. In these circumstances, Hull declared, he would have "real difficulty" persuading his colleagues—let alone anyone else—that Matsuoka's behavior or utterances could be regarded as dependable.

The next day, May 12, Nomura called on Hull again. The Ambassador entered the Secretary's apartment "in some confusion"—apparently concerned about their meeting the previous day. It seems that he had handed over the "wrong" set of documents, including items Hull was not supposed to see. Nomura now wanted these back in exchange for the "right" documents, which he had brought with him.

The Secretary acceded to the Ambassador's request, receiving in turn a draft proposal that was rather curiously entitled "Confidential Memorandum Agreed Upon Between the Government of the United States of America and the Government of Japan." Attached to this document was an annex labeled "Oral Explanation for Proposed Amendments to the Original Draft."

A perusal of these items indicated that the words "Original Draft" referred to the "Draft Understanding," the document Drought had handed to Hull on April 9 and that Nomura had cabled to Tokyo on April 17. Japan's "Confidential Memorandum" of May 12 therefore amounted to a major overhaul of the earlier proposal. As such, it might more accurately have been entitled "Draft Understanding—Revised."

*

As these developments were taking place in Washington, progress was being made in Berlin toward assessing the "agreement" the American Government had reportedly offered to Japan in April. Although Ott had been unable to obtain the text from Matsuoka, the Ambassador had nevertheless managed to send his government a summary of the terms. This material had now come under the scrutiny of Hans Heinrich Dieckhoff, a former ambassador to the United States.

Roosevelt's proposals are not sincerely intended [Dieckhoff informed Ribbentrop] and cannot be sincerely intended.* It is not conceivable that the United States honestly wishes to abandon the stand she has persistently taken in the Manchukuo question for 10 years. . . . What the President really wants is, first of all, to gain time. He wants to lull Japan to sleep until . . . he can intervene in the fight for England with a war industry operating at full capacity and with full mobilization, especially with a larger navy. If Japan were now to play his

---

* Dieckhoff had no way of knowing the true state of affairs. The proposals he was attributing to Roosevelt were not from the American Government at all. They were from the John Doe Associates.

game, Roosevelt could turn with all his force against the Axis Powers, since he would be free to the rear. Later on Roosevelt would not keep his promises to Japan; on the contrary, it would then be Japan's own turn.

Dieckhoff believed the German Government "should strongly caution the Japanese against acceding to the American proposals." If Tokyo felt it could not flatly refuse the offer from Washington, the Japanese should at least "make such counterproposals as Roosevelt could not possibly accept."

The State Secretary of the German Foreign Office, Ernst von Weizsäcker, was in full accord with these views. "I agree with Herr Dieckhoff," he wrote. "What the U.S.A. demands of Japan is an unequal deal at our expense. U.S.A. is helping England on a very large scale; Japan on the other hand is to remain immobilized. I can scarcely conceive that Matsuoka would not realize this."

Weizsäcker had no need to be concerned, for Matsuoka had already formed a similar estimate of the situation and was as anxious as his German allies to frustrate any such scheme. There were certain limits, however, beyond which he could not go if he wished to remain in charge of the Foreign Office. Although he had wanted to postpone action until Ott could obtain instructions from Berlin, this did not prove to be possible. "Much as he regretted it," Matsuoka found it necessary to unleash Nomura in Washington prior to the arrival of Ribbentrop's recommendations.

When a copy of Japan's proposal of May 12 was subsequently shown to Ott, he found the form and content "most surprising." He felt the Japanese had transmitted "a definitive text" to the American Government. This text constituted a "complete instrument"; it seemed to lack nothing but the signatures.

In talking with Ott at this time, Matsuoka declared that he had been unable to put off sending a "conciliatory" reply to Washington; he knew, however, that it was "incumbent upon him under the Tripartite Pact to do everything calculated to keep the United States from entering" the war in Europe.

In attempting to explain his position, Matsuoka used virtually the same words he had recently employed in Moscow, while talking with the American ambassador there. Matsuoka had said then, "I wish Roosevelt and Hull would trust me." Now, in speaking to Ott, Matsuoka was asking his German friends to have confidence in him.

Rules of thumb in international relations do not differ greatly from those that function well in ordinary human affairs. Men who are trustworthy need not plead for trust. Since Matsuoka was forever making contradictory promises, his success as Foreign Minister depended on his ability to avoid having his bluff called, and yet this was something over which he could not hope to maintain control indefinitely.

Matsuoka's arguments failed to impress Ott. In Berlin his report caused Weizsäcker to tell Ribbentrop that the proposal Tokyo had sent to Washington, if put into effect, would mean a disengagement by Japan from her commitments to Germany. Although damage had already been done, an effort should still be made "so to encumber" the contemplated treaty with the United States that it would never be signed. "If the treaty cannot be stopped even in this way," Weizsäcker wrote, "it is essential to take steps to ensure Japan's realignment with us in practical matters."

*

The arrival in Washington of Japan's "Confidential Memorandum" of May 12 (the "Draft Understanding—Revised") brought the long period of waiting and uncertainty to an end. Within the State Department there was a spurt of activity. "We analyzed each point in itself," Hull subsequently wrote, "and in its relation to the other points. We sought to ascertain what we could accept outright, what we had to reject outright, and what lay in the twilight zone where the change of a word or a phrase would mean the difference between acceptance or rejection."

The Secretary felt that "very few rays of hope shone from the document." The Japanese Government maintained that the Axis alliance was "defensive" in nature—it had been "designed" to prevent nations that were not "directly affected" by the war in Europe from engaging in it. The American Government was supposed to renounce any thought of "aggressive measures." Japan did not spell out what she meant, but presumably aid to Britain would fall into this category.

In regard to China, Japan wanted Washington to advise "the Chiang Kai-shek regime" to enter into negotiations for peace on terms laid down by Tokyo. If the Generalissimo refused, the American Government would have to discontinue the assistance it had been giving to Nationalist China.

Japan also wanted the United States to help her procure and produce, in Southeast Asia, the various resources she needed, especially oil, rubber, tin, and nickel. Missing from the "Confidential Memorandum," however, was a guarantee found in the original "Draft Understanding" —a guarantee to the effect that Japan would not resort to arms in the course of her expansion into that area. The only explanation offered was that a pledge of this type was "inappropriate and unnecessarily critical," especially since "the peaceful policy of the Japanese Government" had already been made clear on numerous occasions.

Also absent from the "Confidential Memorandum" was an idea Father Drought had been advocating for months—namely, a Konoye-Roosevelt meeting at Honolulu. This had been the keystone of the "Draft Understanding," the feature that held everything else together because it permitted Drought to argue that any problems remaining at issue could be resolved when the two leaders finally came face to face in Hawaii.

In explaining why the conference proposal had been deleted, the authorities in Tokyo did not entirely rule out the possibility of a meeting, but they put it rather far into the future and completely altered the character of the original proposal: "We consider that it would be better to arrange, by an exchange of letters, that a conference between the President and the Premier or between suitable representatives of theirs will be considered when both the United States and Japan deem it useful to hold such a conference after taking into due consideration the effect resulting from the present Understanding."

As seen by the State Department, Japan's "Confidential Memorandum" of May 12 was "dead on arrival" in Washington, but Roosevelt and Hull—upon viewing the corpse—decided to try artificial respiration. Representations had been made to the American Government to the effect that a Japanese-American settlement would give such a psychological "lift" to the Japanese people that they would readily support programs of peace.

This had been one of Drought's standard arguments. Although the validity of his assurances could be questioned, the President and the Secretary of State were very sensitive to what was taking place elsewhere in the world. Great Britain needed all the help the United States could extend in the Atlantic and in the Near East. With this as a preoccupation —and with Burma, Malaya, North Borneo, the Netherlands East Indies, and Australia "extremely vulnerable" to a Japanese attack—Roosevelt and Hull desired to avert, if they could, any move by Japan that would result in a two-ocean war.

The "Confidential Memorandum" of May 12 "offered little basis for an agreement" in Hull's judgment, "unless we were willing to sacrifice some of our basic principles, which we were not." And yet it was "a formal and detailed proposal from Japan." "To have rejected it outright," Hull wrote in his *Memoirs*, "would have meant throwing away the only real chance we had had in many months to enter with Japan into a fundamental discussion of all the questions outstanding between us. The

President and I figured that if there were the slightest possibility of in-
ducing Japan to withdraw from the Axis alliance, we should pursue it,
for this would be a sharp blow to Hitler and a fillip to the Allies. Even
a gradual withdrawal of Japan would have had its worth. Consequently,
we decided to go forward on the basis of the Japanese proposals and seek
to argue Japan into modifying here, eliminating there, and inserting
elsewhere, until we might reach an accord we both could sign with mutual good will."

In Tokyo, however, Foreign Minister Matsuoka was adopting a tough
posture. He wanted Washington to be told that there was "no room for
further amendment" in the proposals contained in the "Confidential
Memorandum." To underscore this point, he sent Nomura—on May 13
—a new "Oral Statement" to be handed to Hull forthwith:

> Really I feel it hardly necessary but in order to leave no room whatever for
> any misapprehension I wish to put the following on record at this juncture. It
> must have been clear [to the American Government] from what I have often
> stated publicly or otherwise that my decision to follow the pourparler between
> Your Excellency and Ambassador Nomura and open the present negotiation
> was based on the premises that the United States would not enter the European
> war and that the United States Government [would] agree to advise Chiang
> Kai-shek to enter into a direct negotiation with Japan with a view to bring
> about peace between Japan and China at the earliest possible date. Of course
> it must have been plain from the start that on no other premises would or
> could Japan possibly come to any understanding of the sort held in view in
> the present negotiation.

Upon reading this communication, Nomura decided not to deliver it.
When Matsuoka repeated his instructions two days later, Nomura still
refrained from carrying them out.

The records available for this period do not reveal whether Matsuoka's afterthoughts of May 13 reached the Secretary of State through
"Magic," but Hull was so *au courant* in other ways that he had no illusions about the nature of Japan's foreign policy.

One of Hull's sources of information was the American Embassy in
Tokyo. While Matsuoka had been keeping his German allies posted—
incurring their distrust and displeasure by what he told them—Ambassador Grew had been looking forward to the time when he would be
able to confer once again with the Foreign Minister directly. As soon as
Matsuoka had returned to Japan, Grew had written to ask for an appointment at the Minister's convenience. Because Matsuoka had suffered
an attack of bronchitis and had then been busy with various affairs, it
was May 14 before the Ambassador finally obtained the interview he had
been seeking.

What occurred on this occasion, and over the next few days of "not quite orthodox diplomacy," provided Hull and his advisers with some pertinent reading material in the category of "current non-fiction" at the very moment when they were immersed in studying the "Confidential Memorandum."

Grew found Matsuoka to be "in an extremely bad humor"—more "caustic and bellicose" than ever before. He told the Ambassador that Hitler had been very patient and generous thus far, despite the way in which the American Government had been supplying Britain with the materials she needed to carry on the struggle. If German submarines were to sink American vessels in the Atlantic, and if the United States struck back, this would be an act of American aggression that would undoubtedly lead—under Article 3 of the Tripartite Pact—to war between Japan and the United States. The solution to this problem lay exclusively in the hands of President Roosevelt. The "manly, decent, and reasonable" thing for the United States to do was to come right out and declare war openly on Germany instead of engaging in hostile acts under the cover of neutrality.

Grew immediately launched into a rebuttal. He explained American policy at length, saying he "emphatically resented" the charge that his country was guilty of unmanly, indecent, and unreasonable conduct. Grew also reminded Matsuoka of the assurances the Foreign Minister had repeatedly given in regard to Southeast Asia, and yet many highly placed Japanese were openly advocating the use of force in that part of the world.

Matsuoka had an answer for this: the southward advance was to be carried out only by peaceful means "unless circumstances [rendered] this impossible." He was thinking, in particular, he said, of "the concentration of British troops in Malaya" and of "other provocative British measures."

When Grew endeavored to argue that such moves were purely defensive in nature, and that London was merely responding in this limited way to the beating of war drums in Japan, Matsuoka declared that the Japanese masses felt Britain was threatening their security. The day might consequently come when the Japanese Government would be under pressure to act.

In words similar to the ones Dooman had used in talking with Vice-Minister Ōhashi in February, Grew insisted it would be "utter folly" for the United States to send supplies across the Atlantic in support of Great Britain while at the same time complacently watching the British go down to defeat in the Pacific because their Far Eastern lifeline had been severed. The potentialities of this situation were of grave concern to the United States. This concern would now be increased as a result of the Foreign Minister's remark to the effect that Japan's peaceful intentions were wholly dependent upon "circumstances." The Ambassador hoped the Minister would keep in mind that Japanese-American relations would henceforth hinge not on what Japan might say but on what she would do.

Grew had barely returned to the Embassy from his meeting with Matsuoka when a messenger arrived with a note written in the Foreign Minister's own hand:

Dear Mr. Ambassador:

...I was wondering, to be frank, why you appeared so disturbed when I referred to the American attitude and actions. After Your Excellency's departure, it all on sudden dawned on me that I misused a word (of course I was not speaking in my own language and you must make some allowance for my occasionally making mistake in choosing words, particularly when I speak off-hand). Of course, I didn't mean to say "indecency," no! I wanted to say *indiscretion*. What I wished to say (and that not as Foreign Minister but as a man who regarded himself a quasi-American and felt could talk almost as if he were an American) was that I should have like to see the American Government exercise more discretion and be careful to give an appearance of *reasonableness*; in a word to be more cautious and careful.

I write you the above in order to remove any misapprehension; I'd feel very sorry if caused any.

Very sincerely yours,

Y. Matsuoka

In replying to this note, Grew indicated a desire for "further talks in due course." The Minister quickly responded with a very long letter in which he said at the beginning, and again at the end, that he would be glad to have another leisurely and frank conversation with the Ambassador, "preferably sipping tea together" at home. "I wonder if Your Excellency can understand," Matsuoka inquired, "how intensely my innermost soul is troubled and even agonized these days. Ever since I was running about in my knee-pants in your country, I have been dreading that modern civilization, which with all its good points smells of rank materialism, will one day be condemned to destruction unless we retrace our steps and mend our ways so that human society could be placed upon a higher spiritual plane. That day of doom is, to my mind, actually approaching, although I still dare to cling to hope and earnestly desire to contribute my little bit towards preventing it."

"I am praying to God day and night," Matsuoka informed Grew, "that the President of your country may realize the great responsibility he owes to God and humanity and refrain from exasperating Germany by further acts of provocation, finally exhausting the patience of Herr Hitler." A world war would be so destructive that there would no longer be any question of "defending democracy or upholding totalitarianism"—at least not until several thousand years had passed, when "a new kind of civilization" would arise on the debris of the old.

"I often indulge," Matsuoka added, "in thoughts in terms of one thousand or two or even three thousand years. It may strike Your Excellency as if it were a sign of insanity but I cannot help it as I am made that way. Perhaps [a] man like Herr Hess belongs also to the same category.* Of course, it is very hard to judge whether or not a man is truly unsound in his mind. Only I should say I may be regarded sane in the opinion of the average man for the fact that I have not yet flown to Washington or Chungking. Whatever opinion Your Excellency may entertain about my mental state, I am sincerely and fervently praying to God to avert the impending crisis."

Three days after this letter was written Grew called on Matsuoka, by prearrangement, at the Foreign Minister's private residence. After drinking tea together, they strolled in the garden, smoking their pipes and chatting freely. Matsuoka said he had not really been speaking formally to the Ambassador on May 14, even though their meeting had taken place at the Foreign Office. "Never have I imagined you would cable our talk to the State Department," he told Grew, "or else I would have been more careful and have taken a correct attitude."

Grew thereupon repeated the statements that had caused him to regard his earlier conversation with the Foreign Minister as containing "grave and far-reaching implications." Matsuoka did not question the accuracy of the Ambassador's version, but merely smiled and said "that while his words might have been bellicose his heart and thoughts were peaceful."

As the two men were saying goodbye to each other after nearly two hours of discussion, Grew—with tongue in cheek—commented on the collection of inscribed photographs on Matsuoka's mantelpiece: Hitler, Mussolini, Ribbentrop, Ciano, and "in the far corner," bearing the words "As a memento of our first meeting, March 1933," Franklin D. Roosevelt. Matsuoka replied that he soon hoped to add Stalin's photo to the group, and that he thought it would be an excellent idea if he

---

* Reich Minister Rudolf Hess, deputy leader of the Nazi Party and a Hitler confidant of many years standing, had just landed in Scotland by way of a parachute after a solo flight from the continent. His sudden arrival in the United Kingdom could not easily be explained. Was it a madman's caper, an act of treason, or the opening move in a high-level effort to end the war?

could assemble all of these gentlemen in Tokyo for they would undoubtedly succeed in settling the affairs of the world.

*

In a summary dispatch sent to Washington by pouch later in the
month, Grew was charitable in evaluating the way in which Matsuoka
had handled himself throughout this affair. The Ambassador apparently
felt that measured judgments delivered in a spirit of good sportsmanship
would be the best way of closing the door on the whole episode. In the
privacy of his diary, however, he was far more critical and succinct. The
letters he had received from Matsuoka, Grew noted, "might be regarded
as merely laughable if the situation were not so terribly serious," but in
such a situation to have a man in charge of the Foreign Office who "by
all criteria" could only be considered "mentally ill-balanced" was "a
profoundly dangerous thing."

It was indeed, for the possibility that Matsuoka was an emotionally
disturbed individual cannot be dismissed lightly. And yet there was another aspect of the Japanese-American confrontation in the spring of
1941 that was equally dangerous: despite the relationship that existed
between the John Doe "Draft Understanding" sent by Nomura to Tokyo
in mid-April and the "Confidential Memorandum" cabled by Matsuoka
to Washington in mid-May, a fundamental misconception with regard
to who was offering what to whom was already firmly implanted in the
thinking of everyone concerned at the official level on both sides of the
Pacific.

The two governments were looking at the same document, but they
were seeing it in an entirely different light.

Since the information passed along by Nomura, Iwakuro, and Wikawa had been misleading, Konoye and Matsuoka regarded the "Confidential Memorandum" of May 12 as merely *Japan's answer* to the
"American proposal" Nomura had cabled to the Foreign Office on April
17. The State Department, on the other hand, not knowing that the
Japanese Ambassador had been doctoring his reports to Tokyo to convey
the impression that Washington had taken the initiative in suggesting
an agreement, treated the "Confidential Memorandum" of May 12 as
Japan's initial offer to the United States.

In electing to proceed with an attempt "to argue Japan into modifying here, eliminating there, and inserting elsewhere," Roosevelt and
Hull were thus inadvertently providing Iwakuro, Wikawa, and Drought
with what amounted to a new mandate to continue their manipulations
behind the scenes. The many ramifications that resulted from the fur-

ther activities of the John Doe Associates greatly complicated the task to which the Secretary of State and the Japanese Ambassador devoted their energies in the months ahead. This fact helps to explain why these two men accomplished so little despite the many conversations they had with each other. Not only were the problems confronting them complex, but the circumstances in which they were attempting to deal with these problems were as far from ideal as anyone could possibly imagine.

CHAPTER FOURTEEN

Pushing and Pulling for Peace

THE WEEKS THAT followed the delivery in Washington of Japan's "Confidential Memorandum" of May 12, 1941, were weeks of endless talk—mostly courteous and dignified in tone but occasionally punctuated with annoyance and frustration; sometimes short and simple, sometimes long and complex talk; repetitious, confusing, to the point and pointless; expressions of hope vying with a sense of hopelessness. And then suddenly, in midsummer, there was action—action of a type that brought all of this talk to an end, at least for the time being.

The meetings that occurred during this period involving the Secretary of State and the Japanese Ambassador generally took place at night in the study of Hull's apartment at the Wardman Park Hotel. Hull had agreed to this arrangement because Nomura wished to avoid the publicity that would result if he were to be seen constantly going to the State Department. Calling on the Secretary at home not only guaranteed greater privacy, but also gave Nomura an opportunity to converse with Hull at considerable length and without interruption—an impossibility during regular hours.

Included, now, in a number of these discussions, and in others involving Maxwell Hamilton and Joseph Ballantine, were Colonel Iwakuro and Tadao Wikawa. A note written by Father Drought on a piece of Wardman Park stationery suggests one reason for their presence: "Paul: Recent events are giving the impression that the Admiral & yourselves are in disagreement. To overcome this, he should introduce you. He is obligated to do this since relying on your word I have reported things to Mr. Hull which he contradicted."

Although it was Nomura's responsibility to take care of the formalities, Drought was determined to help matters along in any way he could. Telephone calls, oral advice, written exhortations, and revised drafts followed one another in rapid succession as this self-appointed masterplanner endeavored to shape the will of each government to his conception of what it should be:

May 12 Almost whole day with F.W. [Frank Walker]. Wrote Explanations & Agreement in his office until 6 P.M.
Saw Wikawa & told him about terrible misunderstanding.*
Sent special memo of explanation etc. to White House for R. & H. [Roosevelt and Hull].
Phoned H. at 4:30 P.M. & explained further.
Saw H. at 8:15—joined at 9 by Nom. & remained until 10 with F.W. also present.
10 P.M. went with Nom. to Walker's until midnight. . . . Walker & I should see Hull often. . . . Extraordinary compliment paid us by Hull. . . .
May 13 Great mix-up over appt. to-night. Ambassador did not appear while we were there. Walker asked me to leave when Paul & Colonel were leaving. . . .
May 17 Oral Statement & Suggestions given [to Nomura by Hull] at 3 P.M. on Friday [May 16]. . . . I [was] invited [by the Japanese] to interpret & explain it [to them] at 9 P.M.
Apparently [they were] satisfied at One A.M. at which time I was asked to compose in English the points of their response which they desired to have prepared before a conference scheduled in the morning at 10 A.M. . . . I finished my draft at 4 A.M. [Saturday, May 17]. Discussed it . . . again at 9 A.M. Went over it at the Embassy at 11 A.M. with attachés, counsellors, Ambassador, etc. Then dictated the full explanation to Miss King.† Had copies ready at 3 P.M. & remained until 8 P.M. [At] 11 P.M. revised draft was brought back to me, and [I] finished it at 1:30 A.M. [Sunday] May 18th.
All this to answer questions [from the State Department] that need never have been asked—& if asked could have been answered in 10 minutes.

While composing "the points of their response" that the Japanese had asked him to prepare for them in English, Drought produced a very long draft of an "Oral Statement," marked "Strictly Confidential—Informal and Unofficial," which he wanted the Japanese Ambassador to give to the Secretary of State.

Using the voice and the hand of Nomura, Father Drought—an American citizen—was about to usurp the functions of the Japanese Government. He was going to offer assurances and suggestions to Hull as though they represented the will of the decision-makers in Tokyo. Drought was even going to reword significant portions of Japan's "Confidential Memorandum" of May 12 in order to get around some unacceptable American revisions that Hull had conveyed to Nomura on May 16.

Needless to say, the authorities in Tokyo were not told anything about

---

* A notation for May 11 reads: "Answer [from Tokyo]. . . . Day & night in translating etc. Nom[ura] brings wrong documents & creates complete confusion."
† Walker's private secretary.

this John Doe maneuver, even though it was carried out with the full knowledge of the Japanese Ambassador.

*

While Father Drought was thus engaged in Washington, Bishop Walsh was getting ready to leave Maryknoll for another visit to the Far East. His purpose was to resume the tour of inspection he had interrupted in December 1940 in order to help Drought persuade the American Government that influential elements in Japan were sincerely seeking a peaceful solution. Although Walsh was anxious to be on his way, he was prepared to delay his departure if Iwakuro and Wikawa thought his continued presence in the United States would be advantageous.

"The guiding principle with me," the Bishop advised Drought on May 17, "is to be governed by their desires in the matter, and I will postpone the trip until Christmas if they say the word." Three days later, Walsh wrote: "Your 'phone message yesterday confirmed my own optimism and I will be much surprised if a little further patience is not crowned by happy results. . . .* I have definitely changed my plan and am now pointing for the June 3rd Clipper. This means that I can, if necessary, remain in New York until practically the end of the month. . . . Let us know if we can do anything for you up here. We are continuing the prayers, as that is about all we can contribute at this stage."

Drought himself clearly believed, at this moment, that success was within reach. In a letter to Hull on May 20, his enthusiasm played leapfrog with his imagination: "I shall not attempt to convey the deep gratitude, and admiration, with which I shall always associate your name. Soon, millions of poor human beings will honor that name, whether you wish them to or not. And, the gratitude of the poor and simple is Life's greatest, and most terrifying, gift. Divine Providence surely chose yourself and Mr. Walker for the task."

At the same time, Drought felt he had made a mistake ("due partly to the Admiral") in not bringing Iwakuro, Wikawa, and Hull together sooner.† He therefore decided to try to arrange an "exchange of verbal agreement" in order to stop the "fifth columnists" in Tokyo. This might mean "playing a bit of a trick on Matsuoka," but something had to be done to prevent the Foreign Minister—a man who loved "to dabble & get his hand in"—from wrecking everything. If only Hull would per-

---

* Drought had talked with Hull on May 19, and had then placed a call to Maryknoll.
† The Colonel had been introduced to Hull by Nomura on May 16; Wikawa was brought in four days later, on May 20.

sonally endorse the "Confidential Memorandum" of May 12 by immediately "initialing" it in Washington, Iwakuro and Wikawa could then return to Japan to carry the matter through "by explaining the whole background to Prince Konoye."

"The Government of the United States," Drought wrote as though he were the President or the Secretary of State, "considers the basic terms . . . offered [by Japan] for the peaceful settlement of the China Affair [to be] just and equitable; and extends to the Government of Japan congratulations for the successful application [to the Far East] of the Good Neighbor principle. . . . The Government of the United States accepts, on behalf of President Roosevelt, the request [for] 'Cooperative defense against communism' [and] entertains no doubt whatever that the Government of Japan will negotiate this term [with China] in such a manner as to realize complete harmony with the other basic terms of national sovereignty and withdrawal of troops."

The fact that Roosevelt and Hull did not hold these views or share Drought's confidence in the Japanese Government did not disturb John Doe. He believed he could create a "proper" official attitude simply by writing such sentences and by urging their inclusion in supporting documents.

In formulating new arguments on May 25 to present to Frank Walker, Drought pressed for quick action: "Rests with our people to really get a move on. From what I saw to-day, the [State] Depart. is hedging—because they guessed wrong. Think it could be finished to-day and our modifications cabled to Tokyo for approval—where they will meet with some more changes . . . Visit with you—tea with Hull & finish the whole thing? Trouble with the document [the "Confidential Memorandum" of May 12] was that it did not come through me. They expose their complete hand to me—but I am not entrusted with [the] document beforehand. Why can't we say that we consider the terms just, and let it go at that? Are we fighting for Chiang Kai Shek at any cost? China [is] the greatest beneficiary. . . . Japan is not capitulating: it is offering terms—if not accepted then we should not continue to help Chiang Kai Shek. Trying to get Chinese consent is probably useless & time wasting. We must pass our judgment on whether or not we consider the terms to be fair. This 'Understanding' is our best guarantee against a radical gov't in Japan."

As Drought's ideas took shape on paper, his pen produced a freewheeling denunciation of the State Department that he later edited out of his text but presumably not out of his mind: "Having studied the original drafts of agreement weeks before the Japanese government ever saw them; having studied them for three weeks more while the Japanese were considering them; having said the cabled draft was substantially acceptable to us;* and having said that we would require only a few days to suggest unessential modifications—now, two weeks after receiving the Japanese government's approval, for which we waited impatiently, and to obtain which we worked day and night, the U.S. State Dept. [has] not yet succeeded in drafting three relatively simple modifications. Instead we seem to be going back to the beginning to argue questions that have been answered about ten times each during the last two months. Having said that we would [limit] the deliberations [to] the heads of our Government, we are now waiting for Hamilton, Ballantine, and the various clerks of our legal department to submit their suggestions on points concerning which a whole library of books has been written already. Meantime, the Japanese who favor an [agreement with the United States] have to contend not only with delays and domestic suspicions but with the mounting persuasion of German victories—the Balkans, Libya, Greece, Iraq, Crete, the Hood, etc.—all since we started our negotiations."†

Even if these complaints had reached the State Department, Drought would not have succeeded in "shaming" Hull into a speedy decision, for the Secretary and his advisers remained deeply suspicious of Japanese intentions. Stanley Hornbeck had already noted the salient point of this whole business thus far: "We have clear indication that Admiral —————— is having to try to 'sell' to his Government (at least his Foreign Office) the project for an agreement between Japan and the United States, to which project the John Doe associates have been telling us that the Japanese controlling authorities (the backers of Colonel ——————) are already committed in principle."

Hornbeck had come to the conclusion that objectionable aims lurked behind the smiling assurances being conveyed to the American Government by Nomura, Iwakuro, and Wikawa. He thought "*these* Japanese" were trying to use the conversations in Washington to get the better of the United States: "The Japanese have made a treaty with Germany. Do the Germans trust Japan? They have made a treaty with the Soviet Union. Do the Russians trust Japan? *These* Japanese want a treaty with us. Do *these* Japanese represent Japan? Do they represent . . . the Japa-

---

* Drought's assertion to the contrary notwithstanding, Hull had carefully avoided making any such statement.

† H.M.S. *Hood*, Britain's largest vessel of war, was blown up in the North Atlantic on May 24, 1941, by the Nazi battleship *Bismarck*. Three days later the Royal Navy took its revenge by sending the *Bismarck* to the bottom of the sea.

nese people? Do they represent the Emperor? Whom do they represent? What do they want to deliver? What do they expect and intend that Japan . . . shall and will deliver? To what extent will Japan . . . perform on the basis of a treaty which *these* Japanese may conclude with the United States, if and when?"

The question of "performance" that Hornbeck was raising here was a critical one; it had been hovering in the background for a long time. At the American Embassy in Tokyo at this moment, Grew and Dooman were in favor of adopting a policy of conciliation toward Japan. They both thought that if it were attempted it might work. They were not calling for appeasement, however, for they felt that the chauvinists would then run wild.

This was a classic problem to which there was no simple or certain solution. Unrelenting pressure by one side might drive the other side to extreme measures, but a friendly approach might be misconstrued as timidity and could thus lead to dangers of comparable magnitude. This was an aspect of the Japanese-American confrontation that seems to have escaped Father Drought; it did not go unnoticed, however, within the State Department or in the Cabinet Room at the White House.

*

Two weeks had now elapsed since the arrival in Washington of Japan's "Confidential Memorandum" of May 12, but the State Department had still not indicated what its reaction would be. This was absolutely inexcusable from John Doe's point of view. "Hull apparently doesn't know F.E. affairs very well," Drought wrote on May 28. "This is a grave difficulty. [Does he] expect [the Japanese] to publicly renounce the Axis? I told the answer to this last January. [Hull] does not know how to handle them. . . . *We* must not miss this chance. . . . Why doesn't he get on with it—& write his treaty later. . . . *Really* something must be done. [Hull is] jeopardizing their position. . . . Why does he not call in the Colonel & the Admiral for about three hours & finish the business? We expect them to take our word—why not take theirs? *Why can't he say what he wants & be done with it?* He does not *know*—& listens to too many people."

"It is nearly *three weeks* since the Japanese gov't sent in their approval," Drought noted on May 29. "The only thing [Hull] sent was a silly 'Oral Statement' [on May 16] and 3 inept 'Suggestions' which I exploded in three minutes. Then I worked with Hamilton (last Thursday) to reword these three things—apparently satisfactorily. Since then—only silence. Accordingly, the Japanese say it appears that they have been led on to expose their whole position in a promise of agreement—and then [have been] betrayed—by our withdrawal, or rather, pretense that we never seriously considered the proposed Understanding. Nomura reported along this line to his gov't to-day. I informed Mr. Walker & asked if I might not see the President or at least Hull. He said he thought it would do no good. . . . Told Walker I was disgusted & was going home to-morrow."

Drought was so exasperated by the conduct of certain State Department officials that he was ready to unburden himself to Walker even more: "They are making liars out of us. [The Japanese] feel we have betrayed them. We talked [in terms of] Roos., Hull and you. Now it is Hamilton and the legal [department].* Bound in conscience to make the facts known to Roosevelt and then to the Press. The truth is more important than an individual's contemptible vanity. Obligation to humanity is greater than any false obligation of protecting a bureaucratic hypocrite. . . . My advice is he better not send that fool paper from our legal department.† Playing right into Hitler's hands and there goes the war. No wonder the Germans are winning. We have misled shamefully the Japanese. In a couple of hours with Mr. Hull or any other real American I can patch up that document to Mr. Hull's and Mr. Roos. and the Amer. people's satisfaction—though never to the satisfaction of the State [Department]. The history of diplomacy is a history of complete failures —through legal departments. No will to find a way."

Drought's diary-type notes for May 30 and 31 also reflect the state of his mind at what seemed to him to be a moment of crisis:

May 30th 10 A.M. Phoned Hamilton—met Ballantine. . . . Insisted that this kind of delay imperils the very power [of the Japanese] to do anything. Also, it is, however unconscious, a treachery to those who have entrusted to us a knowledge of their aims & domestic political situation.

Asked *him to phone* me what was going to be done *to-day*. I am afraid that if I leave Washington (1) there will be no one to cushion the shock for the Japanese (2) the Japanese will feel that I have deserted the ship. The real move is to try to get Iwakuro in direct contact.

12:30. No word from State Depart. Called Paul & told him what I did.

No word from Walker—who is angry & hurt by Hull's conduct of affairs. If he had more gumption he would have gone to Roosevelt long ago.

The settlement of this "Understanding" should be so simple that our [State Department] people are either (1) prodigiously stupid or (2) deceitful.

---

* The chief of the Far Eastern Division had just given Drought a copy of a memorandum in which the State Department's legal adviser had outlined his views regarding Tokyo's insistence that Japan be permitted to maintain troops in China for "joint defense against communism."

† The "he" in this sentence presumably means Secretary Hull.

3 P.M. Meeting arranged, at my apartment, for Iwakuro, Wikawa, Hamilton, Ballantine. Place was suggested by Hamilton-Ballantine.

Info. given [by me] to Colonel, May 30th:

Hull has been on the point of complete agreement for over two weeks.

Hull [is] being told (1) that if he agrees Matsuoka will leave him holding the bag (2) that if once out of China Japan will move to the S.W.* (3) that you three [Nomura, Iwakuro, Wikawa] will prove ineffective & that someone else will have to come in before results can be obtained.

Financial interests in Japan & U.S. want to delay negotiations until they can move in & take the credit. Therefore, they are trying to shake the confidence of the U.S. Gov't in your ability to get results.

The U.S. Gov't—Pres. & Hull—are completely ready to go ahead but they don't know whom to believe—us or the other people.

May 31st They . . . told their Gov't that the [Draft] Understanding as first submitted was substantially agreeable to the U.S. Their Government, incl. the Emperor, formally approved it.† Now, after 3 wks, our Gov't seems [to be following] a tactic of delay which their Gov't interprets as insincerity and evidence that our Gov't has no serious intention of approving the Understanding which they had encouraged. They have virtually decided to break off negotiations. P & C‡ paid me an official visit of farewell. C had decided to commit suicide.

2:15 P.M. Phoned Hamilton to inform him of this. Out—left my number. I called him again at 4 P.M. Told him as above—he said papers were going over [to the Japanese Embassy]—including explanations—he said papers that were going were "substantial." [I] informed Japanese but they were not particularly enthusiastic as they have lost confidence (and no wonder). Papers were delivered about 5:30—meeting at 7:30 at Embassy—phoned Wikawa at 10:30—he was not pleased & said that many changes had been introduced. Said he would see me tomorrow. I said I thought he (I) could get further changes made, if necessary.

Tried to sleep—then went for a walk—no use—back again in an hour. Am wildly exhausted.

The "papers" that went over to the Japanese Embassy on Saturday, May 31, were indeed "substantial," for they consisted of a complete American redraft of Japan's "Confidential Memorandum" of May 12, three annexes dealing with key sections of the new proposal, an "Oral Explanation" that discussed (in writing) the amendments Washington was suggesting to the Japanese Government, and a one-sentence reminder that "at some appropriate stage prior to any definitive discussion" the United States would consult the Chinese Government concerning the general subject matter, particularly as it pertained to China.

Here, at last, was a definite proposition from the United States—in fact, the first and only one to come from the American Government thus

---

* That is, toward the southwestern Pacific—another way of saying that Japan would move into Southeast Asia.

† Drought may have thought so, but this was not the case.

‡ Paul Wikawa and Colonel Iwakuro.

far. The process of modifying here, eliminating there, and inserting else-where (a process Hull had earlier described to Nomura) had produced a text—"Unofficial, Exploratory and Without Commitment"—that the American Government was now ready and willing to convey to the authorities in Japan. This proposal, which was in the form of a "Joint Declaration," was Washington's answer to Tokyo's May 12 revision of the John Doe "Draft Understanding" of April 9.

*

The fatigue that had overcome Father Drought on the evening of May 31 passed quickly, but a feeling of frustration remained: "Appears that agreement is really reached but attempt is being made to manoeuvre present agents out of position so that others may receive the credit. . . . Delay has enabled others to learn enough to see vast opportunities and the skulduggery period has set in. . . . Idealism is going to have some hard going."

"Really very close," Drought explained for Walsh's benefit, "but legal-ists have begun to haggle and unless bosses step in [it is] difficult to say if and how much longer talks will continue.* Our lesser officials think it is time I stepped out and let final stages proceed directly: this opinion is based partly on considerations you can guess: certainly not gratitude. Our friends [Iwakuro and Wikawa] have become very disquieted again. Suspicion seems their stultifying fault. I gave them a long lecture on the sin of suspicion. Anyway we did what we could and far more than we ever bargained for."

From San Francisco on June 2, Walsh replied: "Remind friends stake for humanity too great to lose. Little extra patience will crown efforts with success that future generations will bless."

This message arrived at a time when Drought himself may have been in need of some "extra patience," for he was wearing out his welcome at the State Department. "Asked for interview," a note in his handwriting reads. "Went to explain some small points—and set-up on procedure. We don't want to accept any more papers this way—they say. Let [the Japanese] come themselves—whatever the difficulties; better than through an intermediary."

"I did not mention in my telegram that I was sending you this," Drought wrote to Walsh on the evening of June 3, "because telegrams are 'open'—I have been constantly watched—all my phone calls have

---

* In using the word "bosses" here, Drought probably had Roosevelt and Hull in mind (rather than Roosevelt and Konoye).

been checked etc.—and if I mentioned a 'letter' in the telegram, some-one might have been watching your mail at San Francisco."

Sometimes I think I understand our [Japanese] friends [Drought complained to Walsh]—sometimes I am helplessly confused by them. I don't really under-stand why they could not have accepted what was officially offered them—and let time take care of the little differences which I note in my "Comment."*
This afternoon, I went over the enclosed ["Comment"] with our people [at the State Department]—who, I must say, were very attentive. But it was made crudely clear to me that it was no longer desired that I should act on behalf of our friends: it was stated that they should act for themselves. I am now trying to have them do this. N. saw white-hair [Nomura saw Hull] this evening and asked for two roundtable discussions by persons with authority to settle up formulas of expression that will coalesce both [sides] on the few points of out-standing differences. Our friends are satisfied with the enclosed: it still remains to be seen if our people will accept it. Some of our people think I am too pro-Japanese: I think I am just pro–common sense.
After consulting F.W. (who is in N.Y. to-night) I think I should leave here to-morrow. Not being the President, there is nothing more I can do. And so I leave it—sincerely to God. Both groups seem to hold me responsible for every difference of opinion: both hold me in some suspicion: F.W. bawls me out for every delay: our friends think I am too weak and complaisant: no one ever says "thank you" except white-hair! So, the thing may succeed after all.

The possibility of success—of achieving a settlement through diplo-macy—was also being anticipated by Nomura at this moment. He had already told Hull that he "and his associates" were "in agreement with" the American draft proposal of May 31 except for "some of the phrase-ology." He was going to be out of town for a few days, but he hoped that during his absence his subordinates would have an opportunity to talk matters over with Hull's staff.

As a consequence of this request, a meeting was scheduled for the afternoon of June 4. On the morning of the fourth, Wikawa (who was now staying at the Hotel 2400 with Iwakuro) tried repeatedly to get in touch with Drought. Ultimately Wikawa went to the Wardman Park in person, but there he learned that his friend had checked out. After reserving a room to be used for the "final drafting," Wikawa returned to his hotel "with a solitary feeling." To his surprise, he found that a note had just arrived from Drought.

"I was deeply impressed," Wikawa immediately wrote in reply, "by your noble attitude, which seeks nothing but to serve God and save humanity from its destruction. I am rather ashamed of the tactics played

---

* The reference here is to an analysis, by Drought, of the American "Joint Declara-tion" of May 31.

by our comerades [sic], especially those vanity seeking folks. I am sure the results will be a great success, though I only regret that I cannot [return] to Japan by tomorrow's boat, though I am glad that this will give me another chance to see you before I sail for my home country."

The meeting that afternoon at the Wardman Park Hotel proved to be as disappointing as all previous sessions had been. Minister Wakasugi frankly told Hamilton and Ballantine that Japan did not want to be bound by the American interpretation of self-defense. When Hamilton said the American Government had been given to understand by "certain persons" that Japan desired to move away from the Axis and that one purpose of the proposed "Understanding" was to create an atmosphere conducive to such action on the part of Japan, Wakasugi "stated categorically that if [the State Department] had received any such impressions they were not in accord with fact."

Colonel Iwakuro agreed. It was entirely incorrect, he declared, to assume that the purpose of the proposed "Understanding" was to enable Japan to drift away from the Axis alliance. The most that could be expected was that the "Understanding" would improve the atmosphere between Japan and the United States, thus enabling them to collaborate with each other in efforts to restore peace.

When the discussion turned to China, Wakasugi proposed a formula thoroughly unlike the one that had been written into the American draft. Substitutions were then offered for other key sections of the document, until it seemed as though the two sides were not only as far apart as ever but possibly even more at odds than before.

"From my conversations with both groups," Drought informed Walker on June 4, "I am convinced that the whole thing, unfortunately, now seems to hang on what is really a very minor issue, particularly for us—the stationing of [Japanese] troops along the northern border of China to resist invasion. I should think we'd be glad to have anybody resist invasion by the Communists."

The Japanese were proposing terms "for negotiation with the Chinese—not for negotiation with the United States." Japan's intentions should be explained to Roosevelt and Hull "orally and authoritatively" so they could satisfy themselves that her conditions were "just, fair, equitable, and designed for future peace." If Roosevelt and Hull reached such a conclusion, they would not need further assurances.

"Personally," Drought wrote, "I believe that any peace terms which do not provide for the retention of some Japanese troops in the northern area [of China] will not be terms 'designed for peace'; they will be designed for the renewal of disorder."

If only "the *right* people on both sides" would go over the draft "for a final meaning," Drought was certain the whole matter could be settled successfully. "But the mere presence, on either side, of emotional characters, or of individuals who either can't think or are unable to express what they think, will flatten, as it always does, the level of thought and destroy perspective. Did you ever try to explain the power and glory of the terse Constitution of the United States to a gimlet-eyed lawyer whose only perception of law was precedent?"

Drought found it "inconceivable" that the American Government planned to confer with the authorities in Chungking before agreeing to the proposed Japanese-American "Understanding." The Japanese Government did not want the people of Japan to think that the United States was dictating "the terms of the China peace." It was up to the American Government, therefore, to exercise "subtlety in avoiding the issue."

To help matters along, Drought now submitted *a new draft* that he had personally prepared "to bridge over the differences." This draft, he told Walker, was "acceptable to the other people." "It remains to be seen," Drought added, "if it will be acceptable to ours."

Privately he was pessimistic. "Will probably not be approved," he wrote on one copy of the document, "though only the angels (fallen) will know why."

Two days later, on June 6, unaware that Drought had in the meantime returned to the Wardman Park Hotel, Wikawa sent a telegram to Maryknoll: "Emergency call. Your immediate trip here would highly be appreciated."

Wikawa was upset over a front-page story in the *New York Times* by Hallett Abend, a veteran Far Eastern correspondent who was now on assignment in Washington. "For nearly two months," Abend reported, "Japan has been attempting to induce the United States Government to conclude with her a neutrality and non-aggression pact similar to that recently concluded between Tokyo and Moscow. So far the reactions of the State Department have been unenthusiastic and at present there appears little likelihood that Japanese hopes will be fulfiilled."

"As I told you last night," Wikawa wrote to Walker on June 6, "the [Abend] despatch, which, according to our information, was derived from your State Department sources, finally appeared in this morning's edition. What I am afraid of is the shocks and reaction it may give to our Government and people, menacing to undermine our noble effort of these months, to a great satisfaction of some third powers."

Only the "following immediate steps to be taken by Mr. Secretary

[Hull]" could prevent disaster: "1) A flat denial of the report; 2) Disciplinary punishment of the responsible officials who dared to leak your Government secrecy; 3) Immediate acceptance of our proposed amendments at the day before yesterday's drafting committee meeting."* Wikawa was "quite confident" that the last of these steps would be the most effective: "it would enable us to refer back to Tokyo for their final approval of the Understanding and [would thus permit] us to make a startling announcement contrary to the Times despatch."

That evening, Nomura called at Hull's apartment accompanied by Iwakuro and Wikawa. Feeling the time had come to bring matters to a head, Hull had armed himself with an "Oral Statement," which he now proceeded to hand to the Ambassador.

Nomura and Wikawa took time out to read this "Statement," summarizing it for Iwakuro's benefit as they went along. It clearly came as a surprise to the Colonel. He had thought that the two sides had already crossed "the mountain and the valley" separating them, and that "only a ditch remained to be bridged." Now he was forced to ask himself whether the mountain and the valley had indeed been crossed at all. Nomura also was at a loss to explain what had gone wrong, but he said he would consult Father Drought, "who . . . understood Japanese psychology," and Mr. Walker, who had been "helpful" on various occasions.

"What had happened thus far," Hull later wrote, "was the opposite of what the President and I had hoped would happen. We had been willing to accept the Japanese proposals of May 12 as a basis for discussion, knowing full well they could not be accepted as they stood, but hoping that our subsequent discussion would bring about modifications that would make them acceptable. But as soon as the Japanese Government realized we were willing to use the May 12 proposals as a basis for discussion, they began instantly to move, not in our direction with more conciliatory proposals, but in the opposite direction with changes that brought the proposals more into line with their imperialistic ambitions and their Axis alliance."

Hull believed that the "more grudging" attitude now being displayed had resulted from instructions Nomura had received from Tokyo, but the truth lies elsewhere. The Ambassador had not even cabled the American "Joint Declaration" of May 31 to his government, nor had he bothered to keep the Foreign Minister up to date on developments in Washington—an extraordinary departure from standard diplomatic practice. Nomura had let himself be persuaded instead (presumably by Drought, speaking through Iwakuro and Wikawa) that the U.S. Gov-

* The meeting held on June 4 at the Wardman Park Hotel.

ernment did not want him to forward the "Joint Declaration" since it was "unofficial" and subject to further revision. He had been advised to wait until he could send the final version to Tokyo. As a consequence, the Ambassador had decided not to do anything at all unless the John Doe Associates proved able to eliminate the main differences between the Japanese proposal of May 12 and the American redraft of May 31.

It was not until June 9 and 10 that Nomura reluctantly cabled the text of the State Department's "Joint Declaration" to the Foreign Office. His action then came only after he had received specific orders from an irate Matsuoka, who had in the meantime indirectly learned of the existence of the proposal.

Matsuoka would very likely have been much more incensed had he realized that unauthorized revisions had been offered to the American Government on June 4 by Nomura's agents; that Father Drought—working behind the scenes—had already prepared a new draft designed "to bridge over the differences" between the two governments; and that Nomura—employing his "discretion"—had pocketed Hull's "Oral Statement" of June 6 instead of cabling it immediately to the Foreign Minister.

Thus, it was Ambassador Nomura and the John Doe Associates who were responsible for the "more grudging" attitude noted by Hull; the Japanese Government in this instance was not at fault.

Through all these developments, Drought remained steadfastly critical of the State Department. He felt that Hull and his advisers had reacted negatively from the very beginning because they were laboring under the misapprehension that the "Draft Understanding," which he had delivered in April, had been "proposed and composed by the Japanese," whereas the truth was that it had been "entirely composed"—with the exception of two sentences—"by an American mindful of American world interests & just peace."

Drought himself had never divulged this, and was not going to do so now, but by coincidence news of comparable import had just reached Hull from the Department of the Navy, where Drought's friend Lewis Strauss was currently on duty as a lieutenant commander. Following a talk with Tadao Wikawa, Strauss had prepared a summary of their conversation for the director of Naval Intelligence. Upon reading a copy of this report, which had been sent over to State, Stanley Hornbeck picked out a revelation that spoke volumes in regard to "the John Doe matter": Wikawa had told Strauss that the man responsible "for the whole idea" was the Reverend Father James M. Drought of Maryknoll!

Around this revelation Hornbeck proceeded to write, on June 10, a most interesting letter to Hull, damning John Doe and all of his works: "Drought has taken upon himself and is playing the role of a promoter and salesman. My conjecture is that he first 'sold' the idea of a negotiation and if possible an agreement to certain Japanese and that he has been since and is [still] doing his utmost to 'sell' the idea to you (and through you to the President): Drought is the pushing and the pulling agent. . . . He has enlisted as his aides the Postmaster General and the three Japanese [Nomura, Iwakuro, and Wikawa] with whom you have been and are conversing about this matter. As a go-between, he has brought these gentlemen and you (with your aides) into what amounts . . . to a negotiation."

In Hornbeck's opinion, the "Understanding" Drought had been advocating was not something that either the Japanese nation or the American people would want. If it were consummated, it would probably be "distasteful" to both. Hornbeck was certain such an agreement would not benefit either China or Great Britain. He also thought it would work against a number of the basic objectives of American foreign policy.

"I feel it my duty in fairness to you and to others here who are intimately concerned with the matter," Hornbeck added, "to let you know that to the best of my knowledge every officer of the Department who has been associated with or who has close knowledge of the progress of the conversations shares in the misgivings to which I have been and am giving expression."

On the evening of the day on which Hornbeck wrote these words to Hull, Nomura and Iwakuro privately discussed—"with much indignation"—a telegram that had just arrived from Tokyo. The next day, still rankled by the contents of the message he had received, Nomura prepared a reply.

It seems Matsuoka had finally learned that appearances and reality had long since parted company so far as the Japanese-American conversations were concerned. He had thereupon castigated Nomura by cable, and the Admiral—already adrift with a broken rudder—had become incensed over the Foreign Minister's reprimand. After further consultation with Iwakuro, however, Nomura decided against sending the reply he had drafted. He stowed it away, instead, in the pages of his diary—a fragment of history that is all the more tantalizing because it survives only in a very shaky postwar translation:

For Your Excellency's information only:
I had a dream last night. You must be well aware that I, who have been your friend for thirty years, am not a man who would act *ultra vires* or who would

do anything that hurts others. Nevertheless, picking up a roadside rumour, you demanded my explanation of it. . . . The words you used . . . were such as one would not dare to use in talking to even a common [sailor]. I obey your instructions to the end, but in carrying them out I am only using my discretion as to the order in which they should be put. . . .

Another world developed before me [in my dream] and there appeared God. "I sympathize with you in your predicament," said He. "You have lost your prestige toward your subordinates, and, moreover, you look very tired. But remember, now that you have been despatched [by Imperial command] to a foreign land as an envoy with a great mission . . . you should with patience and prudence try not to fail in the fulfillment of the Imperial order, even at the risk of injuring your fair name as a man of spotless integrity, [a reputation] which you have enjoyed for the past fifty years."

To this, I answered: "I will always keep Your advice in my mind and I promise You that I will not do anything that will [fail to pass muster in the eyes of] heaven and earth."

This was the end of Nomura's dream, though not of the John Doe endeavor for peace. Some avenues of approach still remained open to Iwakuro, Wikawa, and Drought, but the potential they had once possessed had been so seriously impaired by this time that only a miracle would be able to keep their dying effort alive.

As almost everyone involved in this affair soon learned, however, miracles were in rather short supply in the summer of 1941.

CHAPTER FIFTEEN

Between Scylla and Charybdis

IN REVIEWING THE political picture in Tokyo as the summer of 1941 approached, the German Ambassador to Japan, Major General Eugen Ott, reported to Berlin that various pressures had forced Foreign Minister Matsuoka "to respond for the time being to the American initiative for a kind of neutrality pact."* A Japanese attack on the British at Singapore would consequently have to be postponed. In the event of war between Germany and the Soviet Union, however, Japan would be unable to stay out. Matsuoka had offered the "purely personal opinion" that his country would join Germany in the fight; it would be a case of natural necessity.

Matsuoka wanted to be briefed on German relations with the Kremlin so he could evaluate rumors to the effect that Hitler was getting ready to strike at the Soviet Union. Matsuoka needed to know what was going to happen in Europe in order to undertake appropriate preparations at his end of the Axis alliance. "I consider compliance with this request," Ott informed Berlin, "within the limits of the discretion which is always advisable with respect to Japan, to be an important means of strengthening the Foreign Minister's position in the Cabinet."

The basic message conveyed by Ott to his superiors was that they had a friend in Matsuoka and that they should therefore do whatever they could to help him pursue his pro-German policies.

From an American point of view, this was a deplorably accurate description of the Japanese Foreign Minister. Grew was warning Washington at this time that Matsuoka was "undoubtedly very much in the pocket of the Axis and largely amenable to Axis pressure." In addition, the Foreign Minister had "consistently shown an almost total disregard and discounting of the risks of forceful action by the United States to curb Japan's expansionist ambitions."

* The initiative had come from Matsuoka, not from the American Government.

On June 11, the day on which this observation reached the State Department, the counselor of the Japanese Embassy in Berlin called at the German Foreign Office to convey a message from Matsuoka addressed to Hitler and Ribbentrop. Translating on the spot, word-for-word, the counselor reported that the Foreign Minister had not yet received any answer from the American Government to the Japanese proposal of May 12; he did not intend to ask for one, but when it arrived he would discuss the matter with the German Government before responding to Washington.

In Matsuoka's opinion (the counselor declared) Roosevelt's aim was to destroy the Tripartite Pact. The President wanted to create the impression that it was "still not quite certain" Japan would go in on Hitler's side in case hostilities broke out between the United States and Germany. Washington wanted to force the Germans "to fire the first shot" in order to claim "self-righteously" that Germany had attacked the United States. This would get votes in the Senate and would make the American people believe they had no choice but to defend themselves. Roosevelt was determined to participate in the fighting; American entry into the war was "only a question of time."

In Washington on this same day (June 11), a memorandum was prepared in the Far Eastern Division of the State Department summarizing the situation prevailing at the moment. It appeared from statements made by the Postmaster General that Drought's Japanese friends might be ready to bring their latest proposal (a John Doe draft dated June 8) into closer conformity with the policies of the United States than they had previously been willing to do. Walker was not certain of this, but he wanted to talk to Hull about the matter nevertheless.

This news came at a time when the State Department was still waiting for the Japanese to respond to the various points that had been raised with them earlier. In addition, Joseph Ballantine had just reported that a conversation he had had with Iwakuro and Wikawa over lunch at their apartment had proved unprofitable. As a result, the prevailing opinion within the Far Eastern Division was that the Department "should await a direct approach by the Japanese" before making any further move in their direction.

Over the next week and a half, from June 11 to June 22, the existing impasse continued, despite repeated consultations between Drought and Walker, Wikawa and Walker, Walker and the State Department, Walker and Nomura, Nomura and Drought, Nomura and Hull—and between the John Doe Associates and the Hamilton-Ballantine team. This went on day after day, by telephone and in person, with messages passing back and forth, suggestions being followed by countersuggestions and drafts by counterdrafts, while tedium alternated with excitement, excitement with disappointment, disappointment with chagrin.

Apparently the only person concerned with this whole affair who was able to relax during this period was Bishop Walsh. He had given up his earlier intention to fly to the Far East and was now spending "lazy days of loafing" on board the *Tatsuta-maru*, bound for Yokohama. Having received "nice telegrams" of bon voyage from "Paul and the Sailor," he was not worried about the situation. He was simply going to take things in stride.

But Father Drought did not have the Bishop's gift for detachment— he was constitutionally incapable of letting events follow their natural course. "Every single word of the enclosed document has been agreed to by our State Department," he informed Walker on June 14, "subject to the 'Points of Discussion.' "* He had written these "Points," Drought said, in a way that Hull would have to find acceptable. If only the Secretary would now tell the Ambassador—"at long last"—to advise Tokyo that an agreement had been reached along the lines of the new draft, everything would turn out all right in the end.

To these "urgings" from Drought, Wikawa added some words of his own in a letter to the Postmaster General written at midnight on June 14. "All we have to do now," Wikawa declared, "is to spead [*sic*] up, as judging from every circumstance, I think we should prefer a rough-and-ready method to elaborate and slow execution. . . . I therefore earnestly hope that Mr. Secretary [Hull], when he sees Admiral Nomura tomorrow morning, may ask him to refer the draft just as it is to our Government for their prompt final approval. If so, that will enable either the Colonel or myself to make a hurried trip to Tokyo in order to make the Understanding a real success in modern diplomacy, in other words, to erect on a rough foundation laid by the so-called shirt sleeve diplomats an elaborate palace of peace."

The following morning, Sunday, June 15, Nomura met with Walker and Drought prior to calling on Hull, who was sick in bed at the Wardman Park Hotel. There—in the presence of Iwakuro, Wikawa, and Ballantine—the "Sailor" endeavored to convince the Secretary that the Japanese Government was sincerely desirous of concluding the proposed "Understanding." Nomura wanted to be clear in his own mind, how-

---

* The "enclosed document" was a redraft of the John Doe proposal of June 8; it was informally submitted to the State Department on June 15 by the "associates" of Ambassador Nomura without the knowledge of the Japanese Government. Drought's assertion that the Department had "agreed" to "every single word" should not be taken at face value.

ever, regarding the points on which the Japanese and American sides were in agreement and the points on which they were still at odds.

Hull told Nomura in reply that the procedure he was suggesting might give rise to misunderstanding in Tokyo, and that it would consequently be preferable, and in the interest of the Japanese themselves, if the Ambassador were to use his own judgment concerning anything he might desire to report to his government about the progress of the conversations to date—conversations in which the American attitude toward various matters had already been made clear.

Nomura seems not to have heard the squelch in these remarks, for when he was asked whether he thought the Chinese would be inclined to respond favorably to Japan's terms, he replied that Chungking would collapse, were it not for American help; if the United States withdrew this help, Chiang Kai-shek would be "obliged to accept" Japan's conditions, whether he wanted to do so or not.

In talking with Nomura a few days later, Frank Walker complained that while the United States had been considerate of Japan there was no evidence of any reciprocal goodwill; in fact, the statements being made by the Foreign Minister were rather in the other direction.

They certainly were, for Matsuoka simply did not tone down his pro-Axis pronouncements. Nothing was to be gained by asking Nomura to explain the Foreign Minister's provocative utterances, for in all likelihood the Ambassador would merely smile in reply, as he had done in the past, and mumble something about Matsuoka talking for home consumption because he was ambitious politically and liked to use "big words."

Although the chances were slim of achieving a settlement of the type the John Doe Associates had proposed, Drought and his friends kept trying to bring pressure to bear on the State Department. "We talked the matter over," Wikawa informed Walker by letter on the morning of June 18, "and came to the conclusion that all we have to do now is to get as soon as possible a tentative, so-to-speak, semifinal draft, adequately phrased ... and report it to Tokyo for their final approval.... The State Department representatives [Hamilton and Ballantine] are really very friendly and diligent, our appreciation of which is increasing day by day. Only thing we are afraid of now is that they may go on too slowly.... Under such circumstances, I presume, it would not be too much for us to ask you kindly to take the trouble of advicing [*sic*] them to concentrate their effort for drafting, so that we may be able to report it to Tokyo by this week-end."

From Maryknoll that afternoon Drought dispatched a radiogram to the *Tatsuta-maru* to let Bishop Walsh know, prior to his arrival in Yokohama, the way the wind was blowing back home: "Conversations increasingly difficult. Growing lack of confidence rather alarming. Our own people are contemptible."

"We have in vain followed your kind advice," Wikawa notified the Postmaster General on June 19. "Yesterday's meeting was postponed for the reason that they have to consult with Mr. Secretary [Hull]. It was postponed again this morning for the same reason; and thrice, this afternoon, with an excuse that they had not yet been able to see Mr. Secretary!"

A "faint suspicion" had entered Wikawa's mind: "I wonder whether the Secretary really wants it. If not, was it on account of the State Department people's bitter feeling against us, or was it due to their sympathy with our diplomats who, according to some rumor, are trying to halt the negotiation until it falls into their hands?"*

Drought himself could not have been more annoyed with the Department's handling of the "negotiations." On June 20 he decided that a letter he had just received from Wikawa should be seen by Walker. Prior to putting it in the mail, Drought underlined certain passages because he was "confident" the Postmaster General would find them "very significant."

Dear Father:

All of us are very worried about you, as we have not heard from you for several days. You certainly must be worn out, maybe in sick bed. That is the way we think.

As I told you by telephone, the *situation was quite strained on account of the ill-feeling of leaders of our politics* caused by such an unreasonable delay. I am really having hard time to calm them.

Your good friend here [Walker] advised us quite recently to tell the old man [Hull] that there is no difference of opinion in our basic idea on the three major subjects in question. *We followed it, as we thought such might help in ironing out the situation, but the old man is not yet convinced, as his subordinates had not reported to the same effect!*

So *we are now back* to the March or *April stage of our talks*, with two differences, that is, Hotel 2400 instead of Berkshire, and Mr. Hamilton and Ballentime [*sic*] in lieu of you! It is worse than that! *They are bringing out one after another old controversies, such as complaints made by Americans during the China conflicts, including bus-line franchise in some town of North China, waste-silk purchase in South China districts and what not. Apparently, the negotiation have diverted from its lofty aim of preservation of Pacific peace and contribution to humanity to laying a foundation for future American com-*

---

* The reference here is probably to Minister Wakasugi and other members of Nomura's regular staff, who had been cool to Wikawa from the very beginning (though the phrase, "our diplomats," could also include Matsuoka).

mercial claims in China, though under coats of very idealistic international doctrines, some of which they frankly admitted are not yet practised by the preachers. *I am, however, determined not to criticize them,* for such might only result in a failure, as always is the case with spoilt children.

I have shared with you every hardship and agony caused by both sides. Indeed, I have gone through everything, even sacrificing my main source of income for the sake of humanity. Then why not more, for I am quite confident that our Almighty God would fairly see to it!

What I am afraid of now is, as I wrote to your good friend this morning, while they are indulging in such hypocritical theoretical discussions, there might come out such a stage as "the operation is perfect, but the patient is dead!"

You can easily imagine how much I am disillusioned by the fact that the almost unprecedented diplomatic negotiation should finally have its destiny held in the hands [of a] *few bureaucrats!* Where comes in your great President! God save him and his countrymen from repetition of old diplomacy!

Under such circumstances, I do earnestly pray that you may keep on praying for His wise guidance on him!

With highest respects,

Yours sincerely in *Him*
Paul

In a covering note appended to this letter, Drought called Walker's attention to the words, "Yours sincerely in *Him*." "I think this little phrase," he wrote, "more than anything else, shows the quality of the people we are dealing with."

"No matter what the excuse," Drought added, "I think it is contemptible that our people should manifest what Mr. Ballantine calls frankly a selfish spirit. Talking of such nonsense as bus line franchises and silk purchases in China—this sort of thing will do more harm to the Chinese than it will to the Japanese. It makes us look perfectly ridiculous. . . . I find it difficult to believe that certain members of the Department are not working at cross purposes to your own."

"I have been again informed by our friend," Drought advised Wikawa by telegram the next day, "that the delay is really being caused by people on the other side and that certain conversations here are not to be taken too seriously. Of course our friend really may be mistaken but that is his statement and I would suggest that you investigate it."

The "delay" that Wikawa and Drought were both trying hard to explain was not really so mysterious after all. The John Doe Associates had been in a great hurry from the very beginning; they had repeatedly tried to badger the State Department into making an on-the-spot decision, a rather unrealistic goal but one they had consistently pursued. Hull and his advisers had just as consistently taken their time, turning everything over in their minds, more than once, in an effort to discover what might lie beneath the curiously phrased proposals being put forward by Nomura and his agents.

Despite some misgivings, the Secretary of State had handed the Japanese Ambassador a tentative draft agreement on May 31 for submission to his government. Nomura—keeping his own counsel—had refrained from cabling this document to Tokyo until ordered to do so by Matsuoka, who had learned of its existence in a roundabout manner. Nomura had then told the Foreign Minister that further changes were being made in the proposal, and that a revised text could be expected fairly soon.

The conversations Hull and his staff had held with Nomura, Iwakuro, and Wikawa had been unproductive. The various drafts that had been funneled into the State Department by the John Doe Associates through the Postmaster General had widened the area of incompatibility instead of narrowing it down. In their recent meetings with the Colonel, both Hamilton and Ballantine had found him as candid as ever, but his frankness had further confirmed a realization of considerable import: a Japanese-American settlement was by no means in sight. The Colonel had emphatically stated that Japan could not repudiate the Tripartite Pact. He had also brushed aside American complaints about restrictions imposed by Japan on American business operations in China.

This was very inhospitable ground for negotiation—ground the State Department had repeatedly endeavored to cultivate, only to see each new attempt end in frustration. And yet on June 21, the day on which Drought informed Wikawa that Washington was blaming Tokyo for the delay, Hull made a calculated move. He handed Nomura "a complete rewrite of the draft proposal" that had been under discussion since mid-April.

Accompanying this new "Joint Declaration" was the usual "Oral Statement." After Nomura had read this, Hull began to elaborate on the major points it contained. He drew attention, in particular, to certain remarks by Matsuoka to the effect that measures of resistance by countries facing the threat of invasion would call for action by Japan under the terms of the Tripartite Pact. "This would be like saying," Hull observed, "that if a tiger should break loose in the countryside and if a villager living a mile or so away from where the tiger is committing depredations . . . should go out and attack the tiger in order to protect his own family the action of the villager would constitute aggression."

The next day, June 22, Nomura turned up at Hull's apartment greatly concerned by what he had in the meantime absorbed from the documents Hull have given him the day before. Although word had already been received that Hitler had launched an invasion of the Soviet Union, Nomura ignored this startling news. He concentrated instead on Hull's "Oral Statement" of June 21, which plainly said the American Government "must await some clearer indication" than had yet been given that the Japanese Government, "as a whole," desired "to pursue courses of peace." Until Tokyo had manifested such an attitude, no agreement could be signed.

The assurances that Nomura had repeatedly offered over the past several months had been entirely at variance with the words and deeds of the Japanese Government, and yet in his meeting with Hull on June 22 the Ambassador professed to be unable to understand why there should be any cause for concern regarding the attitude of Japan. Nomura even claimed he had been acting, all along, in accordance with the instructions he had received from his government.

Having made this assertion, Nomura proceeded to hand over a brief "Oral Statement" of his own—one that had been written in Washington, not in Tokyo! In it he expressed the opinion that certain points contained in three letters that had been appended to the American draft of June 21 would be "difficult to recommend to his Government for approval." He therefore suggested that the letters "either be omitted or suitably modified."

Two of these letters, couched in the form of a Hull-Nomura exchange, dealt with the policy the Japanese Government would adopt in the event the United States, acting to safeguard her own security, became involved in the European war. The third letter (from Hull to Nomura) contained a number of questions touching on the principle of nondiscrimination in international commercial relations, with particular reference to the practices Japan would employ in transactions with China. The purpose here was to obtain confirmation of the various assurances the Ambassador and his "associates" had offered to date.

Nomura's dissatisfaction with these letters is interesting, for they had evolved from an idea Father Drought had been promoting—namely, that certain issues would cause less trouble if they could be kept out of the formal text of the contemplated settlement.

When Nomura objected to the letters appended to the American "Joint Declaration" of June 21, Hull disavowed any desire to embarrass Tokyo. He said he might have difficulty, however, in winning acceptance for the proposed "Understanding" among his fellow Americans unless Nomura's government "could find some way of clarifying its attitude."

"I wonder," Hull suddenly asked, "whether Germany's declaration of war against the Soviet Union might not affect the situation in such a way as to render it easier for the Japanese Government to find some way of doing this."

Nomura rejected this feeler immediately by unequivocally declaring that Tokyo did not want to be placed in the position of repudiating its obligations under the Tripartite Pact.

The next day, as Hitler's forces were penetrating the Soviet frontier along a line extending from the Baltic to the Black Sea, Hull departed for White Sulphur Springs, West Virginia, to take a much needed rest—for reasons of health—that kept him away from Washington for a good six weeks. Throughout this period, however, the "old man"—as Wikawa had called him—remained continually in touch with his responsibilities through messages transmitted over the telephone and by pouch, while Sumner Welles "held the fort" as Acting Secretary of State.

Hull had barely left town when Nomura received some "incredible news." He learned that Matsuoka had accused him of exceeding his authority in Washington; the Foreign Minister consequently planned to "torpedo" whatever agreement resulted. This had been reported to the State Department by Grew.

"I think it was very regrettable," Wikawa informed Drought on June 27, "that we did not notify . . . the Tokyo people that the matter which was first handled by three big statesmen [Roosevelt, Hull, and Walker] was handed down to the State Dep't and that he [Matsuoka] should bear the fact in his mind when he was approached by Mr. Grew on this matter. Faithful to our former advice, he and his associates there must have played innocent or indifferent and caused awful lots of misunderstanding. You know, they are known to keeping secrecy with death."

The time had passed when fanciful schemes could be paraded in the clothes of plausibility, but Drought immediately rushed to the fore with the strutting step of a drum major determined to regroup a straggling line of marchers by striking up a stirring tune.

On July 1, 1941, only twenty-four hours before the leaders of Japan secretly committed their people to a do-or-die attempt to construct a "co-prosperity sphere" in Greater East Asia, Drought provided the Post-master General with a new set of documents that allegedly took into account "every single suggestion made by the United States Government in its most recent memorandum."*

Having found this American proposal unacceptable in a number of

* By "most recent memorandum" Drought meant the "Joint Declaration" of June 21, together with supporting annexes and supplements. He had copies of all of these documents.

respects, Drought had personally made changes wherever he felt they were needed. He had inserted his own ideas in red ink "for purposes of easy reading." He had also appended some notes to explain why certain State Department suggestions were "unnecessary."

According to Drought, every point Hull and his staff had raised had now been answered. "I will try to 'sell' this document to the Japanese," Drought informed Walker, "if I can be assured that our people will not do any more second guessing."

"The State Department has made no concession whatever on any point asked for," Drought wrote. "The State Department is not negotiating; it is legislating. However, all that should be over now since everything asked for has been given [by the Japanese]."

In reality, the two sides were not even close to a settlement. During a conversation on July 2, Iwakuro and Wikawa insisted that an "Understanding" should be concluded first, and detailed questions resolved later. Hamilton and Ballantine argued just as vigorously that no "Understanding" could be reached until the American Government had been given "some practical evidence of Japan's peaceful intentions."

Iwakuro and Wikawa emphasized again and again that the Japanese Government was unanimous in supporting the proposed "Understanding." Hamilton just as repeatedly tried to convince them that "this was not the point" of Hull's "Oral Statement" of June 21. The essence of that document was very simple: there were definite indications that certain important elements in the Japanese Government did not favor courses of peace but were committed instead to continued and close association with Hitler in a program of world conquest; unless Hull could be persuaded that this was not the case, the United States would remain wary of entering into an agreement with Axis Japan.

Two days later, on the evening of July 4, Nomura handed Ballantine a one sentence note, requesting that it be conveyed to Hull in West Virginia by telephone as soon as possible. "My dear Mr. Secretary," the message read, "I am glad to inform you that I am now authorized by the Foreign Minister to assure you that there is no divergence of views in the Government regarding its fundamental policy of adjusting Japanese-American relations on a fair basis. Yours very sincerely, K. Nomura."

At a meeting with the Ambassador the following day, the Chief of the Far Eastern Division—acting on Hull's orders—informed Nomura that his note of July 4 could not be regarded as responsive to the Secretary's "Oral Statement" of June 21.

Hull had also asked Hamilton to "run down" a report, communicated orally by Drought through Walker, to the effect that Japan was now willing to remove her troops from China within two years. When Hamilton brought up the subject, however, Nomura's answer proved that Drought's information was incorrect.

Between June 21 and July 5 the State Department had tried, time and again, to get Nomura to explore the possibility of putting Japanese-American relations on a new footing by dealing concretely with the most critical issues, but discouraging replies had been received on each and every occasion. Despite this record, the pessimism that currently prevailed within the American Government in regard to the prospects of reaching a settlement did not arise from attempts to second-guess the "true intentions" of Japan's leaders or from invidious judgments based on superficial evidence. That pessimism arose from intelligence information of an ominous nature.

As reports came to hand "from a variety of sources" that Japan was contemplating an invasion of the Soviet Far East, the President ordered a message sent to Premier Konoye expressing the "earnest hope" of the American Government that these reports were unfounded. The language was courteously firm: "Should Japan enter upon a course of military aggression and conquest it stands to reason that such action would render illusory the cherished hope of the American Government, which it understood was shared by the Japanese Government, that peace in the Pacific area, far from being further upset, might now indeed be strengthened and made more secure."

Upon receiving this communication in Tokyo, Grew immediately asked for an appointment with Konoye. The Ambassador's request was made in a letter that was hand-carried to the private residence of the Premier. In this letter, Grew indicated his willingness to call on Konoye wherever the Prince felt disposed to meet him.

Early the next morning, Sunday, July 6, Konoye's confidential secretary, Tomohiko Ushiba, appeared at the Embassy. Ushiba summarized the situation from the Premier's point of view: Konoye was afraid of the publicity that would result if the Ambassador were to visit him in the "open," but perhaps they could arrange to bump into each other while playing golf; it being Sunday, however, all the courses would be crowded; the Premier would be busy the next day with ceremonies marking the fourth anniversary of the outbreak of the "China affair" in 1937; he would therefore probably not be able to get together with Grew before Tuesday or Wednesday.

Since the matter was urgent, Grew felt he could not accede to this proposal. He decided, instead, to give Ushiba the President's message and to remain at the Embassy the rest of the day to await the Premier's reply.

That evening Ushiba reappeared with a note from Konoye addressed to Grew: "May I express my sincere thanks for your courtesy of communicating to me the message sent by the Secretary of State at the specific request of the President of the United States. My answer to it will be given by the Foreign Minister as soon as possible after he has returned from Gotemba."*

Ushiba expressed his regret over the incomplete nature of this response, but he reminded Grew that there was no precedent in Japan for a Premier to deal directly with an Ambassador in the field of foreign affairs. Grew was polite but emphatic. He asked Ushiba to tell the Prince that it would be "erroneous" to assume the Ambassador had been trying to go "over the head" of the Foreign Minister. The procedure that had been adopted in this instance was "closely in line" with the practice being followed in Washington, where the President had made it plain he would be happy to confer with Admiral Nomura at any time.

In reporting these developments to the State Department, Grew did not interpret Konoye's action as an intentional rebuff; the Premier's handling of the matter, the Ambassador said, simply showed the strength of tradition in Japan.

There was much truth in this, but Konoye's desire to avoid stepping on the toes of his "pathetically jealous, painfully ambitious" Foreign Minister could not alter the fact that a secondhand response from Matsuoka could not be compared in value with a communication bearing the Premier's signature.

The Foreign Minister's reply to the President two days later brusquely informed him that Japan had "not so far considered the possibility of joining the hostilities against the Soviet Union." "Incidentally," Matsuoka added, "the [members of the] Japanese Government would like to avail themselves of this opportunity for definitely ascertaining whether it is really the intention of the President or the American Government to intervene in the European war as they are naturally and very deeply concerned at the prospect, disturbed as they sincerely are by reports reaching them from a variety of sources."

This tit-for-tat approach elicited a stiff answer: American policy toward the Nazi movement of world conquest was based on "the inalienable right of self-defense"; the measures needed for this purpose would "be determined by the acts of ... the aggressor nations"; infor-

* A well-known resort area in the vicinity of Mount Fuji, only hours away from the capital.

mation that might be available to Tokyo concerning any further encroachments contemplated by those nations "would assist the Japanese Government in reaching an estimate" in regard to the action the United States might be compelled to take to safeguard herself in the future; it "should be obvious" in the light of the experience of some fifteen European countries, all of which had been given categorical assurances they would not be molested, that "it would be suicidal and absurd of the American Government to neglect any reasonable precaution necessary to insure the present or future security" of the American people; the United States could not be expected to stand idly by, while Germany obtained control of the high seas or accumulated other strategic advantages that directly threatened the United States; any intimations that the American Government should desist from its policy of self-defense would range those who made such suggestions on the side of those who favored or facilitated "the aims of the aggressor nations to conquer the world by force."

Swept by a powerful current of developments of increasing complexity toward the narrows lying between a Scylla and Charybdis of policy options that offered a choice of dilemmas, the leaders of Japan and the United States now faced a grim reality. Like countless captains of the past who had been forced to attempt a passage on storm-tossed seas, they found themselves in a decision-making situation that provided little room to maneuver.

At the farewell luncheon for Admiral Nomura held in Tokyo under the auspices of the America-Japan Society in December 1940, Ambassador Grew had publicly charted the bearing: "Let us say of nations as of men: 'By their fruits ye shall know them.' "

In the intervening six months, relations between Japan and the United States had gone from bad to worse despite the presence in Washington of a sailor-diplomat who was supposed to inspire "trust and confidence." Around the corner of the present lay a future of new and direct action on the part of the Japanese Government to impose its will on "Greater East Asia," regardless of the consequences. Against the desire of the John Doe Associates for "a rough-and-ready method" of solution, it was thus indubitably right that Secretary Hull should stand firm in demanding a carefully formulated agreement backed by clear evidence of a fundamental change in Japanese policy away from courses of aggression—*an agreement that would speak for itself*. In the circumstances then prevailing, this was the only sensible alternative to a Far Eastern Munich, on the one hand, or war in the Pacific on the other.

CHAPTER SIXTEEN

The John Doe Associates Depart

W ITH BOTH THE Japanese and American governments temporarily immobilized in late June by the incompatibility of their views concerning the proper route to a settlement, Father Drought had found it comparatively easy, despite the State Department's negative attitude toward him, to intrude further upon the Japanese-American conversations. His first step in the direction of reasserting himself had been to rewrite the so-called Joint Declaration that Hull had handed to Nomura on June 21. Two days after sending his revision of this proposal to the Postmaster General, Drought had conferred with the Japanese Ambassador and had then boarded the afternoon "Congressional" for New York, together with Walker's special assistant, William F. Cronin. That same day (July 3) the Postmaster General had telephoned the State Department and had later talked with Admiral Nomura. Sumner Welles had tried to return Walker's call but had not found him in.

From Maryknoll, where he was spending the Fourth of July weekend, Drought had sent a telegram to the Hotel 2400 directing Wikawa's attention to a message awaiting him at the Japanese Embassy: "Be sure you receive it."

The message in question informed Wikawa of the results of Drought's most recent contact with Walker: "Our friend advises that the document should be delivered personally and not through any department.* These are his exact words to me. Therefore you would be at liberty to follow my suggestion and deliver the document personally and state that you were advised to do so by our friend. If possible you could then take the occasion to explain thoroughly the points which we went over today.

---

* The "document" in this instance is Drought's revised version of the American "Joint Declaration" of June 21. He had sent this to Walker on July 1, but the Postmaster General had refrained from forwarding it to the State Department (presumably because he knew the Department desired to deal only with Nomura or with a fully empowered member of his staff).

You could then arrange for [a] personal meeting for your companions [Nomura and Iwakuro]. Kindest regards. James."

Despite this advice, Drought knew there were problems. In a July 7 letter to Walker, who was then en route to Butte, Montana, Drought expressed his annoyance with the way Hamilton and Ballantine were conducting the conversations. He was afraid Nomura, Iwakuro, and Wikawa would conclude that the Americans were "stringing them along."

"Our people must be following purposes and aims," Drought informed Walker, "which they have not confided to us."

Moreover, while relying on our silence, which I scrupulously kept until about three weeks ago, they have felt free, to my certain knowledge, to inform other nationals and certain Americans, journalists among them, of the attitude they were taking and the character of the proposals made. Such inconsistency only fortifies the opinion that an extensive effort is being made to contravene what I know to be your own true purposes, shared by the two others [Roosevelt and Hull].

So far as the document itself is concerned, I'm sure you realize there are so few differences that goodwill and some intellectual competence should be sufficient to eliminate them in an hour's discussion. That these differences should be given greater prominence and significance every time they are talked about, makes me, I think properly, look about to find the "joker."

Three days later, Drought telephoned Cronin to say he was now back at the Wardman Park Hotel in case the Postmaster General wanted to get in touch with him. The following day, July 11, Drought stopped by Cronin's office to deliver his latest revision of the "Joint Declaration," together with a number of related items. In a covering note addressed to Walker, Drought declared: "If the Secretary of State could indicate to yourself that this document in its present form will now be acceptable to him, you could manage then to get the consent of the Japanese Ambassador (and the war in China would stop!)."

Drought claimed Nomura's position was "weakened" each time he obtained approval for successive changes that were later rejected by the State Department. "If agreement on a text is now reached," Drought told Walker, "with yourself continuing as intermediary, further misunderstanding will be avoided and Admiral Nomura will not repeatedly lose face."

Drought had earlier been thinking of trying to "sell" his doctored version of the "Joint Declaration" of June 21 to the Japanese, but he was currently endeavoring, instead, to pawn it off on the State Department via the office of the Postmaster General. The effort proved unsuccessful because Hull's advisers reacted negatively to this new attempt by

John Doe to dictate a settlement. They were concerned about the "mode of presentation" and judged that the contents of the proposal received from Drought, through Cronin, did not afford a sound basis for carrying the discussions forward. The Department had always dealt with Nomura directly, but these July 11 papers had come "through an indirect channel and without definite indication of sponsorship on the part of the Japanese Ambassador."

No one felt that the Japanese Government had as yet demonstrated a desire to pursue courses of peace in the Pacific. In fact, Tokyo still seemed bent on acting in a manner inconsistent with the spirit of the proposed "Understanding."

In a memorandum addressed to the Secretary of State, the chief of the Far Eastern Division—speaking not only for himself but for several of his colleagues—recommended that no action be taken for the time being. "It is suggested further," Hamilton added, "that if Mr. Walker should raise with you, or if Father Drought should raise with us, the subject of these documents, reply be made to the general effect that while we appreciate Father Drought's desire to be of help, the general situation has now progressed to such a point that we feel that in the best interests of all concerned our conversations and any presentation of documents should be directly between the Japanese Ambassador or his associates and the Secretary of State or his associates."

Hull's advisers wanted to short-circuit the informal and unofficial approach being made by Drought; they wanted to deal with Nomura personally or with members of his staff; only in this way could the "conversations" ultimately be transformed into "negotiations."

The prospects were no brighter now, however, than they had been earlier in the year. While Drought had been trying to save the day for Japan by making commitments for the Japanese Government without its knowledge or authorization, Foreign Minister Matsuoka's conflicting promises had been rising to haunt him like witches springing up in the night to dance around a boiling cauldron.

As soon as he had learned of the German attack on the Soviet Union, Matsuoka had discarded any thought he might once have had about honoring the Soviet-Japanese Neutrality Pact of mid-April, supposedly one of his proudest achievements. He had arbitrarily expounded his views to the Emperor, without prior consultation with the Premier, and had subsequently told his fellow decision-makers he would never have concluded such an arrangement in Moscow if he had known that Germany and the Soviet Union would go to war. Now he was in favor of an aggressive policy, apparently without realizing that the Imperial

Army and Navy were not ready to resort to the kind of direct action he was advocating: a commitment of Japanese troops, planes, and warships to an invasion of the Soviet Far East.

Matsuoka wanted to "stop building a fire" in the south by postponing the projected occupation of southern French Indochina until the end of 1941 so that Japan could immediately proceed northward instead. The Supreme Command, however, wanted to move southward now so that Japan would be able to deal with the north later (preferably after the Germans had finished off the Russians).

Matsuoka and his colleagues also differed over policy toward the United States. At Liaison Roundtable Conferences held on July 10 and 12, the Foreign Minister conducted a full-scale offensive against the American "Joint Declaration" of June 21, which he described as "worse than the first proposal."* He lashed out at Hull's accompanying "Oral Statement," calling it "outrageous"—a blatant attempt to interfere in Japan's internal affairs (by implicitly recommending the removal of pro-Axis leaders from positions of authority).

Of great assistance to Matsuoka at this moment was Yoshie Saitō, one of his confidants. Speaking as a Foreign Office adviser, Saitō offered many reasons why the "Joint Declaration" could not be considered seriously as a basis for an agreement. He depicted key terms in the worst possible manner. He also misrepresented the "Oral Statement," putting words and phrases into Hull's mouth that cannot be found in the Secretary's note. The feeling Saitō conveyed to Japan's top civil and military leaders was that Hull had displayed contempt for Japan.

In this atmosphere Matsuoka called for a strong stand; Japan could not be treated, he said, like a protectorate or a dependency; Roosevelt was "a real demagogue"; cooperation between Japan and the United States was a hopeless dream; Hull's "Oral Statement" should be returned to Washington immediately and the conversations broken off; the only question at issue was when and how this should be done.

The military authorities refused to fall in with Matsuoka's demands. They argued in favor of adhering to the Japanese proposal of May 12 while leaving some room for negotiation. They wanted to maintain the status quo at least until southern Indochina was in their hands. They also wanted time to strengthen the Kwantung Army against the day when it might be sent across the Manchurian frontier into the Soviet Union.

After much argument, and perhaps because his will to resist was

* The "Draft Understanding" of April 9.

weakened by tuberculosis, Matsuoka finally consented to the preparation of a counterproposal to the United States that would reflect the views of the Army and Navy. He let it be known, however, that he would first reject Hull's "Oral Statement" of June 21; then, after a few days had elapsed, he would order Nomura to deliver the new Japanese proposal.

This idea did not appeal to either Konoye or the Army and Navy authorities. They knew the Foreign Minister's rejection of Hull's "Oral Statement" might trigger serious repercussions; they consequently did not want any time lag to occur between the return of the "Oral Statement" and the presentation of the message outlining their ideas for a settlement.

Matsuoka's colleagues thought they had obtained his concurrence, but in fact they had not. On the evening of July 14 the Foreign Minister cabled instructions to Nomura regarding the rejection, without sending the text of the counterproposal (Matsuoka did indicate, however, that such a document was in the offing). The next day he directed one of his subordinates to inform the German Ambassador confidentially of the contents of Japan's "Final Plan," which had not as yet been dispatched to Washington.

For several weeks now, Nomura had been waiting for some response from Tokyo to Hull's "Joint Declaration" of June 21. The Ambassador believed that if his government decided to terminate the conversations, the Americans would in all probability retaliate either by freezing Japanese assets or by adopting other measures of a similar nature. He had warned Tokyo that an accommodation through diplomacy would be rendered impossible if force were used against Southeast Asia. He had also passed on to the Foreign Office a comment by a certain member of Roosevelt's Cabinet (probably Frank Walker) to the effect that further delay would be very prejudicial.

Instead of receiving his government's reaction to the American proposal of June 21, however, Nomura had been instructed to send Minister Wakasugi back to Japan to report on the conversations. Nomura had immediately pointed out to Matsuoka that this procedure would result in so much additional delay a rupture might take place while Wakasugi was on the high seas. If Tokyo was determined to have a personal report, then Nomura wanted to return home for that purpose himself, especially since he could not accomplish anything by staying where he was.

An answer had come from Matsuoka within twenty-four hours. Wakasugi was to leave for Japan as ordered; Nomura was to remain in the United States.

The Ambassador had thereupon admitted to feeling that his amateurishness had been a source of trouble to his government. He had also indicated—on July 14—that he desired to relinquish his post as soon as possible.

In Tokyo, meanwhile, Matsuoka had been told by his doctor that he must refrain from all activity if he wanted to be able to resume his duties in the near future. The Foreign Minister was thus confined to bed when the policy conflicts that had developed between him and his colleagues led to a decision, on their part, in favor of a Cabinet resignation. Matsuoka had only recently seemed to be on the threshold of the Premiership, but now he found himself suddenly forced to bid farewell to the world of politics at a moment when his eagerness to follow the lead of Nazi Germany had earned him the unenviable reputation of being Herr Hitler's "office boy."

*

The political demise of Yōsuke Matsuoka in mid-July 1941 was greeted with enthusiasm by Wikawa and Drought. The good news seemed even better when dispatches from Tokyo revealed that the mandate to form a new Cabinet had been bestowed once again on Prince Konoye.

"Things are moving in our favor," Wikawa informed Drought on July 16. "If those people [in the State Department] still have doubt about our ability then we will be through with them. Frankly speaking, I never knew any responsible person was bothered so much with hearsays, etc., to our great dissatisfaction. Now all I want is their showing of great statesmanship. I wish they would exhibit their complete co-operation with the in-coming foreign minister. If they could, at this particular moment, express their utter confidence and trust in him by accepting without any alteration his new proposal, it will do more good than anything else."

"Respectfully suggest to our friends," Drought wired the Postmaster General, "that we have again been one hundred percent right. Much suffering would have been spared if they had believed us in the first place and acted with some resoluteness. New situation will favor us very much and perhaps now our people will come to a decision quickly."

Two days later, on July 18, Drought sent a follow-up telegram to Walker, who was then in Salt Lake City: "Developments over there are in our favor. If our people cooperate immediately with [the] new man as they expect us to, we can achieve a great lasting success. The changes have been [managed] from here to suit our desires. Wish you were back."

A few hours after dispatching this message, Drought filed still another telegram to Walker containing news of seemingly vital importance: "New Minister is great personal friend of [the] Sailor and his appointment and the reappointment of others friendly to us should be seized upon. Our man over there should take advantage of this before the others again confuse the issue. Could you convey this information to the others as it is important they should be correctly and promptly informed."*

Drought was speaking with conviction at a time when even a member of the Japanese Embassy in Washington quite frankly admitted to an officer of the State Department that Nomura and his staff were currently having as much difficulty as any foreigner would have in discovering the true nature of the policy Japan was pursuing.

In Tokyo itself, with nine years of residence behind him, the American Ambassador felt he was on very shaky ground in offering comments to the State Department at this particular moment. "I make no pretensions at being able to predict the future course of events in Japan," Grew wrote in his diary. "In my long experience here I have never before encountered greater difficulty in presenting reasoned estimates and views of Japanese policy."

The Ambassador's uncertainty with regard to what might happen next lasted only a short while, for both Grew and the Department soon learned that Japan, which already had troops garrisoned in northern French Indochina, was about to establish a military position in the southern part of that country. The meaning of this seemed obvious. Indochina, in Hull's graphic phrase, pointed "like a pudgy thumb" toward the Philippines, Malaya, and the Netherlands East Indies. If Japan was going to set up bases in southern Indochina, then the United States was going to place obstacles in the way of further Japanese conquests in Southeast Asia.

As Hull saw it, Japan was not being threatened by anyone. She could bring prosperity to her people simply by concluding a peaceful settlement with the United States. He would then encourage similar settlements between Japan and Britain and between Japan and the Netherlands. If the authorities in Tokyo were demanding a foothold in southern Indochina, they must be planning to go farther south later on.

Maxwell Hamilton, playing the devil's advocate, told the Secretary "it would be very difficult to convince Japanese leaders that they were not in danger at this time as a result of political and military developments in the Far East which some of them viewed as steps directed toward the encirclement of Japan."

---

* The new Foreign Minister was Admiral Teijirō Toyoda, who had been influential in the fall of 1940 in urging Nomura (the "Sailor") to accept the ambassadorship in Washington. "Our man over there" is a reference to Ambassador Grew. By "the others" Drought meant Hull's advisers in the State Department.

Hamilton thought that perhaps the President should speak to Admiral Nomura, but Welles and Hornbeck disagreed. Hornbeck argued that Roosevelt should not take the initiative in matters where the chances were against his approach having the desired effect.

In this situation Hull decided that at the very least either Hamilton or Welles should have "one more talk" with the Japanese Ambassador. This might help keep the record clear, even if no practical results were obtained. If Nomura claimed that the political situation in Japan would not permit Tokyo to effect a drastic change in policy at this time, the American Government could indicate a willingness to wait while the leaders of Japan developed public opinion "by their own means and in such ways as the [Japanese] Government thought best." If Japan wanted to go along with us, Hull declared, even if only gradually, "we could be very patient and collaborate in all practical ways."

It so happened, however, that the Japanese Ambassador was away from Washington at this moment. Welles consequently conveyed Hull's thoughts to Minister Wakasugi instead, informing him on July 21 that a Japanese "occupation of Indochina" would be "so utterly at variance with the foundation stones of the agreement which had been under discussion" in Washington that it was necessary "frankly to ask" the Minister "what the real facts might be."

Looking Welles "squarely in the eye," Wakasugi said that the Embassy had no knowledge whatever of any intention on the part of the Japanese Government to occupy the French colony.

This denial came only one day after Nomura had spoken very candidly to Rear Admiral Richmond Kelly Turner, the director of the War Plans Division of the Navy Department. Turner had prepared a memorandum of the conversation for the benefit of Admiral Harold R. Stark, the chief of naval operations, and he in turn had forwarded this memorandum to both the President and the Secretary of State. Included in Turner's account was the revelation, straight from the Japanese Ambassador, that Japan would move into Indochina within the next few days.

Perhaps Nomura knew what Wakasugi did not, or perhaps the Minister's disclaimer turned on the Acting Secretary's choice of terms—on his use of the word "occupation."

Hornbeck advised Welles the following day that the Japanese had developed "a very clever setup." They were "requesting" certain facilities in Indochina for military purposes; they were telling Vichy that if these "requests" were granted, French sovereignty in Indochina would be respected. Hornbeck believed the French would yield; the whole transaction would be consummated "with due respect for legal technicalities";

Secret Document.

1 This "Secret Document," in the handwriting of Father James M. Drought, led to the John Doe "Draft Understanding" of April 9, 1941

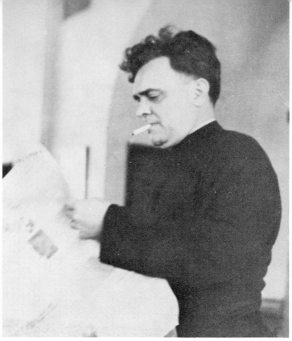

2 Drought during a
moment of relaxation while
"on station" in South
China (around 1925)

3 Drought in a characteristic pose
in the late 1920's (at Maryknoll)

4 Bishop James E. Walsh as
he appeared at the time of
the Hong Kong Chapter (1936)

5 President Franklin D. Roosevelt
congratulating the new Postmaster
General, Frank C. Walker
(September 1940)

6 Foreign Minister Yōsuke Matsuoka, sporting the "national uniform," countersigns an imperial rescript

7 Prince Fumimaro Konoye, whose position as Premier in 1940–41 made him an object of John Doe attention

8 Matsuoka "lecturing" Ambassador Joseph C. Grew at the America-Japan Society luncheon in the Imperial Hotel, December 19, 1940

9 Ambassador Kichisaburō Nomura arriving at the White House to present his credentials, February 14, 1941

10 Banker Tadao (Paul) Wikawa, one of the John Doe Associates

11 Colonel Hideo Iwakuro, another of the John Doe group, is shown here in the spring of 1941 with Drought, Nomura, and Walsh

12 Secretary of State Cordell Hull, who wanted "an agreement that would speak for itself"

13 Stanley K. Hornbeck, Hull's principal adviser on relations with the Far East

14 Matsuoka in Berlin during a European junket that included visits to Moscow and Rome (spring 1941)

15 Maxwell M. Hamilton, Chief
of the Division of Far Eastern
Affairs, Department of State

16 Joseph W. Ballantine, who
assisted Hull during most of his
meetings with Nomura in 1941

17 Admiral Teijirō Toyoda, who succeeded Matsuoka as Foreign Minister
in mid-July 1941, is shown here chatting affably with Grew

18 Shigenori Tōgō, Foreign
Minister of Japan at the
time of Pearl Harbor

19 Special Envoy Saburō Kurusu
on his way to the White House
with Nomura and Hull,
November 17, 1941

20 Eugene H. Dooman,
Counselor of the American
Embassy in Tokyo, 1937–41

21 The two Japanese representatives waiting to be received by
the Secretary of State, Sunday,
December 7, 1941

Seventy-seventh Congress of the United States of America;

At the First Session

Begun and held at the City of Washington on Friday, the third day of January, one thousand nine hundred and forty-one

JOINT RESOLUTION

Declaring that a state of war exists between the Imperial Government of Japan and the Government and the people of the United States and making provisions to prosecute the same.

Whereas the Imperial Government of Japan has committed unprovoked acts of war against the Government and the people of the United States of America: Therefore be it

Resolved by the Senate and House of Representatives of the United States of America in Congress assembled, That the state of war between the United States and the Imperial Government of Japan which has thus been thrust upon the United States is hereby formally declared; and the President is hereby authorized and directed to employ the entire naval and military forces of the United States and the resources of the Government to carry on war against the Imperial Government of Japan; and, to bring the conflict to a successful termination, all of the resources of the country are hereby pledged by the Congress of the United States.

Sam Rayburn
Speaker of the House of Representatives.

H A Wallace
Vice President of the United States and
President of the Senate.

Approved
Dec. 8 - 1941 4:10 P.M. E.S.T.

Franklin D Roosevelt

22 The President, signing the declaration of war against Japan (the armband indicates that he is in mourning for his mother)

force would not be used; there would be no "occupation" in the strict sense of the word.

Hornbeck did not need to say what everyone already knew: the morning after this consummation the rest of the world would awaken to find a victorious Japan standing astride the body of a helpless Indochina.

Unofficial confirmation of the progress Tokyo was making in this direction came on July 23, when Wikawa telephoned Ballantine to report "that the Japanese Embassy had been informed by the Japanese Government that all their negotiations with the Vichy Government had been peacefully settled."

This would give the lie, Wikawa thought, to propaganda harmful to Japan. He said fifth columnists in his country had been trying to cast Japan in a bad light by sending telegrams in simple codes that could be easily broken, thus purposely leaking all sorts of damaging information. Since the negotiations with Vichy had been amicably settled, however, it would now be possible to proceed speedily with the proposed Japanese-American "Understanding."

It was the fashion of the times to claim that hostile acts carried out by "peaceful means" could not be called "aggression," but Hull would have none of this. In a telephone conversation with Welles that same day (July 23), the Secretary declared that if the Japanese Ambassador tried to describe the Indochina situation in this way, then he should be told such "peaceful means" were completely contrary to the spirit of the discussions that had been in progress ever since his arrival in Washington. In such circumstances the American Government could only conclude that these discussions had been "wiped out" by the latest Japanese action in Indochina.

"The Secretary said," Welles subsequently wrote, "that if we waited until he came home [from White Sulphur Springs] to tell Ambassador Nomura the foregoing, then it would come too late as a warning to Japan. We must let them see the seriousness of the step they have taken and let them know that such [a step] constitutes an unfriendly act because it helps Hitler to conquer Britain. The Secretary said that if we did not tell the Ambassador all this, he would not sit down with Admiral Nomura when he came back to Washington. It would be a farce to do so."

That afternoon Nomura turned up at the State Department with various explanations prefabricated in Tokyo. The dispatch of military forces into southern Indochina, he declared, was designed to assure Japan an uninterrupted flow of rice and raw materials; Gaullist agents and Chinese agitators had been stirring up trouble there; unless Japan stepped in, she might one day find her supplies suddenly cut off.

Nomura told Welles that Japan had also acted out of her need to safeguard her security. Tokyo believed that certain powers were endeavoring to encircle Japan; the action taken in Indochina was simply a precautionary measure. The American Government should not jump to "hasty conclusions" but should permit a little time to elapse instead. A friendly adjustment might then be possible after all.

Welles was under orders from Hull to adopt a firm line. He consequently informed Nomura that the Secretary of State could not currently see any basis on which to pursue the conversations he had been having with the Japanese Ambassador.

That evening, in an effort to solicit the help of the Postmaster General, Wikawa described Japan's move into southern Indochina as an "act of self-defense . . . and by no means for any territorial design." "Of course," he wrote, "even such could have been avoided, if there were any understandings in existence between [the] U.S. and Japan!"* "Now . . . all we, the lovers of peace, justice and humanity, have to do," Wikawa added, "is to spare no effort, and to waste no time for the happy conclusion of our protracted negotiations, which, due to some third nations' trick, is threatened to be broken off!† . . . Casting aside all of the misunderstandings and misinterpretations caused by such tricks, we must immediately take the final decisive step for the preservation of peace in the Pacific and save the modern civilization from destruction."‡

The following afternoon, July 24, the President received the Japanese Ambassador, at the latter's request, for an "off-the-record conference" in the Oval Room at the White House. For more than two years, Roosevelt told Nomura, the American Government had been acting in the interest of maintaining peace in the Pacific by permitting the exportation of oil to Japan—a country that had given every indication of pursuing a policy of force in conjunction with the program of world conquest being carried out by Hitler. The shipment of oil to Japan had been allowed to continue—in the face of bitter criticism—largely to deny Japan any pretext for seizing the Netherlands East Indies. Current Japanese policy toward Indochina, however, had created an extremely serious problem for the United States. Surely the Japanese Government could not really believe that China, Britain, the Netherlands, or the United States had any territorial designs on Indochina or were in the slightest degree threatening Japan. The American Government could only assume that

---

* Nomura had made a similar statement to Welles that afternoon.

† Nomura had told Welles that "third powers" were doing everything they could to prevent Japan from reaching an agreement with the United States.

‡ The "preservation of modern civilization" had been one of Matsuoka's favorite arguments.

the occupation of Indochina was being undertaken by Japan for the purpose of further offensive action elsewhere at a later date.

An idea had occurred to him, the President said, just before the Ambassador had come in. There had not been time to talk it over with Mr. Welles, but the idea was simply this: If the Japanese Government would refrain from occupying Indochina, or, in case an occupation had already commenced, if Tokyo would withdraw its military and naval forces, the President could assure the Japanese Government he would do everything in his power to obtain a solemn and binding declaration from China, Britain, and the Netherlands to regard Indochina as a neutralized country in the nature of Switzerland—it being understood that the United States and Japan would join in this declaration. The President would also ask Britain and the other nations concerned for a guarantee to the effect that the local French authorities would be allowed to continue to administer Indochina for the duration of the emergency without having to contend with attempts to dislodge them on the part of Gaullist or Free French agents.

If these steps were taken, the President told Nomura, unequivocal proof would exist that no other power had any hostile intentions in regard to Indochina. In addition, Japan would be afforded the fullest and freest opportunity to obtain access to the food supplies and raw materials available in the French colony.

The Ambassador seemed to understand all of this fully, for he "reiterated concisely and quite clearly what the President had suggested." Nomura then added something that was "not quite clear," but he seemed to be saying that only a very great Japanese statesman would be able to reverse a policy the government had already set in motion.

Sumner Welles, who was present throughout the interview, concluded that Nomura was in no sense optimistic. Secretary Hull, who telephoned Welles the next day from White Sulphur Springs, was expecting the worst: "My judgment is that the State Department and the Government should not say too much on this Japanese question. The first thing we know we will run into a storm. It is so delicate and there are so many angles to it. I am sure Japan is going on unless something happens to stop her."

The news from Colonel Iwakuro at this moment, when everything seemed to be going "hellward," was far from encouraging. On July 25 he told Joseph Ballantine that Tokyo wanted to reopen the conversations Hull had suspended. A resumption would not cause the Japanese Government to revoke what it had done in Indochina, the Colonel said, but the conclusion of an "Understanding" at this time would at least keep

Japan from moving farther south. If the United States imposed embargoes or froze Japanese assets, however, Japan would then have no alternative but to turn sooner or later toward Malaya and the East Indies to obtain essential raw materials.

Iwakuro indicated that he and Wikawa had decided to return home; they had already booked passage, in fact, on the *Tatsuta-maru*, which was scheduled to leave San Francisco on July 31. He would be willing to stay longer, however, if the American Government wanted to continue the conversations; indeed, he would be happy to talk with the Acting Secretary of State or with the President if the American side should desire such a meeting.

The next day, July 26, 1941, as an Executive Order freezing Japanese assets in the United States went into effect, Hamilton noted for the record that both he and Ballantine were of the opinion that "no reply to Colonel Iwakuro's approach [was] called for and that the matter should rest with the statements made by Mr. Welles and by the President to the Japanese Ambassador."

In a letter to Drought written on Sunday, July 27, Wikawa revealed that his spirits were low: "Indeed, I feel quite flat now! After all, as I predicted, 'the operation was perfect, but the patient, Miss Peace, is dead.' ... All we can do now is to pray God to limit the catastrophe the minimum possible."

Wikawa advised Drought that the captain of the *Tatsuta-maru* was afraid to enter San Francisco Bay because of the new situation; he thought he would not be allowed to leave again. "You know what the results would be, especially its bad impression to our fellow countrymen! I can not help but to deplore it!"

"The Reds in your Treasury," Wikawa added, "must certainly be taking this opportunity to embitter us! All they want is to upset the existing social order and to have [a] new one like they have in Russia!"

When Drought subsequently learned that Iwakuro and Wikawa were having difficulty making cross-country travel arrangements, he interceded with Frank Walker to secure air reservations that would permit the two men to reach San Francisco in time to board the *Tatsuta-maru*, the captain having decided in the meantime to bring his ship into port after all.

Although there seemed to be little likelihood that Colonel Iwakuro would be invited to the White House to confer with the President, Wikawa and Drought kept in close touch with the Postmaster General throughout the next few days on the chance an interview might be granted at the last moment. When their hopes were dashed, Wikawa wrote to Walker on July 31 asking him to do whatever he thought best with some souvenirs from Japan—souvenirs that had been intended for Walker's "great friend" in the White House.

Another letter, written that same day and co-signed by the Colonel, took care of the amenities toward Hull:

July 31, 1941

Dear Mr. Secretary:

It has been our earnest wish to call on you there [at White Sulphur Springs] once before our departure and express our heartfelt thanks for all the kindness you have extended to us during our stay here. We have found it impossible for us, as we have suddenly to fly over to San Francisco this afternoon in order to catch our boat sailing therefrom tomorrow noon. We deeply regret it.

Though apparently unsuccessful be our mission, we are quite confident that the seeds planted by informal talks between you and us shall never fail to grow fruits in the future.

With our highest esteem and hearty prayer for your quick recovery,

We remain, Mr. Secretary, always,

Very peacefully yours,
H. Iwakuro
T. Wikawa

Father Drought had by now decided to accompany his two colleagues as far as San Francisco. While traveling across the country he found time to draft several telegrams that he thought Iwakuro and Wikawa should send as a farewell gesture.

For Maxwell Hamilton, Drought recommended an analogy: "An acquaintance well begun should produce good fruit as it ripens into understanding. We hope time will prove that the cordial goodwill, which we share in your regard, shall not be weakened by difficulties created by others."

A brief maxim seemed appropriate for Joseph Ballantine: "Great issues depend on such little things."

For Cordell Hull, however, a more elaborate message was needed. Drought's first draft gave way to a second draft, and even this underwent some further changes. The final, "definitive" version—signed "Two Friends for Peace"—was delivered in White Sulphur Springs on the morning of August 2:

Before sailing we wish to convey to Your Excellency, and through you to the President of the United States, our respectful greetings and the renewed assurance that whatever may be the final outcome of our conversations, we shall never fail to remember with admiration your patient endeavor to overcome the obstacles that have been placed in the way of a lively friendship between us. Our purposes remain unchanged and our convictions unshaken that this goal shall not be difficult to realize. Our Understanding would have made certain things unnecessary and eliminated the possibility of unfortunate incidents. Confident in your peaceful determination we are not without hope that our Understanding may still be gloriously realized.

Hull did not know that Drought was the author of these words. The Secretary of State quite naturally thought this parting message had been written by Iwakuro and Wikawa.

In San Francisco, meanwhile, Drought had missed the plane on which he had intended to return to the East Coast. He was therefore forced to cross the country by train, encountering in the process "a pompous Western ass talking his head off—and saying nothing at all."

Knowing that the departure of the *Tatsuta-maru* had been delayed, Drought drafted still another telegram: "Best wishes for a pleasant voyage home. . . . May the calm waters of the Pacific and the wide horizon help you to forget and to forgive the petty selfish motives which deprived your noble efforts of success. Shall always treasure your friendship in devoted remembrance. . . . Still difficult to believe that our dream was ended by the ambition and hypocrisy of politicians. Your strong character will surmount this disappointment & your idealism will conquer in the end. I shall miss you very much."

From San Francisco, on August 3, Iwakuro and Wikawa wired their reply to a John Doe they would never see again: "Before sailing we wish to thank you for your kind messages and would like to assure you our great admiration of wonderful brain and superhuman energy. We earnestly pray that our joint efforts shall not be in vain."

CHAPTER SEVENTEEN

Toward an "Unbridgeable Antagonism"

I N HIS LAST DAYS as Foreign Minister, Yōsuke Matsuoka had come to realize that something was very wrong at the Japanese Embassy in Washington. The wording employed in Hull's "Oral Statement" of June 21, which contained three separate references to "the Japanese Ambassador and his associates," had increased Matsuoka's suspicions. A subsequent cable from Nomura explaining that "associates" referred not only to Minister Wakasugi and other Foreign Service personnel, but also to Iwakuro and Wikawa, had stirred Matsuoka's anger. He had pounced on this information, upbraiding Nomura in rigorous terms. The gist of the scolding was that the members of an Embassy constituted an Ambassador's "staff," not his "associates." Colonel Iwakuro had never been authorized by the Foreign Minister to engage in negotiations; in addition, Nomura had specifically been instructed to steer clear of Wikawa, a private individual of questionable reputation who had absolutely no authority to speak for Premier Konoye or anyone else. It was "extremely deplorable," Matsuoka had told Nomura, that the State Department should be laboring under the impression that such persons were the Ambassador's "associates." Nomura was to set matters straight immediately.

In responding to Matsuoka's reprimand, Nomura had defended his use of Iwakuro and Wikawa by asserting that relations between Japan and the United States were so strained at the time of his arrival in Washington that he had recognized the futility of relying solely on negotiations conducted directly with the State Department; in resorting to behind-the-scenes activities, however, he had always remained in close touch with developments; nothing had been done without his knowledge and approval; no one in Washington was operating under the delusion that Iwakuro and Wikawa had any right to speak for the Japanese Government; there was no point in arguing about technicalities; such "matters of detail" ought to be left to the discretion of the Ambassador.

By the time Nomura had sent this message, Konoye had begun moving toward a Cabinet resignation. Unaware of this and temporarily incapacitated by his illness, Matsuoka had asked his confidant Saitō to make certain representations to Konoye concerning Hull's "Oral Statement" and "Joint Declaration" of June 21. Matsuoka had also unburdened himself in regard to Nomura, laying bare the Ambassador's sins of omission and commission in damning detail. Nomura was so anxious to conclude an "Understanding" in Washington, the Foreign Minister charged, that he was hiding from the Japanese and American governments whatever he believed each might regard as objectionable. Matsuoka felt that in all probability Nomura was not passing along to the State Department even half of what he was supposed to convey to Hull.

When Saitō could not obtain an interview with Konoye, he put into a letter what Matsuoka had wanted him to tell the Premier in person. If Konoye read this letter, he did nothing about it. The Ambassador was thus able to continue to employ his "discretion" in carrying out the orders he received from Tokyo. Needless to say, Nomura remained what he had always been—a naval officer who was completely out of his element trying to navigate across the dry land he had to traverse as a diplomat.

In mid-July 1941, as the transition from one Konoye Cabinet to the other was taking place, the American Government had accepted the return of the "Oral Statement" to which Matsuoka had objected so strenuously. Nomura had by then received Japan's "Final Plan" of July 15, but he had already decided not to deliver it to the State Department. He was clearly hoping the change in Foreign Ministers would result in new and more conciliatory instructions.

Nomura was determined to do his very best—to exert himself as though he had been "revived from the dead"—but his very best in this instance was to deny the American Government the important knowledge that Tokyo had responded in mid-July to the initiative taken by the Secretary of State on June 21. Thus Hull and his advisers were left with only the very curious documents Father Drought had delivered to Frank Walker's office on July 11, documents that were of no value whatsoever because they did not come from the Japanese Government at all.

Nomura's reason for disobeying his instructions should not be permitted to obscure the fact that he had arrogated to himself a power of decision that ought not to rest with any ambassador.

Soon thereafter, Nomura had committed another serious mistake. In reporting on his conversation with the President on July 24, the Ambassador had made only a perfunctory reference to FDR's Neutralization Proposal.

Ambassador Grew, on the other hand, after reading a briefing cable from the State Department, had judged the White House offer to be of "such prime importance" that he had sought an "off-the-record" interview with the Foreign Minister at once. When this conversation took place on July 27, Grew was amazed to discover that Matsuoka's successor, Admiral Teijirō Toyoda, knew nothing about Roosevelt's suggestion.

Grew had immediately illuminated the subject, arguing that the Neutralization Proposal "clearly and directly met the Japanese contention that the occupation of bases in Indochina was caused by the necessity of ... forestalling an alleged encirclement of Indochina by third countries."

"I ... urged the Minister," Grew later wrote, "with all the strength and earnestness at my command to take advantage of the President's statesmanlike and far-seeing suggestion."

In international affairs the frontier of possibility is forever changing, but never vanishes. Events may sometimes take a surprising turn; a move will be made that is totally unexpected while a predicted response fails to materialize. No one can say what might have happened if Nomura had immediately sent a complete report to Tokyo concerning the President's Neutralization Proposal, but one fact is clear: the Ambassador's failure to do so kept vital information from his government at a decisive moment and for a significant period of time, information that should have been cabled at once in full and untrammeled detail.

The thought that Nomura might be the culprit in this affair had briefly crossed Grew's mind, but he had dismissed the notion as "incredible." He had therefore jumped to what seemed to be the only other conclusion. "The suggestion is unavoidable," he had informed the State Department, "that extremist elements in the Foreign Office may have withheld the President's proposal from the Foreign Minister."

Grew believed it would be a good idea to check with Nomura to determine why Toyoda had been so completely in the dark on July 27. Hamilton and Hornbeck advised against doing so, but they were overruled by Welles. When the Acting Secretary subsequently talked with Nomura, the Ambassador "did not look particularly surprised." He said that on July 24 he had cabled a brief summary of the President's proposal, that he had then gone to New York, and that on the evening of July 27 he had transmitted a very detailed account to his government.

This was three days after the Ambassador had seen the President. No wonder Grew got to the Foreign Minister before Nomura's belated account reached Tokyo. Grew's initiative had in fact impelled Toyoda to instruct Nomura to send a full report at once. It was only when Nomura received this order on July 27 that he finally acted.

Just what emerged even then can be judged from a conversation Minister Wakasugi had with Welles a week later, on August 4. Wakasugi, who was to leave that night for Tokyo, revealed "that he had been unable to understand at all from his Ambassador the proposal which the President had made." The Minister asked whether Welles would clarify the matter for him. Welles immediately obliged, repeating what Roosevelt had told Nomura on July 24. Wakasugi then said that he now understood clearly, *for the first time*, exactly what the President had in mind!

*

With the return of the Secretary of State to Washington from White Sulphur Springs at the beginning of August, the meetings that he had had with Nomura during the spring of 1941 were slowly resumed, but Tokyo remained committed to an "immutable" policy that left little room for compromise. The decisions that had been made earlier in the summer were treated as "irrevocable" by the members of the Japanese Government. And so the President's Neutralization Proposal, which had in the meantime been broadened to include Thailand, was rebuffed.

Perhaps "ignored" would be a better word, for the authorities in Japan did not address themselves directly to Roosevelt's offer but dilated instead upon a scheme of their own—a scheme designed to secure a diplomatic victory for Japan at the expense of the United States.

Despite this bad beginning, Konoye's new Foreign Minister quickly made a good impression; he appeared to be "very frank, honest, and communicative." He had been Vice-Minister of the Navy when the Tripartite Pact was concluded, but he was not known to have any pro-Axis leanings. Although he was lacking in diplomatic experience, he would presumably be able to work well with Nomura. The fact that Toyoda had been chosen to replace Matsuoka could even be regarded as "an example of Prince Konoye's famous policy of appointing men popular with the extremists to carry out moderate policies." And yet Ambassador Grew was pessimistic.

"As in every previous step in the southward advance," he noted in his diary, "the Japanese support their action by . . . the patently baseless charge that Japan is threatened by encirclement by the ABCD powers, American, British, Chinese, and Dutch. [The Japanese] announce that they have gone in to 'protect' Indochina, and that they have no territorial ambitions nor the intention to interfere with French sovereignty. Yet . . . when the time comes for them to get out they will hold that 'circumstances have altered' and they will stay. We know their technique by long experience. It is simply the usual technique of the totalitarian powers."

Grew had already talked with Toyoda about this problem: "I simply told him," the Ambassador wrote, "of my bitter experience with every Foreign Minister since coming to Japan nine years ago: Hirota had given me the most categorical assurances that the Open Door would be scrupulously maintained in Manchuria whether we recognized Manchukuo or not; then when the door was slammed in our face, 'circumstances had altered'; similar assurances were given regarding North China, with similar results; Admiral Nomura [when he was Foreign Minister in the fall of 1939] had promised the opening of the Yangtze to foreign navigation within about two months, but it has not been opened to this day. How could my Government or I myself accept any promises or assurances whatever from any Japanese Government? I said I knew that every Foreign Minister had acted in good faith at the time, just as Toyoda was no doubt acting in good faith now; but in Japan the Government proposes, the army disposes."

The Foreign Minister had offered little by way of reply. He had not attempted to refute Grew's remarks but had earnestly begged the Ambassador to believe him. He had insisted that Japan's intentions were peaceful, but he had also appealed to Grew to tell the American Government how very important it was to avoid provoking the people of Japan.

Toyoda might just as well have been sitting on the outer end of a limb while sawing it off at the trunk. He could hardly be a success as Foreign Minister if he failed to appreciate how greatly Japanese policies in Asia had provoked the people of the United States.

Why had Toyoda agreed to take charge of the Foreign Office at a time when he was likely to reap the whirlwind that would result from Japan's move into southern Indochina?

"My impression for what it may be worth," Grew informed Washington, "is that the Japanese, including the Foreign Minister, have always discounted the possibility of serious retaliation by the United States and that our retaliation has now taken them completely by surprise. Whether this is due to inadequate comprehension of American public opinion by Japanese officials in the United States, or whether their reports have failed to convince the Japanese Government, I cannot say. I myself have constantly tried my best to enlighten them. But of one thing I am sure: the astonishment and profound concern of the Japanese at the turn of events are unmistakably genuine, as is the bitter resentment engendered by the action of the United States."

In contrast to the rasp of indignation heard in Japan there was a ring of jubilation in certain sectors of the American press. "They are asking for it, let's let them have it!" seemed to be a popular view not only in San Francisco, America's "gateway to the Orient," but in other parts of the country as well.

In an editorial entitled "War Has No Boundary," the *New York Times* declared that the President's order freezing Japanese assets had reemphasized an important fact: "This world of ours has become an inextricably bound-up entity. . . . Peace is now indivisible. . . . Resistance is perilous but neutrality is death. We are opposing Hitler's will in Europe. We must oppose the Japanese translation of it in the Pacific. They are . . . part of the same black conspiracy against the happiness, the lives, and the freedom of all humanity."

From Princeton, New Jersey, George Gallup reported that a "momentous" change had taken place since 1937 in the thinking of the average American with respect to the Far Eastern situation: "Four years ago . . . Americans as a whole were little concerned about the fighting in the Orient. While American 'sympathies' were with the Chinese, at least half the country believed the outcome would make little difference to us. . . . Today a new survey shows that while the majority of Americans do not wish to get into a shooting war with Japan now, nevertheless an outright majority believe the United States should impose checks on Japanese power 'even if this means risking war.' "

There were writers who suggested that the Japanese might "bluster and retaliate" at first but would "whimper and capitulate" in the end. Wilfrid Fleisher, however, clearly saw the significance of the American action Japan had brought down upon herself by moving into southern Indochina. "The Japanese," he informed his readers, "are now with their backs to the wall and they must carry on with the struggle they have so rashly embarked upon or renounce their dreams of empire in Asia. The die has been cast."

In a dispatch to the *New York Times* Otto Tolischus warned, " 'Peace' in the Pacific hangs by a thread and there are few optimists left who dare hope that the thread will hold."

Although deeply concerned about the consequences that might result from the order freezing Japanese assets in the United States, Secretary Hull nevertheless felt there was no alternative. He believed—apparently on the basis of Grew's reporting—that the President's Neutralization Proposal had been sidetracked in Tokyo by opponents of the idea; the "military crowd" had gotten "the upper hand" and had "pushed the others" into the Indochina venture. Soon the Japanese would be on the move again, perhaps into Thailand. "They will take us by surprise," Hull said, "if we are not careful."

"They swear every day," the Secretary told Sumner Welles, "that they are going forward and they are fitting their acts to their words. The only time they modify their policy of overt, unfriendly acts is when they make false and fraudulent avowals of peace and friendship. This they do until they get ready to go forward [again]. . . . Nothing will stop them except force. Unless we figure that they are going to turn back, we should not figure that they are going to be satisfied to stop where they are. The point is how long we can maneuver the situation until the military matter in Europe is brought to a conclusion."

In Hull's view there would always be "an element of risk and danger" in any American policy "sufficiently firm and extensive" to "checkmate" the Japanese. "I just don't want us to take for granted," he declared, "a single word they say but [we can] appear to do so, to whatever extent it may satisfy our purpose to delay further action by them."

Secretary of War Henry L. Stimson, who had long advocated more positive measures toward Japan, was pleased to find that a change had taken place in Hull's thinking. "He has made up his mind," Stimson wrote, "that we have reached the end of any possible appeasement with Japan and that there is nothing further that can be done with that country except by a firm policy"—perhaps even the use of force itself.

To Ambassador Grew the outlook was grim: "The vicious circle of reprisals and counter-reprisals is on. *Facilis descensus Averno est.*" Unless radical surprises were to occur in the world, Grew could not see how the momentum of the current "down-grade movement" in Japanese-American relations could be arrested. There was no way of telling how far it would go. The "obvious conclusion" was "eventual war."

Hull himself later summed up the situation: "This first act of the drama of our dialogue with Japan ended in failure, just as the second act was destined to end. It showed us, however, what we had to face. Japan would readily and instantly have signed a straight non-aggression pact with the United States. She would as readily have signed a general agreement with us on the basis of her own proposals. But neither pact would have given us peace for more than a short time. And either one would have meant a betrayal of China, Britain, Russia, and The Netherlands, and of our own future security."

"From now on," Hull added, "our major objective with regard to Japan was to give ourselves more time to prepare our defenses. We were still ready—and eager—to do everything possible toward keeping the United States out of war; but it was our concurrent duty to concentrate on trying to make the country ready to defend itself effectively in the event of war being thrust upon us."

In Tokyo at this very moment a decision was emerging in favor of spurring military preparations while the search for a diplomatic solution continued. Since winter was only a few months away, the pressure for quick action increased as one week followed another. Soon, a lemming-like march toward destruction would draw to its ranks even those Japanese leaders who were least anxious to plunge their country into war in the Pacific. A great chasm of enmity—an antagonism of possibly unbridgeable proportions—was about to open up between Japan and the United States.

PART FOUR

DISASTER

CHAPTER EIGHTEEN

Sounds of War Amid Talk of Peace

B Y THE LATE summer of 1941 the United States and Japan were already too close to the legendary "brink" for anyone to contemplate the future with equanimity. It is a precipice that works a fateful fascination on those whom it attracts. Once at the edge, nations seldom shy from the plunge. In matters of high policy, therefore, it is essential to the maintenance of peace to stay as far away from the brink as possible at all times.

This is easier said than done, even under the best of circumstances. In Washington and in Tokyo one complication had been piled upon another as a result of the partnership that had developed between Ambassador Nomura and the John Doe Associates, thus rendering the situation even more perilous.

The Japanese move into southern Indochina and the possibility that Japan might be on the point of invading the Soviet Far East left American leaders gravely worried about the future. The gods of war seemed to be lurking in the wings, awaiting a predetermined cue to dash forth spreading death and destruction.

At the end of July, in the midst of the Indochina crisis, a situation had arisen of the type that had worried Ambassador Grew more than any other problem since he had taken up his post in Japan nearly a decade before. In another of those "So sorry, mistake" episodes that had already caused considerable anger in the United States, Japanese naval aviators had come within eight yards of scoring a direct hit on the American gunboat *Tutuila* as it lay moored at Chungking in a "safety zone" recognized by the Japanese Government.

"Remember the *Maine!*" "Remember the *Panay!*"

The incident was all the more maddening because similar attacks earlier in the summer had resulted in assurances from Tokyo that the Imperial Army and Navy were taking every precaution to prevent "accidents of this nature." Grew thought it preposterous to believe that Japanese pilots could be so lacking in skill that they would repeatedly bomb, inadvertently, the very targets they were supposed to avoid at all cost.

Nomura informed Welles that henceforth there would be no more strikes against "the city area of Chungking," but the raids began again within a few days, and apparently with greater intensity. All the Ambassador could then say by way of explanation was that Tokyo had promised to suspend the attacks temporarily, not indefinitely. He thought he had made this clear, but perhaps he had failed to get his meaning across. In any event, that was the situation.

Stanley Hornbeck was indignant. The State Department had found it necessary to repeat the original oral protest to Nomura three or four times before he had understood what was being said. Now the Ambassador was claiming he had not expressed himself correctly, and yet when he had promised the bombing would be halted he had read aloud from a statement that had purportedly originated with the Japanese Government. He had even permitted the Under Secretary of State to take notes from the document.

The United States had expected "a pledge of honest intention given in good faith and a performance that would demonstrate such intention and such faith." It had been treated instead, Hornbeck wrote, to another example of "the hazardous futility of placing any reliance upon a pledge given by Japan's diplomats that Japan will desist from pursuit of an objective to which the Japanese nation is committed (and to which we know that it is committed)."

Hornbeck was not the only American who was angered by the behavior of Japan at this time. Editorial comments appearing in the press during the first half of August revealed "the same insistent demand for a firm and unyielding policy" that had been voiced throughout July, with the belief being "increasingly expressed" that such a response was the best way to avoid war. If Japan chose to pick a fight with the United States (the editorials proclaimed), the American people were ready to do battle.

The *Milwaukee Journal* thought that economic measures, if fully implemented, would compel Japan to come out from behind "the fence of deception" that had been shielding her activities to date.

The *News-Tribune* in Waltham, Massachusetts, felt the best way to halt further Japanese penetration of Southeast Asia might be for the Americans, the British, and the Dutch to warn Japan publicly that a single step beyond Indochina would mean war: "Weakness is the one fatal error. It is time to wake up. There is a point where patience ceases to be a virtue and verges on sheer stupidity."

"There need be no qualms about public opinion," the *Washington*

Post informed its readers; the latest Gallup poll had shown that Americans were now "thinking in oceans." A majority of citizens wanted action that would keep Japan from becoming more powerful. They wanted this "even at the risk of war."

The *New York Herald Tribune* argued that "a showdown with Japan" would be better than further procrastination: "No one in this country or in Great Britain, or anywhere else but in Berlin, wants war in the Pacific. But if Japan is set on it, it is folly to leave the timing of it to her discretion and convenience."

*

Although feeling in the United States had turned more decidedly against the Japanese following their move into southern Indochina, voices of dissent could still be heard. Included among those Americans who remained critical of the policies of their own government was Father Drought, who continued to watch developments closely even though his two Associates, Iwakuro and Wikawa, were now on their way back to Japan.

An editorial Drought clipped from the *New York Journal American* early in August suggests the trend of his thinking at this time:

> Well, we were not able to pick a fight with Japan after all.
>
> We cut off hundreds of millions of dollars of trade with Japan (highly profitable to us). We imposed all sorts of sanctions and interdictions—and prohibitions and preventions on that unhappy country. We demanded apologies and indemnities because one of our gunboats, wandering in Oriental waters, intercepted a stray Japanese shot.*
>
> Then we exacted promises and securities that nothing of the kind, intentional or unintentional, preventable or unpreventable, would ever happen again. We paraded around with a chip on each shoulder, spoiling for a fight.
>
> But Japan would not fight. She would not agree to make our bellicose politicians war heroes. She apologized, she promised indemnities, she gave every requested pledge and a few more besides. . . .
>
> So our truculent politicians had to accept the apologies and keep their belligerent shirts on. It was a great disappointment. The military fame with which they had hoped to stain the pages of history has gone glimmering.

Soon after reading this editorial, Drought became so exercised over an article in the *Herald Tribune* that he immediately sent a two-page letter of protest to the author of the piece, Walter Lippmann. The gist of the article was that Herbert Hoover and some other Republicans had recently placed themselves publicly in the position of "seeking to prevent

---

* The *Tutuila* was not "wandering" anywhere; it was virtually marooned at Chungking as a consequence of the war the Japanese were waging in China. Not only that, but the vessel was lying dead in the water at its mooring when it came under aerial attack.

war in the abstract" by warning against activities that might lead to American involvement in the fighting in Europe. As Lippmann saw it, these men had irresponsibly closed their eyes to the "desperately real problem" posed by Japan in the Pacific, the "most immediate and the most likely" area of the world in which the United States might become "directly and deeply engaged" in hostilities.

This was too much for Drought. "There seems to be a conspiracy," he complained to Lippmann, ". . . to entice Japan into actions which may be characterized as aggressive in order that advantage may be taken of public opinion to enter the war against Hitler through the back door of the Far East. I say that a conspiracy seems to exist because an accurate knowledge of Far Eastern conditions reveals no menace to the interests of the United States. On the contrary, our recent policy in the Far East has been aggressive. . . . It is a poor diplomacy that can find no solution but war; it is a wretched morality that forces a war with a disguised purpose."

In writing to Frank Walker some days later, Drought revealed that he now felt "like a rooster on a back fence crowing his head off." "The announcement that Vichy will fully collaborate with the Nazis," he declared, "offers a complete answer to the dullards at the State Department who pretended to wonder why Japan was taking over bases in Indochina."

"I noticed yesterday," Drought informed Walker, "that Jimmy Wadsworth had to use 'the yellow peril' scare to get a couple of votes for the extension of the draft of a land army."*

And yet, our respected President says that we (you and I) were mistaken; the truth is that he has been very badly misled. Yesterday's Congressional vote indicates as clearly as anything could that the President will find it difficult, if not impossible, to obtain a supporting public opinion in favor of intervention in Europe.†

Those who want intervention badly enough are now trying to effect it through the back door of the Far East—realizing that the American people largely have soured on the whole European situation.

Roosevelt "ought to have known," Drought argued, that his Far Eastern policy was "completely wrong" when Senator Burton K. Wheeler of

---

* James W. Wadsworth, a Republican Congressman from New York, had received a standing ovation in the House after a speech in support of the bill in question. He did not use the phrase "yellow peril," but he did say that the vital interests of the United States were being threatened not only by developments in Europe but also by Japanese actions in the Far East.

† Drought was referring here to the nip-and-tuck vote, 203 to 202, by which the House passed an Administration-supported bill that extended the term of service required of men who had been called to the colors.

Montana, an isolationist opponent, "announced that he agreed with it!" The "smell of that agreement" should have reached even the White House.*

"If the President has a spare moment," Drought added, "maybe he would like to read this letter. (I intend that remark quite respectfully.)"

Respectful or not, Drought was being very shortsighted. Only a week earlier, on August 6, Nomura had handed a formula to Hull that totally ignored the President's Neutralization Proposal with regard to Indochina and Thailand. This formula asked the United States Government, *inter alia*, to remove the restrictions it had imposed upon trade and to suspend its "military measures" in the southwestern Pacific. Tokyo also asked for American good offices to initiate direct negotiations between Japan and "the Chiang Kai-shek regime" (it being understood that the United States would in the meantime refrain from sending any aid to the Nationalist Government and the Chinese people).

In return, Japan was thinking of pulling her troops out of French Indochina on a "contingency" basis, but there would be no withdrawal until after a settlement had been reached between Japan and China. Even this very limited concession would become operative only if the United States agreed to pay further compensation: recognition of Japan's "special status" in Indochina following the proposed withdrawal of Japanese troops.

Other provisions were equally restricted in scope or were couched in terms that would have permitted Japan to decide later whether she wanted to abide by her formula or not. Confronted by such an approach to negotiation, the American Government was in an unenviable position.

Several days prior to the receipt of this formula, the President had left Washington ostensibly for a week-long fishing vacation off the New England coast. Actually his destination was Argentia, Newfoundland, where he was to rendezvous with Prime Minister Winston Churchill of Great Britain—a meeting "at sea" that would soon capture headlines as the Atlantic Conference.

Churchill believed that Japan might be discouraged from expanding into Southeast Asia if the President took the lead in issuing a stern warning to Tokyo concerning the consequences Japan would face if she proceeded on her present course. The President did not share Churchill's confidence that a warning would work, but it seemed worth a try. He therefore decided to have a talk with Nomura immediately upon returning to Washington.

* Wheeler had expressed his approval of the Executive Order freezing Japanese assets. "I think the President did the right thing," the Senator declared. "You may say for me that I agree with him—for the first time."

Roosevelt planned to tell the Ambassador that if Tokyo would undertake not to send any more troops into the southwestern Pacific, and would further undertake, "specifically and not contingently," to withdraw those already stationed in French Indochina, the United States Government—despite the general unacceptability of the Japanese formula (of August 6)—would nevertheless be willing to explore the possibilities inherent in the various proposals Japan had made.

The President also planned to tell Nomura that if Japan refused to consider this offer, and instead resorted to new military action, the United States Government would have to respond with various steps of its own, even though these steps might result in war between their two countries.

The President estimated that the net effect of adopting the course he had outlined would be to delay—for at least thirty days—any further act of aggression on the part of Japan that might result in armed conflict.

Churchill felt that if conversations were held with Japan on the basis developed at Argentia perhaps a war in the Pacific could be averted altogether. The Prime Minister realized that the State Department might try to soften the phraseology of the proposed warning to Japan when the President got back to Washington, but against this risk stood Roosevelt's promise to use "hard language."

As matters turned out, the Department did intervene. Upon seeing the declaration that FDR was planning to hand to the Japanese Ambassador, Hull found it to be "dangerously strong, and in need of toning down." He felt that a specific reference by the President to the possibility of war "might be misinterpreted in Japan and treated as a challenge."

Hull and his Far Eastern staff thereupon redrafted the declaration so that it would be far less explicit. Even so, they ended up with a text that still appeared "too provocative." They therefore decided to split the substance of the declaration into two "Oral Statements." One would consist of the diluted warning; the other would indicate the willingness of the United States to resume the Hull-Nomura conversations, which had been suspended at the end of July, following Japan's move into southern Indochina.

When Hull explained all this at the White House on Sunday morning, August 17, the President "readily agreed" to the changes that had been made. That afternoon he proceeded to read both "Oral Statements" to the Japanese Ambassador, to whom he then handed written texts for transmission to Tokyo. It is clear from Nomura's reports to his government, however, that the comparatively weak tone of the so-called warning to Japan, as well as Roosevelt's manner of presenting it—soft-pedaling as he went along—downgraded the President's declaration to the level of a diplomatically phrased admonition handed over for reference purposes in an atmosphere of cordiality.

The President was in such a good mood in fact, having enjoyed life at sea and his encounter with Churchill, that Nomura decided to reiterate an idea he had already laid before Secretary Hull, on instructions from Tokyo: might it not be possible for the responsible heads of the two governments, Roosevelt and Konoye, to meet at some halfway point in the Pacific—like Honolulu—with a view to discussing the means whereby an adjustment of relations between Japan and the United States could be achieved?

Nomura was emphatic in declaring that Konoye was so anxious to preserve amicable relations with the United States he would be disposed to meet Roosevelt midway, geographically speaking, to talk things out in a peaceful spirit.

The President's reaction to this proposal was sufficiently positive to cause Nomura to inform his government that Roosevelt appeared to be favorably inclined toward the idea but would prefer, for various reasons, to substitute Juneau, Alaska, for Honolulu.

This marked the beginning of a marathon diplomatic minuet of more than six weeks' duration—a prolonged effort by Japan to lead the United States toward a bilateral conference at the highest level of statesmanship. Despite the interest initially shown by the President, however, the Japanese Government soon discovered that it could not work out the necessary arrangements. This was largely because the State Department believed the Chief Executive should look before he leaped.

After months of inconclusive Hull-Nomura parleying, the Secretary and his staff wanted a prior agreement in principle on the major questions outstanding between the two nations before endorsing a top-level conference of the type desired by Konoye.

Nomura had warned Toyoda earlier in August that the American Government would not budge from the position it had taken unless Japan renounced the use of force. Without a change in Tokyo's policies, nothing could be accomplished. Nomura had suggested, however, that the Foreign Minister might be able to make use of Ambassador Grew to help sell the conference proposal to Washington.

When Toyoda acted on this advice (on August 18), he stressed to Grew the absolute necessity of not giving the impression that Japan was bowing to American pressure. He consequently suggested that the United States either should terminate the various economic measures she had already invoked or should at least greatly moderate them.

Several days later, Nomura told Hull that the Japanese Government hoped the President would meet with Konoye as soon as possible. Tokyo had learned, the Ambassador said, that "military and other conferences" were to be held in Moscow in the near future; decisions might be reached there that would be detrimental to Japan.*

Hull replied that the Soviet-Japanese Neutrality Pact concluded by Matsuoka in April "would undoubtedly give all of the assurance of Russia's peaceful attitude towards Japan" that Japan could conceivably desire. "I made no promises of any kind," Hull noted after Nomura had left, "in regard to a meeting of responsible heads of the American and Japanese Governments or when it would be held, if it should be held at all."

As August began drawing to a close, American support for the Soviet Union seemed to be developing in ways that would further irritate Japanese-American relations. Ambassador Grew was informed that Foreign Minister Toyoda was "much disturbed" by the strong feelings of resentment with which certain elements in Japan were reacting to the anticipated passage, "through waters contiguous to Japan," of American tankers bound for Vladivostok with supplies of oil that "might be employed against Japan." Nomura had been instructed, Grew was told, "urgently to request" that these tankers be recalled pending a decision on the proposed Konoye-Roosevelt meeting.

In carrying out his instructions on August 27, the Japanese Ambassador encountered a very caustic Secretary of State. Hull was annoyed that a government with a record of aggression in the Far East as long and varied as the one Tokyo had compiled could make such a "fuss" over this matter.

"Intentional provocation of Japan!" yelled the Japanese press.

"A mountain out of a molehill," said Hull.

There were only two tankers en route to Vladivostok. The amount of oil they could deliver to the Russians was "microscopic"—perhaps 200,000 barrels—compared with "the hundred million barrels and more" that Japan had imported from the United States during the preceding four years.

"I . . . inquired of the Ambassador," Hull later wrote, "just what they wanted us to do, whether in fact they were asking us to turn the ships squarely around and sail them back to the United States, and I proceeded to answer for him by saying that would be preposterous."

---

* Washington was planning to send a mission to the Kremlin to determine Soviet defense needs and to make various Lend-Lease arrangements. The British were going to dispatch a mission of their own at the same time.

The "temperature" of Japanese-American relations had suddenly become uncomfortable, and yet it was on this very day that Nomura gave Hull a copy of a "Message" from Konoye to Roosevelt, which the Ambassador wished to deliver to the White House at the earliest opportunity. Nomura was also under orders to hand over a "Statement" from the Japanese Government replying to the various points the President had made during his meeting with the Ambassador on August 17.

Hull found the Konoye "Message" to be a clear expression of the idea that the proposed Konoye-Roosevelt meeting should be held as quickly as possible, and that negotiations for an agreement should follow rather than precede the Honolulu conference. Konoye was afraid that "unforeseen contingencies" might otherwise arise.

"In the second communication," Hull wrote, ". . . the Japanese Government assured us of its peaceful intentions and of its search for a program for the Pacific consistent with American principles." There were several qualifications, however, amounting to sleights of tongue that time and again transformed the promises made by Tokyo into a frustrating combination of meaningless words: "Japan would withdraw her troops from Indochina 'as soon as the China Incident [had been] settled or a just peace . . . established in East Asia.' Japan would take no military action against Russia so long as Russia observed the Neutrality Pact and did 'not menace Japan or Manchukuo.' Japan had no intention of using 'without provocation' military force against any neighboring country."

The Ambassador indicated to Hull that this new "Statement" represented the maximum in concessions the Japanese Government was currently in a position to make.

Twenty-four hours later, on August 28, notwithstanding the emphasis Tokyo had consistently placed on the need for secrecy, a smiling, jovial Nomura—upon leaving the White House—told members of the press that he had just delivered a "Message" from Prince Konoye to the President! Although the Ambassador stopped short of revealing the contents, it was "generally assumed," the *New York Times* reported, that Konoye's "Message" was conciliatory in tone and was meant to indicate that Japan was ready to modify her aims in the Orient.

The authorities in Tokyo were dismayed when they learned what Nomura had done. They did not want Konoye's overture to become a matter of public knowledge, but now the news spread quickly throughout Japan.

Why had Nomura destroyed the secrecy his government wished to maintain? Certain evidence—largely circumstantial—suggests that the Ambassador may have seen method where others saw madness.

Having been left high and dry by the sudden departure for Japan of Iwakuro and Wikawa, Nomura had called upon Drought for help. Hurrying to Washington from Maryknoll, Drought had arrived in the capital in mid-August. After a quick trip back to Maryknoll, he had settled into the Hotel 2400, remaining there until nearly the end of the month. He had thus been very much on hand during the eleven-day period (August 17–28) when Roosevelt and Hull were being asked to respond promptly to Konoye's proposal for a leaders' conference.

In a "Strictly Confidential" memorandum written as though he could speak for Nomura's superiors in Tokyo, Drought had told the Ambassador what he should say, on behalf of his government, in response to the position taken by the President following his return from Argentina. Drought had offered the most positive of assurances, insisting that Japan "would be proud to make sacrifices" for a "lasting and extensive peace in the Pacific." He had let his imagination run wild:

> The Government of Japan, with lively appreciation, endorses as its own, without qualification, the cogent "program attainable by peaceful methods" [outlined by the President on August 17].... The Government of Japan prefers a policy of cooperation and desires to sincerely respond to the cordial, penetrating proposals of the President...and the Secretary of State by the rapid conclusion of our informally negotiated, and almost completed, Understanding. The meeting [at Honolulu] of the responsible heads of our respective Governments would confirm and give such sanction to our purposes that peace in the Pacific would be instituted with the date of that meeting. It is with great goodwill that the Government of Japan anticipates the complete resumption of the historic friendship with the United States.... In an atmosphere of world crisis and international confusion, [however,] it is difficult to ascertain whether an event is a cause or a consequence.... With admirable modesty of mind, the Government of the United States has seemed, frequently, unaware that its words of policy are weighted with the immense power of America's natural endowment and potential might. The President of the United States, and the Secretary of State, in their own unquestioning adherence to the ways of peaceful procedures, might find it difficult to believe that other nationals, anywhere, could consider themselves threatened by the United States.

Nomura had cabled the text of the "Strictly Confidential" memorandum to Tokyo, but he had not revealed that Drought was the author of the piece. Since the authorities in the Foreign Office thought they were dealing with a memorandum prepared by the Embassy in Washington, they made use of Drought's concoction in formulating their own reply to the President.

This was extraordinary enough, but the full reality was even more fantastic. When Nomura went to the White House on August 28, he delivered documents that did not accurately convey what the Japanese Government wished to say to the American Government. This can be explained, in part, by the inability of the Embassy to resolve certain complexities of language in the Japanese texts that Nomura had received from Tokyo. There is, however, another reason why the Ambassador failed to pass along what his government wanted him to hand over: the translations he took to the White House contained revisions made by Drought without reference to the Japanese originals from which the translations had been made.

It was not until a week after these documents were left with Hull and the President that Nomura even bothered to tell Tokyo *he* had considered it "proper" to make a number of changes. In forwarding copies of what he had actually given to the American Government, however, Nomura transmitted only the amended English translations, thus making it difficult for the Foreign Office to pinpoint the changes or to evaluate their significance.

Upon emerging from his meeting with Roosevelt on August 28, Nomura may have decided to confide in the press because Father Drought had in the meantime advised him to take his case "to the people." This was a form of pressure John Doe had advocated in the past. During his visit to Japan in December 1940, for instance, Drought had put the matter squarely to Matsuoka and others: "If the United States Government refuses to move . . . toward an Understanding, we could then reveal our proposed Agenda [for a plenipotentiary conference] to the American Press and thereby embarrass the American Government and weaken proportionately the fast-growing American sentiment that war with Japan may prove inevitable."

Several months later Drought had repeated much the same thought while defending the section of his "Preliminary Draft of 'Agreement in Principle' " entitled "Rules for Nations."

"If you really push the acceptance of these 'Rules,' " Drought had written for Colonel Iwakuro's benefit, "and the Americans refuse to accept them, you will have established a most excellent bargaining position; the Americans have preached these things for years but they have never applied them to Japan and if they refused to do so now you could very calmly, but clearly, indicate that you might give them to the Press. If these 'Rules,' etc., were published in the American Press, and it was told that the Americans refused to accept them, the American State Department would be excoriated, and so would the President of the United States."

By the end of May Drought had become so annoyed by the Department's handling of the "negotiations" that he had advocated making "the facts" known to Roosevelt "and then to the Press."

Drought's assumption that the hand of the American Government could be forced through selective revelations to the news media may thus be one of the clues needed to explain why Nomura violated the secrecy his government had steadily insisted on maintaining throughout the conversations with the United States. In any event, upon coming out of the White House on August 28, the Ambassador—in the idiom that best describes the scene—publicly "spilled the beans."

When Hull emerged fifteen minutes later, he played his part impeccably. In response to a question concerning the nature of the message delivered by Nomura, Hull said "he thought he should leave that for the Ambassador to handle with the press as his Government desired it to be handled," for "he had not conferred with [the Ambassador] on that point." When the reporters still tried to find out exactly what the Premier's communication contained, Hull terminated the interview by insisting once again that this was a matter between the newsmen and Nomura.

"It seems ironical," Grew later commented in his diary, "that while our ... Government was doing everything possible to avoid such publicity, Japan's own Ambassador ... informed the press that he had delivered a ... message to the President from Prince Konoye, which of course simply poured fuel on the extremist fires here. At first the Japanese Government assumed that this information ... had been given out by the White House or the State Department, and when I sent to the Foreign Minister via Terasaki [the chief of the American Bureau of the Foreign Office] Mr. Hull's statement in press conference, to the effect that this was a matter lying exclusively between Admiral Nomura and the press, underlining in red the pertinent passages, there was consternation and chagrin. Terasaki, being slippery as an eel, at first tried to bluff it out and to assume that Mr. Hull had released the information at the same time as Nomura, but I became so angry that he quickly climbed down from that perch and acknowledged that when he had conveyed my information to Admiral Toyoda, the Minister was appalled at the *faux pas* of their own Ambassador. I asked if they had not enjoined secrecy on him, and they said that they had. . . . If Prince Konoye should be assassinated, it would surely be Nomura who had signed his death warrant."

*

Reportorial appetites having been whetted by the Nomura announcement, newsmen immediately began craving a more substantial meal. It took Wilfrid Fleisher, who was now covering the Washington scene, only a few days to assemble quite a feast. In an article in the *New York Her-*

ald Tribune, Fleisher scooped his colleagues by revealing that even before Konoye's "Message" was delivered to the White House the Premier of Japan had proposed to the President "that they meet aboard a Japanese warship somewhere in the Pacific for a personal discussion of Japanese-American relations in an attempt to reach a settlement."

At a press conference the next day, Stephen Early, speaking for the "Boss," scoffed at the idea:

The President has no invitation.

If the *Herald Tribune* had seen fit to check with the White House before publication of the story, I would have told them that.

The only plan the President has, involving a trip on the water in the immediate future, is a cruise from Annapolis on Chesapeake Bay and on the Potomac River. If the *Herald Tribune* cares to follow the President to Annapolis, they will readily see the falsity of this story.

In answer to a question put to him by a reporter, Early said he did not believe that anyone would be able to spot the Premier of Japan sailing up the Bay to greet the President!

The Fleisher report "stirred intense interest in the capital," but diplomatic circles quickly noted that a high-seas conference between Roosevelt and Konoye, especially one held on board a Japanese warship, was "improbable." Secretary Hull was noncommittal. He simply repeated what he had been saying all along: there was nothing new to report in the discussions between the two countries. The Japanese Embassy in Washington declared that it had "no information." Thousands of miles away, in Tokyo, His Imperial Majesty's Government belittled Fleisher's account. A spokesman said "he had no knowledge of another 'meeting at sea' involving Mr. Roosevelt."

Despite these denials, the idea that a mutual desire for peace was fathering thoughts of "constructive conciliation" did not seem far-fetched. What was actually occurring, however, was something else again, and much less encouraging than any of the optimistic guesses being bandied about in print.

Beside a photograph of an ebullient Nomura emerging from the White House on August 28, the *New York Times* ran a picture of a different sort: Japanese soldiers passing through Saigon on their way to an undisclosed destination in French Indochina, advancing the cause of Dai Nippon while riding side by side on that extraordinarily useful but nevertheless incongruous means of military transportation, the unpretentious bicycle.

The *Herald Tribune* also paired the news of Konoye's overture to Roosevelt with a graphic reference to what was currently taking place in the Far East: a revealing shot of Japanese troop transports tied up alongside the docks of Saigon to disembark the men who would occupy the bases in Indochina that Japan had obtained under an "agreement" with Vichy.

In an editorial that same day—read and clipped by Father Drought— the *Herald Tribune* declared that the talks being held with Japan should consist primarily of "polite but insistent reminders" of certain facts. Tokyo should be told that the damage done to the independence, integrity, and commercial opportunities of China "must be undone," that the Japanese program of imperial expansion southward "must be abandoned," and that "Japan's spiritual entente with the recrudescence of barbarism in Europe must be renounced."

Although Grew had thought that Konoye might come to harm as a result of Nomura's action at the White House, newspapers in Japan were currently praising the Premier for having launched a "final" diplomatic offensive. They were in favor of avoiding war with the United States and Britain, if this could be done "with honor." But at the same time, they did not want their government to make any concessions that might threaten Japan's position as the dominant power in the Far East.

This could only mean that the United States would have to back down, since anything short of an American acceptance of the "New Order" in East Asia would be interpreted by Japanese nationalists as harmful to the dignity of the armed services and destructive of the prestige of His Majesty's Empire.

"It would be the height of folly," Colonel Hayao Mabuchi, the chief of the Army Press Section of Imperial General Headquarters, was quoted as saying, "to look on with folded arms while the forces bent on defeating [Japan] are at work. The situation will compel us to stake all to save ourselves as a nation."

A few days later, Konoye called for a total mobilization of the nation's resources. Other Japanese—more "positive-minded" than the Premier—were urging the establishment of a "safety zone" around Japan, a zone in which the armed services would be required to interdict American oil shipments to Vladivostok.

In an editorial reaction to the news from the Far East, the *New York Times* declared: "We do not want to fight Japan. We do not want to waste in the Pacific weapons and ammunition that ought to go to the more important battlefield in the Atlantic. But we will fight if Japan pushes us too far. . . . We have reached a point at which we are no longer willing to buy off Japan from new excursions at the price of helping her to finish up old ones. . . . Our position in the whole Pacific area is stronger than it was a year ago. Our eyes are better, too. We can see now that it is wiser to show our strength than to pretend that we are helpless."

Several days later, new evidence appeared concerning the mood prevailing in Japan. The government had moved in the direction of placing the country on a full wartime footing by invoking a law that gave it control over the principal industries of the nation. The Finance Ministry was about to examine a proposal to establish a corporation that would facilitate the flow of goods needed for wartime production. The Agriculture and Forestry Ministry had announced that all essential foodstuffs would henceforth come under state jurisdiction.

Meanwhile, behind the scenes and in the utmost secrecy, the Japanese Navy was getting ready to test Admiral Isoroku Yamamoto's plan to attack Pearl Harbor in case Japan decided on war with the United States.

*

With an atmosphere of crisis enveloping the Japanese homeland, it is hardly surprising that Iwakuro and Wikawa, who had arrived at Yokohama on board the *Tatsuta-maru* in mid-August, should have found themselves unable to make much headway in reporting privately on conditions in the United States.

All segments of the ruling elite were reached, especially by the Colonel. Premier Konoye and the Emperor's closest advisers were interested in Iwakuro's views, but he did not get very far with officers of rank in the Army and the Navy. They seemed impervious when he tried to tell them that the United States excelled Japan in material resources and industrial strength. Practically the only officer who was willing to listen was the chief of the Military Affairs Bureau of the War Ministry, General Mutō, under whom Iwakuro had served prior to his tour of duty in Washington.

Even at the Foreign Office, where a more searching inquiry into the American "problem" might have been expected, Iwakuro found aimlessness and lack of confidence in the very officials, including Foreign Minister Toyoda, who should have been developing new policy positions. Talking with them was like trying "to plow furrows in a field of sand"— an impression made one moment disappeared the next because the grains all ran together.

Iwakuro was warned on several occasions that he should be "careful." People were saying that he had been "pro-German" when he went to the United States, but that he had come back "pro-American."

When the Colonel suddenly received orders placing him in command of the Fifth Infantry Regiment of the Imperial Guards Division stationed in Indochina, he judged that he had outlived his usefulness in terms of playing any further role in Japanese-American relations.

At Tokyo Station on the day of his departure, scores of friends and acquaintances gathered for the second time within six months to bid him farewell. While waiting for his train to leave, Iwakuro had a premonition that if he should ever return home he would probably find himself standing on the same spot, surrounded by the rubble of burnt-out ruins, with not a soul on hand to greet him—a premonition that proved remarkably accurate four years later, when he at length reached the end of the line in Tokyo from what had been the fighting front in Burma.

*

Although the posting of Colonel Iwakuro to Indochina inevitably drained strength away from the John Doe Associates, James Drought and Tadao Wikawa were not without resources. Bishop Walsh, who was still "working for religion," had recently settled down in western Japan —writing, resting, and "waiting." In between visitation duties in the Kyoto area, he had been enjoying the delights afforded by a Maryknoll retreat on the shores of Lake Biwa, especially the opportunity to swim every day and to read some Dickens. Suddenly, much to his surprise, a "health recovered" cable had arrived from Drought. To the Bishop's even greater surprise, Wikawa had appeared on the scene almost immediately thereafter.

Hopes and plans had filled the day, as can be seen from a radiogram that Walsh promptly sent to Frank Walker at the Wardman Park Hotel: "Paul approached me with his Boss's request asking you urge your Boss for immediate response to new proposal leaving details to further discussion after personal talk which his Boss feels certain will be very satisfactory to your Boss. Time counts, humanity waits, God blesses."*

Walsh had learned from Wikawa "that the peace proposals had encountered difficulties but that there was still some hope of a successful termination." Wikawa had asked the Bishop to lend his assistance "in continuing the negotiations, particularly in the matter of helping to get messages to and from the State Department in Washington and to and from the American Embassy in Tokyo."

After giving the matter some thought, Walsh had replied that he would cooperate to the extent he considered proper, if Ambassador

* Walsh was saying that Wikawa had come to him with a request from Premier Konoye asking Walker to urge the President to reply immediately to the Premier's desire for a meeting at Honolulu to work out a settlement.

Grew had no objections. Consultation at the Embassy subsequently produced the permission Walsh had stipulated, and so he undertook "to perform this little function of helping to transmit information" whenever the need arose.

During the weeks that followed, Walsh stayed first at the Fujiya in Miyanoshita, near Lake Hakone, and then at a beach hotel in Kamakura on the shores of Tokyo Bay. From time to time he was joined by Wikawa, who would convey news intended either for the American Embassy in Tokyo or for the State Department in Washington.

Both Miyanoshita and Kamakura were recreation areas of considerable charm and beauty, far enough removed from the capital to provide a holiday atmosphere and yet easily accessible by rail within a few hours or less. "If a man were to make a practice of spending his vacations in these resort hotels," the Bishop noted in his "line-a-day" diary, "he could hardly help meeting all the princes, barons, elder and younger statesmen, and business tycoons in the land."

Because of police surveillance and government censorship, Walsh knew he would have to be careful in transmitting the information Wikawa obtained "from higher up." As a result, the Bishop occasionally used Biblical references or other cover words that were supposed to conceal but not destroy meaning. This goal was sometimes hard to achieve in practice, as can be seen from a radiogram that reached Frank Walker at the Wardman Park Hotel on August 28, the day on which Nomura delivered Konoye's "Message" at the White House: "Trust you realize latest proposal straight from horse's mouth, including Gog and Magog, Tyre and Sidon. Carries utmost pledge. No power can give more and surely no wise architect can expect more. Kindly convey every regard [to] your esteemed colleague in which Paul joins explicitly. Walsh."*

During the next few days, messages passed back and forth in rapid succession:

Walsh to Drought, August 29: "Satisfactory issue guaranteed on all mutually known vital points but impossible clarify all details without [Konoye-Roosevelt] meeting. Need prompt answer. Last call for dinner otherwise die is cast. Please urge haste, vision, and divine charity."

Walsh to Hull, August 29: "Conversations here assured me success of the Message's idea [the proposed meeting between Konoye and Roosevelt], if carried out promptly, miraculously solving all pending prob-

---

* The Old Testament refers to two mythical kings, Gog and Magog, who failed in their attempt to conquer the people of God (Israel). The ancient cities of Tyre and Sidon, which were near the Holy Land, were often cited by Jesus as the embodiment of paganism. "Your esteemed colleague" means Secretary Hull—not the President.

lems. Your immediate cooperation urgently requested for humanity's sake. With highest regards of Colonel and Paul."

Drought to Walsh, August 29: "Everyone happy and satisfied. I expect [to] see Paul soon. Delirious congratulations. Psalm one one seven Verse twenty-four."*

Walsh to Drought, August 31: "What is true state [of affairs]? When [do] you expect [to] see Paul? Congratulations on what? Official information indicates continue circumlocution office, nothing about rendezvous. Meanwhile we die by inches as long-suffering patient expires. Beg some definite word."†

Three days later, on September 3, Walsh sent Walker a warning that he immediately passed along to Secretary Hull: "Only possibility of success left have resumption talk simultaneous with Message's objective. Latter is imperative account necessity handling vital items firsthand. Also time element anguishingly crucial. Don't you realize proposed move only way unify domestic elements, nullify counteraction, [and] commit [our Japanese] friends [to the] broad path desired?"‡

On the day this telegram was dispatched, Wikawa persuaded Walsh to leave Miyanoshita for the "safer" surroundings of Kamakura. According to Wikawa, certain extremists might make trouble for them if they remained where they were. Walsh understood this to be a reference "to the militaristic and pro-Nazi elements in the Government or the Army or both." Walsh later distinctly recalled that Wikawa had said on this occasion that General Mutō himself was protecting their activities and would continue to do so to the best of his ability. Wikawa had also said, however, that it was not possible to provide safeguards against every eventuality.

Although Walsh had no direct contact with Mutō at this time, the Bishop subsequently expressed his conviction that he would not have been able to communicate so openly with Drought during the autumn of 1941, had it not been for the "active help" of this influential officer.

Censorship was then the rule in Japan rather than the exception; the danger from "foreign spies" had been drilled into the Japanese masses;

---

* "This is the day which the Lord hath made: let us be glad and rejoice therein."

† "Continue circumlocution office, nothing about rendezvous" signified that Walsh had been informed by Wikawa that the State Department was still "talking in circles" and had thus far avoided making any commitment with respect to the proposed conference at Honolulu.

‡ Walsh was arguing that a settlement with Japan could be reached only if Washington agreed to a Konoye-Roosevelt meeting and to a simultaneous resumption of the Hull-Nomura conversations, which had been suspended in July. The Bishop did not know that the Secretary of State was already fully engaged, once again, in talking to the Japanese Ambassador.

and yet Walsh was able to send and receive messages with impunity. Perhaps he was right in believing that he would not have been able to do this without the protection of someone in a position of authority.

Far away, in the very different atmosphere of the United States, Father Drought believed that the John Doe effort for peace was moving into the homestretch. Choosing the right people to attend the Honolulu meeting, drawing up an agenda for the conferees, and taking care of the publicity "angle" were all matters that occupied Drought's attention at this time. "After [Konoye-Roosevelt] meeting arranged," he wrote, "still so much to be done that [the Japanese] can not do—that it is better to be quiet now. They will commit themselves without [our] doing anything. So big—must expect jockeying. Give them [their] head. . . . Coding group are Nazis. Everything directly to Roosevelt. . . . Keep me very far away—no mention to Hull. . . . Need of meeting soon—very important. . . . Reply form sent—doubtful if given over. [Konoye-Roosevelt] statement as prepared. . . . Importance of staying in—no matter what."

Hull and his Far Eastern advisers may have thought that the door had already been closed and bolted against further intrusions by the John Doe Associates, but Father Drought was not a man who could easily be locked out. The departure of Iwakuro and Wikawa, followed by the return to Tokyo of Minister Wakasugi, had given Drought a new opportunity to influence Ambassador Nomura. The reunion in Japan of the ingenuous Walsh and the clever Wikawa also meant that Drought would come to the fore once again.

While time counted and humanity waited, the Japanese and American governments remained mired in the same impasse that had immobilized them for months on end. Amid talk of peace, sounds of war could be heard rumbling in the background, forecasting the disaster that would engulf the Pacific if diplomacy failed to provide a solution acceptable to the nations concerned. Although the decision-makers on both sides knew that the situation was far more critical now than ever before, they did not realize that their long-standing attempt to resolve their differences—short of war—was being hopelessly compromised by the activities of a group of private individuals who firmly believed that they were exerting an influence for good rather than for ill.

With this erroneous conviction as their guiding light, the newly reconstituted John Doe Associates went marching, arm-in-arm, down the darkening road to Pearl Harbor.

CHAPTER NINETEEN

Hope of a Successful Issue Fades

E VEN IF ABSORBED only in snatches, the conversations in Washington and in Tokyo that sustained a waning hope, through August and September and into October, that a peaceful solution for the Pacific could yet be devised have the quality of grinding monotonously on and on and on, always in the same vein: arguments pro and con, assurances, denials, appeals to reason, warnings of approaching disaster, a neat turn of phrase, an awkward silence, nuances of language and of mood, and from beginning to end haunting questions relating to intentions, questions broad enough to last a lifetime of inquiry. One must explore the primary sources to obtain the full effect. To do so, however, is to suffer a feeling of vexation akin to the annoyance caused by a worn phonograph record endlessly repeating itself.

Far more significant than anything that was said during the official exchanges of this period is a critical fact that deserves a special place in the history of Japanese-American relations: the idea of convening a leaders' conference did not originate with Premier Konoye in August 1941, or with anyone else in the Japanese Government either then or earlier; the initiative seemingly taken by the Prince was not a dramatically new development capable of exciting an affirmative response within the State Department; the proposal for a Konoye-Roosevelt meeting in the Pacific was actually a stale suggestion left over from the Walsh-Drought visit to Japan in late 1940, a belatedly salvaged brainchild of none other than Father James M. Drought of Maryknoll, New York. It was an idea Drought had personally spanked into life—a scheme that he had subsequently fostered in Washington throughout early 1941 until the Japanese Government had suddenly turned its back on the proposition in mid-May, at a time when Tokyo thought (quite incorrectly) that it was dealing with a "Draft Understanding" officially put forward by Secretary Hull, acting on behalf of the President of the United States!

It was only when Japan's move into southern Indochina in July had brought Japanese-American relations to the brink of disaster that Konoye suddenly resurrected the very proposal the Japanese Government itself had earlier disdained—a mid-Pacific conference with Roosevelt.

The Premier was sanguine about the chances of obtaining a favorable response from Washington, because the idea of holding a leaders' conference had been part of the "original Draft Understanding"—a document that Konoye regarded as an official proposal to Japan from the United States Government (why shouldn't the President agree in August to a meeting the Americans had suggested in April?).

Hull and his advisers, however, knew that the Honolulu conference idea had been one of the main features of the private proposal for peace that had been brought to their attention in the spring by several American and Japanese individuals who claimed to be acting on behalf of influential interests in Japan. No one at the State Department could consequently see any reason to become excited now over a proposition from Tokyo that the Japanese Government itself had eliminated from consideration earlier in the year, just as the Hull-Nomura conversations were getting under way.

Stanley Hornbeck, for one, remained sharply critical of "the mettle of Japan's diplomacy." He was bothered by the "great solicitude for the Japanese point of view" that Ambassador Grew seemed suddenly to be exhibiting in his telegrams to Washington. Hornbeck was also far from pleased with the tendency of the Far Eastern Division to take the position that a certain action on the part of the United States might "cause Japan to become more aggressive and that, therefore, the said action should *not* be taken."

In Hornbeck's view Japan was "already more than half beaten." She was not in a position to attack the Russians, the British, the Dutch, or the Americans with any expectation of success. The eagerness with which "one element" was seeking a meeting with Roosevelt was an indication of weakness. There was political confusion in Japan; the leaders of the country were bickering among themselves; they were "uncertain and fearful." "Although we should take no unfair advantage," Hornbeck wrote, "we have everything to gain and little or nothing to lose by standing firm on our principles and our policies."

Hornbeck did not want the American Government to do anything that would give "a terrific jolt" to the Chinese, the British, the Dutch, or the Russians—the people who were holding the line against the Axis powers. He felt that the President should refrain from any commitment to confer with Konoye until a "meeting of the minds" had been reached by the two governments at a lower level of negotiation.

The views held by Joseph Ballantine ran parallel to those expressed by Hornbeck. Ballantine believed Tokyo would seek a settlement "couched in general terms," thus leaving the application of those terms "wide open." The Japanese would call for "speedy action"; they would claim that only in this way could the danger be averted of having their government fall into the hands of the "extremists." The Japanese would probably also want to limit points of agreement to broad questions, thus postponing the disposition of specific details to some other occasion. "It will be recalled," Ballantine noted, "that these are the very tactics which the Japanese Government has employed with the proposals for an understanding which were presented to our Government last spring." Ballantine consequently echoed Hornbeck's conclusion that a meeting of minds between the two governments was an essential first step toward a Konoye-Roosevelt conference.

Even Maxwell Hamilton, who generally seemed inclined to give Japan the benefit of the doubt, was unable to offer any encouragement to the Secretary of State.

The President himself had some doubts. Although he had complimented "the tone and spirit" of Konoye's personal "Message," Roosevelt had asked Nomura, on August 28, whether Japan might use the occasion of a mid-Pacific conference to move into Thailand, just as she had gone into French Indochina in July while the Hull-Nomura conversations were in progress.

In subsequently talking with Nomura about the proposal, Hull had emphasized the desirability of reaching *a prior agreement in principle* concerning the main questions at issue between the two nations—a clear reflection of the advice the Secretary had received from Hornbeck and Ballantine.

Less than a week later, on September 3, the President handed Nomura the text of an "Oral Statement" replying to the communication from the Japanese Government that had accompanied the Konoye "Message." The Four Principles Hull had enunciated to Nomura in April, at the very outset of the conversations, were now repeated word for word, the Japanese Ambassador being told once again "that only upon the basis of these principles could an agreement be reached which would be effective in establishing stability and peace in the Pacific area."

Since Nomura had assured Tokyo in the spring that he had talked the American Government into shelving these abstractions while negotiations proceeded on concrete issues, one can well imagine the impact the Four Principles now had upon Japan's leaders as they very belatedly learned from the President's "Oral Statement" of September 3 that Hull's formulation—far from being pigeonholed at all—was still regarded by Roosevelt as "the foundation upon which all relations between nations should properly rest."

Both in the "Oral Statement" and in a separate reply to Konoye's "Message" handed to Nomura at the same time, the President revealed that the American Government wanted a clearer expression of Japan's position than had yet been received. He emphasized that a prior meeting of minds on basic principles was a necessary condition precedent to the conclusion of a Japanese-American "Understanding." Otherwise, he would not participate in a conference with Konoye.

And yet the President made it equally clear that the American Government desired to collaborate with Japan in working out a constructive solution. He even reminded Konoye that Tokyo had made the following declaration: "The Japanese Government wishes to state that it considers these principles and the practical application thereof, in the friendliest manner possible, are the prime requisites of a true peace and should be applied not only in the Pacific area but throughout the entire world. Such a program has long been desired and sought by Japan itself."

One can only wonder what the President and the Secretary of State might have thought if they had somehow discovered that this declaration from Tokyo owed much of its inspiration to assurances of a similar nature written by Drought—assurances Nomura had forwarded to his government without revealing that Drought was involved.

Surely Roosevelt and Hull would have had reason to question the worth of this declaration (and of other "promises") if they had known that Nomura had failed to convey, word for word, what the Japanese Government wanted him to say—a failure that can be attributed, at least in part, to further meddling by Drought.

Only occasionally did some disturbing sign appear—a vague indication of problems not clearly perceived but known to exist—as when Nomura gave Hull a new draft of proposals on September 4 and then suddenly withdrew the document from consideration because it had been submitted without the knowledge of the Japanese Government. In this instance, as in some others, Nomura's action caused a variety of unnecessary and time-consuming difficulties—a frustrating jumble of crossed wires.

Who could possibly have seen in any of this the hand of James Drought?

No one really—at least no one who did not have Nomura and Drought under constant surveillance.

And yet the unauthorized proposals submitted by the Japanese Ambassador on September 4 were simply a revised version of the earlier "Draft Understanding" that the John Doe Associates had persistently tried to persuade the two governments to use as a basis for an agreement.

In Tokyo on this same day, September 4, Toyoda was handing Grew an entirely different proposition, one that set forth, provisionally, a number of reciprocal undertakings designed to serve as a basis for discussion when the President and the Premier met with each other in the Pacific.

Toyoda urgently requested that the document in question, which represented the latest thinking of the Japanese Government with regard to a settlement, be conveyed to Washington in the Ambassador's "most secret code." The proposal had already been cabled to Nomura, the Foreign Minister said, but he hoped the American Embassy would also transmit the text. This was "to obviate any possibility of inaccuracy which he feared might arise through [a] misunderstanding of the English language."

Forty-eight hours later, on Saturday, September 6 (the day on which an Imperial Conference in Tokyo established an early-October deadline for a decision in favor of war or peace), Nomura gave the Secretary of State a copy of the Toyoda proposal, which Hull had already received from Grew. Hull promised that he and his staff would study the document over the weekend. He was anxious, he said, to proceed as rapidly as possible in this matter.

So, too, was Prince Konoye, for that very evening he finally adopted a course of action he had earlier avoided. He had previously refrained from playing a direct role in international affairs, refusing even to receive any members of the diplomatic corps while he was Acting Foreign Minister during Matsuoka's junket to Europe in the spring. Now the Premier was suddenly entertaining the American Ambassador at dinner, exercising great care to ensure that their three-hour meeting would remain secret. In subsequently reporting to Washington what occurred on this extraordinary occasion, Grew put the most important point first— *as he had understood it*: "Prince Konoye, and consequently the Government of Japan, conclusively and wholeheartedly agree with the Four

Principles enunciated by the Secretary of State as a basis for the rehabilitation of relations between the United States and Japan."

The theme that ran through Konoye's entire presentation was that a way could be found to a rapprochement if only the will to seek it were present. Hull and his advisers, however, did not believe that the situation warranted nearly so much optimism as the Premier of Japan—and the American Ambassador—were projecting. Konoye's affirmation of adherence to Hull's Four Principles looked to the State Department like an attempt to make the Premier's other proposals "more palatable." The program of reciprocal undertakings that Toyoda was currently sponsoring remained disappointing.

There was also another problem. The parleying with Japan now entered a phase in which the Foreign Minister adopted a new procedure that did not always work out well in practice. He would hand a copy of this or that proposal to Grew for transmission to Washington, and at the same time would cable the text to Nomura with instructions to deliver the document in question to the Secretary of State. "Owing to the necessity for paraphrasing in both cases," Hull later wrote, "we in Washington found ourselves scrutinizing documents that were intended to be identical but contained serious differences of words and phrases."

An example of this occurred early in September, when Nomura handed Hull a "Draft Proposal" containing the following guarantee: "Japan will not make any military advancement from French Indochina against any of its adjoining areas, and likewise will not, without any justifiable reason, resort to military action against any regions lying south of Japan."

When this sentence was compared with the corresponding one in the text Grew had received from Toyoda, the State Department found a curious discrepancy. The wording in the Grew copy, though substantially the same with regard to the disclaimer involving areas adjoining Indochina, nevertheless ended on an entirely different note by declaring that the Japanese Government would not resort to military action against any regions lying to the *north* of Japan.

Which version was correct? Hull and his advisers sought clarification, but the replies they received from members of the Japanese Embassy seemed to be personal opinions rather than authoritative answers.

Only now, many years later, when the point is purely academic, is it possible to learn from reading the Japanese original that the guarantee delivered by Nomura was inaccurate. Tokyo had offered an undertaking that covered not only the areas adjoining French Indochina, but also the Far Eastern territories of the Soviet Union. In the document given to Hull by Nomura, however, the scope of this undertaking was enormously reduced through the extraordinary substitution of one word for another: north in the original had been transformed into south in the translation.

Textual discrepancies of this magnitude were bad enough, but other factors—on both the Japanese side and the American side—must also be taken into account. Hull had been "conditioned" by the earlier statements of the John Doe Associates (and by the assurances contained in Konoye's "Message" to the President) to expect much more than Japan was currently offering. He now felt that the Japanese were presenting a far narrower program of settlement than before. Toyoda, on the other hand, argued that he and his colleagues were doing just the opposite; they were widening the basis of their commitments.

The Japanese Government believed that "a tentative agreement" had already been reached in Washington in regard to certain sections of the proposed "Understanding," including one that envisaged American "good offices" to settle the war in China, but the American Government thought Tokyo had turned its back on that particular idea.

The document Toyoda had given to Grew on September 4 differed in this respect from the unauthorized draft Nomura had delivered to Hull that same day; in addition, Toyoda's text departed in format from the standard introduced by the John Doe Associates in the spring— a standard that had subsequently been employed by the Japanese Government whenever it had sent proposals to the United States. The net result was further misunderstanding on each side.

Behind these difficulties in the conversations hovered a cloud of threatening developments in the Far East that looked exceedingly black.

Just prior to the delivery in Washington of Konoye's "Message" to the President, Grew had reported that "a psychology of desperation" was beginning to appear within Japan largely as a result of "the throttling effect on Japan's economy" of the freezing of assets. "In Japan," Grew had warned, "a psychology of despair leads characteristically to a do-or-die reaction."

Two days later Grew had reported that an extensive mobilization of men and materiel had recently taken place. Restrictions and prohibitions were increasing on all sides. Queues of people seeking the necessities of life were "a common sight on every street." The press was hammering home the theme of ABCD encirclement: the Americans, the British, the Chinese, and the Dutch were accused of endeavoring to limit Japan—like a dwarfed tree—to a potted-plant existence. Air raid shelters were being built, along with gun emplacements for anti-aircraft weapons; barrage balloons were appearing in the skies over Tokyo. To reassure the people, newspapers were making soothing claims: experience elsewhere showed that enemy planes seldom scored direct hits; casualties would therefore be light; there would be no need to evacuate the cities; indeed, it would be unpatriotic and cowardly to do so.

Grew had also reported on this occasion that Foreign Minister Toyoda was concerned over the effect in Japan of the disclosure in Washington that Konoye had sent a "Message" to Roosevelt. Toyoda was afraid it would now be impossible for the Premier to reach an understanding with the President unless the American Government proved amenable to taking certain steps that would alleviate the situation. Among the steps Toyoda had in mind was a suspension of the Executive Order that had led to the freezing of Japanese assets.

The bleakness of the outlook at this time may help to explain why Grew and Dooman, sitting in grandstand seats at the American Embassy in Tokyo, interpreted the proposal for a Konoye-Roosevelt meeting as an unparalleled opportunity to secure a settlement in the Far East.

Grew had assured Toyoda ("a sympathetic and very human type," who seemed more likable than any other Foreign Minister he had known) that he would personally support the proposal "in the interests of peace." In his initial telegrams to the State Department on the subject, the Ambassador had recommended that further economic measures against Japan be held in abeyance. He had urged "with all the force at his command" that "this Japanese proposal not be turned aside without very prayerful consideration." The good that might flow from a Konoye-Roosevelt meeting, he had declared, was "incalculable."

Having adopted this position, Grew never budged from it. He was aware of the "grave dangers" involved in embarking upon official negotiations prior to the establishment through preliminary talks of "an adequate and agreed basis," but he had by now reached a point where such considerations were no longer paramount in his thinking.

As September progressed, Grew advised the State Department that the Japanese Government was "becoming increasingly restive" over the approach of the anniversary of the signing of the Tripartite Pact. He cited Colonel Iwakuro and Tadao Wikawa as his authority for a warning that further delay "would gravely endanger the position of the Cabinet." He urged the Department to expedite its study of the available material so that an answer could be communicated to the Japanese Government within a matter of days.

The Ambassador realized that a Japanese-American settlement at this juncture might merely provide "a breathing spell" during which Japan would be able to "recoup and strengthen her forces" for further aggression "at the next favorable moment," but he was desperately trying to bring "constructive conciliation" into play. He admitted there was danger in whatever course the United States pursued, but he believed an opportunity now existed, through the medium of a Konoye-Roosevelt meeting, to halt the Japanese program of expansion. If this opportunity was missed, Grew warned, the American Government and people would have to face "the greatly increased risk of war."

The Ambassador wanted to build a permanent structure of peace in the Pacific on a secure foundation, and yet he felt there could be no compromise with the fundamental principles on which American policy was based. The methods of building that structure, however, should be flexible. If "constructive conciliation" failed, the United States could always fall back upon "progressive economic sanctions."

Perhaps Grew would have obtained more of a hearing for his views in Washington if he had recommended a specific course of action. In the absence of such a recommendation, however, the Hull-Nomura conversations continued to follow the same pattern as before. Explanations were requested and replies were given, but the participants did little more than repeat old positions with dull regularity.

The United States was not going to ask the Nationalist Government of China to accept, under diplomatic duress, terms that would bestow upon Japan the victory she had been unable to win by force of arms.

Japan was not going to offer a settlement to Chungking that would amount to an admission of defeat in China at the hands of Chiang Kai-shek and the various elements allied with him.

The American Government was told that the stationing of "required armed forces" (shoyō heiryoku) for "a necessary period" (shoyō kikan) in "certain prescribed areas" of China (ittei chiiki), even after the restoration of peace between Japan and China, was an "absolute necessity" (zettai hitsuyō) from the point of view of Japan.

Tokyo spoke of cooperating with the Chinese to restore peace and order on the mainland, but everyone knew that "cooperation" in this context meant the suppression of the Chinese Communists and other "dissident" groups. In addition, Tokyo claimed that Japan's security could be ensured only if the Japanese Army remained in China.

The Japanese Government went even further, ruling out an idea that might have kept alive the hope of arriving at a solution: "The stationing of international armed forces [in China for the purpose of maintaining peace in that country] is unacceptable [to the Japanese Government] because of public opinion in Japan and also because of the direct and vital bearing the internal conditions of China have upon Japan."

As the month of September began drawing to a close, the State Department received, first from Grew and then from Nomura, a document that Tokyo had prepared "for the convenience of the American Government." A study of this latest Japanese offering, which was a redraft of the American proposal of June 21, revealed that Japan was now backing away from some of the limited guarantees Tokyo had offered early in September.

"We have already said that we have said all that is to be said," a member of Nomura's staff now informed the Foreign Office. "To keep submitting notes after notes thereafter, which do not always run in sequence with the previous note, is not good, for it causes confusion and further delays. . . . For the past six months, we have been holding talks here [in Washington] during which the attitude and stand of the United States has been set down clearly. We feel confident that you are aware, through our various reports on the subject, that it is exceedingly unlikely that the United States has any intention of backing down from those established stands. We feel that there must be a tendency in Tokyo to view the United States statements too optimistically. It is imaginable to us that there are those who approach the Premier with a little too much 'wishful thinking.'"

*

While Toyoda, Nomura, and Grew had regularly been pressing the American Government to respond quickly and positively to Konoye's desire for a mid-Pacific conference with Roosevelt, John Doe and his friends had persistently been trying, behind the scenes, to encourage a favorable answer from Washington. Telegrams had passed back and forth between Walsh in Japan and Drought in the United States, and both Nomura and Drought had kept in touch with Frank Walker. He in turn had communicated to Secretary Hull various John Doe approaches designed to encourage the President to meet with the Premier of Japan without delay.

Soon after Grew had talked with Konoye over dinner on September 6, Walsh had sent several telegrams to Drought that were difficult to decipher. This was partly because of errors in transmission but mainly because of the codelike devices, including Biblical quotations, he employed as cover and concealment.

On September 11 Walsh had asked Drought, by telegram, to "wire back fixed dates as successful solution . . . can be expected only by [Konoye] Message objective for thousand reasons many insuperable as often explained." Walsh had learned from Wikawa that the American Government wanted the Japanese Government to be more precise in describing its position, but that Tokyo would not confide in Ambassador Grew ("Remember Topsy well") because "four winds of heaven pervade every encyclical thence": Grew's communications were not secure; his telegrams to Washington were being intercepted, decoded, translated, and read by the enemies of peace.

On September 13 Walsh and Wikawa had joined forces in a telegram to Walker that came to rest on Hull's desk: "World is too large to be microscoped by those who see only their own sphere of business. Kindly let your wide-visioned Boss and his chief adviser telescope whole situation from humanity's standpoint same as handled here. Key protagonists only. I make this last request as wasting time in details will soon ruin our cherished aim."*

A week later, just after Grew had urged Washington to reply speedily to the Konoye overture, the Bishop had again sought a specific commitment from Roosevelt and Hull with regard to the proposed meeting. "Have Joe [Grew] instructed," Walsh advised Drought, "[to] approach [the Japanese Government] with date leaving sacramentals for synod. Make sure latter include you and friend. . . . Disregard returning pastor pure face."†

During a brief visit to the American Embassy the next day, September 21, Walsh had passed along some news to Dooman that Grew had immediately repeated to Washington, citing as his source a contact in whom he had "complete confidence." The gist of the news was that the Konoye Cabinet had formulated the basic terms of a statement to be communicated to the American Government, that these terms had already been shown to the Emperor by the Foreign Minister, that a definitive text would soon be handed to Grew, that it would contain everything Japan could say in advance of the proposed Konoye-Roosevelt meeting, that "more could not be disclosed for fear of leakage of information," but

---

* "Your wide-visioned Boss and his chief adviser" meant Roosevelt and Hull. "Key protagonists only" signified a desire to have all decisions made by the highest authorities (thus sidetracking the members of Hull's Far Eastern team—Hornbeck, Hamilton, and Ballantine).

† The idea here, probably inspired by Wikawa, was to get the President to bring Drought and Walker to the "synod" with Konoye. "Returning pastor" is a reference to Minister Wakasugi, who had been summoned to Tokyo but who was now en route back to Washington.

that the Premier "would be prepared to present directly and personally to the President further clarification and definition of Japan's policies and objectives."

That very evening, however, Walsh had struck a pessimistic note in a "swan song" night letter to Drought asking him to tell Walker that "all even remotely concerned" believed that it was "impossible [to] pass Saint Michael," and that the "patient" would succumb. Walsh meant that a decision in favor of a Honolulu conference had better be made in Washington by September 29 (the feast day of St. Michael), or the cause of peace would suffer a mortal blow. "Please realize this and consider if sensibilities of few involved in little hitch outweigh halcyon blessed Easter for all."

The following afternoon Wikawa had dispatched his own "swan song." "And that means," Walsh wrote in his diary, "[our swan songs] will never end until the last trumpet."

On September 24, during another visit to the American Embassy, the Bishop had reported that Wikawa was greatly concerned over the lack of progress to date in the informal conversations in Washington. Nobufumi Itō, the head of the Cabinet Board of Information, had said the same thing. Both he and Wikawa had asked Walsh to determine whether the Embassy could hold out any hope that the conversations would eventually prove successful.

Dooman had told the Bishop he might want to inform his Japanese friends that the two governments seemed to be approaching the question "from somewhat different angles." Japan was emphasizing her sincerity and good faith in seeking an adjustment of relations, whereas the United States apparently wanted Tokyo to set forth, as clearly as possible, its future policies and objectives.

Later that same day Walsh had reappeared at the Embassy. The Japanese Government, according to Itō, had already told Ambassador Grew everything that could be disclosed in advance of the proposed Konoye-Roosevelt meeting. Itō wanted to know exactly what more could be done to clarify matters.

The answer Dooman gave Walsh this time reveals that the American Embassy was "wholly confused" concerning the precise position of the Japanese Government. A large number of papers had passed back and forth over a period of three or four months, but the commitments that Tokyo was prepared to undertake remained obscure. The best thing the authorities could do now (Dooman believed) was to draw up a document along the lines of the American draft of June 21. Once this had been done, perhaps some of the confusion could be eliminated.

"I am satisfied with our little people here," Walsh wrote to Drought on September 25, "and even proud of them, but I am sorely puzzled and a little mortified at the Potomac response or lack of it. If the thing is finally done, it will not be due to their good management, but to the superhuman miracle of holding out all this time over here under the most cruel pressure. If the thing isn't done, my last words were God bless Maryknoll and here goes nothing. I went into it with my eyes open and every time I think of a little peace for our millions in the Orient I am glad of it."

*

Although many weeks had now passed, the views expressed earlier by Hull's Far Eastern advisers had not undergone any change. Hornbeck, Hamilton, and Ballantine continued to adhere to the stand they had maintained from the beginning: the President should not confer personally with Konoye until the two governments had reconciled their differences through regular diplomatic channels. "As for me," Hull later declared, "I was thoroughly satisfied that a meeting with Konoye, without an advance agreement, could only result either in another Munich or in nothing at all. I was opposed to the first Munich and still more opposed to a second Munich."

Writing from Hyde Park on September 28, the President confirmed a decision that had been emerging within the State Department for some time: "I wholly agree," he informed Hull, "with your pencilled note—to recite the more liberal original attitude of the Japanese when they first sought the meeting, point out their much narrowed position now, earnestly ask if they cannot go back to their original attitude, start discussions again on agreement in principle, and reemphasize my hope for a meeting."

A "comprehensive communication" prepared by the State Department for this purpose (in the form of an "Oral Statement") was handed to the Japanese Ambassador on October 2, Hull's seventieth birthday. The Secretary told Nomura the United States wanted "an agreement that would speak for itself: one that would on the face of it make manifest the purposes of both Governments consistently to pursue courses of peace." Proceeding indirectly rather than directly, or resorting to some kind of "patchwork arrangement," would serve no useful purpose. Only "a meeting of minds on essentials" could lead to success.

Several days later, in Tokyo, Konoye's private secretary, Tomohiko Ushiba, advised Eugene Dooman that an increasing number of officials were now beginning to believe that Japan had fallen into a trap. The American Government (they were saying) had never had any intention of concluding an agreement with Japan; Washington had recently obtained from Tokyo an exposition of Japanese policies and objectives; these were not in line with American policies and objectives; as a consequence, the United States was now claiming that there was ample justification for refusing to enter into an agreement with Japan.

The October 2 "Statement," Ushiba said, was "extremely disagreeable"—it was argumentative, preceptive, and quite uncompromising. He regarded it as completely devoid of any suggestion that would be helpful to the Japanese Government in meeting the desires of the United States. The Japanese had shown their hand, but Washington had not put any of its cards on the table.

At the Japanese Foreign Office at this moment Admiral Toyoda found himself caught in a predicament that was not of his own making but for which he would be held accountable nevertheless—a predicament that would cause further damage to Japan's already battered reputation as a giver of promises that no one could be sure would ever be kept. In a conversation with Grew on October 7, the Foreign Minister revealed the nature of the problem: the conception the American Government had of what Konoye had said to Grew during their secret dinner meeting on September 6 was incorrect.

According to Toyoda, Konoye had accepted the Hull program "in principle" but had clearly specified that adjustments would be necessary in applying that program to actual conditions. Despite this qualification, the American Government had now declared in its "Oral Statement" of October 2 that Konoye had endorsed Hull's Four Principles. Since this was not the case, the Japanese Government had instructed Nomura to inform Hull that the October 2 memorandum should be revised. Instead of asserting that the Premier of Japan had "subscribed fully to the Four Principles," the memorandum ought to state that the Premier had "subscribed in principle" to those four points.

The comments Konoye had made during his dinner meeting with the Ambassador on September 6, Toyoda told Grew, had been purely private and informal in nature. They had been intended merely to acquaint the Ambassador with the personal views of a man who occupied an important position in molding the decisions and policies of the Japanese Government. Konoye had not anticipated having his remarks turn up later in an official document from Washington—a document that would be seen by various persons in Tokyo who did not even know that such a meeting had taken place.

Grew listened quietly to this explanation but did not find it convincing. There was "no doubt whatsoever" in his mind that Konoye's observations, which had been made in Japanese and translated on the spot by Dooman, "were correctly and accurately set forth" in the report the Embassy had cabled to the State Department. Thus, Grew adhered to his original conception of what had been said; he dismissed from his mind Toyoda's assertion that Konoye had been misquoted.

In another meeting with Grew a few days later, the Foreign Minister reverted to the subject of the American "Oral Statement" of October 2. Toyoda had experienced some difficulty in understanding that note, but he had come to the conclusion that three matters remained unresolved: the presence of Japanese armed forces in China; the respective attitudes of the United States and Japan toward the war in Europe; and the question of equal opportunity in China.

Toyoda said that he had instructed Nomura on October 3 to ask Secretary Hull whether the American Government would set forth, in precise terms, the obligations it wanted Japan to undertake in regard to those three matters. Having heard nothing from Nomura, Toyoda had again instructed him on October 6 to approach the Secretary of State. On October 9 Nomura had finally replied that he had seen Hull that day but was unable, despite their meeting, to provide the information Toyoda had asked him to obtain. Thus, a week of very valuable time had been wasted in a fruitless endeavor to elicit information through the Japanese Ambassador in Washington—information that would have "measurably accelerated" the conversations if only an answer had been received promptly.

Toyoda told Grew on this occasion that Nomura seemed to be "very tired." Serious consideration was therefore being given to the possibility of sending an experienced diplomat to Washington to assist the Ambassador in the conversations.

Three days later, Minister-Counselor Wakasugi, who had only recently returned to Washington from Tokyo, called upon Under Secretary of State Sumner Welles to express, on behalf of Premier Konoye, the same perplexity that Toyoda had exhibited in talking with Grew.

The Welles-Wakasugi interview of October 13 was one of the most revealing of the sixty-odd conversations held in Washington during 1941 concerning Japanese-American relations. It was also one of the most frustrating—for both sides. Each repetition of the familiar sounded ominously like a final position—the irreducible essence of national policy. It was as though these two men could already see, in the mind's eye, the samurai sword of war being drawn at any moment from the scabbard of diplomatic palaver in which it had thus far been so discreetly hidden that only the hilt, with its subtle embellishments, served as a reminder that a nation of artists was also a nation of warriors.

According to Wakasugi, the Japanese Government had made every effort to come to a friendly understanding with the United States and yet an interminable time had elapsed and still no agreement had been reached. As far back as July, Konoye and his colleagues had believed that the fundamental principles necessary for an understanding had already been found. Later, however, the authorities in Japan had discovered that they could not determine the desires of the American Government. Acting under personal instructions from the Premier, Wakasugi now hoped to learn exactly why there had been so much delay. What were the points that Washington still wanted Tokyo to clarify?

Welles replied that it was impossible for him to believe that the Japanese Government did not already comprehend very clearly and specifically the position of the American Government; the Secretary of State and the Japanese Ambassador had held innumerable conversations in this regard; documents setting forth the American position had been handed to the Ambassador on June 21; thereafter, the American Government had believed that very satisfactory progress was being made; then suddenly, early in September, the Japanese Government seemed to be restricting, limiting, and modifying very materially the broad principles on which the American Government thought that a basis for an understanding had been reached; since then, Secretary Hull had met with Ambassador Nomura several times to discuss the issues; on October 2 the American Government had again very lucidly set forth its views in an "Oral Statement"; nothing could be added now that would clarify the issues in any useful way beyond the explanations already offered.

There was, of course, the matter of Japan's military activities in French Indochina and "in the north." It was unfortunate, Welles said, that the overt actions of Minister Wakasugi's government did not correspond to the purposes Tokyo had assertedly been seeking in the conversations with the United States.

In attempting to answer Welles, Wakasugi suggested that the American Government had reacted negatively to the Japanese proposals of early September because unfortunate phraseology had been employed. He said his government was completely willing to commit itself not to undertake any aggressive moves either to the south or to the north. The one reservation that had been stipulated by the Japanese Government in regard to possible action against the Soviet Union—action "for justifiable reasons"—was entirely unnecessary and could readily be dropped.

Wakasugi also declared that his government was willing to withdraw all of its troops from China, but Welles could not believe his ears. Thinking he had misunderstood, he asked the Minister to repeat what he had just said. Wakasugi complied, using the very same words over again—

not just once but twice. He noted, however, that it would be impossible for the Japanese Government, after four years of military operations in China, to pull all of its forces out within twenty-four hours. Welles replied that "nobody expected miracles in this modern age."

*

Minister Wakasugi's assertion to the effect that his country was willing to leave China to the Chinese proved to be empty of meaning, as political developments in Japan soon demonstrated. The inexorable pressures exerted by the early-October deadline the Japanese Government had already secretly imposed upon diplomacy now helped to bring the Kono-ye Cabinet to the end of the road.

Close to the scene of what was happening, though perhaps not realizing that a political crisis was so imminent, Bishop Walsh had again reached out across the Pacific for a helping hand from Father Drought: "Does real sincerity exist?" he had asked on October 6. "Is there any way regain viewpoint God and angels as originally? Puzzle what more to do."

Drought's reply had been pessimistic and rather surprising in its assignment of the blame: "Discouraging. Paul's friends have made too many changes."

On October 12 (Konoye's fiftieth birthday, and the day on which his position began to crumble) Walsh had decided to try once more to obtain "some real evidence" that the President would be willing to meet with the Premier after all. "Council approving," the Bishop's cable read, "please ask Cincinnati Detroit [approach] synod committee chairman interest Easter promise. Explain no reasonable fear good essentials spite confusions. Some necessity some [red] tape. Pity lose so much for so little."*

Drought replied two days later: "Positively known that many changes have caused difficulty and disappointment here. Use June twenty-first as basis and action will follow. Convinced we can do no more."†

That same day, October 14, Walsh abruptly delivered to the American Embassy "a paper containing observations" that had been made to him by a group of Prince Konoye's "personal advisers." The Bishop wanted

---

* Walsh was apparently thinking along these lines: If the Archbishops in Cincinnati and Detroit (with whom he was on good terms) were to approach Roosevelt, urging him to meet with Prince Konoye, perhaps the President would agree to do so. Father Drought was to discuss this idea with the other members of the Bishop's Council at Maryknoll in order to obtain their approval before he did anything about carrying out this plan.

† "June twenty-first" is a reference to the draft proposal Hull had handed to Nomura on that date.

the Ambassador to relay to Roosevelt and Hull everything these men had told him.

Grew realized, and so informed Washington, that this might merely represent a continuation of the diplomatic pressure to which he had been subjected for some time, the purpose being to hasten arrangements for the proposed meeting between the responsible heads of the two governments, but he nevertheless believed Walsh's "paper" contained "an accurate presentation of existing facts."

The "observations" that Konoye's "personal advisers" were offering at this moment were a repetition, for the most part, of the remarks Ushiba had made to Dooman a week earlier: the American "Oral Statement" of October 2 had been "a grave disappointment" to the Japanese; they now thought that "sincerity" was "entirely lacking on the American side with regard to either holding a meeting or otherwise reaching an understanding"; the Japanese therefore felt that any further suggestions from them "would serve no useful purpose"; not only would a continuation of the conversations be "impossible," but a "very unfortunate and serious deterioration of the situation" in the Pacific might ensue unless the American Government provided "some counteracting indication"; if "a gesture of an encouraging character with regard to the proposed [Kono ye-Roosevelt] meeting were forthcoming," however, the suspicion of "having been deceived" that currently existed in official Japanese quarters would be effectively removed, all factions would be reconciled, their confidence in Premier Konoye would be strengthened, and the Prince would then be able "to moderate measures" that had been "dictated by recent practical necessities," even though these measures were not in line with the principles he supported; the Prince would also be able, concurrently, to stop "the seesaw performance in the regions to the south."

As Grew and Dooman both knew, there were other "existing facts" that could not be ignored. Some of these were called to Walsh's attention —in particular the substance of a telegram from Saigon indicating that facilities had already been completed to take care of "a minimum of 100,000 [Japanese] troops in southern Indochina."

What the Bishop thought about *that* is not known. He was out of his element in matters of this nature, and yet he now found himself more deeply immersed in the muddy waters of international politics than he had ever wanted to be.

Walsh was on the point of leaving Tokyo by air for Canton. From there he would proceed to Manila, via Hong Kong, to catch the next Pan American Clipper to the United States. He had been asked by Wikawa and other Konoye "advisers" whether he would be willing to go to Washington to explain in person the situation confronting the Japanese Government. He had at first been reluctant to do this, but after clearing with the American Embassy he had agreed to serve in the manner suggested.

It was a memorable experience for Walsh, on the evening of October 14, 1941, to hear Premier Konoye recite words intended for the ears of President Roosevelt—a *viva voce* message that was immediately rendered into English for the Bishop's benefit by Nobufumi Itō:

From the beginning of these negotiations, I and my Government have had nothing but a sincere and wholehearted desire to conclude an agreement that would result in the peace of the Pacific, and we have worked very hard to bring this about.

I regret very much the delays and misunderstandings, some of them due, I believe, to the maneuvers of Third Powers, that have operated to retard the negotiations and render difficult the attainment of their important aim.

I still entertain hope of a successful issue, and I will continue to work for the attainment of the object sought, namely, an agreement that will establish friendly relations between our two countries, restrict the scope of the war, pacify and stabilize the Pacific region, and contribute to world peace. And now that the terms have been discussed as completely as is practicable under present conditions, it is my confident belief that a meeting between the heads of the respective governments would readily bring about a completely satisfactory understanding that would insure the great objectives we mutually seek.

The sudden resignation of Konoye's Cabinet two days later, however, was to drain this statement of whatever positive influence it might otherwise have had upon the American Government.

By that time Bishop Walsh was already en route to Japanese-occupied Canton, having left Tokyo by air on October 15. Paul Wikawa had given him a ticket that had been obtained with the help of Colonel Iwakuro's former chief, General Mutō. The General had also supplied a "safe-conduct" letter in which "Mr. Walsh" was described as "an American" traveling on "special business of an important nature."

Walsh had quickly discovered the value of this document in clearing the way of difficulties. Officials in southern Japan, who had wanted him to turn back, had changed their minds when he had produced Mutō's letter. The same thing happened in Canton two days later. Without the letter, the Bishop would not have been permitted to proceed to Macao (and thence to Hong Kong and Manila).

It was in Canton that Walsh learned of the resignation of the Konoye Cabinet. He immediately sent a telegram to Wikawa asking whether any new decisions had been made that "would affect the validity of the message" he was carrying to the President. Wikawa's reply was reassuring:

"Bon voyage with Flowers. No substantial change. Urgently persuade speedily respond our reasonableness thus avoid worst."

Since Walsh and Wikawa had previously agreed that "Flowers" would be their code word for Mutō, the Bishop naturally assumed Wikawa was repeating what the General had said.

"If I were asked to interpret the meaning of the Cabinet change," Walsh wrote at this time, "I would surmise that it means a shift in attitude rather than a change in policy. It is a signal that some definite move is imminent, but that its direction will depend on the circumstances that the immediate future will reveal. It seems to say: We still want peace, but if we are to have it, it must come without further delay. We cannot wait any longer. Therefore we are putting our house in order to move in the other direction, if necessary. Much as we want peace, we must have a prompt and definite decision. Please speak, and speak quickly."

In Washington, the news of Konoye's fall inevitably raised questions with regard to what the American Government should do at this juncture. Consideration was briefly given to the advisability of sending a Presidential message to the Emperor of Japan. A text prepared at the White House envisaged having FDR declare, "I personally would have been happy even to travel thousands of miles to meet with your Prime Minister, if one or two basic accords could have been realized so that the success of such a conference would have been assured."

The White House draft also included a passage asking Japan, in effect, to think twice before starting "new wars" in the Pacific—north or south.

Hull's Far Eastern advisers were unenthusiastic. "Mr. Hamilton does not recommend taking the proposed action," Hornbeck informed the Secretary of State. "Mr. Ballantine feels that it is premature to come to any decision on the matter. I feel strongly that this proposed message in the form in which it stands should not at this time be sent."

The President was so advised, and there the matter rested.

Further conversations with Wakasugi immediately following the demise of the Konoye Cabinet convinced Hull that the Minister was trying to stay in line with what he had said to Welles on October 13, but that he was nevertheless hedging on various issues. His efforts to provide interpretation were labored. No new points emerged, only a "rehash" of everything that had been said time and again throughout the spring, summer, and autumn months. As a consequence, the Secretary recorded "his definite impression" that there were "no signs of any disposition on the part of the Japanese Government to revert even to a position approximating that which it had taken" prior to the move into southern Indochina. Hull believed, in fact, that the "area of difference" between the

United States and Japan was "wider" at this moment than it had been at the start of the discussions in April.

Although the Secretary was prepared to afford the Japanese every opportunity to present their proposals, he "entertained increasingly serious doubt whether further conversations would be productive of an agreement."

It was now Japan's turn, Hull felt, to speak up and say something.

CHAPTER TWENTY

Tension Increases as Urgency Prevails

THE NEW JAPANESE Cabinet (with General Hideki Tōjō as Premier and Shigenori Tōgō as Foreign Minister) lost no time in emphasizing that it wanted to keep the Japanese-American conversations going in the hope of reaching an agreement with the United States. Beneath the surface of this expressed desire, however, Secretary Hull found the situation ominous. There was no indication that the Japanese were prepared to modify their position to bring it into line with American views regarding the basic principles on which peace in the Pacific would have to be constructed. On the contrary, it seemed to Hull and his Far Eastern advisers that Tōjō was likely to insist on even stiffer terms than the ones proposed earlier. Hull also detected "a sense of urgency" in the Tōjō-Tōgō attitude toward the conversations—an "almost frantic effort" to rush Washington into an agreement that would give Tokyo everything it wanted.

It was "imminently desirable," Wakasugi told Under Secretary Welles on October 24, "that the conversations be pressed to a satisfactory conclusion speedily." He had instructions from the Foreign Office, the Minister said, to inquire whether the American Government had anything to offer in response to the proposals Japan had made in late September.

Since Hull had handed Nomura a comprehensive "Oral Statement" on October 2, Welles felt a vigorous reply was necessary. He reminded Wakasugi of the seven or eigth months that had already been spent in seeking an equitable agreement. Despite this long search for a solution, there had recently been very few pronouncements, if any, by high authorities in Japan that could be interpreted to mean Tokyo sincerely desired to reach a settlement.

In the course of the discussion that followed, Wakasugi referred indirectly to the John Doe Associates. He revealed that as far back as April he had urged Ambassador Nomura to try to find some practical and concrete grounds for an agreement with the United States, but certain

American gentlemen, who had no official standing, and certain Japanese, who were also "unofficial," had stepped into the picture. In devising various formulas, these men had undoubtedly been sincerely trying to further the cause of friendly relations. Instead of clarifying the issues, however, they had plunged everything into obscurity, causing in the process a good deal of delay.

Wakasugi now thought a fresh approach should be made through new formulas that would take into consideration the principles set forth by the American Government.

If the Minister would prepare these formulas, Welles replied, they would receive "immediate consideration."

Ambassador Nomura, who had once thought that a solution was within sight, was now in a pessimistic mood. He had recently advised Tokyo that his expectations had not been realized; his judgments about the predicament facing the United States and about the way in which the American Government would react to that predicament had been wrong. He was in the dark in Washington; he was afraid that if he were to remain at his post he would either accomplish nothing or even do some harm; he wanted to return home to report personally on the situation and to decide whether he should resign; he thought it would be better for him to retire from the field; Roosevelt and Hull believed in his sincerity, but they knew he lacked influence in Tokyo; he was already "the bones of a dead horse" (*shiba no hone*); he did not want to continue such a sham existence, deluding himself and others into thinking he could be useful when he was not.

This news—no matter how disturbing—may not have come as a complete surprise to Foreign Minister Tōgō. One of the first things he had done upon taking charge of the Kasumi-ga-seki had been to review the records on file there concerning relations with the United States. What he had learned as a consequence, and what Nomura was now saying in his telegrams to Tokyo, convinced Tōgō that the Admiral needed professional help.

Since time was of the essence, Tōgō sought the assistance of the American Embassy, explaining through one of his subordinates that he wanted to send a Special Envoy to the United States. The man chosen for this assignment was Saburō Kurusu, an experienced diplomat with a good command of English. According to Tōgō, Kurusu had to be in Washington by November 13 "for technical reasons."

Acting on Grew's instructions, Eugene Dooman immediately telephoned Maxwell Hamilton, getting him out of bed late on the night of November 3. The Japanese Government wanted to know, Dooman explained, whether arrangements could be made to obtain passage for Kurusu on the Pan American Clipper scheduled to leave Hong Kong on the morning of November 5. This would entail delaying the departure of the airplane for about two days to give Kurusu time to make the connection. An alternative would be to have him proceed to Saipan, where he could board a Japanese vessel—probably a destroyer—so that he would be able to meet the Clipper when it landed at Guam.

Hamilton warned that it might be hard to accomplish anything on such short notice, but he promised to do what he could. Dooman relayed to Hamilton, in turn, a message Grew had received from Tōgō: "Delay in bringing the conversations to a speedy conclusion will only aggravate the situation which is already tense. Please accept this as though it were a message communicated by the Minister of Foreign Affairs to Mr. Hull in person."

A similar note of urgency ran through a long telegram from Grew that had been received by the State Department earlier in the day. If all efforts at conciliation failed, the Ambassador declared, Japan would probably not yield to foreign pressure; she might even risk national suicide in order to render herself impervious to economic embargoes; it would be shortsighted to base American policy on the belief that Japanese preparations for war were nothing more than a saber-rattling attempt to support Tokyo's high-pressure diplomacy; action by Japan that might make hostilities with the United States inevitable could come "with dramatic and dangerous suddenness."

Stanley Hornbeck did not find Grew's arguments convincing. "The reasoning in this telegram," Hornbeck wrote, "as in many which have preceded it, runs to the general effect that, although Japan misbehaves, we must not apply strong pressures to Japan—because that would probably cause Japan to do things which would bring on war, in which case the fault would be ours; rather, we must conciliate Japan, by making concessions; but in doing this, we must not recede one inch from our fundamental principles."

Hornbeck thought it might be appropriate to ask the American Embassy to forward its conception of the provisions of a settlement between the United States and Japan that would be in harmony with such a contradictory recommendation.

Grew, for his part, believed he had sent "a very strong telegram." He did not want the United States to get into war with Japan through any possible misconception of what the Japanese, especially the men of the Army, were capable of doing "contrary to all logic and sanity."

What Japan might do next, whether insane or not, was a subject that was then uppermost in Hull's mind. On the evening of November 3 he had dispatched a telegram to the American Ambassador in China seeking clarification of several contradictory reports that had recently come to hand: the U.S. military attaché in Chungking had conveyed "the official Chinese view" that Japan would begin an offensive in eastern Siberia before November 4; he had also declared, however, that the "official view" in Indochina was that Japan would invade Thailand on or about November 15; subsequently, word had been received from Chiang Kai-shek, who claimed to have "definite information" that the Japanese intended to strike Yunnan province sometime in November.

Hull was annoyed by the "variety" of possibilities contained in these reports. He wanted to know just how many attacks the Japanese were on the point of making and where they were going to make them.

Chiang was currently arguing that Chinese resistance would collapse if Kunming (the capital of Yunnan and the terminus of the Burma Road) were to fall to the Japanese. He wanted the Americans and the British to warn Japan that their governments could not view an attack on Kunming with indifference. He also wanted a commitment of British and American air power to bolster Chinese defenses.

At the Atlantic Conference Churchill had tried to persuade Roosevelt to "lay it on the line" for the Japanese in no uncertain terms. Now, three months later, the Prime Minister was in favor of sending the kind of warning the Generalissimo had in mind. This idea also appealed to Hornbeck because he shared Churchill's assumption that speaking up to the Japanese would cause them to back down. Hull, however, was not persuaded that this was the best course.

What would be the point of issuing a warning that the United States could not enforce? The Pacific Fleet was inferior to the Japanese Navy. To acquire enough strength to carry out unlimited operations in the western reaches of that mighty ocean would mean such an enormous withdrawal of naval and merchant tonnage from the Atlantic that the United Kingdom might well lose the battle there as a consequence.

In case of war with Japan in the Far East, American military plans envisaged fighting on the defensive in cooperation with the British and the Dutch. The Philippines were being reinforced, but several more months would be needed to increase American air and naval power to the point where the United States might be strong enough to deter Japan from undertaking hostilities in that part of the world.

Current American military estimates suggested that the Japanese did not have enough men in Indochina to launch an immediate attack on Yunnan, that they would need at least another two months to complete preparations for such an attack, that they might have to weaken themselves in other areas in the meantime in order to accumulate the necessary troops, and that once the Japanese got into Yunnan they would probably bog down there because the terrain was inhospitable to the kind of operations they would have to conduct.

General George C. Marshall, the Army chief of staff, and Admiral Harold R. Stark, the chief of naval operations, were opposed to dispatching American soldiers, sailors, or airmen to China for the purpose of intervention against Japan. They recommended instead that material assistance to the Chinese be speeded up, "consonant with the needs" of Russian, British, and American forces, and that aid to the "Flying Tigers," a group of volunteers who were still in training at a base in Burma, be "accelerated to the maximum practicable extent." Marshall and Stark also went on record against the idea of sending an "ultimatum" to Japan.

On November 5, 1941—the day on which these views were put into a memorandum to the President—a conference of the top civil and military leaders of Japan, held in the presence of the Emperor, endorsed a previously formulated agreement to the effect that if diplomacy failed to produce a settlement by December 1, the Japanese Government would make a final decision for war regardless of the state of the negotiations at that time.

Immediately following this conference, at which the Emperor was a spectator rather than a participant, a top secret order was given to the Combined Fleet authorizing the implementation of all necessary operational preparations for hostilities against the United States, Britain, and the Netherlands. Similar orders were issued by the Imperial Army the next day.

The American Government knew nothing of these orders, but on November 5 a deadline appeared for the first time in the "Magic" intercepts: Tōgō informed Nomura that all arrangements for the signing of an agreement with the United States had to be completed by November 25.

On the heels of this news came word that Toshi Gō of the *Japan Times and Advertiser* had just unburdened himself in an editorial in which he listed seven points he wanted the American Government to adopt, on its own initiative, by way of "restitution to Japan." As recorded by Grew in his diary, these points were: cessation of all military and economic assistance to Nationalist China; advice to Chungking to make peace with the Japanese; termination of American military and economic encirclement of Japan; acknowledgment of the Co-prosperity Sphere and of

Japan's leadership in Southeast Asia; diplomatic recognition of Manchukuo; an immediate and unconditional rescinding of the Presidential order freezing Japanese assets; and the restoration of trade treaties along with the abolition of all restrictions on commerce. In short, the United States must "undo everything wrongfully done in the name of peace but with the design of war, whether economic or military."

American correspondents in Tokyo, having been told about this broadside in advance, immediately passed the word to their papers in the United States.

"If anything could render utterly hopeless the prospect of our coming to an understanding with Japan," Grew wrote, "this editorial, from a newspaper known to be the organ of the Japanese Foreign Office, would appear to do it, and my guess is that the American people will not be sympathetic to further efforts toward conciliation. This sort of stuff is as stupid as it is discouraging. It certainly affords no help to Kurusu, if it hasn't wrecked his mission in advance."

Two days later, during a reception at the Soviet Embassy, Grew had an opportunity to chat with a number of Japanese, including Editor Gō and Foreign Minister Tōgō. The Ambassador adopted the same line with everyone—he denounced the editorial.

In a subsequent conversation, Tōgō categorically assured Grew that the Foreign Office had not known anything about the matter beforehand, but in the light of this incident, he said, he was considering the possibility of having the paper placed under supervision. He had already suggested, in appropriate quarters, how undesirable it was to publish material that was needlessly provocative. He wished to remind the Ambassador, however, that "violent language" had been employed against Japan by American newspapers and by individuals who held responsible positions in the United States. Unless such language could be toned down, no one could expect the papers in Japan to remain quiet.

Surveying the situation from his command post in Washington, Secretary Hull saw clouds of war boiling up in the Orient. "From the tone of the intercepts," he later wrote, "from the inflamed statements made in Tokyo, from the unyielding and drastic nature of the Japanese demands, and from constant reports of Japanese military activity, it was now obvious to me that Japan was rapidly veering toward further aggressive advances in the South Seas, including war with the United States, if we did not sign the agreement she required."

At a Cabinet meeting held on Friday, November 7, 1941, just one month prior to the attack on Pearl Harbor, Hull delivered "a solemn warning of the dangers ahead." There was a moment of silence when he concluded his statement with the words: "We should be on the lookout for a military attack by Japan anywhere at any time."

That evening, Ambassador Nomura and Minister Wakasugi called at Hull's apartment in the Wardman Park Hotel to hand over a document that supposedly contained new formulas. Upon reading what they had brought, however, Hull felt he was looking at nothing more than a re-wording of earlier proposals—there were no real concessions.

The methods of diplomacy were still being employed, but the "Magic" intercepts that were being secretly delivered to the few men in Washington who were privileged to see them were keeping suspicions very much alive. The President and his top civil and military advisers now knew, more positively than ever before, that a Japanese resort to force—somewhere, somehow, sometime—was an imminent possibility.

CHAPTER TWENTY-ONE

"The Head of a Dragon, the Tail of a Snake"

SOON AFTER Bishop Walsh had departed from Japan in mid-October 1941 with Konoye's verbal message to Roosevelt tucked away in his mind, he had discovered that obtaining passage home from the Far East was not going to be an easy matter. He had consequently sent a telegram to Father Drought asking him to solicit Frank Walker's help in reserving space on the first available Clipper, but despite Drought's answering promise to try everything possible in the way of assistance Walsh had become stranded in Manila. The number of persons desiring to return to the United States by air was greater than the supply of seats provided by Pan American's service. It was thus nearly the end of October before Walsh could report: "Clipper leaves Manila [November] third. Have good story. Full concurrence Joseph [Grew]. Expect hearing. Apologies to nobody. Will meet you East."

In replying to this message, Drought had suggested that "obstacles" had been placed in the way of a Japanese-American settlement "by Paul's friends." "Frank and I have lost face here," he had added, "and our advice is now unwelcome."

Several days later, Walsh himself had found it necessary to convey discouraging news of a different sort: "Another week lost. California Clipper left today. No place for me spite government reservation. Next chance China Clipper leaving Manila eighth maybe. [I and] Joseph think mission vital. Have direct message but don't know if Boss [Roosevelt] wants, tolerates, or ignores it. Can only come when they find me place."

On November 7, the day on which Secretary Hull warned his colleagues that the United States might be attacked by Japan "anywhere at any time," Bishop Walsh tried to cover the possibility that the November 8 plane might leave without him. "I am taking the liberty," he said in a letter to the Postmaster General, "of sending you the enclosed memorandum that I have prepared at the request of the Japanese Government and the American Embassy in Tokyo for the eye of the President. May I request that you get in touch with Father Drought and pass over to him the problem of filing the memo with the proper authorities."

"Since the memo contains a direct message for the President," Walsh informed Drought, "I have prepared my whole statement for his eye. I think the natural and best thing would be for you to take it to him directly for two reasons: (1) because I could thus feel that I have performed my commission as it was entrusted to me and (2) because you know my mind and that of the men with whom I dealt and are thus the best fitted to interpret the memo and clarify any questions that may arise in connection with it. However, use your own judgment as to the best procedure. I put the matter entirely in your hands. Of course, it would be particularly satisfactory to follow any procedure that Mr. Hull might desire in the matter."

In Tokyo, at this moment, the thoughts of Tadao Wikawa were also tending in the direction of Washington. "As your yearlong collaborator for peace," Wikawa cabled Walker, "[I] earnestly pray for superior's act of great statesmanship saving not faces of dew but modern civilization from merciless destruction."

Wikawa felt greatly encouraged by Foreign Minister Tōgō's decision to dispatch a Special Envoy to the United States. "Looking forward pinch hitter's homer in last inning," he informed Walsh. "Hush them yelling fouls for flies. Accepted by captains."

As matters turned out, Walsh need not have worried about missing still another plane, for he managed to board the November 8 Clipper after all. Through pure coincidence, he was thus able to share his weeklong journey across the Pacific with none other than Saburō Kurusu.

*

In Washington, meanwhile, both Father Drought and the Japanese Embassy had been keeping in close touch with the Postmaster General. Despite Nomura's insistence that his government was seeking an amicable settlement, Walker knew that the barometer of Japanese-American relations being watched by Roosevelt and Hull was predicting the onset of foul weather.

Ambassador Grew was currently finding the new Foreign Minister "grim, unsmiling, and ultra-reserved," not a good omen. "He speaks English well enough," Grew wrote in his diary, "but talks so low that few can understand him and I not at all, so I'm glad that he is using an interpreter [who] speaks very distinctly and in perfect English, so nothing will be lost."

Tōgō had learned a great deal from studying the files at the Foreign Office pertaining to relations with the United States, but he had fallen victim, in the process, to several misconceptions: he thought the United States and Japan had already reached an agreement of views concerning Japan's obligations under the Tripartite Pact; he also thought Japan's latest proposition in regard to the principle of nondiscrimination in economic matters adequately covered the desires of the American Government. In Tōgō's view, therefore, only the problem of Japanese troops in China remained to be settled.

Tōgō was confused for a very simple reason: over a period of months Ambassador Nomura and the John Doe Associates had introduced imprecise and awkward formulas into the record; they had sponsored stipulations that were entirely unrepresentative of official thinking; they had consistently endeavored to put "a good face" on everything; they had encouraged Tokyo to believe that greater progress was being made toward a settlement than was actually the case.

During a meeting at the White House on November 10, Nomura tried very hard to convey to the President the attitude prevalent within the Japanese Government: time was very precious; Japan had made a number of concessions but the United States had shown "little sign of reciprocation"; skepticism had consequently arisen in certain quarters concerning the "true intention" of the American Government ("Personally I do not like to say it," Nomura told Roosevelt, "but it is true"); the freezing of assets amounted to the imposition of an economic blockade; if Japan and the United States were to reach an understanding, the "psychological effect" on the Japanese people would "mean much more" than the actual terms of the agreement (an argument that Drought had also offered on occasion).

In Tokyo two days later, the new chief of the First Section of the American Bureau of the Foreign Office, Toshikazu Kase, informed Grew that Tōgō had been "shocked" to learn that the American Government did not fully grasp the urgency of reaching a settlement in the shortest possible time. Not only had the "conversations" become "negotiations," in Tōgō's view, but these negotiations had, in his opinion, reached the final stage. There was considerable opposition within Japan to the attempt currently being made by the Tōjō Cabinet to come to terms with the United States. A very critical and dangerous situation would therefore arise if any appreciable delay were now to occur.

In a conversation with Hull on November 15, Nomura repeated Tōgō's assertion that the stage of actual negotiations had been reached, but the Secretary snapped back at this immediately. He insisted that only exploratory conversations had taken place to date; these "conversations" would continue, he said, until the attitudes of Japan and the United States had progressed to a point where "negotiations" could begin. Once that point had been reached, he would then have to consult the British, the Chinese, and the Dutch.

Hull pursued this argument at length, once again denouncing Japan's "fighting alliance" with Hitler—"the most flagrant aggressor" this planet had seen "in the last two thousand years."

Nomura tried to suggest that the American people would follow the Secretary of State wherever he led, but Hull knew better. "If we were to go into an agreement with Japan," he replied, "while Japan has an outstanding obligation to Germany that might call upon Japan to go to war with us, it would cause so much turmoil in the country that I might well be lynched."

"What I want," Hull insisted, "is a clear-cut, unequivocal agreement which will remove doubts that Japan is trying to face two ways at the same time."

The day on which Hull made these comments to Nomura happened to be the day on which Bishop Walsh finally reached Washington. He was very tired from all the traveling he had done, but he turned up that evening at the Wardman Park Hotel to keep a previously arranged appointment with the Secretary of State.

The asperity Hull had displayed that morning, in talking with the Japanese Ambassador, was not now in evidence, but the Secretary did remark (as he had to Nomura) that "he would be lynched" if he approved any agreement that was not clearly recognized by the people of the United States as constituting a complete severance of Japan's ties with the Axis.

Walsh could not understand why Hull was placing so much stress on the "Axis formula." Like Tōgō, the Bishop thought this particular "difficulty" had already been resolved.

When Hull turned to the "North China formula," Walsh was again at a loss. He wanted to say as little as possible about the Japanese presence in China, since he believed this to be "the real stumbling block." He therefore handed over a copy of the memorandum he had earlier prepared "for the eye of the President," explaining that it contained everything he knew about the situation.

The "whole sum and substance" of the message he had been asked to bring to the President, Walsh declared, was "that the Japanese Government must have a quick decision, and could not, and would not, wait."

The Bishop was unable to remember later whether he specified "that the alternative would certainly be war, and probably an immediate one," but the matter was "so elementary" and of "such universal and common knowledge" that he "scarcely would have thought it worth mentioning at this or at any other time." He probably did say, however, that if an agreement were not reached promptly, "the Japanese would go 'the other way,' meaning, of course, that there would be war."

After handing over his memorandum, Walsh made a request. "I would like to see the President," he told Hull, "and deliver my little message in person to him." The Secretary advised Walsh to consult Walker; ask him (Hull said) to make the necessary arrangements. When Walsh did this, the Postmaster General replied that he would "check back" with Hull and would let the Bishop know. Walker later informed Walsh, however, that "it was not considered wise [for him] to see the President" at this juncture.

Hull had quite properly insisted from the very beginning of the conversations with Nomura that the American Government would deal only with and through the Japanese Ambassador. Special Envoy Saburō Kurusu had now arrived in Washington; he also wished to talk with Hull and with Roosevelt. It would hardly have been proper to usher the Bishop into the White House ahead of the new emissary from Japan. What could Walsh say in person that he had not already recorded in his memorandum or told Secretary Hull? What could the Bishop reveal to the President that was of any current significance? The Japan of Prince Konoye belonged to the past; it was the Japan of General Tōjō that mattered now.

Perhaps the memorandum Walsh had left with Hull also had a dampening effect. It illustrates (as perhaps no other document so clearly can) how thin the line is between fact and fiction where private efforts for peace are concerned. It also shows how easy it is for one individual to influence another by offering arguments in the name of the state or or on behalf of humanity at large, and how plausible many of these arguments can sound when they are repeated to the other side by private brokers for peace acting with all of the intensity that their sense of mission can muster in such circumstances.

Walsh had essentially three things to report: the first was that the American "Oral Statement" of October 2 had reduced the authorities in Tokyo to "desperation"; the second was that trust should be reposed in "the sincerity of the Japanese Government"; the third was that Japan could "negotiate no longer, but must now have either a decision as to an agreement and/or a meeting [with the President], or at least a set of concrete and final terms."

The Bishop did not know the nature of Japan's plans, but he had obtained the impression that they would lead her, sooner or later, into hostilities against the United States. "Does this mean," Walsh had asked in his memorandum, "that if a meeting [with the President] is not promptly arranged, on the basis of the terms already agreed upon and without further specification as to detail, the Japanese Government will abandon the negotiations at once and proceed with other plans?"

"Substantially that is what I was given to understand," Walsh had written in reply to his own question, "but with one important reservation. The reservation is that the Japanese Government will be glad to consider once more—and once more only—any set of terms or conditions the American Government may declare [to be the] essential prerequisites to an agreement and/or a meeting, *provided they are specific, complete, final, and prompt.*"

*

Despite Foreign Minister Tōgō's decision to dispatch a Special Envoy to Washington to assist Ambassador Nomura in the conversations, the prospects for peace in mid-November 1941 remained unpromising. While en route to the American capital, Kurusu had told the press he hoped for a "touchdown" in the talks; he believed he would have a "fighting chance" of succeeding in his assignment, if the American people remained sympathetic.

In the actual parleying, however, Kurusu's fluency in English did not make the same old arguments any more palatable than they had been when they were uttered less smoothly by Nomura. All the while that Kurusu was talking, the President and the Secretary of State were secretly listening to the voice of "Magic." The intercepted messages and other incoming intelligence information had much more impact on them than anything the Special Envoy from Japan had to say.

Kurusu had been in Washington only three days when Hull, his legendary patience wearing thin, flatly declared: "We can go so far, but rather than go beyond a certain point it would be better for us to stand and take the consequences."

It was during this particular conversation that the possibility of returning to the *status quo ante* was raised on Japanese initiative, the idea being to go back to the situation that had prevailed prior to the Indochina crisis in July. Big ships cannot be turned too quickly, Nomura pointed out; they have to be eased around slowly and deliberately.

Hull seems to have assumed that Nomura and Kurusu were acting on instructions from Tokyo in making this proposal, but they were not;

they were embarking entirely on their own, pursuing an idea that had been presented to them the previous evening by the Postmaster General of the United States.

This purely private excursion on their part soon brought an admonition from the Foreign Minister, who insisted that they abide by the instructions they had already received.

Two days later, on November 20, Nomura and Kurusu gave Hull a document from their Foreign Office that was in the nature of a *modus vivendi*—an interim and partial agreement to tide over the situation until a long-term, general settlement could be reached. Hull and his Far Eastern advisers found the contents to be "utterly unacceptable"; the commitments the United States was being asked to make would have amounted (they felt) to surrendering to Japan. The proposals from Tokyo were "of so preposterous a character," in Hull's opinion, "that no responsible American official could ever have dreamed of accepting them."

In order to avoid giving Japan any pretext for walking out of the conversations, however, Hull decided not to be too severe in his reactions. At the same time, he redoubled his earlier efforts to warn his colleagues in key positions of authority in Washington that Japan might attack at any time.

The American Government had just learned from the Dutch that a Japanese force had arrived in the vicinity of Palau, the point in the Japanese Mandated Islands closest to the Netherlands East Indies. Hull had also received reports from the American consuls at Hanoi and Saigon concerning new and extensive landings of Japanese troops and equipment in Indochina. He therefore judged that "the zero hour was approaching."

From a diplomatic point of view, the Secretary felt the situation was "virtually hopeless," and yet the American Government wanted to avert, or at least delay, the outbreak of hostilities in the Pacific. The Secretaries of War and of the Navy, the Army chief of staff, and the chief of naval operations were all pleading for more time to prepare American defenses. In these circumstances, the only practical choice was to try to obtain a reprieve by presenting counterproposals to Japan.

While these were being worked out within the State Department, Hull and his staff—acting on suggestions made by the President—also turned their attention to drafting an American *modus vivendi*. Hull felt there was "very little possibility" that the Japanese would agree to any temporary arrangement other than the one they themselves had proposed on November 20, but he had reasons for wanting to proceed with the *modus vivendi* plan nonetheless: a rejection by Tokyo, on the one hand, would "further expose the Japanese determination to make war"; an acceptance, on the other hand, would mean more time in which to prepare for the blow "in case Japan attacked at the expiration of the temporary agreement."

The idea was to offer not only a *modus vivendi* covering the next three months, but also a more comprehensive proposal—a ten-point peace settlement that would incorporate formulas drafted within the State Department, earlier in November, with suggestions recently made by the Secretary of the Treasury. Hull hoped, in this way, to keep the conversations going, but he and his advisers felt they had reached the stage of "clutching at straws."

On Saturday, November 22, the Secretary called in the British, Chinese, Dutch, and Australian representatives to discuss with them in detail the Japanese proposal of November 20 and the American *modus vivendi* that he desired to substitute in its place. Hull emphasized to his visitors "there was probably not one chance in three" that Tokyo would accept his offer.

Indirect confirmation of this pessimistic estimate came that same day through "Magic": Foreign Minister Tōgō was now informing Nomura and Kurusu that if a settlement was not reached by November 29 *things were automatically going to happen.*

A few hours later, Nomura and Kurusu appeared at Hull's apartment to keep an appointment that had been requested by the Ambassador. "It was almost unreal," Hull wrote in his *Memoirs*, "to see these representatives come to my home smiling, courteous, and outwardly friendly. It was a strain to talk to them in the same tone and on the same level, knowing what I did of Japan's nefarious plans from the intercepted messages, and knowing that Nomura and Kurusu had the same information. There they sat, bowing agreeably, Nomura sometimes giggling, Kurusu often showing his teeth in a grin, while through their minds must have raced again and again the thought that, if we did not say Yes to Japan's demands, their Government in a few days would launch new aggressions that sooner or later would inevitably bring war with the United States and death to thousands or millions of men."

On Monday, November 24, Hull called the British, Chinese, Dutch, and Australian representatives back to his office. They spent an hour reading the latest draft of the Department's proposed *modus vivendi*, taking notes as they went along so that they would be able to brief their governments.

Hull explained the obvious: the purpose of the *modus vivendi* was to gain time. If three months of grace could be obtained by this means, then all of the nations concerned would profit from the opportunity thus provided to make further defensive preparations against Japan. "The envoys seemed gratified at the thought," Hull later wrote, "but they seemed to be thinking of the advantages to be derived from the *modus vivendi* without being willing to make concessions in return."

Hull soon learned that his analysis was correct. The response of Chiang Kai-shek to the State Department's *modus vivendi* plan was "violent." Shooting from the hip in all directions, the Generalissimo declared that any relaxation of American restrictions against Japan would mean the collapse of the Chinese Army and of Chinese morale. To Chiang it looked as though the American Government was moving in the direction of appeasing Japan at the expense of China, and he was determined to do what he could to prevent that from happening.

The Generalissimo was not alone in expressing opposition. Upon reading a memorandum outlining the views of the British Government, Hull concluded that London was offering only limited approval. The response of the Dutch Government was also less than enthusiastic.

With these reactions in mind, Hull told the President's so-called War Council on November 25 there was "practically no possibility of an agreement being achieved with Japan"; there were likely to be "new acts of conquest by force" at any time; American defense planning should therefore proceed on the assumption that "the Japanese might make the element of surprise a central point in their strategy."

When Secretary Stimson returned to the War Department from this meeting, he found news awaiting him that he promptly conveyed to the President and the Secretary of State: the Japanese were embarking a large force at Shanghai, some thirty to fifty ships; the first elements of this expedition had already been sighted sailing south of Formosa, along the China coast.

During the afternoon of November 25, and again that evening, Hull discussed the *modus vivendi* approach with his Far Eastern advisers. Although the prospects were slight that the Japanese would accept the proposal, Hull thought the United States should present it anyway. During the course of these discussions, however, advance notice was received of the lukewarm reaction of Prime Minister Churchill to the *modus vivendi* idea. A message was about to arrive from the "Former Naval Person," addressed to the President, succinctly expressing Churchill's position: "Of course, it is for you to handle this business, and we certainly do not want an additional war. There is only one point that disquiets us. What about Chiang Kai-shek? Is he not having a very thin diet? Our anxiety is about China. If they collapse, our joint dangers would enormously increase. We are sure that the regard of the United States for the Chinese cause will govern your action. We feel that the Japanese are most unsure of themselves."

With the knowledge in hand that the President would be receiving this message from London, Hull decided to "cancel out" the *modus vivendi* plan. Although it contained only a little "chicken feed" (a carefully controlled resumption of trade in certain categories of goods, including petroleum for civilian needs), Hull believed there would be "widespread opposition" among his fellow Americans to making a "deal" with Japan—especially one that involved sending that nation "even limited quantities of oil." With the people of the United States withholding their support, and with America's potential allies entirely unreceptive, Hull felt the risks were too great to warrant proceeding along the lines he had planned.

The following morning, November 26, the Secretary briefed the President. Roosevelt promptly agreed that a *modus vivendi* should not be offered. The Japanese Government would be given instead a comprehensive proposal for a broad agreement—the ten-point peace settlement that would have been presented along with the *modus vivendi*, if that idea had managed to survive the tests to which it had been put.

The pertinent documents were handed to Nomura and Kurusu that very afternoon "with the forlorn hope [as Hull later described it] that even at this ultimate minute a little common sense might filter into the military minds in Tokyo."

Although the terms contained in the Hull note of November 26 were stiff, the Secretary of State was not asking Japan to take unilateral action in a vacuum. He was prepared to reciprocate in various ways: by working for the conclusion of a multilateral agreement providing for equality of economic opportunity in French Indochina; by negotiating a new trade treaty with Japan based on most-favored-nation treatment and the reduction of trade barriers; by lifting the order freezing Japanese assets in the United States; and by adopting "practical measures of financial cooperation."

It was Hull's intention also to buttress his program with a multilateral, nonaggression pact embracing the British Empire, China, Japan, the Netherlands, the Soviet Union, Thailand, and the United States.

Ambassador Grew, in talking with various prominent Japanese at this time, emphasized his personal view that Hull's ten-point plan was "a broad-gauge, objective proposal of the highest statesmanship," offering their country "a reasonable and peaceful way of achieving her constantly publicized needs."

At this particular moment in history, however, the civil and military leaders of Japan were caught up in a suddenly accelerating current of past imperatives that swept them relentlessly on toward disaster. They consequently chose to interpret the Hull overture as an "ultimatum" that they could not possibly accept. Such qualms as had once existed in regard to fighting the United States were either forgotten or suppressed. No one spoiled the awesome unanimity with which the top-ranking members of the Japanese Government secretly agreed, on November 27, that their decision for war would be confirmed at an Imperial Conference to be held on December 1.

*

The countdown on peace in the Pacific that now began in Tokyo coincided with a desperate, last-minute search, conducted mostly in Washington, for some way of avoiding what already appeared to be inevitable. Just before reporting on Hull's ten-point peace plan, Nomura and Kurusu had dispatched an urgent, top-secret telegram to Foreign Minister Tōgō recommending an exchange of messages between the President and the Emperor as the only means of "breaking the impasse" and of "changing the atmosphere." If Roosevelt could be persuaded to take the initiative in this regard, Nomura and Kurusu hoped their government would respond by calling for the neutralization of French Indochina, Thailand, and the Netherlands East Indies. By reminding Tokyo that a similar plan had been proposed by the President several months earlier, Nomura and Kurusu implied that the United States might react favorably if only Japan would make such an offer. They asked the Foreign Minister, in effect, not to reject their suggestion out of hand but to take the matter "at least as far as the Lord Keeper of the Privy Seal," the eyes and ears of the Throne.

The notion that the Emperor might be brought into play on the side of peace, if an appeal were made to him personally, had been studied by the White House and the State Department at the time of Konoye's resignation, but action had been deferred pending further developments. Now, some six weeks later, this idea was about to receive a more favorable hearing.

No one knew better than General Marshall and Admiral Stark just how desperately the armed services of the United States still needed more time to develop enough strength to deal effectively with whatever the Japanese Government might be planning in the way of hostilities in the southwestern Pacific—the area where the Imperial Army and Navy were most likely to strike. On November 27 Marshall and Stark formally advised the President and the Secretary of State of this need. A critical requirement was the reinforcement of the Philippines. Until this could be completed, the two officers recommended that military counteraction against Japan be considered only if Japan attacked or directly threatened American, British, or Dutch territory.

In case Japan moved against Thailand, Marshall and Stark thought the ABD governments should warn Tokyo that an advance west of 100° east longitude or south of 10° north latitude might lead to war. Their reasoning was that a Japanese advance of this magnitude would threaten Burma and Malaya. Prior to the issuance of such a warning, however, Marshall and Stark urged that "no joint military opposition" be undertaken against Japan.

In his office at the State Department on November 27, Stanley Hornbeck composed a long memorandum in which he "made the mistake [as he later explained] of yielding to an emotional urge" that took the form of committing himself "on the record" in terms of "wishful thinking and gratuitous predicting."

As Hornbeck saw it, the Japanese Government did not intend, desire, or expect to have armed conflict with the United States *here and now*. If it were a matter of placing bets, he would offer "odds of five to one" that Japan and the United States would not be at "war" on or before December 15. He would give "three to one" that they would not be at "war" on or before January 15. He would wager "even money" that they would not be at "war" on or before March 1.

While Hornbeck was thus plunging into a prophecy that burned all bridges behind him, Secretary Hull was telling the press that the crisis was at hand: Japanese troops were pouring into Indochina; an attack might come within a few days.

The reporters concluded from Hull's remarks that the United States, although gravely threatened, would not be a party to a Far Eastern Munich.

At a meeting of the "War Council" the next day, Friday, November 28, Hull repeated almost word for word what he had said on November 25: there was "practically no possibility" of reaching a settlement; the Japanese were likely to break out at any time with new acts of conquest; safeguarding the security of the United States was now in the hands of the American Army and Navy; the two services should bear in mind that the Japanese might resort to surprise attacks at various points simultaneously.

The President and his advisers spent a great deal of time discussing the issues posed by the Japanese expedition that was already on the high seas, proceeding south of Formosa. No one knew what Japan was going to do. She might be about to attack the Philippines, land further troops in Indochina, strike at Thailand, invade the Netherlands East Indies, or hit the British at Singapore.

The President pointed out that the Japanese might even be bound for the Kra Isthmus, with Rangoon as their ultimate destination. If they could establish themselves there, they would be able to cut the Burma Road at its beginning.

Everyone agreed that the British would fight if the Japanese got into the Kra Isthmus. Everyone also agreed that the United States would have to fight if the British did. A rounding of the southern tip of Indochina by the Japanese expeditionary force would thus touch off a chain reaction, with one calamity following another.

Something had to be done. The United States could not sit still while Japan proceeded, unopposed, to carry out her secret plans. A counter-attack directed against the Japanese expedition might be emotionally appealing, but it was out of the question politically. The idea of sending a warning to Japan, perhaps through a Presidential message to the Emperor, appeared to be the only alternative. In the meantime, Congress and the public would have to be brought into the picture—they would have to be told what to expect if Japan resorted to overt action.

The drafting of a message to the Emperor, and of another to the Congress, was to be completed over the weekend while the President was away from Washington fulfilling a long-standing promise. He had intended to spend Thanksgiving with the patients of the infantile paralysis center at Warm Springs, Georgia—just as he had done for a number of years—but his duties had kept him in the capital. Although the Far Eastern crisis had now deepened and Thanksgiving had passed, Roosevelt was still anxious to go to Warm Springs. His doctor had been saying that a few days of rest in the sunshine was just what he needed.

The President had scarcely arrived at his destination, however, when the Secretary of State personally telephoned to ask him to move up the date of his return to Washington. In making this request on Saturday, November 29, Hull was influenced in part by reports he had received of further Japanese troop movements in Indochina. He had also seen the "Magic" version of a message from Tōgō to Nomura and Kurusu, informing them that an answer to the American ten-point plan would be forthcoming in two or three days; the "negotiations" would then be ruptured—in fact if not in name—but Nomura and Kurusu were to avoid giving the impression that the talks were being terminated.

While the President was en route back to Washington, Hull learned through the British Ambassador that London had important information indicating that Japan was about to attack Thailand and that a seaborne expedition would seize strategic points in the Kra Isthmus.

When Nomura and Kurusu turned up at the State Department the next day (December 1), Hull gave them "the devil" for what their country was doing. With "a good deal of bark" in his voice, he told them that the United States did not propose to enter into a partnership with the military leaders of Japan. Not one whisper of peace had been heard from them—only bluster and bloodcurdling threats. With Japan tied in with the Axis, Tokyo might just as well ask Washington to stop helping Britain as to stop aiding China; the United States was not going to allow herself to be kicked out of the Pacific.

From the very beginning of the conversations, Hull declared, the American Government had stood squarely on the fundamentals contained in his note of November 26; everything that Japan had been doing and saying, however, was in precisely the opposite direction; there was no reason for conflict between the two nations—there was no real clash of interests; Japan did not have to use a sword to get a seat at the head of the table.

Having delivered himself of these and other sentiments at great length, Hull proceeded to the White House to confer with the President. Up for consideration were the two messages that had been drafted as a result of the decisions made by the "War Council" on November 28: a message to Congress outlining the dangers that seemed about to engulf the United States in the Far East and a message to the Emperor of Japan appealing for peace.

The President also had on his desk at this moment a cable from Prime Minister Churchill reiterating an idea he had first advocated during the Atlantic Conference in August:

It seems to me that one important method remains unused in averting war between Japan and our two countries, namely a plain declaration, secret or public as may be thought best, that any further act of aggression by Japan will lead immediately to the gravest consequences. I realize your Constitutional difficulties, but it would be tragic if Japan drifted into war, by encroachment, without having before her, fairly and squarely, the dire character of a further aggressive step. I beg you to consider whether, at the moment which you judge right, which may be very near, you should not say that "any further Japanese aggression would compel you to place the gravest issues before Congress," or words to that effect. We would, of course, make a similar declaration or share in a joint declaration, and in any case arrangements are being made to synchronize our action with yours. Forgive me, my dear friend, for presuming to press such a course upon you, but I am convinced that it might make all the difference and prevent a melancholy extension of the war.

That such an extension might come very soon was apparent from an intercepted message in which Foreign Minister Tōgō instructed the Japanese Ambassador in Berlin to pay a visit to Hitler and Ribbentrop. "Say very secretly [to them]," this message read, "that there is extreme danger that war may suddenly break out between the Anglo-Saxon nations and Japan through some clash of arms, and add that the time of the breaking out of this war may come [more quickly] than anyone dreams."

At the Japanese Embassy in Washington, Nomura and Kurusu were still looking for a way to bring about a peaceful settlement. On December 1 they sent a telegram to Tokyo in which they tried to reactivate the idea of a mid-Pacific conference. The purpose of such a meeting would be to reach an agreement on the basis of the latest proposals submitted by the two countries—Tōgō's *modus vivendi* of November 20 and the Hull note of November 26. In the Japanese capital, however, December 1 was the day on which Japan's decision for war was secretly confirmed in the presence of the Emperor.

Available records do not reveal whether Nomura and Kurusu were acting under the influence of Father Drought, but here was one of his ideas—a bilateral conference at the highest level of statesmanship—cropping up at the last moment. Ever since Bishop Walsh's return from the Far East in mid-November, Drought had tried to keep abreast of the rapidly developing situation. When a copy of Hull's ten-point peace plan had come into his hands, he had characteristically reacted by drafting, and then redrafting, a lengthy memorandum that seems to have been intended for the Secretary of State (with Nomura serving as the agent of transmission). Included in this "proposed reply" to the Hull note of November 26 were all sorts of statements, made in the name of the Japanese Government, for which there was no basis whatsoever except Drought's own erroneous conception of the nature of that government and of the program it was prepared to pursue.

Walsh, for his part, had advised Wikawa by telegram, on November 27, to impress upon the highest authorities in Tokyo that the Hull offer was intended to be a "friendly cooperative [gesture] toward [a] complete understanding." The situation was urgent: "Realize choice you make now determines all."

Twenty-four hours later, the Bishop had sent still another plea: "Public opinion now convinced both sides sincere. Will welcome and support friendship with dignity and honor. God will bless victorious statesmanship. If this fails, lasting deterioration seems inevitable."

On December 1 Walsh received Wikawa's reply: "Regret your messages seriously contradict [Hull] offer which nullifies mutual year-old effort. Federal's great statesmanship, concentrating North Carolina, only can prevent worst. Recommend tournament for relaxation."*

Two days later, Walsh sent an answering message: "Appreciate your cable and made it known. Necessary Rock Quarter brake hard give Sailor quiet week revive hope."†

The crisis in Japanese-American relations had now reached a point where a "quiet week" would not have made any difference. A telegram from Tōgō informed Nomura and Kurusu that it would be "inappropriate" for Japan to suggest a leaders' conference "at this time." Acting on orders from Tokyo, Japanese Embassy personnel were in the process of destroying a number of their codes, along with one of the two cryptographic machines with which they were equipped. To members of the War Department General Staff, who had secret knowledge of this activity, the Embassy's action meant "at least a break in diplomatic relations and probably war" in the near future.

On Friday, December 5, Nomura and Kurusu gave Secretary Hull their government's reply to a formal inquiry from the President—an inquiry in which Tokyo had been asked to explain the purpose behind "the very rapid and material increase" of Japanese strength in Indochina that had recently been taking place in violation of the limits set by the so-called Protocol of Joint Defense Japan had concluded with Vichy France.

The Secretary of State was greatly annoyed by the Japanese answer, which attempted to relate what was happening in the French colony to Chinese troop activity "along the northern frontier." Denying that there had been any transgression of the agreement with Vichy, the Japanese Government claimed that the American Government had apparently paid too much attention to "an exaggerated report."

This was "a specious statement," in Hull's view, "unworthy of a child's intelligence." In speaking to Nomura and Kurusu about the

* In an earlier message Wikawa had indicated that he was hoping to see the Bishop at a "Federal golf tournament," which he described as "recommendable for recreation." This suggests that Wikawa was still thinking in terms of a top-level conference at Honolulu, or some other mutually convenient place, where "Federal's great statesmanship" could be brought into play. The phrase "concentrating North Carolina" is more difficult to explain, but at the time in question U.S. Army maneuvers were in progress in North and South Carolina. Wikawa may therefore have been trying to emphasize that a Japanese-American settlement would be meaningless unless it had the support of the Japanese Army.

† "Rock Quarter" was a reference either to Colonel Iwakuro (who was in Indochina) or to the Japanese Army as a whole. "Sailor" was the John Doe code word for Nomura.

matter, Hull was sarcastic: he had heard that the Chinese had been concentrating forces in Yunnan province as a response to the massing of Japanese troops in Indochina; it was his understanding that Japan was planning to *attack* the Chinese; he had never been told that it was the other way around, that the Japanese were reacting to a Chinese "threat"; this was the first time anyone had said to him that Japan was on the *defensive* in Indochina.

The following day, December 6, reports reached the American Government that thirty-five Japanese transports, eight cruisers, and twenty destroyers were steaming in the direction of the Kra Isthmus. The moment had now come, the President felt, to appeal directly to the Emperor of Japan.

In Tokyo, however, His Majesty's "servants"—the civil and military leaders of the country—were unanimous in their judgment that going to war with the United States represented the only alternative to committing national suicide. In such a situation, the Emperor could not effectively set himself against the men who had made this decision; the President's appeal could not trigger a reversal of the consensus that had already been reached.

"Nomura's last meeting with me," Hull later recalled, "was in keeping with the ineptitude that had marked [the Ambassador's] handling of the discussions from the beginning. His Government's intention, in instructing him to ask for [a] meeting at one o'clock [on Sunday, December 7], had been to give us their [final] note a few minutes in advance of the attack at Pearl Harbor."

The Japanese Embassy, however, bungled the processing of the note and thereby caused unanticipated delays. It was consequently past two o'clock when Nomura, accompanied by Special Envoy Kurusu, finally arrived at the State Department. Hull had by then read the "Magic" version of the message that was now being delivered more than an hour after the time specified by Tokyo.

Skimming through the text Nomura handed to him—pretending to read it so as not to reveal that he already knew what it contained—Hull allowed the accumulated tensions of a year of frustration to explode in a tongue-lashing that was all the more severe because the President had just advised him, over the telephone, of an unconfirmed report that the Japanese had attacked Pearl Harbor!

Looking straight at Admiral Nomura, Hull transfixed the hapless Ambassador with these barbed words: "I must say that in all my conversations with you during the last nine months, I have never uttered one word of untruth. This is borne out absolutely by the record. In all my fifty years of public service I have never seen a document that was more crowded with infamous falsehoods and distortions—infamous falsehoods and distortions on a scale so huge that I never imagined until today that any Government on this planet was capable of uttering them."

Exactly one year earlier, on December 7, 1940, John Doe's friend Tadao Wikawa had mentioned a possibility to Prince Konoye that had now become a reality: no matter how promising the prospect might be of working through Drought to rehabilitate relations with the United States, an attempt to reach a settlement by this means might fizzle out in the end.

Wikawa had used a picturesque combination of ideographs to express his concern: *ryūtō dabi*, "the head of a dragon, the tail of a snake."

By December 7, 1941, only the surprise attack at Hawaii was needed to confirm the bankruptcy of Japanese-American diplomacy and the failure of Father Drought's conspiracy for peace. After having searched endlessly for an amicable solution through the Hull-Nomura conversations—conversations that had been rendered ever more complicated, confusing, and meaningless by the activities of the John Doe Associates—the United States and Japan were now at war.

In the Fullness of Time

A READER OF provocative bent might ask here, toward the end of this account: What is the point of unraveling the secrets of a group of men who did not accomplish what they set out to do?

Part of the answer lies in the nature of diplomatic history: exploring a classic failure in the field of international relations can be as meaningful as investigating a notable success.

The world is very different now, and the times completely changed, but man himself remains, from age to age, a creature of unaltered passions. Reviewing what has happened in the past—what earlier generations have thought and said and done—can yield a wealth of experience that we might not otherwise be able to accumulate readily on our own.

There is also another factor: the innumerable backdoor incursions into policy formulation and decision-making that have been brought to light in these pages constitute a hitherto unseen view of the diplomatic prelude to Pearl Harbor, thus adding a new dimension to our understanding of a crisis of cataclysmic proportions.

These answers, in combination, provide reason enough to retrace the steps of the John Doe Associates, even though the trail they left behind them in pursuit of their goal is not marked by the milestones of positive achievement they had hoped to establish along the way.

Other readers might ask other questions: How did Father Drought himself see the situation? What did he think he was doing? Was Bishop Walsh aware of the role his right-hand man was playing?

In going to Japan in late 1940, Drought had several purposes in mind: he wanted to help find a way for Maryknoll to continue working effectively within the Japanese Empire despite official efforts to hamper foreign missionary activity; he wanted to do whatever he could "for the relief of China and the defeat of the Nazis"; he also wanted to combat the spread of communism in Asia.

By 1940, as Drought saw it, the war in China had become a "determinant" of Japanese life. Japan had won the battles, but she "could not win the kind of triumph that would justify" those battles, "nor could the Army as the dominating political agency in the Empire accept that failure and continue to enjoy its possession of power."

Drought recognized that some Japanese had an "affinity" for the ideology of Nazi Germany and that others wanted to join Hitler in exercising dominion over the world, but the "real leaders" of Japan (he argued) intended to keep the European war as far away from the Far East as possible. If they had to employ threats to do this, they would.

Many Japanese in 1940 attributed the sorry state of Japanese-American relations to "the mistaken diplomacy of Matsuoka," but Drought believed that the Foreign Minister had been misunderstood. When he spoke of the Tripartite Pact as a "pivot," he was trying to indicate that Japan could turn either toward the European war or away from it. Matsuoka failed to get this idea across, and so his pivot concept "was taken to mean that the Tripartite Pact was the foundation of Japanese diplomacy."

In Drought's judgment, the people of Japan "sincerely believed that the United States . . . had virtually drawn the sword" against their country. The masses felt there was "very little disposition" on the part of the American Government "to encourage a realistic solution" of Far Eastern problems. Even many persons in high places thought that Washington was determined to take advantage of Japan's involvement in China, "not only to prevent further territorial expansion . . . but to bring about the political and economic impairment of [the Japanese] Empire." From their point of view, "the United States had become the aggressor."

Drought found that his assertions to the contrary, and those of Bishop Walsh, "were met with cautious, yet hopeful, disbelief."

In this situation Drought saw an opportunity to bring his own powers of persuasion to bear. Immediate action was needed to correct existing distortions and to establish a new perspective. The Japanese had to be convinced that the door to a resumption of friendly relations with the United States "had not been entirely closed"; the Americans had to be convinced that the Tripartite Pact was merely a "countermove" on the part of Japan, and that in reality she was ready and willing to "talk things over."

The "Working Analysis" that Drought prepared soon after his arrival in Tokyo was a combination of his own ideas and of suggestions passed along to him by his new Japanese friends. It was an outline of an "optimum" international program for Japan, "which, if carefully managed, might obtain some of the desired objectives, and if only partially realized, would do much to prevent a War with the United States."

During his sojourn in Japan, Drought made every effort to get Matsuoka "to commit himself and his Nation to a peace diplomacy." Drought thought the Foreign Minister's response was encouraging. Matsuoka personally offered fervid assurances in this regard. His staff at the Foreign Office (and other prominent persons) scoffed at the idea that Japan had obligations under the Tripartite Pact committing her to war. They said that this was an exaggeration perpetrated by Hitler and Chiang Kai-shek for their own reasons—chiefly to prevent a rapprochement between Japan and the United States.

Everything was going well, Drought felt, until Ambassador Grew took it upon himself to rebut the speech given by the Foreign Minister at the America-Japan Society luncheon honoring Nomura. Once this had happened, Matsuoka and Vice-Minister Ōhashi began expressing the view that further efforts would be useless. The Foreign Minister complained "that the Americans were either unwilling to understand [Japan] or [were] following a determined policy of forcing an action." Drought argued, in turn, that the Japanese had not done enough to counteract the effect of Japanese activities elsewhere or to combat "the anti-Japanese propaganda" that was prevalent "in all the Allied countries."

It was then that Matsuoka said "he wished it might be possible for him to speak with President Roosevelt—if only for an hour." Subsequently, the Foreign Minister asked Walsh and Drought to bring Japan's desire for a resumption of friendly relations with the United States to the attention of the President. Still later, General Mutō "expressed the same idea" by saying that Japanese-American problems could best be settled at a conference table.

Despite these statements by Matsuoka and Mutō, Walsh and Drought found the atmosphere in Tokyo to be one of discouragement and resentment. Ōhashi and others at the Foreign Office argued that Japan's "offer" to the United States, as conveyed by Matsuoka in his speech, had been summarily rejected. They might still be willing "to talk things over," but as far as they were concerned the next move was up to the American Government.

In leaving Japan to return home, Drought decided that he must somehow bring the two countries together. In his opinion, the statements Matsuoka and Mutō had made (and other remarks attributed to Konoye) could properly be interpreted as amounting to a secret, last-ditch attempt on the part of Japan to avert the disaster of war.

And so this tireless priest, who had in the meantime become John Doe, pursued that elusive goal throughout 1941, working closely over a period of months with Iwakuro and Wikawa—two very ambitious men who became, in effect, the members of a plot within a plot.

Bishop Walsh lent his support to Drought's activities from the beginning, but the Father General did not know that the peace efforts of the John Doe Associates were largely a creation of Drought's own imagination—an imagination that was fired and fed by the encouragement he received from his Japanese friends.

Over the years, the Bishop had relied on Drought in the administration of Maryknoll, allowing him considerable freedom in the exercise of his duties on behalf of the Society. During their visit to Japan in 1940, each had operated in his usual fashion. While Walsh had concerned himself with problems of a religious nature, Drought had plunged into political questions. He had kept the Bishop posted in a general way but had not spelled out the details. By the end of their stay in Tokyo, Walsh had come to believe in a Japanese "peace movement" that did not in fact exist. When Wikawa ("the peace treaty envoy," in Walsh's mind) turned up in the United States, followed closely by Iwakuro (the so-called Army representative), Walsh quite naturally concluded that Drought should continue to do whatever he could to help bring about a Japanese-American understanding.

The Bishop was unaware of the role Drought was playing—a role very similar to the one he had perfected in 1935 and '36, when he had organized Philippine Day at Notre Dame and had masterminded the sending of a goodwill cable to the Premier of Japan.

When Walsh returned to the Far East in the summer of 1941 to resume the visitation he had interrupted in December 1940, he again devoted himself primarily to Maryknoll's missionary work. He knew that Iwakuro, Wikawa, and Drought had been trying for months to forge a Japanese-American settlement; he thought that "a little further patience" would very likely be "crowned by happy results"; he was ready to offer his assistance in case of need.

By the time Wikawa sought him out in August, however, the chances of averting war through diplomacy were no longer as good as they had once been. Two months later the situation was worse. In asking Walsh to convey a verbal message to Roosevelt in mid-October, Konoye was grasping at straws. Even if the Bishop had been able to fly at once to Washington, the Prince's message could not have had much impact. Within forty-eight hours after talking to Walsh, Konoye resigned; the Premiership was then placed in Army hands. Konoye could not speak for Tōjō.

The Bishop's mid-November prediction that Japan would go to war with the United States, if a settlement was not reached soon, was hardly "news" to the State Department. The problem was *where* would the Japanese initiate hostilities? And *when*? The best guess, based on intelligence reports from a number of sources, was that Japan would strike *some-where in Southeast Asia sometime in the near future*—possibly even by-passing the Philippines, thus making it difficult for the United States to intervene.

Walsh's limited knowledge of Drought's activities behind the scenes helps to explain why the Bishop could subsequently say in good faith: "While Father Drought and I surely took an active part in these peace negotiations, neither of us did anything at any time that we were not specifically requested to do either by the [Japanese and American governments or by] the American Embassy in Tokyo. . . . We considered our role as that of messengers, no more, no less. We thought this was within our province and, indeed, that it was little [enough] to do in view of the possible objective—a peace that would restore China to the Chinese, put Japan on a law-abiding basis and deprive the Axis of an ally at the same time."

Men are able to entertain such dreams while their nations march toward war.

Thirty years after the event, the Bishop added this comment: "I learned later that the Japanese had . . . reservations about some of the terms in the proposed treaty that spoiled the whole project. And that our own government had consequently refused to conclude an agreement with them. As Father Drought afterwards explained the failure to me, the Japanese had hedged on the two principal points that they had first advocated; namely, the withdrawal of Japan from the Axis Pact and the withdrawal of the Japanese Army from China."

It is doubtful that anyone in a position of authority in Tokyo had ever *advocated* such policies, but talk is cheap and there had been plenty of it. It is not hard to believe that the men with whom Drought conferred tended to stress Japan's willingness to be "reasonable"—an essential ingredient whenever negotiations for peace are in prospect. Some of Drought's contacts may even have been quite specific, planting ideas in his head that he could repeat to others—to the Bishop, to the President, to the Secretary of State. Since Drought was uncritical in his approach to the Japanese, he accepted what he was told at face value. Later, he added his own estimates of the situation—estimates based on what he had observed during his brief stay in Japan and on current information supplied by Iwakuro and Wikawa. In the role of John Doe, James Drought could be very convincing.

*

But one further question needs to be asked. It is perhaps the most pertinent of all, and the most difficult: did the presence of Drought, Iwakuro, and Wikawa on the diplomatic front make any difference in the outcome of events?

This question may be unanswerable in a definitive sense, but it is not imponderable. Nor should it be sloughed off quickly with dogmatic pronouncements. To look this question in the eye is to stare into a deep pool, eddying with crosscurrents. Images seen one moment are gone the next, only to reappear later in slightly different form. They are readily discernible to the constant observer but not easily conveyed to anyone who has not peered into that pool himself, in search of meaning.

Out of such observation, however, comes an abiding thought: the significance of the John Doe Associates lies in the damage they did to the cause of peace in the Pacific in 1941 (though this was certainly not their intention).

The issues that separated the United States and Japan were complex; developments in Europe and in Asia did not make the task of reaching a settlement, short of war, any easier. Even under the best of circumstances, statesmen and diplomats would have been hard-pressed to develop acceptable compromises, but the Japanese and American authorities who had to meet this challenge were operating under the worst of circumstances. Premier Konoye and the Japanese Foreign Office were misled by the activities of Drought, Iwakuro, and Wikawa to a much greater extent than President Roosevelt and the State Department, but American diplomacy did not escape unscathed. Its practitioners were adversely affected, in many subtle ways, by the clandestine manipulations of these three men.

Hull and his Far Eastern advisers were quite right to be circumspect in reacting to the John Doe approach to the President in January; they were eminently prudent in their determination to await the arrival of the Japanese Ambassador, and thereafter to deal only with him or with fully empowered members of his staff. This made perfect sense. But when the State Department saw that Nomura had come empty-handed, that he had nothing to offer in the way of a proposal that might lead to a settlement, the Secretary and his staff should not have waited for the Ambassador to get around to exploring "points of divergence" with *them*. They should immediately have prepared a proposal of their own for submission to *him*. Instead, they were cautious and hesitant—too committed to the idea that Tokyo had to be the one to make the first move toward reconciliation. By failing to seize the initiative, they inadvertently helped to perpetuate a void that Drought, Iwakuro, and Wikawa were able to fill. The "Draft Understanding" of April 9 was the culmination of this phase of the John Doe operation.

It was the end of May before the State Department produced an "Unofficial, Exploratory, and Without Commitment" proposal. Something similar in nature but entirely free of John Doe influences—a document specifically responsive to legitimate Japanese concerns—could easily have been laid on the table, face-up, in February or March. Early action of a type designed to stimulate the interest of the Japanese Government might have given the leaders in Tokyo a meaningful alternative to a policy that envisaged continued adherence by Japan to the Tripartite Pact, prolongation of the war in China, and ultimately debouchment into Southeast Asia. A disclosure of the trend of American intentions, a disclosure handled primarily through Ambassador Grew, would have given hope to the Japanese people, and might possibly have brought public opinion into play. Explicit action by the President and the State Department along these lines would very likely have smothered the John Doe effort before it could have gained the strength that sustained it through the remainder of the year.

Ideas are said to have their time and place, but some of the conceptions that came to mind later (a cease-fire in China; the neutralization of French Indochina; a Japanese-American *modus vivendi*) could have been developed earlier, and in an atmosphere more conducive to acceptance by Japan than the one that prevailed after the crisis in relations had deepened. A brief moment of opportunity was lost by both governments in late June and early July when they failed to take advantage of the extraordinary change in circumstances precipitated by Hitler's invasion of the Soviet Union, but there were also other moments when something positive could have been done.

Professional diplomats may not have all of the answers, but they generally have more and better answers than amateurs are likely to provide. From the spring of 1941 on, however, the trouble for the future lay in the erroneous conception of the Roosevelt-Hull position that resulted from the assignment of a false value to the "Draft Understanding" by the decision-makers in Tokyo. Once that spurious document had come into their hands, they regularly used it thereafter as a yardstick against which to measure the genuine proposals that were subsequently put forward by the State Department. From incorrectly judging, in April, that Washington's attitude was more favorable than it was, Japan's leaders moved toward the argument, in June, July, and August, that the American mood was stiffening and that the terms then being stipulated were far harsher than those originally suggested.

This alleged "change in the American attitude" was confirmed in Japanese eyes by the contents of the "Joint Declaration" of June 21 and by the emphasis given to Hull's Four Principles in the President's "Oral Statement" of September 3—principles, incidentally, that need not have hindered the forging of an agreement acceptable to the parties concerned. Neither Japan nor the United States ever attempted to reduce these abstractions to definable terms, and yet this was not only necessary but possible. Hull had sidestepped the question Nomura had put to him in April concerning the future of "Manchukuo." This left the door open to a settlement of the issue at a later date. Even Hornbeck, for all of his belief in the need for firmness, was thinking in terms of "a fair deal" for Japan. Although the Japanese presence in China proper was a formidable obstacle, no one at the State Department was demanding that Japan remove her forces lock, stock, and barrel overnight. Hull and his advisers knew they would have to be patient. They could easily have sponsored a withdrawal by stages in accordance with a prearranged schedule. The price each party might have had to pay to achieve a compromise on this problem (and others like it) could not have been as barbarous and self-defeating as the cost, in lives and treasure, of war in the Pacific.

In Tokyo, however, the dreary distance that now stretched between appearances and reality seemed too vast to cross. Disappointment and dissatisfaction went hand in hand. The idea that Japan might be able to retain the essence by compromising on the form could no longer be sustained. The result was a hardening of the government's negotiating position. Men who had been suspicious of Washington's motives from the outset, or who were opposed to even the slightest diplomatic concessions, began finding it easier to be obstructionistic. One method was to attack the sincerity of the United States by pointing to the marked differences between the "initial American offer" (the John Doe "Draft Understanding" of April 9) and the so-called second proposal of June 21 (actually the first draft-agreement from the State Department to be fully scrutinized by Japan's leaders).

Needless to say, the authorities in Tokyo might never have become the victims of such confusion if they had not chosen, from the beginning, to be represented in Washington by a man who knew virtually nothing about the art and practice of diplomacy. Nomura was dispatched as a pawn in a game of international chess that the Foreign Minister of Japan was going to play by remote control. Matsuoka misjudged his own powers and also the nature of his agent. Nomura was not satisfied with the role he had been assigned; he wanted to be instrumental in bringing about a Japanese-American understanding. Lacking diplomatic experience, he needed help. He was grateful to the John Doe Associates when they provided it early in his mission. They were his "rescuers," and he followed them through thick and thin thereafter. He was consequently *their man*, not the Foreign Minister's. No one in Washington or in Tokyo ever realized the extent to which the Japanese Ambassador was under the malignant influence of these three "patriots for peace."

International confrontations are all too often regarded as unsolvable, until they have been solved; then everyone can see that a solution was possible all along. War in the Pacific was not inevitable in 1941, but the backdoor diplomacy of the John Doe Associates made an amicable settlement of the Far Eastern crisis harder to obtain. Drought, Iwakuro, and Wikawa were a distracting and disruptive element. Their will-o'-the-wisp activities ate into the time and energy of men with professional training and experience who might otherwise have been free to develop, on their own, workable formulas of compromise. Instead of *acting*, the authorities in Washington and Tokyo were *reacting*; instead of *being in favor of*, they were *taking positions against*.

The psychological emphasis was negative—not positive. This was the case in February and March, following Nomura's arrival; it was the case in April and May, when the John Doe Associates were increasing the pace of their effort; it was the case again, in June and July, as the Germans and the Japanese marched in distant lands; and finally it was the case once more, in August, September, and October, when an idea left over from the Walsh-Drought visit to Japan at the end of 1940 John Doe's "plenipotentiary conference" proposal—was belatedly being served up by Konoye as a means of dealing with the drastic deterioration that had recently occurred in Japanese-American relations as a consequence of the move into Indochina, the first step in Japan's drive southward.

By the time the Premier got around to showing interest in Drought's brainchild, the damage done by the John Doe Associates was extensive. The fundamental misconception that had been planted in the spring, in regard to the "Draft Understanding," had become a tangled, impenetrable growth by autumn. In Tokyo, the Premier and the Foreign Minister could see no reason why the President should reject an idea that had been part of "the original Draft Understanding"—a proposal that had been made to Japan, so far as they were concerned, by the American Government. In Washington, the Secretary of State and his advisers could see no reason to become excited over a proposition that the Japanese Government itself had regarded unfavorably earlier in the year— a proposition contaminated by association with Drought, Iwakuro, and Wikawa, men whose individual and collective efforts on behalf of peace had consistently been found wanting in terms of claims made versus results delivered.

The pernicious effect exerted on Japanese-American relations over a period of months by the machinations of the John Doe Associates, working behind the scenes, suddenly becomes visible here. The various arguments the State Department assembled in August and September against the Honolulu conference idea—arguments that were used to persuade the President to dawdle with the Konoye overture, neither accepting nor rejecting the invitation—acquire new significance when they are read within the context of the John Doe origins of the conference proposal and within the context, as well, of the Japanese Government's own earlier, negative response to that proposal.

The sad irony in this situation is that a "summit meeting" in the Pacific would have been a better policy choice than no meeting at all, for who can say with certainty that a conference would have been unproductive in every respect? There are times when personal contact between the highest political leaders of the contending sides can encourage decisions that protracted discussion at lower levels of competence and responsibility might not otherwise produce. It is difficult to believe that an abortive tête-à-tête would have resulted in any irreparable damage to the United States or that failure at Honolulu would have led to a graver international crisis than the one already in existence.

In playing the part of private brokers for peace, Drought, Iwakuro, and Wikawa enormously complicated the Hull-Nomura conversations, making them more muddled and ineffectual than they would otherwise have been. In the end, the old and battered and already foundering ship of Japanese-American relations went plummeting to the bottom of the sea—not simply a victim of dastardly destruction from without, as the President saw it, but also of unintentional scuttling from within—a tragedy that might more easily have been averted if only the John Doe Associates had never been permitted to set foot on board that already badly listing vessel at such a critical moment in world history.

Appendixes

Appendix A

The "Working Analysis of Our (Japanese) Position & Policy in the Far East, With Particular Reference to the United States" *(written by Father James M. Drought at the Imperial Hotel, Tokyo, in late November and early December 1940, as though he were a Japanese)*:

Present attitude in the United States. The current attitude among the American people and government is no longer related to points of conflicting interests. Nor is it merely a response to the propaganda of pressure groups. It has deteriorated below the level of argumentation: it has become an emotion of antipathy, and, by a complicated psychological process, a means of release for the inability of the American people to take a unified, national attitude on the Germano-British War.

Japan is so far distant, its actions have been so grossly misrepresented, its policy so badly understood, its incidents of diplomatic conflict so frequent, that the United States Government shrewdly estimates what its people unconsciously feel, viz. that a relieving explosion of sentiment against Japan will compensate for their own lack of unified and decisive action toward Europe and thereby unite them on at least one aspect of foreign policy.

To point out that this antagonistic sentiment is not wholly formed by discontent with Japanese-American relations is not to minimize it: rather, this fact emphasizes strikingly that, for the first time in our history, the United States may go to war with us without fully realizing exactly *why* it is going to war. In the United States, sentiment is surprisingly more powerful than money, more powerful even than the Government itself. This sentiment requires cautious treatment and emotional rather than legal diplomacy, if it is to be overcome.

For Japan, there are many serious disadvantages in an emotion that creates moral embargoes, and may create war. But, if properly handled, there is also one great advantage to be gained. When, as now, relations have moved beyond the cool mathematics of diplomacy, one can accomplish, by dramatic reversal, more in a short time than could be gained

---

The text reproduced here is from the definitive version in the JMD papers.

by years of normal effort. An emotional atmosphere renders possible, even necessary, a radical solution in either direction.

Opportunity for direct, bilateral action. Accordingly, for the Japanese, the present American attitude is not only a danger but an opportunity. Insensibly, and as one result of an impasse that may prove a benefit in disguise, Japan has obtained a new, higher, more individual and separate place in the American mind than ever before. If Japan has assumed today, in the American mind, a threatening attitude, she has also assumed, by the same token, a position of equality from which we can quite naturally treat with the United States entirely apart from other nations. For the first time, our mutual relations are not entangled by the necessity of sharing our deliberations with Europeans. The United States, by sponsoring Chiang Kai-Shek's China, has eliminated China as an equal. Moreover, the tactical silence of the European powers at the present moment has left the United States as outstanding protagonist. We should take advantage of this to attempt a settlement of differences before any decisive action has been reached in the European War. Even if our main objective fails, we can hope reasonably so to alter American public opinion as to allay much of its present emotional heat. (The procedure for this will be discussed below.)

The Far East as a region:

(a) Geographic & military. Japan's position, to which her Far Eastern policy conforms, is determined by geographic, economic and political factors of unequal constancy. At this time, we need consider, with an eye to the future, only those factors which are of present influence. It should be our aim to impart such geographical definiteness to the Far Eastern region that it will be accepted as being bounded on the east by 180°L.; on the north, by the arctic zone with eastern limits at 180°L., and western limits at 120°L.; on the south by the Dutch East Indies and New Guinea; on the west by Thailand, Tibet, Sinkiang, Mongolia and Soviet Siberia at 90°L. Soviet Siberia and the United States are the only nations that *now* project territorially into this area. Accordingly, they are now the only nations which could carry on a military war with Japan.

(b) Our economic position. Economically, our territorial position, productive-cost capacity and transportation facilities favor our trade in this area. At present, no one can compete with us except through finance capital. Therefore, we have a choice of obtaining capital cooperation for our development of this Far East, or of setting up a regional, closed economy that will induce and perpetuate, for many years to come, a relatively low standard of living. We need capital to break down our own economic embargo on the imports so necessary for improved material welfare in Japan; we need capital for the rapid and profitable development of the Far East, which will thereby obtain a self-containment that will be its best protection. Due to the compulsion of circumstance, our own lack of capital finance and the tenacity of European politics, we have had to employ military power, to establish, before it was too late, our politic-economic position in relation to Far Eastern countries.

(c) Our political position. Though less rapidly than some anticipated, our political position has been established, if not yet consolidated, in our mandated areas of the South Seas, in the South Sakhalin, Jehol, Inner Mongolia, Manchukou [*sic*], Korea, North and East Central China. We should push through to a satisfactory settlement of the China Incident. In any event, it is apparent that if we obtain a position in South China we will have closed off the West Central territory of Chiang Kai-Shek, and we can quite afford (if other circumstances indicate the prudence of such a course) not to bother too much about that territory, for some years to come. We must aim by political and economic means, or, these failing, by military methods, to establish and strengthen our position in Indo-China, Thailand, Malaya (?) and the Dutch East Indies.

(d) Philippines, Hong Kong & Singapore. If the United States will agree to resist forcibly the efforts of any third power to establish political sovereignty in the Philippines: and agree forcibly to resist the establishment there of any communistic government, we can afford, profitably, to leave the Philippine Islands in statu quo. Moreover, it would be distinctly advantageous to leave Hong Kong, and Singapore also, their present political status. (It has proved helpful to the United States to confirm, under the Monroe Doctrine, small colonial possessions of European powers in the Western Hemisphere. Instead of being focal points of conflict these possessions have become bands of attachment.)

(e) Stabilization of our position by Far Eastern Monroe Doctrine. The manoeuvre for the remaining stabilization of the Far East region might best be accomplished by political and economic means since a too great extension of our military fronts may render difficult the retention of a highly mobile and powerful reserve which may be needed for quick action at a crisis. We must carefully determine at what point we can suspend military action and attempt to consolidate our position by diplomatic action which will result in the effective proclamation, and acceptance by the United States, of a Far Eastern Monroe Doctrine.

(f) Our power of maintaining order in [the] Far East. In exercising what will really be political hegemony over this area, we must recognize that we cannot afford to permit, in any considerable or important section, such political or economic weakness as would entice European powers to a resumption of extra-continental imperialism, or as would dispose any section toward communism which is not a political form of government but a corroding social disease that becomes epidemic. Accordingly, we must establish, and have acknowledged, the power to intervene for the preservation of our Monroe Far Eastern Doctrine. Realistically, such power would proceed automatically from the recognition of the Doctrine and would require no constant military or police surveillance. Our dominant political and economic powers would be effective instruments of normal control: exactly as such are, and have been, for the United States with respect to the Western Hemisphere.

(g) The *real* significance for the U. S. It can correctly, though very secretly, be pointed out to the United States

1. that the above described condition of Far Eastern political affairs is, and will be, by our determination, an effective barrier to the political imperialism of any European power in the Far East: no matter who may win the present struggle:

2. that such a condition conforms to the ideals and interests of the United States better than would a European colonization of the Far East, such as might have been looked for if Japan had not acted:

3. furthermore, and of inestimable world significance, such a condition, which the United States must desire but was in no position to effect, places both our countries, if effectively cooperating, in so dominant a position as to minimize the importance of the European area for years to come.

Results of a true understanding. Could such a cooperative understanding be reached, we would not only prevent the Far Eastern extension of the European conflict, but we would *immunize the Far East against it.* It is even possible that our two countries might become the final arbitrators of the outcome of the European War. Moreover, by such common action and agreement, we would create a friendly and intimate American relationship which would eliminate the likelihood of armed conflict with the United States and thereby strengthen our position against Russia which will remain, for years or generations, a doubtful quantity.

The European War: our position & the U. S. position:

(a) If Germany wins. If Germany wins the present war, England may be reduced to the condition of France: but the fruits of German victory will be restricted by Russia, allied with Turkey, to Western and Central Europe. Africa and some of the Near East will be shared with Italy. We have already, though not yet completely, withdrawn the Far East from the category of "war spoils." If Germany wins, the United States will support our Far Eastern position just as the United States will resist any German advance in the Western Hemisphere. What the German politic for the Dutch East Indies will be, is difficult to guess. Probably, the Germans will mark time until the threat of American opposition has been clarified. If they did not fear the United States, then we should have a politico-economic competitor in the Far East at a strategic source of vital commodities: or we would have to fight Germany for the Dutch East Indies. Finally, if Germany wins, the United States will fight her sooner or later, but surely. (The anti-Nazi sentiment in the United States is the same as was the anti-Kaiser sentiment. Nothing can change it. The United States has been amazed but not chagrined by Nazi victories, which, if continued, will only challenge them more to conflict than to caution. The Americans fought in the World War, and they will not permit Germany to win it now by delayed action.) Meanwhile, Canada will seek some form of union with the United States: so, possibly, will Australia.

(b) If England wins. If England wins, the United States cannot be counted upon to support our Far Eastern policy or position unless, before such a victory, we have already established our position with the United States. An English victory would constrict Russia, destroy Nazi Germany, restore Scandanavia [*sic*] and establish British hegemony over Continental Europe. It would strengthen the units of the Commonwealth and reaffirm the traditional British position in the Far East.

(c) Our protection against either eventuality. Consequently, only an entente cordial with the United States can confirm, in international politics, our Far Eastern position, irrespective of which country may win the European War. Meanwhile, by singularly resisting our present actions, the United States is unwittingly setting up a situation which eliminates European Powers from the Far East. This is of considerable advantage to Japan: it brings closer, because of its very intensity, a possibility of complete adjustment.

A diplomatic stroke. Despite appearances to the contrary, and almost because of the present actions of the United States as well as the condition of Europe, the stage may well be set for the greatest diplomatic stroke in a generation. Toward this end, we should move with a carefully designed strategy, the elements of which we will now consider.

SUPPORTING STRATEGICAL PROCEDURE

We should be clearly aware that, whatever steps are taken, our tactics should be as carefully interrelated and coordinated as are fingers in relation to a hand gathering up diversified threads.

We must plot the cumulative effect of our actions and time them accordingly.

Retain our bargaining position. As items of bargaining strength in a conference designed for the settlement of all our outstanding differences, we need to keep in reserve, and make no present concessions on, our military and political position in China, opening the Yangtse Valley, the Open Door, our intentions relative to the Dutch East Indies, the Philippines, American airways and communications development in the Far East; our Axis Alliance and any other European relationship. Nor should we answer, one way or another, Mr. Stimson's statement of

December 1st concerning American rights and interests in the Far East. Actually, *with our position established,* we can ultimately, though not quickly, concede the Open Door as an American diplomatic victory since it would involve no real competition in our trade. We can use the American doubt about the Philippines to manoeuvre the United States into a commitment of an alliance with respect to any third power. We can consider our positions in East, Central and North China as faits accomplis, though we could, without any loss whatever, permit the Americans to talk of some sort of political structure which would leave our position substantially unchanged but which could be presented acceptably to American public opinion. In confidential conference, we could consider Indo-China, the Dutch East Indies, etc., as war areas of doubtful allegiance and consequently inherently menacing to the Far Eastern situation from both the American and Japanese points of view. The Stimson shibboleth of "territorial integrity of China" could neatly be conceded to him as not involving, for the sake of China and the Far East, a restoration of the purely nominal, political unity, which only existed in diplomatic conversations. *Territorial* integrity is rather a natural fact which no one can change. It is the politico-economic integrity that we wish to establish. Stimson, of course, would have to abandon the pretense that Manchukuo pertains to the territorial integrity of China.

American proposals for China. If the Americans attempt to insist on the relinquishment of the rest of China to the political sovereignty of the Chiang Kai-Shek Government, we do not need to entertain their suggestion. *But* it would be embarrassing to them, and conceivably afford a tactical advantage to us, if we were to ask them if they could suggest any practical politico-economic structure other than what we have developed in China

1. which would be acceptable politically to the Chinese and not a signal for another civil war or provincial division by war lords or the resumption of chaos:

2. that would not be partly communistic:

3. that would be organized with a state economy capable of procuring national development, escape from famine and elevation of the cruelly low Chinese standard of living:

4. that by European entanglements, by incurable Chinese venality and by endemic political disorder (which it is utopian to hope can be changed over-night) would not bring continued misery to China and become a standing enticement for the imperialistic or communistic ambitions of other powers:

5. that the United States would guarantee and *forcibly* prevent from becoming a menace to the peace, order, and security of the Far East. If they are at all fair (and Americans, when not emotionally aroused,

are inclined to be very fair) the Americans will admit that they have run into a cul-de-sac and be prepared to accept provisional plans for setting up really independent governments and the lifting of martial law as conditions warrant within the territory comprised by the phrase "territorial integrity of China." (The Americans could be reminded that under somewhat similar, but much less grave provocation, President Wilson set up the Carranza Government in Mexico, they could be reminded of Nicaragua, Puerto Rico, etc.)

Silence as an instrument. But of such attitudes on our part, we should at the present time give no *slightest indication* if it is our aim to so manoeuvre the present situation as to render necessary and acceptable to both peoples a friendly conference for the settlement of all outstanding differences. It would seem advisable that such a conference should take place before there has been decisive action in the European War.

Agreement with the U. S. It should be our aim to so dispose affairs that the calling of a plenipotentiary Japan–United States conference at Tokyo, or at Honolulu (but not at Washington) would seem reasonable and desirable in the mind of American public opinion: if not in the mind of the Roosevelt Government.

That the United States should move to revive the commercial treaty by sending a "commission": or that the United States should lift the moral embargoes as a gesture of goodwill would not be a prudent suggestion because

1. it might easily be met with a downright refusal:

2. even if accepted, it would leave the main issues unchanged and continuing sources of future and deeper misunderstandings.

At this time, a bold manoeuvre that comprehends all issues

1. will be difficult to resist, as American opinion would favor it if rightly made: and

2. if even moderately successful, it will break down the present tension *and permit Japan to consolidate her position, with or without American approbation.*

The tactics of a special address:

(a) Setting. It would seem strategically advisable that the Prime Minister, or his Minister of Foreign Affairs, should make an address to the Diet, or to some large representation of the government, military, navy, business, etc. In this speech, he would outline Japan's position in phrases and manner of thought that would arrest the attention of the American public. (We shall submit a draft for such a psychological and diplomatic speech.)

(b) Time. This speech should be made before Mr. Nomura arrives in the United States and preferably about December 20th when the Christmas spirit of "peace on earth to men of goodwill" is prevailing in the

United States. If given too near Christmas time, the people will be preoccupied and will not read it. At the present moment, and for the first time in years, they will read any authoritative statement from Japan which has become a subject of major national interest.

(c) Publicity. Careful preparation should be made to obtain widest possible publicity for this address in the United States. The press associations should be advised, twenty-four hours in advance, of the imminence of an important address. This will guarantee wide attention. Also, the Japanese diplomatic representative at Washington should advise the State Department twenty-four hours in advance but not any sooner lest the State Department devise some counter-publicity. The character of the speech should be so thorough and moving as to insure favorable comment. News reels should be made, in English, with excerpts of the speech and with the conclusion. The news reels should be forwarded immediately for release in the United States.

(d) Desired effect. The desired effect of such a speech will be to force the hand of the American Government to a bilateral conference: the bases for which will be arranged diplomatically in accordance with our policy as outlined above.

(e) Related propaganda. Meanwhile,

1. propaganda should be started to counteract Mr. Stimson's adverse interpretation of our Far Eastern Monroe Doctrine.

2. The idea of a Pan-Asian defense paralleling the present United States policy of Pan-American defense should be developed politically and widely publicised. Negotiations for such parallel agreements should be begun at once with Far Eastern governments. This would strengthen our position at any conference.

3. Propaganda should be developed (as emanating from American sources) to show that the present forcing diplomacy of the American Government will, if continued, compel Japan, regardless of its preference, to establish a non-capitalistic economy which will close the door to American capital opportunity in the Far East and react most unfavorably on the domestic economy of the United States.

On the other hand, the revival of distributive capitalism in the Far East would greatly benefit the United States and surely benefit the Far East more than would distributive communism or distributive "commodityism" which are the only alternatives. It can be pointed out that it is idle to talk of the preservation of American rights and interests unless we retain the same basis of economic and financial structure. It can be emphasized, in this connection, that Japan is not only the best customer of the United States but it is the only nation (except deceased Finland) that has never defaulted its obligations. Through Japan, American business and finance can realize its long sought dream of economic opportunity in the Far East: this time to our *mutual* advantage. Billions of dollars could be, and should be, immediately needed for capital uses. We may feel confident that American business and financiers would prefer such an arrangement to the "dole" loans now being made by the United States Government to China.

Axis Alliance in American opinion. Our propaganda respecting the purpose and implications of our Axis Alliance would better, at this time, be carried out by silence than by further explanation. It is perfectly true that Japan, since she is not equally favored by natural resources, etc., as the United States, cannot prudently entertain involvement in the European War nor can we ignore the possibility of an aftermath to that war that would disrupt the order of the Far East. We must take into account the possibility that Germany as well as England may win the war. The United States refuses to entertain the possibility that Germany can win the war, at least ultimately. Accordingly, however realistic our purposes for the alliance may have been, the American mind is disposed to interpret the Alliance as a participation in Nazi ideology and as indicative of intended participation in the Nazi political and economic aggression. The Americans have interpreted our participation, not as a defensive move on our part, but as a challenge: and they would not be disposed to interpret correctly its defensive features even if the Axis had been extended to include France, England and all South America.

We can let the United States maintain its attitude toward the Germano-English War: but we can, and must reasonably demand, at the same time, a cool appreciation of our more prudent though different, attitude. With this understanding, we could proceed wisely with the new elaboration of our American relations.

PLENIPOTENTIARY CONFERENCE

Recognizing the strategic value of our current status and acting on the basis of our position and policy as outlined in our "Working Analysis," we might aim to have a conference called *by simultaneous and similar announcements by both governments.*

Identic statements. Both governments should agree to make only identic statements before and during the conference and also after (if agreement is reached). Let us remember

1. that our consent to the Washington Conference, 1922, was misrepresented before our delegates arrived at Washington:

2. that our protest of the Exclusion Act was misconstrued. Etc.

Veto courtesy. Both governments should agree to grant to the other the veto courtesy accorded in the designation of ambassadors. The names of the members proposed as delegates should be submitted for acceptance by each government—it being clearly understood that no information shall be given to the press respecting names proposed or rejected. The press shall be given only such names as are agreed upon.

Exception to this regulation shall be made, if desired, for our Minister and Vice Minister of Foreign Affairs, the President of the Diet and of the House of Peers: for the American Secretary and the Assistant Secretary of State, the Speaker of the House of Representatives and the President of the Senate. The present Ambassadors of Japan and the United States shall also be excepted from the veto courtesy.

Members. The composition of the conference members should reflect, not only political interests, but military, business and financial, as well. We would handicap ourselves if we agree to receive a commission of such personnel as the United States sent to Havana this year.

Agenda. The conference agenda should be announced as including all outstanding, present points of difference: but on no account should these points be antecedently specified to the press of either country. If kept general in character, public opinion would be favorably impressed: if specified, pressure groups will foment arguments. As between the governments, however, a confidential list of subjects should be agreed upon in advance. Keeping in mind our own "Working Analysis," it would seem that we can profitably discuss the whole structure of our position as well as every conflicting interest with the United States. The Americans would be unprepared for such a wide scope of subject and, though we desire it, we can make it appear as if it were, in part, a concession.

Prominent items of agenda would be:

The Far East as a region.
The Far Eastern Monroe Doctrine.
Pan-Asian Defense.
Armaments (since there can now be no question of limitation and we have everything to gain and nothing to lose by discussion of this subject).
Political situation in territorial China.
"Territorial" integrity of China.
The 9 Power Pact and why it *could not work.*
The Philippines, Dutch East Indies, etc.
Embargoes and Government loans.
Exchange and censorship.
Financial cooperation.
Trade agreement.
Substitution of a quota for the Exclusion Act (to be proposed by the Americans).
The Open Door.

Realistically, we are in a strong position for the conference discussion of such subjects and policies which could be improved diplomatically where they most need improvement.

A constructive discussion of such agenda should force the United States to discontinue their "rear-guard action" diplomacy: and force them, also, to abandon their tactic of trying to fit new circumstances into old legal phrases. In any event, the mere fact of discussion will serve to advance our position.

Time. Such a conference should be projected as soon as possible after the proposed speech of December 20. As from the date of the conference announcement, both governments should agree to refrain, so far as may be conformably to national interests, from further involvement in any controversial action. This would immobilize the United States until the conference had been concluded. Provided announcement is made as soon as possible, the conference itself could take place in February or March, 1941. It *should not* take place during the summer months (remember Versailles).

Place. It would be very advantageous to us if the Americans could be persuaded to come to Tokyo. As such a concession might be represented in America as "appeasement" we must be prepared to *make every effort* to overcome objections by pointing out the propriety of our acting as the conference hosts for a Far Eastern bilateral conference. It would be a diplomatic victory, and assure a good start, if we can secure Tokyo as the place of meeting. To this end, we must take the practical, though not the diplomatic, initiative. Japanese courtesy, cherry-blossom time, a fine hotel, golf courses, the moving pageantry of kimonos against the backdrop of national sacrifice—all of these should prove helpfully disposing circumstances. If we fail to agree on Tokyo, we could reluctantly accept Honolulu because of its symbolic significance and as a subtle indication of our own policies.

Notification to other governments. It would seem inadvisable that either the United States or Japan should inform other nations of a projected conference. If it is successful no one would dare to object; and if it fails, no one will quarrel with us.

Appendix B

The John Doe "Draft Understanding" *(written by James M. Drought, Hideo Iwakuro, and Tadao Wikawa at the Wardman Park Hotel, Washington, D.C., in early April 1941):*

The Governments of the United States and of Japan accept joint responsibility for the initiation and conclusion of a general agreement disposing the resumption of our traditional friendly relations.

Without reference to specific causes of recent estrangement, it is the sincere desire of both Governments that the incidents which led to the deterioration of amicable sentiment among our peoples should be prevented from recurrence and corrected in their unforeseen and unfortunate consequences.

It is our present hope that, by a joint effort, our nations may establish a just Peace in the Pacific; and by the rapid consummation of an entente cordiale, arrest, if not dispel, the tragic confusion that now threatens to engulf civilization.

For such decisive action, protracted negotiations would seem ill-suited and weakening. We, therefore, suggest that adequate instrumentalities should be developed for the realization of a general agreement which would bind, meanwhile, both Governments in honor and in act.

It is our belief that such an understanding should comprise only the pivotal issues of urgency and not the accessory concerns which could be deliberated at a Conference and appropriately confirmed by our respective Governments.

We presume to anticipate that our Governments could achieve harmonious relations if certain situations and attitudes were clarified or improved, to wit:

1. The concepts of the United States and of Japan respecting international *Relations and the Character of Nations*
2. The attitudes of both Governments toward the European War.
3. The relations of both nations toward the China Affair.
4. Naval, aerial and mercantile marine relations in the Pacific.

The text reproduced here is from the file copy in the archives of the State Department.

5. Commerce between both nations and their financial cooperation.

6. Economic activity of both nations in the Southwestern Pacific area.

7. The policies of both nations affecting political stabilization in the Pacific.

Accordingly, we have come to the following mutual understanding subject, of course, to modifications by the United States Government and subject to the official and final decision of the Government of Japan.

I. *The Concepts of the United States and of Japan Respecting International Relations and the Character of Nations*

The Governments of the United States and of Japan might jointly acknowledge each other as equally sovereign states and contiguous Pacific powers.

Both Governments assert the unanimity of their national policies as directed toward the foundation of a lasting peace and the inauguration of a new era of respectful confidence and cooperation among our peoples.

Both Governments might declare that it is their traditional, and present, concept and conviction that nations and races compose, as members of a family, one household; each equally enjoying rights and admitting responsibilities with a mutuality of interests regulated by peaceful processes and directed to the pursuit of their moral and physical welfare, which they are bound to defend for themselves as they are bound not to destroy for others.

Both Governments are firmly determined that their respective traditional concepts on the character of nations and the underlying moral principles of social order and national life will continue to be preserved and never transformed by foreign ideas or ideologies contrary to those moral principles and concepts.

II. *The Attitudes of Both Governments Toward the European War*

The Government of Japan maintains that the purpose of its Axis Alliance was, and is, defensive and designed to prevent the extension of military grouping among nations not directly affected by the European War.

The Government of Japan, with no intention of evading its existing treaty obligation, desires to declare that its military obligation under the Axis Alliance comes into force only when one of the parties of the Alliance is aggressively attacked by a power not at present involved in the European War.

The Government of the United States maintains that its attitude toward the European War is, and will continue to be, determined by no aggressive alliance aimed to assist any one nation against another. The United States maintains that it is pledged to the hate of war, and accordingly, its attitude toward the European War is, and will continue to be, determined solely and exclusively by considerations of the protective defense of its own national welfare and security.

III. *China Affairs* [i.e., *"The China Affair"* or *"The China Incident"*]

The President of the United States, if the following terms are approved by His Excellency and guaranteed by the Government of Japan, might request the Chiang-Kai-Chek regime to negotiate peace with Japan.

a. Independence of China

b. Withdrawal of Japanese troops from Chinese territory, in accordance with an agreement to be reached between Japan and China

c. No acquisition of Chinese territory

d. No imposition of indemnities

e. Resumption of the "Open Door"; the interpretation and application of which shall be agreed upon at some future, convenient time between the United States and Japan

f. Coalescence of the governments of Chiang-Kai-Chek and of Wang-Ching-Wei

g. No large-scale or concentrated immigration of Japanese into Chinese territory

h. Recognition of Manchukuo

With the acceptance by the Chiang-Kai-Chek regime of the aforementioned Presidential request, the Japanese Government shall commence direct peace negotiations with the newly coalesced Chinese Government, or constituent elements thereof.

The Government of Japan shall submit to the Chinese concrete terms of peace, within the limits of aforesaid general terms and along the line of neighborly friendship, joint defense against communistic activities and economic cooperation.

Should the Chiang-Kai-Chek regime reject the request of President Roosevelt, the United States Government shall discontinue assistance to the Chinese.*

IV. *Naval, Aerial and Mercantile Marine Relations in the Pacific*

a. As both the Americans and the Japanese are desirous of maintaining the peace in the Pacific, they shall not resort to such disposition of their naval forces and aerial forces as to menace each other. Detailed, concrete agreement thereof shall be left for determination at the proposed joint Conference.

b. At the conclusion of the projected Conference, each nation might despatch a courtesy naval squadron to visit the country of the other and signalize the new era of Peace in the Pacific.

c. With the first ray of hope for the settlement of China affairs, the Japanese Government will agree, if desired, to use their good offices to

* This stipulation was deleted from the text of the "Draft Understanding" *before* Nomura cabled it to Tokyo.

release for contract by Americans certain percentage of their total tonnage of merchant vessels, chiefly for the Pacific service, so soon as they can be released from their present commitments. The amount of such tonnage shall be determined at the Conference.

v. *Commerce Between Both Nations and Their Financial Cooperation*

When official approbation to the present understanding has been given by both Governments, the United States and Japan shall assure each other to mutually supply such commodities as are respectively available or required by either of them. Both Governments further consent to take necessary steps to the resumption of normal trade relations as formerly established under the Treaty of Navigation and Commerce between the United States and Japan. If a new commercial treaty is desired by both Governments, it could be elaborated at the proposed Conference and concluded in accordance with usual procedure.

For the advancement of economic cooperation between both nations, it is suggested that the United States extend to Japan a gold credit in amounts sufficient to foster trade and industrial development directed to the betterment of Far Eastern economic conditions and to the sustained economic cooperation of the Governments of the United States and of Japan.

vi. *Economic Activity of Both Nations in the Southwestern Pacific Area*

On the pledged basis of guarantee that Japanese activities in the Southwestern Pacific area shall be carried on by peaceful means, without resorting to arms, American cooperation and support shall be given in the production and procurement of natural resources (such as oil, rubber, tin, nickel) which Japan needs.

vii. *The Policies of Both Nations Affecting Political Stabilization in the Pacific*

a. The Governments of the United States and of Japan will not acquiesce in the future transfer of territories or the relegation of existing States within the Far East and in the Southwestern Pacific area to any European Power.

b. The Governments of the United States and of Japan jointly guarantee the independence of the Philippine Islands and will consider means to come to their assistance in the event of unprovoked aggression by any third Power.

c. The Government of Japan requests the friendly and diplomatic assistance of the Government of the United States for the removal of Hongkong and Singapore as doorways to further political encroachment by the British in the Far East.*

* This stipulation was deleted from the text of the "Draft Understanding" *before* Nomura cabled it to Tokyo.

d. Japanese Immigration to the United States and to the Southwestern Pacific area shall receive amicable consideration—on a basis of equality with other nationals and freedom from discrimination.

Conference

a. It is suggested that a Conference between Delegates of the United States and of Japan be held at Honolulu and that this Conference be opened for the United States by President Roosevelt and for Japan by Prince Konoye. The delegates could number less than five each, exclusive of experts, clerks, etc.

b. There shall be no foreign observers at the Conference.

c. This Conference could be held as soon as possible (May 1941) after the present understanding has been reached.

d. The agenda of the Conference would not include a reconsideration of the present understanding but would direct its efforts to the specification of the pre-arranged agenda and drafting of instruments to effectuate the understanding. The precise agenda could be determined upon by mutual agreement between both Governments.

Addendum

The present understanding shall be kept as a confidential memorandum between the Governments of the United States and of Japan.

The scope, character and timing of the announcement of this understanding will be agreed upon by both Governments.

Appendix C

Some readers may wish to know what happened to John Doe and his friends after Pearl Harbor. This postscript was written with that thought in mind:

The sudden and drastic shift from peace to war that occurred at Pearl Harbor on Sunday morning, December 7, 1941, left millions of Americans in a state of shock, stubbornly picking up the pieces of a way of life that could never be the same again. For the Maryknoll Society new problems arose at home and abroad that quickly absorbed the attention of Walsh and Drought. They scarcely had time to look back at the shambles of a year that had come so mercilessly to a close. And yet the past could not be dismissed entirely, or old friends forgotten, even if some of them now belonged to the ranks of "the enemy."

During the early months of the conflict, Drought tried repeatedly to obtain permission to call on Admiral Nomura (the Ambassador had been interned —together with other members of the Japanese Embassy —immediately after the commencement of hostilities). The American authorities with whom Drought dealt seemed to be "sympathetic," but they steadfastly refused to allow a meeting to take place. Finally, toward the end of April 1942, Drought decided to commit to paper the thoughts he would not be able to express in person: "I do not feel that the fact of war alters in the least the deep esteem with which I regard you who strove so honorably and honestly for the restoration of friendly relations between our peoples."

"Since it appears that I cannot visit you," Drought added, "I hope this letter may reach you to assure you of my prayers and of my unchanging confidence in your great personal integrity."

It was the middle of May before Drought received Nomura's warm reply, written in the Admiral's own hand:

My dear Father Drought!
I think of you and the Bishop very very often and needless to say, am most anxious to see you, but it might be impossible to see you these days.
Your indefatigable endeavor for the betterment of mankind, I understand

and know to appreciate from the bottom of my heart. It looks to me as if I can imagine what you are thinking of these days. May your noble service as a teacher of the Gospel of the All-mighty for the interests of mankind be continued!

I expect to leave your country soon, and say good-bye, hoping to meet you again some time.

With deepest respects and best wishes,

Yours very Sincerely

K. Nomura

By the time this letter arrived at Maryknoll, Drought had completed work on a project involving another old friend—one who was soon to be awarded an honorary Doctor of Laws degree at Georgetown University. Drought had already written an acceptance speech for the recipient, Frank Walker, and was now thinking of ways to obtain "a good press" for the occasion.

The Postmaster General would thus have an opportunity to tell the American people what Drought was currently thinking: "We were unprepared for war because we were unprepared for malice—the deep, planned malice of an evil soul. Ready to argue our rights, we were unready to fight for our lives. Our enemies . . . will be satisfied with nothing but our destruction. . . . We could not appease them even if we supinely would. Their hands . . . are now grasping at the throat of our civilization. We are at last aware that this has always been their aim. . . . We are in critical danger."

The members of the Georgetown graduating class of 1942 dutifully listened to the Postmaster General's speech, accepted their degrees, and then went their separate ways, many of them into the armed forces of the United States.

Summer came, and Father Drought began getting ready to leave for Lima, Peru, where Bishop Walsh was awaiting his arrival. To his amazement, he suddenly learned that he would not be given a passport. He immediately tried to reach the Secretary of State by telephone, but had to be content with talking to an administrative assistant instead.

Over a week ago [Drought subsequently informed Frank Walker] I phoned Mr. Hull, who asked Mr. [Cecil] Gray to take the call. I told Gray what I had learned from other sources in the State Department, and Gray said such a thing was "contemptible" and that the "Chief" would be greatly displeased. I waited ten days for the "Chief" to show some evidence of his displeasure, and when none was forthcoming, I wrote him a letter, copy of which I enclose for your information. . . .

Personally, as I am sure you know, the opinions of the individuals at the State Department would mean very little to me but, under the circumstances, it may mean a great deal to our Society, and to the work of the Church. Instead of getting the Congressional Medal of Honor (which, if the Department wants to be technical, we richly deserve) we are being thrown . . . "a dead cat."

An official of the State Department blandly informed me that space [on flights abroad] was difficult to obtain. An hour later I proved the contrary, and in the daily paper on the same day I noticed that space was provided for the wife, servant, and Saint Bernard dog of the 77th Assistant on the British contingent of the Lend Lease Program.

Although a member of Walker's office was able to help Drought obtain tentative reservations from Pan American, the State Department still refused to give him a passport. Drought vowed to get "a clear answer and a clear apology" even if he had to go "to the President himself."

Drought believed that he was being denied a passport because of his association with "Japanese officials" during the "exploratory conversations" in 1941. "The President and the Secretary of the United States are well aware," Drought declared in his letter to Hull, "that it was by their own encouragement and direct request that I participated so actively in the successful manoeuvre of delay, and in the unsuccessful effort for Pacific peace."

Drought was putting the best face on matters that he could; he was also allying himself with an incorrect assumption that ultimately achieved wider currency—namely, that Hull's primary purpose in holding so many conversations with Nomura during 1941 had been to stall for time.

In mid-1942 Drought wanted to be praised for having facilitated that "purpose," but more than a year earlier, when he had first gone to the White House to outline the steps the Japanese Government was allegedly prepared to take to achieve a settlement with the United States, he had been advised to reduce to writing what his Japanese contacts had in mind. No one had asked him to take part in any "manoeuvre of delay."

If Hull was surprised to learn that Drought now saw himself as having participated in such a stratagem, one can only wonder what went through the Secretary's mind when he read Drought's next assertion: "Actually, no other citizen of our country accomplished so much; no one else was in a position to do so, since with the exception of the stupid documents of November and December 1941, I myself composed most of the communications, as a test of Japanese good faith, and in an effort to meet the requirements of the President and of yourself."*

Drought's recollection was that he had repeatedly tried after April 1941 to relinquish the role he had been playing, but that he had been "discouraged, by both parties, from doing so." He had therefore "continued to act obediently, as a 'very patriotic citizen' and was so described to others by the Honorable Secretary of State."

"I was well aware," Drought insisted, "that some individuals in our State Department were curiously antipathetic. Such things happen in

---

* The phrase "stupid documents" is presumably a reference to the proposals from Tokyo that were submitted to Hull on November 7 and 20, and to Japan's final note of December 7.

human life. But that their attitude should have been formulated into a recorded opinion which prejudices my reputation is a development that I cannot permit to occur. It is a malicious injustice."

"I realize that the Secretary of State is much occupied," Drought added, "but I will not believe that he is too occupied to correct, decisively and with finality, the false accusations against one who, at great cost to himself, was, intimately and by request, associated with the highest officials of the United States Government, and shared their confidence in an effort to win a war without the shedding of blood."

Hull replied promptly and patiently, indirectly touching on the fact that Drought's connection with the Japanese-American conversations had been purely "private and unofficial." "It was my understanding," the Secretary wrote, "that you preserved entirely your status as a loyal patriotic American citizen, while, as a friend of peace and of peace groups and officials in Japan, you sought a number of times to aid and facilitate the conversations between the duly authorized officials of the two governments. I at no time considered or treated you as representing any other attitude."

Hull's answer was not entirely satisfactory from Drought's point of view. "This . . . does not acknowledge," he wrote at the bottom of the letter, "(perhaps for diplomatic reasons) that we acted on his behalf also —many times. On the other hand, it does not deny my letter's assertion of that fact."

"I was not surprised [to learn]," Drought subsequently informed the Postmaster General, "that the letter as read to you was not [the one they] sent to me. That sort of thing happened many times during our conversations last year. Things explained to you one way were explained differently to somebody else—but you were understandably loathe to believe it."

Mr. Hull's answer . . . evades the whole point of my letter; nor was his answer backed up with action—since I am still at Maryknoll, while movie actresses, journalists, and even dogs obtain priorities to travel not only to South America but even to England and China (where, by the way, Protestant missioners still go though Catholic missioners are refused transportation).

To say that I feel personally offended would be to say too much; but to say that I am disappointed and pained to receive evidence of a lack of grateful appreciation, would not be to say too much. It would be to say too little.

Personal persistence and influential connections permitted Drought ultimately to obtain some satisfaction, but if anyone in Washington had wanted to be "technical" Drought might have had to answer for his actions—as "a friend of peace"—under the provisions of the Logan Act. This legislation, which had been "on the books" since 1799, made it unlawful for any citizen of the United States, wherever situated, to commence or carry on, either directly or indirectly, without the permission or authority of the American Government, "any verbal or written correspondence or intercourse with any foreign Government or any officer or agent thereof, with an intent to influence the measures or conduct" of the same "in relation to any disputes or controversies with the United States."

Any citizen found guilty of having counseled, advised, or assisted "in any such correspondence with such intent," or of having endeavored "to defeat the measures of the Government of the United States," was to be "fined not more than $5,000 and imprisoned not more than three years."

Although no one had ever been brought to trial on such charges, Drought could have been accused of violating the Logan Act as a consequence of his activities in late 1940 and early 1941. His involvement thereafter would have been another matter, for he could always have claimed in his own defense that the President of the United States had personally asked him, on January 23, 1941, to find out what the Japanese had in mind.

*

The difficulties Drought encountered in obtaining a passport from the State Department did not dampen his enthusiasm for "causes" or affect his relationship with Frank Walker. Even before the matter was resolved, Drought was forwarding the draft of another speech, "The Fullness of the War Effort and Aims," that Walker was to make before a Knights of Columbus convention at Memphis, Tennessee, in August 1942.

Since Drought had "long felt an impatience with words and a fatigue with oratory as a substitute for action," it seems rather remarkable that he should have spent so much of his time composing addresses for other men to deliver, but perhaps he saw his ghostwriting as a necessary first step toward later, direct, personal involvement in the decision-making process. In the meantime, he was able to propagate his ideas through the platform performances of men who commanded the attention of audiences that he might not otherwise have reached.

Drought did not suffer from a lack of opportunities. After giving Walker a hand in August, he began drafting a speech for Manuel Quezon, the President of the Philippines, whom he hoped to influence through his old friend Carlos P. Romulo. "Our enemies are not united," Drought wanted Quezon to tell the world. "They hate each other in their hearts. They attacked us for different reasons but with the same motive of murderous conquest. They are without honor: they are without humanity: they are villainously cruel even to their own citizens. I do not know *when* we will destroy them, nor by what strategy of warfare. I only know we will destroy them if we have to track them down to the ends of the earth."

Later in the year Drought had more to say about the Japanese enemy. The man on the platform this time was Romulo himself, appearing before the Economic Club of Detroit: "The bombing of Pearl Harbor shook the foundations of civilization: the whine of the shells was the tocsin of a global war: the flames of burning battleships emblazoned, across the Pacific sky, the epitaph of isolation. . . . At Pearl Harbor, on December 7th, 1941, the Japanese might have captured Hawaii. Instead, we captured there a vision which we had long sought through the turbulent years of the 1920's: *we captured* a vision of spiritual decency, of human liberty and of divine purpose in life. . . . *On that day*—whatever may be the interval of struggle—*on that day, we won the war.*"

Although Franklin D. Roosevelt had never been one of Drought's favorite people, by February 1943 John Doe was seeing matters differently. When the Postmaster General asked, "Would you like to look this over and do a job on it for me?" Drought responded with slightly more than twelve, single-spaced typewritten pages entitled "Memo on the 1944 Campaign."

Whereas Drought had previously exerted himself to elect a Republican President, he was now telling Walker that as chairman of the Democratic National Committee he should "come out openly from the very beginning and say" (or better still—"get some prominent non-partisan to say") that in war and in peace Roosevelt was "the choice of the Democratic Party" because he was "the choice of the Nation." The President was a man of "magnificent accomplishments," a man whose humanitarian aims and policies would continue to earn him worldwide admiration "for generations to come."

Drought was looking to the future, to the years that would follow an American victory in Europe and the Far East. It was a future, however, in which he would play no part. He had never fully recovered from the effects of the injuries he had sustained in the Mediterranean in 1936. In 1940 he had been afflicted with a severe kidney ailment, and in 1942, as he was busily writing speeches, he had experienced a number of minor heart attacks. His doctors had warned him that he could scarcely expect to enjoy a normal span of life, but with characteristic determination he had closed his mind to his condition and had continued to operate at his usual hectic pace. As 1943 had progressed, he had been forced to take an extended rest in the south, but when he returned to Maryknoll for Holy Week he seemed to be in excellent health—excellent, that is, for a man of forty-six with serious medical problems.

On Saturday, May 1, after watching Frank Walker's son get married at St. Patrick's Cathedral, Father Drought went to the Hotel Commodore to pick up railroad reservations to Chicago. He was talking to a friend in the lobby when he collapsed. The physician who was called to the scene learned from the stricken priest that this was his second heart attack in four days. All efforts to assist him proved unavailing; the hand of death could not be stayed.

"May God give him the rest," Bishop Walsh wrote, "[that] he scarcely took for one hour while there was work to be done for Maryknoll."

At a Pontifical Requiem Mass celebrated in the Maryknoll Chapel several days later, Walsh delivered a tribute to his friend and assistant of so many years standing: "All who knew Father Drought personally—and well—will always regard him as one of those very unusual characters that we encounter once in a lifetime. His natural gifts from God were striking . . . gifts of mind, of heart, and of character. It is not likely that many of us have known many individuals who possessed his extraordinary mental powers, and it is very unlikely that we have known many who possessed with it the same strength of character and bigness of soul. He was evidently fashioned by God to understand everybody's needs, to sympathize with everybody's problems, to bear everybody's burdens. He had the strength and the bigness of mind and heart and soul and, I will add, the deep and exquisite charity to carry a major and giant share of all that could help Maryknoll and its missions and its members and its large circle of friends during his lifetime. . . .

"We will pray for him," the Bishop added, "because, like every human being, he had his frailties. We must remember, above all, that we have been blessed by the vocation of Father Drought, and it will remain always one of Maryknoll's treasures. May God receive him. May Christ Our Savior welcome him. May Mary Immaculate smile upon him. May he rest in joy and peace."

A very large gathering of persons attended the Mass that Bishop Walsh said for Father Drought—archdiocesan officials, representatives of missionary orders, the entire Maryknoll community, and many members of the laity, including Frank Walker. They listened to the eulogy and then walked in a long procession to Maryknoll's own cemetery, where interment took place.

*

Of the men who had cooperated with Father Drought in 1941 in his effort to bring about a Japanese-American settlement, all without exception survived the war he had hoped would never break out.

Tadao Wikawa was appointed to the House of Peers in June 1946, having in the meantime become Secretary-General of the "Japan Cooperative Party"—a post in which he maintained contact with the Occupation authorities.

According to Harry Emerson Wildes, who was a member of General Douglas MacArthur's "Government Section," Wikawa and a number of other English-speaking politicians who provided such liaison were essentially propagandists who trotted into headquarters with supposedly "confidential" information. This generally boiled down, however, to nothing more than the news that anyone with a knowledge of Japanese could read any day of the week in the vernacular press. Wildes regarded Wikawa as a master of the method—as a man who regularly spoke of a party made up of old-line, fascistic, political bosses as though he were talking about a democratic youth group following in the footsteps of the Danish and Dutch cooperative movements.

How well Wikawa might have fared under the rapidly changing conditions of the middle and later years of the Occupation can only be surmised, for he died of a heart attack early in 1947, a few days before his fifty-fourth birthday.

Frank Walker, who had been of so much help to Father Drought in earlier years, resigned as Postmaster General in 1945 to return to the practice of law and to the management of various business interests. When death came at the age of seventy-three in 1959, Walker left behind him the reputation of having been "one of the finest men" in the Roosevelt entourage: "People knew he had no axe to grind and wanted nothing personal in return for the loyal and devoted service he gave to the Boss and the nation. He was kindly, soft-spoken, self-effacing and answered every summons to duty and served in any post where the President needed his talents most." It is easy to understand how Walker could have become "a conduit for passing along information" obtained by Drought concerning the possibility of achieving a peaceful solution of Japanese-American differences.

Kichisaburō Nomura, who had tried to do his best under extremely difficult circumstances, died in 1964 at the age of eighty-six. Whenever he was asked about his experiences in Washington, he always claimed he had felt "shocked and surprised" upon learning, after he had left Hull's office on December 7, that planes of the Imperial Japanese Navy had hit Pearl Harbor without warning, and that this had occurred *before* he had delivered Japan's final note.

"I must have been the worst-informed ambassador in history," Nomura said over and over again on a visit to the United States in 1953. "I told the American authorities [in 1941] that I might be called back at any time, but that there would only be talk and more talk. I said I was certain there would be no attack."

No evidence has come to light to cast doubt upon the Admiral's insistence that the war plans of his nation were never disclosed to him, nor is there any reason to believe that his colleague, Special Envoy Saburō Kurusu, knew anything more than that war with the United States was a distinct possibility (an "open secret" at the time).

Hideo Iwakuro, who was demobilized in 1945 as a major general, turned his back upon the past to pursue new interests in the field of education in a nation reborn—like the legendary phoenix—from the ashes of its own destruction. A man of engaging personality, he conveyed the impression, years later, that some of his seemingly boundless energy must be absorbed by other, less public concerns. Friends in Tokyo in a position to know more than generally appears in print have taken issue with this judgment. They say that Iwakuro, who died in 1970 at the age of seventy-three, did not participate in the political or military life of postwar Japan.

James Edward Walsh, whose heart had always been in missionary endeavors, left Maryknoll in 1948 to work personally once again in fields afar that he hoped would produce a bountiful harvest. His destination was the city of Shanghai, where he was to serve in a post that made him the coordinator of all the missionary, cultural, welfare, and educational activities of the Catholic Church in China, a country in which he had first labored as a young priest in the year 1918. In the 1950's, however, Walsh found that the new rulers of China had no intention of allowing him to pursue the goals he had in mind. He was told he could go home, but he decided to remain at his post. Only if he were specifically ordered to leave by his superiors in the Church would he depart voluntarily.

Suddenly, in the autumn of 1958, Walsh was arrested for "infringement of Chinese law." For a while nothing was known of his whereabouts. Then, in March 1960, a Chinese Bishop was sentenced in Shanghai to life imprisonment for treason. Twelve other Chinese Catholics drew terms of varying duration on similar charges.

The day after this story appeared in the *New York Times*, Walsh made the front page. A dispatch from Hong Kong revealed that he had been given a twenty-year sentence for having led a group of Chinese priests in plots, espionage, and other counterrevolutionary activities against the Chinese state.

As time passed, it seemed less and less likely that Walsh would ever emerge from China alive. Occasionally his name would appear in the news of the day, but for long periods there was little or no word about his condition or prospects. Then, on July 10, 1970, a report was flashed from Hong Kong that the Bishop had arrived in the British Crown Colony.

Walsh had endured twelve years of imprisonment in Shanghai, much of it spent in a room in the hospital section of the Ward Road jail. He had received no intimation that he would be released. He had simply been told, early one morning, to "pack his bags" at once; two hours later he was on a train bound for Canton, accompanied by a Chinese doctor, two interpreters, a photographer, and several policemen.

After crossing the border into British territory, Walsh said merely that he was "glad to be out." Later he admitted to feeling "a bit like Rip van Winkle waking up after a long sleep."

Emphasizing that he had not been a spy either for the American Government or for the Vatican, the seventy-nine-year-old Walsh declared that he had been treated with "basic human dignity." He was not bitter about his imprisonment; in fact, after so many years of work among the people of China, he "could just never feel angry with any Chinese."

*

The world in which the Bishop "awoke" in 1970 was a very different world from the one he had known at the time of his arrest; politically, and in other ways, it was entirely unlike the planet he had traversed in 1940 and '41. The Japan of Konoye and Matsuoka, of Iwakuro and Wikawa, seemed to belong to another age. Only those persons who had spent their lives in the "land of the gods" when the Imperial Army had held sway—sublimely confident of its ability to make the impossible possible—could perhaps still conjure up meaningful scenes of the past. And yet those scenes—however hazy they may appear to later generations—intrude upon us nevertheless.

The inability of the Japanese and American governments to find a way out of the impasse of 1941 through the time-honored methods of diplomacy led ultimately to a sudden shattering of the peaceful relations that had previously been maintained in the Pacific through nearly a century of Japanese-American contact. What Ambassador Nomura had once called "the only bright light of hope . . . left to mankind" was blown out. Across that vast ocean, and through the lands bordering upon it, swirled the "fearful vortex of a great war," leaving death and misery in its wake, and hazards for the future of a type never before imagined by man.

Notes

Notes

Full information concerning the sources is given in the Bibliography, pp. 461–68. Romanization throughout the book is based on the 1954 edition of Kenkyūsha's *New Japanese-English Dictionary*. Where special usage intrudes, exceptions occur. All dates in the notes are for 1941, unless otherwise specified. I have employed the following abbreviations:

DGFP	*Documents on German Foreign Policy*
FDR	Franklin D. Roosevelt (in the case of his papers, references to OF, PPF, and PSF are to the Official File, the President's Personal File, and the President's Secretary's File)
FR 1941	*Foreign Relations of the United States: Diplomatic Papers, 1941*
FRJ	*Papers Relating to the Foreign Relations of the United States: Japan, 1931–1941*
FW	Frank Walker
IMTFE	International Military Tribunal for the Far East (page references are to the "Transcript of Proceedings")
JMD	James M. Drought
JTA	*Japan Times and Advertiser*
LC-JFOA	United States, Library of Congress, Microfilm Collection of Japanese Foreign Office Archives (followed by Reel No. and Doc. No. respectively)
NBKK	*Nichi-Bei Kōshō Kiroku* (all page references are to the "Shiryō" sections)
NYHT	*New York Herald Tribune* (Late City Edition; alternately, Late City Lift of the Late City Edition)
NYT	*New York Times* (Late City Edition)
PHA	*Hearings Before the Joint Committee on the Investigation of the Pearl Harbor Attack*
PMG	Postmaster General
SKH	Stanley K. Hornbeck
State 711.94/ 1973-1/3	General Records of the Department of State, Record Group 59, File No. as indicated
TA Log	Telephone and Appointment Log
TSM	*Taiheiyō Sensō e no Michi* (esp. the portion of Vol. VII written by Jun Tsunoda; also material in the *Bekkan*: a volume of documents)

"In the Midst of Swift Happenings"

1–2 Willkie and Kennedy: *NYT*, Jan. 17: 1, Jan. 19: 1, 35 (also Jan. 13: 1, 4), Jan. 20: 16, Jan. 22: 1; *Washington Post*, Jan. 19: 1, 6, Jan. 20: 10; *Life*, Jan. 27: 27; U.S. Congress, *Hearings on H.R. 1776* (Congress 77, 1941), 221–315.

2 "A damp squib": *NYT*, Jan. 20: 2 (also Jan. 19: 34).

2 Aroi on Kennedy: *NYT*, Jan. 23: 6.

2–3 Nazi flag incident: *NYT*, Jan. 19–22, 24, 26, *passim*. See also *Washington Post*, Jan. 19: 1, Jan. 20: 7; *Newsweek*, Jan. 27: 18; *Time*, Jan. 27: 14; *JTA*, Jan. 19, even. ed.: 1, Jan. 22, morn. ed.: 1; *FR 1941*, II: 634; and U.S. Dept. of State, *Bulletin*, Jan. 25: 108–9.

3 Inaugural address and parade, Jan. 20: *NYT*, Jan. 21: 2; *Washington Post*, Jan. 21: 1.

3–4 Air Defense Command test: *NYT*, Jan. 19–25, *passim*; *Life*, Feb. 3: 24–25.

4–5 Developments in Europe and the Mediterranean: *NYT*, Jan. 19–25, *passim*.

4 "Moral embargo": Hull, I: 636, 706–7, 709, 729–30, 744, 901–2, and II: 969; Langer and Gleason, 336–40; Feis, 19 n3, 44 n7; Butow, *Tojo*, 188–89; *DGFP*, D.XI: 1181–83.

5 "A conjunction of Mars and Saturn": *NYT*, Jan. 21: 20.

5 Lindbergh's testimony: U.S. Congress, *Hearings on H.R. 1776* (Congress 77, 1941), 371–436, esp. 378–81, 385, 389, 419, 427, 435; *NYT*, Jan. 24: 1, 7; *Washington Post*, Jan. 24: 1, 2, 7, 8; *Life*, Feb. 3: 18.

5–6 Reactions to Lindbergh: *NYT*, Jan. 25: 2, 14 (also Jan. 22: 4, Jan. 24: 7, 16); *Washington Post*, Jan. 24: 8.

6 Hull to the Foreign Affairs Committee, Jan. 15: U.S. Congress, *Hearings on H.R. 1776* (Congress 77, 1941), 2–51, esp. 2–7; Hull, II: 982; *FRJ*, II: 131–33, 329–30; *NYT*, Jan. 16: 1, 8.

6 The Tripartite Pact, Sept. 27, 1940: For the text, see *DGFP*, D.XI: 204–8; Gaimushō, *Shuyō Bunsho*, II: 459–62; and LC-JFOA, WT 90, IMT 662, 95–103.

6 Konoye and Matsuoka in the Diet: *NYT*, Jan. 21: 1, 14 (AP, UP items), Jan. 22: 8, Jan. 23: 5, Jan. 24: 4. See also Hull, II: 983–84; *FRJ*, II: 330; and *NYT*, Jan. 20: 4 (AP, UP items).

7 Five-child families: *NYT*, Jan. 23: 5, Jan. 24: 16 (edit.); *Japan Weekly Chronicle*, Jan. 16: 47; *JTA*, Dec. 24, 1940, morn. ed.: 8.

7–8 A German Foreign Office blast: *NYT*, Jan. 25: 2.

8 The designation of a new ambassador to the U.S.: Matsuoka offered the post to Nomura in late Aug. 1940, but the Admiral declined. Various friends—naval officers in particular—then attempted to change his mind. In early Nov. he finally indicated that he might be willing to go to Washington. By then he had come to believe that the authorities in Tokyo were sincerely desirous of improving relations with the U.S. and that the American Govt. would ultimately compromise with Japan rather than choose to fight in the Atlantic and the Pacific at the same time. Although Nomura prided himself on being "an old friend" of FDR, it would be wrong to place too much emphasis on this relationship. The two men had first encountered each other during World War I, but despite an occasional exchange of letters in later

years they were hardly more than "acquaintances." Nomura, 12–25, 180–92, esp. 184–86; FDR papers, PSF, Box 11, and OF 197, Box 1; Kiba, 417–22; Yabe, II: 242–44; Harada, VIII: 361, 362–64, 377–78, 387–92, 397–98; *FRJ*, II: 123–24, 128–29, 517; Moore, 142, 174; Grew papers, "Diary," Jan. 1941: 4725 and Feb. 6 memo of conv. with Terasaki (following p. 4866); Butow, "Hull-Nomura Conversations," 824; Grew, *Ten Years*, 350, 351; *NYT*, Aug. 23, 1940: 1, Aug. 24, 1940: 4, Dec. 11, 1940: 10, Dec. 21, 1940: 6; *JTA*, Nov. 26, 1940, morn. ed.: 1, even. ed.: 1, 2, Nov. 27, 1940, morn. ed.: 4; *Japan Weekly Chronicle*, Dec. 5, 1940: 695, 710–12; *FR 1940*, IV: 981–82; *FR 1941*, IV: 355; *TSM*, VII (Tsunoda): 127–33, 155–56; *Sugiyama Memo*, I: 55; Nomura, "Chū-Bei Ninmu Hōkoku," Sects. 1 and 3. Also Tsunoda intv.

8 "Gloomy mood" and "program": *NYT*, Jan. 23: 5, Jan. 24: 4. Also *TSM*, VII (Tsunoda): 129.

8–10 Walsh and Drought at the White House, Jan. 23: JMD papers, a 1st draft written in pencil on Maryknoll stationery and multiple typewritten copies of a JMD memo, "Verbal Statement made to Pres. Roos. & Mr. Hull on Jan. 23rd"; Walsh papers, the Bishop's "Confidential Memorandum" of Dec. 11, 1945, and his Sept. 15, 1971, account of the "peace treaty negotiations"; FW papers, misc. items, incl. "Daily Memo Calendar, 1941," and a copy of the above-mentioned "Verbal Statement" bearing the title "Political Summary"; FDR papers, "Appointment and Desk Diaries," and pertinent items in PSF, Box 27, and OF 197-A Misc., Box 1; Hull papers, "Desk Diary," Folder 295-I; Hull, II: 982–86; *FRJ*, II: 328–31; U.S. Dept. of State, *Peace and War*, 114–15; *FR 1941*, IV: 14–16; *PHA*, XX: 4291–93; IMTFE, 32978–85 (Walsh affidavit).

10 The FDR-Hull response: Hull, II: 982–86; *FRJ*, II: 325–31. See also *FRJ*, II: 173–81, esp. 178, 181; *FR 1941*, IV: 6–8; Grew, *Ten Years*, 357–63, and *Turbulent Era*, II: 1254–61; and *PHA*, II: 407–18. Hull thought Walsh and Drought had been in touch with "several members of the Japanese Embassy" prior to the interview at the White House, but this is not borne out by any of the material in the JMD papers. Drought was suspicious of the Embassy and was quite anxious to keep the regular staff there in the dark. His Japanese contacts, at this stage, were all still in Japan.

A Bid for a Friendly Settlement

13–14 The "Strictly Confidential Memo for Pres. Roosevelt": FDR papers, OF 197, Box 1, Folder "Japan, 1941," and PSF, Box 27; JMD papers, Drought's handwritten draft of the Memo and a revised, typewritten version; FW papers, a copy; *PHA*, XX: 4291–93; *FR 1941*, IV: 14–16 (14 n31 incorrectly describes James Edward Walsh as the founder of Maryknoll, a distinction that belongs to his predecessor, the late Bishop James Anthony Walsh).

13 "Conservative authorities" in Tokyo: According to the Memo: "Prince Konoye, Mr. Matsuoka, Count Arima, General Muto, etc. and the Emperor." Count Yoriyasu Arima was Secretary General of the Imperial Rule Assistance Association, an organization that was regarded in some quarters as the spearhead of the totalitarian movement in Japan. Maj. Gen. Akira Mutō was chief of the Military Affairs Bureau of the War Ministry, a bureau that played an important role in the drafting of national policy.

13 The remarks attributed to Konoye and Matsuoka: The names of the two men, though omitted from the text of the Memo, were divulged during the White House interview. JMD papers.

13 The Treaty with Wang Ching-wei, Nov. 30, 1940: See *FRJ*, II: 117–23; and Gaimushō, *Shuyō Bunsho*, II: 466–74.

14 Walsh to Walker, Jan. 27: JMD papers; FDR papers, PSF, Box 27; State 711.94/1973-1/3; *FR 1941*, IV: 17–18; *PHA*, XX: 4285–86.

14 FDR to Hull, Feb. 3: FDR papers, PSF, Box 27; State 711.94/1973-1/3; *FR 1941*, IV: 17 n37 (which incorrectly substitutes "shall" for "should"); *PHA*, XX: 4284.

14–16 Three State Dept. memos: FDR papers, PSF, Box 27; *FR 1941*, IV: 21–27; *PHA*, XX: 4284, 4287–91.

16 Nomura's arrival: Kiba, 423–25, 427–29, 431–33; Nomura, 26–28; Moore, 158–66; *NYT*, Feb. 7: 5, Feb. 12: 1, 10; *Washington Post*, Feb. 11: 3, Feb. 12: 11; *JTA*, Feb. 14, morn. ed.: 1, Feb. 15, morn. ed.: 5; *Life*, Feb. 24: 28–29; *Time*, Feb. 24: 30; Ballantine and Burman corresp.

16–17 The Zacharias-Nomura conv., Feb. 8: FDR papers, PSF, Box 11; *PHA*, XVIII: 3258–64; Nomura, 27; Zacharias, 225–32.

17–18 Byas on Nomura: *NYT*, Feb. 9, Sect. 7: 14 (as corrected in Feb. 23, Sect. 7: 18).

18–19 Nomura's initial call on Hull, Feb. 12, and on FDR, Feb. 14: *Time*, Feb. 24: 15, 30; *NYT*, Feb. 13: 5, Feb. 15: 1; *Washington Post*, Feb. 15: 1; *JTA*, Feb. 14, morn. ed.: 1; *PHA*, XX: 4293–96; Nomura, 35–37; Kiba, 429–31; *FRJ*, II: 387–89; Hull, II: 985–88; *FR 1941*, IV: 39–41. See also State 711.94/2039 and 2193.

18 Preliminary conversations vs. negotiations: See *PHA*, XX: 4294; *FRJ*, II: 398, 402, 405, 407; IMTFE, 11024 (Ballantine testimony); Ballantine, "Reminiscences," 41–42. Also Hornbeck corresp.

18 "Speak softly": *PHA*, XX: 4294.

19 The state of Nomura's English: See Grew, *Ten Years*, 367; Hull, II: 987; and Moore, 170–71. Even when formalities had broken down somewhat, communication between Hull and Nomura still proved difficult. This situation did not change until May 16, when Hull brought Joseph W. Ballantine, a Japanese-speaking Foreign Service officer, into the conversations so that he could repeat, in Japanese, "some of the vital points" Hull was making. Prior to that date Hull and Nomura got along as best they could, talking slowly to each other and reiterating key statements so that their meetings grew longer but did not necessarily cover more ground. See Hull, II: 996; Nomura, 29–30; *FRJ*, II: 388, 389, 404–5, 409–10, 427 n25 and n26, 434 n32, and *passim*; *NYT*, Feb. 20: 4, Nov. 19: 1; and Butow, "Hull-Nomura Conversations," 829 n19.

Many years later, I asked Shigeyoshi Obata about the language problem. Obata, who was educated in the U.S., was regarded as the top English translator in the employ of the Foreign Office in 1941 (he spent most of that year assigned to the Japanese Embassy in Washington). Mulling the matter over in 1963, Obata offered this opinion: Nomura probably missed a good deal of what Hull said to him, at least during the early stages; while Hull was talking, Nomura may not always have been listening; instead, he may have been formulating in his own mind what *he* would say in reply when Hull relinquished the floor; ultimately (in Sept.) Obata was told to accompany Nomura as a sort of "listening post"; the staff at the Embassy hoped, in this way, to obtain a better understanding of what Hull was saying than Nomura was able to convey on his own. Obata intv.

Drought was aware of the language barrier. In April he wrote that Hull could not negotiate with Nomura "because the Admiral only half understands"; in May he noted that Nomura was "completely incapable" of long discussions. JMD papers.

19 Nomura to Hull several weeks later (Mar. 8): *FRJ*, II: 393–94.

19 The "John Doe Associates": *FR 1941*, IV: 120–22; Butow, "Backdoor Diplomacy," 48 n1.

19–20 Potential "competitors": E.g., Tetsuma Hashimoto, Roy Howard, E. Stanley Jones, Toyohiko Kagawa, Jiuji Kasai, and Max Kleiman. One man— a Russian émigré named Ivan Lebedeff—thought it would be a good idea to render Japan militarily impotent "by a surprise attack upon ships of the Japanese Navy in advance of a declaration of war." State 711.94/2045; SKH papers, Box "League of Nations—Lebedeff," "Ivan Lebedeff" folder.

Envoys Extraordinary in Washington

21 Walker's letter, Jan. 28: JMD papers.

21 Walsh and Drought were back in town: JMD papers, a 1st draft as well as revised copies of the Feb. 28 memo; FW papers, a copy; Hull papers, "Desk Diary," Folder 295-I; *FR 1941*, IV: 54.

21–22 Hornbeck's reaction: *FR 1941*, IV: 55, 57–58 (the cryptic reference to Hull's "impending conversation set for 4 o'clock this afternoon" is to a Mar. 4 appointment with FW, as is revealed by an entry in Hull's "Desk Diary").

22–23 Calls and callers, Mar. 4–5: FW papers, TA Log; Hull papers, "Desk Diary," Folder 295-I.

23 The "Principal Items" memo, Mar. 5–6: JMD papers, a draft written in ink by John Doe on Mayflower Hotel stationery and a typewritten copy; FW papers, a typewritten copy and a copy in ink on Mayflower stationery; *FR 1941*, IV: 61 ("Political *sterilization* of Far Eastern countries" is a mistake for "political stabilization." John Doe's handwriting was so hard to read that errors were often made in transcription).

23–24 Smith on Wikawa, and word from Grew: I have used the form "Wikawa" because that is how he spelled his name in his letters to JMD and FW. *FR 1941*, IV: 51–53 (not all of the information pertaining to Wikawa is correct, but Smith presumably reported what he had been told); Smith and Dooman corresp.; State 711.94/2005-2/14. See also State 711.94/1971; Grew papers, "Diary," Feb. 1941, 4791–92, 4838; Kiba, 459; Iwakuro ms., 53–58, 63–65; *NYT*, Mar. 5: 8; *JTA*, Feb. 14, morn. ed.: 3; and *FR 1941*, IV: 63–64, 80–81.

23 "Apparently a sincere and ardent Christian": The nature and extent of Wikawa's faith remains in doubt. I once thought he was a Catholic (on p. 12 of his "Higeki no Nichi-Bei Kōshō Hiwa," he uses the "non-word" Katorishian to describe his religious affiliation, whereas the usual term would be Katorikku kyōto). Walsh has stated, however, that Wikawa was a "Protestant Christian." Walsh papers, "peace treaty negotiations" account, Sept. 15, 1971; Coleman corresp.

23 Central Bank of Co-operative Societies: Wikawa's office letterhead reads

"Sangyo-Kumiai Chuo-Kinko (The Co-operative Central Bank)." Sangyō Kumiai is a term used for "Industrial Associations"; Chūō Kinko means "Central Cash Office."

24 Col. Hideo Iwakuro: References to "Takao" or "Takeo" Iwakuro in some of the sources for this period are incorrect.

24–25 The Mar. 7 memo: *FR 1941*, IV: 63–64; JMD papers, handwritten drafts on Hotel Washington stationery, typewritten copies, and misc. handwritten notes; FW papers, a copy; State 711.94/2005-3/14 (virtually the same as the printed version).

25 Minister-Counselor Kaname Wakasugi: Wakasugi was assigned to the Embassy at Nomura's request because the Admiral regarded himself as an "amateur" in diplomatic matters and was not well posted on developments in the U.S. Wakasugi was *au courant* by virtue of having recently completed a tour of duty as Consul General in New York. Ōhashi, 109; Ōhashi intv.; *NYT*, Dec. 11, 1940: 10.

25 Hornbeck to Hull (and Hamilton's concurrence), Mar. 7: *FR 1941*, IV: 62–63; State 711.94/2193.

26 A man "given to sifting a difference": Feis, 39, 172, 173–74. Although writing as a historian, Feis could speak with particular authority, having served as Hull's Adviser on International Economic Affairs.

27 "There was not one chance of success in twenty": See Butow, *Tojo*, 239–40. Hull's estimate was made during discussions with FDR prior to Nomura's arrival in Washington.

27 The identification of James Drought as John Doe: See Butow, "Backdoor Diplomacy," 48. I have used Hornbeck's phrase (the John Doe Associates) to refer to Drought, Iwakuro, and Wikawa. It would be a mistake to think of Walker and Walsh as members of the group.

27 Drought as the author of the memos delivered by Walker: The proof of this lies in the JMD papers, which contain the drafts—in Drought's handwriting and in his style of expression—that led to the final, typewritten versions FW passed along to Hull (see *ibid.*, 53 n11). Only in one instance (the Feb. 28 memo) is there clear evidence—at Maryknoll—that Walsh went over JMD's draft, suggesting changes in the wording of it.

"The End of the Axis Alliance! Alleluia!"

28–30 The Hull-Nomura meeting, Mar. 8: *FRJ*, II: 389–96. See also Hull, II: 988–90; *FR 1941*, IV: 64–68, 80–81; Nomura, 39–41; and Kiba, 433–35.

28 Nomura merely bowed in reply: On the basis of the information available to them, Langer and Gleason, 466–67, concluded that Nomura was "patently mystified" by Hull's reference to the private persons who were endeavoring to be of help. More recent evidence indicates that Nomura was not in the dark; he simply thought it best to say nothing.

30–31 Drought's "Berkshire" memo: JMD papers, a handwritten original on Berkshire stationery and a typewritten version with a notation indicating that the memo was written on Mar. 10 and delivered on Mar. 11; FW papers, a copy; *FR 1941*, IV: 69–70.

30 "Don't worry": When Iwakuro was asked about this in Tokyo in 1965, he had no recollection of ever having sent such a telegram. In fact, he even

suggested that Wikawa might simply have said something of the sort on the spur of the moment while talking to JMD. Iwakuro intv.

30–31 John Doe's contention: See *FR 1941*, IV: 15, 54, 61, 63.

31 Berlin's view of Matsuoka's forthcoming visit: *JTA*, Mar. 11, even. ed.: 1.

31 Drought took a different position: *FR 1941*, IV: 70.

31–32 Drought's lengthy memo of Mar. 13: JMD papers, drafts and typewritten copies; FW papers, a typewritten copy; State 711.94/2005-6/14; *FR 1941*, IV: 71–74. SKH mistakenly believed that this memo was the work of Walsh.

32 Drought's personality and nature: My comments here, and *passim* hereafter, are based on impressions gained from a reading of the sources, supplemented by characterizations obtained during interviews with the following men (all of whom knew JMD): Ballantine, Bauer, Collins, Considine, Iwakuro, and Sawada. Also Coleman corresp. and enclosures, incl. this pertinent observation: "JMD was a very controversial character within the Society right up to the moment of his death, so much so that little he did was beyond criticism, thanks to his high-handed methods. Doubtless his mode of operation . . . in the peace negotiations [in 1941] will be accepted by anyone who knew him as 'typically Drought.' . . . [His] operations were often characterized as 'jesuitical' after the old slur that whereas the Jesuits did not preach that the end justifies the means they often practiced it!"

32–33 Drought's "Special Memo," Mar. 13: JMD papers, a handwritten draft in ink and a typewritten copy; FW papers, a copy; *FR 1941*, IV: 74.

33 The FDR-Nomura meeting, Mar. 14: *FR 1941*, IV: 75–79; *FRJ*, II: 396–98 (the omissions resulting from wartime publication are covered by the preceding *FR 1941* citation); Hull, II: 990–91; Nomura, 42–46; Kiba, 437–41; Gaimushō, *NBKK*, 5–9. It was on this date that the letter Zacharias had sent to Stark from San Francisco, more than a month earlier, at length reached FDR's desk.

33 The Drought memo of Mar. 14: Both the JMD and the FW papers contain copies of this memo, but it is not among the items published in *FR 1941*, IV. I could find no trace of it in the archives of the State Dept.

33–34 Drought's "Alleluia" memo, Mar. 16: JMD papers, several typewritten copies; *FR 1941*, IV: 95–96 (the attribution to Walsh in n46 is incorrect).

34 "Renouncement" of the Axis: *Not* "announcement" as in the text given to Hull.

An Excess of "Plenipotentiaries"

35–36 Walker delivered two communications (JMD memos, Mar. 17 and 18): *FR 1941*, IV: 96–97, 111–12 (supplemented by State 711.94/2005-8/14 and 11/14). Typewritten copies (with slight textual variations) can also be found in the JMD papers, together with some scribbled notes that are pertinent.

35–36 The "Preliminary Draft of 'Agreement in Principle'": This Mar. 17 document is printed in *FR 1941*, IV: 97–107; it was delivered in Washington on the 19th. Multiple typewritten copies, with numerous revisions, and a considerable amount of pertinent handwritten material can be found in the JMD papers.

35 Konoye and other leaders in Tokyo: JMD again mentioned Arima, to whom he had referred in the "Strictly Confidential Memo" of Jan. 23, and

to Arima's name he now added that of Marquis Kōichi Kido, Lord Keeper of the Privy Seal (the Emperor's closest adviser).

36 Hull and his advisers were not going to be rushed: State 711.94/2005-9/14; *FR 1941*, IV: 64–65 (the reference in n29 to "the Japanese with regard to whom the Postmaster General had spoken" is to Wikawa); Hornbeck corresp. After suggesting that nothing further be done until Iwakuro had arrived, Hamilton went on to say that if Nomura's "compatriots" did not wish to wait, Hull might speak with them himself or might "arrange for someone in the Department of State or someone outside the Department ... to talk with them, all this in order that they might have full opportunity to present their views." Such an arrangement would be made, however, only if Nomura introduced his compatriots to Hull "either in person or by written communication, officially or privately."

36 Drought was currently seeking a personal meeting: JMD and FW papers; *FR 1941*, IV: 112.

36–38 The Ballantine-Drought conversations, New York, Mar. 24, Mar. 27, and Ballantine's meeting with Wikawa, Mar. 27: *FR 1941*, IV: 113–17; Ballantine "Reminiscences," 33–35; Ballantine intv. and corresp.; Hornbeck corresp.

37 Wikawa's account of his career: I have been unable to find any evidence to support his claimed relationship with Wakatsuki. Perhaps they were "cousins"; perhaps they were not.

38 American action against Japan: Berlin's special representative, Minister Plenipotentiary Heinrich Stahmer may have used the arguments attributed to him by Wikawa (the termination of the Treaty of Commerce and Navigation and the inauguration of restrictions on exports to Japan), but upon reading this portion of Ballantine's report SKH noted that the U.S. had actually imposed very few limitations prior to the conclusion of the Tripartite Pact in Sept. 1940. *FR 1941*, IV: 116 n68.

38 Wikawa's criticism of Wakasugi: The hostility that was being expressed here can be traced in part to Wikawa's negative view of career diplomats in general (a view that was shared by JMD), and in part to Wakasugi's direct efforts to prevent amateurs like Wikawa and Drought from intruding upon matters of high policy.

39–40 Sequence of events on Apr. 3, and the Apr. 4 memo: FW papers, TA Log; Hull papers, "Desk Diary," Folder 295-I; JMD papers, a handwritten draft and a typed carbon of the memo; *FR 1941*, IV: 119–20.

39 "After some delays": JMD's 1st draft began, "After some delays caused by a certain Mr. Matsuoka ... ," but he revised this sentence to read as shown in the text.

40 Hornbeck's analysis: *FR 1941*, IV: 120–22.

40 "A super-colossal political bombshell": When I asked SKH in 1965 whether he had been thinking of possible Anglo-Chinese reactions to an announcement that the U.S. and Japan were negotiating "for the establishment of peace in the Pacific," he replied: "Your assumption is correct—as far as it goes; but I was thinking not alone of the probable British and Chinese interpretations but of reactions in and of various quarters within the U.S.A. itself: in the Department, in other Departments and agencies of the government, in the press, among the people, etc. Why make such a commitment and/or

announcement at that stage and in the circumstances then prevailing?" Hornbeck corresp.

40 Calls and callers, Apr. 5: FW papers, TA Log and an unsigned and undated memo on notepaper from the Office of the PMG paraphrasing the statements made by Hull over the telephone; Hull papers, "Desk Diary," Folder 295-I. For the text of the document Hull received on that day, see State 711.94/2066-5/9.

40–41 Ballantine at the Wardman Park, Apr. 7: *FR 1941*, IV: 127–28; State 711.94/2066-2/9. The historian must sometimes be a detective, pursuing leads that take hours to trace—hours that stretch into days, into weeks, into months —with no larger reward in sight than the prospect of tracking down some small but possibly significant clue, a piece of evidence that may not be provable in the end. The "prearrangement" mentioned in the text is a case in point. On Saturday, Apr. 5, the following telegram was sent to Ballantine: "Tried to reach you by phone this afternoon. Will phone again Monday morning and make engagement to suit your convenience with the two visitors. Kindest personal regards. Donaldson." State 711.94/2066-2/9.

When I first saw this message, I assumed that the two visitors were Iwakuro and Wikawa, but I was puzzled by the signature. Investigation led to Jesse M. Donaldson, Dep. First Asst. PMG. It seemed likely that he had simply acted for Walker in this instance, at the latter's request. This conjecture appeared to be confirmed by a statement in *FR 1941*, IV: 123 n78, to the effect that Donaldson had delivered a key John Doe document to the State Dept. on Apr. 9. In an effort to learn more, I sent an inquiry to Donaldson in the spring of 1965. His reply was interesting: "I did not call at the State Department or send any [such] telegram."

When I consulted Hornbeck and Ballantine, they had no recollection of any involvement by Donaldson. I therefore concluded that the "delivery man" on Apr. 9 had been someone other than Donaldson—the most likely candidate being Drought. I already knew that Hull's "Desk Diary" for 1941 showed a 3:35 P.M. appointment for him on that day. I was also struck by the fact that both Donaldson and Drought had exactly the same initials—JMD. None of this, however, would explain the Donaldson signature on the telegram to Ballantine.

Several months after reaching this impasse, I happened on a draft of a telegram addressed to Sumner Welles at the State Dept.: "Have not reported further because other parties here while substantially in agreement desire to make draft of their own within next few days." This message, which predated the one to Ballantine, was written on a piece of Wardman Park stationery and was signed Donaldson. The phrase "other parties here" immediately brought Iwakuro and Wikawa to mind. Since both Walker and Hull had been out of town for some time, liaison between Donaldson (acting for Walker) and Welles (representing Hull) was certainly a possibility. The only trouble was that Donaldson had already disclaimed any connection whatsoever with the John Doe affair. There was also this remarkable fact: the entire text of the draft telegram to Welles, including the Donaldson signature, was in the handwriting of Fr. Drought (I had found the item in question among his papers at Maryknoll).   (*continued*)

It began to look very much as though James M. Drought had been using Jesse M. Donaldson's name as a "cover." If so, then the message to Welles and the telegram to Ballantine had been written by one and the same man—the ever-present but not always clearly visible "John Doe."

Soon after reaching this conclusion, I remembered a sentence in a letter from Drought to Hull, dated July 23, 1942, that I had found at Maryknoll during an earlier stage of the research process. In retrospect, the sentence seemed to be pertinent to the "Donaldson" puzzle. It read: "I did not communicate, except twice during your absence, with Mr. Sumner Welles; though he had asked me to do so and had given me a code name to use for telephone calls."

I checked all of this through once again (in the spring of 1966) with Donaldson, Hornbeck, and Ballantine, but I was unable to learn anything substantially new. It seemed that I had reached the end of the trail, but it then developed that one of the file copies of the proposal delivered to the State Dept. on Apr. 9 (State 711.94/2066-6/9) bore an SKH notation: "Left w. Secy by Donaldson IV-9-'41" (hence the reference in *FR 1941*, IV: 123 n78, mentioned above). When I asked Hornbeck for clarification, he replied that this was his reporting of the information given to him at the time "presumably orally and by Mr. Hull or someone in his office," but that the actual leaving of the document might have been carried out "by someone who identified himself as Donaldson and who handed it to someone in the Secretary's office for delivery to the Secretary," and this person "might readily have been Drought."

41 A premature leak might endanger their lives: JMD had been emphasizing since January that the members of the so-called peace party might be assassinated. In talking with Ballantine in New York on Mar. 27, Wikawa had claimed that he was risking death by divulging certain information. See *FR 1941*, IV: 14–15, 16, 63, 96, 97, 111, 115.

41 The delivery of the "Draft Understanding": As noted previously, *FR 1941*, IV: 123 n78, incorrectly names Donaldson as the "carrier." *FR 1941*, IV: 143 n91, however, properly names Drought as the man who brought the "Draft Understanding" to Hull. Along with it, JMD submitted a summary of the main terms. This can be found in *ibid.*, 132–34. The FW papers contain an onion-skin copy.

41 The Hull-Drought meeting, Apr. 10: Hull papers, "Desk Diary," Folder 295-I.

41 A "Far East" memo of comment, Apr. 10: *FR 1941*, IV: 135–39.

41 Hornbeck's tentative counterdraft, Apr. 11: *Ibid.*, 142–46.

42 Hornbeck's second memo of Apr. 11: *Ibid.*, 147–48. That same day, Hamilton outlined an "Oral Statement" Hull could make whenever he got around to discussing the John Doe matter with Nomura. *Ibid.*, 146–47.

42 "A fair deal" for Japan: *Ibid.*, 148. Probably everyone in Washington who knew SKH would agree that he scrutinized documents sent to him for analysis with the meticulousness of a pathologist. He was generally regarded as "a friend of China," and by extension this placed him under the suspicion of being anti-Japanese. And yet there is evidence to suggest (as in this instance) that despite his predilections, he tried to maintain an open mind. This aspect of the man was noted by Frederick Moore, who was then serving as a Coun-

selor to the Japanese Embassy in Washington: "Hornbeck I had known well for many years. I had felt that he had been too pro-Chinese in [the] past. But I had seen him develop—as we all had done with maturing years—and I knew him in this crisis [mid-1937 to late 1941] to have leaned back, so to speak, in efforts to be fair in his dealings with the Japanese." Moore, 282.

42 "Father Drought phoned": Coleman corresp. and enclosure. The reference to Walsh's governing council is to the General Council, which was responsible for administering the affairs of Maryknoll.

42 Drought drafted a telegram to Wikawa: JMD papers, a handwritten draft. This item bears the date April 14, but this may have been added later; in any case, it appears from the context to be incorrect. The telegram was probably sent on Easter Sunday, Apr. 13.

42 Walker telephoned Hull over "the White House line": FW papers, TA Log. Louise Hachmeister, who was Chief Operator at the White House at the time, has stated that the only line that fits this description was one linking the White House with the desks of members of the Cabinet. Hachmeister corresp.

42 "Little token" of souvenirs: FW papers, Wikawa's Apr. 13 covering note.

43 Changes made by Hornbeck on Apr. 14: *FR 1941*, IV: 148–50.

43 Calls and callers, Apr. 14–16: Hull papers, "Desk Diary," Folder 295-I; FW papers, TA Log.

43 The briefing of Hull: *FR 1941*, IV: 152–61.

43 "The Japanese draft of April 9": This was the way in which Hamilton and Ballantine now referred to the John Doe "Draft Understanding." They knew that this proposal had been presented to Hull "through the medium of private American and Japanese individuals," but both Hull and his advisers believed that the proposal reflected the thinking of peace-minded elements in Japan, and could therefore be described as a "Japanese draft."

43 The Iwakuro-Wikawa letter to Hull, Apr. 17: *FR 1941*, IV: 161 (supplemented by State 711.94/2066-8/9). An expression of appreciation was extended orally by Ballantine on Apr. 23, speaking on Hull's behalf.

43 "In a spirit of high resolve": *FR 1941*, IV: 98.

44 In a moment of zeal: The reference is to a claim made by JMD in his Mar. 16 "Alleluia" memo.

44 At least sixty substantive meetings: Several technicalities make it difficult to offer definitive figures, but the reckoning in the text is based on material in the pertinent *FR* volumes and in Nomura's *Beikoku ni Tsukai Shite*. The figure forty-five does not include Nomura's initial 4-minute call at the State Dept. on Feb. 12 or his final encounter with Hull on Dec. 7, nor does it include any of the interviews with FDR that Hull also attended. The two occasions (Aug. 23 and 27) on which Nomura saw Hull twice on the same day have been counted as two meetings—not four. In the case of Nomura and Welles, I have used the figure six rather than eight because two of their conversations dealt with special problems that were not directly pertinent to the search for a peace formula.

State Dept. records reveal that in addition there were at least six meetings between Wakasugi and Welles (with Hull sitting in twice), to say nothing of a number of sessions between Nomura, or members of his staff, and various officers of the Dept. (principally Hamilton and Ballantine). Iwakuro was present at five of the Hull-Nomura conversations that were held in May and June; Wikawa at four. Iwakuro and Wikawa also conferred with Hamilton and Ballantine a number of times.

On eight of the forty-five occasions on which Nomura saw Hull, the Ambassador was accompanied by Saburō Kurusu, who was sent from Tokyo in Nov. 1941 as a Special Envoy. Kurusu also joined Nomura in two of his nine visits to the White House and made one call on Hull entirely on his own.

44–45 The direct relationship between the "Draft Understanding" of Apr. 9 and each and every subsequent proposal: The calculation in the text (fourteen documents in seven months) embraces draft agreements presented on the following dates: May 12, 31; June 4, 8, 15, 21; July 11, 15; Sept. 4, 6, 25; and Nov. 7, 20, 26. Omitted here are the President's Neutralization Proposal of July 24 (a special offer prompted by Japan's move into southern French Indochina) and Japan's rejection thereof and counterproposal of Aug. 6. Also omitted from consideration are all exchanges that involved only a few portions of a particular document rather than the document as a whole (e.g., the revised drafts of Sections II, III, and V, which Hull handed to Nomura on May 16); and all tentative drafts that did not actually change hands from one side to the other (e.g., the American redraft of May 23, which led to the American draft proposal of May 31; also, some documents JMD sent to FW on July 1, which were replaced on July 11 by a new set without the originals ever having been sent to the State Dept.).

45 Each a self-appointed diplomatic "Mr. Fix-it": Hornbeck intv. SKH used this term while referring to "peace brokers" in general.

45 Three "patriots for peace": In a conversation with Nomura on Apr. 16, Hull is said to have referred to Drought, Iwakuro, and Wikawa as "three patriots" (Iwakuro ms., 130)—a phrase that FDR himself had supposedly used (Wikawa, 21). Since there is no equivalent statement in Hull's memo of this conversation (*FRJ*, II: 406–10), the attribution is probably based on a misunderstanding of certain remarks made by Hull to Nomura on Mar. 8 and Apr. 14. See *ibid.*, 389, 403.

The Historical John Doe

49 Drought's early life: JMD papers, "Autobiographical Notice" (written ca. 1920, when JMD became a Maryknoll seminarian) and Walsh letter, May 1, 1943, to the Maryknoll community. Also misc. items from the Maryknoll Archive (I am indebted to Fr. William J. Coleman for this material and for additional information, oral and written, which he obtained from Fr. Thomas V. Kiernan, who was very close to Drought).

James M. Drought was the son of Anna Etchingham and Michael J. Drought. At the Catholic University of America, where JMD obtained a Master's degree ca. 1924, Education was his major. Despite this, "he took all knowledge for his province!" Coleman corresp.

49 Financial negotiations in Rome: As a consequence of JMD's involvement in this matter (from 1929 on), he had become acquainted not only with Lewis L. Strauss of Kuhn, Loeb and Co., but also with Sir William Wiseman of the same firm. Coleman corresp. and enclosures.

50 A diplomatic hullabaloo: *FRJ*, I: 223–29; Grew, *Ten Years*, 128–34, and *Turbulent Era*, II: 957–62; Borg, 75–83. The spokesman was Eiji Amau.

50 "Deep sea conferences": Grew, *Turbulent Era*, II: 965.

50 Drought to the Foreign Policy Assoc. president, Aug. 28, 1934: JMD papers.

50–51 Naval conversations in London, Oct.–Dec. 1934: Grew, *Ten Years*, 142–52, and *Turbulent Era*, II: 966–67, 974 n32; *The Moffat Papers*, 115–23; *FRJ*, I: 249ff.

51 Drought on naval parity: State 500A 15A 5/237 and 238; FDR papers, OF 404, Box 1, "General Correspondence" folder.

51–52 "It would be helpful": Grew, *Ten Years*, 145–53, and *Turbulent Era*, II: 974 n32.

52–55 Philippine Day at Notre Dame, Dec. 9, 1935: JMD papers. Unlike the hundreds of items relating to 1941, a body of material that was in utter disarray when I first came to it, everything pertaining to the Notre Dame affair is conveniently filed in a single folder.

55 Drought chain-smoked through many a night: This caused Fr. Kiernan concern in later years when JMD's health was in decline. If he did not appear in the morning, Kiernan would go to his room half expecting to find him dead. JMD showed no regard for his physical condition, "worked at high tension all the time," and remained a heavy smoker. Occasionally he would fall asleep in his chair, never getting to bed at all. Coleman corresp. and enclosures.

55–60 The goodwill cable to Premier Hirota: JMD papers (everything pertaining to this episode is filed in a single folder). See also the *Congressional Record (Senate)*, Feb. 10, 1936: 1703–8; *Time*, Feb. 24, 1936: 23, 26; *NYT*, Mar. 26, 1936: 17; Grew, *Ten Years*, 162–65; and the *Japan Times and Mail*, Mar. 27, 1936: 1, 8.

56 "The friendly statement issued by President Roosevelt in 1934": I have been unable to find anything of this nature, but JMD may have been referring to the American response to Amau (delivered to the Japanese Foreign Minister by Grew on instructions from Hull). *FRJ*, I: 231–32; Grew, *Turbulent Era*, II: 961–62.

61 Drought's accident, Aug. 22, 1936: State 368.1115—Drought, James M./1–6, and 341.1141—Drought, James M./1–9; JMD papers; Coleman corresp.

61 Drought and the 1936 Presidential campaign: JMD papers.

62 The state of Drought's health (Nov. 1938): Coleman corresp. and enclosures, incl. a JMD note from Caracas, Dec. 1938 (in which he describes himself as "a fast-driving dray horse—racing above his normal speed").

62 Drought and the "Social Service Commission" to Venezuela: Coleman corresp. and enclosures; Gannon, 344–45; Moll, 521–25; *NYT*, May–July 1939, *passim*.

62–63 Maryknoll and the war in China: Coleman corresp. and misc. items in the Maryknoll Archive, esp. "Confidential Council Bulletin No. 53," Oct. 2, 1937; Byrne to Walsh, Nov. 21, 1937, and reply, Dec. 16; Walsh to Council, Dec. 1, 1938; Fr. John J. Considine's "Memo for Council," Dec. 11, 1938; Council minutes, Dec. 17, 1940; and Superior General's report to the 1946 Chapter. See also JMD papers, misc. corresp., esp. Walsh to Hull, Jan. 16, 1940, and JMD to Horinouchi, Feb. 12, 1940, and reply, Feb. 13.

63–65 Drought and the 1940 Presidential election: JMD papers; Coleman corresp.

65 Drought to Walker, Sept. 5, 1940: FW papers.

To "The Land of the Gods"

67 New worries and old ambitions: The following postwar comment by a former Imperial Japanese Army officer succinctly summarizes the point being made in the text: "Underlying the conclusion of the Tripartite Pact lurked a fear of 'missing the bus' on the part of the High Command, which was dazzled by the brilliant military successes of the German Army at the outset of World War II. An atmosphere of great worry prevailed lest Japan lose her chance if she maintained a cautious policy 'with her hands in her pockets' while Germany was stripping the world of its choice treasures. Within the High Command, the feeling rapidly gained sway that Japan should derive great advantage from the Tripartite Pact by carving out her own sphere of influence in East Asia." Hayashi, 18.

67–71 The 2,600th anniversary: Grew papers, clippings, CIX–CX (Nov.–Dec. 1940); Grew, *Ten Years*, 352–53; *Asahi*, Nov. 10–12, 1940, *nikkan* and *yūkan*, *passim*; *Japan Weekly Chronicle*, Nov. 14, 1940: 598–601; *Japan Advertiser*, Nov. 9–13, 1940, *passim*.

68–70 There was little room in wartime Japan for frivolity: Grew, *Ten Years*, 327–28; *Pictorial Orient*, VIII, 10–11 (Oct.–Nov. 1940): 346–47, 388–89, 390–91; Grew papers, clippings, CX (Dec. 1940), Fleisher article, *NYHT*, Dec. 1, 1940; Argall, 113–20, 197; *Japan Weekly Chronicle*, Aug. 22, 1940; 223, Aug. 29, 1940: 257, and Nov. 7, 1940: 566 ("Off with the Dance"). See also Fleisher, 112–14 (foreigners in Japan jokingly referred to the "new structure" as the "new stricture" because it was accompanied by endless prohibitions of the type associated with the dictatorships in Europe).

70 "Ancestor worship": *Japan Weekly Chronicle*, Nov. 14, 1940: 598, quoting Dr. Inazō Nitobe.

71 The Emperor nods his approval: Grew, *Ten Years*, 352–53; Grew papers, "Diary," Nov. 1940: 4634, and clippings, CIX–CX (Nov.–Dec. 1940).

71–72 The origins and background of the Walsh-Drought visit to Japan: Coleman corresp. and enclosures, incl. a Walsh memo for Council, Nov. 27, 1939; the Most Rev. Paul Marella, Apostolic Delegate, Tokyo, to Msgr. Patrick J. Byrne, Prefect Apostolic, Kyoto, Sept. 23, 1940, and reply, Oct. 1; Walsh to Byrne, Oct. 5, 1940; Walsh to Cardinal Prefect of Propaganda, Rome, Oct. 25, 1940, and reply, Nov. 13; Walsh to the Most Rev. Francis J. Spellman, Nov. 2, 1940; Walsh to Fr. John J. Considine, Nov. 30, 1940; and Council minutes, Nov. 28, 1939; Jan. 9, Aug. 7, Oct. 14, Oct. 25, Oct. 28, Nov. 6, Dec. 17, 1940. Also a 6-page statement, written by JMD in the autumn of 1940, analyzing "the Japanese edict"; Walsh papers, a "Confidential Memorandum" of Dec. 11, 1945, the Bishop's report to the 1946 Chapter, and his "peace treaty negotiations" account, Sept. 15, 1971 (as qualified by Kiernan's note to Coleman, Sept. 23, 1971, and reply, Sept. 28); and FW papers, "The 'X' Memorandum."

72 "The only consolation prize": Coleman corresp. and enclosures, Walsh to Byrne, Oct. 5, 1940.

72 The Japanese Government had announced a change in policy: The requirement that Christian institutions in Japan be headed by Japanese was part of a general effort to force all religious bodies (including indigenous organizations) to conform to the demands of the new national structure. There

was talk of forming an *"Imperial* Christian Church" or a *"Genuine Japan* Christian Church" (with the Emperor assuming the functions of a Pope). For a time it looked as though there would be a "Missionaries Must Go!" movement, but the problem was solved when one foreign group after another proceeded to comply with the new policy. The Salvation Army, for example, changed its name to the "Salvation party [or body]," abolished all military titles, severed relations with British headquarters, and dismissed all foreign officers. *NYT,* Aug.–Oct. 1940, *passim; Time,* Sept. 30, 1940: 36; Argall, 195–206; Fleisher, 125–27.

72–73 Drought's preparations for the trip to Japan: JMD papers and Coleman corresp., misc. items incl. tips from Fr. John C. Murrett, who also reported on the N.Y.K. arrangements; a Nov. 2, 1940, note to Fr. Hugh T. Lavery asking for "a list of influential Japanese now in Japan whom you think it would be helpful for us to see," and his Nov. 11 reply, "Japanese Friends in Nippon"; carbon copies of the JMD letters quoted in the text; and a Nov. 9 radiogram from a colleague at Maryknoll informing JMD that Kennedy did not have any Japanese connections.

73–74 The arrival in Japan of Walsh and Drought, Nov. 25, 1940: Coleman corresp. and enclosures, esp. Walsh's so-called line-a-day "Japan Diary—1940"; JMD papers, misc. items incl. a rough-draft chronology, press releases for use in the U.S. and Japan, clippings from the *JTA,* Nov. 13, 26, and 28, 1940, and a copy of *Japan News-Week,* Dec. 7, 1940. The statements attributed to Walsh in the text are a composite of the quotations found in the clippings.

74 "Et surtout, messieurs": "And above all, gentlemen, not too much zeal." I have drawn on an observation made by Joseph Ballantine in Nov. 1962. Ballantine corresp.

74–75 Ackerman to Takaishi, Nov. 7, 1940: JMD papers.

75 Ackerman to Horinouchi, Nov. 7, 1940: *Ibid.*

75–76 A special packet of nine letters and the Drought-Strauss connection: JMD papers, misc. letters and telegrams; Strauss, 82–83, 121–23 (Strauss's account is incorrect here; he has described what he learned *after* Walsh and Drought returned from Japan as though he had been told all this *before* they left); Strauss corresp. and intv.; Coleman corresp. and enclosures. Copies of the Strauss and Drought letters to Wikawa, retyped on his own letterhead, are in the Konoye papers, having been sent by Wikawa to the Prince on Dec. 7, 1940; the originals are in the FW papers, together with various other Wikawa items (see my Note on the Sources).

76–77 A partial log: The record presented in the text was pieced together from various items in the JMD papers, incl. scribbled notes and carbon copies of correspondence, and from entries in Walsh's "Japan Diary—1940." I have done some paraphrasing for the sake of clarity, and have omitted many details. For a general sense of what was taking place, I have also drawn—here and elsewhere in the text—on the following accounts (even though some of them are irreconcilable and others abound in inaccuracies): the 1945, 1946, and 1971 Walsh items cited in the Note for pp. 71–72 (The origins and background of the Walsh-Drought visit to Japan); Sawada ms.; Wikawa, 12–15; Iwakuro, "Amerika ni okeru Nichi-Bei Kōshō no Keika," 288–91; JMD papers, Drought ms. (an untitled and undated 24-page, typewritten account describing the 1940 visitation to Japan), Walsh's statement on behalf of Mutō; FW papers, "The 'X' Memorandum," "The Japanese Negotiations— 1941"; Konoye papers, Wikawa's letters to Konoye; Iwakuro ms., 1–13; *TSM*, VII (Tsunoda): 133–36, and *Bekkan*, 394–95; "Matsuoka Oboegaki"; Ōhashi, 107–9; Strauss, 121–23; and Yabe, II: 237–42. Also Iwakuro, Sawada, Tsunoda, and Ushiba intvs.

77 Drought's further efforts to gain access to Matsuoka: JMD papers, a draft of the cable to Sawada and instructions pertaining thereto, Lavery's "Japanese Friends" memo, a Nov. 10, 1940, telegram from Fr. Considine reporting to Walsh and Drought that word had been received, via Cuddihy, that Sawada would be "glad [to] welcome and introduce them to Government authorities," and a carbon of a JMD letter to Ōhashi, Dec. 26, 1940; Sawada ms. (some of the dates are wrong and his recollections occasionally contradict other evidence); Ōhashi, 107–9 (Ōhashi's memory may not be correct in all details). Also Hasegawa, Hirasawa, Ōhashi, and Sawada intvs.

78 Drought to Terasaki, Dec. 4, 1940: JMD papers. Tarō Terasaki's younger brother, Hidenari, served in the Japanese Embassy in Washington in 1941 as First Secretary.

78 "Mr. Kabayama will prepare the translation": Drought was referring to Sukehide Kabayama, a member of the Foreign Office in 1940. See LC-JFOA, WT 77, IMT 576, 296–322, for his unsigned Japanese translation of JMD's "memo on policy and strategy." Kabayama's widow positively identified her husband's calligraphy when I showed her the document in 1965 without prior explanation of its nature or significance.

78 The Walsh-Drought meeting with Matsuoka, Dec. 5, 1940: The text is based on Walsh's Sept. 15, 1971, account of the "peace treaty negotiations."

78–79 Drought's "Summary of Our (Japanese) Plan": JMD papers, a 1st draft in ink and a revised, typewritten version bearing the handwritten notation "to Matsuoka."

79 Drought to Matsuoka, Dec. 6, 1940: JMD papers, a copy of the original and a slightly altered version incorporated in the JMD ms.

80 Wikawa's reputation: Kase, 45, describes Wikawa (without identifying him by name) as "an ex-official of the Japanese Treasury Department whose integrity was rather dubious." See also *TSM*, VII (Tsunoda: 136, 145–46; Hull, II: 1003; Ballantine, "Reminiscences," 33, 34, 41. Also Ballantine, Iwakuro, Tsunoda, and Ushiba intvs.

80 Differences in personality: Wikawa, 12. "Though a rugged realist as an old China hand the bishop is also quite pious and even ascetical in temperament and thought—NOT the JMD type!" (Coleman corresp.) Also Ballantine, "Reminiscences," 35; Iwakuro ms., 73–74; Yabe, II: 241; Iwakuro and Sawada intvs.; Ballantine and Dooman corresp.

80–81 The "protection" sought by Wikawa and his Dec. 7, 1940, letter-report to Konoye: Konoye papers; *TSM*, VII (Tsunoda): 133–34, and *Bekkan*, 394– 95; Yabe, II: 237–39. Also Wikawa, 12–14; Strauss, 82–83, 122–23; Iwakuro intv.; Ushiba corresp. and intv.; Tsunoda corresp.

81 Wikawa to Strauss, Dec. 8, 1940: FW papers, Wikawa items.

81 Developments, Dec. 11–14, 1940: Konoye papers; *TSM*, VII (Tsunoda): 134, and *Bekkan*, 395; Wikawa, 13–14; Yabe, II: 238–39; Tsunoda intv.

81–84 Drought's "Working Analysis of Our (Japanese) Position & Policy in the

Far East, With Particular Reference to the United States": JMD papers, multiple typewritten copies, some of which are incomplete, and a copy in ink in Drought's hand—probably his 1st draft—bearing the title "Analysis of Japan's Position & Policy in the Far East—With Particular Reference to the U.S."; Konoye papers, a copy of the "Working Analysis" typed on Wikawa's office letterhead (except for a few unimportant typographical differences, this copy is exactly the same as the final version in the JMD papers); LC-JFOA, WT 77, IMT 576, 296–325 (a provisional translation into Japanese under the title "Tōa ni Okeru Nihon no Seisaku no Kaibō—Toku-ni Tai-Bei Kankei ni Tsuite" and stamped *Gokuhi*—top secret; this is the translation to which JMD referred in his Dec. 4, 1940, letter to Tarō Terasaki; also a copy of the English text of the "Working Analysis" with the handwritten English words "strictly confidential" and the Japanese characters for Vice-Minister; there are some slight differences in this version that suggest it may be a somewhat earlier draft than the one given to Wikawa); *TSM*, VI (Fukuda): 352–54, in which the "Working Analysis," which consists of three major sections, is treated as three separate documents: "Tai-Bei Kankei kara Mita Nihon no Tachiba to Seisaku no Jissai-teki Bunseki," "Suishin Hōhō," and "Zenken Daihyō-kaigi"; *TSM*, VII (Tsunoda): 134–35, and *Bekkan*, 395–403, an unofficial, postwar translation of the "Working Analysis" prepared by the Senshi-shitsu under the title "Toku-ni Beikoku to no Kankei ni Okeru, Kyokutō ni Okeru Ware-ware (Nihon) no Chii to Seisaku no Jissai-teki Bunseki"; the English text, as found in the Konoye papers, is reproduced at the end of the *Bekkan*, following p. 617; Yabe, II: 238–41, wherein JMD's "Working Analysis" title is rendered as "Beikoku to no Kankei ni Tokubetsu-ni Ronkyū Shitaru Waga (Nihon no) Kyokutō ni Okeru Chii to Seisaku no Jikkō-teki Bunseki." Three typewritten copies of the "Working Analysis" (one copy is on Wikawa's office letterhead) can also be found in the FW papers. The final version of the text (as found in the JMD papers) is printed in the Appendixes, pp. 323–33 (Appendix A). Some minor typographical refinements have been added for ease of reading.

84–85 Editor Spinks on the nature of the problem: *Japan News-Week*, Dec. 7, 1940: 4 ("An Opportunity"). Also Spinks corresp. and intv.

85 "The cool mathematics of diplomacy": JMD papers, "Working Analysis," 1.

The Language of Diplomacy Unveiled

86 Matsuoka to the press, July 18, 1940: *Japan Weekly Chronicle*, July 25, 1940: 99.

86 Matsuoka's "extreme loquaciousness": The evidence is overwhelming on this point, but the specific statement quoted is that of the British ambassador. Craigie, 107. On Matsuoka's reputation as a conversationalist, see Sheba, "Yosuke Matsuoka," 300. Katō, 20, describes Matsuoka as "ordinarily an extremely talkative person who dominated every conversation and with whom as a rule it was extremely difficult to get a word in edgewise."

86 Matsuoka, a product of two cultures: Yōsuke Matsuoka was born in Yamaguchi Prefecture in 1880. He went to the U.S. at an early age, enrolled in the public schools, and later entered the University of Oregon from which he received an LLB on June 14, 1900. During World War I, when Nomura was the Japanese naval attaché in Washington, Matsuoka served as second secre-

tary of the Embassy and then as first secretary. The two men were also colleagues in Shanghai in 1932. Butow, *Tojo*, 75 n52; Sheba, "Yosuke Matsuoka,"
300–301; Kiba, 417; FDR papers, OF 197, Box 1, and PSF, Box 11. The young
Matsuoka's sojourn in Oregon, where he helped put himself through school
by working as a busboy in lumber camps, coincided with a period of agitation
in the western states against Chinese and Japanese nationals. Sokolsky, "Why
Matsuoka Hates the United States," 10ff (Drought sent this article to Walker).
See also Kase, 43; Craigie, 106; Shigemitsu, *Japan and Her Destiny*, 196–97,
and *Shōwa no Dōran*, II: 8–9; Moore, 130–31, 134; Katō, 117–18; *NYT Magazine*, Mar. 23, 1941: 6 (Byas on Matsuoka); and *NYT*, June 27, 1946: 21
(Matsuoka's obituary).

86 Matsuoka as "Refuter-in-Chief": Young, 165.

86 Matsuoka's readiness to be Konoye's *zōri-tori*: Ushiba intv.

87 "If Konoye was a shy squirrel": Kase, 43. Also Moore, 116–17; Katō, 119.

87 A Japanese reporter's view of Matsuoka: Katō, 118–19.

87 The problem posed by the prolixity of Matsuoka's language: Grew, *Ten
Years*, 344, 374; *FR 1941*, V: 80.

87 The effect of German victories on the Japanese: Grew, *Ten Years*, 325;
Presseisen, 236; Meskill, 12. The "wave of pro-Axis enthusiasm" sweeping
Japan was one of the particularly striking changes noted by A. T. Steele,
Far Eastern correspondent for the *Chicago Daily News*, on his return to
Tokyo in Aug. 1940 after an absence of four months. *PHA*, IV: 1712–15.

87 Matsuoka to Fleisher, July 21, 1940: *FR 1940*, IV: 966–67.

87–88 The "Matsuoka cyclone": *NYT*, Aug. 23, 1940: 1; *Japan Weekly Chronicle*, Aug. 29, 1940: 253–54, Nov. 7, 1940: 577; Sugiyama, 14–15; Sheba, "Yosuke Matsuoka," 300–301, and "Diplomats," 374–75; Moore, 116–19; JMD
papers, pertinent articles in the morning editions of *JTA*, Dec. 21–22, 1940;
FR 1940, I: 644, 650; *Asahi*, Dec. 20, 1940, *nikkan*, 1; Shigemitsu, *Shōwa no
Dōran*, II: 22; Craigie, 107; and Tsunoda intv.

88 "Hell-bent toward the Axis": See Grew, *Ten Years*, 321–22, 324–27; and
Craigie, 102–6.

88 Dooman's estimate of the situation: *FR 1940*, IV: 414–16.

88 Tying a Japanese tail to the German kite: I have rephrased a remark Grew
made to Matsuoka in Sept. 1940. Grew, *Ten Years*, 333–34.

88–89 Matsuoka's article (the original appeared in the Aug. 1940 issue of *Gen-
dai*): State 711.94/1718.

89 Matsuoka—a practicing Christian: In an article written for the July 22,
1933, issue of *Liberty Magazine*, Matsuoka declared: "Let me say right here
that I am a Christian, and if I have any prejudice it is in favor of spreading
the gospel of Christ throughout the world. Let me say also that there are
many honorable and able American missionaries and philanthropists in
China. But as a whole the body of missionaries has become a group of
propagandists among Americans in behalf of China and opposed to Japan.
There are too many of them who know nothing of Japan, who blind themselves to the faults and facts of China, who are uninformed and unqualified
to speak with authority." Grew papers, clippings, CX (Dec. 1940). Matsuoka
was greatly impressed by Pope Pius XII, with whom he had an audience during his visit to Europe in the spring of 1941. Although he may subsequently
have implied that he was a Catholic, Matsuoka's actual conversion did not

take place until later, perhaps not until 1945 or '46. Hasegawa, Matsuoka (Kenichirō), and Ōhashi intvs. See also Kase, 43.

89 Matsuoka's failure to foresee the U.S. reaction to Japan's alliance with Hitler and Mussolini: See FDR papers, PSF, Box 11; *PHA*, XX: 4300; *FRJ*, II: 114–15; and Katō, 20.

89–90 Article 3 of the Tripartite Pact: Implicit in this stipulation was the idea of automatic action on the part of the signatories, but a "strictly confidential" letter from Ambassador Ott to Matsuoka, dated Sept. 27, 1940, contained the following qualifier: "Needless to say, the question, whether an attack within the meaning of Article 3 of the Pact has taken place, must be determined through joint consultation of the three contracting parties." Germany, on the other hand, according to Ott's letter, would remain bound to "consider it a matter of course to give Japan full support and assist her with all military and economic means" in case she found herself attacked "by a power so far not engaged in the European War or the China conflict." *DGFP*, D.XI: 205–7. No one in Washington—or even in Berlin—was aware of the existence of this letter. The matter was handled by Ott and Stahmer (Ribbentrop's special representative) entirely on their own responsibility.

Ott's letter made it easier for Matsuoka to "sell" the Tripartite Pact to reluctant elements at home. Now he could argue, with some validity, that Japan retained her "freedom of action." Whether Tokyo would in fact have been able or willing to pursue an independent course in an actual test-case, with Berlin and Rome applying pressure under the terms of Article 3, is a debatable proposition. See Feis, 119–21; Langer and Gleason, 31–32; Trefousse, 71; *TSM*, V (Hosoya): 202–4, 213–14, 216–19, 222, and *passim*; Meskill, 18–20, 193–94, 197, 207, 230–31; Presseisen, 262–64; Schroeder, 119–22; Iklé, 181; Ike, 9; *NYT*, Sept. 28, 1940: 1; *DGFP*, D.XI: 204–5, 206, 261–62; *FRJ*, II: 145–46; *FR 1940*, I: 651, 663–64, 665, 666, 669; *FR 1941*, IV: 187–88, 194–96, 205, 971; Gaimushō, *Shuyō Bunsho*, II: 460; and Grew papers, "Diary," May 1941: 5114, 5125. Also pertinent here is Point 7 of the instructions Matsuoka handed to Nomura on Jan. 22. See Gaimushō, *NBKK*, 1–2; Gaimushō, *Shuyō Bunsho*, II: 479; Shigemitsu, *Japan and Her Destiny*, 221, and *Shōwa no Dōran*, II: 61.

90 Craigie on Matsuoka's primary purpose: Craigie, 101–2.

90 Grew's "Green Light" telegram (no. 827-30, Sept. 12, 1940), and his diary entry: Grew papers, "Diary," Nov. 1940: 4613–27. See also Grew, *Ten Years*, 332–39, and *Turbulent Era*, II: 1223–33; *FR 1940*, IV: 599–603 (the text of the telegram); *PHA*, II: 584–85, 621–25, 633–43, and IV: 1712–15 (Peiping's 300, Aug. 31, 1940, to which Grew referred in his 827-30); and U.S. Dept. of State, *Peace and War*, 569–72 (an extract in paraphrase). The "Green Light" telegram was so named because it represented a reversal of Grew's earlier "Red Light" position on American employment of retaliatory measures against Japan. Grew, *Ten Years*, 334.

90–91 Grew on Japan's word of honor: At the urging of his wife, Grew subsequently qualified his condemnation somewhat: "There is a difference between Hitler's word of honor and Japan's. Hitler's promises are made with his tongue in his cheek, knowing in advance that he will break those promises as soon as it suits his convenience. Japan's promises are made to us through the Foreign Minister, I believe in good faith, and when broken their breach has generally if not always been due to the refusal of the military to implement those promises. [Foreign Minister Kijūrō] Shidehara's promises with regard to the occupation of Manchuria, Hirota's promises to respect the principle of the Open Door in Manchuria and China, Nomura's promises to open the Yangtze to foreign navigation, were, I believe, made in entire good faith with every intention of carrying them into effect. But in Japan the Foreign Minister proposes, the Army disposes. Matsuoka has made promises that *he will do his best* to clear away the grounds for our complaints with respect to interference with American rights and interests in China but he has not promised that he will be successful. Perhaps he doesn't yet realize what he is up against. He told me that Admiral Nomura's reluctance to accept the post in Washington was the Admiral's fear that such promises as he might make would not be implemented at home." Grew papers, "Diary," Nov. 1940: 4623, 4626–27, 4635–36. See also Grew, *Ten Years*, 344.

91–92 The "special address": JMD papers, Drought ms., multiple typewritten copies of the speech, incl. some suggestions in Walsh's hand, and a considerable amount of 1st-draft material written by JMD—some of it on Imperial Hotel and Kyoto Hotel stationery; Walsh's "Japan Diary—1940"; Ōhashi, 108–9; Sawada ms.; Ōhashi and Sawada intvs.

The "special address," which was untitled, began with the following words: "This will not be an address in the veiled language of Victorian diplomacy. I am conscious of it. My speech is rather in the tradition of 'open covenants openly arrived at'—a phrase of hope which we cling to though it has been buffeted by disaster." JMD had the entire piece translated into Japanese, but no copies have come to hand.

92 Drought's desire to obtain a "substantially acceptable" commitment from the Japanese Govt.: A statement from the Foreign Minister, for example, to the effect that the proposals contained in JMD's "Working Analysis" were "substantially acceptable" would have added weight to the arguments Drought planned to use in Washington on his return. His failure to secure such a commitment in Tokyo helps to explain why he later made such strenuous efforts to get a corresponding assurance from FDR and Hull.

92 Matsuoka's reaction to the speech Drought had written for him: Ōhashi, 108–9. Also JMD papers, Drought ms.

92–93 Japan, Germany, and Italy (three partners with a common aim): Matsuoka had introduced this theme during a radio address on Sept. 27, 1940, marking the conclusion of the Tripartite Pact. *FRJ*, II: 166–68. The idea that Japan, Germany, and Italy had "the same aspirations and policy" was reiterated frequently thereafter.

93–94 Grew to FDR, Dec. 14, 1940: Grew, *Turbulent Era*, II: 1255–58, and *Ten Years*, 359–61; *FR 1940*, IV: 469–71; *PHA*, II: 615–19, 639–42; FDR papers, OF 197-A Misc., Box 1, and PSF, Box 11.

94 The dissimilarity between the address Matsuoka delivered and the "psychologically-American speech" Drought had drafted for him: JMD later wrote: "It will be observed . . . that Mr. Matsuoka followed the thought sequence and the general line of argument as developed in [my] prepared address, or if he did not, he thought he did, because he said so." JMD papers, Drought ms. Although a rather superficial comparison can be made here and there, the differences in style, content, and phraseology are rather striking. Such similarities as do exist (e.g., references in both texts to China being of "vital"

interest to Japan, to minding one's own business, to "sentimental" attachments, and to the absence of imperialistic motives in regard to the war in China) could indicate that Matsuoka influenced JMD rather than vice versa. In any case, subsequent developments support the judgment that Drought did not gain any ground with the Foreign Minister.

94–96 Matsuoka to the America-Japan Society, Dec. 19, 1940: I have quoted only part of the original address, using for this purpose a mimeographed version that was distributed to the luncheon guests; I have also consulted a typewritten copy of the speech (with a few marginal notes by JMD) and other pertinent material in the JMD papers, incl. *JTA*, Dec. 19, 1940, even. ed., Dec. 20, 1940, morn. ed., and *Japan News-Week*, Dec. 21, 1940. In summarizing Matsuoka's remarks, I have rearranged the order of his presentation slightly to bring his views on the Axis alliance and the conflict with China into clear focus. See also Grew papers, "Diary," Dec. 1940: 4687–90, and *passim*; *FRJ*, II: 123–28; and the following files (all 1940): State 711.94/1881–84, 1886–87, 1889, 1939.

95 The tantalizing obliteration: The wording in the text, which is taken from JMD's copy of the mimeographed handout distributed at the luncheon, was verified with the aid of a strong light. The phraseology used in a "clear," typewritten copy that turned up in the JMD papers is slightly different. In his ms. account of the 1940 visit to Japan, JMD wrote: "On the night of the 15th [18th?] [a] copy [of Matsuoka's speech] was sent to the American Embassy and to ourselves. Early in the morning of the 16th [19th?], we persuaded Mr. Matsuoka (by telephone conversation) to change a phrase and to omit another in the speech as prepared, particularly the intendedly [*sic*] humorous as well as threatening reference to a struggle in the Pacific between Admiral Nomura and President Roosevelt.... The American Embassy was much puzzled by the omission of this phrase from the Speech that was later given to the Press. Apparently Mr. Grew prepared his response either not realizing or ignoring what Matsuoka had intended as a diplomatic invitation to a fresh discussion of Japanese-American relations." JMD papers. Drought's contentions are based on supposition rather than on any positive evidence. In this connection, see also Grew papers, "Diary," Dec. 1940: 4689–90; and State 711.94/1939.

95 Some Americans "wilfully or otherwise": Grew informed Washington that Matsuoka's phrase had appeared in the vernacular press as "wilfully or maliciously." State 711.94/1939.

95 The Tripartite Pact as the "pivot" of Japan's foreign policy: A marginal comment by JMD (on a typewritten copy of Matsuoka's speech) notes that this "pivot" concept was "objected to by many." In his ms. account, Drought later wrote: "Frequently Matsuoka tried to say that this Pact was a pivot upon which the diplomacy of Japan would turn, whether in the direction of the European War or away from it. Unfortunately, his idea of pivot was taken to mean that the Tripartite Pact was the foundation of Japanese diplomacy." JMD papers. This strained explanation flies in the face of all of the evidence, including a number of specific statements by Matsuoka in which he emphasized that the alliance with Hitler constituted the "keystone" of Japanese policy, and that close cooperation with Nazi Germany and Fascist Italy would be Tokyo's "guiding principle."

96 Matsuoka's view that "the fate of China" was largely a matter of "sentiment"

to the American people: In the "special address" Drought had written for Matsuoka, JMD had declared: "We [Japanese] can understand the sentimental attachment of many persons [in the U.S.] for the cultural history and the attractive moral qualities of the simple Chinese people. We share that admiration. But the Chinese apathetic subservience to chaotic tyranny brings consequences no less evil to our people than to the Chinese themselves." Later, in his ms. account, Drought wrote that Matsuoka's attempt to dismiss American interest in China as sentimental was "unfortunate" and failed to take into consideration that "if it was sentimental, it was by that fact the more serious."

97 Nomura to the America-Japan Society: See *FRJ*, II: 128–29. Nomura spoke first in Japanese in an impromptu manner, and then formally in English. "Admiral Nomura's speech was a gem," Grew wrote. "But his command of English and pronunciation are poor and he is very difficult to understand." Grew papers, "Diary," Dec. 1940: 4689.

97–98. Grew's thoughts and reactions (incl. his rebuttal of Matsuoka's speech): Grew papers, "Diary," Nov.–Dec. 1940; 4659, 4687–90, 4704, and *passim*. The full text of the rebuttal is given in State 711.94/1939; and in *FRJ*, II: 129–30. In selecting material from his diary for publication, Grew inadvertently added part of his Dec. 19 rebuttal (the last three paragraphs) to an entry dealing with another clash at a farewell luncheon Matsuoka gave for Nomura on Jan. 18, 1941 (Grew, *Ten Years*, 366; Grew papers, "Diary," Jan. 1941: 4757), but the diary itself leaves no doubt about what was said on each occasion.

99 Grew on Terasaki's gibe: Grew papers, "Diary," Dec. 1940: 4689.

99–100 Drought's presence in the banquet room and his reactions to the proceedings: JMD papers, Drought ms. In the role of toastmaster, Grew had introduced several guests of "high distinction," among them Walsh and Drought. State 711.94/1939.

99 Grew's judgment that "even the missionaries" wholeheartedly supported his response to Matsuoka: Grew papers, "Diary," Dec. 1940: 4689.

100 The coverage of Matsuoka's speech by the vernacular press (as reported by Grew): State 711.94/1939. See also *Asahi*, Dec. 20, 1940, *nikkan*, 2, *yūkan*, 1, 2; Grew papers, clippings, CX (Dec. 1940), misc. items from the English-language press in Japan, incl. some translated comment from the vernacular; and JMD papers, *JTA*, Dec. 20, Dec. 21, 1940, morn. eds., *Japan News-Week*, Dec. 21, 1940.

100 The reaction of the *Mainichi* and the *Nichi-Nichi*: Grew papers, clippings, CX (Dec. 1940).

100 Grew's concern about press coverage in the U.S.: State 711.94/1882–83.

100 Drought's cable to Maryknoll, Dec. 19, 1940: JMD papers.

100–102 Far-reaching coverage in the U.S.: Grew papers, clippings, CX (Dec. 1940); State 711.94/1883. See also Grew papers, "Diary," Jan. 1941: 4727; State 894.24/1194A; *Seattle Times*, Dec. 19, 1940: 4; and *Seattle Post-Intelligencer*, Dec. 20, 1940: 1.

101 "Joseph Grew 'Tells 'Em' in Tokyo": This was the editorial lead in the *Knoxville Journal*, Dec. 21, 1940. The other captions, in the order quoted: *Milwaukee Journal*, Dec. 21, 1940; *Louisville Courier Journal*, Dec. 21, 1940; and *St. Louis Globe-Democrat*, Dec. 25, 1940. Grew papers, clippings, CX (Dec. 1940).

101–2 The clippings Grew received (all 1940): *Columbus Dispatch*, Dec. 20

("Grew's Warning to Japan—A Surprisingly Blunt Statement"); *Canton Repository*, Dec. 20 ("Making Friends with the Japanese"); *Philadelphia Inquirer*, Dec. 20 ("Mr. Grew Tells It to Japan"); *Washington Star*, Dec. 20 ("Mr. Grew Speaks Out"); *Greenville News*, Dec. 21 ("Reiteration of Absurdities"); and *Milwaukee Journal*, Dec. 21 ("Straight Talk to Japan"). *Ibid.*

An Impresario from Abroad

103 Drought's interview with Wakatsuki: JMD papers, a Dec. 4, 1940, letter from the chairman of the board of the Kokusai Bunka Shinkō-kai, setting up the appointment; Wakatsuki, 406–9 (this must be used with care since the Baron's recollections, which were published in 1950, reveal the effects of age on memory; he refers to Walsh by name, but he is in fact talking about Drought); Yabe, II: 241–42; Strauss corresp.

103–4 Ogura's approach to Drought: JMD papers. The letter quoted in the text was written on Jan. 8, 1941. In the spring of that year, Ogura was named Minister Without Portfolio (in the second Konoye Cabinet); several months later he became Minister of Finance (in Konoye's third Cabinet).

104–6 Some revealing glimpses of Axis Japan at work and at play: I have used, in particular, JMD's copy of *JTA*, Dec. 20, 1940, morn. ed.; and three items in the Grew papers, clippings, CX (Dec. 1940): *NYHT*, Dec. 21, Dec. 25, 1940; and *NYT*, Dec. 21, 1940. *JTA*, Dec. 21, 1940, morn. ed., and *Japan News-Week*, Dec. 21, 1940, both of which are in the JMD papers, are also instructive.

104 The *Japan Times and Advertiser* (a Foreign Office "rag"): Argall, 153–54; Grew papers, "Diary," Dec. 1940: 4691; Eric Fleisher corresp.

105 Ōshima's reappointment as ambassador to Germany (and his pro-Axis sympathies): See *DGFP*, D.XI: 863–64. Ōshima had previously served in the post from Nov. 1938 to Dec. 1939. He returned to Berlin in Feb. 1941, the same month that Nomura took up his duties in Washington.

106–7 Walsh and Drought to the Pan-Pacific Club: JMD papers, misc. items, incl. the full texts of the remarks the two men made. Grew felt "a definite antipathy" toward the Pan-Pacific Club for luring newly arrived Americans onto the speaker's platform, where they frequently gave "a totally wrong impression of opinion in the United States" by saying the sort of thing—"often far from the truth"—that they thought the Japanese wanted to hear. Grew papers, calls and callers, June 13, 1941: 5243.

107–10 The final week of the Walsh-Drought visit to Japan, Dec. 21–28, 1940: JMD papers, Drought ms., carbon copies of the letters mentioned in the text, Walsh's statement on behalf of Mutō, misc. items incl. some random thoughts jotted down on the spur of the moment; FW papers, "The 'X' Memorandum," "The Japanese Negotiations—1941"; Konoye papers, Wikawa to Mutō, Dec. 31, 1940 (this item can also be found in *TSM, Bekkan*, 403–4); Walsh papers, "Japan Diary—1940," the Bishop's Dec. 11, 1945, "Confidential Memorandum," and his Sept. 15, 1971, account of the "peace treaty negotiations." Some of the items cited contain contradictions that I have endeavored to resolve.

107 The Walsh-Drought view of Wikawa as Konoye's "confidential agent": *FR 1941*, IV: 529. According to Tomohiko Ushiba, the Premier's private secretary, Wikawa was not a close friend of Konoye's. Ushiba corresp. and intv. Iwakuro expressed the same opinion. Iwakuro intv.

107 The Japanese had two basic proposals in mind: Despite Walsh's impression,

which derived from information supplied by JMD, the Japanese Govt. was not in fact prepared in Dec. 1940 to offer any such "guarantees." If the leaders of Japan had been willing to turn their backs on the Tripartite Pact (a commitment they had made just three months earlier) and to withdraw their armed forces from China (where the war was already into its fourth year), Tokyo would have been able to reach an understanding with Washington quite easily (and, presumably, also with Chungking).

Shigenori Tōgō, Foreign Minister at the time of Pearl Harbor, expressed his astonishment when he learned after the war that Walsh had returned home with such a conception of Japan's intentions: "Where the bishop could have acquired such erroneous ideas, I do not know. If these reported terms had been the policy of the Japanese government, an understanding with the United States could readily have been reached without recourse to any negotiations or to employing anyone as go-between. In any event, it is sure that this misunderstanding was conveyed to the American authorities, and possibly led them to entertain the belief that Japan would, if pressed, recede to these terms; and the later negotiations were certainly complicated thereby." Tōgō, *The Cause of Japan*, 68 (for the corresponding passage in Japanese, see his *Jidai no Ichimen*, 160).

Tōgō's statement helps to correct a "revisionist" view published by Tansill in 1952, from which it would appear that Walsh and Drought were given a polite brush-off at the White House in Jan. 1941, when they presented far-reaching proposals that (allegedly) emanated from Matsuoka. "And thus ended," Tansill wrote, "an anxious effort on the part of the Japanese Government to find a path to peace even though this path led to a renunciation of Japan's objectives in China and a tremendous loss of face. It seems quite possible that the Far Eastern Military Tribunal brought to trial the wrong persons. It might have been better if the tribunal had held its sessions in Washington." See Tansill, 628–29.

109 Having already pledged themselves to secrecy: In his Dec. 11, 1945, "Confidential Memorandum," Walsh wrote: "We did not consult the American Embassy [in Nov.–Dec. 1940] because we were asked specifically not to do so by the Japanese officials [*sic*] who were sending the message [*sic*]. Their reason, as explained before, was because the American Embassy insisted (as they alleged) on believing that [its] secret code was unknown, and would consequently be almost certain to make some reference to the plan that would disclose its nature."

Despite the reference to "officials who were sending the message," Walsh and Drought did not bring home any proposal, in writing, from anyone authorized to speak for the Japanese Government. What they did bring back was a grab bag full of impressions gathered from conversations with Matsuoka, Wikawa, and other Japanese of varying importance.

If Walsh and Drought did not inform Grew, how much did they disclose to the Apostolic Delegate in Tokyo, Archbishop Paul Marella? There is conflicting evidence in this regard, but the answer may be "very little." See *ibid.*; a June 4, 1941, note by Walsh summarizing his briefing of the Archbishops in the U.S.; Walsh's Sept. 15, 1971, account of the "peace treaty negotiations"; and a Sept. 27, 1973, letter from Walsh to Fr. Coleman responding to some questions I had raised on a related matter.

109 Drought's farewell letters: JMD papers. Drought also wrote to a number of other people, including Wikawa.

109 Iwakuro was not present at the interview: When I asked Iwakuro about this, he replied that there was no reason for him to be present. The idea of his going to the U.S. developed later. He consequently did not meet Walsh and Drought until he reached New York in Mar. 1941. Iwakuro intv.

109 Konoye was out (when Walsh and Drought called): A statement by Konoye at an Apr. 18, 1941, Liaison Roundtable Conference (*TSM, Bekkan,* 389; Ike, 18) to the effect that he had met the "two American missionaries" in late 1940 should be disregarded, for he did not in fact have any such encounter. This is quite clear from Walsh's "Japan Diary—1940"; from materials in the JMD papers, esp. the Drought ms. and Walsh's statement on behalf of Mutō; and from a careful investigation into the matter by Tsunoda (*TSM,* VII: 136, and Tsunoda intv.). Also Ushiba intv.; "Matsuoka Oboegaki"; a Mar. 17, 1941, telegram from Matsuoka to Nomura indicating that Konoye did not see Walsh and Drought during their visit to Japan; and Coleman corresp. and enclosures, Walsh to Coleman, Nov. 19, 1971.

Two items in the FW papers, "The 'X' Memorandum" and "The Japanese Negotiations—1941," contain assertions to the effect that Konoye assured Walsh, during a brief meeting in the autumn of 1941, that the 1940 "message" had been conveyed at his "request," and that Walsh (and Drought) had indeed been "negotiating for him," but there is no evidence to support these claims.

110 "A peaceful day for a peaceful mission": FW papers, a Nov. 8, 1940, letter from JMD.

110 FDR's fireside chat, Dec. 29, 1940: *FRJ,* II: 173–81. Also Grew papers, clippings, CX (Dec. 1940), a Dec. 31, 1940, *NYT* edit.; Stimson and Bundy, 366.

110 Drought was alive to the Nazi menace: The JMD papers contain much evidence in this regard. The letter quoted in the text was written on Sept. 2, 1940, to Dean James E. McCarthy of the University of Notre Dame.

110–11 The situation in Japan as seen by an alert American Consul in Osaka (Walter Patrick McConaughy): *FR 1940,* IV: 978–81.

111–12 Grew had advised FDR against harboring any illusions on this score: See the Note for pp. 93–94 (Grew to FDR, Dec. 14, 1940).

112 Grew on the fireside chat (and related subjects): Grew, *Ten Years,* 357–59, 364, and *Turbulent Era,* II: 1258; Grew papers, "Diary" and misc. notes, Jan. 1941: 4716–17, 4769–72. Six months earlier, in June 1940, Grew had privately expressed the hope that FDR would run again. If he did not, then Grew believed that Willkie would be the right man for the job. It was in this context that Grew saw himself as "an original Willkie man." Grew, *Ten Years,* 318–19.

112 The messages drafted by Drought on board the *Nitta-maru:* The originals, written in pencil, are in the JMD papers.

112 Drought's long-distance call to Strauss: Strauss, 123; Strauss corresp. and intv. Strauss believes that Walsh and Drought called on Hoover personally (he was then living on the campus of Stanford University, close to San Francisco), but there is no material in the JMD papers on this subject. When Walsh was asked about the matter in 1971, he wrote: "Whether Father Drought went to Stanford U. to see Hoover, tried to see him, actually did see

him, or had any sort of communication with him I cannot recall and simply do not know. . . . I only know that I myself never saw Hoover. And I feel fairly certain that I never went to Stanford U. in an attempt to see him." Coleman corresp. and enclosures, Walsh to Coleman, Nov. 19, 1971.

112–13 The way in which Drought arranged an interview at the White House: FW papers, TA Log, plus "Personal Notes" item, Mar. 10, 1949, "Japanese Negotiations" item, July 12, 1954, "The 'X' Memorandum," and "The Japanese Negotiations—1941"; JMD papers, Walsh's statement on behalf of Mutō, and misc. notes and papers, incl. copies of the telegrams quoted in the text; FDR papers, PPF 1–o: (1), (2), and (3), Boxes 186, 191, and 200, respectively; *NYT*, Jan. 17: 1; Coleman corresp. and enclosures.

The "fragmentary reconstruction" in the text (as seen from Walker's desk) is a paraphrase of material in the FW papers rather than a direct quotation from the TA Log.

When I sent an inquiry to Joseph P. Kennedy in 1965, I was informed by a member of his staff in New York that no one in the organization had any recollection or record of the events enumerated in my letter, and that Mr. Kennedy could not take up the matter personally for reasons of health.

113 Kennedy on Lend-Lease: In a Mar. 3, 1941, letter to Fr. Byrne in Kyoto, Fr. Kiernan wrote: "Had not Jim [Drought] seen Joe Kennedy when he did [on Jan. 16], two days prior to Joe's radio blast, it would have been much worse. Jim gave Joe some new ideas and even some hope. It was Joe that got the entrée to our Socialist Number One. Moreover, Jim succeeded in cutting out a lot of bitterness that Joe had planned for his radio blast. So you see there are still some Council members who aren't carrying a tombstone where the head ought to be." Coleman corresp. and enclosures.

113 The "Good" and "Satisfactory" messages, Jan. 19, Jan. 20: JMD papers.

113 Walsh to Kennedy, Jan. 20: *Ibid.*

114 A simple, homemade code: A copy of Wikawa's Dec. 31, 1940, letter to Mutō describing the code arrangement is in the Konoye papers. This suggests that the Premier was *au courant* at the time. Also Yabe, II: 242; *TSM*, VII (Tsunoda): 136, and *Bekkan*, 403–4; Tsunoda intv.

114–15 Wikawa's Jan. 22 cable and Jan 23 letter: JMD papers.

114 "I lost no time": Wikawa wrote to Konoye on Jan. 21, informing him of the arrival of the "Good" and "Satisfactory" cables. Konoye papers; *TSM*, *Bekkan*, 403.

116 The snatches of conversation, etc., jotted down by Drought: There is a voluminous amount of material of this nature in the JMD papers. Although undated, most of the items quoted in the text are written on Willard Hotel stationery (JMD stayed there from Jan. 21 to Jan. 23). I have made a few minor typographical changes in the interest of clarity and have occasionally supplied some missing words. These additions are indicated by brackets in the text.

116 The "Agreement" outlined in Drought's "Strictly Confidential Memo": See *FR 1941*, IV: 15–16.

117–18 An early draft of the "Strictly Confidential Memo": JMD papers. The revised text, which was handed to FDR on Jan. 23, is printed in *FR 1941*, IV: 14–16.

118 The meeting with the President: FDR papers, PPF 1–o: (1), (2), and (3),

Boxes 186, 191, and 200, respectively, and the appointment book kept by the Office of Social Entertainments; Hull papers, "Desk Diary," Folder 295-I; FW papers, "Daily Memo Calendar, 1941"; Drewry corresp. FDR had been scheduled to see various visitors at fifteen-minute intervals beginning at 11:00 A.M. He was to have lunch at one o'clock, and the Cabinet would convene at two.

119 Drought to Wikawa, Jan. 24: JMD papers. Wikawa wrote to Konoye the next day to report the receipt of this cable, which he rendered into Japanese as *"Daitōryō ōhō no kekka yūbō shinchoku-chū, tenkai kitai seraru."* Yabe, II: 242; *TSM*, VII (Tsunoda): 136, and *Bekkan*, 403; Tsunoda intv. According to Tsunoda, Wikawa also conveyed the news to Matsuoka, Mutō, and others.

119 Drought to Joseph P. Kennedy, Jan. 24: JMD papers.

119 The Wikawa-Drought exchange of cables: *Ibid.*

119 Walsh to Walker, and Drought's earlier recommendations to FDR: See text, pp. 13–14, and the pertinent notes.

120 The "ideal" Presidential representative: Although Wikawa later got the impression that Drought had been asked to represent FDR in the "preliminary negotiations" because Harry Hopkins could not be spared from other duties, I do not believe that JMD ever considered "Harry" for the job. Hopkins was too close to FDR to be acceptable, and probably of too independent a mind. Drought wanted someone he could "steer" in the "right direction." Walker was made to order for Drought's purposes: the PMG did not have any diplomatic experience and would therefore have to rely on JMD.

120 Wikawa to Drought, Jan. 31: JMD papers.

120 "Our consul in New York": Sadao Iguchi. When I talked with Iguchi about the matter in 1965, he did not recall the cable or cables that he presumably sent in this regard, and the material has yet to be found in the archives of the Foreign Office. Also Suma intv.; JMD papers, Drought to Setsuzō Sawada, Feb. 12.

120–21 Wikawa to Drought, Feb. 5: JMD papers.

120 Wikawa had previously noted: The reference here is to his Jan. 31 letter to JMD.

121–22 Sir William Wiseman: His activities during World War I are discussed in Willert, 1, 15–16, 25–26, and *passim*. See also Fowler, esp. 8–25, on the beginnings of the Wiseman-House relationship.

122 Drought to Wiseman, Feb. 3: JMD papers. Also Strauss corresp. I am indebted to Wilton B. Fowler for copies of several pertinent Wiseman-Drought items from the "New Wiseman ms" (Yale University).

122 Drought turned once again to Walker: FW papers, TA log; JMD papers. He did not get through to the PMG until Feb. 6.

122 Drought to Wikawa, Feb. 6, and Wikawa's Feb. 7 reply: JMD papers. Wikawa, 15, and *TSM*, VII (Tsunoda): 136, refer to a cable (supposedly received on Jan. 28) that read: *"Saku-ya futatabi bosu* ["boss" here signifies FDR] *to kyōgi, ichijirushiku yūbō nari."* This is undoubtedly a rendering (perhaps from memory) of Drought's Feb. 6 message—a message Wikawa received on Feb. 7. To the best of my knowledge, Walsh and Drought did not have a second meeting with FDR. Perhaps JMD's Feb. 6 message was based on an optimistic interpretation of something Walker said over the telephone that day.

"Harsh Talk Is for Home Consumption"

123 Hornbeck's view of Japanese aims and intentions, Jan. 28: State 894.00/1008.

123 Sounds suggestive of compromise and conciliation: See *FR 1941*, IV: 8–10; Grew papers, "Diary," Jan. 1941: 4734–35, 4777–78; and Grew, *Ten Years*, 365–66, 368–71. See also State 711.94/1964; and Grew papers, "Diary," Nov. 1940: 4626–27.

124 "Dangers that were real and those that were imaginary": Craigie, 133.

124 Grew on the possibility of "a surprise mass attack on Pearl Harbor": Grew's 125 was received in Washington at 6:38 A.M., Jan. 27. The following day the State Dept. sent paraphrased copies (a security precaution employed in the handling of coded messages) to the Office of Naval Intelligence and to the Military Intelligence Division of the Army. See *FR 1941*, IV: 17 (the cable as sent by Grew); and *FRJ*, II: 133 (for the paraphrased version). See also Grew, *Ten Years*, 368, and *Turbulent Era*, II: 1233, 1283; Grew papers, "Diary," entry for Jan. 27; Wohlstetter, 386; Millis, 35.

After the war, in Nov. 1945, Grew was badgered by a Congressman from North Carolina, who wanted to know why he had not made an effort to obtain more details at the time. He replied: "I think in all probability if I had asked my colleague for the source [of his information] he probably would have felt that he could not give it to me. In any case, it is a rather difficult thing to do, to ask for such a thing as that." *PHA*, II: 571–73. My efforts to get in touch with Grew's Peruvian colleague of 1941, Dr. Ricardo Rivera Schreiber, all ended unsuccessfully. Eugene Dooman, who was on home leave at the time, was later unable to add to the record except to say: "In diplomacy as it used to be practiced, it was not 'good form' to ask colleagues about sources of information." Dooman corresp.

124 The Japanese people were determined to proceed: See *FR 1941*, IV: 16–17.

124 Matsuoka had just told a committee in the Diet, Jan. 26: The sentences quoted in the text are Matsuoka's words as cabled by Grew. No official text was available, and newspaper accounts were not entirely in agreement. See *FRJ*, II: 133–35, 136; and *TSM*, VII (Tsunoda): 124.

124 Matsuoka in reply to interpellations in the Diet, Jan. 29, Feb. 4: *FR 1941*, IV: 18–20; *FRJ*, II: 135–36. See also Grew papers, "Diary," Jan., Feb., 1941: 4780–82, 4846–48.

124–25 Matsuoka "emphasized that his statements were not irresponsible remarks": *FRJ*, II: 135.

125 The "southward advance" was being pushed: Grew papers, "Diary," Jan. 1941: 4715–16. See also Butow, *Tojo*, 195–201.

125 The outlook for the future had "never been darker": This observation, which appears in the "introduction" to Grew's "Diary," Jan. 1941: 4715–16, is printed in Grew, *Ten Years*, 369, under the date Feb. 1, 1941. The "introduction" for that month ("Diary," 4789) contains a reference to Mar. 7. This means that the "introduction" for each month was written retrospectively, at the end of the month, and was then put at the beginning of the "Diary" for that month as a matter of style. The comment quoted in the text is therefore applicable to late Jan. and early Feb. 1941.

125–26 A serious case of war "jitters": Langer and Gleason, 319–31. See also

FR 1941, V: 103–6; Churchill, 176–82; Eden, 354–59; Pogue, 180–81; and *DGFP*, D.XII: 139–51, esp. 144–46.

126 The importance of Singapore: See the Note for p. 130 (The danger of a concerted Japanese drive to the south).

126–27 The Drought-Nomura exchange of telegrams: Feb. 11, Feb. 13: JMD papers. Also FW papers, "The 'X' Memorandum"; *TSM*, VII (Tsunoda): 136; Sawada ms.; Tsunoda and Sawada intvs.

127 Drought to Sawada, Feb. 12: JMD papers; Sawada intv. Drought's letter was very misleading, for it suggested a much more dynamic participation by FDR and Hull in his enterprise than the facts justified. When Sawada gave copies of JMD's letter to his friends in Tokyo, he found that they were "glad to get it." Apparently Matsuoka, Ōhashi, and Tarō Terasaki all read Drought's report. LC-JFOA, WT 73, IMT 557, 25–26; Matsuoka to Nomura, Mar. 15 (I am indebted to Jun Tsunoda for a copy of this telegram).

127–30 Grew's feeling that he was "out on a limb," his efforts to obtain a White House interview for Dooman, and the Dooman-Ōhashi conv. of Feb. 14: Grew papers, "Diary," Jan.–Mar. 1941: 4736–37, 4789–91, 4857–58, 4937; Dooman corresp. (esp. in regard to his experiences in Washington while he was on home leave); *FR 1941*, IV: 37–39, 53–54; *FRJ*, II: 137–43; *PHA*, II: 671–72, 673–76, 705–6, 726–28, III: 1384–87, IV: 1715; Langer and Gleason, 325–26; Grew, *Turbulent Era*, II: 1261; Hull, II: 983.

There is no doubt that Grew felt cut off in Tokyo—isolated and left to fend for himself, so to speak—but it is also clear that his complaints in this regard, which intensified during 1941, loomed larger *after* the Japanese attack on Pearl Harbor. See his "Diary," Apr. 30, 1941: 5005–6; and his later reflections in *Turbulent Era*, II: 1272–76. Also Dooman corresp.

SKH later offered this observation: "The simple fact was that the Department of State had never developed machinery such as apparently had been developed in the British Foreign Office for distributing information wholesale or in particular to the diplomatic missions. We ... were no less eager than was [Grew] that he be fully informed; but we had not the personnel nor did the Department have the practice necessary for serving that purpose. . . . [We] repeatedly brought this need to the attention of our superiors—but without, in those days, effective results." Hornbeck corresp.

128 Dooman's "long experience in Japan": Grew, *Ten Years*, xii.

129 "The frankest and most direct admonition": See Langer and Gleason, 319–26.

129 The "spineless program": *Ibid.*

130 The danger of a concerted Japanese drive to the south: *FR 1941*, IV: 29–30, 36–37, 41–42, 43–49, and *passim*, V: 52, 60–99 *passim*; *PHA*, XIX: 3442–54; Grew papers, "Diary," Jan., Feb. 1941: 4715–16, 4789–91, 4859–66, 4904–9; Grew, *Ten Years*, 354–55, 365, 369–72, 373–74, and *passim*; Eden, 354–59; Shigemitsu, *Gaikō Kaisō-roku*, 279–93; Gaimushō, *Shuyō Bunsho*, II: 482–87; LC-JFOA, WT 38, IMT 261, 130–32, 134–35, 138 (some of these items were cabled to the Japanese Embassy in Washington); Langer and Gleason, 322–31. See also State 711.94/2193 ("The Program of Japan," 11–13); FDR papers, PSF, Box 27, a Butler-Hamilton conv., Feb. 7; *FR 1940*, IV: 599–603; and *PHA*, XIX: 3492–94.

130 Japan's nibbling movement toward the south: This description was coined

by A. T. Steele. Grew papers, "Diary," Nov. 1940: 4615; *PHA*, IV: 1712–15. See also Spotswood, "Japan's Southward Advance as an Issue in Japanese-American Relations."

130–31 Nomura's press conference, Feb. 19: *NYT*, Feb. 20: 4. Nomura conversed in Japanese, using a member of his staff as his interpreter. The correspondents were told that the Ambassador understood English but did not speak it "readily."

131 Matsuoka to the British Govt., Feb. 17: LC-JFOA, WT 38, IMT 261, 131–32 (and related items); *FR 1941*, V: 80, 84–86; Craigie, 114; Grew, *Ten Years*, 372; Langer and Gleason, 328; *NYT*, Feb. 18: 1, Feb. 19: 1, Feb. 20: 4. See also LC-JFOA, WT 37, IMT 261, 27–33, 47–53, and *passim*.

131 "We have no recourse": *FRJ*, II: 134.

131 Matsuoka, a dynamic but erratic genius: Kase, 43. See also Grew papers, "Diary," Mar. 1941: 4917.

131 "As crooked as a basket of fishhooks": Hull, I: 902. Hitler's opinion proved to be equally harsh. Matsuoka, he said, possessed "the hypocrisy of an American Bible missionary." Compton, 190.

The John Doe Associates Converge

133–34 The problems Wikawa faced and the assistance he received from Iwakuro: Iwakuro ms., 17–26, 44–51; Yabe, II: 244–45; Ōhashi, 109–10; FW papers, Wikawa items, esp. his application to the Finance Ministry, the permit that allowed him to obtain foreign exchange, and a National City Bank receipt covering his transactions at the Tokyo branch on Feb. 12, 1941. Also Iwakuro, Ōhashi, and Tsunoda intvs. The sources cited in this note are not in agreement on all points.

133 Iwakuro consulted two businessmen: Shigeru Suzuki and Kunitoshi Dobashi of Nihon Shōkai and Nihon Kōshūha Jūkōgyō, respectively. Wikawa may also have received some monetary "send-off gifts" from others, but he was not on the Foreign Office payroll (a point Matsuoka made to Nomura in a Mar. 6 telegram, a copy of which was sent to me by Jun Tsunoda). In a letter to Drought dated Feb. 5, Wikawa had suggested that he would be traveling at his own expense.

134 "Extra Secretary of the Ministry of Foreign Affairs": State 711.94/2178-6/18. Despite this designation, Wikawa did not have diplomatic standing in the U.S.

135 Wikawa went to see Konoye, Feb. 12: As in the case of their first meeting, on Jan. 11, virtually nothing is known about this second encounter. *TSM*, VII (Tsunoda): 137; Wikawa, 17; Tsunoda intv. There was adverse criticism of Wikawa in various quarters. Konoye knew this, but he seems to have felt Wikawa might prove "useful" nevertheless. A similar thought appears to have crossed the minds of both Iwakuro and Nomura at one time or another.

135 Wikawa was not empowered to act for the Japanese Govt.: There is a great deal of general evidence in support of this point, but it has been specifically confirmed by Iwakuro and Tsunoda. Arita, 105, a former Foreign Minister, describes Wikawa as "the self-styled representative of Prince Konoye." Ushiba believes that Wikawa, in talking with Hull and other State Dept. officials, "must have freely posed himself as the Prince's personal representative." Ushiba corresp.

135–36 Wikawa to Drought, Feb. 14, and JMD's reply, Feb. 24: JMD papers.

136–37 Efforts to expedite Wikawa's arrival in the U.S.: JMD papers, the messages exchanged between the principals; Tibesar intv.; FW papers, Wikawa items. "This took 21 telegrams!" Walsh wrote. "But I think it is worth the trouble." Drought replied: "Quite a chapter—Thanks."

137–38 Nomura's outlook during his first weeks in Washington (Feb. 14–Mar. 8), esp. the slowness with which he entered upon his mission: Yabe, II: 246–47; Nomura, 28–32, 37–38; Kiba, 460; *JTA*, Mar. 5, morn. ed.: 1 ("Nomura Biding Time to Better Relations"); *TSM*, VII (Tsunoda): 169; *NYT*, Feb. 20: 4; Iwakuro ms., 27–29; Wikawa, 19. See also *PHA*, XX: 4296–98; and Moore, 143–56, 161, 170, 174, 175–76, 201–4.

137 The instructions Nomura had received from Matsuoka (Jan. 22): See Gaimushō, *Shuyō Bunsho*, II: 478–79, and *NBKK*, 1–5; Shigemitsu, *Japan and Her Destiny*, 220–22, and *Shōwa no Dōran*, II: 60–62.

137–38 FDR's reaction: The President sent this note to Sumner Welles on Feb. 20: "I have just read the purported instructions from Foreign Minister Matsuoka to Ambassador Nomura dated February 14. Please read them. These instructions seem to me to be the product of a mind which is deeply disturbed and unable to think quietly or logically." *PHA*, XX: 4296; *F.D.R.: His Personal Letters, 1928–1945*, II: 1126. With the help of the various custodians of the records mentioned below, I have engaged in a long and fruitless search for the instructions "dated February 14." They are apparently not at Hyde Park, or in the archives of the State Dept., or in the "Magic" files in the custody of the U.S. Navy, or among the records that remain in the Japanese Foreign Office.

Despite the apparent conflict in dates, I am inclined to think that the instructions FDR read on Feb. 20 were the ones Matsuoka handed to Nomura on Jan. 22. The Feb. 14 date FDR used in his note to Welles happens to correspond to the day on which Nomura paid his first visit to the White House. Perhaps he gave the President a copy of Matsuoka's intructions; if so, FDR might have assigned the Feb. 14 date to these instructions when he got around to reading them on Feb. 20. The idea that Nomura would divulge material of this nature may seem implausible, but a few months later—on May 12, 1941 —he asked Hull to return some documents (incl. instructions from Tokyo) that he had mistakenly handed over the day before.

Another possible explanation is that FDR read a "Magic" version of some supplementary instructions from Matsuoka to Nomura dated Feb. 14. The fact that no one has been able to find anything of this nature does not necessarily mean that such instructions were never sent.

138 Nomura knew his Govt.'s attitude but he disagreed with it: See *TSM*, VII (Tsunoda): 123–25, 129–33. Also Tsunoda corresp.

138 Trying to chase two rabbits at the same time: Nomura, 12; Kiba, 417. See also Katō, 20–21.

138 "The tightrope of diplomacy": Nomura employed this phrase in a slightly different context in his Dec. 19, 1940, speech at the America-Japan Society luncheon. *FRJ*, II: 128–29.

138–39 Wikawa's initial visits to the Japanese Embassy in Washington and the part he played in bringing about the meeting at the Carlton: Wikawa, 16–19; Iwakuro ms., 27–33; Nomura, 39, 41; LC-JFOA, WT 38, IMT 265, 227–28;

Yabe, II: 246–47; *FRJ*, II: 389; Hull, II: 988. Also Iwakuro intv. Although I have summarized the Nomura-Wikawa-Iwakuro version of what happened, I doubt that the arrangements were quite as melodramatic as their memories suggest. My own guess is that the idea of holding a "backstairs meeting" came originally from Drought and Wikawa, and that Walker and Hull were innocent parties to the whole thing. The PMG was probably told that Nomura desired an off-the-record meeting (to keep it out of the press); this was passed along to Hull and he agreed to devote a Saturday morning at his apartment (not evening, as in some accounts) to what he hoped would be a heart-to-heart talk with the Ambassador.

139 "Although the store was open it wasn't doing any business" (*kaiten kyū-gyō*): Wikawa, 18. This was still the situation a month later (in early April). Iwakuro ms., 80–85.

139–40 Wikawa's initial contacts with Walker: Both the JMD and the FW papers are barren in this regard, but a brief account can be found in Wikawa, 16–19.

141 The memoranda barrage, Mar. 5–19: See *FR 1941*, IV: 61, 63–64, 69–74, 95–107, 111–12; the originals, incl. an unpublished memo dated Mar. 14, are in the JMD papers; typewritten copies are in the State Dept. files and in the FW papers.

141 Wikawa planned to consult Iwakuro immediately: The text draws on Drought's "Berkshire" memo of Mar. 10–11 (JMD papers; *FR 1941*, IV: 69–70); and on statements in a Mar. 14 memo submitted to Walker for transmission to FDR and Hull (JMD and FW papers).

141–45 The posting of Iwakuro to Washington, his reactions to the assignment, and his arrival in the U.S.: Iwakuro, Ōhashi, and Tsunoda intvs.; FW papers, Wikawa items; JMD papers, misc. notes, letters, and telegrams; Iwakuro ms., 34–68, 71–73; Nomura, 51 (Nomura's brief tribute contains only the barest hint of the very large role played by Iwakuro and Wikawa); Kiba, 458–59; Ōhashi, 109; IMTFE, 32992–33003 ("Sokki-roku," 312: 13–15); *TSM*, VII (Tsunoda): 147–48, 153 (where Iwakuro is described as a "born plotter"), 165–66; State 701.9411/1374 and 1387; corresp. with the office of the chief of Military History; Yabe, II: 245; Arita, 104–6; Aoki, III: 100–101; Nakamura, Part 2, 983; Saitō, 101, 180; Storry, 247, 277 n4, 286 n1, 315; *JTA*, Mar. 28, morn. ed.: 2.

142 The "nucleus clique" of officers: *Chūken shōkō* (see as indexed in Butow, *Tojo*). Coox, 49–50, gives Iwakuro's own description of how this group operated.

142 Iwakuro's visit to the American Embassy, Feb. 27, and his conv. with Dooman: *FR 1941*, IV: 53; State 711.94/1971; Grew papers, "Diary," Feb. 1941: 4838; Iwakuro ms., 53–56.

142 *Bōryaku no meijin*: A phrase used by Chūichi Ōhashi during an interview I had with him in Tokyo in 1965.

143 Katō on Iwakuro: Katō, 21–22.

143 A front-page story: When Iwakuro learned that the "flag of truce" account was based on a report from Washington, he remembered that shortly before leaving Japan, while he was visiting the offices of the Army General Staff, he had been shown a Japanese translation of an American Embassy telegram to the State Dept. commenting on his influence in the Army and on his forth-

coming trip to the U.S. This telegram, which Grew had sent in code, had been intercepted and deciphered by Japanese Military Intelligence. Upon being approached by the press in Hawaii, Iwakuro assumed that the Embassy's telegram had caused the U.S. Govt. to regard his assignment to Washington as a matter of importance, leading in turn to the newspaper story that had caught the eye of the reporters in Honolulu. Iwakuro ms., 56–58, 63–65. See *FR 1941*, IV: 53, for the telegram in question (p. 75 is also pertinent, esp. when supplemented by State 711.94/2004).

143–44 The *Hawaii Hōchi* article, Mar. 15: I am indebted to Minoru Shinoda and Mitsugu Matsuda for searching the Hawaii newspapers on my behalf, and to George Akita for a photostatic copy of the article in question. There is also a brief but pertinent mention of Iwakuro in the *Nippu Jiji*, Mar. 14: 6.

144–45 The messages exchanged by Wikawa and Drought, Mar. 20–25: JMD papers; FW papers, Wikawa items. Iwakuro did not need a rest; he was not tired or ill. He wanted time to think matters through. He also wanted to see the country (this was his first visit to the U.S.). Iwakuro ms., 71–72; Iwakuro intv.

144 "Party came to New York today to meet you": Ballantine's memo covering his visit to New York indicates that he arranged to see Drought on the morning of Mar. 24, but JMD's telegram to Wikawa is dated the 25th.

145 The suspicion with which Wikawa was regarded by Wakasugi and the other Embassy "regulars": Yabe, II: 247; *TSM*, VII (Tsunoda): 146; Kiba, 460; Iwakuro ms., 33, 81–85; Gaimushō, *NBKK*, 111; Nomura and Iwakuro intvs.

145 Slighting references to members of the Japanese Embassy: See text pp. 25, 32–33. Wikawa's Mar. 27 statement to Ballantine (text p. 38) is also pertinent.

145 The Nishiyama channel of communications: See LC-JFOA, WT 73, IMT 557, 32–38; *Gendai-shi Shiryō (13)*, xix, 663–64. To date, only two of Wikawa's reports, Special Nos. 8 and 9, have been found. The Finance Ministry apparently did not retain copies of the telegrams in this series because they did not bear upon the work of the Ministry. One might have expected something to turn up in the Konoye papers, but much of the material, which the Prince kept in his possession upon relinquishing the Premiership, went up in flames as the result of an American air raid. Konoye had instructed a member of his staff to take special precautions to guard against such an eventuality, but the man in question failed to follow through, and so the papers were lost. Tsunoda corresp.

146 Nomura had reported to Matsuoka, Mar. 1: LC-JFOA, WT 38, IMT 265, 227–28; Kurihara corresp.

146 Matsuoka's warnings to Nomura concerning Wikawa, Mar. 6, Mar. 15, Mar. 17: *TSM*, VII (Tsunoda): 145; Tsunoda corresp.; Nomura, Iwakuro, and Tsunoda intvs. (I am indebted to Jun Tsunoda for copies of the three telegrams.) Mamoru Shigemitsu has criticized Nomura for disregarding his instructions and for relying on Iwakuro and Wikawa rather than on his staff. Shigemitsu notes that "divided diplomacy" was the result, and that historical criticism should focus on the circumstances surrounding the commencement of the conversations in Washington rather than on developments thereafter. *Japan and Her Destiny*, 222–23, and *Shōwa no Dōran*, II: 62–63.

146–47 The Mar. 17 cable to Nishiyama (from the Finance Minister): LC-JFOA, WT 73, IMT 557, 27–31; *TSM*, VII (Tsunoda): 146; Tsunoda corresp.

147 If Matsuoka's postwar recollections are correct: The text is based on a memo by Matsuoka ("Matsuoka Oboegaki"). The Foreign Minister's response to JMD's request helps to explain why Drought, who had previously been so anti-Wakasugi in tone, also began making disparaging comments about Matsuoka—a man who had figured prominently in JMD's Jan. 23 report to FDR.

147 Nomura's optimistic outlook: See Moore, 170, 174, 201–2.

147 Iwakuro's position as a "Special Adviser": In a Mar. 11 communication to Hull, Nomura described Iwakuro as a "newly appointed Assistant Military Attaché." State 701.9411/1374. In April, the U.S. War Dept. extended the "usual courtesies and facilities" to Iwakuro in view of his position at the Embassy. State 701.9411/1391. One of Iwakuro's calling cards (vintage 1941), which I found in the FW papers, also describes him as an "Assistant Military Attaché." Despite all this, he did not actually function as an assistant to the military attaché. He played the part of a "Special Adviser." During his tour of duty in Washington, he remained attached to the Military Affairs Bureau in Tokyo. Iwakuro intv.

148 If the Foreign Minister had adhered to what seems to have been his original plan: At various times during Matsuoka's tenure at the Foreign Office (July 1940–July 1941), he indicated to Grew and others that he regarded himself as the ideal man to go to Washington. He also felt, however, that he could not be spared from Tokyo. Grew, *Ten Years*, 350; *TSM*, VII (Tsunoda): 127–29. Also *Sugiyama Memo*, I: 55.

148 Japan's "last trump card": *Asahi*, Dec. 20, 1940, *nikkan*, 2; JMD papers, *JTA*, Dec. 21, 1940, morn. ed.: 5.

Shirtsleeve Diplomats at Work

149 Wikawa to Drought (from San Francisco), Mar. 21: JMD papers.

149–50 Drought had just submitted several memos: See *FR 1941*, IV: 95–97, 111–12.

149 Konoye and several other like-minded men: In addition to the Premier, Drought specifically mentioned Marquis Kido and Count Arima. As a matter of fact, however, Wikawa did not send the text of the "Preliminary Draft" to Konoye until Mar. 22. Since it then went by sea, the Prince could not have received it until around Apr. 5 at the earliest. *TSM*, *Bekkan*, 404–7 (the original is in the Konoye papers); Tsunoda intv.

In a covering letter, Wikawa advised Konoye not to show the "Draft" to any of the authorities in Tokyo who would normally be consulted; the reason given was that it would probably be amended in the near future.

Although the State Dept. had been told that the "Agreement in Principle" was the joint work of Drought and Wikawa (see *FR 1941*, IV: 69–70, 95–97, 111–12), Wikawa referred to the document as though it were an American proposal that had been handed to him by a source close to FDR.

Four days before Wikawa dispatched the "Draft," Drought prematurely advised the State Dept. through Walker that a copy had been sent to Konoye "unknown to [the] Japanese Embassy." *FR 1941*, IV: 96 n48.

149 The risk of assassination: During the period in question, Konoye and other

Japanese leaders could have been attacked by fanatics at any moment, but it is farfetched to claim, as Drought did, that Iwakuro and Wikawa were in danger at this time.

150 The excuse Drought offered to Ballantine, Mar. 27: See *FR 1941*, IV: 114–15.

150 Iwakuro's objections to the "Agreement in Principle": The JMD papers contain an item dated Mar. 27 with a notation in Drought's hand identifying it as "Japanese Comments" on the "Preliminary Draft of 'Agreement in Principle.'" Circumstantial evidence suggests that these "Comments" were Wikawa's version of the objections Iwakuro had raised in San Francisco.

150–52 Drought rushed to the defense of his brainchild: Several typewritten copies of his Mar. 27 memo, which is addressed to Wikawa, can be found in the JMD papers; there is also an early, handwritten draft on RCA radiogram blanks.

151 The eleven "Rules for Nations": *FR 1941*, IV: 98–99.

151 Some corresponding "Aids to Peace": *Ibid.*, 99–100.

153 Drought's Mar. 29 memo, "written exclusively from the Japanese viewpoint": There are several copies in the JMD papers, incl. one bearing a notation in his hand: "sent to Prince Konoye." Drought probably asked Wikawa to forward this piece to the Premier, but whether Wikawa did so or not is uncertain. I did not find it among the Konoye papers.

153 It appears that Iwakuro held his ground: Iwakuro intv.; Iwakuro ms., 71–77 (although the time reference is later, see also 108–14); *TSM*, VII (Tsunoda): 149; Kiba, 460.

154 Drought's Apr. 4 memo: *FR 1941*, IV: 119–20.

154–58 The origins and authorship of the "Draft Understanding" (of Apr. 9): Drought, Iwakuro, and Wikawa produced a 1st draft at the Wardman Park Hotel over a period of several days (Apr. 2–5); the "Draft Understanding" of Apr. 9 was a refinement of the earlier text (and was therefore in the nature of a 2d draft). See Butow, "Hull-Nomura Conversations," 823–24, 826, and *passim*. Several years after this article appeared, Iwakuro told me that he did not have a Japanese "text" in the sense of a piece of paper on which he had recorded his ideas; rather, he developed each major point orally at the Wardman Park, his statements were translated by Wikawa for Drought's benefit, the three of them talked the matter over until agreement was reached on the wording, and Drought then composed an English text for that particular point before they went on to the next one.

The term Draft Understanding, which derives from Japanese references to the "Ryōkai-an," "Nichi-Bei Ryōkai-an," or "Nichi-Bei Ryōkoku Ryōkai-an," is the most convenient designation for the untitled proposal (State 711.94/2066-6/9; *FRJ*, II: 398–402) that reached Hull on Apr. 9 and Konoye on Apr. 18. Most Japanese accounts, however, refer to this document as the "Draft Understanding" *of Apr. 16* because that is the date on which Hull and Nomura agreed that the proposal might serve as a basis for further conversations in certain circumstances. The text (as found in the archives of the State Dept.) is printed in the Appendixes, pp. 334–38 (Appendix B). Some minor typographical refinements have been added for ease of reading. A Japanese translation can be found in Gaimushō, *Shuyō Bunsho*, II: 492–95; *TSM, Bekkan*, 390–92; and Gaimushō *NBKK*, 10–16; and in many primary and secondary accounts. These Japanese versions of the document must be used with caution, however, for they do not accurately reflect what was handed to Hull on Apr. 9. In this connection, see the Note for pp. 336–37 (Deletions made in the text of the "Draft Understanding" *before* Nomura cabled it to Tokyo).

The following sources are also applicable: Iwakuro, "Amerika ni okeru Nichi-Bei Kōshō no Keika," 297–98, 303–4, and *passim*; Iwakuro ms., 85–130; JMD papers, misc. handwritten and typewritten items, incl. a great deal of material showing the evolution of the Apr. 9 proposal from a 1st draft, labeled "Secret Document," through the final version, which was a revision of a draft marked "Confidential Memorandum to the Honorable Secretary of State, Cordell Hull" (the final draft bears a notation in Drought's hand to the effect that this "revised form" was submitted to Hull and Nomura and that "no substantial changes" were made); Wikawa, 20–21; Yabe, II: 247, 251–53; *TSM*, VII (Tsunoda): 135, 149–53 (in referring, on p. 150, to the Apr. 9 proposal as the "Iwakuro draft," Tsunoda acknowledges the very large role played by the Colonel in the formulation of the "Draft Understanding," but the two telegrams quoted by Tsunoda on pp. 150–51 date from the autumn of 1941 rather than from the spring; see text p. 280 and the pertinent note: Walsh to Drought, Oct. 6, and Drought's reply, Oct. 10); State 711.94/2066-5/9 (the incomplete, 1st draft proposal of Apr. 5) and 711.94/2066-6/9 (the "second draft" given to Hull on Apr. 9; see *FRJ*, II: 398–402); *FR 1941*, IV: 173–74 (Hornbeck's reference to "an earlier draft" is to the "Preliminary Draft of 'Agreement in Principle' ").

Japanese accounts of the evolution of the "Draft Understanding" must be used with caution. They generally claim that the "U.S. side" actively participated in the drafting process, that the final version was not completed until Apr. 16, and that the document Nomura cabled to Tokyo was a proposal from the U.S. Govt. All of this is quite incorrect.

154 The military and naval attachés and an Embassy treaty expert: Maj. Gen. Saburō Isoda, Capt. Ichirō Yokoyama, and 2d Secy. Kōtō Matsudaira.

155 Hull and his Far Eastern advisers were men of more than ordinary prudence: Thumbnail sketches of Hull and his "Japanese" negotiating team (Hornbeck, Hamilton, Ballantine, and Max W. Schmidt) can be found in Feis, 172–74. "With these four men to help him," Feis wrote, "the Secretary of State could have worn out even the voluble Matsuoka, had he been there." Also Acheson, 9–12, 19–20, 741–42; Davies, 210–12; and the essay by James C. Thomson, Jr. in *Pearl Harbor as History*, 81–106.

155 Hornbeck "[did] not for one moment believe": See *FR 1941*, IV: 120.

155–56 Hornbeck's analysis of the John Doe material he had read thus far: *Ibid.*, 123–26. The John Doe document in question (State 711.94/2066-5/9) was in reality a portion of the "first draft" of the proposal that became the "Draft Understanding" of Apr. 9.

156 Hornbeck's desire to test Japan's good faith: *FR 1941*, IV: 125, 130–31. Washington was in turn to give its word that American armed forces would not launch any "offensive move" against Japan. SKH also added the following stipulation: "The two Governments to promise, reciprocally, that neither country will make an armed attack upon the other or upon possessions or

interests of the other without due notice in the form of a declaration of war by the highest authorities given at least 24 hours in advance of the striking of the first blow." *Ibid.*, 131.

A Mission Is Placed in Jeopardy

159–61 A week of extraordinary activity, Apr. 9–16: The eight memos and three counterdrafts mentioned in the text can be found in *FR 1941*, IV: 135–39, 142–50, 152–61.

159 Hull and his staff felt keenly disappointed: I have drawn on Hull, II: 991–94; on the many State Dept. memos of comment prepared between Apr. 9 and Apr. 16; and on Ballantine, "Reminiscences," 35–37.

159 The assurances that had been given earlier: Drought had claimed, in one memo after another, that Japan was willing to divorce herself from the Axis alliance. See, for example, *FR 1941*, IV: 15, 54, 61, 63, 70, 72, 95, 96. He seemed to be hedging somewhat in the "Preliminary Draft" of mid-March, and by Apr. 9 he was heading in an entirely different direction. Compare *ibid.*, 100–101, with *FRJ*, II: 399–400.

159–60 The "Draft Understanding" and China: *FRJ*, II: 400. For some pertinent earlier statements by Drought, see *FR 1941*, IV: 15–16, 54, 61, 72–73, 95, 101–2, 119.

159 "Joint defense against communistic activities": These were "words of ominous connotation" from the Dept.'s point of view. See *FR 1941*, IV: 135.

160 The time had come to raise "certain fundamental questions": *Ibid.*, 136–39.

160 "Negotiations of any sort": *Ibid.*, 142–43.

160 Hornbeck's Apr. 11 counterdraft of the John Doe "Draft Understanding": *Ibid.*, 142–46. A note in brackets reads: "This is based on and follows the set-up, as to form, of the draft submitted by *D*." SKH revised his draft on Apr. 14; further changes were introduced by Hamilton and Ballantine on Apr. 16 (*ibid.*, 148–50, 154–61). All of these counterdrafts began with Section I of the John Doe proposal of Apr. 9, thus passing over the untitled "Preamble," which bears the unmistakable imprint of Drought's style. On Apr. 16 Hamilton and Ballantine wrote: "With regard to the introductory statement in the Japanese draft, there is perceived no need for including such statement and it is doubted whether the Japanese contemplate that such statement be included. If, however, the Japanese should desire some such statement, it is believed that the substance of the Japanese statement could be readily rephrased so as to be mutually satisfactory." *Ibid.*, 155.

160 Hornbeck's belief that a firm attitude was needed: *Ibid.*, 142–43, 147–48.

160 Hamilton's attitude: See *ibid.*, 135–39, 146–47.

160–61 "The state of our relations with Japan": Hull, II: 994. Hull wanted to reach a settlement if at all possible. He was not planning to use the conversations with Nomura to buy time for America to arm herself against Japan. Hull's primary purpose, from beginning to end, was to keep war out of the Pacific; the sooner an agreement could be signed with Tokyo that would accomplish this purpose, the better it would be for the U.S.; if such an agreement could not be negotiated, war would probably result; until this issue was decided, American defense preparations had to be pushed with all possible speed; thus, even in the worst eventuality, the effort spent in seeking an agreement with Japan would serve the secondary purpose of giving the U.S. a last chance to do what should have been done much earlier in the domain of national security.

161 Secret Anglo-American staff conferences: See Langer and Gleason, 285–89, 307–11, 470.

161–64 The Hull-Nomura conversations, Apr. 14 and 16: The two men met at Hull's apartment because Nomura wanted to avoid being questioned by the press. This might not have been possible if he had gone to the State Dept. *FRJ*, II: 331–32, 402–10 (supplemented by State 711.94/2112); *FR 1941*, IV: 135–39, 146–47, 152–54; Hull, II: 994–96; Nomura, 47–51; Kiba, 455–58; Butow, "Hull-Nomura Conversations," 826–29; and Nomura, "Chū-Bei Ninmu Hōkoku," Sect. 5.

161 "Certain of the Ambassador's compatriots": *FRJ*, II: 403.

161 "A first step in negotiations": Hull's memo of the conversation shows that he immediately qualified this as follows: "I again cited those phases previously referred to, which called for preliminary conversation on certain subjects before a stage of negotiations could be reached, and which discouraged the immediate presentation of the document by the Ambassador in an official way." *FRJ*, II: 403. Two days later Hull reminded Nomura that they had "in no sense reached the stage of negotiations." *Ibid.*, 407, 410.

162–63 Hull's statements to Nomura on Apr. 16: *Ibid.*, 406–7.

162 Hull's Four Principles: *Ibid.*, 407. The wording Hull employed represented a refinement of phraseology suggested to him in an unsigned memo dated Apr. 15–16. *FR 1941*, IV: 153–54 (see also 136–39, 147).

162 "You can answer [these] questions or submit them to your Government": Most of the memos of conversations between Hull and Nomura are paraphrases of what was said, but in this instance Hull's wording is quoted directly in the original—an indication that he attached special importance to this statement. *FRJ*, II: 407. In response to a question I asked in this regard, Ballantine wrote that he was "inclined to believe that the statement in direct quotes . . . was prepared in advance and read [verbatim] to Nomura without giving him a copy."

162 "You tell me that you have not [yet] submitted the [April 9] document . . . to your Government": Langer and Gleason, 470, state that Hull "made a rather serious mistake in requesting Nomura to send the informal program to Tokyo with the inquiry whether the Imperial Government would accept it as a basis for negotiation." The record shows that Hull was very careful in choosing his words, and that he did not in fact make any such request (Japanese claims to the contrary notwithstanding).

In talking with Nomura on Apr. 14 and 16, Hull unequivocally indicated that the next move was up to Japan. Nomura could send the "Draft Understanding" of Apr. 9 to Tokyo or not, as he saw fit. The authorities there could order him to submit this document to Hull or not, as they saw fit. The Secretary of State was not offering proposals to anyone at this stage, nor was he making any commitments. If the Japanese Govt. was willing to subscribe to his Four Principles, and if Tokyo, as a consequence, instructed Nomura to present the "Draft Understanding" officially to Hull, then further conversations could be held in the hope that an earnest discussion of the issues would produce an acceptable basis for negotiations.

163 Nomura studied the text of the Four Principles: Hull had handed this formula to him on a plain sheet of paper devoid of any legend, letterhead, or insignia, in order to emphasize the informal and exploratory nature of the proceedings. *FRJ*, II: 407; Ballantine corresp.

163 The "Declaration of American Principles," Lima, Dec. 24, 1938: U.S. Dept. of State, *Peace and War*, 440–41. Hull, I: 535–38, contains a brief summary of the background and development of his views on foreign policy and international relations. Especially pertinent here is the statement he issued as a press release on July 16, 1937. *FRJ*, I: 325–26.

163 Hull's status quo principle and the situation in Manchuria: *FRJ*, II: 409. When I asked SKH about this matter, he replied: "You will note that what Mr. Hull said about 'non-recognition' came not on his initiative but after Nomura had mentioned 'the Manchurian situation.' I doubt whether Mr. Hull had envisioned what might be the position which the American government would take if and when at some future date the Manchurian situation should become a subject for negotiation." Hornbeck corresp.

163–64 Nomura's attempt to obtain Hull's approval of the Apr. 9 proposals and Hull's refusal to oblige: *FRJ*, II: 409–10.

164 Nomura made it plain (or so Hull thought): Hull never imagined that Nomura might fail to perform in accordance with the only logical expectation in the circumstances. Hence, this postwar comment: "Nomura duly sent to Tokyo the document of April 9, along with my four points and other observations, and we sat down to await the Japanese reply." Hull, II: 996.

165 Nomura let himself be persuaded: Iwakuro ms., 128–32; Iwakuro intv. The Colonel appears to have encouraged Nomura to report as he did by arguing that only thus would it be possible to "unify" opinion at home (an essential step toward achieving success in their endeavor).

165 Nomura to the Foreign Office (in regard to the "Draft Understanding"): Butow, "Hull-Nomura Conversations," 829–36; Gaimushō, *NBKK*, 9–16, 24–27; Konoye papers, Tels. 235, 237, Apr. 17; Nomura, 47–51; Iwakuro ms., 128–32; Iwakuro intv.

165 Nomura's passing reference on May 8 to the Four Principles: Gaimushō, *NBKK*, 41–44. It was early Sept. before the Japanese Govt. learned how critically important the Four Principles were in the thinking of Roosevelt and Hull. See *ibid.*, 236–42 (Tel. 777, Sept. 3; received in Tokyo the following afternoon).

165–66 Iwakuro to the military authorities in Tokyo, Apr. 18: The Colonel's telegram, which was sent through the military attaché, was addressed to the War Minister, the chief of the Military Affairs Bureau of the War Ministry, and the chief of the Operations Bureau of the Army General Staff. *TSM*, VII (Tsunoda): 154–55, 467 (n2 of section 5), and *Bekkan*, 392–94. See also Tanemura, 53–54.

166 The "first draft" (according to Iwakuro) had been written by the "U.S. side" (*Beikoku-gawa*), which had accepted most of the demands lodged on behalf of Japan: These statements, which bear no relationship to reality, were inserted in the telegram because Iwakuro wanted to convey the impression that the "Draft Understanding" was an American proposal being offered to Japan by Hull. Iwakuro intv.; Iwakuro ms., 128–32; *TSM*, VII (Tsunoda): 467 (n2 of section 5). Iwakuro's further statement that the "U.S. side" had "in

general no objections" and his assertion that Presidential approval had already been given were also entirely incorrect.

166 A section-by-section explanation: Gaimushō, *NBKK*, 24–27. In this connection, see the Note for pp. 336–37 (Deletions made in the text of the "Draft Understanding" *before* Nomura cabled it to Tokyo).

167 Konoye and his colleagues decided to study the matter further: The Foreign Office began receiving the pertinent telegrams from Nomura (Nos. 233, 234) on the afternoon of Apr. 17, but it was the morning of the 18th before everything was in hand. At 11:00 A.M. Vice Minister Ōhashi interrupted a Cabinet meeting in order to convey the news privately to Konoye. The Premier, who was concurrently acting as Foreign Minister during Matsuoka's absence in Europe, was given the decoded Japanese text of the "Draft Understanding" in the late afternoon. At 8:00 P.M. the matter was placed before a Liaison Roundtable Conference. Of all the men present, perhaps only Konoye had some idea of what had transpired in the U.S., and yet his conception of what had occurred there was quite erroneous because it was based on the reports Wikawa had been sending through Nishiyama in New York. Although Konoye offered some background information orally that evening, his remarks scarcely clarified anything (in fact, they may actually have reinforced some optimistic illusions). Since Konoye and his colleagues did not realize the truth in regard to the John Doe affair, they were at a disadvantage in dealing with the "Draft Understanding." See Butow, "Hull-Nomura Conversations," 832–33; Konoye, 62–65; Yabe, II: 255–60; *TSM*, VII (Tsunoda): 165–73, and *Bekkan*, 389–90; Ike, 17–19; Tanemura, 53–55; Kiba, 474–75; Tomita, 135, 139–40; Ōhashi, 111–12; Saitō, 176–77; Wikawa, 22; Iwakuro ms., 137–39; and *PHA*, XX: 3985–86. On the role of Liaison Conferences in the decision-making process, see Butow, *Tojo*, 149–50. The nature of Wikawa's reporting is revealed in two telegrams dispatched through Nishiyama on Mar. 11. See LC-JFOA, WT 73, IMT 557, 33–38; and *Gendai-shi Shiryō* (*13*), xix, 663–64. Of historical interest here, but clearly not applicable to the events of Apr. 18, is a letter Wikawa wrote to Konoye on Apr. 16; it presumably did not reach Tokyo until sometime in May. Konoye papers; Yabe, II: 253–54; *TSM*, VII (Tsunoda): 152, and *Bekkan*, 408.

167 Clarification would be sought from Nomura: Konoye followed through on this the next day. See Gaimushō, *NBKK*, 27–28.

167 The Admiral stood squarely behind the "Draft Understanding": See *ibid.*, 29–31.

167 The Soviet-Japanese Neutrality Pact, Apr. 13, 1941: For English versions of the text, see Degras, III: 486–87; and *FR 1941*, IV: 944–45. The Japanese text is printed in Gaimushō, *Shuyō Bunsho*, II: 491–92.

Into a Quagmire of Confusion

171 The reaction in Japan to Matsuoka's return from Europe: Konoye, 65–67; *TSM*, VII (Tsunoda): 176; Wikawa, 22; Iwakuro ms., 139–45; Craigie, 116; *JTA*, Apr. 22, morn. ed.: 3, 4 (edit.), Apr. 23, morn. ed.: 1, 2, even. ed.: 1, 2; *Nippon*, No. 26 (1941): 58; Grew papers, "Diary," Apr. 1941: 5053–57.

171 Matsuoka to the foreign press: *JTA*, Apr. 23, even. ed.: 1.

171–82 Matsuoka's attitude toward, and handling of, the "Draft Understanding" (ca. Apr. 20–May 12): Kase, 44–46; Konoye, 65–77; Tomita, 140–45; Yabe, II: 260–65; *FR 1941*, IV: 921–23, 932–37; Gaimushō kiroku, "Nichi-Bei Gaikō Kankei Zassan," Hizuke-jun, I, Tatekawa's 422, Apr. 9, and "Tai-Bei Chūkan Kaitō-an Yōshi"; LC-JFOA, WT 22, IMT 98, 33–37; *TSM*, VII (Tsunoda): 128–29, 173–90, and *Bekkan*, 409–12, 414–15, 416–17; Ike, 19–34; "Matsuoka Oboegaki"; Tanemura, 55–56; Butow, "Hull-Nomura Conversations," 833; *DGFP*, D.XII: 711–15, 723–25, 743, 745–46, 749–50, 751–55, 777–80, 794, 806–10, 818–22, 847–48; Gaimushō, *NBKK*, 31–39, 45–57, 157–59; Tsunoda and Ushiba corresp. The Ott-Matsuoka conversations and the discussions that took place at the Liaison Roundtable Conferences held on Apr. 22, May 3, May 8, and May 12 are especially pertinent to an understanding of what occurred during this period.

172 Several trial balloons: In particular, Matsuoka's feelers to Roy Howard in the U.S. and to Laurence A. Steinhardt, the American Ambassador in Moscow.

173 Matsuoka's remark to Konoye, Apr. 23: "Shibaraku Yōroppa no koto wo wasurete kara handan sasete moraitai." Konoye, 67.

173–79 The mood and activities of Nomura and the John Doe Associates, while they waited for Tokyo's reaction to the "Draft Understanding": Wikawa, 21–24; Iwakuro intv. and ms., 132–37, 145–72; JMD papers; *TSM*, VII (Tsunoda): 146, 170; Nomura, 52; and as noted separately hereunder.

173 A cable from the Navy (to the naval attaché, Capt. Ichirō Yokoyama): Wikawa, 22, states that a telegram from Vice-Minister Ōhashi indicated that the Japanese Govt. had "no objections" to the "Draft Understanding," and that an answer would be forthcoming after Matsuoka's return, but this does not accord with the generally accepted version of what happened at the time, and no such telegram has been found. It seems, rather, that Tarō Terasaki, the chief of the American Bureau, after conferring with representatives of the Army and the Navy (Muto and Oka), proposed sending an "agreement in principle" cable to Nomura with instructions to pass this information along to the American Govt. but that Ōhashi argued against doing anything of the kind prior to Matsuoka's return. Konoye could have overridden Ōhashi, but the Prince did not do so. Thus Nomura was left in the dark by the Foreign Office, although both Yokoyama and Iwakuro received reassuring telegrams from their respective services. See Konoye, 65; Tomita, 140; *TSM*, VII (Tsunoda): 173.

173 Iwakuro's telegram of welcome: State 711.94/2244-1/11; Iwakuro intv. The translation in the text is from an enclosure to a special report received by the State Dept. several months later from a "very reliable" source.

173 Matsuoka warned Nomura: Gaimushō kiroku, "Nichi-Bei Gaiko Kankei Zassan," Hizuke-jun, I: Matsuoka's 176, Apr. 23.

173 An attack of chronic bronchitis: Some of Matsuoka's colleagues thought, at the time, that he was feigning illness in order to postpone having to deal with the "Draft Understanding," but Grew, who saw him on May 14, noted that he was still coughing badly. Grew papers, "Diary," May 1941: 5113.

173–74 Nomura to Tokyo, Apr. 28: *TSM*, VII (Tsunoda): 162.

174 Matsuoka's reply to Iwakuro: The Foreign Minister wanted him to tell Nomura not to bear down too hard in Washington; he was to take it easy—

not overdo it. The wording in Japanese has sexual connotations: "Nomura ni amari koshi wo tsukawanu yō chūi shite oke." Iwakuro ms., 148.

174–76 Drought's mood and activities during the latter part of April: I have drawn on a great deal of handwritten material in the JMD papers. Most of the items are undated and are very difficult to read, but when separate comments pertaining to the same subject are brought together, as in the text, they reveal rather clearly what Drought was thinking and planning at the time. Also FW papers, TA Log.

174–75 In roughing out a letter: JMD may have thought better of the idea, for nothing corresponding to this item has turned up in the FW papers.

175 Drought had "literally imposed the whole thing on [the Japanese] government": He had, indeed, but neither Washington nor Tokyo was aware of this.

176 "Matsuoka wants the credit": JMD and FW papers. Although this memo is undated, internal evidence suggests that it was written on or about Apr. 29. Walker may have passed it along to Hull, but I have been unable to find a copy in the archives of the State Dept.

176 JMD's May 1 memo: *FR 1941*, IV: 172–73; JMD papers.

176–77 Nomura on Matsuoka: *FR 1941*, IV: 172. The comment was made to Adm. William V. Pratt on Apr. 28.

177 Nomura to Hull, May 2: *FRJ*, II: 411; Hull, II: 997; Nomura, 51–52.

178 Matsuoka sent instructions, May 3: Gaimushō, *NBKK*, 31–37.

178 The chief of the European and Asiatic Bureau to the German and Italian Ambassadors, May 4: *TSM*, VII (Tsunoda): 185–86; Gaimushō, *NBKK*, 37–39; *DGFP*, D.XII: 711–12.

178 Ott immediately cabled a report to Berlin: See *DGFP*, D.XII: 711–15; p. 712 n1 incorrectly attempts to link the "four principal proposals" mentioned by Ott with the "four points" (i.e., the Four Principles) Hull handed to Nomura on Apr. 16, but they are in no way related to each other.

178 Matsuoka's plans, as divulged to Ott by the Foreign Minister: Esp. pertinent here is the conv. they had on May 9 (*DGFP*, D.XII: 749), but see also *ibid.*, 723–25, 753–54, and D.XIII: 84–86.

178 Ott tried to obtain the text of the mid-April "agreement": See *ibid.*, 745–46, 753–54.

178 "In consequence of the promise of secrecy": As a result of the reports sent by Nomura, Iwakuro, and Wikawa, the authorities in Tokyo believed that only two or three Cabinet members close to the President knew about the "Draft Understanding," and that the maintenance of secrecy was so essential that even Ambassador Grew should not be told anything in this regard. Konoye papers, Nomura's 235, Apr. 17; *TSM, Bekkan*, 394 (the concluding portion of Iwakuro's cable); *Gendai-shi Shiryō (13)*, 663 (Special No. 8 from Wikawa through Nishiyama). See also Gaimushō, *NBKK*, 38, 45–46; *TSM, Bekkan*, 414; and Ike, 29.

Although the Japanese Government had its own reasons for not wanting to divulge too much, the emphasis on secrecy—in this instance—had originated with Drought and his Associates (they were afraid that obstacles would be placed in their way if too many persons learned what was taking place). Despite the assertions made in the Japanese sources cited, Grew was fully informed by the State Dept. of developments in regard to the "Draft Under-standing." See *FR 1941*, IV: 163, 173–74.

178–79 Drought was reporting to Hull: JMD papers, a May 6 memo; *FR 1941*, IV: 179–80.

179–81 The Hull-Nomura conv., May 7: *FRJ*, II: 411–15; Hull, II: 997–99; Nomura, 52–53; Gaimushō, *NBKK*, 39–40 (Nomura's 273 of May 7); *TSM, Bekkan*, 414 (Matsuoka's May 8 report to his Liaison Conference colleagues concerning a telephone conversation he had had with Nomura in regard to the "Oral Statement" and Neutrality Pact proposal of May 3); and as noted separately hereunder.

Matsuoka was misled by Cable 273 (and the subsequent telephone conver-sation) into believing that Nomura had at least adhered to the spirit if not the letter of his instructions. Hull's memo of the conversation shows that this was not the case. A cryptic reference in Cable 273 to the way in which Nomura learned the intentions of American leaders at this time suggests that he was relying on information supplied by the John Doe Associates.

179 Matsuoka did not want a nonaggression clause to be included in his Neu-trality Pact proposal: See Gaimushō, *NBKK*, 32; and *TSM, Bekkan*, 411.

179–80 "Something in the way of a manuscript" (i.e., the "Oral Statement" Matsuoka had mentioned to his colleagues on May 3): The text that was cabled to Nomura for transmission to Hull is the same, except for a few minor differences, as the one sent by Ott to Berlin. An effort, on my part, to obtain a copy of the "Magic" intercept read by Hull proved unsuccessful. See Gaimushō, *NBKK*, 31–37, 39–40; LC-JFOA, WT 73, IMT 556, 819–21; and *DGFP*, D.XII: 713–14.

On May 5 Ott informed Berlin that Matsuoka's "Oral Statement" had been presented to Hull by Nomura. This was a logical assumption—similar in nature to Hull's belief that Nomura had promptly sent the text of the Four Principles to Tokyo in mid-April. Like Hull, Ott simply overlooked the possibility that the Japanese Ambassador might fail to do what he was sup-posed to do. In the earlier instance, Nomura may have used his "discretion" in deciding not to mention the Four Principles until a later date; in this in-stance, however, he was clearly disobeying his instructions.

179–80 "Magic": See Hull, II: 998; Butow, *Tojo*, as indexed; Wohlstetter, esp. Ch. 3; and Kahn, Ch. 1. Over a period of time, the "Magic" intercepts tended to show that Tokyo was going ahead with its plans for conquest in Southeast Asia even while talking to the American Govt. about the maintenance of peace in the Pacific. Hull consequently looked upon these purloined messages as he "would upon a witness who was testifying against his own side of a case."

Needless to say, every effort was made to preserve the secrecy of the "Magic" operation, but Hans Thomsen, the German chargé d'affaires in Washington, sent the following telegram to Berlin on Apr. 28 (the message was received there on the 29th): "As communicated to me *by an absolutely reliable source*, the State Department is in possession of the key to the Japanese coding sys-tem and is therefore also able to decipher information telegrams from Tokyo to Ambassador Nomura here regarding Ambassador Oshima's reports from Berlin." *DGFP*, D.XII: 661 (italics mine).

In response to an inquiry I made in 1966, the German Foreign Office replied that copies of the clear text of Thomsen's telegram were circulated to Foreign Minister Ribbentrop; State Secretary Weizsäcker; the chief of the Political Department; the Office of the Reich Foreign Minister; and "Pers. Z." (Ciphers and Communications). Of these five copies, only the one sent to Weizsäcker remains extant.

On May 3, four days after the receipt of Thomsen's warning, Heinrich Stahmer told Ōshima that it was "fairly reliably established," on the basis of information received from Germany's Intelligence organization in the U.S., that the American Govt. was reading Nomura's "code messages," and that "drastic steps" should therefore be taken regarding this matter. Ōshima's cable reporting this to Matsuoka was intercepted, decoded, and translated by "Magic," which also picked up a May 5 telegram from Japan's Foreign Minister advising the Embassy in Washington that it appeared "almost certain," according to "a fairly reliable source," that the U.S. Govt. was reading "code messages" from the Embassy. Nomura's immediate reply to the effect that "the most stringent precautions" were being taken "by all custodians of codes and ciphers" also passed through "Magic." Nomura asked that he be informed of "any concrete instances or details" that might turn up. Since these and other related messages dealing with the tightening of Japanese security were all transmitted in a cipher called "Purple" (to which "Magic" gave top priority), Matsuoka, Nomura, and others who were involved at this time obviously felt confident that "Purple" was unbreakable. If they had entertained any doubts, changes would have been made immediately. The Foreign Office and its embassies abroad, however, continued to use this cipher, and "Magic" kept right on reading it throughout the remainder of 1941. See Wohlstetter, 178–79; and *PHA*, IV: 1859–63, and V: 2069–70.

181–82 The Hull-Nomura convs., May 11 and 12: *FRJ*, II: 415–19; Hull, II: 999; Nomura, 53–55.

182 The "wrong" set of documents: *FRJ*, II: 415, 418–19; State 711.94/2086.

182 The "right" documents (i.e., the "Confidential Memorandum" of May 12 and the "Oral Explanation"): See *FRJ*, II: 420–25 (note also the "Explanation" on p. 426 and the "Errata" on pp. 439–40). The "Oral Explanation" was later marked "Annex and Supplement." *Ibid.*, 436, 438. Also Gaimushō, *NBKK*, 47–58; Nomura, Furoku No. 2, 11–20; LC-JFOA, WT 38, IMT 265, 180–81; *TSM, Bekkan*, 416–17.

The text of the "Confidential Memorandum" of May 12 had been cabled to Nomura in advance; he had been told that he would be advised, in a separate telegram, when to hand over the proposal and begin negotiations. This instruction was not dispatched from Tokyo until shortly after twelve noon on Monday, May 12 (the evening of May 11 in Washington). *TSM, Bekkan*, 416; Ike, 32.

182 A summary of the terms: Ott had informed Berlin that "the proposal of the Washington Government for the conclusion of a secret agreement between the United States and Japan" contained "four principal proposals": (1) the U.S. and Japan would exchange pledges not to enter the European war on their own initiative; they would restrict their policies exclusively to defense; (2) the U.S. would influence Chiang Kai-shek to come to a direct understanding with Japan; (3) normal trade relations would be restored between the U.S. and Japan; they would cooperate with each other in the ex-

ploitation of raw materials in the South Pacific; (4) the U.S. would recognize Manchukuo and, together with Japan, would guarantee the status quo in the Philippines. See the Note for p. 178 (Ott immediately cabled a report to Berlin).

Since the Japanese Foreign Office had been misled by Nomura into thinking that the proposed agreement was from the authorities in Washington, Ott had no way of knowing that he was actually summarizing the John Doe "Draft Understanding" of Apr. 9—a proposition that was completely unrepresentative of the views of the American Govt. Ott's report, in turn, inadvertently misled Dieckhoff and others in Berlin.

Later in the month (on May 23 and 24), the British ambassador in Washington, Lord Halifax, informed the American Govt. that London was in possession of information in regard to what appeared to be a peace maneuver toward Japan initiated by the U.S. (in actuality, the John Doe "Draft Understanding" that Ott had ascribed to the "Washington Government" in reporting the matter to Berlin). Hull rejected the representations made to him at this time by the British Govt. In doing so, he offered "some rather vigorous comment" to Lord Halifax regarding an *aide-mémoire* in this connection that Hull considered "wholly inaccurate and unsound in its chief meaning and implications." The British Foreign Secretary (Hull later wrote) "had all of his facts wrong." See *FR 1941*, IV: 210–12, 234.

Thus, by May 1941, the activities of the John Doe Associates had already created a situation in which the Japanese, German, and British Govts. had an entirely erroneous conception of what had transpired thus far (they all believed that Washington had offered an "agreement" to Tokyo). In addition, the American Govt., which thought it had the facts straight, was itself completely in the dark, for it did not know that Nomura had treated the "Draft Understanding" in his telegrams to Tokyo as though that document were a proposal from the authorities in Washington (when, in fact, it was not).

182–83 Dieckhoff's assessment and Weizsäcker's endorsement: *DGFP*, D.XII: 751–53 (a May 10 memo that was shown to Ribbentrop).

182 "It is not conceivable": Ott had already informed Berlin that he was going to tell Matsuoka that "the offer to recognize Manchukuo" was "a worthless gesture." *Ibid.*, 715. As noted previously, all of the parties concerned were unknowingly dealing here with a John Doe proposal that actually contemplated "recognition of Manchukuo" by the "Chiang-Kai-Chek regime." *FRJ*, II: 400. Since the John Doe Associates also contemplated obtaining Presidential approval of the various peace terms they had outlined on China, a willingness by FDR to cooperate in this regard would presumably have meant an eventual recognition of Manchukuo by the U.S. as well. Drought had certainly been thinking along these lines in March. See *FR 1941*, IV: 102.

Hornbeck's draft of April 11 contains nothing at all on the "recognition of Manchukuo." In his redraft of Apr. 14, SKH wrote: "The question of the future of Manchuria to be dealt with by negotiations, without duress, to which China, Japan and 'Manchukuo' shall be parties." *Ibid.*, 149. On Apr. 16, Hamilton and Ballantine revised Hornbeck's wording slightly. *Ibid.*, 156, 159. All of these drafts were for State Dept. use only.   *(continued)*

Hull's comment to Nomura on Apr. 16 has already been noted (see text p. 163). On May 15 Hornbeck sent a memo to Hull containing some "brief observations" on the "Manchukuo" issue. After referring to the long-standing American formula ("the principle of non-recognition of situations *de facto* which have been brought about by acts contrary to law and/or to express agreements"), SKH declared that it would be "unwise, inexpedient, and of doubtful morality" for the American Govt. to associate itself with any effort to undermine the principle of nonrecognition. *FR 1941*, IV: 193–94.

The U.S. Govt. subsequently limited itself to an occasional restatement of the view that "the question of the future of Manchuria" should "be dealt with by friendly negotiations" between Japan and China (*FRJ*, II: 433), or that "the question of the independence of Manchuria" should "be dealt with by friendly negotiations" (*FR 1941*, IV: 217), or that "amicable negotiations" should take place "in regard to Manchoukuo" (*FRJ*, II: 449, 490). See also Butow, "Backdoor Diplomacy," 71–72.

183 Matsuoka had already formed a similar estimate of the situation: *TSM*, VII (Tsunoda): 185–86; Gaimushō, *NBKK*, 38.

183 Matsuoka had wanted to postpone action: See *DGFP*, D.XII: 724, 749, 755, 777–80, 794. Also *TSM, Bekkan*, 416; Ike, 31–34.

183 Ott found the form and content "most surprising": *DGFP*, D.XII: 806–10.

183 Matsuoka-Ott conv., May 13: *Ibid.*

183 "I wish Roosevelt and Hull would trust me": *FR 1941*, IV: 922.

184 Weizsäcker to Ribbentrop, May 15: *DGFP*, D.XII: 819 (see also pp. 820–22, 847–48).

184–86 The reaction in Washington to Japan's "Confidential Memorandum" of May 12: Hull, II: 1000–1001; *FRJ*, II: 332–35, 420–25 (the pertinent documents); Feis, 199–201. Wikawa, for his part, thought that the prospects now were much better than before. "Fine weather today," he cabled Konoye. "Not a cloud in the sky. Appreciate all you have done." Konoye papers.

During a telephone conversation with Wendell Willkie on May 15, Hull made the following remark: "What seems to be happening in Japan is a close struggle between the Matsuoka extreme pro-German elements, to control foreign policy, and business people and more or less liberal statesmen, including [Premier Konoye] and the heads of the Army and the Navy, for a readjustment in the opposite direction. Now . . . I am trying to maneuver so as . . . to let them have a chance to assert themselves at Tokyo and see whether that crowd can succeed in controlling the situation. . . . Of course, I'm watching with all of the anxiety that a person can to see some daylight . . . in the Pacific. It's an awfully delicate thing."

"And if it were removed," Willkie interjected, "it would make you so much stronger—"

"Oh, my good fellow," Hull replied, "it would make a noise that could be heard on the northeast corner of the moon." Hull papers, "Japan–General," Folder 309. A typescript of the entire conversation was prepared in the Secretary's office, and was subsequently circulated to Hornbeck and "Far East" for their information. Slight adjustments have been made in the punctuation for ease of reading.

184 The Japanese Govt. maintained that the Axis alliance was "defensive" in nature: See *FRJ*, II: 421. The wording of this clause was changed slightly on May 23, when Nomura handed Hull an "Errata" sheet. *Ibid.*, 439. Both versions derived directly from a similar stipulation in the John Doe "Draft Understanding" of Apr. 9. *Ibid.*, 399.

185 Tokyo's deletion of the "Honolulu conference" proposal—an idea Drought had been advocating for months: See Butow, "Backdoor Diplomacy," 48–58. In eliminating the "Honolulu conference" idea, which had been set forth in a section of the "Draft Understanding" marked "Conference," the Japanese authorities overlooked a passing reference to the proposal that Drought had written into the "Preamble" section. *FRJ*, II: 398–99. The "Confidential Memorandum" of May 12 therefore retained JMD's wording: "It is our belief that such an understanding should comprise only the pivotal issues of urgency and not the accessory concerns which could be deliberated at a conference and appropriately confirmed by our respective Governments." *Ibid.*, 420. In its counterdraft of May 31 the State Dept. virtually repeated this phraseology through the word "conference" but eliminated the remainder of the sentence. *Ibid.*, 446. On June 4, however, Wakasugi informed Hamilton and Ballantine that the word "later" should be substituted for the phrase "at a conference." The Japanese were afraid that they might otherwise find themselves committed to participating in a conference. See *ibid.*, 456.

185 Representations had been made: See *ibid.*, 334.

186 "No room for further amendment": *TSM*, *Bekkan*, 416; Ike, 32. Nomura was informed of this by telephone on May 12.

186 Matsuoka's "Oral Statement" of May 13: Gaimushō, *NBKK*, 58–59; *DGFP*, D.XII: 808 n4. The texts are the same in these two sources except that the copy given by Matsuoka to Ott for transmission to Berlin begins with the word "Really." In a typewritten copy of the English text, found in the Konoye papers, the word "Really" appears at the beginning of the "Oral Statement" as a handwritten addition to the text.

186 Nomura decided not to deliver it: See Gaimushō, *NBKK*, 59–60. There is nothing in the American records for this period to indicate that Nomura ever handed over Matsuoka's "Oral Statement" of May 13. The Ambassador apparently simply buried it in his files. There is no mention of it in his final report.

186–90 The Matsuoka-Grew conv. of May 14 and their subsequent exchanges: Grew papers, "Diary," May 1941: 5096–97, 5097–98, 5099–5100, 5106–10 (quoted in Grew, *Ten Years*, 388–92), 5111–41. A great deal (though not all) of this material, which also covers a rather heated conv. between Matsuoka and the British ambassador on May 14, can be found in *FRJ*, II: 145–48, and *FR 1941*, IV: 187–88, 189–90, 194–96, 198–200, 201–6, 234–38. See also as noted separately hereunder.

Grew's initial report, covering his May 14 conv. with Matsuoka, led to a brief exchange between Hull and Nomura on the subject of the Foreign Minister's "more or less offensive . . . references" to the U.S. See *FRJ*, II: 426.

On May 19, Matsuoka gave Grew the following memo, written in pencil—in English—on five small slips of paper (Grew papers, "Diary," May 1941: 5099–5100, 5141):

I want to be exact; so I put it down in writing.

In one of the cables from Ambassador Nomura, it was stated that Mr. Hull told Nomura that I intimidated (Jap. word Kyōi which means "to intimidate") Your Excellency. So I cabled back to Nomura to tell Mr. Hull when he happens to see him again that I *neither intended* ever to intimidate or ever actually intimidated Mr. Grew, but that I merely stated, in connection with his queries and arguments, honestly & straight as is usual with me.

I want to make it clear to Your Excellency that I always think it best to lay aside as far as possible all formalities pertaining to our official positions & talk very frankly. Never have I imagined you would cable our talks to the State Dep't. or else I would have been more careful & have taken a *correct* attitude.

187 An act of American aggression (as defined by Matsuoka): This remark, which was first made on May 14, was confirmed by Matsuoka five days later. *FRJ*, II: 145–46; *FR 1941*, IV: 205. He then told Grew that Japan would have to consult her allies (concerning the applicability of Article 3 of the Tripartite Pact) if the U.S. went to war with Germany; in such a situation, Japan would have *only one out of three votes*. In this regard, see the Note for pp. 89–90 (Article 3 of the Tripartite Pact).

187 "Unless circumstances [rendered] this impossible": This was an old argument—one that Grew and Hull found particularly annoying. See Grew, *Ten Years*, 384–85; Grew papers, "Diary," Apr. 1941: 5002; and Hull, II: 1002.

188 Matsuoka's handwritten note to Grew, May 14: Grew papers, "Diary," May 1941: 5119. The version in *FRJ*, II: 148, contains editorial corrections.

188 Grew's reply, May 15: Grew papers, "Diary," May 1941: 5121; *FR 1941*, IV: 189–90. In talking with the German Ambassador on May 15, Matsuoka conveyed some idea of what had transpired on the 14th; he also let Ott see Grew's letter. *DGFP*, D.XII: 818–19.

188–89 The Minister quickly responded (Matsuoka to Grew, May 16): Grew papers, "Diary," May 1941: 5129–31; *FR 1941*, IV: 198–200. I have added some punctuation but have otherwise thought it best to allow Matsuoka's text to stand as he wrote it.

189 The Hess incident: See Douglas-Hamilton, *Motive for a Mission*. Also Churchill, 48–55; Sherwood, 293–94, 374, 390; Langer and Gleason, 528–29.

189–90 The Matsuoka-Grew meeting, May 19: See the Note for pp. 186–90 (The Matsuoka-Grew conv. of May 14 and their subsequent exchanges).

189 Matsuoka said he had not really been speaking formally: Matsuoka saw himself both as Japan's Foreign Minister and as "a world citizen"; he regarded Grew not only as the U.S. envoy in Tokyo but also as "an American friend." Matsuoka argued that it was unfair and improper to accord official standing to remarks made by him at times when he was speaking as a citizen of the world to a fellow human being rather than as a Foreign Minister to an ambassador. Grew's position was that such a distinction could not in fact be made—that all exchanges between the two of them, "however unorthodox," could only be regarded "in an official light" and placed on the record for the benefit of the American Govt. See *FR 1941*, IV: 236–37.

190 In a summary dispatch sent to Washington by pouch: No. 5641, of May 27; it did not reach the State Dept. until July 5. See *FR 1941*, IV: 234–38. A copy of the original can be found in the Grew papers, "Diary," May 1941: 5106–10 (quoted in Grew, *Ten Years*, 388–92).

190 In the privacy of his diary: See Grew papers, "Diary," May 1941: 5097–98.

190 The possibility that Matsuoka was an emotionally disturbed individual: The sources for this period contain a number of references to the state of the Foreign Minister's mental health—some of them by Matsuoka himself (as in his letter to Grew of May 16: "It may strike Your Excellency as if it were a sign of insanity.").

Ten months earlier, in July 1940, while talking with Wilfrid Fleisher, Matsuoka said that he had seen the European war coming as far back as 1934; he had consequently begun to advocate a single-party system for Japan, but his was a voice crying in the wilderness; people thought that he was crazy. *FR 1940*, IV: 967.

In an episode in Oct. 1940 involving some statements attributed to him in regard to the Tripartite Pact, Matsuoka claimed that the man who had interviewed him had "mangled" his words. "No Foreign Minister would ever say anything so challenging or sensational," he declared, "unless he was out of his mind." Grew papers, "conversation," Oct. 5, 1940: 295–96. It was in Oct., also, that Baron Kumao Harada told Prince Kinmochi Saionji that some people were questioning Matsuoka's sanity. Saionji replied that it would be better if the Foreign Minister were crazy, for then there might be some chance that he would recover his senses ("Ki de mo kuruyaa sore wa ii hō da. Kaette kondo wa shōki ni kaeru ka mo shirenai yo!"). Harada, VIII: 360.

On Dec. 7, 1940 (which, by coincidence, was two days after Walsh and Drought had their first meeting with Matsuoka), Grew sent the following report to Washington: "Informant added that the 'thinking' people in Japan are convinced that Mr. Matsuoka is rapidly losing his mind. From other sources I have been told that the Foreign Minister is on the verge of a nervous breakdown but in my personal contacts with him I have seen no indications to confirm such an allegation. The wish is probably more father to the thought." *FR 1940*, IV: 459.

Later that month, in relaying some information obtained from an influential Japanese, Grew described his source as one of many persons who were working to bring about the fall of Matsuoka. The Foreign Minister's "recent provocative utterances," Grew added, "and especially the ineptness of his speech before the America-Japan Society [on Dec. 19] as a prelude to Admiral Nomura's mission to the United States, have led to grave doubts as to the Foreign Minister's balance." *Ibid.*, 983.

In Feb. 1941, as noted earlier in the text (pp. 137–38), FDR privately expressed the belief, after reading some instructions from Matsuoka to Nomura, that the Foreign Minister's mind was "deeply disturbed."

During his visit to Germany in the spring of 1941, Matsuoka told Hitler's interpreter: "There are many people in Japan who say . . . 'Matsuoka is crazy!' " Schmidt, 229–30.

Upon seeing a copy of Matsuoka's letter to Grew of May 16, the British Ambassador in Washington, Lord Halifax, told the Under Secretary of State "that the letter bore evidences of lunacy." Sumner Welles then remarked that he had "formed that impression himself, but that this might be due to the fact that Mr. Matsuoka was understood to be drinking extremely heavily at this time and the mental state apparent in the writing of this letter might be momentary rather than permanent." *FR 1941*, IV: 200 (see also p. 175 for a May 2 report from Grew stating that Matsuoka, on the evening of his return from Europe, had called on the Premier "in an intoxicated condition" and had proceeded to reveal that during the negotiations in Moscow for a Neutrality Pact he had, on his own responsibility, given the Soviet Govt. an undertaking that had not been authorized by the Konoye Cabinet).

At a Liaison Roundtable Conference held on May 22, Matsuoka presented views that prompted the Navy Minister to remark: "The Foreign Minister is crazy, isn't he?" ("Gaishō wa atama ga hen de wa nai ka?"). *TSM, Bekkan*, 418; Ike, 39; Butow, *Tojo*, 208. See also Tanemura, 58, for a comment to the effect that Matsuoka had appeared to be saying and doing "abnormal" (or "erratic") things recently—a judgment also expressed by Col. Iwakuro. Iwakuro ms., 140. In later recalling his Apr. 29 telephone call to Matsuoka from New York, Iwakuro came to the conclusion that the Foreign Minister's attitude could perhaps be explained in terms of his "abnormal psychology." *Ibid.*, 153–54.

In a book published in 1942, Frederick Moore, who had known Matsuoka for a number of years, expressed the thought that the Foreign Minister's "grand coup" (the alliance with Hitler and Mussolini) had been "a stroke of either genius or madness," as time would tell. "In my opinion," Moore declared, "it was the latter, and I have persisted in that view." Moore, 123–24.

Writing in 1950 with reference to the period from Feb. to May 1941, Herbert Feis offered these observations: "About the direction of Matsuoka's mind at any given moment any guess seemed to be as good as another—so like a twisted rope was he"; "There is another interpretation of his conduct not to be dismissed; that his mind by then was in disorder"; "[His letter to Grew of May 16] revealed a most upset and wandering mind"; "No matter what he intended, his unbalanced antics could end only in war." Feis, 161, 186, 202, 203.

Despite the circumstantial nature of the evidence, I do not think that it is farfetched to believe that Matsuoka may have been an emotionally disturbed man. This would be the most logical explanation of his conduct in 1940 and '41 and of the policies he pursued as the Foreign Minister of Japan.

190 A fundamental misconception: See Butow, "Hull-Nomura Conversations," 822–36.

Pushing and Pulling for Peace

192 Weeks of endless talk: See Hull, II: 997–1015; Nomura, 51–81; Iwakuro ms., 172–73; Langer and Gleason, 479–82, 484–85; Feis, 199–201, 203–5; and the voluminous memoranda of conversations and the many pertinent documents printed in *FRJ*, II; and *FR 1941*, IV.

192 The meetings at Hull's apartment: Hull, II: 988; Ballantine, "Reminiscences," 29–31, 33, 37–40, 42–43, 206; Ballantine and Ōi corresp.

192 The inclusion of Iwakuro and Wikawa in a number of these discussions: Iwakuro went with Nomura to see Hull on May 16, 20, and 21, and again on June 6 and 15; Wikawa was present on all but the first of these occasions. Between May 30 and July 25, Hamilton and Ballantine had at least 13 meetings with the Japanese Ambassador or with members of his official family. Iwakuro and Wikawa were present at eight of these sessions (May 30; June 4, 9, 15, 16, 17; July 2, 25).

Nomura's decision to introduce Iwakuro and Wikawa to Hull did not surprise the Secretary of State, for he had been aware of their presence in Washington for some time. Hull thought that Iwakuro had the authority to represent the Japanese Army, that Wikawa was "close to the most influential civilian group" in Tokyo, and that both men "had been sent especially from Japan" to take part in the conversations. Despite these mistaken beliefs, Hull did not go astray. He saw in Iwakuro "all the virtues and shortcomings" of a man who had spent his life in the Imperial Japanese Army. "He was a very fine type," Hull later wrote, "honest, calmly poised, very sure of himself without being annoyingly self-confident. He could, of course, see only his Army's viewpoint, not ours or the real interest of Japan." Wikawa, on the other hand, struck the Secretary of State as being "of the 'slick politician' type whom the Japanese themselves did not seem to respect for integrity." Hull, II: 987, 1003.

192 A note written by Father Drought: JMD papers. Another reason why Iwakuro and Wikawa began appearing in the conversations is that Nomura preferred employing these two men to using his regular staff, from which he was gradually becoming alienated. Katō, 23.

192 Drought was determined to help matters along in any way he could: Although he knew that Nomura had handed the pertinent materials to Hull, JMD took the precaution of giving Walker copies of Japan's "Confidential Memorandum" and "Oral Explanation" of May 12. Along with these documents, Drought supplied a "Private Explanation" of his own that contained a number of fanciful ideas. The PMG transmitted this memo to the Secretary of State. *FR 1941*, IV: 184–86; JMD papers, handwritten drafts; FW papers.

Drought was concerned about the procedure the two governments would follow in reaching an accord based on the "Confidential Memorandum." As a result, he produced a statement worded as though it were from Nomura personally. A revised version of Drought's rather garbled original was handed by Nomura to Hull "about May 12, 1941," under the curious title "Project." JMD papers (Drought's draft is written on two sheets of paper of the type used by the Japanese Embassy in preparing telegrams for transmission to Tokyo); *FR 1941*, IV: 186.

Drought now began to increase the tempo of his activities. He had spent 16 days in Washington during the first three months of 1941, but between May 12 and July 23 he stayed in the capital for a total of 69 days. His papers reveal that during this time he always had at his disposal copies of the proposals that were being discussed by the two governments. He probably obtained these items from Nomura and Iwakuro (through Wikawa) rather than from the State Dept.

Referring to this same period (May–July 1941), Iwakuro later recalled that Drought devoted himself so wholeheartedly to working out a settlement "for the sake of both countries" that it seemed impossible to tell any longer whether he was an American or a Japanese. Iwakuro ms., 221.

193 Drought's activities, May 12–17: JMD papers, a diary-type record written in Drought's hand on pieces of Wardman Park stationery; I have supplied some punctuation for the sake of clarity; omissions are indicated in the usual manner, and all insertions are enclosed in brackets.

193 "Almost whole day with F.W.": Various items in the JMD and FW papers

(esp. the TA Log) reveal that this marked the beginning of a period during which Drought was consulting Walker constantly. From May 13 to May 31, for example, JMD visited the PMG or spoke with him by telephone on all but three days—and often several times per day.

193 "Wrote Explanations & Agreement": This entry suggests that Drought may have been asked by his Japanese friends to proofread and correct the English translations of the documents from Tokyo that Nomura was about to deliver to the Secretary of State.

Shigeyoshi Obata told me (in 1963) that documents to be handed to Hull were transmitted by the Foreign Office in Japanese. Corresponding English texts were not cabled from Tokyo but had to be prepared within the embassy (the major exception being Japan's final note of Dec. 7, which was dispatched from Tokyo in English). When the Japanese originals were found to be worded in a stiff or harsh manner, Nomura assumed responsibility for changes in translation that eliminated the grating tone.

193 "Special memo of explanation": The reference here is to the "Private Explanation" mentioned earlier. *FR 1941*, IV: 184–86. In it, Drought claimed that the "Confidential Memorandum" of May 12 was "a virtual treaty *sanctioned* by the Prime Minister, the Home and Foreign Ministers, the Chiefs of the War and Navy Departments, the Imperial Household *and the Emperor himself.*" A "revolution" had occurred in Japanese politics; the liberals had triumphed over the "militaristic forces"; Col. Iwakuro had demonstrated "his great political power." JMD may have believed all this, but none of it was true.

193 "Saw H. at 8:15—joined at 9 by Nom. & remained until 10 with F.W. also present": The following undated letter, written at two o'clock in the morning, may pertain to what happened on the evening of May 12:

Dear Mr. Postmaster General and Statesman Extraordinary:
  You really did a magnificent "job of work" to-night on both individuals. The meeting was an alarmingly critical one and your invitation to the Admiral, and your talk, dispelled what would have been only further confusion. Forgive my own simplicity, but I was proud to think that you were a Catholic!
  The thing now rests with the U.S. government. Your "hunch" has come "under the wire" and to-night, you delivered by hand to our friends that which others said could never be obtained. They were the "smart boys" and they have been proved wrong. Bp. Walsh says *God* was on our side.

Respectfully,
JMD

I found this letter (marked "A") among the FW papers. Attached to it was a May 20 letter from JMD to Hull (marked "B"). This does not necessarily mean, however, that these two letters belong together, or that they were written at the same time (Walker or one of his assistants may merely have thought so when they were sorting things out, after the war).

193 "Oral Statement & Suggestions": The reference here is to an "Oral Statement" marked "Informal and Unofficial" that Hull gave Nomura on May 16. *FRJ*, II: 428–30; a copy of this "Statement," with marginal notes written in JMD's hand, can be found among his papers. Hull also handed over some extracts from a speech he had recently delivered before the American Society of International Law and three annexes (Draft Suggestions A, B, and

C) that dealt with Sections II, III, and V of Japan's "Confidential Memorandum" of May 12. *Ibid.*, 430–34. In other words, within four days of the receipt of the Japanese proposal of May 12, the State Dept. had already rewritten certain sections of that proposal, and Hull had handed these drafts to Nomura for his consideration.

193 The "Oral Statement" drafted by Drought (for submission by Nomura to Hull): The JMD papers contain a handwritten draft in pencil on ruled sheets of yellow paper, a revised typewritten version of the same, and a further revision—also typewritten. This last document, which presumably postdates changes made at the Japanese Embassy, is full of emendations made by Drought in red pencil, to say nothing of marginal comments in ink for good measure. This necessitated typing up another clean copy, which is also among the JMD papers.

The "Oral Statement" then underwent alteration at the Japanese Embassy, and further changes were introduced by JMD as well. In the end, the State Dept. was given only a drastically whittled-down version of the original, but the document the Dept. received through Drought on May 17 nevertheless amounted to a revision of the sections of Japan's "Confidential Memorandum" of May 12 that dealt with such paramount issues as the European war, relations with China, and economic activities in the southwestern Pacific. See *FR 1941*, IV: 200–201; a copy can also be found in the FW papers.

194 Walsh to Drought, May 17 and 20: JMD papers. See also Hull papers, "Desk Diary," Folder 295-I. A round of golf with "Francis of Montana [the PMG]," Walsh advised Drought on May 17, "might not be without its effect in the minds of our friends across the sea. The major doubt in their minds was whether or not we would ever get to first base, and although there has been every indication of putting the ball across the plate, yet every little item that adds to this impression will have its value."

194 Drought to Hull, May 20: This letter, together with the envelope (which is addressed "To the Honorable Cordell Hull, Secretary of State, Wardman Park Hotel"), can be found in the FW papers. This could mean that Walker was supposed to give the letter to Hull but did not do so. Another possible explanation is that Hull read JMD's letter and then passed it along to the PMG (his neighbor at the Wardman Park) because it contained a reference to Walker. Drought believed, at this moment, that his own "little contribution" had been "mainly psychological" and that a "magnificent accomplishment" was in the offing. He was so certain the U.S. and Japan were on the verge of an agreement that he was even thinking of calling the next baby boy he baptized "Cordell," and the one after that "Frank." JMD papers, an early draft of the letter to Hull.

194 Drought felt he had made a mistake: I have drawn on some cryptic notes written in Drought's hand on a piece of Wardman Park stationery (the draft of his May 20 letter to Hull is on the reverse side of the sheet) and on another similar item in the JMD papers.

195 The attitude of the U.S. Govt., as portrayed by Drought (writing as though he were the President or the Secretary of State): JMD called at the State Dept. on May 21 and 24 to offer various recommendations and to hand over some rather curious documents in which, having already spoken for the Japanese Govt., he now proceeded to extend his services to the American

Govt. as well. Drought did this primarily in the form of several declarations, written by himself, that he felt Hull should adopt as part of an "Annex" to Japan's "Confidential Memorandum" of May 12. JMD hoped in this way to bring various conflicting opinions close enough together so that no major rewriting of the proposal received from Japan would prove necessary. See State 711.94/2133-8/18; and *FR 1941*, IV: 221–24.

195 Drought's new arguments, May 25: JMD papers.

195–96 Drought's freewheeling denunciation of the State Dept., ca. May 25: *Ibid.*, a handwritten draft and a later typewritten version. For a general sense of Drought's views at this time, I have also drawn on a JMD memo (ca. May 25) in which he reported on current developments and offered his advice to the American Govt. on how to proceed. JMD and FW papers; see also Hull to Nomura, May 28, *FRJ*, II: 440, supplemented by State 711.94/2133-15/18.

196 "We have clear indication": *FR 1941*, IV: 179. The file copy of this May 6 memo (State 711.94/5-641) contains a second sheet on which SKH quoted a number of statements made by Nomura which indirectly supported Hornbeck's argument that the true intentions of the Japanese Govt. were quite irreconcilable with the claims made by the John Doe Associates.

196–97 Hornbeck on "*these* Japanese," May 23: *FR 1941*, IV: 212–15 (see also pp. 190–94 and 224–25).

197 Grew and Dooman were in favor of adopting a policy of conciliation: There is a great deal of general evidence to support this view, but see specifically Grew, *Turbulent Era*, II: 1267–68, 1270–71, 1296–99; *FR 1941*, IV: 231–32; and Grew papers, "Diary," May 1941, 5100–5101.

197 The Cabinet Room at the White House: Some of Hull's colleagues—notably Henry L. Stimson, Henry Morgenthau, Jr., and Harold L. Ickes of the War, Treasury, and Interior Depts.—had long since come to wish that the Secretary of State would adopt sterner measures against Japan, but Hull persisted in trying to keep the door to negotiation open by refusing to recommend any form of economic pressure that might tip the balance against the "moderates" who Grew and Dooman hoped would emerge in Japan.

197 The State Dept. had still not indicated what its reaction would be: The record shows, however, that Hull and his advisers had not been idle. A few days after the delivery of the "Confidential Memorandum" of May 12, Hornbeck had composed a draft agreement that he thought might provide a basis for a settlement. See *FR 1941*, IV: 196–97. Although much briefer and simpler than either the John Doe concoction of Apr. 9 or Tokyo's rejoinder of May 12, Hornbeck's proposal was clearly an outgrowth of the earlier documents (his phrases even contained traces of JMD's prose). By May 23 an American redraft of the "Confidential Memorandum" of May 12 had been prepared for use within the State Dept. and had been discussed by Hull with the President. Serious reservations on the part of Hornbeck, however, led to further textual changes. The end-product was an American draft proposal that was handed to Nomura on May 31. See *ibid.*, 215–21; and *FRJ*, II: 446–54.

197–99 John Doe's attitude and activities, May 28–31: I have drawn on some diary-type notes in the JMD papers written in Drought's hand on yellow, ruled, legal-size paper. Part of this record is in the nature of a summary, indicating what JMD planned to say (or had already said) to FW.

A May 29 memo by the State Dept.'s legal adviser (*FR 1941*, IV: 239–41) and JMD's May 30 criticism of the views expressed in that memo (State 793.94/16641-2/4) are also pertinent here. Hull's "Desk Diary" shows a noon appointment for Drought on May 31, followed by a 1:00 P.M. meeting with Hamilton, Ballantine, and the legal adviser. Hull papers, Folder 295-I. While at the State Dept., Drought handed over a memo in which he outlined what he thought the American Govt. should say to the Japanese Govt. about the issues under consideration. State 793.94/16641-3/4.

199 "Meeting arranged, at my apartment, for Iwakuro, Wikawa, Hamilton, Ballantine": *FRJ*, II: 444–45, contains a memo of a conversation on May 30 in which these men participated.

199–200 The "papers" that went over to the Japanese Embassy, May 31: *Ibid.*, 446–54; Hull, II: 1007. On the use of the term "Joint Declaration," see *FRJ*, II: 446, 455; and *FR 1941*, IV: 155.

200 Drought's analysis of the situation: JMD papers.

200 Walsh to Drought, June 2: *Ibid.*

200 "Asked for interview": *Ibid.*

200–201 Drought to Walsh, June 3: *Ibid.*

200–201 "I have been constantly watched—all my phone calls have been checked": The JMD papers contain the following note written in Drought's hand on a piece of Wardman Park stationery (probably during the latter part of April): "F.W.: any chance that my phone is being tapped?" Iwakuro and Wikawa were aware that Drought thought he was under surveillance. Iwakuro ms., 221–22.

201 Nomura to Hull (regarding the American draft proposal of May 31): *FRJ*, II: 337–38, 454–55; Hull, II: 1007; Nomura, 60, and "Diary," June 3.

201–2 Wikawa's activities on June 4 and his letter to Drought: JMD papers. Walker, who was in New York on June 4, also tried to reach Drought (in Washington) but was told that he had departed the preceding evening. FW papers, TA Log.

202 The June 4 meeting at the Wardman Park Hotel: *FRJ*, II: 455–64 (supplemented by State 711.94/2162-1/14); Hull, II: 1008; Iwakuro ms., 207–16.

202–3 Drought to Walker, June 4: JMD and FW papers.

203 *A new draft* "to bridge over the differences": JMD papers. Drought sent this proposal to the PMG on June 4, together with a copy of the American "Joint Declaration" of May 31. To save Walker the trouble of comparing the two texts, JMD enclosed a copy of the "Comment" he had mailed to Walsh on June 3. Drought may also have sent a copy of his "bridging" draft to Sir William Wiseman.

203 "Will probably not be approved": There is also a note in Drought's hand reading, "Final draft prepared by me—in an effort to make both official drafts successfully meet." JMD papers.

203 Wikawa sent a telegram to Maryknoll: The message was relayed from there to Drought at the Wardman Park. JMD papers. Ambassador Nomura had, in the meantime, personally telephoned Drought and had "begged" him to return. "I told [Nomura]," Drought informed Walker on June 5, "that I had left [Washington] because I believed the affair was virtually concluded successfully." FW papers.

203 A front-page story: JMD papers, clipping; *NYT*, June 6: 1 ("Japan Asking U.S. for No-War Pact").

203–4 Wikawa to Walker, June 6: FW papers. A June 5 note in the TA Log reads: "Mr. Wikawa, Japanese Embassy, anxious to get in touch with Mr. Walker. May try to contact him at the hotel this evening."

204 The June 6 meeting at Hull's apartment and his "Oral Statement" of that date: *FRJ*, II: 338, 465–68 (supplemented, with reference to the omission on p. 467, by State 711.94/2162-2/14); Hull, II: 1008–10. Also Nomura, 60–61, and "Diary," June 7 and 9; Gaimushō, *NBKK*, 64–66. The "Statement" delineated the State Dept.'s reactions to the revisions proposed by Nomura's agents on June 4.

204 "What had happened thus far": Hull, II: 1009–10.

204 The "more grudging" attitude: See *ibid.*, 1008.

204 Nomura's failure to cable the American "Joint Declaration" of May 31 to Tokyo immediately: Nomura, "Diary," June 9; *TSM, Bekkan*, 422–23, and Konoye papers (Iwakuro to Mutō, received June 3); Gaimushō, *NBKK*, 64–66 (an unnumbered telegram from Nomura to Matsuoka dated June 8), 160; LC-JFOA, WT 38, IMT 265, 100–118, 121–30 (Nomura's 378, 379, 380, and 384, of June 9–10, and an unnumbered telegram of June 10).

Matsuoka had learned of the existence of the "Joint Declaration" of May 31 through remarks made at a Liaison Roundtable Conference by members of the Army General Staff and through brief references to the proposal in a telegram sent by Nomura on June 8. The Army's more complete knowledge in this regard had come from information Iwakuro cabled to his superiors in Tokyo through the Japanese military attaché in Washington.

Because of Nomura's handling of the matter, the American proposal of May 31 never attained a separate existence of its own insofar as the Japanese Govt. was concerned. Since so much time had elapsed without any response from Washington to the Japanese proposal of May 12, the feeling had spread in Tokyo that the American Govt. was procrastinating in the most flagrant manner. The real problem, of course, was that Nomura had been conducting "flanking maneuvers" (*sokumen kōsaku*) through the John Doe Associates because he did not think that ordinary diplomatic procedures were equal to the task. He admitted as much to Matsuoka on June 8.

205 Nomura had pocketed Hull's "Oral Statement" of June 6: The records of the Foreign Office for this period are incomplete (various documents were destroyed as a result of wartime air raids; other items disappeared during the brief period between Japan's decision to surrender and the beginning of the American Occupation), but my inability to find any trace of Hull's "Oral Statement" of June 6 could mean that Nomura never transmitted it to Tokyo.

How poorly informed and "out of date" the Japanese Govt. was, as a consequence of Nomura's handling of his mission, is reflected in Matsuoka's statements to Ott as reported to Berlin on June 6 (*DGFP*, D.XII: esp. 968), in Matsuoka's message to Hitler and Ribbentrop dispatched June 9 (*ibid.*, 1016–17), and in a summary of the Japanese-American negotiations that was released to the public on Dec. 8, 1941 (Gaimushō, *NBKK*, 558–78). This summary refers to the John Doe "Draft Understanding" of Apr. 9 as *an informal draft from the American Government* ("*Beikoku seifu yori hi-kōshiki shian*") and describes the "Confidential Memorandum" of May 12 as Japan's counterproposal (*"taian"*). According to the summary, a revised draft (*"shūsei-an"*) was presented by the American Govt. in the latter part of June (i.e., June 21). There is no mention of Hull's "Oral Statement" of May 16, the "Joint Declaration" of May 31, or the "Oral Statement" of June 6.

205 The truth concerning the "Draft Understanding": On June 10 JMD wrote a letter to FW but then decided against sending it. The original, written in Drought's hand on Wardman Park stationery, is among the JMD papers. There is also another version, on ordinary, ruled binder-paper, that is virtually the same. Nothing is attached to either copy, though one purpose of Drought's letter was to forward his "honest comment" on a State Dept. "Memorandum of Comment" (*FR 1941*, IV: 260–62) that had come into his hands. I did find, however, two drafts that seem to be a fairly reliable guide to the contents of the final version of JMD's "honest comment" (both drafts bear misleading dates that were probably added later). The "truth," as quoted in the text, is from this material, which also contains the following statement by Drought: "Curiously, yet correctly, the Jap. Govt. at Tokio thought [the "Draft Understanding"] was an American document and they studied it accordingly."

205–6 Strauss to the director of Naval Intelligence, May 22, and Hornbeck to Hull, June 10: *FR 1941*, IV: 263–64. The original report has either been lost or misplaced for neither Strauss nor the Navy Dept. could find a copy when I inquired about the matter.

206–7 A telegram from Tokyo, and the reply Nomura drafted but did not send: Nomura, "Diary," June 10–11.

Between Scylla and Charybdis

208 Ott to Berlin, June 6: *DGFP*, D.XII: 967–70.

208 Matsuoka's "purely personal opinion": *Ibid.*, 968–69. A month earlier Matsuoka had been equally specific. He had told Ott then that no Neutrality Pact could change anything in this regard. *Ibid.*, 724–25 (see also p. 809).

208 Grew was warning Washington, June 10: *FR 1941*, IV: 264–65; Grew, *Ten Years*, 392–93.

209 Matsuoka to Hitler and Ribbentrop: The views conveyed by the counselor had been dispatched from Tokyo on June 9. *DGFP*, D.XII: 1016–17 (see also pp. 973–74, 1057–59).

209 The situation in Washington, June 11: *FR 1941*, IV: 265–66.

209 A John Doe draft dated June 8: State 711.94/2162-3/14; *FR 1941*, IV: 256–62. The JMD papers contain a preliminary draft dated June 7 and a copy of the June 8 document. The latter contains changes introduced by Drought after he had seen a State Dept. analysis entitled "Memorandum of Comment on Japanese [*sic*] Suggestions of June 8" (*FR 1941*, IV: 260–62); there are also two pages of suggestions added by JMD sometime between June 8 and June 15 (these two pages are not in the State Dept.'s file copy).

In forwarding the John Doe proposal of June 8 to Hull, Walker wrote: "I am of the opinion that the enclosed draft is approximately that which will be presented to the Secretary [by the agents of the Japanese Ambassador]. I have examined it with care. The sense of my limitations in this field makes me hesitate to venture an opinion, but from my understanding of conversations had, it seems to state the principles involved quite satisfactorily. If [it is agreeable to the Secretary], I would like to discuss it with him before the final draft is submitted. I venture the suggestion only in the hope that I may be helpful." FW papers.

Hull was on the point of taking an extended rest from his duties for reasons of health. Hull, II: 1012. He therefore instructed Hamilton to show the PMG the "Memorandum of Comment" mentioned above. Hull's thought was that the analysis presented in this memo might be of assistance to Walker and Drought in comprehending the Dept.'s view and in conveying that view to the Japanese concerned. Although Hull specified that the memo was not to be given to the Japanese, it nevertheless ended up in their hands. Either Walker failed to understand that the Dept.'s comments were not for distribution or Drought (having obtained the memo from the PMG) decided to give a copy to his Japanese friends. *FR 1941*, IV: 260 n33.

When Walker asked Drought what he thought of the Dept.'s "Memorandum," the PMG apparently took JMD's reply personally. "Certainly, nothing was further from my mind," Drought wrote on June 10, "and when you closed my comment off, as you did, you obviously left me no response. I am extremely sorry if I displeased you—even though I do not know why you were displeased. Perhaps I was too frankly critical." JMD papers (this letter was not sent).

209 Ballantine's conv. with Iwakuro and Wikawa over lunch, June 9: *FRJ*, II: 468–70. When the Colonel endeavored to "smoke out" the Dept.'s reaction to the John Doe draft of June 8, Ballantine replied that *Secretary Hull* was the State Dept.—*he* spoke for the American Govt. on matters of foreign policy. Ballantine assured his hosts that he personally would be happy to go over anything that was not clear in what the Secretary had said to the Colonel and the Ambassador on June 6, so long as they understood that he "could not undertake to express an attitude on any points which they might bring up"; in short, he was not in a position to add to the statements Hull had already made.

209–10 Calls and callers, June 11–22 (esp. Walker's involvement): FW papers, TA Log.

210 Walsh on board the *Tatsuta-maru*: JMD papers, esp. a June 9 letter from Walsh. On June 13, as Walsh entered his second week at sea, Drought dispatched a telegram in care of the Maryknoll mission in Kyoto: "Patient improving but still needs confidence."

210 Drought to Walker, June 14: JMD and FW papers, the first draft and final version respectively. According to the TA Log, "Mr. Walker tried to reach Father Drought [on June 14] but he was out of the hotel; Mr. Hamilton and Mr. Ballantine saw Mr. Walker; Father Drought came in and also went into conference with Mr. Walker, Messrs. Hamilton and Ballantine."

Drought's June 14 letter contains the following postscript: "I really must go home [to Maryknoll] but shall return gladly if I can be of any service. I am thoroughly convinced that Hamilton and Ballantine are incapable and a threat to good results." Drought's first draft of this sentence was more impersonal but no less censorious: "I do not consider the silly nonsense of this morning's 'conversations' a service to anyone."

210 "The enclosed document" (a redraft of the John Doe proposal of June 8): *FRJ*, II: 473–76. In forwarding this new draft to Walker on June 14, Drought

wrote: "If possible, Mr. Hull should have this document before tomorrow at 11 A.M. at which time he is to see Admiral Nomura." See *ibid.*, 471–72, for Ballantine's memo of Hull's June 15 conversation with Nomura, Iwakuro, and Wikawa, and 472–73 for a memo covering a subsequent meeting between Hamilton and Ballantine, on the one hand, and Iwakuro and Wikawa, on the other (with Kōtō Matsudaira sitting in). It was at this second meeting on June 15 that Iwakuro and Wikawa handed over the new draft, declaring that they had received it the previous day *from the Postmaster General* (it was actually the work of Fr. Drought). Upon examining this "June 15" document, Hamilton and Ballantine found it to be "a redraft of the Japanese draft of June 8." *FRJ*, II: 472 (supplemented by State 711.94/2162-8/14). Also Hull, II: 1010.

210 Wikawa to Walker, June 14: FW papers. Elsewhere in this letter, Wikawa wrote as though Walker had personally had a hand in preparing the latest John Doe draft, but I believe this is unlikely. Perhaps Drought had conveyed that impression to his Japanese friends, or perhaps Wikawa was simply being lavish in praising the PMG. At any rate, the letter indicated that Walker's "further efforts" would be highly appreciated by his "sincere friend in peace, T. Wikawa."

210–11 Nomura's activities on Sunday morning, June 15 (esp. his meeting with Hull): Nomura, 63, and "Diary," June 15; *FRJ*, II: 471–72 (the visit to Hull was made at the Ambassador's request); Gaimushō, *NBKK*, 67.

211 Chungking would collapse, were it not for American help: This was a thought that Nomura shared with many of his countrymen. In the circumstances of 1941, it was extremely difficult for the people of Japan to determine, let alone judge, what was being done in their name in China (or elsewhere in the Far East). Grew had long since discovered that His Majesty's subjects were in the habit of repeating arguments that were without foundation but to which they tenaciously adhered nevertheless. One of their most frequent charges was the very accusation that Nomura lodged on June 15—namely, that the U.S. was aiding and abetting Chinese resistance to Japan by the sending of supplies to Chiang Kai-shek. Grew had heard this particular complaint so often that he had finally resorted to carrying around in his pocket a document that showed at a glance the total value of exports from the U.S. to Japan, as well as to China, during the two most recent years for which figures were available—1939 and '40. There had been far more trade with Japan than with China even in such strategic commodities as gasoline, iron and steel bars, and petroleum and petroleum products. Grew papers, "Diary," Apr. 1941: 5006–7.

In Washington, a difference of opinion had developed within the State Dept. concerning the effectiveness of American policy to date in sustaining China and in impeding Japan. Hamilton was afraid that the imposition of sweeping restrictions on trade, esp. on items the U.S. was known to have in ample supply, might impel Japan toward accepting "the risks of a military campaign southward." He consequently favored a continuation of the policy that had been followed thus far: "The attrition of Japan's energies and resources by steps undertaken gradually on a basis designed to obviate creating the impression that they were in the nature of overt acts directed primarily at Japan." Hornbeck maintained that the Japanese had been significantly aided since 1937 by the "practically unrestricted access" they had had to "the rich and most helpful markets of the United States." His attitude about this kind of policy, SKH wrote, was that he would "praise the day when it is done." See *FR 1941*, IV: 150–52, 164–67.

211 Walker complained to Nomura: Nomura, 63–64, and "Diary," June 17.

211 Matsuoka simply did not tone down his pro-Axis pronouncements: See, for example, *NYT*, June 15: 6 ("Matsuoka Backs Duce Against U.S."). Also *NYT*, June 16: 3; Hull, II: 1011; *FRJ*, II: 493.

211 In all likelihood the Ambassador would merely smile in reply: See *FRJ*, II: 391; and *FR 1941*, IV: 77.

211 Wikawa to Walker, June 18: FW papers. That same day, Drought telephoned Walker from Maryknoll; later the PMG talked to Hamilton at the State Dept. FW papers, TA Log and "Daily Memo Calendar, 1941."

211–12 Drought to Walsh, June 18: JMD papers. On June 23 Walsh replied from Japan: "Luke twenty-two forty-four ['And his sweat became as drops of blood, trickling down upon the ground'] accounts delay. Interpretation worst possible." JMD papers.

I am indebted to Sister William Mary of Maryknoll for help in identifying the Biblical references that appear from time to time in messages exchanged between Walsh and Drought.

212 Wikawa to the PMG, June 19: FW papers. Also pertinent is a letter Wikawa wrote to Drought on the evening of June 19. JMD papers.

212 Drought's annoyance with the State Dept.'s handling of the "negotiations": There is much evidence for this in the JMD papers, but especially interesting in this regard is a June 16 memo written by Sir William Wiseman, possibly for the benefit of the British Embassy. The original is in the "New Wiseman ms" at Yale; Wilton B. Fowler kindly sent me a copy.

212–13 The letter from Wikawa that Drought forwarded on June 20 to Walker: The handwritten original, dated "June 18, Evening," is in the FW papers; a typewritten copy can be found among the JMD papers.

212 *"They are bringing out one after another old controversies"*: A necessary corrective to the impression of niggling negotiation created by Wikawa in this paragraph of his letter can be obtained by reading the memos of conversations held in Washington on June 15, 16, and 17. *FRJ*, II: 472–73, 476–83.

213 Drought to Wikawa, June 21: JMD papers.

214 Hull made a calculated move: In his *Memoirs*, II: 1010, Hull wrote: "Then on June 21 I handed Nomura a document containing revisions of his draft of June 15 [see *FRJ*, II: 473–76] so as to bring it into focus with our views." Appended to the "Oral Statement" of June 21, however, was the following note (*ibid.*, 486): "In order to bring the current discussions up to date as far as the American attitude is concerned, there is being handed the Japanese Ambassador separately a revision, bearing the date of June 21, of the document marked 'Unofficial, Exploratory and Without Commitment' which was handed the Japanese Ambassador on May 31."

The apparent discrepancy is immaterial, since an examination of the three documents shows how closely interrelated they are (and how much they have in common with the John Doe "Draft Understanding" of Apr. 9 and Japan's "Confidential Memorandum" of May 12). IMTFE, Exhibit 1245A (Ballantine affidavit, Exhibit "D"), contains a table comparing Japan's May 12 proposal with the American draft of June 21; State 711.94/2162-11/14 compares the June 21 draft with the earlier American proposal of May 31.

214 The Hull-Nomura conv. of June 21, the "Joint Declaration" of that date, and related documents: *FRJ*, II: 339–40, 483–92; *FR 1941*, IV: 270–72; Hull, II: 1010–11; U.S. Dept. of State, *Peace and War*, 122–23; Nomura, 65, 66–68, and Furoku No. 7, 57–74; Nomura, "Diary," June 21; Gaimushō, *NBKK*, 67–93 (the pertinent Nomura telegrams are Nos. 424, 425, and 426, dispatched from Washington on June 23; the *besshi otsu-gō* item is incomplete); Gaimushō, *Shuyō Bunsho*, II: 527–30 (also incomplete; see *FRJ*, II: 491–92, for the text handed to Nomura); Iwakuro ms., 189–207. The JMD and FW papers also contain the relevant documents. A copy of the American redraft of June 21 was forwarded to Grew with a letter, dated June 30, from an officer of the Dept. *FR 1941*, IV: 424.

214–16 The Hull-Nomura conv. of June 22 and the relevant "Oral Statements": *FRJ*, II: 485–86, 492–94; Hull, II: 1011; Nomura, 65–66, 67, and Furoku No. 8, 75–78 (containing items that were apparently appended to Nomura's "Oral Statement" of June 22 but are not printed in *FRJ*, II); Nomura, "Diary," June 22; Gaimushō, *NBKK*, 67. A copy of Hull's "Oral Statement" of June 21 with marginal notes by Drought can be found in the JMD papers; the FW papers contain copies of all the pertinent State Dept. materials for June 21 and also a copy of Ballantine's memo covering this conversation.

215 The proposed "exchange of letters" and Nomura's reaction: In Tel. No. 424 of June 23 (Gaimushō, *NBKK*, 67) Nomura reported that he had expressly told Hull that the letters (*FRJ*, II: 490–92) could not be transmitted to Tokyo because certain portions of them would be unacceptable to his government. Despite this, Nomura cabled everything to the Foreign Office. Matsuoka later charged (*TSM, Bekkan*, 477) that he would never have seen the letters if he had not specifically ordered Nomura to send them.

Nomura seems to have been of the opinion that he had taken care of the matter, but Hull had said nothing to indicate that he would eliminate or modify the letters (until and unless the Japanese Govt. recommended specific changes). The Secretary therefore sat back to await Japan's response to the June 21 proposal and to the letters appended to that proposal. When Matsuoka read the letters, he thought they were outrageous. Nomura, meanwhile, having failed to appreciate Hull's intentions in the matter, kept expecting to receive word that the American Govt. either was withdrawing the suggested letters altogether or was preparing new and revised texts for submission to the Ambassador and his govt. In other words, a situation very similar to the one that had existed in Apr. arose again in June, with neither side comprehending the other's position.

215 Drought's connection with the "exchange of letters" idea: JMD papers, suggestions offered by Drought on or about June 10.

216 Hull's departure for White Sulphur Springs: Hull, II: 967, 1012. According to a mid-July press report, Hull had been suffering from "a run-down condition, which at one time was complicated by an attack of bronchitis." *NYT*, July 13: 9. The Secretary returned to his desk on Aug. 4. *Ibid.*, Aug. 5: 6.

During the greater part of July, Walker was also away from the capital, traveling through the American northwest. The JMD papers contain an itinerary showing that FW would leave New York on July 5 and return to Washington on July 24.

216 Nomura received some "incredible news": Nomura, "Diary," June 25 and July 23. Also *TSM, Bekkan,* 474 (a June 28 cable from the naval attaché at the Japanese Embassy in Washington to the Vice-Minister of the Navy and the Vice-Chief of Staff).

216 Wikawa to Drought, June 27: JMD papers.

216 A do-or-die attempt: The reference here is to a decision confirmed at an Imperial Conference held in Tokyo on July 2. See Butow, *Tojo,* 218–20, 222 n65); *TSM, Bekkan,* 463–69; and Ike, 77–90.

216–17 Drought to the PMG, July 1: JMD and FW papers.

217 A conv. on July 2: *FRJ,* II: 495–99 (supplemented by State 711.94/2178-1/18); *FR 1941,* IV: 291–92. Max W. Schmidt and Kōtō Matsudaira were also present.

217 Nomura to Hull via Ballantine, July 4: *FRJ,* II: 499–500, 626; *FR 1941,* IV: 291–92. The FW papers contain an unsigned copy of this same note, and it is printed in Nomura, Furoku No. 9, 79–80. Although Nomura's "Diary," July 4, mentions the receipt of a dispatch from Tokyo that served as the basis for Nomura's note, no cable has been found in the Foreign Office archives that fits the circumstances.

As of July 4 Matsuoka had not replied to the various cables Nomura had sent on June 23 regarding the American offering of June 21. In fact, Nomura did not receive any instructions in this connection until July 15.

217–18 The July 5 meeting between Hamilton and Nomura: *FRJ,* II: 499–502 (supplemented by State 711.94/2178-2/18); *FR 1941,* IV: 290–91; Nomura, 69–70, and "Diary," July 5. Ballantine was also present.

218 Intelligence information of an ominous nature: The American Govt. had been advised that Japan was proceeding with military preparations on an enormous scale, including the calling up of between one and two million reservists and conscripts. All Japanese vessels in American Atlantic-coast ports were under orders to be west of the Panama Canal by Aug. 1. Movement of Japanese flag shipping from Japan was suspended, and additional merchant vessels were being requisitioned. Restrictions were placed on travel within Japan. Censorship of mail and other forms of communication was also imposed. See *FRJ,* II: 339–40; *FR 1941,* IV: 298–99, 300–302, 1004, 1005; Hull, II: 1012–13; and Grew, *Ten Years,* 403–4. U.S. Army authorities were afraid, at this time, that the Panama Canal might be sabotaged by the crews of Japanese vessels passing through that waterway. See State 701.9411/1437 and 894.85/639–40.

218–20 The President's message to Konoye and related exchanges: Hull, II: 1012; *FRJ,* II: 502–4, 509–10, 513; *FR 1941,* IV: 994–95, 997–98, 1002–3, 1004–5, 1006, 1010; Grew, *Ten Years,* 396–400; Gaimushō, *NBKK,* 94–97, 112–15; Ushiba corresp.; and as noted separately hereunder.

The President's message to Konoye, the text of which was approved by FDR on July 3, was cabled by Acting Secretary Welles on July 4. This telegram reached Grew on July 5, and the next morning, Sunday, July 6, he handed a paraphrased version (what Grew calls "the substance of the message") to

Ushiba (paraphrasing was a security measure employed in the transmittal of all items received in code). On Tuesday, July 8, Matsuoka gave Grew "in strict confidence a Japanese text accompanied by a strictly confidential unofficial English translation" of a "Message in Reply," dated July 7, "Sent by H.I.M.'s Foreign Minister at the Request of the Prime Minister for Delivery to the President of the U.S.A."

On July 10, Welles sent Grew instructions that had been approved by the President. This telegram, which reached the Ambassador on the 11th, suggested the general lines of a response to Matsuoka's "Message in Reply." Since the Foreign Minister was ill in bed at the time, Grew did not act on these instructions until July 16. On that day he handed to Vice-Minister Ōhashi what I have called "a stiff answer." The next day, July 17, Ōhashi gave Grew an "Oral Statement" from the Foreign Minister that finally brought this series of exchanges to an end.

219 A note from Konoye addressed to Grew: *FR 1941*, IV: 998. When I asked Tomohiko Ushiba, more than 25 years after the event, whether he could possibly recall any of the circumstances pertinent to this letter, he wrote in reply: "I tried very hard to remember but I don't think that I drafted the letter; from the English of the message, I am almost certain that I did not draft it. . . . I cannot quite get rid of the impression [despite the account given by Grew] that Mr. Matsuoka, upon contact with Prince Konoye, drafted the message and had his secretary bring it to the Ambassador. . . . Prince Konoye could not have written it himself; his English was quite limited: he could read it all right, but he scarcely ever wrote or spoke it."

219 Konoye's "pathetically jealous, painfully ambitious" Foreign Minister: Ushiba corresp.

219–20 A stiff answer, July 16: See *FRJ*, II: 509–10.

220 *An agreement that would speak for itself*: See *ibid.*, 466, 467; and Hull, II: 1009.

The John Doe Associates Depart

221 Drought's first step in the direction of reasserting himself: See text pp. 216–17.

221 Calls and callers, July 3: Nomura, "Diary," July 3; FW papers, TA Log.

221–22 Drought to Wikawa, July 5: JMD papers.

222 Drought to Walker, July 7: JMD and FW papers.

222 Calls and callers, July 10–11: FW papers, TA Log.

222 The documents Drought delivered to Cronin on July 11 and the covering note to Walker: JMD papers. Also *FR 1941*, IV: 303–4, 311–21; State 711.94/ 2178-8/18.

222–23 Hull's advisers reacted negatively: See *FR 1941*, IV: 314–17. The State Dept. treated the July 11 documents as though they constituted a "New Japanese Draft" that had the full backing of Nomura and his govt. See *ibid.*, 311–14, 317–21. In actuality, however, Tokyo knew nothing at all about this John Doe proposal.

223–24 Matsuoka's views following the German invasion of Russia: See Butow, *Tojo*, 208–21, 228–29, 230–33; Ike, 36–90 (the records of policy conferences held between May 22 and July 2; for the Japanese originals, see *TSM, Bek-*

kan, passim); *DGFP*, D.XIII: 1–2, 18–19, 36–37, 41, 73–77, 158–60, 187, 198; and as noted separately hereunder.

224 Matsuoka wanted to "stop building a fire" in the south: The Foreign Minister made this remark during a Liaison Roundtable Conference on June 30. Ike, 72; *TSM, Bekkan*, 460.

224–25 Matsuoka's ideas regarding policy toward the U.S. (and the conflict that ensued with his colleagues): See Butow, *Tojo*, 230–33; *PHA*, XX: 3994–97; Konoye, 86–96; *TSM, Bekkan*, 469–74; Ike, 93–103; and *FRJ*, II: 628–29. Note also *TSM, Bekkan*, 457, 458; and Ike, 65, 67.

224 "Worse than the first proposal": *TSM, Bekkan*, 470, 474; Ike, 94, 102; and *DGFP*, D.XIII: 108–10, 121.

224 Saitō's misrepresentation of Hull's "Oral Statement" of June 21: *TSM, Bekkan*, 470–71; Ike, 94–97. Compare Saitō's remarks, as given in *TSM, Bekkan*, 471, with the Japanese translation of Hull's "Statement" printed in Gaimushō, *NBKK*, 87–89.

224 Roosevelt was "a real demagogue": This remark was made at a Liaison Roundtable Conference on July 12. *TSM, Bekkan*, 473; Ike, 101.

225 Matsuoka's illness: See LC-JFOA, WT 38, IMT 263, 257–58 (the rough-draft translation on pp. 259–60 is quite misleading).

225 The Foreign Minister cabled instructions to Nomura: See Gaimushō, *NBKK*, 100–102.

225 Matsuoka directed one of his subordinates: See *DGFP*, D.XIII: 172–73 (the extract from Tel. No. 1247). Ott was given only the substance—not the exact text—of Japan's counterproposal.

225–26 Nomura's attitude and outlook (while he waited for some response from Tokyo): Gaimushō, *NBKK*, 67–68, 92–93; Nomura, 67–69, 70–71, 181–87, and "Diary," June 28 and July 3, 8, 10, 11, and 14 (see also the entry for July 23).

225 The ordering home of Wakasugi: Nomura received this instruction on July 10; the State Dept. learned of the Minister's impending departure on July 29. Nomura, 71, 182–83; State 701.9411/1420-1/2. See also Matsuoka's remarks in this connection on July 12. Ike, 100; *TSM, Bekkan*, 472.

226 Nomura's desire to resign: See Nomura, 183–87, and "Diary," July 14.

226 Matsuoka had been told by his doctor: See *DGFP*, D.XIII: 172 (the extract from Tel. No. 1247).

226 A decision in favor of a Cabinet resignation: See Butow, *Tojo*, 228–29, 230–33; *FR 1941*, IV: 326–28, 336–38.

226 Herr Hitler's "office boy": See *FR 1941*, IV: 337.

226 Wikawa to Drought, July 16: JMD papers. No "new proposal" had as yet been delivered to the State Dept.

226 Drought to the PMG, July 16: FW and JMD papers.

226 Drought's follow-up telegram to FW, July 18: *Ibid.*

226–27 Drought's second telegram, July 18: *Ibid.*

227 A member of the Japanese Embassy to an officer of the State Dept., July 16: State 894.00/1092.

227 Grew felt he was on very shaky ground: Grew papers, "Diary," July 1941: 5352–55; *FR 1941*, IV: 1006–10.

227 The Japanese move into southern Indochina: See *FRJ*, II: 340–43; Hull, II: 1013–14; Langer and Gleason, 641–42; and Butow, *Tojo*, 209–12, 221–23.

227 "Like a pudgy thumb": Hull, II: 1013.

227 Hull's attitude: See *FR 1941*, IV: 325–26, 329–30. In a postwar statement, Hull declared: "The Japanese move into southern Indochina was an aggravated, overt act. It created a situation in which the risk of war became so great that the United States and other countries concerned were confronted no longer with the question of avoiding such risk but from then on with the problem of preventing a complete undermining of their security. It was essential that the United States make a definite and clear move in self-defense." *PHA*, II: 422.

227 Maxwell Hamilton, playing the devil's advocate: See *FR 1941*, IV: 329.

228 Hamilton thought . . . but Welles and Hornbeck disagreed: *Ibid.*, 330–31.

228 Hull's instructions on having "one more talk" with Nomura: See *ibid.*, 333–35.

228 Welles to Wakasugi, July 21: *FRJ*, II: 520–22. Also Nomura, "Diary," July 21; *FR 1941*, IV: 343.

228 Nomura-Turner conv., July 20: See *FRJ*, II: 516–20 (esp. 518–19).

228–29 Hornbeck to Welles, July 22: *FR 1941*, IV: 335.

229 Wikawa telephoned Ballantine, July 23: *Ibid.*, 338, but see *FRJ*, II: 522 (Nomura attributes the same information to "press reports").

229 Hull's telephone conv. with Welles, July 23: See *FR 1941*, IV: 339–41; *FRJ*, II: 525–26.

229–30 The Welles-Nomura conv., July 23: *FRJ*, II: 522–26 (the details were reported to Grew by telegram), 533; Nomura, 74–76, and "Diary," July 23.

230 Wikawa to the PMG, July 23: FW papers.

230–31 The FDR-Nomura meeting and the President's Neutralization Proposal, July 24: See *FRJ*, II: 341–42, 527–30. Also Hull, II: 1014; Feis, 236–38; Langer and Gleason, 649–51; Nomura, 77–79, and "Diary," July 24; Gaimushō, *NBKK*, 125–28; and Nomura, "Chū-Bei Ninmu Hōkoku," Sect. 4.

"At the time this [FDR-Nomura] conversation was held," Hornbeck later wrote, ". . . we all, including the President, had positive knowledge that the Japanese had demanded of the Vichy Government a new agreement whereby Vichy would assent to a virtual military occupation of southern Indochina by Japanese armed forces. The Japanese had placed Japanese naval vessels, including aircraft carriers, along the Indochina coast, and had given an ultimatum. Vichy capitulated on July 23 and signed the demanded agreement on July 29." SKH papers, Box 254, Folder "Japan-U.S. Conversations" (a memo dated Oct. 28, 1941).

Two days after talking with Nomura, the President sent the following instructions to Harry Hopkins (in London): "Tell Former Naval Person [Winston Churchill] in great confidence that I have suggested to Nomura that Indo-China be neutralized by Britain, Dutch, Chinese, Japan and ourselves, placing Indo-China somewhat in status of Switzerland. Japan to get rice and fertilizer but all on condition that Japan withdraw armed forces from Indo-China in toto. I have had no answer yet. When it comes it will probably be unfavorable but we have at least made one more effort to avoid Japanese expansion to South Pacific." *PHA*, XX: 4379.

231 Hull's telephone conv. with Welles, July 25: *FR 1941*, IV: 341–42. Also *FRJ*, II: 505–9.

231–32 The Iwakuro-Ballantine conv., July 25: *FRJ*, II: 530–32; FW papers, TA Log.

232 The Iwakuro-Wikawa decision to return home: Iwakuro ms., 230–39; Katô, 30–31; IMTFE, 32998–99, 33005 ("Sokki-roku," 312: 14, 15); Iwakuro intv. Also Nomura, 83, and "Diary," July 31.

232 The freezing of Japanese assets in the U.S., July 26: See *FRJ*, II: 264–65, 266–67, 315–17, 342–43; *FR 1941*, IV: 301, 826–27; Grew, *Ten Years*, 408; Feis, 227–41; Langer and Gleason, 649, 651–52; and Butow, *Tojo*, 223. Also Hamilton papers, Box 2, Folder "Japan, 1942–1952" (a July 14, 1942, memo summarizing American policy on the imposition of embargoes against Japan, 1937–41), and Box 1, Folder "China" (a Nov. 11, 1942, memo on the same subject, together with four pertinent annexes).

232 Hamilton noted for the record: *FRJ*, II: 532 n66.

232 Wikawa to Drought, July 27: JMD papers (I have capitalized the word Reds to conform with standard usage).

232 Calls and callers, July 28–31: FW papers, TA Log. Nomura asked Welles, on July 28, whether the President would be able to receive Iwakuro before the Colonel left on the 31st. Welles indicated he would confer with the White House, but he suggested that FDR was far too busy to meet every demand made upon him. Nomura, in turn, was "very emphatic in saying that he by no means wished to intrude upon the President's time." *FRJ*, II: 539.

232–33 Wikawa to Walker, July 31: FW papers.

233 Iwakuro and Wikawa to Hull, July 31: Hull papers, Box 49.

233 The telegrams intended for Hamilton and Ballantine: JMD papers (the messages are written in Drought's hand on Western Union blanks that he was using as scratch paper).

233–34 The "Two Friends for Peace" telegram to Hull: The rough drafts of this message (the first on a Western Union blank, the second on a piece of Hotel Mark Hopkins stationery) are among the JMD papers at Maryknoll, and are in the handwriting of Fr. Drought. The telegram, as received by Hull, is in the Hull papers, General Correspondence, Aug. 2, 1941. Drought's 1st draft contains two sentences that were subsequently eliminated: "[We] understand the American position and honestly wish that our own might be sympathetically appreciated. Frankly, we think it has not been." All other changes are comparatively minor.

234 Drought's return trip by train and the draft of his telegram to Iwakuro and Wikawa (ca. Aug. 2): JMD papers.

234 Iwakuro and Wikawa to Drought, Aug. 3: JMD papers. Despite the reference to "your kind messages," I was unable to find anything more than the draft of the telegram mentioned in the preceding note.

Toward an "Unbridgeable Antagonism"

235 Matsuoka's scolding of Nomura over the "associates" issue: See *FRJ*, II: 485–86 (the "Oral Statement" of June 21); LC-JFOA, Reel UD 40, Doc. UD 63, 216 (Nomura's 479 of July 8 in which the Ambassador explained the meaning of "associates"); *TSM, Bekkan*, 472 (a passing reference by Matsuoka, at a Liaison Roundtable Conference, to the "*taishi oyobi dōryō*" matter); and Gaimushō, *NBKK*, 97–100 (Matsuoka's 356 of July 11, sent in response to Nomura's 479), 100–102 (an unnumbered cable dispatched on July 14, in which Matsuoka briefly referred once again to the "associates" issue).

Hull's "Oral Statement" of June 6 also contained several references to "the associates of the Japanese Ambassador" (*FRJ*, II: 467–68), but Nomura had refrained from forwarding this particular "Statement" to his govt.

235 Nomura's response to Matsuoka's reprimand: Gaimushō, *NBKK*, 109–12.

236 The representations Matsuoka had asked Saitō to make to Konoye, as seen through Saitō's letter (ca. July 17) to the Premier: See *TSM, Bekkan*, 475–78 (esp. 477–78).

236 The American Govt. had accepted the return of the "Oral Statement" of June 21: Since Hull was still at White Sulphur Springs, the matter was handled by Hamilton, who kept in touch with the Secretary in this regard. *FRJ*, II: 485–86, 506–8, 511–12, 513–14; *FR 1941*, IV: 323–24. Also *TSM, Bekkan*, 471, 472–77; Ike, 96–97, 99–103; Gaimushō, *NBKK*, 97–102, 109–12; Nomura, "Diary," July 16.

236 Japan's "Final Plan" of July 15 and Nomura's decision not to deliver it to the State Dept.: The Ambassador was of the opinion that his govt.'s proposal would be unacceptable to Roosevelt and Hull because of its uncompromising nature. See Nomura, 73, and Furoku 10, 81–84; Kiba, 562; Konoye, 91–94, 97–98, 116 (*PHA*, XX: 3995–96, 3997–98, 4003); Gaimushō, *NBKK*, 102–9, 161; LC-JFOA, Reel UD 40, Doc. UD 63, 423–32, and Reel S 539, Doc. S 1.1.3.1-1, 16–17, 20–25, 192–216; *DGFP*, D.XIII: 169–73, 353, 491; *TSM, Bekkan*, 483; and Ike, 109. Also Nomura, "Diary," July 23 (Nomura's desire for instructions) and Sept. 17 (Nomura's 823 informing Toyoda that the July 15 proposal had not been submitted to Hull); *TSM, Bekkan*, 475 (Matsuoka's judgment of the situation as recorded by Saitō); *DGFP*, D.XIII: 173, 198; *FRJ*, II: 626.

236 Nomura was determined to do his very best: Nomura, "Diary," July 23.

236–37 Nomura's handling of FDR's Neutralization Proposal and the action taken by Grew: *FRJ*, II: 529, 534–37, 538, 545; *FR 1941*, IV: 345, 347, 348, 351–52, 353–54, 358, 360–61; Nomura, "Diary," July 19, 23, and 28; Grew, *Ten Years*, 411–13; Gaimushō, *NBKK*, 125–28, 135–39; Konoye papers, a July 30 telegram from Nomura and a paraphrase in English of FDR's July 24 proposal; and as noted separately hereunder. Hindsight suggests that a proposal of such importance ought to have been handed to Nomura in writing and that a copy of the text should then have been cabled to Grew for delivery to Japan's Premier or Foreign Minister. Appending a Japanese translation to the English original might also have been a good idea.

237 Grew's elimination of one culprit in favor of another: See *FR 1941*, IV: 345. Grew was closer to the truth when he subsequently wrote in his diary: "We have all too much evidence that the Japanese Embassy in Washington is half the time asleep at the switch either in failing to understand statements made by our Government or in failing to report them promptly, accurately, and comprehensively. This view, I am confidentially informed, is shared by the Foreign Office here." Langer and Gleason, 651 n57, quoting an entry for Aug. 5, 1941. See also Grew papers, "Diary," Aug. 1941: 5535.

237 The Hamilton-Hornbeck advice to Welles and the action taken by him: *FR 1941*, IV: 347; *FRJ*, II: 538.

238 Wakasugi to Welles, Aug. 4: Wakasugi also said that he could not deny that the President's proposal, if consummated, would give security to Japan. *FRJ*, II: 545.

238 The gradual resumption of the Hull-Nomura convs.: The last meeting had

taken place on June 22, just prior to Hull's departure for White Sulphur Springs. Nomura had made an unsolicited and unannounced visit there on July 13, hoping to see the Secretary, but Hull had demurred. Hull, II: 1013. The conversations had been suspended, in effect, on July 23, as a result of the Indochina crisis (see text pp. 227–30). Hull saw Nomura, at the Ambassador's request, on Aug. 6 (*FRJ*, II: 546–50), and again on Aug. 8, at the Secretary's request (*ibid.*, 550–53), but apparently neither man regarded these meetings as anything more than an extension of the Ambassador's interview with the President on July 24. There was also a Hull-Nomura meeting on Aug. 13 (*ibid.*, I: 724–25) occasioned by the continued bombing by Japanese aircraft of "the city area of Chungking."

On Aug. 16, with peace very much on his mind, Nomura took the initiative by "pointedly" asking Hull whether the conversations they had been having earlier in the year could be resumed, but Hull did not give any sign whatever "of saying anything favorable about [the Ambassador's] request for a resumption of conversations." At the end of their discussion, however, Hull indicated that he would have no objections if Nomura "desired to talk to any others on this subject or to the President." *Ibid.*, II: 553–54. This, in effect, marked the beginning of a new series of sessions between Hull and Nomura that lasted until the attack on Pearl Harbor.

They had three more meetings in Aug. (making a total of six for that month, if the special meeting on Aug. 13 is disregarded), seven in Sept., three in Oct., nine in Nov., and two in Dec. (not counting their final meeting on Dec. 7). In this same period Nomura saw the President six times (Aug. 17 and 28; Sept. 3; Nov. 10, 17, and 27). Hull was present on all of these occasions.

238 Tokyo remained committed to an "immutable" policy: See *FR 1941*, IV: 332, 336–38, 343. Also *DGFP*, D.XIII: 185–86; Ike, 105–6, 113; *TSM, Bekkan*, 480–81, 486; Konoye papers, the demands of the Supreme Command (this document can also be found in *TSM, Bekkan*, 482); Butow, *Tojo*, 233–34.

238 The "irrevocable" nature of Japanese decisions: This theme was constantly heard (as Langer and Gleason, 662, have pointed out). Irrevocable decisions inevitably led to "immutable" policies—hardly an enviable position for any govt. to assume.

238 The extension of the President's Neutralization Proposal to cover Thailand: See Welles to Nomura (July 31) in *FRJ*, II: 539–40. Also, Nomura, "Diary," July 31.

238 The Japanese Govt.'s reaction to the President's Neutralization Proposal: On Aug. 6 Nomura presented a counterproposal. Tokyo thought that this would serve to reopen the suspended conversations. Two days later, however, Hull told Nomura that the document was "lacking in responsiveness to the suggestion made by the President" on July 24. See *FRJ*, II: 343–44, 546–53; *FR 1941*, IV: 360–61; U.S. Dept. of State, *Peace and War*, 127–28; Hull, II: 1016–17; Nomura, 83, 85–86, 87–88, and "Diary," Aug. 2, 6, and 8; Gaimushō, *NBKK*, 143–49, 152–56, 259–60; *PHA*, XII: 10–12; and Konoye, 99–102 (*PHA*, XX: 3998–99). Grew was briefed on the Hull-Nomura conversations of Aug. 6 and 8. *FR 1941*, IV: 379.

238 Konoye's new Foreign Minister (Adm. Teijirō Toyoda) quickly made a good impression (on Grew): *FR 1941*, IV: 328–29; Grew papers, "Diary," July 1941: 5356. Also Grew, *Ten Years*, 416–17. By way of contrast, the German Ambassador in Tokyo found Toyoda "very reserved." *DGFP*, D.XIII: 415.

238 Toyoda's lack of diplomatic experience: *FRJ*, II: 521; *FR 1941*, IV: 343. Also Grew, *Ten Years*, 406.

238 "An example of Prince Konoye's famous policy": *FR 1941*, IV: 354.

238 "As in every previous step in the southward advance": Grew papers, "Diary," July 1941 (introductory summary): 5332–33.

239 Grew had already talked with Toyoda about this problem: *Ibid*. Also *FRJ*, II: 317–19; Grew, *Ten Years*, 406–8.

239 "My impression for what it may be worth": *FR 1941*, IV: 344; Grew, *Ten Years*, 410–11. On the expectations of the Japanese Govt. (esp. the feeling that American measures of retaliation would be more limited), see also Ike, 108–9; *TSM, Bekkan*, 483; and Craigie, 120.

240 A ring of jubilation in certain sectors of the American press: Langer and Gleason, 652–53, 655, supplemented by *NYT*, July 26: 14 (edit.), and Aug. 3: Sect. 4: 4E.

240 George Gallup reported: *NYT*, Aug. 3: 20. In mid-July, just before the American people received the news of Japan's advance into southern Indochina, the Gallup Poll began asking the following question: "Should the United States take steps now to keep Japan from becoming more powerful, even if this means risking war with Japan?" 51% of those polled were in favor, 31% were opposed, and 18% were undecided or had no opinion. Also Grew papers, "Diary," Aug. 1941: 5509–20.

240 Fleisher on the significance of the freezing order: Langer and Gleason, 652, citing an article in the *NYHT* for July 27.

240 The Tolischus warning: *NYT*, Aug. 3: Sect. 7: 10 (see also Sect. 4: 4E).

240–41 Hull's attitude (late July–early Aug.): *FR 1941*, IV: 348–49, 358–59. Also Feis, 248–49; Langer and Gleason, 652–53, 659–60.

241 Stimson on the change in Hull's thinking: Langer and Gleason, 659, citing Stimson's "Diary" for Aug. 7–9.

241 Grew's outlook: Grew papers, "Diary," July 1941 (introductory summary): 5333. Also Feis, 248; Langer and Gleason, 654. Grew repeated his *"facilis descensus"* prediction in a Sept. 22 letter to FDR. *FR 1941*, IV: 468–69.

241–42 Hull's later summation (late July–early Aug.): Hull, II: 1014–15.

242 The decision emerging in Tokyo: See Butow, *Tojo*, 245–59.

242 An antagonism of possibly unbridgeable proportions: In a July 21 telegram to Berlin, Ott reported that Ōhashi had told him that Matsuoka, before resigning as Foreign Minister, had expedited the sending of the "Final Plan" of July 15 to Washington in order to commit Japan to a policy of "unbridgeable antagonism" toward the U.S. *DGFP*, D.XIII: 198. Be that as it may, the crisis in Japanese-American relations deepened enormously after July.

Sounds of War Amid Talk of Peace

245–46 The *Tutuila* episode, July 30: See Grew, *Ten Years*, 413–14; *FRJ*, I: 715–26; *FR 1941*, IV: 352–53, 365–70, and V: 886–91, 894–95; Nomura, 82, and "Diary," July 30–31; *PHA*, XX: 4216–17; *NYT*, June 17: 5, July 31: 1, 10, Aug. 1: 1, 14 (edit.), Aug. 14: 5; State 711.94/2248A; and *Newsweek*, Aug. 11: 15–16.

246–47 Editorial comments appearing in the press: I have drawn on information sent to Grew by the State Dept. State 711.94/2248A.

247 The *Journal American* editorial, Aug. 4: JMD papers.

247–48 Drought to Lippmann, Aug. 7: *Ibid*. For the article in question, "A

Strange Oversight," see Lippmann's "Today and Tomorrow" column in the *NYHT*, Aug. 7: 17.

248–49 Drought to Walker, Aug. 13: JMD papers.

248 The announcement by Vichy: See *NYT*, Aug. 13: 1, 4.

248 James W. Wadsworth and the Congressional vote: See *ibid.*, 1, 10; *Congressional Record*, Vol. LXXXVII, Part 7: 7020–21; and Langer and Gleason, 570–74.

248–49 Senator Wheeler's "agreement": *NYT*, July 26: 7.

249 The formula Nomura had handed to Hull on Aug. 6: See *FRJ*, II: 546–50.

249–50 The Atlantic Conference and the proposed warning to Japan: See Langer and Gleason, 663–98 (esp. 670–77, 693–98); Feis, 255–58; Hull, II: 1017–20; Churchill, 438–41; *FRJ*, II: 345–46, 554–59; *FR 1941*, IV: 370–76, 410–11; *PHA*, II: 423, 458–61, 477–87, 523, 538–39, 627–30, 643–44, IV: 1784–85, 1786–87, 1790, XIV: 1254–1300, and XV: 1682–88; Gaimushō, *NBKK*, 166–80, 182–83; and *NYT*, Aug. 2–19, *passim*. I have also checked some unindexed "Records of the Far Eastern Division" in Record Group 59 at the National Archives: "Superseded Drafts of Documents Handed to Ambassador Nomura by the President on August 17, 1941."

FDR was thinking of linking the proposed warning to Japan to Tokyo's failure to show any interest in his earlier Neutralization Proposal. The draft that Welles brought back from Argentia (*FR 1941*, IV: 370–72) was much more explicit in this regard than the text that was handed to Nomura on Aug. 17 (*FRJ*, II: 556–57), but even in the latter document the connection was made clear. Although Tokyo had ignored Roosevelt's proposition in regard to Indochina, the President nevertheless made a point of securing a British commitment of the type he had said he would obtain when he had first talked to Nomura about the matter on July 24. As a consequence, Churchill promised to provide a statement in writing, declaring that London was completely in accord with the Neutralization Proposal with respect to Indochina, that the British Govt. had no aggressive designs whatsoever on Thailand, and that Britain would not move in the direction of occupying that country. *PHA*, XIV: 1282–83.

250 The role played by Hull and his Far Eastern staff in "toning down" the warning to Japan: See Hull, II: 1017–19. Hull had remained in Washington during the Atlantic Conference.

250–51 The FDR-Nomura conv., Aug. 17: *FRJ*, II: 554–59 (Hull was also present); *FR 1941*, IV: 378–80; Gaimushō, *NBKK*, 166–80, 182–83 ("*saru Kinyōbi*" is a mistake for "*saru Nichiyōbi*"), 260–61; Nomura, 92–96, and "Diary," Aug. 17–19; *PHA*, XI: 5410, XV: 1682–88, and XVII: 2749–56; Konoye, 108–10 (*PHA*, XX: 4001).

251 A diplomatically phrased admonition: The so-called warning to Japan (*FRJ*, II: 556–57) was in no sense an "ultimatum"—Hull's use of this word during a conversation with the British chargé d'affaires on Aug. 30 (*FR 1941*, IV: 410) to the contrary notwithstanding.

251 An idea Nomura had already laid before Hull, Aug. 8 and 16: *FRJ*, II: 550–54; Gaimushō, *NBKK*, 149–50, 152–53, 164–66; Nomura, 87–88, 90–91, and "Diary," Aug. 8 and 16. The sources are not entirely in agreement here.

The concluding paragraph of the second of the two "Oral Statements" FDR handed to Nomura on Aug. 17 (*FRJ*, II: 557–59) had originally been written with the Konoye overture in mind, but all specific references to the possibility of a "summit meeting" between the President and the Premier were subsequently deleted. In the following quotation, the italicized words enclosed by brackets are the ones that were eliminated: "In case the Japanese Government feels that Japan desires and is in position to suspend its expansionist activities, to readjust its position, and to embark upon a peaceful program for the Pacific along the lines of the program and principles to which the United States is committed, the Government of the United States would be prepared to consider resumption of the informal exploratory discussions which were interrupted in July and [*the President of the United States*] would be glad to endeavor to arrange a suitable time and place [*which would be mutually convenient to meet the Japanese Premier and*] to exchange views [*with him*]. The Government of the United States, however, feels that, in view of the circumstances attending the interruption of the informal conversations between the two Governments, it would be helpful to both Governments, before undertaking a resumption of such conversations or proceeding with plans [*for any arrangements*] for a meeting [*between the President and the Japanese Premier*], if the Japanese Government would be so good as to furnish a clearer statement than has yet been furnished as to its present attitude and plans, just as this Government has repeatedly outlined to the Japanese Government its attitude and plans." FW and JMD papers. In this connection, see also Gaimushō, *NBKK*, 167, 176–77; *PHA*, XV: 1686–87, and XVII: 2771; and Nomura, "Diary," Aug. 20–21.

251 The President's preference for Juneau: See *FRJ*, II: 571–72; and Gaimushō, *NBKK*, 167. Nomura kept giving the impression in Washington that the choice of a meeting site was a matter of secondary importance, but this was not the way Konoye and Toyoda felt about the matter. See Gaimushō, *NBKK*, 198, 213, 215; *PHA*, XII: 22, and XVII: 2795, 2798; and *FRJ*, II: 588–89.

251 A marathon diplomatic minuet: The story of *official* Japanese efforts to persuade the American Govt. that a Konoye-Roosevelt meeting should be held can be found in the following: Feis, 248–81; Langer and Gleason, 693–731; Heinrichs, 336–54. The Japanese decision-making context in which the proposal for the meeting was put forward is described in Butow, *Tojo*, 234–61.

251 The State Dept.'s desire for a prior agreement in principle: See Hull, II: 1020–34; *FR 1941*, IV: 384–87, 398–99, 403–5, 412–16, 419; and *FRJ*, II: 576–79. Also Hornbeck and Ballantine intvs. In reciting the reasons why the Dept. had taken this position in 1941, SKH added this thought in 1963: "And we also knew our own President, and we knew Konoye."

251 Nomura had warned Toyoda: This was following the Ambassador's conversation with Hull on Aug. 8. Thereafter Nomura had continued to report in a pessimistic vein. At one point he had ventured to suggest that the personal appearance at Honolulu of even Konoye himself would not be enough to influence the American authorities. Still later, Nomura had forcefully told his govt. that the survival of Japan was at stake. He had pleaded for a heroic decision in favor of a détente that would rescue the Japanese nation from the plight in which it found itself. Gaimushō, *NBKK*, 152–53, 156–57, 163–64, 180–82; *PHA*, XII: 14–15, 17–18.

251 Toyoda to Grew, Aug. 18: See *FRJ*, II: 559–65. Also *FR 1941*, IV: 378, 381,

382–83, 384–87; Grew, *Ten Years,* 416–21; Gaimushō, *NBKK,* 183; PHA, XVII: 2770.

252 Hull-Nomura conv., Aug. 23: *FRJ,* II: 568. Also *ibid.,* 565–67; Hull, II: 1020–21; Nomura, 98–99, and "Diary," Aug. 23; *PHA,* XVII: 2772–73. Nomura took Hull's remark about the Neutrality Pact in good part, laughing very heartily at the Secretary's comment.

252 Missions to Moscow: U.S. Dept. of State, *Bulletin,* V, 124 (Nov. 8, 1941): 364–67; Hull, II: 974–81. On Aug. 26 the White House announced that a similar mission, to be headed by Brig. Gen. John Magruder, would be sent to China. U.S. Dept. of State, *Bulletin,* V, 114 (Aug. 30, 1941): 166.

252 Japanese resentment over American oil shipments to the Soviet Union via Vladivostok: See *FRJ,* II: 566–70; *PHA,* XII: 21; *FR 1941,* IV: 397–98, 400–403, 406–7, 425; Hull, II: 1020–21; *NYT,* Aug. 8: 4, Aug. 12: 4, Aug. 13: 7, Aug. 20: 11, Aug. 22: 3, Aug. 26: 10, Aug. 27: 1, Aug. 28: 1, 3, and 18 (edit.), and Aug. 29: 16 (edit.); *Newsweek,* Aug. 25: 16; and *Life,* Sept. 15: 36. Ribbentrop and Ott tried to take advantage of the situation. See *DGFP,* D.XIII: 351–52, 377–78.

252 A very caustic Secretary of State: See *FRJ,* II: 570. Also *ibid.,* 569, 572; *FR 1941,* IV: 400, 402, 406–7, 429–30, 442–43; Hull papers, Correspondence (1940–41), Folder 146, Green H. Hackworth memo, Aug. 21.

253 Nomura gave Hull a copy of a "Message" from Konoye to Roosevelt: There are some discrepancies in the sources, but Nomura saw Hull at least twice on Aug. 27, and possibly three times. In delivering the English text of Konoye's "Message," Nomura referred to a so-called Statement from the govt. of Japan that was supposed to be handed over in conjunction with the Premier's communication. Since the translation of this "Statement" had not yet been completed, the Ambassador summarized the main points orally. He subsequently called on Hull again, this time with the written text. See *FRJ,* II: 569–71, 572–75; Nomura, 99–100, and "Diary," Aug. 27; and Gaimushō, *NBKK,* 209–10.

253 Hull's view of Konoye's "Message" and of the accompanying "Statement": Hull, II: 1021.

253 The maximum in concessions: *FRJ,* II: 571.

253 The emphasis Tokyo had consistently placed on the need for secrecy: See Gaimushō, *NBKK,* 149–50; *PHA,* XII: 12–13; *FRJ,* II: 560, 569; and *FR 1941,* IV: 381, 382.

253 Nomura to the press (at the White House), Aug. 28: *NYT,* Aug. 29: 1; *NYHT,* Aug. 29: 1.

253 The authorities in Tokyo were dismayed: Nomura was reprimanded on Aug. 29. He was ordered to clear with Tokyo in the future before making any public statements. See *PHA,* XVII: 2797–99. Also *FRJ,* II: 579, 586, 609, 631–32.

254 Nomura had called upon Drought for help: The Ambassador had telephoned JMD on the night of Aug. 14 "to obtain his assistance." Nomura, "Diary," Aug. 15.

254 Drought's return to Washington: JMD papers, esp. an Aug. 15 telegram to Nomura; FW papers, "Daily Memo Calendar, 1941," and TA Log. Close liaison was maintained with the PMG during Aug. by both Nomura and Drought.

254 Drought's "Strictly Confidential" memo written as though he could speak for Nomura's superiors in Tokyo, ca. Aug. 19: JMD papers, several handwritten drafts and a typewritten text (with later changes by hand); I have altered the order of presentation for the sake of clarity. This memo was a reply to the "second" of the two "Statements" the President had handed to Nomura on Aug. 17. *FRJ*, II: 556–59. Although a comment by JMD written in the margin of a related document reveals that he knew of the existence of the other "Statement" (the President's so-called warning to Japan), Drought apparently thought that the best way to deal with this "warning" was to ignore it entirely. He did not consider it to be "the real document," and consequently said nothing about it in formulating his "response."

Drought also prepared at this time a short "Oral Memo" covering the points he wanted Nomura to make to Hull. JMD's main idea was that a prolongation of the conversations would risk "further exposure to the enemies of our peace," who would then "foment new incidents of misunderstanding." JMD papers.

254 "Program attainable by peaceful methods": JMD was here quoting from the "Statement" FDR handed Nomura on Aug. 17. See *FRJ*, II: 558.

254 "In an atmosphere of world crisis": This sentence and the two that follow it (in the quotation in the text) were repeated—almost word for word—in the "Statement" Nomura handed FDR on Aug. 28. See *ibid.*, 573, 574.

254 Nomura had not revealed to Tokyo that Drought was the author of the piece: See Gaimushō, *NBKK*, 191–97; Nomura, "Diary," Aug. 20; Konoye, 109–10 (*PHA*, XX: 4001); and *PHA*, XVII: 2759–69 (these "Magic" intercepts contain a number of translation errors). In reporting to the Foreign Office, Nomura described the "Strictly Confidential" memo as "a tentative draft, for reference purposes, prepared here," but Konoye's account, which may reflect information received later, calls it a "private plan."

254 The use made by the Foreign Office of the "Strictly Confidential" memo: The extent to which the authorities in Tokyo employed Drought's concoction as a rough draft for the "Statement" to be given to the President (along with Konoye's personal "Message") becomes apparent when the texts are compared paragraph by paragraph. There are a number of differences, but there are also some word-for-word concurrences. JMD papers, the "Strictly Confidential" memo; Gaimushō, *NBKK*, 192–97, 199–209.

254–55 The delivery by Nomura of documents that did not accurately convey what the Japanese Govt. wished to say: The Japanese texts of the Konoye "Message" (Tel. 502) and of the accompanying "Statement" (Tel. 503) are printed in Gaimushō, *NBKK*, 197–203. The translations handed to Hull and Roosevelt are in *FRJ*, II: 572–75. The part Drought played in introducing changes is revealed in several typewritten documents in the JMD papers. These are copies of the translations Obata made for the Japanese Embassy following the receipt of the two telegrams. Drought found much that he wanted to change but far more in the "Statement" than in the Premier's "Message." He even went so far as to reinsert, from his own "Strictly Confidential" memo, lines that had been eliminated in Tokyo. He also managed to garble one whole paragraph in the process of rewriting it; see *FRJ*, II: 575, the paragraph beginning "Quite properly..."

The "Statement" delivered to Hull and Roosevelt, a cleanly typed copy of Obata's translation, reflects many of the changes recommended by Drought. In addition to the Japanese original, Gaimushō, *NBKK*, has a so-called Gist (pp. 203–9)—an English translation prepared within the Foreign Office but not cabled to Nomura. The Foreign Office archives also contain another and somewhat smoother English version similar to, but not the same as, the "Gist" (several paragraphs are missing, and there are differences in terminology and word order). See LC-JFOA, WT 73, IMT 556, 828–31.

Even if Drought's alterations are ignored, this "Statement" from the Japanese Govt. provides an excellent example of what can happen in the process of translation. The two Foreign Office texts in English do not agree with each other or with Obata's version, and the largely illegible "Magic" intercept rendition (*PHA*, XVII: 2779–88)—insofar as it can be made out at all—offers still further variation.

In the case of the Konoye "Message," the Foreign Office archives contain a translation of the "Message" done in Tokyo but not cabled to Washington. LC-JFOA, WT 72, IMT 555, 324–25. When this version is compared with Obata's rendition (a copy is in the JMD papers) and with the "Magic" intercept translation (*PHA*, XVII: 2776–78), and when all three texts are compared with the Japanese original (Gaimushō, *NBKK*, 197–98), the degree to which translations can run wide of the mark becomes instantly apparent.

255 Nomura's belated admission to Tokyo, Sept. 3: The excuse he offered, in explaining why he had made changes, was that the documents were intended for a Chief of State, and consequently had to be couched accordingly. He had also been motivated, he said, by his desire to help bring about the proposed meeting between Konoye and Roosevelt. See Gaimushō, *NBKK*, 225–32. From some comparatively minor differences between the English translations handed over in Washington and those later cabled to Tokyo, it would appear that a few additional changes were introduced after Aug. 27. Another possibility is that the transmission on Sept. 3 was done from copies that did not contain all of the changes made prior to Aug. 27. Careless handling, at either end, could also have been a factor.

An incorrect translation by "Magic" (*PHA*, XII: 20) of the concluding sentence of Toyoda's 504 (Gaimushō, *NBKK*, 209) misled Langer and Gleason, 701 n19, into believing that Toyoda had given Nomura permission to use his discretion in the wording of the "Statement" from the Japanese Govt. This is not the case. Konoye, 125, notes that the question of recalling Nomura was discussed as a result of the confusion the Ambassador had caused through what Konoye decribes as "mistakes in translation" made in the text of the "Statement."

255–56 The possibility that Nomura leaked the news of the Konoye "Message" to the press because Drought had advised him to do so: Such an interpretation would explain Nomura's willingness to break the secrecy that Tokyo wished to maintain, that he himself had earlier recommended (Gaimushō, *NBKK*, 182–83; *PHA*, XVII, 2755–56), and that even Drought had generally urged.

In attempting to reconstruct what happened on Aug. 28, I have drawn on the following material: *NYT*, Aug. 29: 1; *NYHT*, Aug. 29: 1; *FRJ*, II: 579–83, 586–87, 592; *FR 1941*, IV: 407, 409; Konoye, 118 (*PHA*, XX: 4004); Nomura, "Diary," Aug. 28 and 30; Grew papers, "Diary," Aug. 1941: 5532; *PHA*, XII: 25, and XVII: 2796–99; Gaimushō, *NBKK*, 232–33.

256 "It seems ironical": Grew papers, "Diary," for Aug. 1941 ("introductory summary"): 5504–5. Also *FRJ*, II: 580.

256 "Hull's statement in press conference": *FRJ*, II: 582–83.

256–57 The Fleisher scoop and the reaction from the White House: *NYHT*, Sept. 3 and 4: 1; *NYT*, Sept. 3: 12, Sept. 4: 8. See also *FRJ*, II: 586; and *PHA*, XII: 25. Grew, *Ten Years*, 445, notes there was a wartime rumor to the effect that the Japanese had planned to kidnap the President while he was meeting with Konoye on board a Japanese battleship.

257 Hull was noncommittal: See *NYT*, Aug. 31: 14.

257 "No information" (according to the Japanese Embassy): *NYHT*, Sept. 4: 2.

257 His Imperial Majesty's Govt. belittled Fleisher's account: *NYT*, Sept. 4: 8.

257–58 What was actually occurring (i.e., the news from the Far East): *NYT*, Aug. 29: 5, Sept. 1: 8; *NYHT*, Aug. 29: 1, 5.

258 An editorial read and clipped by Drought: JMD papers, *NYHT* edit., Aug. 29.

258 Newspapers in Japan were currently praising the Premier: *NYT*, Aug. 29: 5.

258 "It would be the height of folly": *NYT*, Sept. 2: 1; Tolischus, 241–42. Also *NYHT*, Sept. 7: Sect. 2: 1; Gaimushō, *NBKK*, 325–26; *PHA*, XII: 47.

258 Konoye's call for a total mobilization of the country's resources, and the views of other, more "positive-minded" Japanese: *NYHT*, Sept. 4: 1. Also *NYT*, Sept. 3 and 4: 1.

258–59 An editorial reaction to the news from the Far East: *NYT*, Sept. 4: 20 ("Power in the East").

259 New evidence concerning the mood in Japan: See *NYHT*, Sept. 7: Sect. 2: 1.

259 The testing of Yamamoto's plan: See Wohlstetter, 370–71. The table-top test, to which this refers, was conducted during "war games" held between Sept. 2 and Sept. 13.

259–60 Iwakuro's activities following his return to Japan in mid-August, and his departure for Indochina: Iwakuro intv. and ms., 239–310, esp. 289–310. Also Wikawa, 26; Konoye, 110 (*PHA*, XX: 4001, gives a misleading impression because of errors in translation).

259 Officers of rank seemed impervious: A former colonel, writing after the war, has described the atmosphere prevailing among his colleagues in Tokyo in 1941: "The military had a strong tendency to disbelieve—and to treat as astronomical—official United States Government data indicating the rate of production of American industry. In addition, they made light of America's spiritual fiber. The majority believed that the United States would find it difficult to instill a martial spirit throughout the nation as a whole. After all, isolationism was rampant there, and most of the advocates were influential figures. The Army High Command's outlook upon the international situation was therefore remarkable for its tendency to overestimate Germany and to underestimate other countries." Hayashi, 23. Shigemitsu's experiences after returning to Tokyo in the summer of 1941 from his ambassadorial post in London are also instructive. *Japan and Her Destiny*, 238–40; *Shōwa no Dōran*, II: 84–88.

260–63 Walsh in western Japan, the arrival of Wikawa on the scene, and the Bishop's decision "to perform this little function": Walsh papers, "Visitation

Diary—1941" (supplemented by two related items: "Kyoto Visitation—1941" and "Heijo Visitation—1941"), a Sept. 25 letter from Walsh to JMD, Walsh's "Confidential Memorandum" of Dec. 11, 1945, his report to the 1946 Chapter, and his Sept. 15, 1971, account of the "peace treaty negotiations." Also Dooman corresp.; IMTFE, 32976–91 (Walsh's affidavit on behalf of Mutō); Wikawa, 26; Butow, *Tojo*, 310–11.

260 Walsh to Walker, Aug. 22: FW papers. That same day Walsh also cabled Drought: "Wired Frank. Please cooperate for immediate action. Regards [from] Paul." JMD papers.

261 "If a man were to make a practice": Walsh papers, "Visitation Diary—1941," Sept. 11.

261 The information Wikawa obtained "from higher up": The Bishop was under the impression that the messages he was transmitting came from the Cabinet, from the Premier, or from both. JMD papers, a Sept. 25 letter from Walsh.

261 Walsh to Walker, Aug. 28: FW papers. I am indebted to Fr. Coleman for elucidation of the phrase, "Gog and Magog, Tyre and Sidon," and for help with other "curiosities" in the messages exchanged between Walsh and Drought in the autumn of 1941.

261 Walsh to Drought, Aug. 29: JMD papers. Whenever possible, I have used the date of dispatch, but on occasion (as in this case) only the time of arrival can be determined. Often the two dates are the same. I have corrected several minor transmission or typing errors in this message.

261–62 Walsh to Hull, Aug. 29; State 711.94/2244-10/11. This message apparently reached Hull at the Wardman Park on Aug. 30; he passed it along to the Division of Far Eastern Affairs.

262 Drought to Walsh, Aug. 29: JMD papers.

262 Walsh to Drought, Aug. 31: *Ibid.* I have corrected a transmission error, changing "circumlocation" to "circumlocution," a word Walsh used again in a Sept. 23 telegram to JMD.

262 Walsh to Walker, Sept. 3: FW papers. On Nov. 10, Hull wrote to Walker: "I return with thanks the telegram to you from Father [sic] Walsh which I read with real interest."

263 The thoughts and activities of Drought, late Aug.–early Sept: JMD papers.

Hope of a Successful Issue Fades

264–65 The identification of Drought as the man who originated the idea of a Konoye-Roosevelt meeting: Reference has been made elsewhere in the text to Drought's promotion of the "plenipotentiary [or bilateral] conference" concept, but see Butow, "Backdoor Diplomacy," 48–59.

265–66 The position taken by Hornbeck, mid-Aug.–early Sept.: *FR 1941*, IV: 365–70, 384–88, 398–99, 412–16, 419 (for an earlier version of this memo, see State 740.0011-P.W./8-2941), 425–28. For the remarks in the text (in the order quoted), see *FR 1941*, IV: 365, 414, 388, 412, 419, 426, and 387. Also SKH papers, Box 254, Folder "Japan–United States Relations," memoranda dated Aug. 29, Sept. 30, 1941, and Mar. 29, 1943 (with an Apr. 1 chit addressed to Hull).

266 The views held by Ballantine, Aug. 28: *Ibid.*, 403–5 (for later submissions, see 428–29, 458, 470–75, 478–80).

266 Hamilton was unable to offer any encouragement: See *ibid.*, 449–50.

266 FDR's query to Nomura about a possible move into Thailand, Aug. 28: Nomura reported this remark to Tokyo, but there is no mention of it in Hull's memo of the conversation. Gaimushō, *NBKK*, 213; *FRJ*, II: 571–72. The President was moved to speak in this way after reading the following sentence in one of the communications handed to him that day by Nomura: "In an atmosphere of world crisis and international confusion, it is sometimes difficult to ascertain when an event is a cause and when it is a consequence." This sentence had evolved from one written by Drought (see text p. 254), but the authorities in the Foreign Office did not know this. In deciding to use the "cause or consequence" sentence in their response to FDR, they added a line of their own, which was ultimately rendered into English as "A judgment based upon only a certain set of facts is dangerous, and may do great harm to the cause of permanent peace." The President never saw this sentence, however, because Drought crossed it out of the translation prepared at the Japanese Embassy in Washington.

266 *A prior agreement in principle*, Aug. 28: *FRJ*, II: 576–77. Hull repeated this position on Sept. 1. *Ibid.*, 584.

266–67 The FDR-Nomura meeting, Sept. 3, and the communications handed to the Ambassador: *Ibid.*, 347, 588–92, 600–601. Also Hull, II: 1023–26; Gaimushō, *NBKK*, 232–42 (the English texts printed in this source contain some errors); Nomura, 111–15, and "Diary," Sept. 3; *FR 1941*, IV: 423–25 (Hull to Grew). Hull's Four Principles were reiterated on Oct. 2 and Nov. 26. *FRJ*, II: 658, 768.

267 A prior meeting of minds on basic principles: In other words, the President had accepted the State Dept.'s position in regard to the proposed tête-à-tête with Konoye. This position was essentially the same as the one taken by the Japanese Govt. in May 1941. Japan's idea at that time had been an agreement first, then perhaps a conference. See text p. 185.

267 "The Japanese Government wishes to state": See *FRJ*, II: 575, 592.

267 The draft submitted by Nomura on Sept. 4 without the knowledge of his govt.: See *ibid.*, 595, 600, 610–13, 615, 621, 626, 665; Hull, II: 1030; Nomura, 116, and "Diary," Sept. 4; and *FR 1941*, IV: 436, 535–36. Also Grew, *Ten Years*, 442. The authorities in Tokyo apparently first learned of Nomura's unauthorized draft as a result of questions raised in a "Statement" handed to Toyoda by Grew on Sept. 10. See *FRJ*, II: 610–13, 626; Gaimushō, *NBKK*, 324–26; and *PHA*, XII: 46. While talking with several officers of the State Dept. on the tenth, Obata revealed "that the document which Ambassador Nomura had given the Secretary on September 4 represented merely the Ambassador's personal views and had not been referred to the Japanese Government and therefore did not represent, necessarily, the views of the Japanese Government." *FRJ*, II: 615.

267 A variety of unnecessary and time-consuming difficulties: See *FRJ*, II: 610–13, 614–15, 626, 665; and *FR 1941*, IV: 433–34.

268 Toyoda to Grew, Sept. 4, and Nomura to Hull, Sept. 6: *FRJ*, II: 348–49, 593–95, 606–7, 608–9 (the English text of the draft proposal Nomura handed Hull on Sept. 6); Gaimushō, *Shuyō Bunsho*, II: 545–46 (the Japanese text), and *NBKK*, 242–47, 248–50, 274–75; Hull, II: 1027–29; Nomura, 116–17, and Furoku 16, 117–21; Nomura, "Diary," Sept. 6; *PHA*, XII: 25–26.

268 Konoye's refusal to receive any members of the diplomatic corps during Matsuoka's junket to Europe: In the spring of 1941, Grew had wanted to talk with Konoye prior to Matsuoka's return in order to review the conversations Nomura had been having in Washington and to discuss the U.S. attitude toward developments in the Far East, especially Japan's southward advance. But when Grew had asked for an appointment, Konoye had demurred. His reasoning was that he did not want to confer with any members of the diplomatic corps during Matsuoka's absence, for if one chief of mission were received others would have to be accorded the same privilege. On the whole, Grew thought that Konoye, with his heavy duties as Premier, was justified in taking such a stand, but Grew was also very much aware of the contrast between Konoye's response and Roosevelt's far more accommodating approach: the President had opened the door of the White House to the Japanese Ambassador and had expressed a willingness to talk with Nomura at any time. *FR 1941*, IV: 129–30, 139; Grew papers, "Diary," Apr. 1941: 4986, and "letters," CXI, Grew to Shigeharu (Jūji) Matsumoto, Apr. 10.

Konoye had also avoided a meeting with Grew in early July, when the Ambassador wished to deliver a communication from the President addressed to the Premier. See text pp. 218–19.

Konoye's sudden desire to talk with Grew over dinner on Sept. 6 was thus not only a fundamental departure from the Premier's earlier practice but also an indication of how critical matters had become. Prior to sitting down with the Ambassador that evening, Konoye had participated in a conference held in the presence of the Emperor at which the following decision was confirmed as the policy Japan would now secretly pursue: "If, by the early part of October, there is still no prospect of being able to attain our demands [through diplomacy], we shall immediately decide to open hostilities against the United States, Great Britain, and the Netherlands." See Butow, *Tojo*, 241–61, esp. 249–50, 253–59. Also Ike, 129–63; *TSM, Bekkan*, 507–23; Gaimushō, *NBKK*, 255–62.

268–69 Konoye's Sept. 6 endorsement of the Four Principles (according to Grew): *FRJ*, II: 604–6. Also Butow, *Tojo*, 259–61; Hull, II: 1029; Grew papers, "Diary," Sept. 1941: 5643. Tomohiko Ushiba and Eugene Dooman were also present; they served as interpreters for the principals, neither of whom could speak the other's language.

269 The reaction of Hull and his advisers: Hull, II: 1028–31; *FR 1941*, IV: 428–29 (Ballantine memo), 432–34; *FRJ*, II: 348–51. *FR 1941*, IV: 428 n95, incorrectly refers the reader to *FRJ*, II: 597, where he will find the unauthorized document that Nomura submitted on his own on Sept. 4 and later withdrew. Ballantine's memo is not concerned with that document. It deals instead with "the new Japanese proposal"—i.e., with the document Toyoda handed Grew on Sept. 4. See *FRJ*, II: 593–94. This was received in Washington on Sept. 5. Hull, II: 1027. The text cabled by Grew was a "closely paraphrased" version of the text the Foreign Minister had handed to the Ambassador. *FRJ*, II: 593. On Sept. 6 Nomura gave Hull a copy of this same proposal, though with variations in the wording of the text. *Ibid.*, 608–9. In writing his memo on Sept. 5, Ballantine used the paraphrased text that had been received that very day from Grew. This explains why the phrases in quotation marks (*FR 1941*, IV: 428–29) do not agree, word for word, with the cor-

responding phrases in the document printed in *FRJ*, II: 608–9 (the text delivered by Nomura on Sept. 6).

269 The Foreign Minister adopted a new procedure: Soon after taking over from Matsuoka, Toyoda began relying on Grew to an ever-larger extent. Toyoda may have thought that the Ambassador would be a sympathetic advocate in pleading Japan's case with the American Govt. Toyoda may also have hoped that by using Grew in Tokyo the Foreign Office would be able to offset any mistakes Nomura might make in Washington. See *FRJ*, II: 602, 614, 667; *FR 1941*, IV: 434; Hull, II: 1030; and Grew, *Ten Years*, 442–43.

269 "Owing to the necessity for paraphrasing": Hull, II: 1030.

269–70 "Regions lying south of Japan" vs. regions lying to the *north*: The guarantee, as quoted in the text, was handed to Hull by Nomura on Sept. 6. See *ibid.*; and *FRJ*, II: 608. The Japanese original is in Gaimushō, *NBKK*, 246: "*Futsu-In wo kichi to shite kinsetsu chiiki ni buryoku-teki shinshutsu wo nasazu. Hoppō ni tai-shitemo dōyō yue-naku buryoku-teki shinshutsu wo nasazu.*" This was translated by the Foreign Office as "Japan will not make any military advancement from French Indochina against any of its adjoining areas, and likewise will not, without any justifiable reason, resort to military action against any regions lying north to [*sic*] Japan." *Ibid.*, 244.

The Foreign Office would normally have cabled the Japanese text to Nomura. This would then have been translated into English at the Embassy for submission to the American Govt. In this instance, however, that procedure was not followed—presumably because the Foreign Office had in the meantime learned that Nomura had made unauthorized changes in the documents he had delivered to the President on Aug. 28. Toyoda did not want to run the risk of having this happen again, and so he handed a copy of his new "Draft Proposal" to Grew for transmission to Washington. Toyoda then sent the text to Nomura—*in English* rather than in Japanese. *Ibid.*, 244–46.

The precautions taken by the Foreign Minister did not prove effective. The Japanese Embassy in Washington transformed Tokyo's awkward phrase, "regions lying north to Japan," into "regions lying south of Japan." Why? Presumably because someone decided that the curious combination of words, "regions lying north to Japan," must refer *to the area between French Indochina and Japan*—in other words, to the area "south of Japan."

The phrase "*hoppō ni*" in the Japanese text means something entirely different, however. It is, in fact, a reference to the area "to the north" of Japan—in other words, a reference to the Soviet Far East.

269 Hull and his advisers sought clarification: Ballantine called the north-south discrepancy to the attention of Nomura and Obata on Sept. 10. He also requested clarification regarding the applicability, territorially speaking, of the qualifying phrase "without any justifiable reason" (the Japanese wording was *yue-naku*, which literally means "without having a reason to do so," and consequently, by extension, "without provocation"). *FRJ*, II: 615–16. The discussion then turned to other points that the American Govt. felt were unclear. A number of these matters were brought to Tokyo's attention in Nomura's 804 of Sept. 10, including the question Ballantine had raised regarding the phrase "without any justifiable reason," but Nomura did not refer in his telegram to the north-south discrepancy. Gaimushō, *NBKK*, 264–65. *(continued)*

The authorities in Tokyo subsequently had some "second thoughts" about the undertaking not to go north. As a consequence, it was not included in the new proposals presented to the American Govt. toward the end of Sept.— proposals that superseded all earlier submissions. In this way Tokyo reduced its commitment to the areas adjacent to French Indochina ("excluding China"). *FRJ*, II: 640; Ike, 173–76; *TSM, Bekkan*, 525–26.

270 The conflicting views of Hull and Toyoda regarding the scope of the proposals (narrower vs. wider) being offered: See *FR 1941*, IV: 432–34; *FRJ*, II: 613–14, 631; and Gaimushō, *NBKK*, 275.

270 A cloud of threatening developments, Sept. 1941: Hull, II: 1031. Also *FR 1941*, IV: 441–42, 450–51.

270 A "psychology of desperation" within Japan: *FR 1941*, IV: 397–98 (this report was cabled to the Dept. on Aug. 27).

270–71 Japanese preparations for war (as reported by Grew on Aug. 29): *Ibid.*, 408–9.

271 The concern felt by Toyoda: *Ibid.*, 409; *FRJ*, II: 579–82.

271 The way Grew and Dooman interpreted the proposal for a Konoye-Roosevelt meeting: Following the Cabinet change in July 1941, both men had become more actively engaged in the conversations with Japan than they had previously been, but they were not satisfied with the way things were going. The Ambassador—perhaps under Dooman's influence—had become discouraged over what he regarded as "little or no reaction from Washington by way of comment" on his periodic reports. He was later to compare his experience in this regard to throwing pebbles into a lake at night—he was not permitted to see even the ripples. The Ambassador also had the feeling (unjustified it now appears) that he was not being kept fully informed by the State Dept. At least until the end of Aug., however, Grew had remained basically "in accord with the general course and measures of the Administration" as it had endeavored to cope with one Japanese development after another. In fact, he had frequently written and spoken of his "great pride" in his government's conduct of America's foreign affairs. The parting of the ways began when the Ambassador realized that the President might not meet with Konoye. If Grew and Dooman had known about the John Doe origins of the conference proposal, however, they might have been less inclined to believe that any good could come from the scheme. See Grew, *Turbulent Era*, II: 1272–76; Heinrichs, 340; and Butow, "Backdoor Diplomacy," 62–65.

271 Grew had assured Toyoda, Aug. 18: Grew, *Ten Years*, 417; *FRJ*, II: 564.

271 Grew's initial telegrams to the State Dept. concerning the proposed Konoye-Roosevelt meeting: *FR 1941*, IV: 378, 382–83; *FRJ*, II: 565. The views expressed by Grew were given a very cold reception by Hornbeck. *FR 1941*, IV: 384–87. Also SKH papers, Box "Autobiography mss 2," Folder "Autobiography 1941."

271 Grew's awareness of the "grave dangers" involved (as of Sept. 17): *FRJ*, II: 625.

271–72 Grew's advice to the State Dept. as Sept. progressed: *FR 1941*, IV: 463–64, 483–89. Also Grew papers, "Diary," supplement for Sept. 1941: 5743; *FRJ*, II: 645–50; Grew, *Ten Years*, 436–46. Grew endeavored to make a distinction between "constructive conciliation" and "appeasement." See Grew, *Ten Years*, 445–46, and *Turbulent Era*, II: 1267–68, 1270. Also Grew papers, "Diary," Sept. and Oct. 1941: 5790–96, 5838.

272 The American Govt. was told: I am referring here to an "Oral Statement" conveyed to Dooman by Tarō Terasaki on Sept. 23 and cabled by the Foreign Office to Nomura that same day. *FRJ*, II: 634, 640–41; *FR 1941*, IV: 476–77; Gaimushō, *NBKK*, 298–99. The phrases quoted in the text are from a "tentative translation" (*FRJ*, II: 641) supplemented by the Japanese original (Gaimushō, *NBKK*, 299). See also *FR 1941*, IV: 477.

Although Nomura had been instructed to bring the "Statement" to Hull's attention at once, the Ambassador refrained from doing so for four days while he waited for the arrival of a telegram of clarification from Tokyo that he hoped would make the "Statement" more palatable to the American Govt. Nomura, "Diary," Sept. 24. In the meantime Hull had received substantially the same text from Grew, whose Sept. 23 cable contained a transcription of the full notes taken by Dooman during the interview with Terasaki. *FR 1941*, IV: 476–77.

272–73 The Japanese Govt. went even further, Sept. 23: The quotation in the text is from *FRJ*, II: 641, but see also *FR 1941*, IV: 477: "The idea of maintaining internal order in China by the stationing of international forces is not agreeable to Japan in view of the present trend of Japanese public opinion and of the fact that Japan is directly and most vitally affected by the maintenance of order in China." Although the phrasing employed in these renditions is awkward in places, both translations conveyed the substance of the Japanese original: *"Kokusai guntai ni yoru chian iji-an no gotoki wa Nihon yoron oyobi Shina no chian ni chokusetsu katsu 'vaitarī' ni kankei suru Nihon to shite wa judaku shi ezu."* Gaimushō, *NBKK*, 299.

After leaving Japan in Oct., Bp. Walsh had this to say: "I tried very hard to get the Japanese to agree unofficially to something short of actual occupation [of North China] by their troops for an indefinite period. I proposed a time limit, but they demurred. I proposed a Chinese corps directed by Japanese officers, but they again demurred. I proposed the creation of an international police force, but I was informed that they had already anticipated this suggestion and ruled it out as impractical." See *FR 1941*, IV: 536–37.

273 A document Tokyo had prepared "for the convenience of the American Government": This Japanese redraft to the American proposal of June 21 was given to Grew on Sept. 25 and to Ballantine (acting for Hull) on Sept. 27. See *FRJ*, II: 636–41; Hull, II: 1032; State 711.94/2344-90/95; Gaimushō, *NBKK*, 300–314, 318–23; *PHA*, XII, 36–39, 42–44; *FR 1941*, IV: 481–82 (481 n70 is incorrect; the cross-reference should be to *FRJ*, II: 608–9), 490–91; Ike, 173–76; and *TSM, Bekkan,* 525–26. The following statement was made in the name of the Japanese Ambassador when this document was delivered to the State Dept. on Sept. 27: "Decoded and slightly edited at this Embassy, the present text of the document may not agree exactly with the one transmitted directly to the State Department from the American Embassy in Tokyo, though it is not believed there can be between the two any important differences in substance." *FRJ*, II: 636.

273 "We have already said": Sadao Iguchi to Tarō Terasaki. I was unable to find the Japanese original (Tel. 870, Sept. 29), but the "Magic" intercept is printed in *PHA*, XII: 41–42 (see 45–48 for the "Magic" version of the reply Tokyo sent on Oct. 1; the Japanese text of this reply is in Gaimushō, *NBKK*, 324–26). Iguchi's message also contained this report: "Father Drught [*sic*] advises us that a friend of his in Tokyo (probably Walsh) reports that Japa-

nese governmental circles feel that there is absolutely no reason why the United States should not accept the most recent proposals. The fact that she has not done so, must be due to interference from some Washington source, Walsh cables."

273 The contact maintained with Walker: FW papers, TA Log.

273 Several telegrams that were difficult to decipher: JMD papers, Walsh to Drought, Sept. 8 and 9.

274 "Wire back fixed dates," Sept. 11: JMD papers. I have corrected several transmission errors and have been guided, in my interpretation of this message, by some marginal notes on the copy at Maryknoll.

274 "World is too large," Sept. 13: FW papers and State 711.94/2344-11/25. This message, which was signed "Paul [and] Walsh," reached Walker on Sept. 15. The PMG sent a copy to Hull the next day for his "information." I have corrected one transmission error.

274 "Have Joe [Grew] instructed": JMD papers, a night letter dispatched from Japan on Sept. 20.

274–75 Walsh's visit to the American Embassy, Sept. 21: FR *1941*, IV: 467; Walsh papers, "Visitation Diary—1941," Sept. 21. Grew's report to the Dept. did not identify Walsh as the source of the "news" or indicate that the visitor had talked with Dooman, but these details are in the Grew papers, "Diary," supplement for Sept. 1941: 5749. See also Grew's Despatch 5924, Oct. 17, which was not received by the State Dept. until Mar. 31, 1942 (State 711.94/2624), and Despatch 6018, Feb. 19, 1942, which was not filed until after the Ambassador's repatriation (a copy can be found in the Grew papers).

275 Walsh's "swan song" night letter to Drought, Sept. 21: JMD papers; Coleman corresp. The Sept. 21 entry in the Bishop's "Visitation Diary" notes that he spent a "halcyon day" in Tokyo but returned to Kamakura that evening "to waft swan song, parting shot, and last will and testament at James and Francis." Walsh papers. Walsh normally referred to Walker as "Frank," but in this instance (and in a night letter sent two days later) the Bishop employed "Francis" instead.

275 "All even remotely concerned": After his return from Japan in Nov. 1941, Walsh added some marginal notes to the text of this message. His notation for the phrase quoted here reads "including U.S. Embassy."

275 Walsh on Wikawa's "swan song": Walsh papers, "Visitation Diary—1941," Sept. 22. On Oct. 1, Wikawa sent a postcard to Drought reading "Oh! How I wish I could give a punch to those fellows that only try to [save] their own face and not humanity from destruction." JMD papers.

275 The Walsh-Dooman exchanges, Sept. 24: Grew papers, "Diary," supplement for Sept. 1941: 5761–63, and Despatch 6018, Feb. 19, 1942. Also State 711.94/2624; and Walsh papers, "Visitation Diary—1941": "Day in Tokyo—working hard, running in circles, and accomplishing probably nothing. . . . Saw final answer to great puzzle, which seemed to me quite good, and considerably raised my hopes."

276 "I am satisfied with our little people here," Sept. 25: JMD papers. This letter was carried to the U.S. by a member of Grew's staff who was returning home.

276 "As for me": Hull, II: 1025.

276 FDR to Hull, Sept. 28: FR *1941*, IV: 483; FDR papers, PSF, Box 11; *PHA*, XX: 4423–27. Also *FRJ*, II: 351–53; Hull, II: 1023–26, 1035–37.

276 Hull-Nomura meeting, Oct. 2, and the American "Oral Statement" of that date: Hull, II: 1033; *FRJ*, II: 353–56, 654–61; *FR 1941*, IV: 494–97; Gaimushō, *NBKK*, 326–41; Nomura, 125–29, and "Diary," Oct. 2; *PHA*, XII: 50. At one point in the conversation the Ambassador did not appear to understand Hull's remarks, and so Ballantine repeated what the Secretary had said in Japanese.

276 "An agreement that would speak for itself": *FRJ*, II: 655. Hull was reiterating a position he had expressed during a meeting with Nomura on June 6. *Ibid.*, 466. The same point had been made by the President in his Sept. 3 communication to Konoye. *Ibid.*, 592.

276–77 Ushiba advised Dooman, Oct. 7: *Ibid.*, 662–63; *FR 1941*, IV: 500–501 (see also 508–9, 527–28). Foreign Minister Toyoda and Tarō Terasaki, the chief of the American Bureau of the Foreign Office, thought the American Govt. had taken great pains not to specify what it wanted the Japanese Govt. to do. They sought elucidation from Grew and Dooman but learned virtually nothing. The Ambassador insisted that the State Dept.'s communication of Oct. 2 was "friendly in tone and helpful in substance"; it indicated "a clear desire . . . to make progress in the conversations." *FRJ*, II: 663–69. Also *FR 1941*, IV: 501 n97; Gaimushō, *NBKK*, 348–50.

It is quite understandable that officials in Tokyo were dismayed by Hull's "Oral Statement." Upon seeing what it contained, they suddenly realized that their earlier optimism, to which Nomura and the John Doe Associates had greatly contributed through inaccurate reporting and fanciful suggestions, was completely unwarranted.

277–78 The Toyoda-Grew conv., Oct. 7: *FRJ*, II: 350, 663–65; Gaimushō, *NBKK*, 348–50; *PHA*, XII: 54–56; Grew, *Turbulent Era*, II: 1330–32. Prior to this conversation, a briefing document (an undated "Oral Statement"-type of communication in English) was prepared within the Foreign Office for Toyoda's use. See LC-JFOA, WT 72, IMT 555, 480–83. According to this document, Ambassador Nomura—on more than one occasion—had modified "at his own discretion" the instructions he had received from Tokyo. As a consequence, the real intentions of the Japanese Govt. had not been accurately conveyed to the American Govt. In one instance, Nomura had delivered a note containing phraseology—in English—that was not to be found in the Japanese text. As a result, Washington had falsely concluded that Tokyo was in full agreement with the basic principles to which the U.S. had long been committed. This misunderstanding had in turn caused the American Govt. to state, on Oct. 2, that the Japanese Govt., while accepting the principles of the U.S. without qualification in Aug., had subsequently narrowed down the said principles in its later proposals. It was clear, however, that this situation had arisen because Nomura had altered the intructions of the Japanese Govt.

Although the Foreign Office now knew that this had occurred, Nomura was not to be blamed. The officials in Tokyo believed that he had "resorted to such a proceeding out of his eagerness to consummate promptly the readjustment of . . . relations between Japan and the United States." In spite of the "clerical mistakes" Nomura had made, the Japanese Govt. professed to be "rather appreciative of [his] sincere effort" to maintain and improve relations between the two countries.

The briefing document summarized above appears to have been the basis for the remarks Toyoda made to Grew on Oct. 7 (esp. in regard to the Konoye-Grew meeting of Sept. 6), but the Foreign Minister apparently did not elaborate on Nomura's unorthodox handling of his responsibilities; at least, there is hardly anything on this subject in Grew's memo of his conversation with Toyoda on Oct. 7.

277 Konoye had accepted the Hull program "in principle": In the briefing document summarized above, the following passage, couched in the form of a statement in English to be made by Toyoda to Grew, is pertinent: "As Your Excellency is aware, the [Premier] subscribed to these principles simply in principle; and he tried to make clear that, as there should be expected various divergences of opinion to arise between the two countries in the matter of the practical applications of these principles, the coordination and readjustment of such divergences of opinion should be discussed at the occasion of a meeting of the heads of the two Governments." LC-JFOA, WT 72, IMT 555, 482–83.

   On Sept. 13 Toyoda had informed Nomura that the Japanese Govt. could not "swallow" (*unomi*) Hull's Four Principles unless the settlement suggested in Tokyo's proposal of early Sept. (*FRJ*, II: 608–9) was attained. Gaimushō, *NBKK*, 275. See also Gaimushō, *NBKK*, 345–50; and *PHA*, XII: 54–56. The word *unomi* literally means to gulp something down whole, in the manner of a cormorant.

277 The Japanese Govt. had instructed Nomura: For an indication of the way in which the Ambassador and his staff implemented these instructions, see *FRJ*, II: 671, 673, 675. Also Nomura, 131, and "Diary," Oct. 9.

277–78 "No doubt whatsoever" in Grew's mind: See *FRJ*, II: 664–65.

278 In another meeting with Grew, Oct. 10: *Ibid.*, 677–79. See also Gaimushō, *NBKK*, 352–54, *PHA*, XII: 62–64; *FR 1941*, IV: 507–8, 509–11; and State 701.9411/1490. Toyoda did more than simply complain to Grew—he reprimanded Nomura, instructing him henceforth to take along either Wakasugi or Iguchi whenever he went calling on Hull or the President, and to cable immediately to Tokyo the full minutes of such conversations. *PHA*, XII: 62–63.

278 Nomura seemed to be "very tired": *FRJ*, II: 679; Grew, *Ten Years*, 455–56; State 701.9411/1490. Just prior to the Cabinet change in mid-July Nomura had expressed a desire to resign, but the Foreign Minister, the Navy Minister, and the chief of the Naval General Staff had all counseled him to remain in Washington. Nomura, 183–87, and "Diary," July 14. Three weeks later, on Aug. 4, the Ambassador had asked Matsuoka's successor, Admiral Toyoda, to send an experienced diplomat—a man like Saburō Kurusu—to assist him. Gaimushō, *NBKK*, 139–40. It was early Oct., however, before the Foreign Minister began moving in that direction. "We knew from comment made to us by Japanese officials," Grew later wrote, "that the Japanese Government was not altogether happy at Admiral Nomura's handling of the situation. Of the Ambassador's high principles and integrity there could be no doubt, nor could there be doubt as to his earnest endeavors to bring our two countries to an agreement; but there existed a degree of dissatisfaction in Tokyo with his reports in point of promptness, comprehensiveness, and precision; his grasp of the English language was not believed to be wholly adequate, and the lack of satisfactory progress in the conversations had con-

vinced Admiral Toyoda of the advisability of sending a coadjutor to assist the Ambassador in his work." Grew papers, Despatch 6018, Feb. 19, 1942: 3.

Following the formation of the Tōjō Cabinet in mid-Oct., Nomura once again indicated that he wanted to give up the post in which he had proved so ineffective, but he was urged (by the Navy and Foreign ministers) to remain in Washington. Nomura, 189–92, and "Diary," Oct. 18, 20, and 22 (the telegrams Nomura dispatched on these dates were all intercepted by "Magic," as was a reply sent from Tokyo on Oct. 23; see *PHA*, XII: 79–80, 81–82; the "Magic" translations need to be revised).

Thus, it was not until Nov. 4 that Toyoda's successor at the Foreign Office, Shigenori Tōgō, finally informed Grew that the Japanese Govt. wished to send Saburō Kurusu to the U.S. as a Special Envoy. See Grew, *Ten Years*, 470–71, and *Turbulent Era*, II: 1246–47, 1378–79; *FRJ*, II: 704–5; *FR 1941*, IV: 566–67, 570; and Grew papers, "Diary," Nov. 1941: 5939–40.

278–80 The Welles-Wakasugi intv., Oct. 13: *FRJ*, II: 356–58, 680–86. Also Gaimushō, *NBKK*, 360–66; *PHA*, XII: 64–65, 66–68, 69–70; Hull, II: 1034.

On Oct. 15, Grew, who had been kept fully informed of what was being said in Washington, was authorized, at his discretion, to seek an interview with Toyoda in order to review the various statements that had been made in the meantime to Nomura and to members of his staff by the Secretary, the Under Secretary, and other officers of the State Dept. Presumably Toyoda would then be able to comprehend the position of the American Govt. The very next morning, however, Washington learned from Grew that the Konoye Cabinet was no more; the Premier and his colleagues had resigned. *FR 1941*, IV: 509–11 (see also 507–8).

280 The early-Oct. deadline: See the last paragraph of the Note for p. 268 (Konoye's refusal to receive any members of the diplomatic corps).

280 Walsh to Drought, Oct. 6, and Drought's reply, Oct. 10: JMD papers. The handwritten text of both items, unsigned and undated, can also be found in the Konoye papers with a note identifying the "Christians" as the source. *TSM*, VII (Tsunoda): 150–51, quotes both (in Japanese translation) but is incorrect in suggesting that this particular exchange of messages may have taken place in early April.

280 Oct. 12 (the day on which Konoye's position began to crumble): See Butow, *Tojo*, 268–76.

280 Walsh to Drought, Oct. 12, and Drought's reply, Oct. 14: JMD papers. Walsh's message was badly garbled in transmission.

280–81 Walsh's visit to the American Embassy and the information he delivered there, Oct. 14: *FR 1941*, IV: 508–9; *IMTFE*, 32987–88. Included among the "personal advisers" who had asked Walsh to convey their observations to Grew were Nobufumi Itō, Tomohiko Ushiba, and Kinkazu (informally known as Kōichi) Saionji (a grandson of the late Prince Kinmochi Saionji).

The Konoye papers contain a typewritten copy of the "paper containing observations." A handwritten notation in the upper right-hand corner reads: "Drafted Oct. 13th." There is also this heading: "The following observation is that of Bishop W. and it is forwarded with the request that it be called to the immediate attention of the President and the Secretary of State."

281 "Some counteracting indication": Two possibilities were mentioned: a formula capable of removing "the divergencies between the American draft state-

ment of June 21 [*FRJ*, II: 483–92] and the Japanese draft statement of September 27 [*ibid.*, 636–41]"; or "some clear assurance" in the near future by the President, "either publicly or privately," of his readiness to confer with Premier Konoye.

281 A telegram from Saigon: *FR 1941*, IV: 509; State 740.0011 P.W./564.

281–83 Walsh's departure from Japan with a *viva voce* message for FDR from Konoye: JMD papers, misc. items incl. Walsh's statement on behalf of Mutō, the "safe-conduct" letter, and the "Bon voyage" telegram; Walsh papers, "Visitation Diary—1941," the Bishop's "Confidential Memorandum" of Dec. 11, 1945, and his Sept. 15, 1971, account of the "peace treaty negotiations"; IMTFE, 32987–91; *FR 1941*, IV: 508–9, 527–39 (a report written by Walsh on Oct. 18, 1941, and handed by him to Hull on Nov. 15); Butow, *Tojo*, 310–12.

In his Oct. 18 report, Walsh had this to say: "I do not quote the Prince verbatim, as I did not take down his exact words at the time they were uttered. I fixed them in my memory, however, and jotted them down almost immediately after the interview. I am satisfied that I have reproduced here the exact sense of his message and even to a large extent, his very words." *FR 1941*, IV: 529–30.

282 The sudden resignation of Konoye's Cabinet, Oct. 16: See Butow, *Tojo*, 262–309. Also *FR 1941*, IV: 511, 512–13; *FRJ*, II: 689–92; Gaimushō, *NBKK*, 368; *PHA*, XII: 76.

283 "Bon voyage with Flowers": JMD papers. The slightly different text of this message in Butow, *Tojo*, 312, is the version quoted by Walsh (probably from memory) in his Oct. 18 report.

283 Walsh on "the meaning of the Cabinet change": *FR 1941*, IV: 529.

283 Consideration was briefly given to the advisability of sending a Presidential message to the Emperor of Japan, Oct. 16–17: *PHA*, XV: 1727–34; *FR 1941*, IV: 513–15, 520–22. Also Konoye, 141–42 (*PHA*, XX: 4016); Langer and Gleason, 730–31; *PHA*, II: 530–31, IV: 1700–1702, and XIV: 1226–30.

283 "One or two basic accords": The accords FDR had in mind related to "the future integrity of China" and "the assurance that neither Japan nor the United States would wage war to obtain control of any further territory in or adjacent to the Pacific area." *FR 1941*, IV: 514.

283 The President was so advised: The matter "rested" until Dec. 6, when FDR sent an eleventh-hour message to the Emperor of Japan. See Butow, *Tojo*, 387ff.

283–84 Further convs. with Wakasugi, Oct. 16–17, and Hull's analysis of the situation: *FRJ*, II: 358, 687–89; Hull, II: 1035. See also Gaimushō, *NBKK*, 365–66, 368–75; *PHA*, XII: 69–70, 73–75, 76–79; and State 711.94/2406-7/11.

Tension Increases as Urgency Prevails

285 Hull found the situation ominous: Hull, II: 1054–55; *FRJ*, II: 358–59, 692–93.

285–86 The Welles-Wakasugi conv., Oct. 24: *FRJ*, II: 692–97. "Magic" intercepted two Japanese Embassy reports to Tokyo concerning this conversation. *PHA*, XII: 82–84 (Gaimushō, *NBKK*, 381–83), 86–87 (the Japanese original is not available). The State Dept. briefed Grew fully the next day. Grew papers, "Diary," Oct. 1941: 5918–24. On Oct. 30, Grew gave the new Foreign Minister, Shigenori Tōgō, a paraphrase of this briefing telegram. Grew felt that Tōgō "would derive therefrom a clear understanding" of the attitude of the American Govt. toward the conversations. See *FRJ*, II: 700.

286 Nomura's pessimistic mood and his desire to return home: The text is based on several mid-Oct. telegrams that were all intercepted by "Magic" (*PHA*, XII: 79–80, 81–82), supplemented by Nomura, 189–92, and "Diary," Oct. 18, 20, and 22. See also his "Chū-Bei Ninmu Hōkoku," Sect. 8.

286–87 The decision to send Kurusu to Washington and the help solicited from the American Govt.: *FRJ*, II: 362, 704–5; Grew papers, "Diary," Nov. 1941: 5939–40, and misc. telegrams, 6028–32; *FR 1941*, IV: 566–67, 570; State 711.94/2540-1/35; Grew, *Ten Years*, 470–71, and *Turbulent Era*, II: 1246–47, 1378–79; Tōgō, *Jidai no Ichimen*, 219, 222–25, and *The Cause of Japan*, 149–53. Also SKH papers, Box "Krock-Kwantung," Folder "Kurusu, Saburō," a Sept. 1944 memo summarizing "Kurusu's journey to Washington"; *DGFP*, D.XIII: 744–46; and "Kurusu Taishi Hōkoku," Sect. 1.

287 "Delay in bringing the conversations to a speedy conclusion": I am quoting Hamilton's paraphrase of what Dooman told him over the telephone. *FR 1941*, IV: 567.

287 A long telegram from Grew: Tel. 1736, Nov. 3, the substance of which is printed in *FRJ*, II: 701–4, and in Grew, *Ten Years*, 467–70. See also Grew, *Turbulent Era*, II: 1276–82; Hull, II: 1056; Grew papers, "Diary," Oct.–Nov. 1941: 5813–16, 5930, 5935–36 (three paragraphs that Grew deleted from his telegram before sending it to Washington), 5939; *PHA*, II: 672–73, 676–80, and XIV: 1045–57; and Langer and Gleason, 849–50.

287 Hornbeck did not find Grew's arguments convincing: See *FR 1941*, IV: 568–69. Also SKH papers, Box 254, Folder "Japan–United States Relations," a Mar. 29, 1943, memo.

287 Grew's view of his Nov. 3 telegram and his reason for sending it: Grew papers, "Diary," Nov. 1941: 5939.

288 Hull to the American Ambassador in China, Nov. 3: *FR 1941*, IV: 565–66 (this telegram was repeated to Grew). See also Langer and Gleason, 838–40.

288–89 The situation in China as portrayed by Chiang, Churchill's reaction, and the American response (late Oct.–early Nov.): See Langer and Gleason, 710–13, 839–48; Hull, II: 1057; Churchill, 591–93; Hull papers, Japan—General, Folder 309, an Oct. 31 memo by SKH, and Folder 310, the Marshall-Stark recommendations of Nov. 5 entitled "Estimate Concerning Far Eastern Situation"; *FR 1941*, V: 740–44, 747–54, 756, 757–61, 763–64; *PHA*, XIV: 1061–82; Feis, 299–303; and Pogue, 193–95.

289 The Imperial Conference of Nov. 5 and the operational orders issued that day and the next: Butow, *Tojo*, 325–26.

289 A deadline appeared: Hull, II: 1056–57; *PHA*, XII: 100; Gaimushō, *NBKK*, 396–97. For the Tokyo background, see Butow, *Tojo*, 314–26. The deadline was later extended to Nov. 29. See *PHA*, XII: 165; and Gaimushō, *NBKK*, 478–79.

289–90 The Toshi Gō editorial, Nov. 5, Grew's reaction, and Tōgō's response: See Grew, *Ten Years*, 471–76, 478–79; *FR 1941*, IV: 569, 573–75, 576; and *FRJ*, II: 705–6. Also *PHA*, XII: 100–101, 103, 107.

290–91 Hull's estimate of the situation and the warning he delivered at the Cabinet meeting on Nov. 7: Hull, II: 1057–58; Feis, 303; *PHA*, II: 429; *FRJ*, II: 359.

291 The Nomura-Wakasugi conv. with Hull, Nov. 7: Hull, II: 1058–59; *FRJ*,

II: 706–10. Also Nomura, 136–38, and "Diary," Nov. 7; Gaimushō, *NBKK*, 398–99; *PHA*, XII: 104–6, 123. The document Nomura delivered that evening was Japan's so-called Proposal A. It was supplanted on Nov. 20 by "Proposal B," which proved to be equally unacceptable to the American Govt. See Butow, *Tojo*, 321–23, 333–35.

291 The "Magic" intercepts were keeping suspicions alive: Hull, II: 1060; *PHA*, XII: *passim*.

"The Head of a Dragon, the Tail of a Snake"

292 Walsh to Drought asking for Walker's help, Oct. 15, and Drought's reply, Oct. 16: JMD papers.

292 "Clipper leaves Manila" and JMD's (Oct. 29) reply: *Ibid*. I have also consulted the Bishop's "Visitation Diary" for the period in question.

292 "Another week lost": JMD papers. The copy at Maryknoll is undated, but Walsh apparently sent this message to JMD on or about Nov. 3.

292–93 Walsh's letters to Walker and Drought, Nov. 7: FW and JMD papers. Walsh intended to ask the High Commissioner to the Philippines to put these letters into one of the diplomatic pouches destined for Washington.

292 "The enclosed memorandum": I have changed Walsh's "memoranda" to "memorandum" since it is clear that he is referring to a single document (consisting of several distinct sections). This memo, which was written on Oct. 18, was handed to Hull by Walsh on the evening of Nov. 15. See *FR 1941*, IV: 527–39. In the FW papers, the wrong memo is attached to Walsh's letter of Nov. 7. Instead of the Oct. 18 document (copies of which are filed elsewhere in the PMG's papers), I found JMD's "Working Analysis" (typed on Wikawa's office letterhead) clipped to the Bishop's letter from Manila. The two do not belong together even though they were filed together by Walker or one of his assistants.

293 Wikawa to Walker: FW papers. This message, sent as a night letter, arrived in Washington late in the evening of Nov. 7.

293 "Looking forward pinch hitter's homer": JMD papers. Wikawa sent this message to Maryknoll on Nov. 7 in the belief that the Bishop would soon be arriving there, but Walsh was still stranded in Manila.

293 The Walsh-Kurusu journey across the Pacific: The Bishop's recollection is that he chatted with Kurusu but did not say anything about the "peace message" Konoye had asked him to convey to Roosevelt. "I was careful not to mention it," Walsh told Fr. Coleman in 1974. Coleman corresp. When Walsh asked Kurusu whether he thought his mission would be successful, Japan's Special Envoy intimated "that he had no message which would relieve the tension between his country and the United States, but only hoped to find some solution by hard work." SKH papers, Box 254, Folder "Japan–U.S. Conversations," an Apr. 29, 1942, memo.

293 The liaison maintained with the PMG by Drought and the Japanese Embassy: FW papers, TA Log and "Daily Memo Calendar, 1941."

293 Grew on Tōgō: Grew, *Ten Years*, 465–66. Also *FRJ*, II: 699–700; Grew papers, "Diary," Nov. 1941: 6030, 6032; *FR 1941*, IV: 523, 542. Toshikazu Kase, the newly appointed chief of the First Section of the American Bureau of the Foreign Office, served as Tōgō's interpreter. It should be noted, in this connection, that Grew (who had no knowledge of the Japanese language)

was so hard of hearing that he generally missed anything that was not spoken loudly and distinctly in face-to-face conversation. On the Ambassador's deafness, see Heinrichs, *passim*.

294 The extent to which Tōgō was the victim of misconceptions: See Tōgō, *Jidai no Ichimen*, 198–99, and *The Cause of Japan*, 121–22; Gaimushō, *NBKK*, 343; *PHA*, XII: 53; Butow, *Tojo*, 326 n23; *FRJ*, II: 712; and IMTFE, 35699 ("Sokki-roku," 337: 7). Tōgō knew that Nomura had made mistakes, but the Foreign Minister did not appreciate their enormity. Nomura had now been told to obey his instructions to the letter (Gaimushō, *NBKK*, 386; *PHA*, XII: 94), but the pattern of his behavior as a diplomat could not easily be changed this late in the day.

294 Nomura's conv. with FDR, Nov. 10 (Wakasugi and Hull were also present): *FRJ*, II: 715–19; Hull, II: 1059. Also Nomura, 139–41, and "Diary," Nov. 10; Gaimushō, *NBKK*, 401–4; *PHA*, XII: 112–16. The remarks Tōgō made to Grew in Tokyo on Nov. 10 are also pertinent. See *FRJ*, II: 710–14; Gaimushō, *NBKK*, 406–8; *PHA*, XII: 109–11; and Tōgō, *Jidai no Ichimen*, 225–26, and *The Cause of Japan*, 154–55.

294 Kase informed Grew, Nov. 12: *FRJ*, II: 719–22. Kase later changed "shocked" to "concerned."

294 Tōgō's insistence that the Hull-Nomura "conversations" had become "negotiations": See *FRJ*, II: 710, 721–22; *PHA*, XII: 130; Gaimushō, *NBKK*, 443; and Grew, *Turbulent Era*, II: 1247.

294–95 The Hull-Nomura conv., Nov. 15 (Wakasugi and Ballantine were also present): Hull, II: 1061–62; *FRJ*, II: 359–62, 731–37, 748. Also Nomura, 145–46, and "Diary," Nov. 15; *PHA*, XII: 131–32, 134–37, and XX: 4093–95; Gaimushō, *NBKK*, 428–42; *FR 1941*, IV: 576–79, 588–89, 591–98, 599–600.

295 "I might well be lynched": Hull used similar phraseology on Nov. 26 in a conv. with Nomura and Kurusu, but the subject on that occasion was "the oil question" rather than the Tripartite Pact. See *FRJ*, II: 765.

295–96 Walsh's meeting with Hull, Nov. 15: The text is based on a Dec. 15 memo in which the Bishop endeavored to recall the substance of his conversation with Hull a month earlier. JMD and FW papers.

295–97 The memo Walsh left with Hull: *FR 1941*, IV: 527–39 (note the marginal comments by SKH). The FW papers contain several copies of the original.

297 The prospects for peace remained unpromising: Tōgō would later write that the Konoye Cabinet had retired from office leaving behind "the bomb of the Japanese-American negotiations" with the fuse already ignited. *The Cause of Japan*, 115; *Jidai no Ichimen*, 194.

297 Kurusu to the press (while en route to Washington): *NYT*, Nov. 15 and 16: 5 and 1, respectively.

297 "We can go so far": Hull made this remark on Nov. 18. Hull, II: 1065. See also *FRJ*, II: 745.

297 The *status quo ante* proposal made by Nomura and Kurusu, Nov. 18: Hull, II: 1067–68. See also *FRJ*, II: 363–66, 744–53; *FR 1941*, IV: 605–6, 616–22, 626; Nomura, 149–50, and "Diary," Nov. 18–19; *PHA*, XII: 146–50, 152–53, 154, 158; and Gaimushō, *NBKK*, 452–55, 457–59. Hull was cautious in his reply to this overture, but he did indicate that he would consult the British and the Dutch to see what their attitude might be. This was done that same

day and the next, with the Chinese and the Australians also being informed. *FR 1941*, IV: 616–17.

297–98 Nomura and Kurusu were pursuing an idea that had been presented to them by the Postmaster General: See the "Magic" intercept version of Nomura's 1135, Nov. 18, *PHA*, XII: 154.

Langer and Gleason, 872–74, believe that Walker was acting for the President, and that Nomura and Kurusu grabbed the bait FDR was offering through the PMG. It is also possible, however, that Walker was simply trying to be helpful by repeating, on his own responsibility, something he had already heard from either Roosevelt or Hull.

298 The unauthorized nature of the Nomura-Kurusu démarche and the admonition they received from the Foreign Minister: This is much clearer when Tōgō's postwar account (*Jidai no Ichimen*, 228–29; *The Cause of Japan*, 160–61) is read in conjunction with the "Magic" intercepts than when his telegrams are read alone (Tels. 798 and 806, Nov. 19 and Nov. 20, *PHA*, XII: 155–56, 160; Gaimushō, *NBKK*, 467, 470). The fact that these messages were intercepted does not necessarily mean that Hull saw them.

298 The presentation of Japan's *modus vivendi* on Nov. 20 and the reaction of Hull and his advisers: The reference here is to Japan's "Proposal B." Hull, II: 1069–71; *FRJ*, II: 366–68, 753–56. Also Butow, *Tojo*, 322–23, 334–35; *FR 1941*, IV: 633–34; Hull papers, "Japan—General, 1941," Folder 310; Nomura, 150–51, and "Diary," Nov. 20; *PHA*, XII: 161–63; Gaimushō, *Shuyō Bunshō*, II: 558, and *NBKK*, 470–71; Churchill, 595–96; and Berle, 379.

Tokyo wanted Washington to restore commercial relations to the level that had prevailed prior to the freezing of Japan's assets. Tokyo also wanted the U.S. to supply Japan with "a required quantity of oil" and to help her secure the goods and commodities she needed from the Netherlands East Indies. The American Govt. would have to agree, in addition, not to do anything that would be "prejudicial" to the restoration of peace between Japan and China. In return, Japan would undertake not to advance by force of arms beyond French Indochina into the rest of Southeast Asia or the South Pacific. Japan would give this promise only if the U.S. would make a similar commitment. Japan would eventually withdraw her troops from Indochina, but she would not do so until peace had been restored between Japan and China or until "an equitable peace" had been established "in the Pacific area." If the U.S. accepted Japan's *modus vivendi*, however, the Japanese Govt. would "in the meantime" transfer its troops in southern Indochina to the northern part of that country.

"The President and I could only conclude," Hull later wrote, "that agreeing to these proposals would mean condonement by the United States of Japan's past aggressions, assent to future courses of conquest by Japan, abandonment of the most essential principles of our foreign policy, betrayal of China and Russia, and acceptance of the role of silent partner aiding and abetting Japan in her effort to create a Japanese hegemony over the western Pacific and eastern Asia." Hull, II: 1070.

According to Ballantine, it was not until this late in the day (ca. Nov. 20) that the President privately spoke in terms of "babying the Japanese along." See *FR 1941*, IV: 372–74.

298 Intelligence received by the American Govt. concerning Japanese military movements, Nov. 21: Hull, II: 1071. Also *FR 1941*, IV: 633.

298 Hull's judgment of the situation: Hull, II: 1071–72. See also *FRJ*, II: 369–71.

298–301 The FDR-Hull *modus vivendi* idea and the staff work pertaining thereto, Nov. 20–25: Hull, II: 1072–82. Also *FR 1941*, IV: 579–84, 601–3, 626–27, 635–40, 642–46, 661–65, 665–66 (in June 1969 I tried to find the six "not used" drafts mentioned on p. 635, but they were not in the State Dept. files at the National Archives).

The projected American *modus vivendi* called for the withdrawal of all Japanese soldiers and sailors from southern Indochina and the reduction of Japanese military strength in northern Indochina to the number of men (about 25,000) that were believed to have been stationed there just prior to the freezing of Japanese assets by the U.S. Tokyo would also have to promise not to send any additional land, sea, or air forces to Indochina.

So far as the American Govt. was concerned, Japan did not have any right to keep even a single soldier in the French colony, but the 25,000 figure was regarded as part of the price Washington would have to pay to obtain a Japanese acceptance of the proposal as a whole. A garrison of that size, it was judged, would not be able to threaten the nearby Burma Road, a supply line that was vital to the maintenance of China's resistance to Japan.

For its part, the American Govt. was prepared to permit a limited resumption of certain categories of trade with Japan, including the export of oil solely for civilian consumption. The British, the Australians, and the Dutch would be urged to follow the American lead. With reference to China, the Administration's position was that a settlement between Tokyo and Chungking would have to be based on the principles of law, order, justice, and peace.

299 A ten-point peace settlement: See Hull, II: 1071–73; and *FR 1941*, IV: 579–84, 601–3, 606–16, 621–32, 633–40, 642–66. The opening paragraphs of Section I of the Ballantine-Schmidt draft of Nov. 11 (the document that led to much subsequent staff work concerning a peace settlement) were siphoned off, practically word for word, from the "Preamble" section of the John Doe "Draft Understanding" of Apr. 9. Compare *FR 1941*, IV: 580, and *FRJ*, II, 398.

299 Hull's consultation with the British, Chinese, Dutch, and Australian representatives, Nov. 22: Hull, II: 1073–74; *FRJ*, II: 368; *FR 1941*, IV: 640, 650–51; Feis, 312.

299 Indirect confirmation through "Magic," Nov. 22: Hull, II: 1074; *PHA*, XII: 165. Two days later "Magic" intercepted and translated a one-sentence message specifying that the Nov. 29 deadline was "in Tokyo time." *PHA*, XII: 173. The Secretary of State, who was one of the recipients of this intercept, later wrote: "The sword of Damocles that hung over our heads was therefore attached to a clockwork set to the hour." Hull, II: 1077.

299 "It was almost unreal": Hull, II: 1074. Also *FRJ*, II: 757–62; Nomura, 151–52, and "Diary," Nov. 22; *PIIA*, XII: 167–69, 170–71; Gaimushō, *NBKK*, 473–75, 477–78.

299–300 Hull's consultation with the British, Chinese, Dutch, and Australian representatives, Nov. 24: Hull, II: 1076–77; *FR 1941*, IV: 646–47; Feis, 313–

14. In a message to Churchill that evening, describing the *modus vivendi* proposal, FDR declared: "This seems to me a fair proposition for the Japanese but its acceptance or rejection is really a matter of internal Japanese politics. I am not very hopeful and we must all be prepared for real trouble, possibly soon." *FR 1941*, IV: 648–49.

300 The response of Chiang Kai-shek to the State Dept.'s *modus vivendi* plan: Hull, II: 1077–78; *FR 1941*, IV: 651–54, 660–61, 685–86; Feis, 315–17. On Nov. 25 Chiang instructed his brother-in-law T. V. Soong, who was then in Washington, to carry his protests directly to the Secretary of War and the Secretary of the Navy. Chiang also communicated with the British Prime Minister. See Churchill, 596–97, 598–99.

300 The views of the British Govt.: Hull, II: 1078–79; *FR 1941*, IV: 654–57. Also Churchill, 595–97.

300 The response of the Dutch Govt.: *FR 1941*, IV: 651, 658–60.

300 Hull told the President's so-called War Council, Nov. 25: See Hull, II: 1079–80; Feis, 314–15; Langer and Gleason, 885–87; and Butow, *Tojo*, 335–36. In his *Memoirs*, Hull describes the "War Council" as "a sort of clearinghouse for all the information and views" that the President, the secretaries of State, War, and Navy, the chief of staff, and the chief of naval operations had under discussion with their respective contacts and in their respective circles.

300 The news awaiting Stimson, Nov. 25: Feis, 315: Langer and Gleason, 891–92; Wohlstetter, 242–44.

300–301 Developments in Washington from the afternoon of Nov. 25 through the afternoon of Nov. 26: Hull, II: 1080–86; *FR 1941*, IV: 665–66; *FRJ*, II: 764–70; Feis, 317–20; Langer and Gleason, 889–901 (see also 929–32); Churchill, 596–98; Pogue, 205–7; Butow, *Tojo*, 337–38; Nomura, 152–58, and "Diary," Nov. 25–26; *PHA*, XII: 181–85, and XIV: 1300; Gaimushō, *NBKK*, 483–84, 486–89.

   The British, Australian, and Dutch representatives were surprised that Hull had dropped the *modus vivendi* plan, but he in turn found their reactions rather curious in the circumstances. See *FR 1941*, IV: 666–69, 685–87. The Chinese persisted in their view that the "damage" from a *modus vivendi* might be "irreparable." *Ibid.*, 681, 699, 708–9. On Nov. 30 the British Ambassador and the Australian Minister separately emphasized to Hull that their countries hoped that he would keep the conversations going with Japan because they needed more time to prepare their defenses. *Ibid.*, 700.

300 Advance notice was received: The nature of the message Churchill was sending to FDR was apparently conveyed orally to the State Dept. during the afternoon of Nov. 25 by the British ambassador or by a member of his staff. "Formal record came later" in a telegram from the American Embassy in London; this was received in Washington shortly after midnight, Nov. 25/26. See SKH papers, Box "Autobiography mss 2," Folder "Autobiography 1941." Also pertinent is a Dec. 4, 1964, letter from Ballantine to Hornbeck, and his Dec. 18 reply. SKH papers, Box 24.

300–301 "Of course, it is for you to handle this business": Churchill, 596–97.

301 The pertinent documents were handed to Nomura and Kurusu that very afternoon: See *FRJ*, II: 371–75, 764–70. The so-called Hull note of Nov. 26 consisted of an "Oral Statement" and an "Outline of Proposed Basis for Agreement Between the United States and Japan." Also, *FR 1941*, IV: 709–11.

301–2 Grew on Hull's ten-point plan: *FR 1941*, IV: 707 (see also 720–21).

302 The reaction of the leaders in Tokyo to the Hull overture: See Butow, *Tojo*, 337–44. Also *DGFP*, D.XIII: 906–8.

302 Nomura and Kurusu to Tōgō, Nov. 26 (recommending an exchange of messages between the President and the Emperor): *Ibid.*, 399–401; Tōgō, *Jidai no Ichimen*, 232–33, and *The Cause of Japan*, 165–66; Nomura 152–53, and "Diary," Nov. 26; *PHA*, XII: 180–81, 195 (these "Magic" intercept translations are inaccurate; for the original messages, see Gaimushō, *NBKK*, 482–83, 505–6).

302 The notion that the Emperor might be brought into play: Although His Majesty was not in fact endowed with the power to order the government to do anything that it had not already agreed to do of its own accord, the Throne still seemed to a number of men to be a possible court of last resort. Among those who were active in the U.S. in this regard were Langdon Warner of Harvard, a specialist on the art and culture of ancient Japan, and Kan'ichi Asakawa of Yale, a friend of Warner's and an authority on early Japanese history. *FR 1941*, IV: 671; State 711.94/2542 and 711.94/2580. Also involved, but working independently of the Warner-Asakawa effort, was the Rev. Dr. E. Stanley Jones, who had been trying for some time to play the role of an intermediary. See Jones, 609–16, esp. 613–16.

302–3 The Marshall-Stark recommendations, Nov. 27: See Hull, II: 1087; Feis, 322–24; Langer and Gleason, 899–900; Wohlstetter, 246–50; and Pogue, 213.

303 Hornbeck's long memo of Nov. 27: *FR 1941*, IV: 672–75. SKH explained his choice of dates as follows: Dec. 15 was the date by which the chief of the War Plans Division (Army) had "affirmed that we would be 'in the clear' so far as consummation of certain disposals" of American forces were concerned; Jan. 15 was "seven weeks from now"; Mar. 1 was "a date more than 90 days from now, and after the period during which it has been estimated by our strategists that it would be to our advantage for us to have 'time' for further preparations and disposals."

303 Hornbeck "made the mistake": "Both my thinking and my predicting were . . based on my scrutiny of materials which emanated from 'intelligence' services, some British and some American. From the British sources there had emanated false reports regarding the strength of the military establishment at Singapore. I for one had been informed by [U.S.] Navy personnel that the Japanese main fleet—including its heavy air-craft carriers—was in home waters." SKH papers, Box "Autobiography mss 2," Folder "Autobiography 1941."

303 Hull to the press, Nov. 27: Langer and Gleason, 907–8; Hull, II: 1086–87. At a press conference the following morning, the President himself took up the subject of Japan, on the understanding that his remarks were for "background purposes" only. Ever since the spring (he declared)—April to be exact—the Secretary of State ("with more patience than I could possibly have had, which is saying a lot") had been conducting talks with the Japanese Govt. The U.S. had been prepared to make concessions to Japan designed to rehabilitate her internal economic structure and her international trade opportunities. In the midst of these talks, as all Americans were aware, the Japanese had moved into Indochina (which was "getting pretty far afield in the realm of Japanese aggression"). In addition, the safety of the Philippines

had come into question. The Islands were in the center of a great horseshoe opening to the south. To the west, the Japanese were in control of the China coast; to the east, they held the Mandated Islands. This situation could be compared to the German military method of taking a piece here, and a piece there, in carrying out the final encirclement. The U.S., however, was not going to allow itself to be entrapped in this way. FW papers, "Memorandum for Mr. Walker on the White House Press Conference, Friday Morning, November 28, 1941." Also *NYT*, Nov. 29: 1.

303–4 The Nov. 28 meeting of the "War Council": Hull, II: 1087; Langer and Gleason, 911–13; Wohlstetter, 265–67; Pogue, 213–14. See also Hull to Lord Halifax, Nov. 29, *FR 1941*, IV: 686–87; and Berle, 379–81.

304 The President's visit to Warm Springs, Ga., and his sudden return at Hull's request: See Tully, 249–51; Hull, II: 1087–90; Butow, *Tojo*, 348–57, 364–69; *PHA*, XII: 195.

305 Hull learned through the British ambassador: Hull, II: 1090; *FR 1941*, IV: 700, and V: 360; Langer and Gleason, 916–17, 918, 920–21. It has been said that Hull was nowhere to be found on the weekend of Nov. 29–30, but this observation, which is apparently based on a remark by Stimson, does not accord with other evidence—namely, that Hull received the British Ambassador and the Australian Minister separately on both the 29th and the 30th, presumably either at the State Dept. or at his Wardman Park apartment. See Hull: II, 1088–89; and *FR 1941*, IV: 685–87, 700.

305 Hull's conv. with Nomura and Kurusu, Dec. 1: Langer and Gleason, 917 (citing the Berle "Diaries"); Hull, II: 1090–91; *FRJ*, II: 376–77, 772–77; Berle, 381. The dressing-down that Hull gave the two men on this occasion does not come through in any of Nomura's accounts. See Gaimushō, *NBKK*, 511–12; *PHA*, XII: 210–12; Nomura, 161–62, "Diary," Dec. 1, and "Chū-Bei Ninmu Hōkoku," Sect. 5.

305 Hull's conference with the President on Dec. 1, and the messages that were up for consideration: Hull, II: 1091–92; *FR 1941*, IV: 675–80, 688–98, 721–26, 727; Langer and Gleason, 911–21.

305 A cable from Churchill (dated Nov. 30): *PHA*, XIV: 1300; Hull, II: 1092; Langer and Gleason, 917–18; Hull papers, Box 49, Folder 147, "Correspondence—II, Oct.–Dec. 1941"; Churchill, 599–600.

306 The "Magic" intercept of Tōgō's instructions to the Japanese Ambassador in Berlin: Tel. 985, Nov. 30 (translated by "Magic" on Dec. 1). *PHA*, XII: 204–5; Hull, II: 1092. Also Churchill, 600–601. The intercepted message also contained the following passage: "Say [to Hitler and Ribbentrop] that by our present moves southward we do not mean to relax our pressure against the Soviet [Union] and that if Russia joins hands tighter with England and the United States and resists us with hostilities, we are ready to turn upon her with all our might; however, right now, it is to our advantage to stress the south and for the time being we would prefer to refrain from any direct moves in the north."

306 The Nomura-Kurusu effort to reactivate the Honolulu conference idea, Dec. 1: On the assumption that a meeting between Roosevelt and Tōjō might not be feasible, Nomura and Kurusu suggested that the two sides be represented by persons enjoying the "complete confidence" of their respective governments: Vice-President Henry Wallace or White House adviser Harry

Hopkins for the U.S. and former Premier Fumimaro Konoye or Viscount Kikujirō Ishii (a diplomat of World War I fame) for Japan. Tōgō rejected this proposal on Dec. 3. Butow, *Tojo*, 338–39; *PHA*, XII: 213–14, 224.

306 Japan's decision for war was secretly confirmed, Dec. 1: See Butow, *Tojo*, 358–63.

306 Drought had tried to keep abreast of the rapidly developing situation: FW papers, TA Log. The JMD papers show that Drought was at the Wardman Park Hotel from Nov. 2 to Nov. 26, Dec. 3 to Dec. 7, and Dec. 11 to Dec. 12. See also Hull papers, "Desk Diary," Folder 295-I; and Nomura's "Diary," *passim*.

306 Drought's proposed reply to Hull's ten-point peace plan: JMD papers, several drafts in Drought's hand and typewritten copies of the final version (addressed "Excellency," and concluding with the words, "With assurances of highest esteem, etc."). The FW papers contain a copy of the final version.

306 Walsh to Wikawa, Nov. 27: JMD papers. The Bishop sent an identical message to Kinkazu (Kōichi) Saionji.

306–7 Walsh to Wikawa, Nov. 28, Wikawa's reply, Dec. 1, and Walsh's answering message, Dec. 3. *Ibid.* The earlier Wikawa message mentioned in the footnote on p. 307 was sent Nov. 21. It was in answer to an optimistic telegram from Walsh dated Nov. 15. LC-JFOA, WT 21, IMT 90, 1.

307 A telegram from Tōgō: Tel. 876, Dec. 3. *PHA*, XII: 224.

307 The destruction of a number of codes: For the pertinent "Magic" intercepts, see *PHA*, XII: 215, 236, 237, 249.

307 The conclusion drawn by members of the War Dept. General Staff: Butow, *Tojo*, 368–69.

307–8 The Japanese Govt.'s reply (Dec. 5) to a formal inquiry from the President (Dec. 2) and Hull's reaction thereto: Hull, II: 1092–93; *FRJ*, II: 378–79, 778–84. See also Nomura, 163–64, and "Diary," Dec. 2–5; Gaimushō, *NBKK*, 524–28, 532–33; and *PHA*, XII: 221–23, 224, 235–36.

308 The reports that reached the American Govt. on Dec. 6 and the President's decision to appeal directly to the Emperor: Hull, II: 1093–94. Also Churchill, 600–601, Langer and Gleason, 929–32.

308 The situation in Tokyo on the eve of war (with particular reference to the limited role of the Throne): See Butow, *Japan's Decision to Surrender*, 228–33 (1941 compared with 1945), and *Tojo*, 387–401 (FDR's appeal to the Emperor).

308 "Nomura's last meeting with me": Hull, II: 1097.

308 The late delivery of Japan's final note: See Butow, *Tojo*, 371–87. Also *FRJ*, II: 379–85.

308 Hull's prior knowledge (through "Magic") of the contents of Japan's final note: Hull, II: 1095. See also Langer and Gleason, 932–34.

308 The President's telephone call to Hull: Hull, II: 1095–96. The intelligence information received by officials in Washington during late Nov. and early Dec. had pointed to the likelihood of a Japanese attack *somewhere in Southeast Asia*. Stimson and Bundy, 389–91; Langer and Gleason, 926–29, 932, 934–35, 936–37. On Dec. 7 Roosevelt and Hull surmised that the report the President had received concerning Pearl Harbor was "probably true," but they could hardly take it in at first—it was beyond belief. Hull therefore thought that the President should have the report *confirmed*.

308 Hull transfixed the hapless Ambassador: See Hull, II: 1095–97; and *FR 1941*, IV: 786–93. Also Butow, *Tojo*, 401–2, and Nomura, "Chū-Bei Ninmu Hōkoku," Sect. 5.

309 *Ryūtō dabi* (Wikawa to Konoye, Dec. 7, 1940): Konoye papers; *TSM*, *Bekkan*, 394–95.

In the Fullness of Time

311–13 How Father Drought viewed the situation: JMD papers, an untitled and unfinished ms. of 24 typewritten pages. Internal evidence suggests that this account of the Walsh-Drought visit to Japan was written sometime after Pearl Harbor, but many of the views expressed therein can be found in other, earlier items dating from late 1940 through 1941. In his manuscript, Drought used the pronoun "we," thus placing Walsh on a par with himself in regard to the activities described. Since this was largely a polite use of the pronoun, historical accuracy requires a liberal substitution of "I" for "we."

When Drought's account was shown to Bp. Walsh in 1971, he wrote: "This is a memo written by Father Drought, evidently. When? Hard to say. No date on it. I do not recall ever seeing it. Neither do I understand half of it. Yet I must have done both years ago." Coleman corresp.

312 The "Working Analysis": Drought's retrospective conclusion was that his "Analysis" had been used by Tokyo "as a platform from which to move during the subsequent efforts to reach a formula of understanding" with Washington.

314 "The peace treaty envoy": Walsh papers, the Bishop's Sept. 15, 1971, account of the "peace treaty negotiations."

314 "A little further patience": JMD papers, a May 20 letter from Walsh to Drought.

315 "While Father Drought and I surely took an active part": I am quoting from a "Confidential Memorandum" of Dec. 11, 1945, in the Walsh papers. See also Walsh's report to the 1946 Chapter, in which he describes the 1941 peace effort as having been undertaken "at the invitation of the Civil Governments of both Japan and the United States." Also Coleman corresp. and enclosures, esp. a Walsh statement given to United Press on May 23, 1946.

315 Walsh's comment (thirty years after the event): Walsh papers, the Bishop's Sept. 15, 1971, account.

317 A disclosure of the trend of American intentions through Grew: In this connection, see an "eleventh hour" speculation by the Ambassador concerning the effect that publication of the Hull note of Nov. 26 might have in bringing public opinion to bear on the Japanese Govt. *FR 1941*, IV: 720–21 (see also 707).

317 The assignment of a false value to the "Draft Understanding": See Butow, "Hull-Nomura Conversations," 822–36, esp. 834.

318 Neither Japan nor the U.S. ever attempted to reduce these abstractions to definable terms: See Kennan, 38–54, esp. 46–49, 53–54, for an indictment of American policy in this regard.

318 Hull had sidestepped Nomura's question concerning "Manchukuo": See *FRJ*, II: 409.

318 This left the door open to a settlement of the issue: In the opinion of Harry Hopkins, "Hull had always been willing to work out a deal with Japan.

To be sure, it was the kind of a deal that Japan probably would not have accepted but, on the other hand, it was also the type of a deal which would have made us very unpopular in the Far East." Sherwood, 428–29. In this connection, see also Butow, "Backdoor Diplomacy," 70–72; and *FR 1941*, IV: 710 (Hamilton's elucidation of certain portions of the Hull note of Nov. 26, particularly the stipulation calling for the withdrawal of all Japanese armed forces from China—a stipulation that said nothing at all about the question of Manchuria).

318 The so-called second proposal of June 21: A brief review of the documents pertinent to this period may minimize the danger of confusion here. The John Doe "Draft Understanding" of Apr. 9 was the first proposal to be studied by the authorities on both sides of the Pacific. Hull and his advisers looked upon this document as a "proposal presented to the Department of State through the medium of private American and Japanese individuals," but Konoye and the Japanese Foreign Office thought that it was a proposal being offered to them by the American Govt. When Tokyo "responded" with a "Confidential Memorandum" on May 12, the State Dept. then produced an "Unofficial, Exploratory, and Without Commitment" proposition in the form of a "Joint Declaration." This *first American draft-agreement* was handed to Nomura on May 31, but he did not cable it to Matsuoka until June 9–10. Largely because of Nomura's handling of the matter, the State Dept.'s proposal of May 31 did not result in any action by the authorities in Japan. On June 21, less than two weeks after it reached Tokyo, it was superseded by a "second" proposal: a revised "Joint Declaration" also labeled "Unofficial, Exploratory, and Without Commitment." As noted in the text, this June 21 draft-agreement was actually the first proposal from the State Dept. to be fully scrutinized by the leaders of Japan, but Konoye, Matsuoka, and other decision-makers in Tokyo did not see the matter in this light. For them the "Draft Understanding," which had been forwarded by Nomura in Apr., constituted the "initial American offer"; the "Joint Declaration" of May 31 did not figure in their thinking; and so they regarded the "Joint Declaration" of June 21 as amounting to the State Dept.'s "second" bid.

319 An idea left over from the Walsh-Drought visit to Japan: See Butow, "Backdoor Diplomacy," 48–72, esp. 58–59, 66–67, 69–72.

Appendixes

323–33 The "Working Analysis": See the Note for pp. 81–84.

336–37 Deletions made in the text of the "Draft Understanding" *before* Nomura cabled it to Tokyo: In diplomatic transactions involving an exchange of documents it is axiomatic that each of the parties concerned be supplied with exactly the same text—a text that will be used not only as a point of departure but also as a base of reference. This is such an obvious way of starting off on the correct foot that it is universally taken for granted.

In transmitting the "Draft Understanding" to Tokyo, however, Nomura did not forward the English text that Drought, Iwakuro, and Wikawa had prepared at the Wardman Park Hotel (see the Note for pp. 154–58). The Ambassador sent, instead, a Japanese translation. When Matsuoka discovered —toward the end of April—that the Foreign Office did not have a copy of the original, he ordered Nomura to cable it to Tokyo at once. Upon comparing it with the Japanese version, Matsuoka felt that he was dealing not simply with a "surprisingly careless" translation but with one that was meant to mislead—the purpose being to make various points in the "Draft Understanding" appear to be favorable to Japan when in fact they were not. See *TSM, Bekkan,* 477.

By the time Matsuoka reached this conclusion, he was already dissatisfied with Nomura's handling of his mission, and yet the Foreign Minister refrained from ordering the Ambassador home. Matsuoka might have shown less restraint had he realized that Nomura had sent not merely a sloppy translation but a text that could not stand up to a paragraph-by-paragraph comparison with the copy in the hands of Secretary Hull.

Missing from the Japanese version of the "Draft Understanding" was a clause (the last paragraph of Section III) that envisaged a reversal of American policy: "Should the Chiang-Kai-Chek regime reject the request of President Roosevelt [to negotiate peace with Japan], the United States Government shall discontinue assistance to the Chinese."

Also missing was another clause (paragraph c of Section VII) in which the Japanese Govt. was described as seeking American support for "the removal of Hongkong and Singapore as doorways to further political encroachment by the British in the Far East."

How these clauses came to be omitted is not entirely clear, but certain facts are known. Shortly after arriving in the U.S. in March, Col. Iwakuro had expressed reservations about various features of the "Preliminary Draft of 'Agreement in Principle.'" As a result, Fr. Drought had learned, through Wikawa, that the Colonel felt Japan could not be expected to stop aiding Germany economically while the U.S. continued to extend assistance to China. Iwakuro had also talked in terms of an "unconditional approval" by Chiang Kai-shek of peace proposals to be submitted by Japan. Realizing that such an approach would cause trouble, Drought had tried to dissuade Iwakuro from writing these stipulations into the text of the draft agreement. Drought himself was in favor of a more subtle approach that would permit the Japanese to get what they wanted in China "without asking for it and, therefore, without giving anything in return." See text pp. 149–52, esp. p. 152.

In communicating with the State Dept. in early April, however, Drought had warned that it would be "impossible *politically*" to effect a 180° change in Japanese policy unless Iwakuro could demonstrate to Tokyo that Japan would receive "some substantial benefits"—for example, the "removal of Hong-Kong and Singapore as doorways to further political encroachment by the British in the Far East." *FR 1941,* IV: 119.

This provision had been written into the "Wardman Park draft" between Apr. 2 and Apr. 5. The clause calling for the cessation of American aid to China had been added later as a result of revisions made at the Japanese Embassy.

Second thoughts had then prevailed and these two stipulations had been discarded, but where these thoughts originated and how they influenced Nomura are questions that must surrender to conjecture for an answer.

Nomura may have learned directly from Hull, or indirectly through Drought, that provisions of this nature would be unacceptable to the U.S. What would the Ambassador gain by forwarding to Tokyo—as part of an "American proposal"—stipulations that Washington would immediately reject, once negotiations began? If Nomura suppressed these controversial items initially, however, he might be able to work them back into the text later on, especially if a point were reached where some further incentive was needed to persuade a hesitant Tokyo to proceed with the conclusion of an agreement. Being of an optimistic nature, Nomura may have believed that Hull would then be willing to compromise with him simply for the sake of reaching a settlement.

At any rate, the Japanese text Nomura sent to Tokyo did not correspond to the English version in Hull's hands. When Matsuoka instructed Nomura to send the original, the Foreign Minister received a text that was equally incomplete. The "Draft Understanding" on file in the State Dept. during this period, however, remained unchanged. Needless to say, Hull and his Far Eastern advisers were unaware that any of this was taking place.

339 The sudden and drastic shift from peace to war: What were Walsh and Drought doing (and thinking) on Dec. 7, 1941? I was unable to find any contemporaneous material at Maryknoll pertinent to this question. In the spring of 1973, however, Bp. Walsh offered this recollection: "On December 7 . . . Fr. D. and I were in Washington. We had visited Mr. Frank Walker and he sent us to have a game of golf at his Club that afternoon. We were worried and uneasy at the time, as the peace prospect seemed very dubious. But we were still hoping against hope, as it were. Just as we reached the 18th green and were about to finish our game, a man we had met in the golf shop came out and told us the news of the Pearl Harbor attack. We felt stunned. We did not even bother to finish our game. We just returned to our hotel, confirmed the news, and soon after returned to Maryknoll, New York." Coleman corresp. and enclosures.

339 The internment of Nomura: Japanese Embassy personnel were taken initially to the Homestead Hotel in Hot Springs, Va.; later they were moved to the Greenbrier Hotel in White Sulphur Springs, W. Va. The first stage of their repatriation began in June 1942, when they boarded the Swedish liner *Gripsholm* bound for Lourenço Marques, the seaport capital of Mozambique in southeastern Africa, where they were to be exchanged for Ambassador Grew and his staff arriving on the *Asama-maru* from Yokohama. See Terasaki, 79, 86, 93–94; and Grew, *Turbulent Era*, II: 1377–80.

339 40 Drought to Nomura, Apr. 24, 1942, and Nomura's reply, May 14. JMD papers.

340 Drought had completed work on a project: *Ibid.*, a May 11, 1942, letter to Walker enclosing Drought's draft of the Georgetown commencement address, a May 13 letter urging that every effort be made to obtain full publicity, a May 19 letter enclosing a revised draft, and a *NYT* clipping for May 26 ("Georgetown Is Told of Tyranny in Peace; Postmaster General Walker Sees Danger in Pride of Power").

340 Drought began getting ready to leave for Lima, Peru: Maryknoll was currently looking for new stations in Latin America in which to place not only missioners repatriated from the Far East but also a large number of newly ordained priests. Coleman corresp. and Council minutes for June 22, 1942, and July 6, 14, and 16, 1942.

340–42 Drought's passport difficulties: JMD and FW papers. Drought wrote to Hull on July 23, 1942; Hull replied on July 29; in the meantime, Drought had written to Walker on July 27 and was to write again on July 31 and Aug.

2. A note in the FW papers states that after Drought "appealed" to the Post-master General "the matter was finally cleared up," but no details are given. I was unable to pursue this subject in the files of the State Dept. because such information is considered "sensitive" and is therefore in the "closed" category of materials.

342–43 The Logan Act: I am indebted to Professor Joseph R. Strayer of Prince-ton for calling the Logan Act to my attention one day while we were talking about the role Drought had played in 1941. The applicable wording of the Act can be found in *The Statutes at Large of the United States of America* . . . , Vol. XLVII, Part 1, 132–33, and *United States Code*, 1940 ed., 1514: Title 18, Sect. 5. Corresp. with the Internal Security Division of the Dept. of Jus-tice also provided useful information.

343 "The Fullness of the War Effort and Aims": JMD papers, a special delivery letter, Aug. 1, 1942, forwarding the draft, an Aug. 2 telegram, an Aug. 2 letter with a corrected copy of the speech, and a *NYT* clipping for Aug. 19 covering Walker's speech the preceding day.

343 "An impatience with words and a fatigue with oratory": This phrase, which is from the opening sentence of the speech to the Knights of Columbus, ac-curately reflects Drought's own attitude even though he was writing this for the PMG.

343 A speech for Manuel Quezon, Oct. 1942: JMD papers. During this same month JMD asked Bp. Walsh to release him "for chaplain service to the U.S. Air Corps," but the Father General declined to do so. Reminiscing years later, a colleague of Drought's said: "Jim had to be doing something big all the time or he wasn't Jim." Coleman corresp. and enclosures.

344 Drought on the Japanese enemy (in a speech delivered by Romulo on Dec. 8, 1942): *Ibid.*

344 Drought on Roosevelt: *Ibid.*, a Feb. 13, 1943, note from Walker and JMD's Feb. 17 reply (his "Memo on the 1944 Campaign").

344–45 The decline in Drought's health and his death: I have used the follow-ing items at Maryknoll: a May 1, 1943, letter from Bp. Walsh to the members of the Maryknoll community announcing the death of Fr. Drought earlier in the day and describing the important part he had played in the life of the Society, a copy of the Father General's sermon at the Pontifical Requiem Mass on May 4, and a newspaper clipping relating to Drought's death and funeral. Also FW papers, a *NYHT* clipping for May 2, 1943; and several items in the *NYT*, May 2–5, 1943. The inscription on JMD's gravestone reads: "Lucerna Ardens et Lucens." It is from John, V, 35: "He was a bright and a shining light."

345–48 The fate of the men who had cooperated with Drought in 1941: Little is known about Wikawa's wartime activities, but a memo in the archives at Maryknoll, written on or about Dec. 20, 1943, reads as follows: "An inquiry has come [from Wikawa] to know if certain conversations could be resumed, taking into consideration present actualities, and with or without the concur-rence of the Vatican. It is further requested that an answer, definitely nega-tive or affirmative, be communicated by cable through the Swiss Consul to a missionary quarter." The form of "answer" suggested by Wikawa was as fol-lows: (1) "If conversations can be resumed, 'Uncle Vincent died' "; (2) "If conversations cannot be resumed, 'Uncle Robert died.' " Walsh consulted Walker. His advice (on Jan. 11, 1944) was to the following effect: "Do nothing but keep it in mind." Wikawa died on Feb. 18, 1947. Coleman corresp. and pertinent items from the Walsh and FW papers. Also Tsunoda corresp.; Wildes, 29–31.

The details of Frank Walker's postwar career are given in his obituary in the *NYT*, Sept. 14, 1959 (the day following his death). The appreciation of him is from Tully, 183–84 (see also Hull, I: 209); the "conduit" description is from a memo in the FW papers entitled "The Japanese Negotiations—1941." "From words and gestures of Mr. Hull," Hornbeck wrote to Ballantine on Nov. 20, 1962, "I gathered that he . . . was of a divided mind regarding Walker—feeling well disposed toward him as a fellow Democrat but impatient of him because of and in connection with his sponsoring of the trespassers whom he introduced." In another letter sent three days later, Hornbeck added this thought: "I am of the impression that Frank Walker was more than a 'letter-carrier' and that he concerned himself with the efforts of the persons whom he sponsored to an extent which annoyed Mr. Hull." Ballantine acknowledged both letters on Nov. 29. He indicated that he had not had any contact with the PMG in 1941 but that he felt "the same way as you do about [Walker's] interposition." SKH papers, Box 24, Folder "Ballantine, Jos. W., 1955–63."

The *NYT* was also a convenient source for Admiral Nomura's later years; the remarks made by him in 1953 are quoted in an obituary in the May 9, 1964, issue.

I was unable to determine the scope of Hideo Iwakuro's postwar interests, but in several meetings with him in Tokyo (in 1963 and 1965) I found it hard to believe that his service as a trustee of Kyoto Industrial College (Kyōto Sangyō Daigaku) could absorb all of his energy and attention. "The Colonel" (as Drought called him) died on Nov. 22, 1970.

The index to the *NYT* for the postwar years covers developments pertaining to Walsh's life in China from 1948 to 1970. There are a number of references, but I have drawn specifically on the following: Jan. 8, 1956: 34; July 4, 1956: 2; Jan. 14, 1959: 10; Jan. 31, 1959: 5; Mar. 18, 1959: 20; June 7, 1959: 66; Mar. 18, 1960: 3; Mar. 19, 1960: 1, 3; Mar. 21, 1960: 28; Nov. 27, 1965: 23; July 11, 1970: 1; July 12, 1970: 2; July 19, 1970: 6, E5. Also helpful were *The Sun* (Baltimore), Nov. 21, 1965: 10; *The Post-Intelligencer* (Seattle), Dec. 9, 1965: 25; *The Evening Star* (Washington, D.C.), July 10, 1970: 1; and *The Washington Post*, July 10, 1970: 1; July 11, 1970: 1; July 12, 1970: A26.

346 No evidence has come to light: Both Hull and Walker ultimately expressed the conviction that Nomura had sincerely done his best to avoid war in the Pacific. Hull, II: 987; FW papers, "The Japanese Negotiations—1941." See also Ballantine, "Reminiscences," 40, 48–49. With reference to Kurusu, a memo written by Ferdinand L. Mayer shortly after the attack on Pearl Harbor contains an interesting account of two long conversations he had with his "old friend" on Dec. 6. When Mayer talked with Kurusu again, by telephone, on the evening of Dec. 7, "his voice sounded like that of a broken man . . . quite overwhelmed and in the deepest sort of despair." FDR papers, PSF, Japan Folder (Dec. 6, 1941). Also *PHA*, XX: 4528–37, esp. 4537.

348 "The only bright light of hope": This phrase and the following one, "fearful vortex of a great war," are from the speech Nomura gave at the America-Japan Society luncheon held in his honor at the Imperial Hotel on Dec. 19, 1940. *FRJ*, II: 128–29.

Acknowledgments
A Note on the Sources
Bibliography

Acknowledgments

MY INDEBTEDNESS to a number of persons and institutions is very great, and covers more than a decade of involvement in this project. Grants in aid of research came initially from the Far Eastern and Russian Institute at the University of Washington, the Rockefeller Foundation, and the Institute for Advanced Study in Princeton, N.J. Further opportunity to pursue the subject was subsequently provided by the John Simon Guggenheim Memorial Foundation and by the Institute for Comparative and Foreign Area Studies (formerly the Far Eastern and Russian Institute). In connection with these grants, and because the following persons also revealed their interest in other ways, I would like especially to thank George M. Beckmann, Robert E. Burke, Harold F. Cherniss, Frederick S. Dunn, Herbert J. Ellison, Herbert Feis, Gerald Freund, John W. Hall, Donald C. Hellmann, W. Stull Holt, Solomon Katz, George F. Kennan, John M. Maki, Robert Oppenheimer, Otis A. Pease, Kenneth B. Pyle, Gordon N. Ray, Joseph R. Strayer, George E. Taylor, Homer A. Thompson, and Donald W. Treadgold.

I would also like to express my appreciation to the members of the Maryknoll General Council (1956–1966) for permitting me to make use of the James M. Drought papers and related materials. In particular, I wish to acknowledge the consideration shown to me by Thomas J. Bauer, William J. Coleman (who is in charge of the newly established Maryknoll Archive), William J. Collins, Thomas V. Kiernan, and Thomas S. Walsh.

I owe a similar debt to Thomas J. Walker for allowing me to explore the Frank C. Walker papers at Notre Dame.

Wherever I turned in the search for materials, or in an effort to solve problems of one sort or another, I encountered friends, librarians, archivists, scholars, administrators, government officials, and many others who were generous with their time and their suggestions. It is a pleasure, after all these years, to be able to mention each in turn: Thomas E. Blantz, W. H. Bond, Jerome V. Deyo, Patricia G. Dowling, Elizabeth B. Drewry, Donald E. Emerson, Arther L. Ferrill, Wilton B. Fowler, William M. Franklin, Felix Gilbert, Milton O. Gustafson, Marilla B. Guptil, Noburu Hiraga, Masao Inaba, Robert L. Jacoby, Carolyn E. Jakeman, Harry W. John, Arthur G. Kogan, Ken Kurihara, Franz G. Lassner, Thomas T. McAvoy, Joseph W. Marshall, Hideo Masutani, Kiyoaki Murata, Atsushi Ōi, E. Taylor Parks, Judith A. Schiff, William J. Stewart, Carol G. Thomas, Alan E. Thompson, Jun Tsunoda, and Tomohiko Ushiba.

During the many years I have worked on this book, I have been able to rely, seriatim, on some of the best secretaries, research assistants, and "troubleshooters" anyone could hope to find: Peggy Adeboi, Anita Brown, Jean Bruntlett, Linda Cheever, Susan Dubin, Joyce Hollander (who was on board when it all began), Sally Kester, Joanne Miller, Melissa Queen, Carolyn Sforza, and Sheila Wilkins (who has been standing watch during the final stages).

Although I have already mentioned Kenneth Pyle in another connection, I would like to say a word about the role this friend and colleague has played over the years in sharing his perceptions with me. In the present instance, his reactions to the text caused me to take up certain matters that I might otherwise have allowed to lie dormant. The result was a new epilogue that went quite far beyond what I had originally written.

Last but not least, I am happy to find myself once again in the good company of Leon Seltzer and J. G. Bell, Director and Editor, respectively, of Stanford University Press. During the past year, I have also enjoyed the editorial companionship of Associate Editor Barbara Mnookin, who has been in charge of preparing the manuscript for publication. In the process she has somehow also managed to keep the author in a fairly tractable frame of mind.

A Note on the Sources

AMONG the primary materials that were of key importance in the writing of this book are the private papers of Father James M. Drought. It was an exciting day when I first saw them at Maryknoll, N.Y., early in 1963—scribblings in ink and pencil, typewritten letters and documents, telegrams and other messages, newspaper clippings and travel information, all jumbled together in a filing-cabinet drawer that was ready to burst at the seams.

Many of the handwritten items were scarcely legible, for Drought normally produced a scrawl that inevitably got worse whenever he was excited or in a hurry. He had the habit of jotting down thoughts on whatever came to hand, including hotel stationery, telegraph blanks, and even memo slips from the desk of the Postmaster General. Since Drought rarely dated anything—or did so only later—I found that his dates were sometimes wrong or were rendered doubtful by the addition of question marks indicating uncertainty. Personal references were often incomplete and occasionally incorrect, particularly in the case of Japanese nationals. There were also abbreviations and special words or phrases that created problems of interpretation. Deciphering all this and putting it into some semblance of order was a formidable and time-consuming task.

After I had gotten quite far into the research stage of the work, a Maryknoll Archive was established under the direction of Father William J. Coleman. In recent years he has sent me copies of many documents that were not originally accessible. I have thus been able to make use of items at Maryknoll that come from the "Kyoto Mission" file, the "Council Minutes," the "Superiors General" file, and the papers of Bishop James E. Walsh, whose safe return from the People's Republic of China in the summer of 1970 resulted in the opening up of materials of considerable value that would not otherwise have become available.

My visits to Maryknoll in 1963 proved to be merely the beginning of a long search that took me in many directions: to the archives of the State Department in Washington and of the Japanese Foreign Office in Tokyo; to the Franklin D. Roosevelt Library at Hyde Park; to the Yōmei Bunko in Kyoto, where the records of Prince Fumimaro Konoye are kept; to the papers of Joseph C. Grew at Harvard, of Cordell Hull at the Library of Congress, and of Stanley K. Hornbeck at Stanford.

Intercession by Thomas J. Walker on my behalf opened the door to the materials his father gave to Notre Dame. I could therefore browse freely in the Frank C. Walker collection at a time when it was still officially under restriction.

I was also fortunate in being able to draw, some years ago, on the recollections and observations of Joseph W. Ballantine, Eugene H. Dooman, Stanley K. Hornbeck, Hideo Iwakuro, Tomohiko Ushiba, and many others. Much later, I had an opportunity—at long last—to meet Bishop Walsh, and to chat with him about the past.

As I worked my way into the sources, Father Drought's attempt to calm down the waters of the Pacific (to use Tadao Wikawa's phrase) began to emerge more clearly. There were surprises and also disappointments. The papers of President Roosevelt and Secretary Hull did not produce the rich details I had expected to find, but other sources confirmed the nature and extent of their involvement. The archives of the State Department and the Japanese Foreign Office provided valuable background briefing but very little direct information about the John Doe Associates. The Grew papers were equally barren of anything immediately pertinent to the subject of this book, but they were rewarding in other respects, especially in conveying a sense of the crisis that bedeviled Japanese-American relations in 1940 and '41. A diary kept by Kichisaburō Nomura also proved helpful, even though it was available only in the form of an unsatisfactory translation (American authorities obtained the original during the Occupation of Japan, but when Nomura later tried to regain possession he was advised that a search conducted in Washington had failed to reveal any trace of the diary).

While sifting through the Walker papers at Notre Dame, on the other hand, I discovered—quite fortuitously—a Japanese-style briefcase that had once belonged to Wikawa. Tucked inside were letters and telegrams, airline ticket stubs, a curriculum vitae, printed fortunes of the type that are sold at temples and shrines throughout Japan, several tax tokens from the State of Washington, train and bus schedules obtained in California, and a small amount of Japanese currency.

How did Frank Walker come to have Wikawa's briefcase? I can only answer this question with another: Who knows? One possibility is that Wikawa left it behind by accident in the rush of checking out of his hotel in July 1941; it may then have been turned over to Walker because he was known to be a "friend" of Wikawa's. Another possibility is that Wikawa asked the Postmaster General to keep the briefcase for him either as a matter of convenience (he was hoping to return to Washington to resume his activities there) or because he was reluctant to take "incriminating" documents home with him (the Kenpeitai might want to know what he had been "doing" in the United States). The reason why this briefcase ended up in Walker's hands is actually less important than the fact that very little Wikawa material has come to light in Japan.

Chance also played a part during other phases of the research process. In Tokyo, on one occasion, I was told of the existence of a manuscript of considerable value—322 handwritten pages entitled "Watakushi ga Sanka Shita Nichi-Bei Kōshō." At first, this record seemed beyond reach. It was no longer in the possession of its author, for he had given it to an agency of the Japanese Government. With the help of Jun Tsunoda, however, I was eventually able to obtain a photocopy on condition that I agree, for the time being, not to reveal the author's name or other details. It was feared that the acquisition of historical materials from persons who might be willing to be of assistance only if their anonymity were preserved would otherwise be jeopardized. Since this was a valid argument, I undertook to abide by the stipulation. Having recently been released from my commitment, I can now say that the document under reference is the most complete account ever provided by Colonel Iwakuro concerning the part he played in the Japanese-American "negotiations."

*

Although most of my research has been in primary sources, I would like to add a word about certain secondary works that I have used with profit. The most extensive treatment in Japanese of the private effort for peace described in this book is the contribution made by Tsunoda in Volume VII of *Taiheiyō Sensō e no Michi*, which was published in 1963 [a separate volume of documents (*TSM, Bekkan*) contains primary materials from the "Konoye shiryō" (the Prince's papers in Kyoto), the "Gaimushō kiroku" (the files of the Foreign Ministry), and the "Senshi-shitsu shiryō" (the archives of the War History Office of the Defense Agency)]. Also pertinent is the coverage in Teiji Yabe's biography of Konoye, which appeared in 1952. From time to time other Japanese writers have touched on the "Walsh-Drought affair," but they have done so only briefly and without any clear conception of what took place.

Much less attention has been devoted to the John Doe Associates on this side of the Pacific, but they have not gone entirely unnoticed. In *The Lost War: A Japanese Reporter's Inside Story*, which was published in New York in 1946, Masuo Katō identified Colonel Iwakuro as "one of the most important though least known of the men who participated in the negotiations for peace." Katō characterized Postmaster General Walker as "a behind-the-scenes middleman" and noted that "Bishop Walsh of the Catholic Church and a priest named James Drought ... also participated in conferences with Nomura."

The two clergymen from Maryknoll and their Japanese colleagues were mentioned in 1948 by Cordell Hull in his *Memoirs*, in 1950 by Herbert Feis in *The Road to Pearl Harbor*, in 1953 by William L. Langer and S. Everett Gleason in *The Undeclared War*, in 1960 by myself in an *American Historical Review* article and a year later in *Tojo and the Coming of the War*. There have been other references as well, but they have generally been misleading.

By reading the secondary sources and by conferring with various knowledgeable persons on both sides of the Pacific, I became aware of an interesting disparity: the American interpretation that Walsh and Drought had simply "started the ball rolling" at the outset of the talks in Washington (and possessed no significance beyond that) contrasted sharply with the Japanese view that the Bishop and the priest had traveled to Tokyo with the backing of men close to the President (and perhaps at the urging of the Vatican) for the purpose of exploring the chances of achieving a Far Eastern settlement.

Research over a prolonged period on related matters increased my suspicion that there was a great deal more to all this than met the eye at first glance—my main clue being that the assertions Drought made at the White House in January 1941 did not accurately reflect the realities of Japanese foreign policy at that time.

A year at the Institute for Advanced Study in Princeton, N.J., cleared the way to working on the problem in earnest. With the resources provided by the grants in aid of research mentioned in the Acknowledgments, I was eventually able to piece together the activities of the John Doe Associates and could thus ultimately produce the account presented in the pages of this book.

Bibliography

I. *Primary and secondary sources*
(private papers, official records, books, and articles)

Acheson, Dean. *Present at the Creation: My Years in the State Department.* New York, 1969.

"America and Japan" (edited by William P. Maddox), *The Annals of the American Academy of Political and Social Science,* 215 (May 1941).

Aoki, Tokuzō. *Taiheiyō Sensō Zenshi.* 3 vols. Tokyo, 1953.

Argall, Phyllis. *My Life with the Enemy.* New York, 1944.

Arita, Hachirō. *Hito no Me no Chiri wo Miru: Gaikō Mondai Kaiko-roku.* Tokyo, 1948.

Ballantine, Joseph W. Autobiographical manuscript (lent to the author by Mr. Ballantine).

————. "Reminiscences." Columbia University Oral History Research Office, 1961.

Berle, Adolf A. *Navigating the Rapids, 1918–1971: From the Papers of Adolf A. Berle.* Edited by Beatrice Bishop Berle and Travis Beal Jacobs; introduction by Max Ascoli. New York, 1973.

Blum, John Morton. *From the Morgenthau Diaries.* 3 vols. Vol. II: *Years of Urgency, 1938–1941.* Boston, 1965.

Borg, Dorothy. *The United States and the Far Eastern Crisis of 1933–1938: From the Manchurian Incident Through the Initial Stage of the Undeclared Sino-Japanese War.* Cambridge, Mass., 1964.

Boyle, John H. "The Drought-Walsh Mission to Japan," *Pacific Historical Review,* 34.2 (May 1965): 141–61.

Burns, James MacGregor. *Roosevelt: The Lion and the Fox.* New York, 1956.

————. *Roosevelt: The Soldier of Freedom.* New York, 1970.

Butow, R. J. C. "Backdoor Diplomacy in the Pacific: The Proposal for a Konoye-Roosevelt Meeting, 1941," *The Journal of American History,* 54.1 (June 1972): 48–72.

————. "The Hull-Nomura Conversations: A Fundamental Misconception," *The American Historical Review,* 65.4 (July 1960): 822–36.

————. *Japan's Decision to Surrender.* Foreword by Edwin O. Reischauer. Stanford, Calif., 1954.

————. *Tojo and the Coming of the War.* Foreword by Frederick S. Dunn. Original ed., Princeton, N.J., 1961. Reissued, Stanford, Calif., 1969.

Churchill, Winston S. *The Grand Alliance.* Boston, 1950.

Compton, James V. *The Swastika and the Eagle: Hitler, the United States, and the Origins of World War II.* Boston, 1967.

Conroy, Hilary. "The Strange Diplomacy of Admiral Nomura," *Proceedings of the American Philosophical Society,* 114.3 (June 1970): 205–16.

Coox, Alvin D. *Year of the Tiger.* Tokyo, 1964.

Craigie, Sir Robert. *Behind the Japanese Mask.* London, 1945.

Davies, John Paton, Jr. *Dragon by the Tail: American, British, Japanese, and Russian Encounters with China and One Another.* New York, 1972.

Degras, Jane. See *Soviet Documents on Foreign Policy.*

DGFP. See the following entry.

Documents on German Foreign Policy, 1918–1945. Series D (1937–45), Vols. XI–XIII (Sept. 1940–Dec. 1941). Washington, D.C., 1960, 1962, 1964. Cited in the notes as *DGFP.*

Douglas-Hamilton, James. *Motive for a Mission: The Story Behind Hess's Flight to Britain.* Foreword by Alan Bullock. New York, 1971.

Drought, James M., papers. Maryknoll Archive, Maryknoll, N.Y. Cited in the notes as JMD papers. See my Note on the Sources.

Drought manuscript. This item is described briefly in the Note for pp. 311–13.

Eden, Anthony. *The Memoirs of Anthony Eden, Earl of Avon: The Reckoning.* Boston, 1965.

Farago, Ladislas. *The Broken Seal: The Story of "Operation Magic" and the Pearl Harbor Disaster.* New York, 1967.

F.D.R.: His Personal Letters, 1928–1945. Foreword by Eleanor Roosevelt; edited by Elliott Roosevelt, assisted by Joseph P. Lash. Vols. I and II. New York, 1950.

Feis, Herbert. *The Road to Pearl Harbor: The Coming of the War Between the United States and Japan.* Princeton, N.J., 1950.

Fleisher, Wilfrid. *Volcanic Isle.* Garden City, N.Y., 1941.

Fowler, W. B. *British-American Relations, 1917–1918: The Role of Sir William Wiseman.* Princeton, N.J., 1969.

FR and *FRJ.* See U.S. Department of State, *Foreign Relations . . . ;* and *Papers Relating to the Foreign Relations of the United States . . .*

Gaimushō (hensan). *Gaikō Shiryō: Nichi-Bei Kōshō Kiroku no Bu (Shōwa Jūroku Nen Nigatsu yori Jūnigatsu made).* Tokyo, 1946. For a microfilm copy, see LC-JFOA, WT 71, IMT 553, or S 531, S 1.1.3.1-1, 1972-2280. Cited in the notes as *NBKK.*

———. *Nihon Gaikō Nenpyō narabi ni Shuyō Bunsho* (alternatively: *Shuyō Monjo*). 2 vols. Tokyo, 1955. Cited in the notes as Gaimushō, *Shuyō Bunsho.*

Gaimushō kiroku, esp. "Nichi-Bei Gaikō Kankei Zassan: Taiheiyō Heiwa narabi ni Tō-a Mondai ni kan suru Nichi-Bei Kōshō Kankei." Gaimushō, Tokyo, Japan. For a microfilm copy, see LC-JFOA, S 529–33, S 1.1.3.1-1.

Gannon, Robert I. "An American Commission Consults With Venezuela: Catholicism Is the Firmest Link Between the Americas," *America,* 61.15 (July 22, 1939): 344–45.

Gendai-shi Shiryō (13). Tokyo, 1966.

Grew, Joseph C. *Ten Years in Japan: A Contemporary Record Drawn from the Diaries and Private and Official Papers of Joseph C. Grew, United States Ambassador to Japan, 1932–1942.* New York, 1944.

———. *Turbulent Era: A Diplomatic Record of Forty Years, 1904–1945.* Edited by Walter Johnson, assisted by Nancy Harvison Hooker. 2 vols. Boston, 1952.

Grew papers. Houghton Library, Harvard University, Cambridge, Mass. See my Note on the Sources.

Hamilton, Maxwell M., papers. Hoover Institution on War, Revolution and Peace, Stanford, Calif.

Harada, Kumao. *Saionji Kō to Seikyoku.* 8 vols. and a *Bekkan.* Vol. VIII (July 1939–Nov. 1940). Tokyo, 1952.

Hayashi, Saburō (in collaboration with Alvin D. Coox). *Kōgun: The Japanese Army in the Pacific War.* Quantico, Va., 1959.

Heinrichs, Waldo H., Jr. *American Ambassador: Joseph C. Grew and the Development of the United States Diplomatic Tradition.* Boston, 1966.

Hornbeck, Stanley K., papers. Hoover Institution on War, Revolution and Peace, Stanford, Calif.

Hull, Cordell. *The Memoirs of Cordell Hull.* 2 vols. New York, 1948.

Hull papers. Library of Congress, Washington, D.C. See my Note on the Sources.

Ickes, Harold L. *The Secret Diary of Harold L. Ickes.* 3 vols. Vol. III: *The Lowering Clouds, 1939–1941.* New York, 1954.

Ike, Nobutaka. See *Japan's Decision for War.*

Iklé, Frank William. *German-Japanese Relations, 1936–1940.* New York, 1956.

IMTFE. See the next entry.

International Military Tribunal for the Far East. "Transcript of Proceedings" (also called "Record of Proceedings" or simply "Proceedings"), 48,412 mimeographed pages, unpublished but microfilmed by the Library of Congress. Cited in the notes as IMTFE. References in the notes to the "Sokki-roku" are to a stenographic record, in Japanese, consisting of 416 gō, paginated separately (e.g., "Sokki-roku," 312: 13–15).

Iwakuro, Hideo. "Amerika ni okeru Nichi-Bei Kōshō no Keika," May 10, 1946. A copy can be found among the Konoye papers.

———. "Heiwa e no Arasoi," *Bungei Shunjū,* 44.8 (Aug. 1966): 220–40.

———. "Watakushi ga Sanka Shita Nichi-Bei Kōshō." Unpublished manuscript consisting of 322 handwritten pages. Cited in the notes as Iwakuro ms. See my Note on the Sources.

Iwakuro manuscript. See the preceding entry.

Japan, Ministry of Foreign Affairs. See Gaimushō.

Japan's Decision for War: Records of the 1941 Policy Conferences. Translated, edited, and with an Introduction by Nobutaka Ike. Stanford, Calif., 1967. Cited in the notes as Ike.

Jones, E. Stanley. "An Adventure in Failure: Behind the Scenes Before Pearl Harbor," *Asia and the Americas,* 45.12 (Dec. 1945): 609–16.

Kahn, David. *The Codebreakers: The Story of Secret Writing.* New York, 1967.

Kase, Toshikazu. *Journey to the Missouri.* Edited by David Nelson Rowe. New Haven, Conn., 1950.

Kato [Katō], Masuo. *The Lost War: A Japanese Reporter's Inside Story.* New York, 1946.

Kennan, George F. *American Diplomacy, 1900–1950.* Chicago, 1951.

Kiba, Kōsuke (hensan). *Nomura Kichisaburō.* Tokyo, 1961.

Konoye, Fumimaro. *Ushinawareshi Seiji: Konoye Fumimaro Kō no Shuki.* Tokyo, 1946.

Konoye papers. Yōmei Bunko, Kyoto, Japan. Microfilm copies of this material can be consulted at the Far Eastern Library, University of Washington, Seattle, and at the Hoover Institution on War, Revolution and Peace, Stanford, Calif.

Kurusu, Saburō. *Hōmatsu no Sanjūgo-nen: Gaikō Hishi.* Tokyo, 1948.

————. "Kurusu Taishi Hōkoku," June 5, 1942. The original is in the files of the Gaimushō. For a microfilm copy, see LC-JFOA, WT 77, IMT 577, or S 531, S 1.1.3.1-1, 2281–2327.

————. *Nichi-Bei Gaikō Hiwa: Waga Gaikō-shi.* Tokyo, 1952.

Langer, William L., and S. Everett Gleason. *The Undeclared War, 1940–1941.* New York, 1952.

LC-JFOA. See U.S., Library of Congress, Microfilm Collection of Japanese Foreign Office Archives.

Maruyama, Masao. *Thought and Behaviour in Modern Japanese Politics.* Expanded ed., edited by Ivan Morris. London, 1969.

Matsuoka, Yōsuke. "Toward World Peace," *Contemporary Japan*, 9.12 (Dec. 1940): 1507–13.

"Matsuoka Oboegaki" (a brief note on the Walsh-Drought affair apparently dictated by Matsuoka in 1945 or 1946; a copy was sent to the author by Shinichi Hasegawa).

Meskill, Johanna Menzel. *Hitler & Japan: The Hollow Alliance.* New York, 1966.

Millis, Walter. *This is Pearl! The United States and Japan—1941.* New York, 1947.

The Moffat Papers: Selections from the Diplomatic Journals of Jay Pierrepont Moffat, 1919–1943. Edited by Nancy Harvison Hooker; foreword by Sumner Welles. Cambridge, Mass., 1956.

Moll, Aristides. "The United States Social Service Mission to Venezuela," *Bulletin of the Pan-American Union*, 73.9 (Sept. 1939): 521–25.

Moore, Frederick. *With Japan's Leaders: An Intimate Record of Fourteen Years as Counsellor to the Japanese Government, Ending December 7, 1941.* New York, 1942.

Morris, John. *Traveler from Tokyo.* Foreword by Joseph C. Grew. New York, 1944.

Nakamura, Kikuo. "Nichi-Bei Kōshō no Keika to Mondai-ten, Toku-ni Nihongawa kara Mita Baai" (2 parts), *Hōgaku Kenkyū*, 34.9: 1–14 (867–80); 34.10: 22–43 (974–95).

NBKK. See Gaimushō (hensan), *Gaikō Shiryō* . . .

Nihon Kokusai Seiji Gakkai, Taiheiyō Sensō Gen'in Kenkyū-bu (hen). *Taiheiyō Sensō e no Michi: Kaisen Gaikō-shi.* 7 vols. and a *Bekkan.* Esp. Vol. VII and the *Bekkan.* Tokyo, 1963. Cited in the notes as *TSM.*

Nomura, Kichisaburō. *Beikoku ni Tsukai Shite: Nichi-Bei Kōshō no Kaiko.* Tokyo, 1946.

————. "Chū-Bei Ninmu Hōkoku," Aug. 20, 1942. The original is in the files of the Gaimushō. For a microfilm copy, see LC-JFOA, WT 53, IMT 386.

————. "Diary" (June 3–Dec. 31, 1941), International Prosecution Section Evidentiary Document 1686 ("Diary of Admiral Nomura, rough translation"). See my Note on the Sources.

Ōhashi, Chūichi. *Taiheiyō Sensō Yuraiki: Matsuoka Gaikō no Shinsō.* Tokyo, 1952.

The Pacific Rivals: A Japanese View of Japanese-American Relations. Prepared by the staff of the *Asahi Shinbun*; foreword by Edwin O. Reischauer. New York, 1972.

Pearl Harbor as History: Japanese-American Relations, 1931–1941. Edited by Dorothy Borg and Shumpei Okamoto, with the assistance of Dale K. A. Finlayson. New York, 1973.

PHA. See U.S. Congress, Joint Committee on the Investigation of the Pearl Harbor Attack.

Pogue, Forrest C. *George C. Marshall: Ordeal and Hope, 1939–1942.* Foreword by Gen. Omar Bradley. New York, 1966.

Pratt, Julius W. *Cordell Hull.* 2 vols. New York, 1964.

Presseisen, Ernst L. *Germany and Japan: A Study in Totalitarian Diplomacy, 1933–1941.* The Hague, 1958.

The Public Papers and Addresses of Franklin D. Roosevelt. 13 vols. Vol. X: *1941: The Call to Battle Stations.* Compiled with special material and explanatory notes by Samuel I. Rosenman. New York, 1950.

Roosevelt, Franklin D., papers. Franklin D. Roosevelt Library, Hyde Park, N.Y. See my Note on the Sources.

Saitō, Yoshie. *Azamukareta Rekishi: Matsuoka to Sangoku-dōmei no Rimen.* Tokyo, 1955.

Sawada, Setsuzō. "The Maryknoll Peace Negotiators on the Eve of the Pacific War" (an excerpt from the reminiscences of former Ambassador Setsuzō Sawada, translated by his son, Dr. P. A. Sawada). An unpublished, typescript copy of the original sent to the author by Dr. Sawada.

Schmidt, Dr. Paul. *Hitler's Interpreter.* London, 1951.

Schroeder, Paul W. *The Axis Alliance and Japanese-American Relations, 1941.* Ithaca, N.Y., 1958.

Sheba [*sic*], Kimpei. "Diplomats of the Matsuoka Blitz School," *The Pictorial Orient,* 8.11 (Nov. 1940): 374–75.

———. "Yosuke Matsuoka: A Nationalistic Internationalist," *The Pictorial Orient,* 8.9 (Sept. 1940): 300–301.

Sherwood, Robert E. *Roosevelt and Hopkins: An Intimate History.* Rev. ed. New York, 1950.

Shigemitsu, Mamoru. *Gaikō Kaiso-roku.* Tokyo, 1953.

———. *Japan and Her Destiny: My Struggle for Peace.* Edited by Maj. Gen. F. S. G. Piggott; translated by Oswald White. New York, 1958.

———. *Shōwa no Dōran.* 2 vols. Tokyo, 1952.

Shuyō Bunsho. See Gaimushō (hensan), *Nihon Gaikō Nenpyō* . . .

"Sokki-roku." See International Military Tribunal for the Far East.

Sokolsky, George E. "Why Matsuoka Hates the United States," *Liberty Magazine,* 18.27 (July 5, 1941): 10–11, 25.

Soviet Documents on Foreign Policy. Selected and edited by Jane Degras. 3 vols. Vol. III. *1933–1941.* London, 1953. Cited in the notes as Degras.

Spotswood, Rogers Dalton. "Japan's Southward Advance as an Issue in Japanese-American Relations, 1940–1941." Ph.D. dissertation, University of Washington, 1974.

State 711.94/1973-1/3. See U.S. Dept. of State, General Records . . .

The Statutes at Large of the United States of America . . . Vol. XLVII, Part 1. Washington, D.C., 1933.

Stimson, Henry L., and McGeorge Bundy. *On Active Service: In Peace and War.* New York, 1947.

Storry, Richard. *The Double Patriots: A Study of Japanese Nationalism.* Boston, 1957.

Strauss, Lewis L. *Men and Decisions.* New York, 1962.

Sugiyama, Heisuke. "Foreign Minister Matuoka [*sic*]," *Nippon*, No. 24 (1940): 13–15.

Sugiyama Memo: Dai-hon'ei-Seifu Renraku Kaigi Nado Hikki (Sanbō Honbu hen). 2 vols. Tokyo, 1967.

Takaishi, Shingorō. *Japan Speaks Out.* Tokyo, 1938.

Tanemura, Sakō. *Dai-hon'ei Kimitsu Nisshi.* Tokyo, 1952.

Tansill, Charles Callan. *Back Door to War: The Roosevelt Foreign Policy, 1933–1941.* Chicago, 1952.

Terasaki, Gwen. *Bridge to the Sun.* Chapel Hill, N.C., 1957.

Tōgō, Shigenori. *The Cause of Japan.* Translated and edited by Fumihiko Tōgō and Ben Bruce Blakeney. New York, 1956.

———. *Jidai no Ichimen: Taisen Gaikō no Shuki.* Tokyo, 1952.

Tolischus, Otto. *Tokyo Record.* New York, 1943.

Tolles, Frederick B. *George Logan of Philadelphia.* New York, 1953.

Tomita, Kenji. *Haisen Nihon no Uchigawa: Konoye Kō no Omoide.* Tokyo, 1962.

Trefousse, H. L. *Germany and American Neutrality, 1939–1941.* New York, 1951.

TSM. See Nihon Kokusai Seiji Gakkai.

Tully, Grace. *F.D.R.: My Boss.* Foreword by William O. Douglas. New York, 1949.

United States, Congress. *Congressional Record.* Washington, D.C., 1936, 1941.

———, ———, Committee on Foreign Affairs. *Hearings Before the Committee on Foreign Affairs, House of Representatives, Seventy-Seventh Congress, First Session, on H.R. 1776, a Bill to Promote the Defense of the United States, and for Other Purposes.* Washington, D.C., 1941. Cited in the notes as U.S. Congress, *Hearings on H.R. 1776.*

———, ———, Joint Committee on the Investigation of the Pearl Harbor Attack. *Pearl Harbor Attack, Hearings Before the Joint Committee on the Investigation of the Pearl Harbor Attack, Congress of the United States, Seventy-Ninth Congress, First Session* . . . 39 Parts. Esp. Parts II-IV, XI-XII, XIV-XV, XVII-XX. Washington, D.C., 1946. Cited in the notes as *PHA.*

———, Department of State. *Bulletin* (for 1940 and 1941). Washington, D.C., 1940–42.

———, ———. *Foreign Relations of the United States: Diplomatic Papers, 1940.* Vol. I: *General*; Vol. IV: *The Far East.* Washington, D.C., 1959 and 1955, respectively. Cited in the notes as *FR 1940.*

———, ———. *Foreign Relations of the United States: Diplomatic Papers, 1941.* Vols. IV and V: *The Far East.* Washington, D.C., 1956. Cited in the notes as *FR 1941.*

———, ———. General Records of the Department of State, Record Group

59, File No. (as indicated). Diplomatic, Legal, and Fiscal Records Division, National Archives, Washington, D.C. Cited in the notes as State (followed by the pertinent File No.).

———, ———. *Nazi-Soviet Relations, 1939–1941: Documents from the Archives of the German Foreign Office.* Edited by Raymond James Sontag and James Stuart Beddie. Washington, D.C., 1948.

———, ———. *Papers Relating to the Foreign Relations of the United States: Japan, 1931–1941.* 2 vols. Washington, D.C., 1943. Cited in the notes as *FRJ.*

———, ———. *Peace and War: United States Foreign Policy, 1931–1941.* Washington, D.C., 1943.

———, ———. *Register* (for 1941). Washington, D.C., 1942.

———, Library of Congress. *Checklist of Archives in the Japanese Ministry of Foreign Affairs, Tokyo, Japan, 1868–1945, Microfilmed for the Library of Congress, 1949–1951.* Compiled by Cecil H. Uyehara. Washington, D.C., 1954.

———, ———. Microfilm Collection of Japanese Foreign Office Archives. Washington, D.C. Cited in the notes as LC-JFOA.

United States Code, 1940 edition. Washington, D.C., 1941.

Wakatsuki, Reijirō. *Kofūan Kaiko-roku.* Tokyo, 1950.

Walker, Frank C., papers. University of Notre Dame Archives, Notre Dame, Indiana. See my Note on the Sources.

Walsh, James E., papers. Maryknoll Archive, Maryknoll, N.Y. See my Note on the Sources.

Wikawa, Tadao. "Higeki no Nichi-Bei Kōshō Hiwa," *Nihon Shūhō Daijiesuto,* Aug. 1, 1956: 11–26.

Wikawa materials, miscellaneous items among the Walker papers at the University of Notre Dame. See my Note on the Sources.

Wildes, Harry Emerson. *Typhoon in Tokyo: The Occupation and Its Aftermath.* New York, 1954.

Willert, Arthur. *The Road to Safety: A Study in Anglo-American Relations.* London, 1952.

Wohlstetter, Roberta. *Pearl Harbor: Warning and Decision.* Stanford, Calif., 1962.

Yabe, Teiji. *Konoye Fumimaro.* 2 vols. Tokyo, 1952.

Young, A. Morgan. *Imperial Japan, 1926–1938.* London, 1938.

Zacharias, Ellis M. *Secret Missions: The Story of an Intelligence Officer.* New York, 1946.

II. *Interviews and/or correspondence*
  (1962–1974)

Ackerman, Carl W.
Ballantine, Joseph W.
Berle, Adolf A., Jr.
Burman, Roger W.
Coleman, William J.
Considine, John J.
Donaldson, Jesse M.
Dooman, Eugene H.
Feis, Herbert
Fleisher, Eric W.

Gray, Cecil W.
Hachmeister, Louise
Hasegawa, Shinichi
Hirasawa, Kazushige
Hoover, Herbert
Hoover, J. Edgar
Hornbeck, Stanley K.
Iguchi, Sadao
Iwakuro, Hideo
Kase, Toshikazu

Kennedy, Joseph P.
Kido, Kōichi
Kido, Takahiko
Kurihara, Ken
Kurusu, Alice
Matsuoka, Kenichirō
Nomura, Kichisaburō
Obata, Shigeyoshi
Ōhashi, Chūichi
Ōi, Atsushi
Rabbitt, James A.
Renchard, George A.
Sawada, Setsuzō

Smith, Donald W.
Spinks, Charles N.
Strauss, Lewis L.
Suma, Yakichirō
Terasaki, Gwen
Terasaki, Tarō
Tibesar, Leopold H.
Tsunoda, Jun
Ushiba, Tomohiko
Walker, Thomas J.
Walsh, James E.
Welles, Benjamin
Willkie, Philip H.

III. *Newspapers and magazines*
(items found in private papers or in official records are not included)

Asahi Shinbun
Evening Star (Washington, D.C.)
Japan Advertiser
Japan News-Week
Japan Times and Advertiser
Japan Times and Mail
Japan Weekly Chronicle
Life
Newsweek

New York Herald Tribune
New York Times
Nippon
Pictorial Orient
Seattle Post-Intelligencer
Seattle Times
Sun (Baltimore)
Time
Washington Post

Index

Index

All dates are for 1941 unless otherwise specified